FAIL BETTER

FAIL BETTER

Reckonings with Artists and Critics

HAL FOSTER

The MIT Press Cambridge, Massachusetts London, England

The MIT Press would like to thank the anonymous peer reviewers who provided comments on drafts of this book. The generous work of academic experts is essential for establishing the authority and quality of our publications. We acknowledge with gratitude the contributions of these otherwise uncredited readers.

This publication is made possible in part by the Barr Ferree Foundation Fund for Publications, Department of Art and Archaeology, Princeton University.

This book was set in Minion by the MIT Press. Printed and bound in Canada.

Library of Congress Cataloging-in-Publication Data is available.

ISBN: 978-0-262-55235-6

10 9 8 7 6 5 4 3 2 1

Contents

Introduction

Most of the forty essays collected here were published over the last twenty years, but some only recently, so why offer them up again? One reason is that, though several texts can be found online, they are locked behind paywalls, while others are scattered in ephemeral journals or expensive catalogues. A more urgent motive is that I wanted another crack at them. Etymologically, an essay is a trial, and mine were often affected by the contingencies of the occasion—a commission for a special exhibition, say, or a publication with a particular style—or simply by errors of my own. Frequently, then, an essay calls out for another attempt. That's one meaning of the (anti)motto I borrow from Samuel Beckett: try again, fail again, fail better.[1]

I have also reached the point where I want to take stock. I turn seventy in 2025, and my first collection of essays, *Recodings: Art, Spectacle, Cultural Politics*, appeared forty years ago (the "reckonings" in my subtitle is meant to rhyme with "recodings"). Prompted by new practices and theories, *Recodings* mainly looked ahead, whereas this book of reckonings mostly gazes back, revisiting some of the same figures along the way.[2] Most of the artists I term "antecedents" aren't alive, most of the "contemporaries" aren't young, and the "critics" who are still with us are long in the tooth.

My roster is far from comprehensive (I am a situated writer, long based in New York), nor is it very inclusive, and many will rightly object to its lack of diversity. Although several "contemporaries" are key feminists, and difference is a central concern in all three sections, nearly all the "antecedents" are white men. I can't defend this limitation, which may be another version of failure, apart from the fact that I present what I know best, I have published on artists of color elsewhere, and others do this crucial work better in any case (I see criticism as collaborative in this way).[3] Clearly, I write from the center—often about known figures, in established publications, from a privileged university—but I do so in part because value is concentrated there and so might be revised there as well. At the same time the center isn't so central anymore, and what was once assumed as knowledge about postwar practice can't be taken for granted.[4]

The texts vary widely. Some are brief, others extensive. Some tend to the analytical, others to the synthetic. Some concentrate on a single body of work, others review entire careers. Some focus on beginnings, others on midcareer shifts, and a few touch on late styles. In this respect, too, they're not comprehensive, yet each essay does aim to articulate a salient concept of the practice in question.[5] By the 1980s ambitious work in art history was divided between semiotic and social-historical approaches. This was never an either-or for me: I have always focused not only on how art signifies but also on what it says about the conditions that prompt it—on the historicity of the ideas embedded in the practice. For me that's the most productive way to address what Roland Barthes called "the historical responsibility of forms," to come to terms with the work and its moment in one go.[6]

This needn't be an obscure operation. Many of the texts first appeared in the *London Review of Books*, which has implications for readership: I have aimed to contribute to a shared understanding of postwar art and criticism in a way that doesn't depend on inside information, and this is true of the essays written for *Artforum* as well. And yet, though some of the texts are streamlined to suit the speediness of electronic publication, clarity isn't necessarily the enemy of complexity. That said, this book contains little in the way of scholarly apparatus: it is the labor of a critic more than a contemporary art historian (a category that still seems a little oxymoronic to me). There are a couple of reasons for this positioning. First, I am acquainted with a good number of the figures in the book. This is a mixed blessing, since being a participant-observer has its disadvantages; insight can come through proximity, but perspective can suffer as well. Second, many of these practices aren't things of the past for me; many "antecedents" might be historical, but not most "contemporaries." In part that's why I have opted for the two rubrics, inadequate though they are. By "antecedent," which combines "before" and "go" (*ante* + *cedere*), I simply mean an artist who emerged in a historical conjuncture prior to that of my generation. And I intend "contemporary" in the sense less of similar age than of shared history, of inhabiting a fractured time together (*con* + *tempus*).[7] Crucially, the "antecedents" are among the artists who set the terms of art-making for the "contemporaries."

If many readers will view most figures in this book as historical, the question becomes how to position them. Like other critics, I once relied on two concepts to periodize postwar art: postmodernism and the neo-avant-garde. Yet the model of a restrictive (medium-specific) modernism opened up by an expansive (post-medium) postmodernism no longer guides important developments, and the same is true of the schema of a prewar avant-garde recovered by a postwar neo-avant-garde.[8] Although other concepts not so based on Western European and North American practices have come to the fore—concepts like diasporic connections, "archipelagic thought," and global transfers—the old context isn't devoid of paradigms and patterns either.[9] For example, a partial genealogy can be traced through different stagings of the body, from its immediate presence in much art of the 1960s, through its performed abjection in some work of the 1990s, to its partial virtualization in many video installations and digital simulations of late. A second line could be drawn through various conceptions of site over the last six decades—as a matter first of physical location, then of institutional setting, and finally of discursive fields that artists explore in the manner of field research. And a third tale might be told through successive transformations of the image, from the crossing of painting and commodity in Pop art, through the appropriation of mass-cultural signs in postmodernism, to the extensive absorption of art in the vast media market of the present.[10]

As these sketches suggest and my roster makes clear, the afterlives of Minimalism and Pop remain important to me. I agree with Gerhard Richter that Minimalism presented a "new alphabet" for art, and with Charles Ray that it established a new "geometry of viewing" as well.[11] These propositions were soon challenged and extended—extended *because* challenged—by Richard Serra, Eva Hesse, Bruce Nauman, Dan Graham, and others discussed here. Pop art was epochal in other ways. Not long after Richard Hamilton, Claes Oldenburg, Andy Warhol, and others created that language, artists like Sigmar Polke, Ed Ruscha, and John Baldessari adapted it to different concerns, and the same held, a decade or so later, for Pictures artists like Barbara Kruger and Sarah Charlesworth and others like John Miller and Rachel Harrison.[12] At least for my cohort Minimalism and Pop existed on the threshold between the historical and the contemporary; unlike subsequent artists and critics, we had to deal with them directly—to contend with their divergent propositions about artworks, viewers, and the spaces that they share.

Why include a section on critics, especially when it too is neither comprehensive nor inclusive? One reason is simple enough: critical theory was never so influential as it was for the period surveyed here. Certainly, my generation had to sort through many varieties on the fly, including different kinds of Marxist critique, psychoanalytic theory, Foucauldian analysis, feminist and queer critiques, postcolonial discourse, and cultural studies. Poststructuralism constituted a "paraliterary" avant-garde of its own, Rosalind Krauss argued as early as 1981, and the correlating of poststructuralist concepts and postmodernist practices was an initial project of some of my closest colleagues.[13] The ambition of the critics in this section is beyond doubt, but a reckoning with these antecedents and contemporaries is also due, and my offering is meant as a tentative step in that direction.[14]

Criticism and history were long opposed; while the former could be partisan, the second had to be as objective as possible. For my cohort, however, the two weren't held apart so strictly; criticism was taken to focus history, history to ground criticism, and theory to sharpen both conceptually. This wasn't a question of contemporary art history (that field didn't exist as such), but neither was it a matter of criticism disguised as history, as is sometimes alleged. Already two decades ago Howard Singerman asked, with writers associated with *October* magazine in mind, "why—and for how long—1980s art criticism has been taken for history."[15] His answer was that initial interpretations were taken too quickly as settled accounts, and that this state of affairs was the result of "art criticism written by art historians."[16] This isn't quite the case—*October* authors like Benjamin Buchloh, Douglas Crimp, Craig Owens, and myself weren't ensconced in the academy then—but that doesn't vitiate his argument, which is primarily concerned with how "locutions such as 'critical' or 'advanced' . . . assume a narrative trajectory for art and history."[17]

Sometimes critical value was converted into historical value (the Pictures artists would be one instance), at least to an extent (never great, this extent is much diminished today), and such value creation was a by-product of both kinds of criticism during the period. On the semiotic side, there was the aforementioned connection between postmodernist practice and poststructuralist discourse, but just as important was the institutional convergence of the two: by the late 1980s both contemporary art and critical theory were welcomed by the very academy that had long shunned them. Meanwhile, on the social-historical side, the mandate was "Always historicize!," the stirring call with which Fredric Jameson opened his *The Political Unconscious: Narrative as a Socially Symbolic Act* in 1981. How we define that operation, though, makes all the difference. Citing the intellectual historian Sande Cohen, Singerman argued that "the language on art" works "to *historicize* or make contemporary art 'historically significant,'" and "*to historicize is to academicize*."[18] In my view this is to confuse historicizing with historicism. Whereas historicism is a causal account of cultural practices in terms of chains of influence (which can be readily taught), historicizing is a coming to terms with the preconditions of art in order to articulate its inciting contradictions as well as its structuring concepts (this task is far more difficult both to achieve and to teach). For some critics this coming to terms is a necessary task for artists as well, who are asked to grasp their cultural situation as best they can and to find adequate forms not only to comment on it but also to act in it. In this sense, to criticize is indeed to historicize—guilty as charged!—but then what exactly is the crime?[19]

I am in no position to historicize myself. Hardly an insightful reader of my own work, I advise students not to follow my particular leads but to look to the blind spots in the writing of predecessors that most interests them. That said, let me point to a few basic shifts that have occurred since my earlier volumes of essays. The first, obvious enough, is the change in the valence of appropriation—from a strategy in which images were purloined, from mass media, art history, and elsewhere, in order to question claims about originality and property, to a concern about cultural theft that often insists on representation precisely as original property.[20] Another shift involves framings of the real. In the 1980s much art presented reality as a construction, a view that responded to a society shot through with media spectacle. First proposed in Pop art, this symbolic conception of the real was pervasive by the time of postmodernism. However, with the slashing of welfare and the raging of AIDS in the 1990s, the real came to be positioned less as an effect of representation than as a site of trauma, and the damaged human body was often staged as a figure of a broken body politic. In recent years the terms have shifted again: the mediation of the real is accepted as given, and the point is less to deconstruct it than to reground it. Artifice served to make reality appear actual again, to render the real—after all the derealizations of both new media and political lies—effective as such.[21]

Sometimes one senses a utopian impulse in this project, especially with artists discussed here like Jeremy Deller and Adam Pendleton. This signals yet another shift, from an anti-aesthetic position of a generation ago to a renewed insistence on the beautiful, which now appears almost as a space of hope or at least of refuge from an otherwise oppressive web of traumatic histories.[22] However, this move away from an anti-aesthetic position isn't uncritical, as Deller and Pendleton demonstrate. Ed Atkins and Mungo Thomson also make this point: both artists highlight glitches in our media world, gaps that might loosen us from our status as human programs subject to ceaseless testing and technological reformatting, moments where failure is indeed only human.

This brings us back to my title. I suggested that essays are only attempts, more or less failed. Critics also fail artworks in the sense that they can never provide a definitive reading; this surplus of meaning is yet another attribute that sets art apart from other things in the world.[23] But there's also a way—and this goes back to the call to historicize—in which artists can't help but fail their historical moments as well. Like myth according Claude Lévi-Strauss, art can't resolve the contradictions that prompt it for the simple reason that they exist beyond its ambit.[24] Yet in this very failure these contradictions can be glimpsed nonetheless, and in this flash of historical consciousness failure can count as success. There's a double temporality here. On the one hand, this consciousness usually occurs in retrospect, hence the need for "reckonings." On the other, the failure can serve as a prompt for future work, even further illumination.[25] Try again, fail again, fail better. Or, as Beckett also says, "Nohow on!"

I Some Antecedents

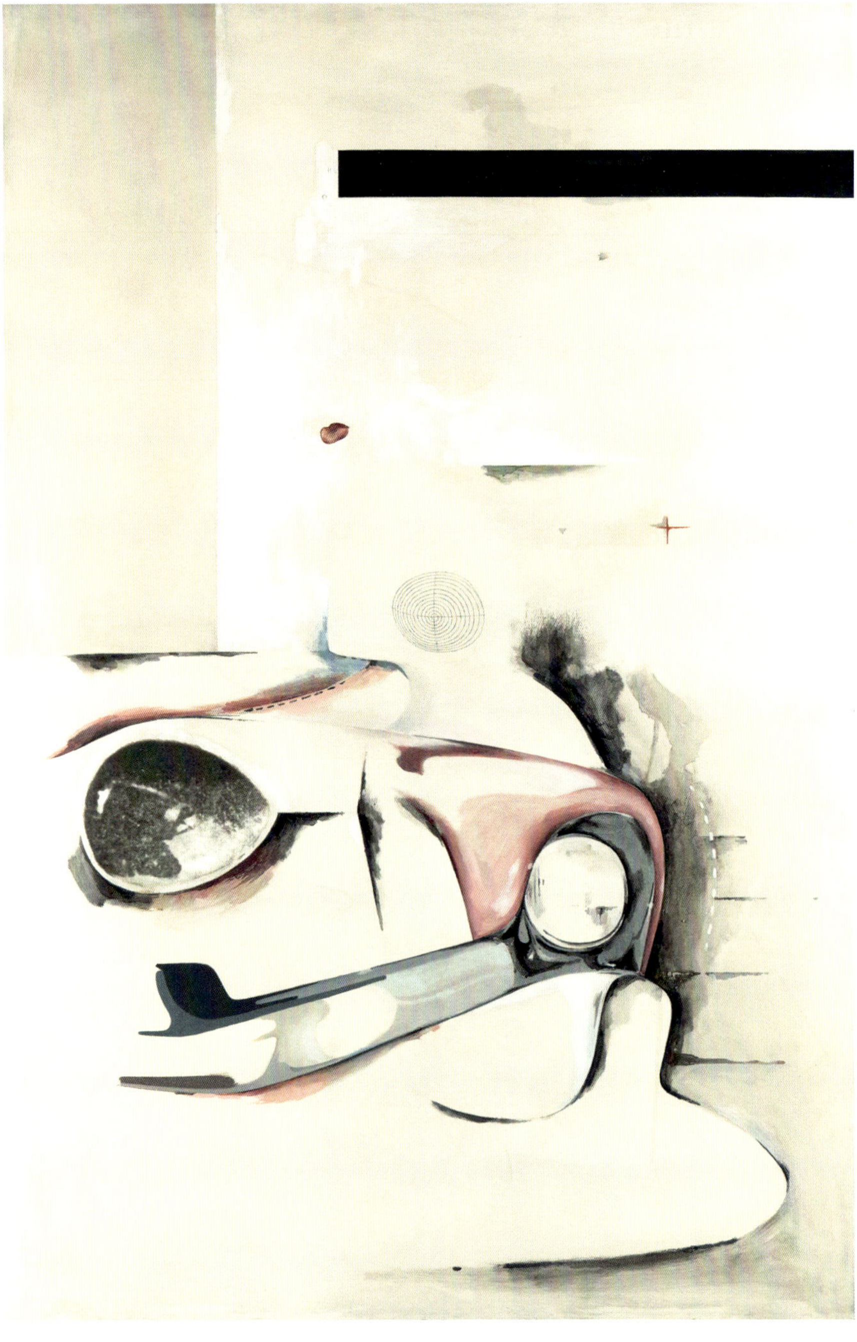

Richard Hamilton, *Hommage à Chrysler Corp.*, 1957. Oil, metal foil, and collage on panel, 48 × 32 inches. Tate. Courtesy Rita Donagh.

1 A Painter of Pop Life

Born in London in 1922, Richard Hamilton talked his way into adult art classes at the age of twelve and entered the Royal Academy of Art at sixteen. However, for all his early training in anatomy and perspective, he was also steeped in modern life: his first memories include riding in sports cars with his chauffeur father and encountering new brands like Pan Yan Pickle at the grocery store. At fifteen, attracted by an abstract facade, Hamilton sought employment at Reimann Studios, an art school cum design company modeled on the Bauhaus, and during World War II he served as a jig and tool draftsman. In short, for Hamilton paintings and products, art and design, were always complements, not opposites, and he always sought ways to fold them together in his work.

Hamilton resumed the Royal Academy in 1946, only to be expelled by a faculty turned reactionary (apparently, he dared to prefer Cézanne to Augustus John). Forced into the army for eighteen months, he read during slack times, Joyce above all, and *Ulysses* became the subject of a first suite of etchings; old media attracted him almost as much as new. "Hamilton was fascinated by the skill, the virtuosity, and the outrageous power of the command of language that gave Joyce the freedom to employ every trick of his trade with a confidence that could absorb parody and pastiche into the poetic flow of words," his biographer tells us. "The question that needed to be asked was, why had such a phenomenal freedom and mixture of styles not appeared in the visual arts?"[1] Hamilton made over a hundred illustrations of *Ulysses* during his lifetime, most of which focused on the "Oxen of the Sun" chapter in which Joyce rehearses the history of English literature in a series of brief imitations. Although Hamilton never completed this project, it supported his burgeoning belief that "the painter need not be committed to a personal style"—a lesson underscored by Marcel Duchamp, his other great inspiration—and that "fragments of image" could be "freely quoted" in a single work. It also announced his commitment to print-making, which Hamilton developed in a recursive relay with painting. ("There is often an interrelationship between a print and a painting for which it serves as a study, or even a copy," his biographer writes, "but occasionally a subject is so firmly bound to the medium of print that it sits in isolation.") Finally, the *Ulysses* project led to his first curatorial effort, a gathering of Joyce materials, in which

Hamilton included some of his etchings, at the new Institute of Contemporary Art (ICA) in 1950, for which he also designed the poster and the catalogue (this too became his customary practice). Hamilton soon treated the exhibition as an art form in its own right, as did other colleagues in the Independent Group (IG), which began to gather at the ICA two years later.

In 1949, in a final foray into formal study, Hamilton entered the Slade School of Art, where he met Eduardo Paolozzi and Nigel Henderson, who joined him in the IG. Hamilton was especially fond of Henderson, whom he found "well educated, quick-witted and street wise, on friendly terms with just about everyone worth knowing in the art world of London, and blessed with a generosity of spirit that he showed by sharing his privileged status with charm and good humour." The son of Wyn Henderson, who oversaw the Guggenheim Jeune Gallery, Henderson introduced Hamilton to Roland Penrose and Lee Miller, an artist power-couple who both supported the IG and exposed Hamilton to Duchamp—most importantly, to *The Green Box*, the book of notes that detail the making of *The Bride Stripped Bare by Her Bachelors, Even* (1915–1923), aka *The Large Glass*. At this time, too, together with Paolozzi and Henderson, Hamilton began to haunt natural history museums, to comb through glossy American magazines, and to look through science publications, all in a search for sources for individual pictures as well as entire shows.

Exhibition-making was central to the IG, especially shows devoted to natural and technological worlds—an enterprise that can be seen as a preemptive counter to the famous "two cultures" thesis about the postwar divide that had opened between the sciences and the arts, as argued by the novelist and chemist C. P. Snow in 1959.[2] In these exhibitions, both staged at the ICA, two treatises were most important to Hamilton: *On Growth and Form* (1917) by the Scottish polymath D'Arcy Thompson, which inspired Hamilton to curate a 1951 display of various images of natural morphologies (he even borrowed the title), and *Mechanization Takes Command* (1948) by the Swiss architectural critic Sigfried Giedion, which prompted Hamilton to undertake a 1955 survey of disparate pictures of human-mechanical hybrids on the ground, in the air, and below the sea (*Man, Machine & Motion*). Such motifs soon appeared in his own work as well: Hamilton produced paintings dotted with organisms like sea urchins drawn from Thompson, and prints devoted to machines like reapers found in Giedion. Hamilton believed, moreover, that the "rigorous causality" evidenced in the evolution of organic and mechanical forms "might be applied to the vagaries of art," that is, that this causality might be used to motivate the pictorial image in new ways. Even as Hamilton acknowledged the breakdown of academic figuration, he couldn't accept the limitations of pure abstraction. A third text,

The Perception of the Visual World (1950) by the American psychologist James J. Gibson, "a study of how motion affects a viewer in a three-dimensional space," also played an important role in his art-making (Duchamp was interested in such questions too). During this period Hamilton spent many hours on the train from London to Newcastle where artist and writer Lawrence Gowing had hired him to teach; this helped Hamilton pay the bills that his art couldn't yet cover. (At this point he had two young children with his wife Terry O'Reilly, who died in a car accident in 1962.)

1956 was a watershed year for Hamilton. The celebrated exhibition *This Is Tomorrow* appeared at the Whitechapel Gallery in London in the summer, and though it wasn't strictly an IG event, it presented the concerns of the group clearly enough. The Brutalist wing of the IG was represented by the team of Paolozzi, Henderson, and the architects Peter and Alison Smithson, who together littered a bare shed on a rough patio with symbolic relics. It looked as though it were "excavated after the atomic holocaust," the architectural critic Reyner Banham, who was also a key IG member, remarked.[3] On the proto-Pop side of the IG were Hamilton, John McHale, and the architect John Voelcker, who contrived a fairground funhouse on the theme of the new sensorium produced by mass media. Among other images and objects, it featured a sci-fi robot, a juke box, "a life-size cut-out figure of Marilyn Monroe in the legendary scene from the film *The Seven Year Itch* in which her dress is blown by the draught from a subway vent," and "a giant papier-mâché bottle of Guinness." The most consequential work associated with the show was also the smallest, the collage *Just What Is It That Makes Today's Homes So Different, So Appealing?*, which Hamilton produced for the catalogue, with the help of his wife Terry and fellow artist Magda Cordell, out of pictures cut from American magazines such as *Life*, *Look*, *Good Housekeeping*, and *Scientific American*. In this tiny tour de force, whose title is a trimming from a full-page advertisement for linoleum that provided the interior setting of the image, a body-building Adam and a hair-perming Eve preside over a paradise of consumer products and mass entertainments. One of the iconic pictures of twentieth-century art, it summed up what "Pop" meant even before the term was in circulation.

This Is Tomorrow marked the end of the IG, but its dissolution allowed Hamilton to focus on his own art-making, and his "tabular pictures," in which "fragments of image" are indeed "freely quoted," soon followed. "1956 was a vintage year for the great names of the American automobile industry," and *Hommage à Chrysler Corp.*, a smooth commingling of curvaceous car and body parts, was his first riff on a new type of commercial styling that spiked commodity fetishism with sexual fetishism. Here, almost literally, "the dream car of the Fifties grew breasts and was judged on its rear end." While *Hommage* presents a luxury product gendered female from the outside, *Hers Is a Lush Situation* (1958)—the title is another line from an advertisement—imagines what it might feel like to drive alongside Elizabeth Taylor in midtown Manhattan (the windshield is a picture of the United Nations Building turned on its side). Hamilton produced a few more semifigurative combinations of sexy commodities and commodified women in a concerted attempt "to capture those moments when the eyes, as in a swoon, lose control." Although he viewed his tabular paintings "as a demonstration of support for feminism," he acknowledged that "feminists were not amused." He also thought that these pictures were more "ingenuous" than ironic: "It looks as though the painting is a sardonic comment on our society. But I would like to think of my purpose as a search for what is epic in everyday objects and everyday attitudes." Here Hamilton aligns his project with "the painting of modern life" according to Baudelaire, whose famous line—"By 'modernity' I mean the ephemeral, the fugitive, the contingent, the half of art whose other half is the eternal and the immutable"—Hamilton updated as his own pictorial credo.[4] Like Paolozzi and McHale, he felt that art had to produce new "archetypes," to reclaim this traditional function from mass culture, or at least to adapt what was already proposed in mass culture for the purposes of art.

The tabular pictures project a theater of heterosexual male desire in which, as in Duchamp, the bride is stripped by her bachelors but never possessed by them. In this way the tabular pictures are an indirect reflection on *The Large Glass*, which preoccupied Hamilton at this time. He devoted no less than three years to the complex task of transliterating *The Green Box* of notes for the *Glass*, which was a key contribution to the frantic reception of Duchamp in the 1960s, and this study confirmed not only his belief in the impersonality of the artist but also his model of the artwork as a "pictorial essay" that the viewer must puzzle out. Well into his eighties Hamilton referred to Duchamp as his "mentor," despite the fact that he veered away from this example often enough. For example, though Hamilton also valued artistic detachment, his hand was "very active in execution," and though he too adopted a cerebral approach, his forte was "retinal" painting, which Duchamp famously eschewed. At the same time they shared an ambiguous attitude toward both fine art and popular culture, which Duchamp termed an "ironism of affirmation" and Hamilton glossed as a "peculiar mixture of reverence and cynicism."[5] The close association of the two artists had other outcomes as well. In 1963 Hamilton accompanied Duchamp to the first retrospective of his work in Pasadena, California, a landmark event where Hamilton met fellow Pop practitioners Andy Warhol and Claes Oldenburg (who became a good friend). And in 1966 Hamilton collaborated on another Duchamp survey at the Tate Gallery, the centerpiece of which was his own painstaking reconstruction of *The Large Glass* (the fragile original, long since shattered, couldn't travel from the Philadelphia Museum of Art).

For a time after his American sojourn Hamilton shifted from passive female figures to active male subjects. In *Towards a Definitive Statement on the Coming Trends in Men's Wear and Accessories* (1963)—another tagline from a magazine, in this case *Playboy*—he reviewed the "different realms" of "space, sport [and] virility," with four pictures of astronaut John Glenn, an American football player, a track and field athlete, and President John Kennedy. What does it mean, this series implicitly asks, that such men are seen as role models? Do they count as sex objects too? (That is, can the lines of identification and desire cross, and, and if so, to what effect?) Next Hamilton moved from individual figures to crowd scenes, as in *Whitley Bay* (1965) and *Trafalgar Square* (1965–1967), both based on enlarged postcards with color overlays and paint daubs added to suggest tentative groupings. The paintings reprise a question that dates to Impressionism: How has modern leisure affected traditional genres like landscapes and urban scenes? And they point to a Pop query as well: Is class consciousness now overwhelmed by mass culture? In one painting, titled simply *People* (1965–1966), the source image is "magnified to a stage where the medium is no longer able to carry the image." Like the Antonioni film *Blow-Up*, which it predates by a few months, *People* questions the truth value of photographic representation in a way that theorists like Roland Barthes had only begun to do.[6]

Hamilton mostly stuck with "classic subjects for art" such as "the interior, the nude, landscape, seascape, still-life, portrait, flower-piece, and mother and child," but he always filtered them through popular forms like advertisements, movies, postcards, and commercial design. How is still life altered by the inclusion of industrial products? How has fashion photography affected the conventions of the nude? In the 1970s this most anal of artists indulged in a "scatological period," dropping images of "gigantic turds" at the bottom of kitschy floral arrangements and resplendent sunsets. If these blobby shapes are playful swipes at the sculpture of Hans Arp and Henry Moore, they also seem to parody the notion that our first painting is our infantile smearing of shit, a psychoanalytic cliché that, thanks to Piero Manzoni and others, had become an avant-garde one as well. Often this collision of high and low realms was a matter of appropriation along the lines of what Duchamp called the "assisted readymade." In *Still-life* (1965) Hamilton took a photograph of an electric mini-oven from a Braun brochure and simply anglicized the brand name to "Brown." In *Toaster* (1966–1967) he claimed another Braun product, added a wash of color, and rechristened it a "Hamilton." In a similar vein he remade a Ricard

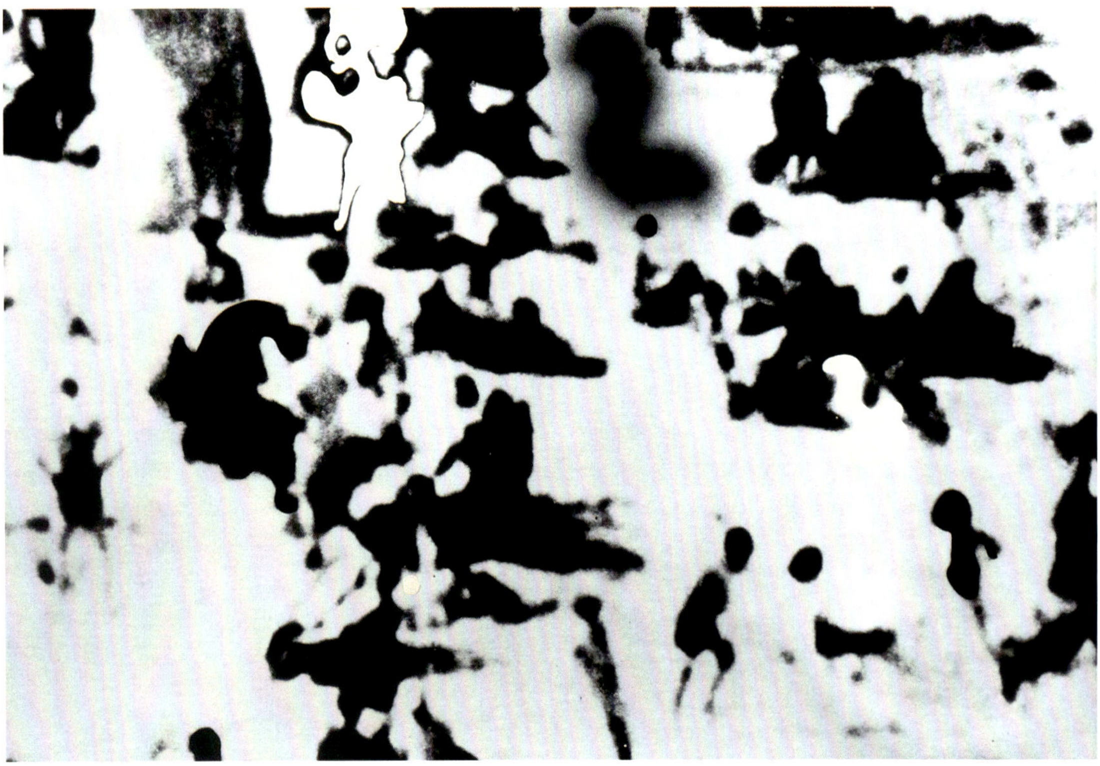

Richard Hamilton, *People*, 1965–1966. Oil and cellulose on photograph on panel, 32 × 48 inches. Courtesy Rita Donagh.

carafe, ashtray, and enamel sign, turning them into "Richards" with the addition of a letter.

This genre of "art as consumer product," which Hamilton celebrated, could also be a complicated affair. His *Lux 50* (1979) is "a two-dimensional image of a radio with components that could function well acoustically and also perform silently as a depiction of itself." On such occasions "he approached an aesthetic problem with recourse to his experience as an engineer." In the mid 1960s Hamilton struggled to transform a favorite advertisement depicting the development of an automobile tire from 1902 to 1950 into an exact perspectival diagram; it took an early computer to complete the task. During the same years he executed a "building portrait" of the great spiral of the Guggenheim Museum in six fiberglass reliefs fabricated with the help of a car part company (five were spray-painted like hoods, but one was gold-leafed like an icon). Always a quick adopter of advanced equipment, Hamilton asked fellow artists to take his picture with the recently released Polaroid. The result, *Polaroid Portraits* (1968–2001), consisted of 128 photographs that "spanned the history" not only of this "instant camera" but also of three decades of his own appearance. He was an early user of computer programs, too, and after 1987 all his "prints and paintings utilized, in a variety of ways, digital image processing equipment."

Throughout his career Hamilton proceeded by way of polarities, a "stratagem of dichotomy" that he also credited to Duchamp, but his purpose was to demonstrate how oppositions such as the epic and the everyday, traditional genres and popular forms, and art and technology were more apparent than real. Hamilton even attempted to ease a contradiction that lay deep in the historical avant-garde, the one between the anti-institutional impulse of Dada and the constructive pedagogy of the Bauhaus. (Apart from Duchamp, Hamilton advocated for Kurt Schwitters, whose Merzbarn in the Lake District he helped to save, and he had close ties to the Bauhausian Hochschule für Gestaltung in Ulm, Germany.) By the same token his practice was animated by such contradictions. For example, for all his intensive work in the studio Hamilton was also responsive to political events in the world, which he addressed from his 1964 portrait of Labour Party leader Hugh Gaitskell as a movie monster, through his iconic image of a fallen student murdered by the National Guard at Kent State in 1970, and on to his extraordinary pictures concerning the Troubles in Northern Ireland in the 1980s, which were influenced by the commitments of his second wife Rita Donagh, an important artist in her own right. This last suite of images—of a hunger striker, an old Orangeman, and a young soldier—counts as contemporary history painting on par with the representations of the Baader-Meinhof gang produced by Gerhard Richter during the same years. In a very late painting

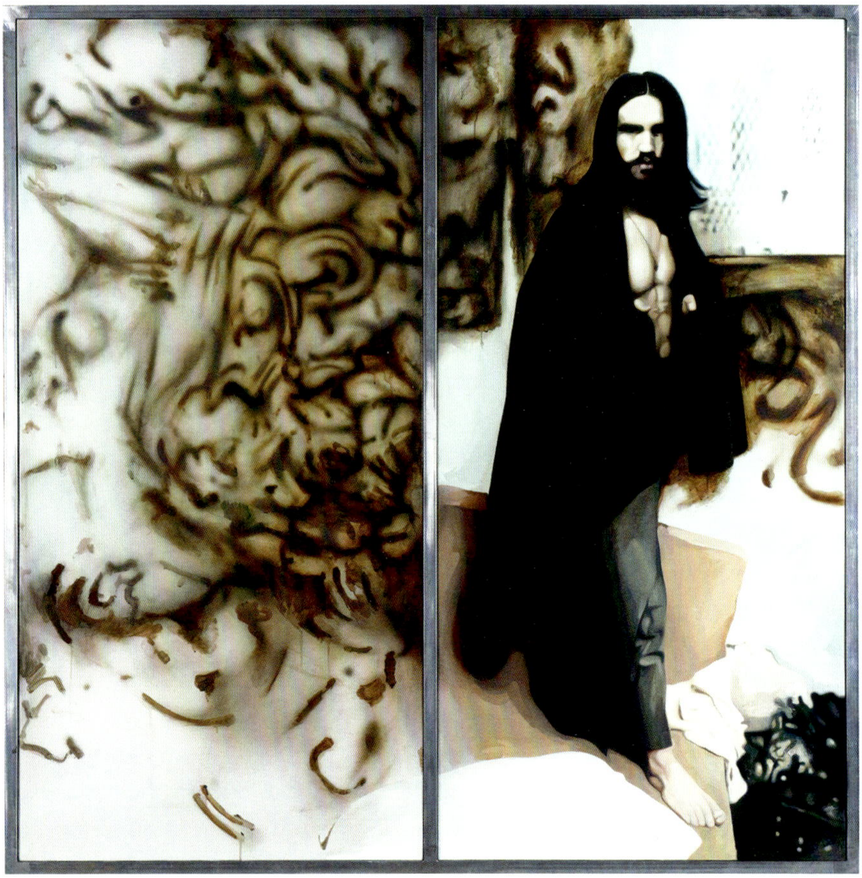

Richard Hamilton, *The citizen*, 1982–1983. Oil on canvas, two panels, each 78¾ × 39½ inches. Tate. Courtesy Rita Donagh.

Hamilton presented Tony Blair as a Wild West cowboy, and he left a project concerning the Occupied Territories in the Middle East unfinished at his death.

In the end Hamilton was animated by this tension above all: even as he embraced the postwar world of spectacle, he aimed to "open up an apparently seamless media image or event to analysis through a variety of print media and painting techniques"; that is, he sought to deconstruct the pictorial construction of such images and events. Neither reverence nor cynicism, then, neither complicity nor critique, but both at the same time. This tension points to a further one between his investigation of many media and his privileging of painting above all, between his eclectic imagery and his singular style, between his career understood as a "succession of projects" and his process given over to self-critical revision. Against all expectations, Hamilton positioned painting not as an outmoded medium but as an ever-new meta-art that could, at once, carry forward precious devices like perspective, raid mass culture for myth-making subject matter, and—because of its static nature, not in spite of it—reflect critically on photography, film, digital images, and other new media. "I've always been an old style artist," Hamilton acknowledged in 1969, "a fine artist in the commonly accepted sense: that was my student training and that's what I've remained." Strange words for a founder of Pop, but true enough.

Then there is his writing. Hamilton authored as well as designed many of his catalogues, and his *Collected Words* (1982) remains the best study of his work to that point in his career. He revised and reused his texts as much as he did his pictures. Hamilton once called them "a poetic parody, a pastiche that attempts to match with words what he had struggled to create visually with paint, collage and photography." To this end, like his friend Reyner Banham, Hamilton produced a distinctive kind of Pop prose, which, even as it resembled the "gonzo journalism" of Hunter S. Thompson, Tom Wolfe, and others, also recalled the rambunctious mix-and-match of images and ideas in the IG, with a lingo that is excessively mimetic of a brash commodity-scape of bright but broken surfaces. In this light Hamilton and Banham were madder men than any copywriters on Madison Avenue of the time.

Hamilton titled his final text *Introspective*, which was edited by one Phillip Spectre. Spectre was in fact an alter ego that permitted Hamilton to write his memoir in the third person. (He once told me that his initial title for the book was *Autofaction*, a nice anticipation of recent autofiction.) This double is also a final nod to Duchamp, who created his female alter ego, Rrose Sélavy, to open a little more space for the staging of his art. Along these lines what might "Phillip Spectre" connote? I doubt Hamilton meant it as an homage to Phil Spector, the record producer turned convicted murderer, though they both liked to lay down complicated tracks in the studio, and this allusion wouldn't be beyond his wicked sense of humor. Maybe Hamilton intended the name to conjure up a "spectre-phile," a lover of ghosts, for there are many spectral figures that float through his work. Certainly, it is like him not only to write his own biography (he was a control freak to the end) but also to haunt his afterlife in this way (modest though Hamilton was, he was confident of his place in art history). The final pages of *Introspective* are indeed spectral: the text breaks off in the 1990s, even as the images run on till his death in 2011. As Duchamp said of *The Large Glass* after it was accidentally cracked, *Introspective* is "definitively unfinished," and there is real pathos in these blank spreads. But then, restless as Hamilton always was, I can imagine him even now tinkering with his *Ulysses* prints, retouching his tabular pictures, seeking out new titles for pieces on websites, trying out the latest computer, or revising this very memoir in that weirdly welcoming bardo that is his art history.

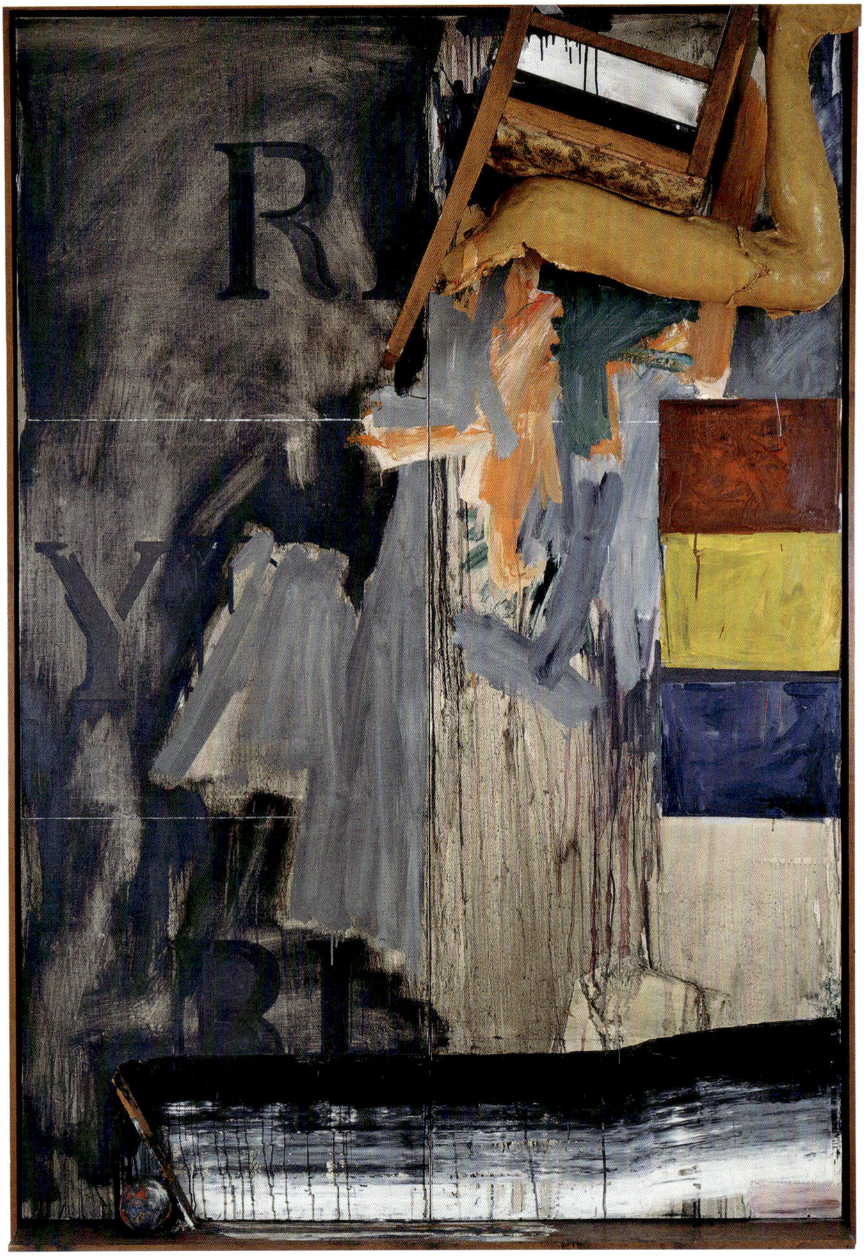

Jasper Johns, *The Watchman*, 1964. Oil on canvas with objects, two panels, 85 × 60¼ inches overall. Broad Museum. © Jasper Johns / Artists Rights Society (ARS).

2 Watchman and Spy

In summer 1953, after a short stint in the army, Jasper Johns moved back to New York; he was twenty-three years old. There, several months on, he met Robert Rauschenberg, with whom he would partner, artistically and romantically, until 1961. He soon befriended composer John Cage and choreographer Merce Cunningham as well, and in this heady company Johns decided, in fall 1954, to destroy all his prior work. He then began the paintings that made his name when they were shown four years later—flags, targets, and numbers crafted in encaustic (pigment mixed in hot wax) with collage (often simply newspaper) on canvas. Johns added alphabets to this repertoire of everyday motifs and, a little later, maps (this last idea came from Rauschenberg). Told that their art was "Neo-Dada," Johns and Rauschenberg traveled to the Philadelphia Museum of Art sometime in 1957 to see its great holdings of Marcel Duchamp, who became an avuncular touchstone for both artists. That the museum also has superb Cézannes wasn't lost on Johns.[1]

Johns made an exceptional entrance with his first show in early 1958. Staged at the new Leo Castelli Gallery, it nearly sold out, with no fewer than four paintings purchased by the Museum of Modern Art, and the unknown artist also appeared on the cover of *ARTnews*. Johns had sized up the New York art world precisely, dominated as it then was by the formalist model of "modernist painting" developed by Clement Greenberg to champion Abstract Expressionism, and deftly deflected its discourse toward what Leo Steinberg would soon term "other criteria." "The subjects which Jasper Johns chose to paint up to 1958," Steinberg wrote in "Jasper Johns: The First Seven Years" (1962), the most influential essay on the artist, "have these points in common":

1. Whether objects of signs, they are man-made things.
2. All are commonplaces of our environment.
3. All possess a ritual or conventional shape, not to be altered.
4. They are either whole entities or complete systems.
5. They tend to prescribe the picture's shape and dimensions.
6. They are flat.
7. They tend to be non-hierarchic, permitting Johns to maintain a pictorial field of leveled equality, without points of stress or privilege.
8. They are associable with sufferance rather than action.[2]

The 1958 show had the force of a brilliant blague: do what modernist painting aimed to do—be at once complete as compositions and flat as objects—and do so with apparent ease, with everyday motifs ready to hand. In effect, after the grand rhetoric of Abstract Expressionism, Johns reintroduced banality into modernist art in the double sense of the word—emphatically common and heretofore banned. A few years later Roy Lichtenstein and Andy Warhol pushed such banality further with borrowings from cartoons and comics, and, along with Rauschenberg, Johns was soon slotted in as a transitional figure between Abstract Expressionism and Pop, an art-historical positioning that always irked him, as though his work could be reduced to a formula of modernist painting combined with its Dadaist opposite, or a recipe of the pigment of Cézanne (or, more proximately, Willem de Kooning) mixed with the wax of Duchamp.

For some critics this turning of serial things into singular paintings was a conservative move, a win for high culture over low. And in 1960, when Johns first made exquisite replicas in painted bronze of trashy things like two Ballantine ale cans or a Savarin coffee jar stuffed with paint brushes, the radicality of the readymade also appeared to be recouped. In his view, however, Johns had simply followed his breakthrough work according to a logic of inversion, which became a signature strategy. "If the painting is an object" like a target, he told the curator Walter Hopps in 1964, "then the object," such as an ale can, "can be a painting," and mundane things can be added to paintings as pictorial elements too. Johns seemed to relish rendering utilitarian items—a drawer, a spoon, a hanger—not only useless but also homeless. "I thought how then to make an object which is not so easily defined as an object," Johns continued, "and how to add space and still keep it an object painting." Sometimes his means were simple, a tin cup or an old ruler attached to a canvas, and sometimes they were complicated, spatial bursts of bright hues stenciled with the names of those colors but in ways that rarely match up. Such developments closed out the first decade of his work, one of the most consequential in the career of any twentieth-century artist.

In the Steinberg catechism on Johns the attitude of sufferance is as important as the use of the commonplace, for it suggests a shift in artistic voice—from the active to the passive, from painting as an arena of existential self-expression (the alternative account of Abstract Expressionism put forward by Harold Rosenberg) to painting as a surface where external signs are impressed. Whereas Rauschenberg played "in the gap" between art and life, a famous motto that suited his rambunctious personality, the taciturn Johns waited for the world to come on to him, commenting obliquely on its particular effects.[3] His encaustic medium was essential here, since it allowed him to suspend his brushstroke, almost to freeze his gesture—a distinctive mark that is another of his innovations—in a way that registers touch but not subjectivity. "I found I couldn't do anything that would be identical with my feelings," as an Abstract Expressionist might. "So I worked in such a way that I could say that it's not me." Put more emphatically: "My work became a constant negation of impulses."

Some commentators ascribe this turn to the negative—in 1961 Johns made austere works with titles like *No*, *Disappearance*, and *Liar*, and his palette darkened to a deep gray—to his breakup with Rauschenberg, a reading that befits our melancholic and memoir-hungry times.[4] Yet the early paintings had already shown a blank face. One well-known target from 1955 is topped by a row of plaster casts of heads cut off at the eyes that are stonier than any death mask. From the beginning, then, Johns was deadpan, the Buster Keaton of postwar art (like Duchamp, he even resembled the silent comedian a little). The demeanor of art and artist alike is blasé—the term that Georg Simmel used long ago to describe the defensive posture of "the metropolitan type" against the shocks of the modern world. Johns extended this blank suspension to his conception of the picture. Duchamp called his *Bride Stripped Bare by Her Bachelors, Even* (1915–1923) a "delay in glass," a field of frustrated desire.[5] Johns, who owned a copy of *The Green Box*, the book of notes that Duchamp assembled for *The Large Glass*, presented his paintings as delays in wax, so many screens where different motifs could be held fast so as to test our responses (or lack thereof). If his voice is mostly passive, his verbs are largely intransitive; *Arrive/Depart* is a typical title.

In a studied phrase Johns spoke of his position as one of "shunning statement." This suggests an aversion to polemics, political as well as artistic, that goes beyond temperament, a fatigue with the heated ideologies of the period (the Korean conflict, the McCarthy hearings, the Cold War). And Johns did muffle his subjects along with his gestures; for example, his large *White Flag* (1955) is literally whited out. Might this intimate a "painting degree zero" in line with the "writing degree zero" that Roland Barthes posed against Sartrean commitment in these same years?[6] "I can't imagine my work being used to accomplish anything socially," Johns averred. This is less an act of negation than a posture of neutrality à la Barthes, for whom "the neutral" was a way to baffle conceptual binaries, to undo ideological oppositions, to mess with "the paradigm."[7] This baffling might also pertain to the guarded language of a gay artist like Johns in a straight (art) world.[8] More generally, the baffling points to an obstructed agency pervasive in the Eisenhower era; "shunning statement" is about feeling stuck historically, not moving forward. And yet, then as now, American flags and maps (not to mention targets) are hardly neutral, even or especially for Johns, who was born in the South and named after a Revolutionary

War hero said to have rescued a flag during a battle. Immediately after Barthes published *Writing Degree Zero* (1953), he began to write the critical essays about everyday life collected in *Mythologies* (1957). Is there a hint of ideology critique in Johns too, who, after all, did witness the rise of both the civil rights movement and the Vietnam War protests? Certainly, *White Flag* makes a statement of its own today, though whether it was the one intended by Johns in 1955, the year of both the brutal murder of Emmett Till and the bus boycott in Montgomery, Alabama, is not entirely clear—another point of ambiguity in a practice riddled with the same.

In 1959, along with stenciled words, Johns introduced different devices to produce his marks. "Find ways to apply/make paint with simple movements of objects—the hand, a board, feather, string, sponge, rag, shaped tools, comb (and move the canvas against paint-smeared objects)." Once again he credited this strategy to Duchamp, who "assimilated process itself into his work." Rotating a ruler in paint around its own axis, as in *Device Circle* (1959), appears simple enough—his new method seems as self-evident as his early motifs—but it too is more complicated than it looks. "What seems literal can twist," Johns warned, "or be twisted into something else." Results can be fudged—the arced swath in *Voice* (1964–1967) doesn't quite line up with the ruler attached to the painting. Or they might be faux—the supposed teeth marks in *Painting Bitten by a Man* (1961) are infant-size. With Johns indexical signs are no more reliable as evidence of procedure than as traces of presence. When he stencils "Liar" on a painting and titles it the same, he does so as the Cretan who declares "All Cretans are liars." In short, what seems obvious in Johns rarely is. "This is a flag," we say, but it is not, and for many early viewers it scarcely qualified as a painting either; as Johns attests, "I'm interested in the area [where it] is neither a flag nor a painting." He told Steinberg that he used "things the mind already knows" because "that gave me room to work on other levels," but it's more accurate to say that the mind registers them without understanding them. (In this same spirit Duchamp dubbed Johns the "Sibyl of the targets.")[9] Such "ambivalence"—his term—is deepened with the addition of words. "My work is largely concerned with relations between seeing and knowing, seeing and saying, seeing and believing." By "relations" Johns means "indecisions" (another of his terms): we toggle between these activities without resolution or rest.

"I'm believing painting to be a language," Johns noted in the early 1960s, or, more precisely, a game in which language might be tested. He read Wittgenstein in summer 1961, *Philosophical Investigations* (1953) in particular, but already by 1959 he had let colors and names slip away from each other, and in 1960 he superimposed numbers 0 through 9 to the point of illegibility. With *Fool's*

House (1961–1962), the curator Scott Rothkopf notes, "the support began to act more like a pegboard, covered with assorted objects and explicit references to prior works."[10] And by the time of *According to What* (1964) category mistakes abound: this multi-panel work has no focal point, and it's very difficult to connect its sundry items (an upside-down chair with a plaster cast of a leg, a vertical row of color names in letter blocks, large abstract rectangles both brushy and matte). "According to what" would we correlate them? Johns comes close to Rauschenbergian randomness here, but he risks it in order "to get rid of (destroy) the language value of anything at all." "What is 'red' out of many shades of red, or which 'red' is the real red, this red or that red?," Johns asked rhetorically in 1964. "When we gradually add yellow, exactly how much yellow will turn 'red' into 'orange'?" In short, "red" is "an agreement." Such conventions are "useful and necessary in our daily life," Johns allows. "If we come closer and closer to that 'something' to identify it, however, we will begin to wonder whether that 'something' is really 'something' or not." Along with this dose of Wittgenstein Johns added a touch of René Magritte to his work (he purchased a Magritte painting, *The Interpretation of Dreams*, in 1965). The unwritten caption of every flag painting is *Ceci n'est pas un drapeau.*

"Include one's looking, 'seeing,' using," Johns wrote in 1960. This note captures the great interest of this reflexive art: it makes one aware of observing and thinking, and, more and more, of feeling too, however muffled this feeling might be. This move "to embody a sense of the experience of looking" in painting often produces a split in viewing, which Johns personified in allegorical figures that he called the Watchman and the Spy: "The Watchman falls 'into' the 'trap' of looking," he semi-explains in 1964. "The 'spy' is a different person. . . . The spy must be ready to 'move,' must be aware of his entrances & exits." In effect, the viewer as watchman is invited to become the observer as spy—that is, to become a voyeur of his own viewing like Johns. This is no longer sufferance, or rather his passive demeanor here discloses an aggressive side. Is seeing also a targeting? Are our own mugs implied in *Target with Four Faces*? Is seeing ever free from desire, for good or bad? (Feminist theory has instructed us on this score, but this wasn't a familiar notion then.) Sometimes Johns sounds a sadistic note, as in *Painting Bitten by a Man* or *The Critic Sees* (1961), a pair of glasses in sculp-metal in which a toothy mouth replaces the expected eyes.

This brings us back to the model of the picture that Johns elaborated from Duchamp—and also, it seems, from Freud. "Devise technique to imitate 'magic picture pad'" reads an obscure note from 1970–1971. "There may be the question of resemblance or substitution (Freud)." Here Johns appears to allude to the "mystic writing pad" that Freud used to describe how the unconscious operates, how it retains inscriptions even when they appear to be effaced.[11] Johns also likens the picture to the dream ("a question of resemblance") and to the symptom ("a question of substitution"), which suggests another connection to Surrealism—quite a reversal for an artist who once aimed to suppress all subjectivity. Likely with Magritte in mind, André Breton once offered the image of "a man cut into two by a window" as the paragon of the Surrealist picture.[12] This is close to what Johns presents: a model of painting that is neither window nor mirror, the traditional paradigms of representational art, but a semi-abstract combination of the two in which what is exterior mingles with what is interior, often to the point of obscurity. Some works even intimate invisibility or blindness, as in the murky *Diver* (1962–1963) and *Periscope (Hart Crane)* (1963), both of which are also associated, via the named poet, with watery suicide.

As this art looks at itself, it folds on itself; it develops by recursion, by "repetition and recombination."[13] Johns first juxtaposes motifs within a painting, then often transposes them from picture to picture and medium to medium. This doubling is intrinsic to printing, which long occupied him, but it is active, from the beginning, in his objects (the double ales) and his paintings (the double flags), as well as intrinsically from his early stenciling to his later silkscreening. Johns also plays on the bilateral symmetry of our bodies, mirroring it with paintings divided into left and right halves. Often, too, he uses actual seams, on either the horizontal or the vertical axis, as formal hinges between disjunct panels, which become more complex with the polyptychs of the mid 1960s onward.

Motifs are also mirrored, as well as rotated and inverted, in the flagstone and crosshatch paintings, begun in 1967 and 1972 respectively. The result of accidental sightings—a patch of wall spotted in Harlem, a pattern on a car glimpsed on a highway—these series involve found images but also foreground traditional devices. The flagstone shapes, in red, black, and white, are glossy in a way that lifts them slightly above the dirty white seams that mimic the cement that holds actual flagstones together, and the patterns hover between the given and the composed, the readymade and the abstract (they are also neither organic nor geometric, the usual categories of abstraction). These paintings rotate what is flat on the floor to what faces us on the wall, and so render basic orientations ambiguous (Rauschenberg and Warhol played with this oscillation too). Floor tiles, if not flagstones, helped late medieval painters to lock in the orthogonal lines necessary for one-point perspective. This allusion, along with others, is active in *Harlem Light* (1967), which juxtaposes, across panels from left to right, a flagstone square, a black-and-white area with an attached ruler, an abstract painting of three stacked rectangles, and a diagrammatic window. The crosshatch paintings, which preoccupied Johns for a decade, center a key device of pictorial illusion, the sign of shadow that gives shape to objects and figures. Here, though, what is often unseen is made blatant, what is usually colorless becomes colorful, and what evokes depth is flattened. The touch is varied, but just as the encaustic suspends gesture, the crosshatch appears semiautomatic. As with the flagstones, we struggle to work out the system that governs color and arrangement—is there one? An untitled triptych from 1972 is an early summa of the two devices with another one thrown in: it presents, from left to right, four panels, one in crosshatch, two in flagstone, and one in wood on which thin planks are nailed askew and cast body parts are attached. Depth, perspective, and figuration are broken up in sequence. The body-part section might suggest that any stretched canvas is already a kind of crucifixion. (If so, this one has gone badly awry.)

"One of the most interesting things one can do is use something in a variety of adaptations," Johns commented in 1978, "and then ask the question 'what does it mean?'" At times, though, this isn't so interesting: the iterative becomes repetitive, the recursive turns hermetic, and as Johns shifts from "commonplaces of our environment" to self-citations in his studio ("studio" crops up in titles from 1964 on), the work gets fussy in its fragments and tasteful in its arrangements. At least for me it becomes involuted. In the process Johns sometimes loses his connection to viewers; there is little address to the world, as there is always in Rauschenberg and Warhol (even if with them it often comes via references to our shared experience of urban junk and capitalist glitter). Here "sufferance" takes on the note of arrogance also buried in the word: Johns suffers the world to come on to him. There is a hint of a crown already in the Savarin can, but it also calls up a fool's cap, and early on Johns was both king and pawn of a New York art world revved up by a new market. (He knew it too: the bronze Ballantines were said to be provoked by a remark from de Kooning that Leo Castelli could sell anything, even two beer cans.) In short, painting as a rebus has its downside: the telling of dreams, let alone symptoms, can be tedious; it's one thing for an artist to ask us to be spies of our own seeing, another to be analysts of the neuroses of others. Are we supposed to "unpuzzle" Johns, to parse his semiprivate iconography, simply because he is a great painter? As usual, Johns was aware of the problem. "Avoid the idea of a puzzle" reads a note from 1968; "I try to be *less* enigmatic," he insists in 1977. Yet he persisted with his semi-Freudian riddles and quasi-Wittgensteinian games. (Sometimes literally so: the visual doubles of the rabbit-duck and the urn-face from *Philosophical Investigations* make repeated appearances.) "The *Glass* is a pun on opaque meaning and transparent material," Johns noted of Duchamp. "He presents in literal terms the difficulty of knowing what anything means." Johns does too—but too often.

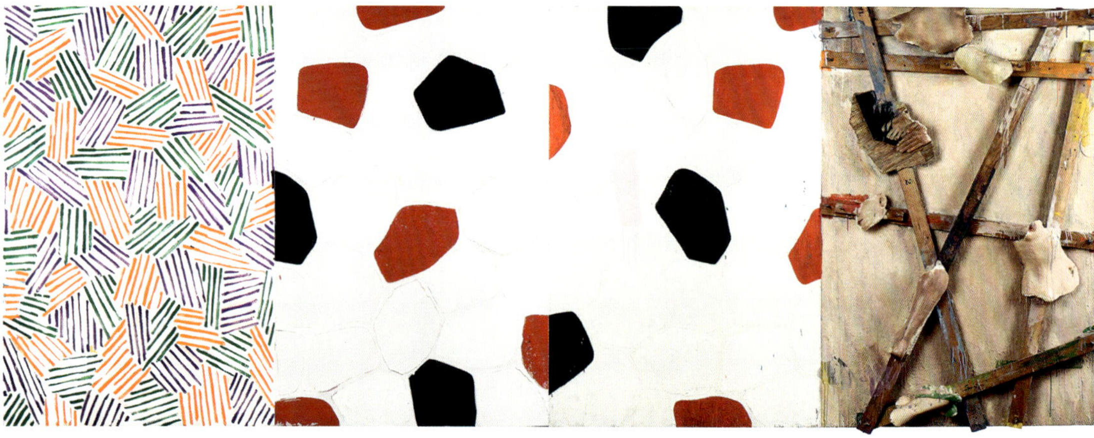

Jasper Johns, *Untitled*, 1972. Oil, encaustic, and collage on canvas with objects, four panels, 6 × 16 feet overall. Museum Ludwig, Cologne. © Jasper Johns / Artists Rights Society (ARS).

Advocates claim enormous range for Johns, but his painting is rather limited in format—primarily portrait and landscape modes, the vertical form of the mirror and the horizontal one of the window, plus assemblages that are partly derived from Rauschenberg. Johns once admitted that he isn't a great colorist, and he's not much interested in sculpture either (again, his objects have a pictorial quality). How then to explain his outsize influence? Johns blazed new paths for other artists, most American but some European (such as Piero Manzoni in Italy and the Nouveaux Réalistes in France). Apart from Pop painters like Warhol, Ed Ruscha, and Vija Celmins, among the indebted are abstract painters such as Frank Stella, Robert Ryman, and Brice Marden; Minimalists like Donald Judd, Dan Flavin, and Robert Morris; Conceptualists such as Sol LeWitt, Dorothea Rockburne, and Mel Bochner; Postminimalists like Richard Serra, Bruce Nauman, and Eva Hesse; and African-American artists such as David Hammons, Glenn Ligon, and Adam Pendleton who play with loaded signs and stenciled texts. Duchamp, Johns wrote, turned art "into a field where language, thought, and vision act upon one another," but that lesson didn't register fully until Johns reinforced it with his own brilliant example.

Perhaps because Johns was so influential early on, he was treated as historical too quickly. (Most of us focus on the early work—I have again here—but there are ample reasons to do so.) Given that he was an art-historical fixture at the age of thirty-five, it's no wonder that he entered his late style prematurely. Can such a style come early, though, and can it be conscious, even calculated, as opposed to the no-holds-barred grappling with art, life, and death that we associate (maybe too romantically) with the notion? There's not much asperity or joy in his work of the last few decades; it has little of the return to fundamentals of the elderly Matisse or the devil-may-care virtuosity of the old Picasso, though Johns alludes to both. Dotted with skulls, skeletons, silhouettes, and stick figures, the paintings are often more morbid than mortal in spirit. (Some paintings include a diagram of a Halloween costume—is Johns having us on here? But then we remember that many of these pieces were produced during the ravages of the AIDS epidemic.) There are exceptions, such as the bracing *Catenary* series, which Johns began in his late sixties. With the odd plank that droops from the support like a loose stretcher bar, or a tenuous thread that sags across the brushy gray expanse of the canvas like a blackboard wiped clean of memory, these paintings convey, without imagistic tricks, the gravity of the aged body and the fragility of all entropic life. But does even a great *Catenary* warrant a subtitle like "I Call to the Grave"? Can an artist celebrated for decades by museum and market alike seriously identify with Job?

On the other hand, Johns did treat loss, and his humor is melancholic, almost from the beginning. A note from 1960–1961 reads, "A DEAD MAN Take a skull cover it with paint rub it against canvas." Perhaps the grave rubbing and the death mask were the secret ur-forms of his pictures and objects all along. Johns acknowledges that some assemblages have the disjunctive composition of the pictorial game known as "the exquisite corpse," and sometimes his work evokes the coffin as well as the crucifix (he quotes the Isenheim Altarpiece by Matthias Grünewald more than once). Two of his most beautiful crosshatch paintings are titled *Corpse and Mirror*, the two sides reflecting each other, and in some languages "cadaver" and "likeness" are indeed the same word. Somehow Johns was able to preserve a gesture in encaustic or to break it up like a fractured cast, that is, to produce marks that seem more dead than alive. For me that's the ultimate puzzle: how Johns could take a medium associated with presence and plenitude and make it signify absence and loss, how he could imbue painting with the mournful temporality that Barthes ascribed only to photography—*this will have been.*

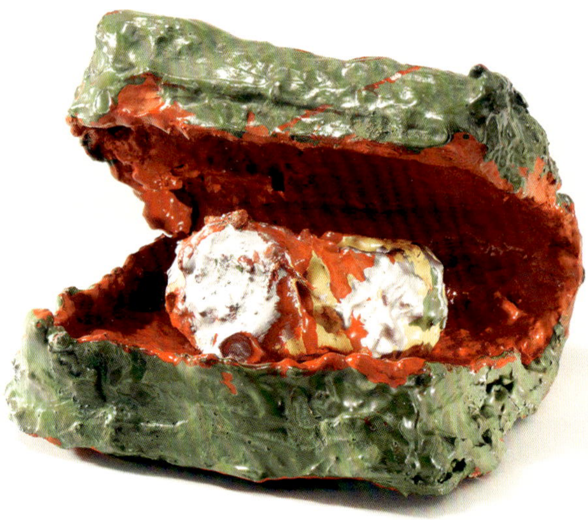

Claes Oldenburg, *Watch in Red Box (in 2 Parts)*, 1961. Muslin soaked in plaster over wire frame, painted with enamel, 5½ × 6½ × 6¼ inches. Photo: Ellen Page Wilson. © Claes Oldenburg. Courtesy Oldenburg van Bruggen Studio.

3 Every Sidewalk Is a Ray Gun Beach

Soon after Claes Oldenburg moved from Chicago to New York in June 1956, the twenty-seven-old wrote this promissory note: "My art strives for a simultaneous presentation of contraries." Among the contraries that animate his two great installations of early objects, *The Street* (1960) and *The Store* (1961–1962), are the found and the handmade, the everyday and the outré, and, above all, the imagistic and the bodily.[1] "These are rips out of reality, perceptions like snapshots, embodiments of glances," the artist remarked of the shirts, cigarettes, cakes, and the like that make up *The Store*, all of which were molded, with the essential assistance of his wife Patty Mucha, into lumpen shapes of muslin, wire, and plaster that were then slopped with bright enamel. And through these "eye-clusters" Oldenburg aimed to present a "formal model for a kind of visual experience," one that involved "fragmentation, simultaneousness, superimposition."[2] This is a mimesis of vision as experienced on the Lower East Side of Manhattan at a time when light industry still mixed with little stores, a mimesis that, even as it tore each "eye-cluster," whether street debris or product display, from its setting, also grounds it both in the materiality of the urban world from which it came and in the corporeality of the individual viewer who snatches it, as it were, with his or her look.[3] "They are shown as fragments (of the field of seeing)," Oldenburg repeated about his objects, and this is how they are presented—as "torn-birth flesh-fragments."[4] Exemplary, in this regard, is *Two Girl's Dresses* (1961), which evokes a sighting of such garments in a store window, but a sighting that seems embodied, almost literally fleshed out (the dresses are white and pink).

If the *Street* and *Store* objects are "embodiments of glances," what kind of body is evoked? "The erotic or the sexual is the root of 'art,' its first impulse," Oldenburg insisted, and, clearly, he wanted to tap that root. At the same time he saw that it was entwined with "fetichistic stuff," an allusion to a fetishism that is both sexual and commercial.[5] According to the art historian Julia Robinson, Oldenburg pits the sexual fetish against the commercial fetish in a way that not only pathologizes commodities but also mimics regression, and he does so in order "to mark out a path back from alienated object relations."[6] I agree with this reading but would inflect it differently. Oldenburg actually compounds the two kinds of fetish, seeking to charge his objects with the "intensity" of both in order to restore a "magic" to materials and things alike.[7] Indeed, two different models fundamental to twentieth-century sculpture, the commodity and the part object, are often combined in his art, and here the fact that the work is crafted is key. In any case, his sculptures don't arrest desire as sexual fetishes usually do. Rather, they remain "constantly elusive," both like and unlike actual objects in the world, which is how Oldenburg wanted them: "It is important to me that a work of art . . . mean many different things to many different people. My work is always on its way between one point and another."[8]

Although his sculptures often have fetishistic associations (this is true of the ray guns above all), the Oldenburg world is finally less phallic than anal, as is the case with other masters of regression, such as Kurt Schwitters before him and Mike Kelley after. "Store is cloaca," Oldenburg once commented, "defecation is passage," and some of his works do appear half-digested, "residual objects" passed through the body. This is especially the case with *Jacket and Shirt Fragment* (1961–1962) with its fecal brown and blood red; *Cash Register* and *Watch in a Red Box (in 2 Parts)* (both 1961) also look as though they were corroded by intestinal acids. The psychoanalyst Ernest Jones once proposed that the prototypical act of art-making is the infantile shaping of shit. Might this be what Oldenburg means by the "first impulse" of art, and what he wishes to reclaim by his "shit view" of aesthetics?[9] "I am for the art of kids' smells," he declaimed in his famous manifesto of 1961. "I am for the art of mama-babble."[10] For Freud this anal zone is one of indistinction—an infant might associate feces with a penis or a baby—and one can only regress there. But might the anal be a site of emergence into difference as well? In this regard Oldenburg treats us less to the collapse of form into formlessness, to the breakdown of language, than to the development of signs from amorphous stuff, from things seen on the street, like a piece of bent metal or scrap wood that might be used to signify a gun or a flag. Or, rather, Oldenburg offers us a range of (a)signifying possibilities. He once described the objects in his *Mouse Museum*, which was begun in 1965 with leftovers from his performances as well as assorted purchases and gifts, as "examples of things that have no form, things that have form, things that are trying for form but dont make it."[11]

There is, then, another tension here, one between the contraries of body and sign, or the material and the semiotic, whereby almost any piece of scrap might become a signifier and vice versa. "I try to have everything equal a 'Ray Gun,'" Oldenburg remarked of this part of his language. "Every sidewalk is a Ray Gun beach."[12] Of course, not everything turns into this one figure; again, that would hardly be "elusive" enough. Rather, Oldenburg is concerned with

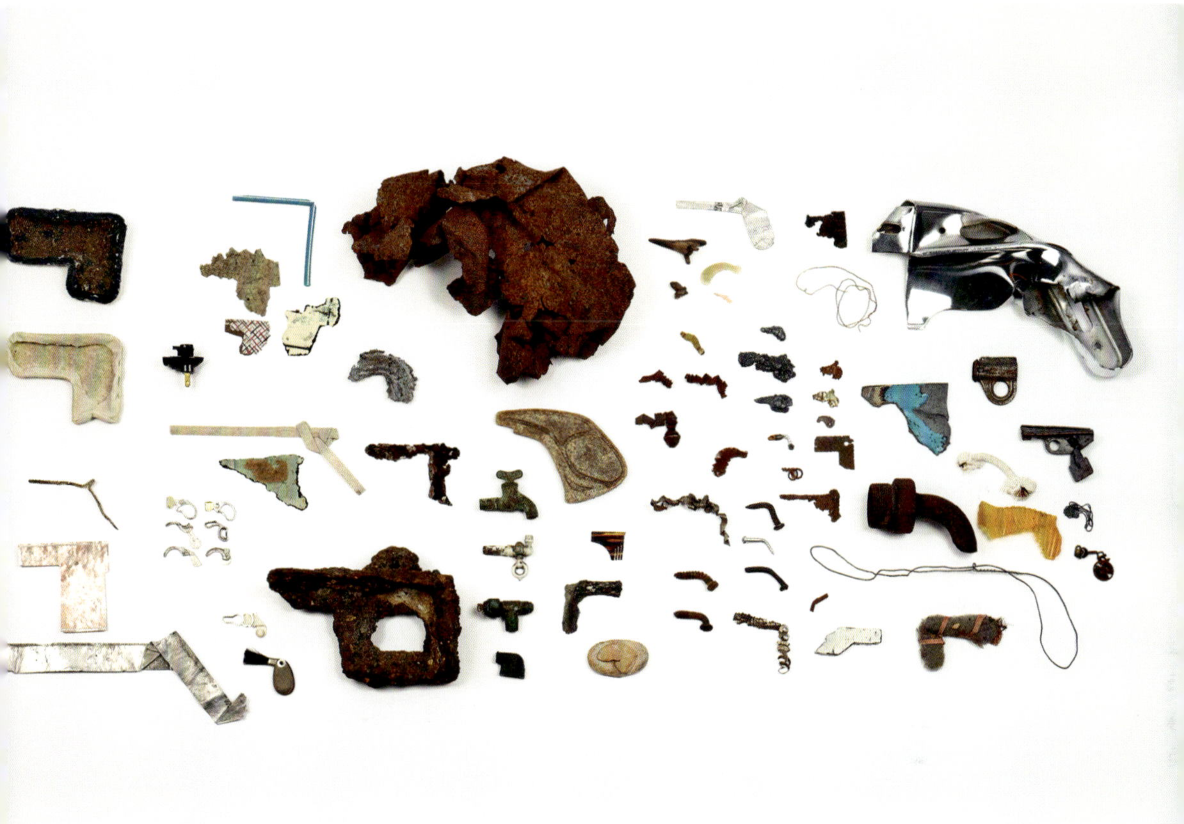

Claes Oldenburg, *Mouse Museum, Ray Gun Wing, Vitrine VI*, 1965–1977. Mixed media, dimensions variable. Museum moderner Kunst, Vienna. Photo: Lisa Rastl and Lena Deinhardstein. © Claes Oldenburg. Courtesy Oldenburg van Bruggen Studio.

the formal-semiotic transit "between one point and another" along a relay of associations, as exemplified in this riff on some of his *Store* objects:

> cock and balls
> cock and balls equals tie and collar
> equals leg and bra equals stars and stripes
> flag equals cigarette package and
> cigarettes
>
> heart equals balls and triangle
> equals (upside down) girdle and stockings
> equals (sidewise) cigarette package equals
> flag.

This free association begins phallically, to be sure, but it quickly opens out to the polymorphously perverse.[13]

The image of a "Ray Gun beach" conjures up Oldenburg as a Robinson Crusoe on the Lower East Side, or, better, a neo-Baudelairean cross between a Beat poet and a Pop artist, strolling through a postwar forest of confused symbols in search of new correspondences in the tacky everyday. At the same time his work calls to mind an even more mythical event—the moment when signification exploded into being. "Language can only have arisen all at once," Claude Lévi-Strauss wrote in an essay on the great sociologist Marcel Mauss (1950). "Things cannot have begun to signify gradually. In the wake of transformation . . . a shift occurred from a stage when nothing had a meaning to another stage when everything had meaning."[14] At this hypothetical origin there was a sudden surplus of signification such that any signifier might float free as "a simple form, or to be more accurate, a symbol in its pure state, therefore liable to take on any symbolic content whatever."[15] According to Lévi-Strauss, such was the case for Mauss with the Polynesian term *mana*. Oldenburg has this *mana* touch; his art is a ray gun of magical transformation.

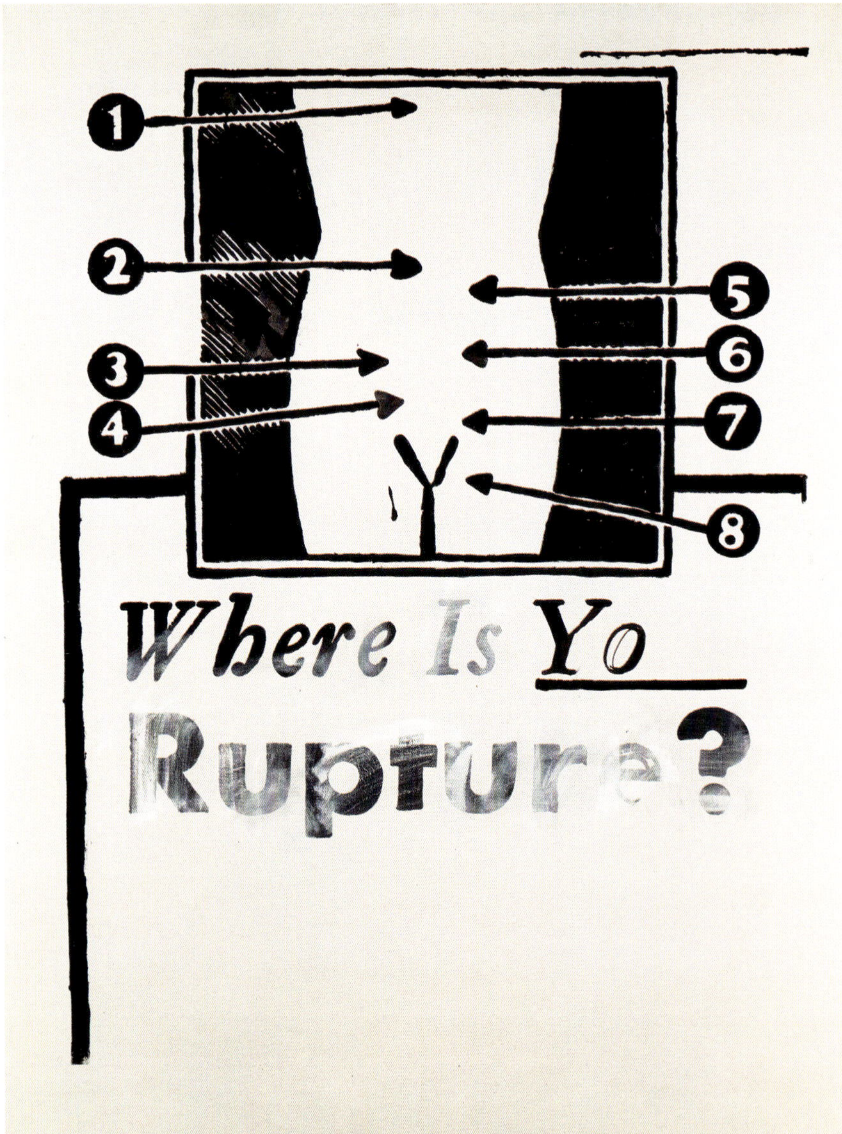

Andy Warhol, *Where Is Your Rupture? [1]*, 1960. Water-based paint on cotton, 69½ × 54 inches.

4 Andy Paperbag

In an influential account Fredric Jameson describes the culture of advanced capitalism in terms of schizophrenia—broken in language, amnesiac about history, in thrall to glossy images, subject to mood swings from speedy euphoria to catatonic withdrawal.[1] No wonder that one exemplar of this culture for Jameson is Andy Warhol. "Warhol distrusted language," Wayne Koestenbaum writes on the first page of his smart biography of the artist; "he didn't understand how grammar unfolded episodically in linear time, rather than in one violent atemporal explosion. Like the rest of us, he advanced chronologically from birth to death; meanwhile, through pictures, he schemed to kill, tease, and rearrange time." Signs of this linguistic disturbance, real or staged, are abundant. There is "virtually no correspondence in his hand"; photographs, audiotapes, and films were his modes of inscription. He couldn't spell to save his life; typographic errors recur in his commercial illustrations of the 1950s (though some were introduced by his mother Julia). And he spoke in a deadpan that extended to the flat tone of his books, which were mostly built up from taped conversations edited by others. All this evidence leads Koestenbaum to his initial diagnosis of Warhol: "Trauma was the motor of his life, and speech the first wound," speech understood here as the medium of "normal" intersubjectivity or reciprocity with the world.

"Trauma" has been a persistent frame of cultural analysis over the last few decades, and it's not new to Warhol studies either.[2] From the colostomy bag of his mother (she had colon cancer) to the brutal scars that tattooed his torso (he was shot, almost fatally, in June 1968), wounds figure literally in Warhol. A 1960 painting, based on a newspaper ad for surgical trusses, asks prophetically "Where is Yo Rupture?," and Warhol always seemed to pick out the telling cracks in images as well as in people, whom he often regarded as another species of image. Metaphorically too, as a breaching of interior and exterior, trauma can be seen as the very operation of his art. "It's just like taking the outside and putting it on the inside," Warhol said early on about Pop, "or taking the inside and putting it on the outside."[3] This elliptical remark might also be understood literally; at one point Koestenbaum interprets his "entire oeuvre as an externalization, crisply distanced and disembodied, of his abject internal circuitry." Or, again, it might be read metaphorically, with his Pop images seen to register the delirious confusions between private and public that first became pronounced in that era, in particular the confusions between the desires and fears of the individual subject and the commodities and celebrities of consumer society, of which Warhol was the great portraitist. In either case he appeared "porous" in a strange, new, near-total way. He was porous in his art, with its steady stream of Pop effluvia (from his early *Campbell's Soup Cans* to his late *Diamond Dust Shoes*). And he was porous in his life, with his studio, dubbed the Factory, set up as an open playground of subcultural denizens and mass-cultural celebs, with superstars of his own making somewhere in between.

At the same time Warhol was the opposite of porous. Especially after his 1968 shooting by Valerie Solanas, a Factory extra who authored the radical *SCUM Manifesto* (1967), he countered his vulnerability with psychological defenses and physical trusses of different sorts—buffering entourages, opaque looks (big glasses, silver wigs), and protective gadgets (omnipresent Polaroid camera and tape recorder). Warhol was also insulated by his weird ability to pass as his own double or simulacrum; even when he was right there in front of you on a New York street, he seemed somehow disembodied or otherwise absent. All his devices became central to his persona, which is sometimes seen as his ultimate work: Warhol as the spectral center of a flashy scene, a kind of blank *Gesamtkunstwerk*-in-person, from the multimedia events of "Exploding Plastic Inevitable" in the mid 1960s to the druggy nightclub world of Studio 54 in the late 1970s. Whereas Marshall McLuhan, a media theorist cum media figure, viewed new technologies as prostheses, Warhol used them as screens. As Koestenbaum notes, the dominant strategy of his Pop was to combine "lurid subject" and "cool presentation," and to translate images from one medium or sphere into another in order to "embalm" them, though this embalming could also infuse his images with a psychic charge, an unexpected *punctum*. Think of the two housewives in *Tunafish Disaster* (1963), victims of botulism taken directly from a newspaper page. Smeared across the silkscreened painting, their smiling faces become piercing in repetition.

From the early days of the Factory on, Warhol always recorded. Visitors were often placed before a movie camera in a "screen test" that served as an initiation rite (these shoots weren't part of any film project). And especially in his last years he collected compulsively. When the going got rough, Warhol went shopping, and his townhouse filled with collections of kitschy things like cookie jars that were auctioned after his sudden death in 1987. For Koestenbaum this endless taping-and-filming and buying-and-bagging point to a subconscious plan to "conquer by copying" or to control by gathering. Here what counts as "putting in" or "taking out," as porous or trussed, open or closed, isn't clear, but that may be the point: like the two states that underlie them, these two strategies are bound up with each other. In this light his collecting was another way of being porous to the world, and his being porous another way to defend against images and objects, that is, to drain them of affect, to close them off again. His sayings on this score are well known: from his early motto, "I want to be a machine," to his late ode to repetition, "I like things to be exactly the same over and over again. . . . Because the more you look at the same exact thing, the more the meaning goes away, and the better and emptier you feel."[4] Perhaps it was to this same end that, after 1974, he diarized the bric-a-brac of his life in time capsules, cardboard boxes filled with mementos and ephemera (there were over 600 in his estate). In a nice twist Koestenbaum adopts a nickname that Warhol picked up and dropped early, "Andy Paperbag," which evokes not only his compulsion to collect but also the fragility of this protective stratagem. More ominously, Koestenbaum writes of the *Campbell's Soup Cans* and *Brillo Boxes* as "simulacra of Andy's body." If Deleuze and Guattari gave us the "body without organs," the subject as a machine of desirous connections, Warhol left us with its quasi-autistic opposite, the "box without openings."

Koestenbaum relates the proclivity for "multiplication and archiving" to gay style in New York, which in "the bleak McCarthy era paradoxically flourished in the home." In this "domestic avant-gardism," public signs were ironized in private ways that "interrupted the distinction" between the two spheres. Such customizing of images is close to camp as defined by Susan Sontag in her celebrated essay "Notes on Camp" of 1964. Alert to the queer dimension of this sensibility (her text reads in part like a field report on the underground of Warhol, filmmaker-performer Jack Smith, and others), Sontag saw camp as dandyism "in the age of mass culture," that is, as a way of wresting the distinctive from the vulgar, of finding feeling in kitsch, of transcending "the nausea of the replica."[5] Some of this spirit, such as the attraction to degraded imagery, is maintained in Pop, but much is not. Pop hardly redeems sentiment, and it doesn't transcend the nausea of the replica so much as rub our faces in it. Here Koestenbaum shifts the lines that have long defined Warhol studies, away from differences in style such as Abstract Expressionism versus Pop, and toward continuities in sensibility across his campy commercial work of the 1950s and his cool artwork of the 1960s.

Trained at the Carnegie Institute of Technology (now Carnegie Mellon University), Warhol moved from Pittsburgh to New York in 1949. He shed his ethnic identity along the way, at least nominally, dropping the final "a" from his patronymic. (Warhol is often called Czech, but his parents, Julia and

Ondrej Warhola, were Carpatho-Rusyns who immigrated in the early 1920s from present-day Slovakia.) He fared well as a commercial illustrator, with advertisements produced for *Harper's Bazaar*, *Seventeen*, the *New Yorker*, and *Vogue*, displays for Bergdorf Goodman, Bonwit Teller, I. Miller, and Tiffany & Co., as well as book jackets, record covers, stationery, and the like. Warhol received three Art Directors Club awards in the 1950s, and he continued in this line of work well into the 1960s—through 1962, when the *Campbell's Soup Cans* appeared, 1963, when the films began, and 1964, when the *Brillo Boxes* were done. Moreover, Warhol was closer to fine art in the 1950s as a commercial illustrator than he was in the 1960s as a Pop artist, if by "fine" we mean art that manifests crafted handwork and subjective expression. And the reverse is also true: his great silkscreens begun in 1962 show great design intelligence, and, as Benjamin Buchloh noted long ago, his Pop art carries over traits of his commercial illustration: "extreme close-up fragments and details, stark graphic contrasts and silhouetting of forms, schematic simplification, and, most important, rigorous serial composition."[6] The imbrication of the two practices was persistent: his first show of Pop paintings occurred in a window display at Bonwit Teller in 1961, and after 1968 he returned to a mode that he never really left—"business art." For years art historians mostly glanced over the commercial design in some embarrassment (at least Robert Rauschenberg and Jasper Johns had the good taste to treat their window displays as rent-money work), sidelined the films, and bemoaned his supposed decline after the 1968 shooting. In the recent literature all three biases have been corrected.

Until recently, too, art historians liked to posit a clean break between the aftermath of Abstract Expressionism and the rise of Pop, and they pounced on a famous anecdote to firm up this stylistic divide. In 1962 Warhol showed two paintings of a Coke bottle, first to the filmmaker Emile de Antonio, then to the dealer Ivan Karp, and asked them which he should exhibit. (This is a classic instance of his deferring of responsibility. Duchamp exacerbated the problems of artistic making and judging with his readymade objects: "Whether Mr. Mutt made the fountain or not had no importance. He CHOSE it."[7] Sometimes Warhol complicated aesthetic choice further by outsourcing it, often to his assistants.) One of the Coke paintings has painterly drips that might read as signs of expressive gestures, while the other is almost as pristine as the commercial original, right down to the registered trademark. His friends opted for the iconic Coke, and Pop was born. Now sealed with the false obviousness of history, this story was always too convenient; at the same time, though Abstract Expressionism had run out of track by then, Warhol did truly derail it. The question is what drove this turn.

Another juxtaposition is telling here. In the early 1960s Warhol continued the drip paintings of Jackson Pollock by other means: he urinated on canvases covered with metallic paint and set on the floor, or had his assistants do so (even here he passed the work on).[8] The paint oxidized into misty veils or, when his female associates did the deed, murky puddles. These spray paintings queered the drip paintings. Suddenly the machismo of the Pollock gesture looked less potent, and the homosocial dimension of the old Abstract Expressionist circle seemed a little like a circle jerk. The piss paintings also forced a double take on the apparent purity of Color Field painting, on the stained grounds of Helen Frankenthaler and the poured veils of Morris Louis. And when Warhol did more of these canvases in the late 1970s, Neo-Expressionist painting looked even more absurd than it had before. As the art historian Richard Meyer has stressed, this queering of art was also a matter of content. If one persona of the Abstract Expressionist was the action painter in existential torment, Warhol put pretty idols of mass culture up front, such as the young Troy Donahue and Warren Beatty, Elvis and Brando, all subjects of early silkscreens. More notoriously, he did the same with the not-so-pretty *Thirteen Most Wanted Men*, the FBI mugshots that he silkscreened for the facade of the New York State Pavilion at the 1964 World's Fair. (They were covered up by order of commissioner Robert Moses, who was not amused when Warhol offered to substitute an image of this infamous powerbroker instead.) As Meyer pointed out, Warhol turned the meaning of "most wanted" inside out: these men might be wanted sexually too.[9]

The queering didn't stop there. As Annette Michelson argued, the Factory was a semiconscious travesty of Hollywood cinema and culture industry alike. For instance, in many Warhol movies "montage" simply means the splicing together of unedited rolls of film; *Empire* (1964) is a fixed stare at the Empire State Building that lasts for over eight hours. Few of the films have stories, let alone scripts, and some verge on porn. Moreover, Michelson sees the Factory as a latter-day experiment in Bakhtinian reversal: with its "parodistic procession of divas, queens, and superstars," and spectacular mixing of uptown society, Forty-Second Street riffraff, and downtown bohemia, it resembled a court turned into a carnival. "In carnival," she writes, "behavior and discourse are unmoored, as it were, freed from the bonds of the social formation. Thus, in carnival, age, social status, rank, property, lose their powers, have no place; familiarity of exchange is heightened."[10] The strategy of the Factory was indeed "super"—to hyperbolize roles in a way that sometimes mocked them. But this parodistic play with the social order was only half-intended. It was also sporadic and short-lived, and by the time of the *Interview* magazine of the Reagan years it had swung over to its opposite: hero-worship of the rich and famous. So, too, the tropes of carnival,

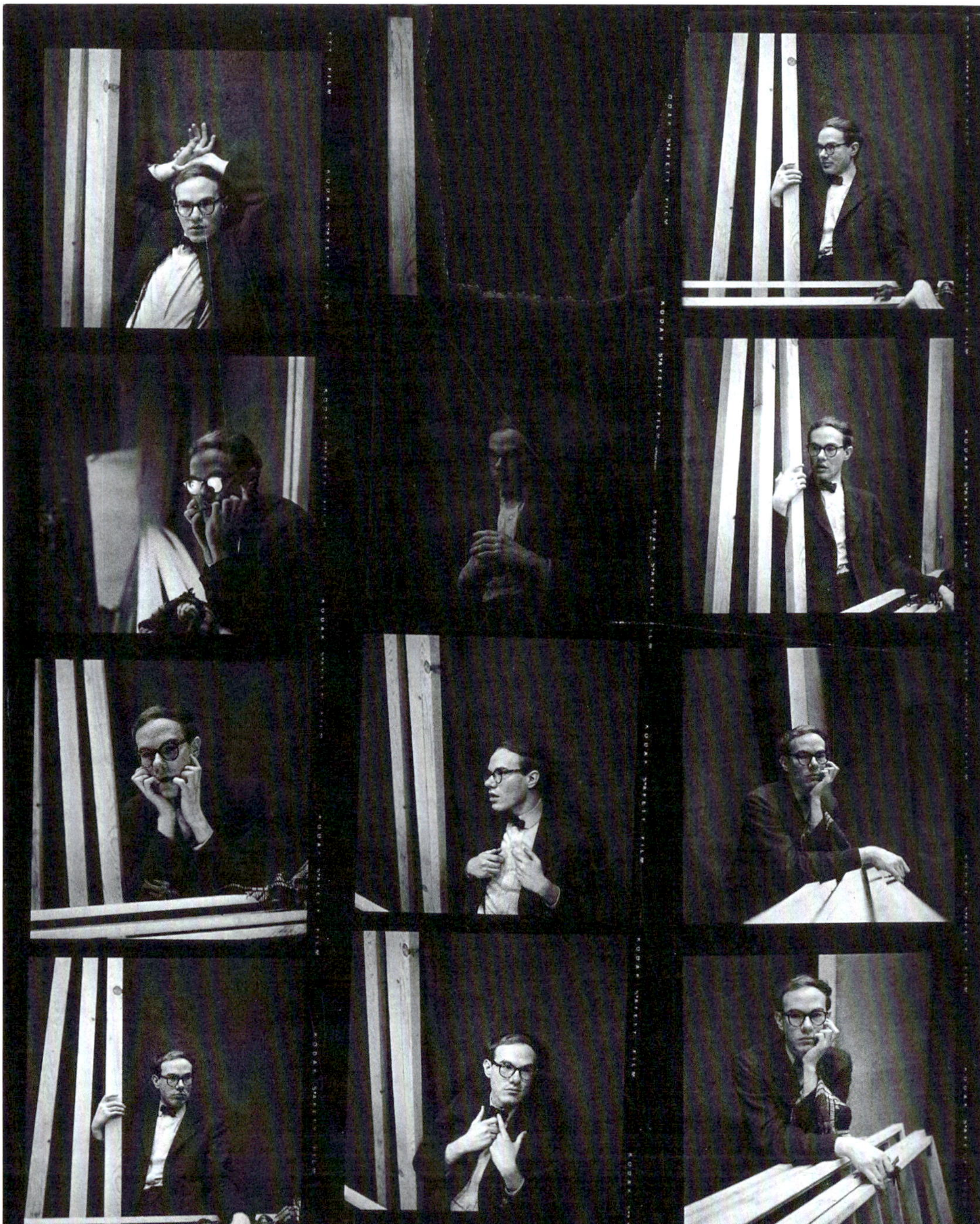

Otto Fenn, *Andy Warhol*, c. 1952–1954. Black and white contact sheet, 10 × 8¼ inches.

"travesty and humiliation" above all, often rounded on Factory dwellers. Very different from the close milieu of the commercial-illustration days, this scene could be cruelly hierarchical.

Koestenbaum sees both continuity and discontinuity here. Even as the Factory "extended the apartment philosophy Warhol first learned from décor-conscious gays," it diverged from the campy sensibility of his design studio. In his *Diaries* (1989) Warhol referred this break to the death of his favorite kitty in the early 1960s: "My darling Hester. She went to pussy heaven. And I've felt guilty ever since. . . . That's when I gave up caring."[11] This is a mock-traumatic account, of course. Affect didn't die with Pop; in fact, it took on a torturous turn in the Factory. In part this happened because the Factory was given over to performance in the sense not only of performance art (all the screen tests and films, the live theater and Exploding Plastic Inevitable events featuring the Velvet Underground) but also of performed identity. "To work for Warhol was to lose one's name," Koestenbaum comments. Billy Linich, the de facto manager of the Factory, became Billy Name; Robert Olivio became Ondine, the heroine of *a: a novel* (1968); Susan Hoffmann became Viva, the star of several films; and so on. This renaming was one prerequisite to superstar status, and it was often bound up with regendering: to swing both ways was to play with sexual as well as semiotic designations. This was the carnivalesque moment par excellence, and it had obvious risks, especially when mixed with pill-popping and vein-poking, bohemian showmanship and media spotlights.

In short, there was a psychological volatility of roles in the Factory, which sometimes approximated a desultory S&M theater, with Warhol as a director both kind and cold, passive and aggressive. He would goad people into defensive or outlandish performances, especially in the films (some of which also thematize bondage), as though to film meant to provoke and to expose, and to be filmed meant to parry this attack as best one could. Koestenbaum detects this "emotional oscillation" between inhibition and excess, "diffidence and exhibitionism," deathly stillness and sexual motility, and argues that it could induce a "paranoid relation" to whomever acted out on the screen or in the Factory at large. But the movies also produce a different sort of connection. The viewer doesn't identify with the filmed subject in the manner of classic Hollywood cinema so much as he or she empathizes with the travails of being before a relentless camera, with the vicissitudes of becoming an image, with wanting or resisting this condition too much.

According to Koestenbaum, Warhol always had a particular target in his sights, masculinity, and a particular way to mess with it, which he terms "twinship." "Masculinity was a subject Warhol failed from the start,"

Koestenbaum writes; his art became "the sexualized body his actual body largely refused to be." In this regard, too, "Andy liked to entrust others with the task of embodying Andy," and often this embodying involved female dopplegängers like Edie Sedgwick whose ambiguity as both femme and boyish did a number on gender. Koestenbaum refers this twinship to a "homoerotics of repetition and cloning," but it might also be seen as a play with kinds of likeness that are only like enough to be subversively other. This doubling-with-a-difference runs throughout Warhol—in his life, where he was mirrored, weirdly, by Edie, Nico, the monotone singer with the Velvet Underground, and others, as well as in his art, where the silkscreens are often instances of image repetition run amok. The films, too, are often double projections in which the scant action in one screen has little or nothing to do with that in the other. Koestenbaum describes this trait as "nonparticipatory adjacency," and in a sense it structured the entire Warhol world. He spent his days at the Factory with image-producers and scene-makers, his evenings first at the bar-and-restaurant Max's Kansas City and later at the club Studio 54 with his entourage, his nights at home on the Upper East Side with his mom and cats, and his Sundays at Mass (Warhol remained a Catholic to the end).

At first Warhol projected onto celebrities; later he painted them; in time "he merely needed to stand next to them . . . his Andyness could *sign* the adjacent presence, make it Andyish." Here, too, doubling was the primary Warholian device. (For me it became delirious one night in the early 1980s at a club called Area, as I watched Jean Baudrillard, the theorist of the simulacrum, watching Warhol posing as "Warhol" in a bare diorama of his own making, as though he had become his own wax replica.) "Pop art rediscovers the theme of the Double," Roland Barthes once wrote, but it has "lost all maleficent or moral power . . . the Double is a Copy, not a Shadow: beside, not behind: a flat, insignificant, hence irreligious Double."[12] This last point isn't so certain. In the Factory Warhol was called "Drella," a fitting contraction of Cinderella and Dracula, for like the former he lived the dream of going to the ball (and sometimes getting the prince), and like the latter he sucked the blood of others in a way that left him ravished. This deathly doubling is one reason why Warhol remains so fascinating: more than anyone else he acted out the strange mass subjectivity of the Pop image-world. As the critic Michael Warner has argued, "To be public in the West means to have an iconicity. . . . In the figures of Elvis, Liz, Michael, Oprah, Geraldo, Brando, and the like, we witness and transact the bloating, slimming, wounding, and general humiliation of the public body. The bodies of these public figures are prostheses for our own mutant desirability."[13] Warhol operated on both sides of this equation. He was a "mutant desirer" first and last, but he also became a

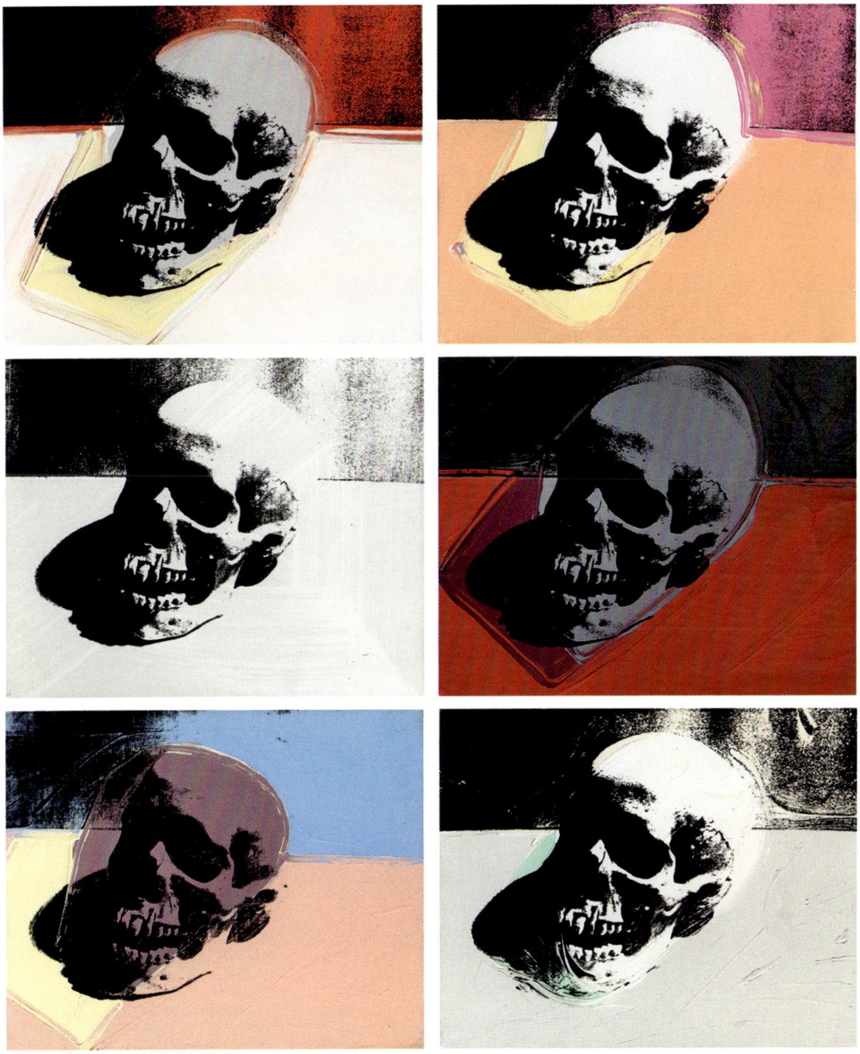

Andy Warhol, *Skulls*, 1976. Acrylic paint and silkscreen on canvas, six panels, each 15 × 19 inches. Tate. © Andy Warhol Foundation for the Visual Arts, Inc. / DACS, London.

mass icon in his own right. In fact, after his shooting he entered the pantheon of martyr-stars (Marilyn, Liz, Jackie . . .) that he also portrayed.

Like Christ, Warhol became more iconic as his body became more ravaged. As Koestenbaum notes, he took on a "revenant appearance" and delivered works possessed of "the shadow aura of bulletins from the afterlife," paintings of *Skulls* (1976) and *Shadows* (1978) in particular. Appropriately, Warhol was at work on a wallpaper version of the *Skulls*—which are portraits of us all, he once suggested—at the time of his death. Unlike much Pop art, his work had teeth, and a great part of its bite lay in its recognition of the deathliness of the mass image. On this score the best remark comes from Deleuze in 1968, in the midst of the Vietnam War, and it is clear he has Warhol in mind:

> The more our daily life appears standardized, stereotyped and subject to an accelerated reproduction of objects of consumption, the more art must be injected into it in order to extract from it that little difference which plays simultaneously between other levels or repetition, and even in order to make the two extremes resonate—namely, the habitual series of consumption and the instinctual series of destruction and death. Art thereby connects the tableau of cruelty with that of stupidity, and discovers underneath consumption a schizophrenic clattering of the jaws, and underneath the most ignoble destructions of war, still more processes of consumption. It aesthetically reproduces the illusions and mystifications which make up the essence of this civilization, in order that Difference may at last be expressed.[14]

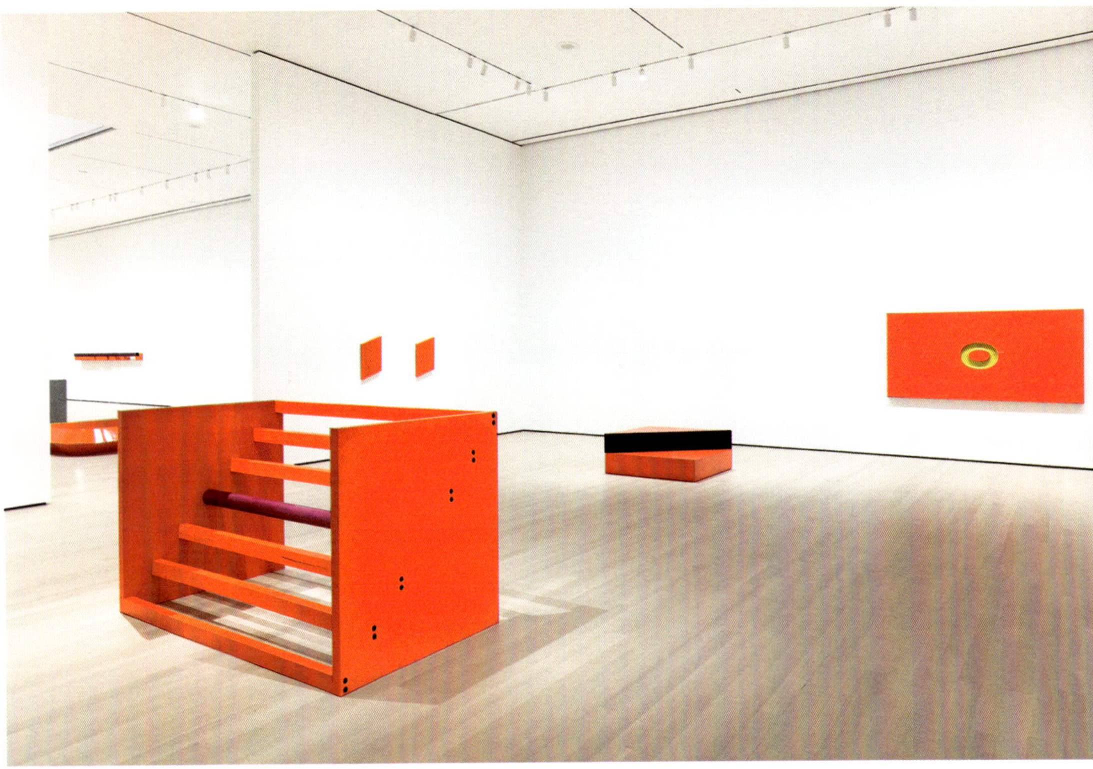

View of the exhibition *Judd* at the Museum of Modern Art, 2020. From left: *Untitled*, 1963/1975; *Untitled*, 1963; *Untitled*, 1963; *Untitled*, 1963; *Untitled*, 1962. Photo: Jonathan Muzikar. © Judd Foundation / Artists Rights Society (ARS).

5 Object Lessons

The art of Donald Judd remains stunning seven decades after its first appearance. The early paintings and objects are especially vivid: the intensity of the cadmium red, often made tactile by roughened surfaces of board and wood; the physicality of the specific shapes, such as a yellow oval carved into the support or a tin pan embedded there; the first tentative moves into actual space with paintings whose metal tops and bottoms curl outward toward us; and then the initial objects, cut in sharp geometries, set boldly on the floor without pedestals or plinths.

Judd had his first solo museum show at the Whitney Museum in 1968. Already then he had begun to repeat elements, as in his "stacks," consisting of identical shelves set on a wall at regular intervals from floor to ceiling, as well as in his "channels," comprised of rectangular frames spaced on the floor so as to describe a perfect square. Other now-familiar series followed, such as his "progressions," made of box and bullnose units sized and arrayed along horizontal bars according to mathematical orders like the Fibonacci sequence (1, 1, 2, 3, 5, 8 . . .). These pieces marked a shift in production from the homemade work of the early 1960s, when Judd was assisted by his father, a skilled carpenter, to the ones fabricated later in the decade, in iron, stainless steel, brass, aluminum, and Plexiglas, by sheet metal specialists. Some of these objects have a fragile finish that, in the 1970s, Judd offset with pieces in unpainted plywood, a move that recovered the crafted hardiness of the early work and allowed him to build larger than he had heretofore.

Along with a few other templates, Judd turned these series into a basic language that he deployed in different materials, colors, and sizes for the next two decades of his life. His work has a final twist, though. In 1984 he began to collaborate with Lehni AG, a Swiss company that helped him assemble long blocks of color units in enameled aluminum. Often set on the wall, these blocks are Judd at his most pictorial (they might call up the color grids of Ellsworth Kelly or Gerhard Richter). Such pieces have little of the austerity usually associated with late style, but then Judd died prematurely, felled by cancer in 1994 at the age of sixty-five.

With Judd it is impossible to separate the artist from the critic, and some of his words remain as forceful as most of his objects. "Half or more of the best new work in the last few years has been neither painting nor sculpture," he stated in the first lines of his famous essay "Specific Objects" (1965). "Much of the motivation in the new work is to get clear of these forms. The use of three dimensions is an obvious alternative."[1] Although Judd appeared to dismiss painting in toto—"the main thing wrong" with it, he remarked in his usual deadpan, "is that it is a rectangular plane faced flat against the wall"—it was Jackson Pollock, Clyfford Still, Mark Rothko, Barnett Newman, and Ad Reinhardt who prompted his shift into three dimensions. Along with a commitment to large scale, unmodulated color, and emphatic materiality, their painting mandated a "sense of singleness" for Judd, who felt that this "wholeness" would have "a better future" outside that medium.

Judd didn't eliminate composition so much as he displaced it from the interior to the exterior of the work, where it became a matter of "symmetry" and "proportion" among the units on a wall or a floor. This was a radical move in appearance but less so in aesthetics, for first and last Judd held "that ultimately one essential of art is unity," a traditional criterion indeed. Hence, unlike many of his peers, he had little interest in chance or any other device of the Duchampian neo-avant-garde. Nevertheless, his shift—from an arrangement of parts within a painting or a sculpture to the wholeness of an object in actual space—was misread by early critics, and Judd responded fiercely. "I object to several popular ideas," he wrote already in 1966. "I don't think anyone's work is 'reductive.'" Far less was Minimalism—a label Judd also abjured—an attack on art: "'Non-art,' 'anti-art,' 'non-art art,' 'anti-art art' are useless. If someone says his art is art, it's art."

For all his resistance to "anti-art," Judd articulated most of his own positions in the negative. Above all he was opposed to "illusionism" and "rationalism," which were closely linked in his view. "Three dimensions are real space," he wrote in "Specific Objects." "That gets rid of the problem of illusionism." Why did Judd object to this "relic of European art" so strongly? Again, his argument was not avant-gardist—that abstraction had voided illusionism once and for all. Rather, the problem was that illusionism was "anthropomorphic," by which he meant not simply that it allowed for the representation of the human body, but that it assumed an a priori consciousness whereby the ideation of the artist always preceded the realization of the object. In short, like composition, illusionism was "rationalistic," a vestige of an outmoded idealism in need of expunging. "There is little of any of this in the new three-dimensional work," Judd insisted. "The order is not rationalistic. . . . [It] is simply order, like that of continuity, one thing after another."[2]

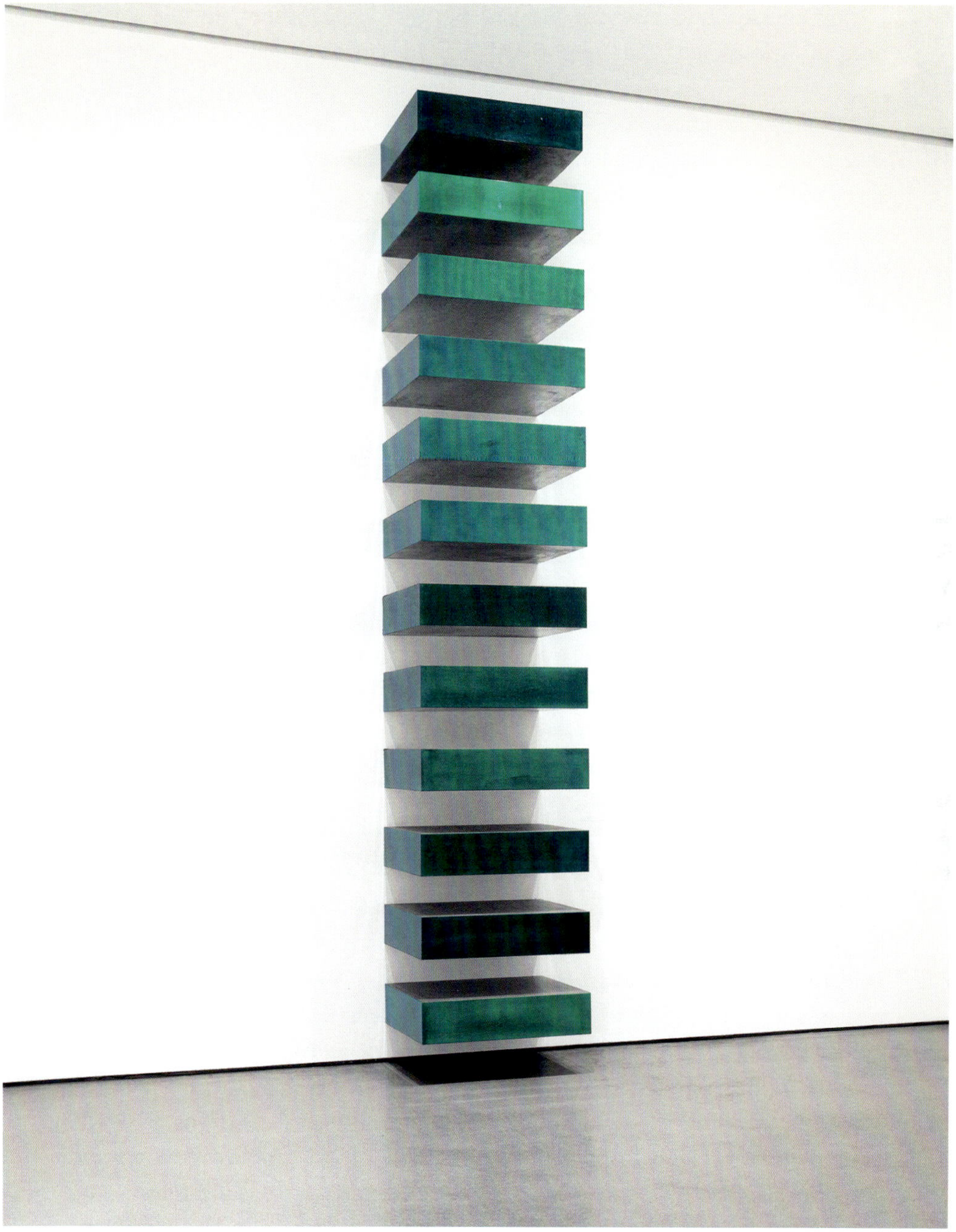

Donald Judd, Untitled, 1972. Lacquer on galvanized iron, twelve units, each 9 × 40 × 31 inches, with 9-inch intervals. Museum of Modern Art. © Judd Foundation / Artists Rights Society (ARS).

Of course, Judd also put forward positive values, especially the related ones of "specificity" and "objectivity," but he did so largely to counter the negative ones. "Materials vary greatly and are simply materials—formica, aluminum, cold-rolled steel, Plexiglas, red and common brass, and so forth," he stated, in his laconic way, about several of his preferred substances. "They are specific. If they are used directly they are more specific." Here "specific" means physically emphatic. His explicit materials and straightforward presentations were intended to focus us on the intrinsic qualities of the former and on our reflexive perception of the latter. At the same time, at least for Judd, most of these substances were unburdened by associations, artistic or otherwise, and this lent them even more objectivity. In his account this specificity and that objectivity supported the autonomy of the artwork, which he prized most of all.

These values are materialist, but what kind of materialism is it? In an incisive critique from 1975, Karl Beveridge and Ian Burn, two members of the Art & Language camp of Conceptual art, called it "middle-class materialist," one that put too much faith in "the supposed 'objectivity' of science."[3] "I leapt into the world an empiricist," Judd stated proudly, and his posture was indeed empiricist, according to which knowledge is derived from the senses, if not positivist, according to which it must be verified there as well. (For a point of comparison, Frank Stella was positivist when he said of his painting of the early to mid 1960s, "What you see is what you see.")[4] Judd moderated his empiricism a little through a reading of Pragmatists such as Charles Peirce. There is also a trace of the Transcendentalists in his writings, especially when he struck his recurrent note of Emersonian self-reliance.

Although Judd was art-historically trained—he did an MA under Meyer Schapiro at Columbia University—he was limited philosophically, and he seemed to like it that way: he thought what he thought, and defiantly so. Judd believed, correctly, that, apart from other vices, "European rationalism" was too dependent on problematic binaries, not only of subject and object and mind and body, but also of thought and feeling, spirit and matter, and form and content, with the privilege granted the first term in each pair. Yet for the most part he couldn't think his way through these oppositions. He didn't have enough Marx to dialecticize them (Judd mentions Marx only twice in his texts), nor did he possess any Derrida to deconstruct them. Arguably, his very insistence on the object removed it from the subject all the more. Certainly Beveridge and Burn thought so: they read the vaunted objectivity of his specific objects as so much "alienability," equally divided between artwork and viewer. (This is what other viewers have long registered as "the coldness" or "the impersonality" of Minimalism.)[5]

Judd didn't oppose the specific to the general; he believed in "generalities," that of art above all (again, "if someone says his art is art, it's art"). If the specific object moves beyond the discrete media of painting and sculpture, it enters the realm of art-in-general, art with a capital A, which was also the conclusion drawn by his Conceptual followers, of whom Judd mostly disapproved.[6] Prominent critics saw the situation very differently. Far from autonomous art, the specific object was, for Clement Greenberg, too close to a mere thing—like "a door, a table, or a blank sheet of paper." It was also too caught up in mundane time: Michael Fried famously termed Minimalist objecthood so much "theater" and opposed it to art in no uncertain terms.[7] Yet Judd insisted on the autonomy of art as much as Greenberg and Fried did, even if, as Beveridge and Burn alleged, his version initially required the art-institutional context of the gallery or the museum for it to be recognized as such. There is a further connection to his two great antagonists. Like Greenberg and Fried, Judd conformed to a conceptual framework that, rather than alien to "European rationalism," might be essential to it. In *The Order of Things* (1966), written in the same years that Minimalism was developed, Michel Foucault argued that modern thought operates as "a strange empirico-transcendental doublet"; that is, however opposed the epistemological orientations of the empiricist and the transcendental might appear, they are actually bound up with each other.[8] Greenberg and Fried put forward such a doublet—medium-specificity on the one hand, autonomous art on the other—and so did Judd with his simultaneous commitment to specific objects and to art-in-general.

To be sure, Judd helped to open up new possibilities for postwar art. "The main thing for anyone now," he remarked in 1966 in the full flush of this expansion, "is to invent their own means." Yet, again, he ruled out some devices from the start, such as chance operations à la John Cage, and shied away from others, such as the found objects of Dada and Surrealism. "I've lived in the shade of a coat hanger and a bed spread," Judd lamented in 1981 in a swipe at Jasper Johns and Robert Rauschenberg. Certainly, after his initial move into three dimensions, Judd did produce brilliant variations, but he held fast to his basic theme. "I want a particular, definite object," he remarked in a 1969 text on Dan Flavin. "I think Flavin wants, at least first or primarily, a particular phenomenon."[9] One can distinguish Judd from his other peers in this way as well. Whereas Carl Andre insisted on given material units, Robert Morris opted for direct bodily engagement, and Richard Serra ventured into emphatic spatial intervention, Judd stuck with his discrete specific object. By and large he supported, even prepared, these other moves, but he didn't join them, not fully.

This point seems clear enough, but it wasn't always evident to artists and critics then or now. For all the visual power of the Judd oeuvre, it doesn't often engage us deeply in a phenomenological way. That it was thought to do so was partly a projection onto his work from that of Morris and Serra, who did delve into the philosophy of Maurice Merleau-Ponty. (Although his *Phenomenology of Perception* was translated into English in 1962, Judd, unlike Morris and Serra, doesn't mention Merleau-Ponty in his writings.) An involvement in phenomenology might have led Judd to probe process and space more deeply than he did; certainly, it supported Morris and Serra to move in those directions.[10] Judd was interested in the effects of fabrication more than the discoveries of making, in the drama of installation more than the articulation of space. In fact, all the reflections of light, transparencies of material, and interactions of color in his work can tend to disembody viewers and to dematerialize space more than the opposite. "Little was done until lately with the wide range of industrial products," Judd stated in "Specific Objects." "Almost nothing has been done with industrial techniques." He did a lot with the products, of course, but not as much with the techniques—a point that Serra underscored with his distinction between the "shiny Minimalism" of Judd and Flavin, centered on objects and effects, and the "down and dirty Minimalism" of his own cohort (among whom he named Robert Smithson, Bruce Nauman, and Eva Hesse), focused on materials and processes.[11]

Is this a fair assessment of Judd when it comes to space? Although his move into three dimensions was hardly unique, it did alter the relationship of art to architecture significantly. Artworks could no longer be seen as a simple matter of rectangles on the wall or things on the floor: his Minimalism altered "the geometry of viewing" in art, making us newly alert to the nuances of its installation.[12] For some critics, however, this awareness had a downside. Beveridge and Burn complained that Judd "choreographed" his objects and "programmed" his viewers.[13] At the same time, though many of his pieces are site-adjusted—including the stacks, the plywood pieces that extend across an entire wall, not to mention multiple works at Marfa, Texas—not many are site-specific, at least in the rigorous sense given the term by Serra ("to move the work is to destroy it"). In this respect Judd was also limited in his outdoor pieces, whose concrete geometries often seem more set on the landscape than sited in it.

Although Judd set up crucial investigations of the 1960s and '70s, one wonders why he didn't take his own radical move further. I've offered a few possible reasons; another concerns his historical resources. In a 1981 text titled "Russian Art in Relation to Myself," Judd admitted, "I essentially missed the Russian work," by which he meant Constructivism above all. "I would like to have known of that interest in the early 1960s," he added, with "the culture of materials" of Vladimir Tatlin in mind. Given his art-historical knowledge, did this work truly escape his notice? Contemporaries such as Sol LeWitt, Andre, Stella, Flavin, and Serra were all aware of the basics of Constructivism, mostly through *The Great Experiment: Russian Art 1863–1922* (1962) by Camilla Gray.[14] In any case, Constructivism could have assisted Judd in his principal aims. Its insistence on construction would have supported his critique of composition, and its understanding of materialism would have deepened his critique of idealism (it might have complicated his empiricism too). The Constructivist principles of *faktura*, tectonics, and construction were dedicated to a Marxist undoing of bourgeois art forms; the goal was to defetishize the work of art by a new transparency of materials and production. Arguably, Judd often did much the opposite, fetishizing facture as techy surface and outsourcing construction as fabrication. Of course, there was no sociopolitical context for any thorough recovery of Constructivism, but that didn't stop Andre, Serra, and others from a partial understanding of its principles.[15]

Perhaps the primary reason Judd held fast is that he rejected anything that looked like compromise to him. In his writings he often railed against wayward artists, obtuse critics, nefarious collectors, bureaucratic museums, untrustworthy foundations, and corrupt governments. His withdrawal to Marfa in the early 1970s was also a defiant stand against any encroachment on his autonomy. Here his liberal belief in self-reliance edged into a Texan brand of libertarianism ("don't tread on me"). Yet, paradoxically, standing his ground could also mean slipping up. For instance, if Judd didn't oppose the specific to the general, he did pit it against the generic, and what is more generic than the commodities that suffuse our everyday world? When repeated, as Judd repeated his boxes, stacks, and other elements, the specific object became less specific and more serial—"one thing after another," as he phrased it, like one product after another. In structural terms, then, the specific object began to approximate the commodity, and often it is as "shiny" as any luxury item, which is not the case with the "down and dirty" version of Minimalism. In this respect, too, Judd came to share a serial logic with his enemy twin Andy Warhol (Judd disdained Pop), the difference being that Warhol owned up to that condition. Rather than deny it only to reproduce it, as Judd sometimes did, Warhol often exacerbated it and so exposed it.

Similarly, even though Judd insisted on the autonomy of art, he also designed furniture and architecture. That was his prerogative, of course, and he kept these ventures separate from his artwork. Yet, intentionally or not, this activity blurred the line between the specific object and the utilitarian thing, the very line that Greenberg condemned Minimalism for crossing. Did Judd thus prepare the repurposing of Minimalism by commercial design, both high and low, from Design Within Reach to IKEA? Whereas "Minimalism" once meant materially emphatic, formally rigorous, and perceptually precise, it now signifies quite differently. To many people it means expensive elegance, to others moral uplift (à la Marie Kondo space management). This not-so-secret sharing between Minimalism and design is hardly the fault of Judd—it's a matter less of production than of reception—and yet, just as Leo Steinberg once pointed to a connection between Color Field painting and Detroit automobile styling, it must be mooted nonetheless.[16] Other possible crossings are no less problematic. For example, if Minimalism initiated a new geometry of viewing for art installation, it might also have paved the way for galleries and museums to entertain the immersive spectacles favored by the culture industry at large.[17]

Finally, there is this turn, for which Judd is responsible. In "Specific Objects" he declared matter-of-factly, "A work needs only to be interesting." Here, consciously or not, he posed the expansive criterion of "interest" against the Greenbergian shibboleth of "quality." Whereas quality was judged by reference to the standards of Old Masters and great moderns alike, interest was prompted by the testing of aesthetic categories and the transgressing of traditional media. In 1984, two decades after that famous declaration, in a two-part essay with the unironic title "A Long Discussion Not About Masterpieces but Why There Are So Few of Them," Judd stated the opposite: "quality . . . is nearly the definition of art." Why did he reject his original position? Given that Judd had ascended to the status of a modern great by then, did he simply want to defend Old Master quality as the ultimate criterion? Or had he held out for it all along? For those of us who, even as we admired Judd, were also quickened by the feminist critique of the idea of male genius in the early 1980s, this was a disappointment. What happened to his caustic skepticism about traditional categories of art?

On the one hand, what Judd initiated is well-nigh epochal. "It's not so far from the time of easel painting," he commented in 1982; it's "still the time of the museum, and the development of the new work is only in the middle of the beginning." Certainly, for my generation he was a key reference, not unlike Pollock for his own generation. On the other hand, how salient is his work for artists and critics today? "The past never stays the same since it is always seen from a new time and place," Judd wrote also in 1987. "The experience, the work, that once could not be seen from outside, is eventually, often sadly, given an outside." Has that "outside" come for his work as well? However fresh it might still look, has it reached that Hegelian condition, at once grand and melancholy, of "a thing of the past"?

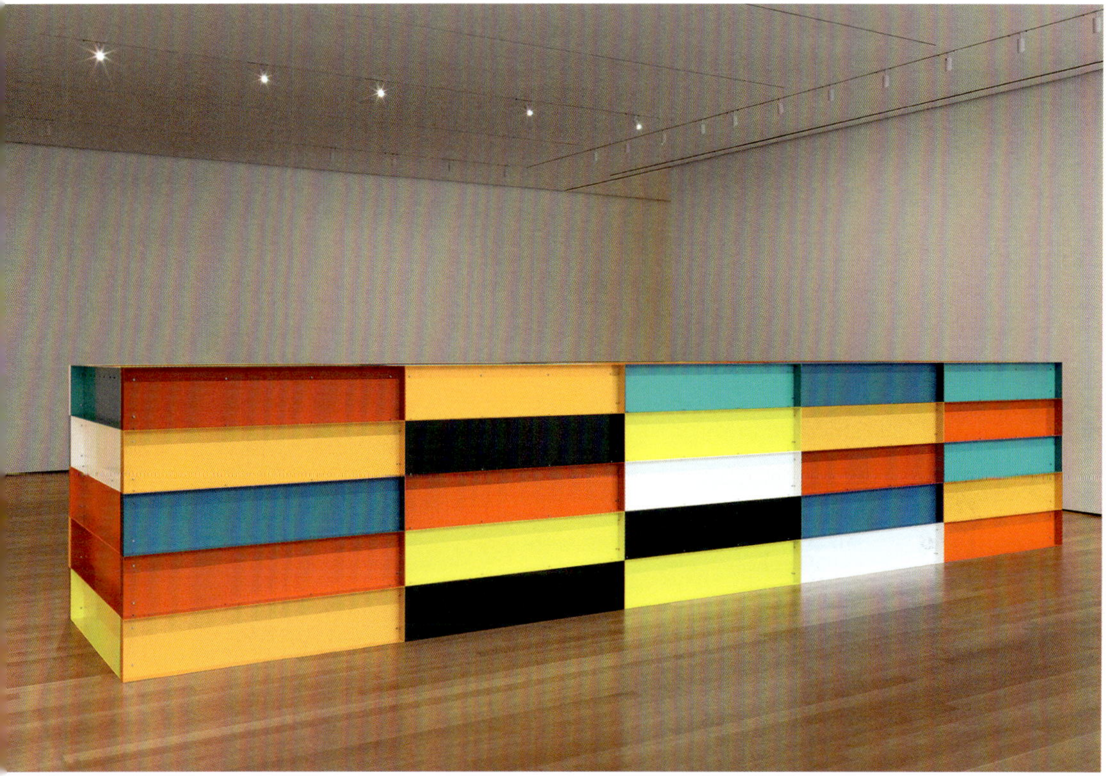

Donald Judd, Untitled, 1991. Enameled aluminum, 59 inches × 24½ feet × 65 inches. Museum of Modern Art. © Judd Foundation / Artists Rights Society (ARS).

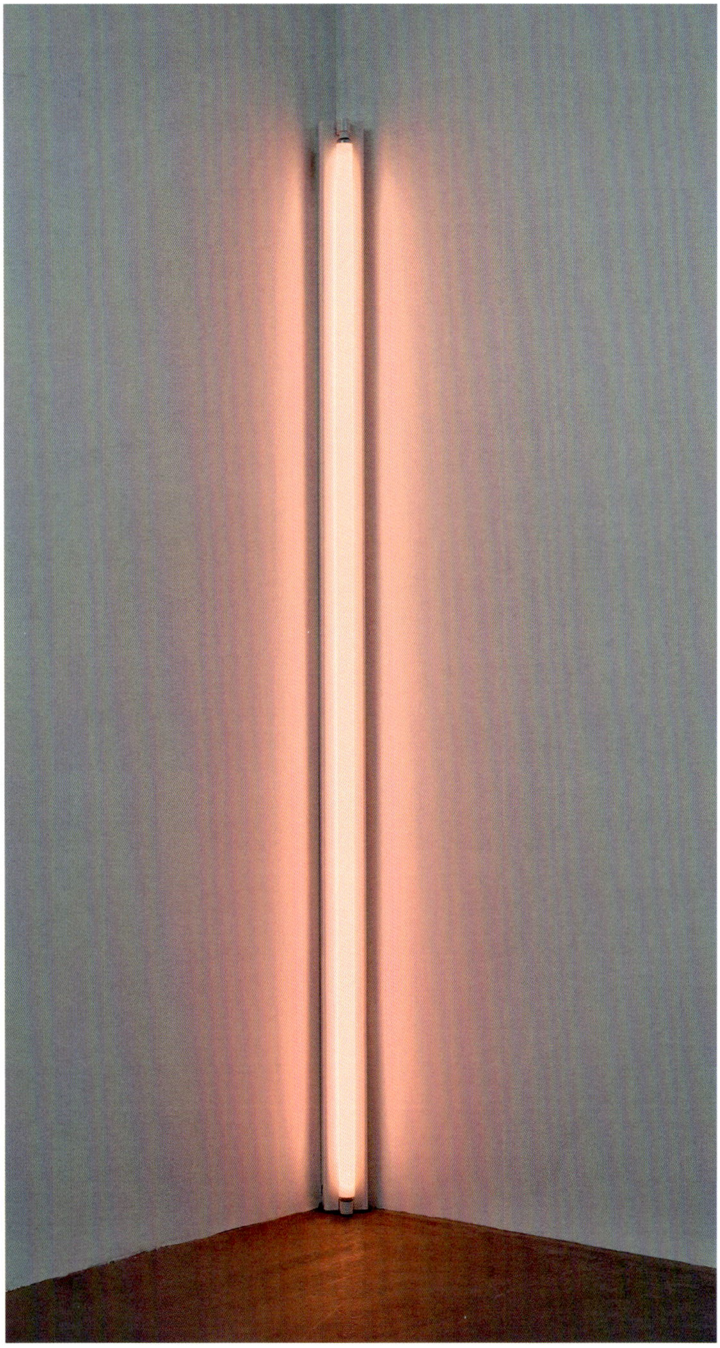

Dan Flavin, *1 pink out of corner (to Jasper Johns)*, 1963. Fluorescent light and metal fixture, 96 × 6 × 5½ inches. Museum of Modern Art. © Estate of Dan Flavin / Artists Rights Society (ARS).

6 Blank Magic

For years I took Donald Judd at his word: that Minimalism was absolutely opposed to pictorial illusionism and virtual space. Why not take a "literalist" (one of the initial labels for the Minimalists) literally? But is this account true to his art, let alone that of his friend Dan Flavin, early or late?[1] What is the fate of the celebrated opposition between "specific object" and illusionist space in the aftermath of Minimalism—and the role of Flavin in that story? Opposed to illusionism in principle, is Minimalism also propped up by it, bound up with it, even invested in it? In my own literalism, which was deepened by that of process, body, and site-specific art, I didn't attend to how illusionism was not only preserved in Minimalism but also expanded by it: consider the reflective surfaces and refractive depths in a typical Judd, or the brilliant color and immersive light in a characteristic Flavin. I also didn't attend to how illusionism was released everywhere, in the dispersive opticality of the Light and Space art that followed on Minimalism (especially on Flavin), with Robert Irwin, James Turrell, and others. Could it be that the Minimalist break from pictorial virtuality into actual space was only partial and temporary, a ruse on the way to the triumph of the virtual (a triumph hardly limited to art)?

For Judd illusionism enfolded much of what he wanted to get rid of in traditional aesthetics. This led him to project illusionism away from his work and, to a lesser extent, Flavin's. "They don't involve illusionistic space," Judd declared in 1964 of the early Flavin pieces called "icons," which Judd described as "blunt" (high praise for him), only to qualify his assessment with the fluorescent lights that followed: "I want a particular, definite object," he wrote in 1969. "I think Flavin wants . . . a particular phenomenon."[2] Although Flavin didn't sign on fully to the program of specific objects, *both* artists entertained a play between "object" and "phenomenon," material support and illusionistic effect, despite the fact that Judd turned this oscillation within each practice into an opposition between them.[3] And, indeed, essential to our experience of a Flavin fluorescent is the relay of our attention among fixture, gas, luminous tube, extended glow of color, and spatial diffusion of light. And Flavin knew it: "The composite term 'image-object' best describes my use of the medium."[4]

However, Flavin struggled to hold "the lamp as image back in balance with [the lamp] as object."[5] This struggle preceded the fluorescent works as well; it was in play ever since he moved, in the late 1950s, from his fussy watercolors to his tins and tools smashed against brushy Masonite grounds (which he called, in a typical riff of Joycean assonance, "plain physical factual painting of firm plasticity").[6] His mix of abstract painting and found object attests to the two principal imperatives in advanced art at the time. On the one hand, like others in his milieu, Flavin was impressed by Barnett Newman; on the other, one couldn't avoid Rauschenberg and Johns. (The latter lineage was underscored in the exhibition *The Art of Assemblage*, mounted at the Museum of Modern Art in 1961 when Flavin was a guard there.) Either of these lines of influence—Newman or Rauschenberg and Johns—might have led Flavin to extrude pictorial space into actual space. Another influence, not represented in the MoMA show or elsewhere in New York in 1961, clinched the move: the Constructivism of Tatlin and Rodchenko. This precedent came by way of a 1962 book by English art historian Camilla Gray, *The Great Experiment: Russian Art 1863–1922*, which was also important to Carl Andre and Sol LeWitt (they alerted Flavin to it). Three years later Flavin looked back on this Constructivist project as the basis of his own "proposal":

> This dramatic decoration has been founded in the young tradition of a plastic revolution which gripped Russian art only forty years ago. My joy is to try to build from that "incomplete" experience as I see fit. *Monument 7* in cool white fluorescent light memorializes Vladimir Tatlin, the great revolutionary, who dreamed of art as science. It stands, a vibrantly aspiring order, in lieu of his last glider, which never left the ground.[7]

Although the recovery of "that 'incomplete' experience" was an important part of the neo-avant-garde project of the early 1960s, it was also an inevitable retreat from the goals of the original avant-garde. What was, for Tatlin, a radical monument that emblematized a new order had become, with Flavin, a "dramatic decoration" that eulogized a failed artist. And the Flavin lights did remain on the threshold between the illusionistic and the actual, the aesthetic and the utilitarian.

"I can abuse lighting in a sufficiently useful way," Flavin once remarked, "and still accomplish what I regard as art."[8] Supplied by "any hardware store," fluorescent lights were deployed, in the early 1960s as they still are today, in workaday spaces: factories, offices, lunchrooms, subways, train stations. (In 1977 Flavin installed his fixtures on two platforms at Grand Central Terminal in New York, almost in a test of whether they would be legible as different from everyday tubes.) Of course, the lights were also used commercially; in fact, beyond workaday, they are a little tacky, and Flavin didn't shy away from this association. He once remarked that the fluorescents evoke a "Brooklyn Chinese restaurant," and an incandescent work like *icon V (Coran's Broadway Flesh)* (1962) has an erotic aspect too (with its fleshy tint and flashy lights, it was titled in homage to "a young English homosexual who loved New York City").[9] On the one hand, then, Flavin held that "there is no room for mysticism in the Pepsi denigration. . . . My fluorescent tubes never 'burn out' desiring a god."[10] On the other hand, the lights are often glorious, the effects even ecstatic, and Flavin used both adjectives almost in the sense of religious transport (he once considered becoming a priest). Here is another instance of different associations held together in tension: evocations of transcendental spaces on the one side (Flavin designed lights for a church in Milan, finally realized in 1997, a year after his death) and of mundane places like train stations and subways on the other.[11]

Flavin engaged other binaries—immediacy and mediation, materiality and immateriality—which were in play elsewhere in advanced art of the 1960s. And he often spoke for both sides of these oppositions. On the one hand, "the physical fluorescent light tube has never dissolved or disappeared by entering the physical field of its own light"; on the other, the "brilliance" of the light can "somewhat betray its physical presence into approximate invisibility."[12] Here again Flavin wanted to hold the effects together, yet this tension was difficult to maintain, and often his work is less site-specific than site-obliterating: "An eight-foot fluorescent lamp . . . pressed into a vertical corner," he admitted about a piece like the one he dedicated to Johns, "can completely eliminate that definite structure."[13] This crucial aspect of his work prompts my principal claim here, which is that, with Flavin, Minimalist anti-illusionism turns into an expanded field of illusionism. Put otherwise, his work moved beyond the frame of painting and off the pedestal of sculpture into a realm less of specific objects than of pictorial space writ large. Might it be that his primary achievement was not only to abstract such pictorialism (that was done before him) but almost to atomize it?[14] In his Minimalism (if that is still the right term to apply), to literalize is also to pictorialize, even to opticalize: illusion is not negated but extruded into space.[15] This diffusion of colored light into actual space, Rosalind Krauss argued in 1969, has "the simultaneous depth and physical inaccessibility of illusionistic space"; in effect "the [real] space 'of the room beyond' . . . bear[s] on the conventions of painting."[16] With Flavin the literal doesn't correct the illusionistic so much as it is subsumed by it. And the same might be said of our own bodies in the midst of his work; at its extreme, his colored light overwhelms our visual apparatus. We are dazzled.

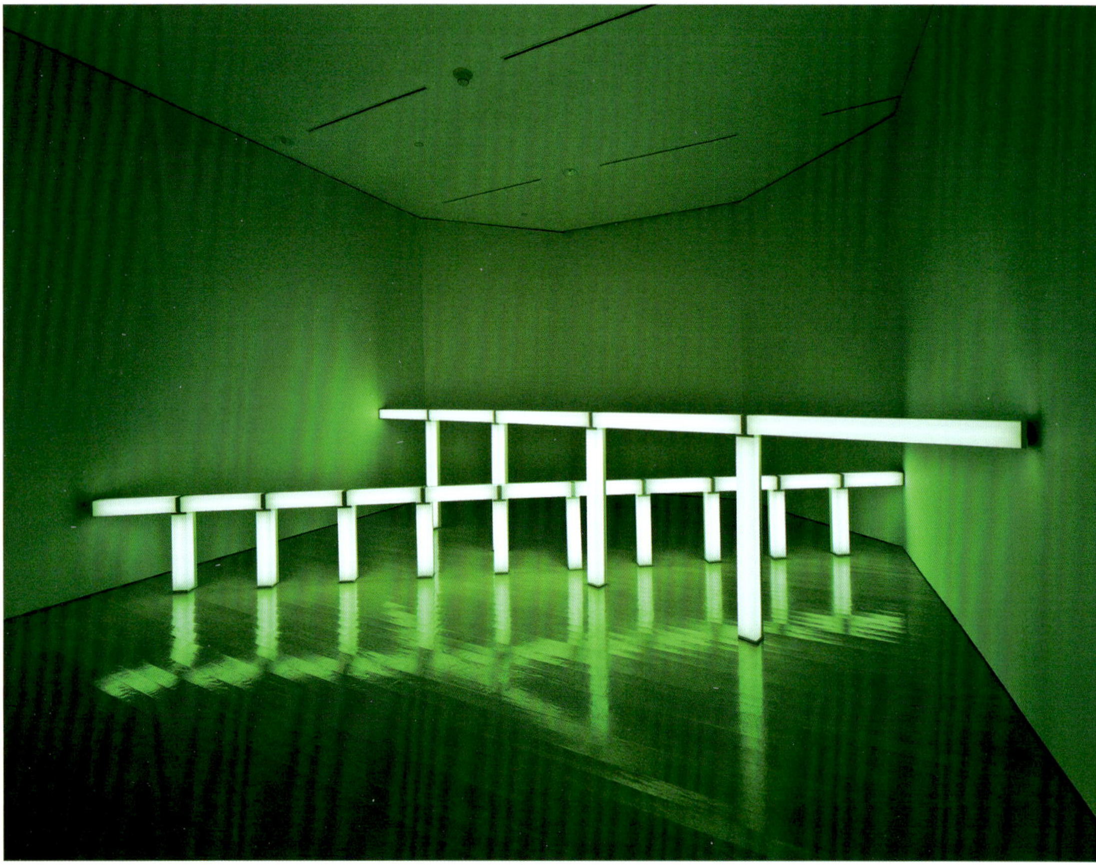

Dan Flavin, *greens crossing greens (to Piet Mondrian who lacked green)*, 1966. Fluorescent light, first section 4 × 20 feet, second section 2 × 22 feet. Solomon R. Guggenheim Museum. © Estate of Dan Flavin / Artists Rights Society (ARS).

"As I have said for several years," Flavin wrote in 1966, "I believe that art is shedding its vaunted mystery for a common sense of keenly realized decoration. Symbolizing is dwindling—becoming slight. We are pressing downward toward no art—a mutual sense of psychologically indifferent decoration—a neutral pleasure of seeing known to everyone."[17] Flavin didn't want to shed this "mystery" altogether; early on he termed his art "blank magic." At the same time "decoration" was not a pejorative term for him, as it was from abstract artists like Kandinsky and Mondrian in the 1910s and 1920s to Greenbergian critics in the 1960s.[18] For decoration is valued negatively only if abstraction is pledged absolutely to medium-specificity and aesthetic autonomy, and for Flavin it was not. "At times," he said of his icons, "they may be lamp blocks losing their identity to a greater ensemble," which is even more true of his fluorescents: "the lights are integrated with the spaces around them."[19] Yet Flavin refused any connection with the emergent practice of installation art: "I do not like the term 'environment' associated with my proposal," he wrote in 1967. "It seems to me to imply living conditions and perhaps an invitation to comfortable residence. Such usage would deny a sense of direct and difficult visual artifice."[20] Despite his move into actual space, he wanted to retain the punctual intensity of late modernist abstraction: "I intend rapid comprehensions—get in and get out situations. I think that one has explicit moments with such particular light-space."[21] This "keenly realized decoration," which releases the opticality of a Color Field painting in the spatial medium of colored light, shifts Flavin away from Judd, Andre, and friends toward Irwin, Turrell, and company. That is, it aligns him with a genealogy of art that often involves conditions of immersion and effects of bedazzlement ("regard the light and you are fascinated").[22] In the 2000s this once-secondary line became dominant, and it effectively undid the materialist dimension of Minimalism—its will to specify object, viewer, and space. This devolution might be understood as a catastrophe (in the etymological sense of a "downturning"): the catastrophe of Minimalism.[23]

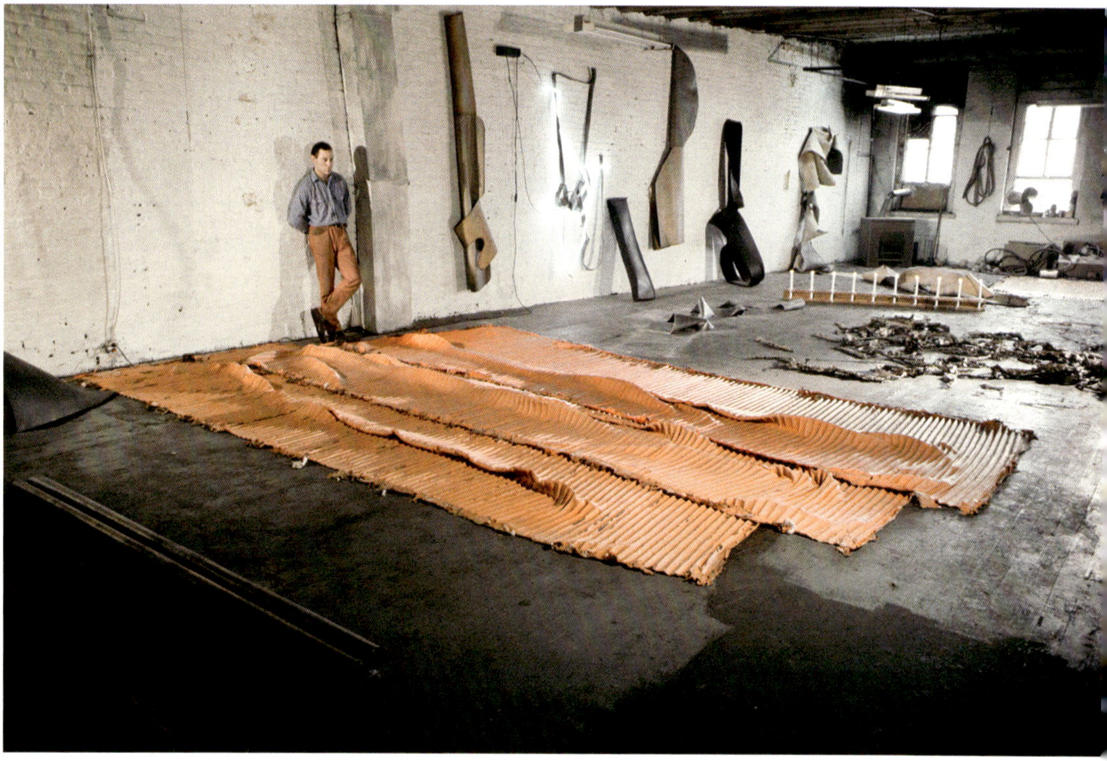

View of Richard Serra in his studio with works from 1966–1968. Photo: Lawrence Fried.

7 To Support

A photograph published in *Newsweek* in July 1968 shows a twenty-nine-year old Richard Serra in his first loft in Lower Manhattan. On the dark wood floor in front of him appear three long sheets of orange latex from 1968 cast from corrugated doors found on a nearby pier; a mess of rubber strips from 1967 that are the beginnings of his first scatter work; a lead sheet titled *Cut and Folded* (1968) that registers just those actions; and a wood plank set with a row of ten candles called *Candle Piece* (1968). Along the white brick wall beside him appear a rubber piece titled *Slant Step Folded* (1967); a work of looping lines in rubber and neon from 1966–1967; a relatively stiff rectangle of rubber called *Chunk* (1967), only half as tall as the first two pieces; a sinuous shape in folded rubber from 1967, the top of which is a folded circle and the bottom a folded parallelogram; two more long works in rubber from 1968, the darker of which leans against the wall while the lighter one droops from it; and, finally, between the two windows, a cluster of rubber loops from 1966–1967 that is the first of the *Belts*. Except for *Chunk* and his *Belts*, these pieces are roughly human scale, and all ask to be seen in some relation to our bodies.[1]

At the time, the old industrial loft was a relatively new space for art-making. A floor in a factory or warehouse turned into a studio, it was still a place of work, but it was also a site of study (such is the etymology of "studio") where an artist such as Serra might develop his language through experiment.[2] As evidenced in the photo, his early work was dominated by rubber pieces—Serra salvaged a great cache of the material when a rubber warehouse on West Broadway closed in 1966—all manipulated according to various actions laid out in his *Verb List* (1967), namely, "to roll, to crease, to fold . . ." Some pieces read more as shapes, others more as objects; some are oriented to the wall, others to the floor. None, however, can be readily designated as painting or sculpture. At this point in his investigations Serra was concerned with the forms that result (or fail to result) from the conjunction of materials and processes, not with any definition of medium per se. "The residues of the activities didn't always qualify as art," Serra remarked in retrospect. "I was primarily interested in the process and it was important that whatever was finally made reveal its making."[3] In this light his choice of materials becomes less strange. Why rubber? It was close to hand in the sense not only of availability but also of manipulability: rubber can be worked so as to articulate line, plane, or volume. "It's an active material," Serra adds. "You can cut it and fold it and unfold it and tie it and string it and unstring it, you can use it for its topology, you can use it for its interlacing, you can use it for its knotting, you can make it free-stand but you can also use it for its instability."[4] We see many of these actions already undertaken in the work in the *Newsweek* photo. In this respect his shift to lead as a basic material was simply the next step for Serra; lead was like "rubber with more mass, more weight, and more gravitational load."[5]

How the artist appears in the photo is also telling, dressed in work clothes, his arms behind his back, his left leg akimbo, his gaze directed at the large rubber lengths in front of him. Serra all but mimics his work: propped against the wall like some of his pieces, he looks to the floor at others as though he were about to step out into space to interact with them once more. Serra has spoken of the importance of Judson Church dance for his early practice, especially that of Yvonne Rainer, and such performance is evoked in the loft setting here (a common one for dance at the time), but even more in the shared protocols of everyday materials and objective tasks taken up to render the work of art less symbolic and subjective. Then, too, there is the disposition of the artist and the art along the wall: they appear almost like dancers at the barre, at rest between exercises, about to leave the vertical support of architecture for the horizontal extension of space. "One performer would fall and another would catch her," Serra commented. "I saw things—in terms of movement and equilibrium, weight and support—that I could use in my sculpture. And I was faithful; I watched it all."[6] Judson Church dance allowed him to imagine new relations among material, space, time, and movement, relations in which, again, the body is the fundamental unit of measure.

Initial responses to Serra tended to follow two lines of thought, the first of which treated the early work as a Duchampian testing of the category of art. Serra resisted this account from the start. "I'm not saying the pig is art or is not art," he remarked of one of his early *Habitats* (1966), which involved live and stuffed animals placed in cages, "but she makes a form."[7] This emphasis on form would persist over the years. "Calling the Splash Pieces a performance is a misnomer," Serra also stated. "These lead pieces were made ladle-full by ladle-full. . . . I took a measured length of the juncture of wall and floor that I wanted to cast. . . . I didn't see that as gestural. . . . I saw it as forming a sculpture through a repetitive process."[8] The second reading—that the work is the product of self-evident materials and processes, which, however foreign to traditional art, are familiar in industrial labor—echoed Serra, and it came to predominate.

This account is accurate, of course, but it might distract us from the centrality, already apparent in the *Newsweek* photo, of the body at work in space.

The fundamental parameters of this interplay are horizontality and verticality, which Serra activates as a physical tension, almost a dialectical struggle. In this regard consider *Doors* (1966–1967), which is a rubber and fiberglass cast of fire doors in four parts, or *Trough Pieces* (1966–1967), which are two forms like troughs cast in the same manner. One might think of the ambiguous relation between the utilitarian and the aesthetic, which Brancusi, a signal precedent for Serra, engaged fifty years before in wood pieces such as *Caryatid* (1914–1926) and *Cup II* (1917–1918). One might also think, in Brancusi, of the pulling down of sculpture from the pedestal of art into the space of our own activities. Yet most salient here is the tension between horizontal and vertical dimensions that follows from this fall, and, importantly, neither axis is privileged: even as the vertical doors are dropped to the horizontal, the horizontal troughs are lifted to the vertical. In other words, form isn't debased here, much less dispersed. Consider two more pieces, both rubber strips on the wall, the one a horizontal work with hanging lines from 1966, the other a vertical cluster of looping belts from 1967. Although both appear "antiformal" in the sense given the term by Robert Morris at the time, Serra articulates the primary line in each piece with a neon tube. He aims to focus our gaze, not to scatter it, as Morris does in such installations as *Untitled (Threadwaste)* (1968). And a field piece of the same moment, *Tearing Lead* (1968), announces that its primary concern is process in time, not dispersal in space; its peripheral strips also remain ordered by the central sheet of lead that is their material source.[9] Nor was Serra as taken with the effects of entropy as was his friend Robert Smithson: he aims to engage natural forces like gravity—to exploit them, even to counter them—not to submit to them. A crucial verb in his list is "to support."

Although Serra is known for his critique of figure-ground compositions, the target of his critique is "the pictorial convention" more than the figure per se.[10] If he questions the figure as image, it is largely to engage the body in other ways (as agent, as gauge, and so on), including the actions announced in some of his titles and in most of his verbs. The early work tests what reads as a figure, and often Serra gives us only the bare minimum to go by. Consider the vertical piece of curvaceous rubber shapes from 1967: it is entirely abstract, but its two parts are stapled together at the middle just as the two main parts of the human body are connected at the waist. The overall form describes curves that carve out slight volumes, and it also hints at contrapposto, which is typically regarded, in the history of Western sculpture, as the epochal move that freed the figure from Egyptian stasis into Greek liveliness. So, too, with its shapes and its folds, the piece evokes a template such as those used in the making of clothes. In fact, this allusion to the figure is explicit in the title of *Template* (1967), a rubber piece whose limp form hangs down from the wall like a hooded cape on a hook. Of course, it's not a cape, no more than the sinuous piece is a kouros; the point is that both works play with an abstract reference to the body, as do other rubber pieces that droop from the wall or lean against it like figures in states of exhaustion or rest.

As the early work developed, it became involved with the question of what counts as a structure—bodily, built, or both—and here again Serra sometimes tested us with a bare minimum. Will a sheet of rubber, lifted at one edge, continue to stand? Will four plates of lead, 500 pounds each, stay upright if propped against one another without additional support? Will a sheet of lead, rolled up into a pole and leaned against another sheet left flat on the wall, keep it in place? Will a similar pole, wedged across a corner of a room and set atop a lead plate in open space, suffice to maintain it upright? Will it keep up two such plates abutted at a right angle? Can the pole support, by way of such capping, ever more plates in ever more arrangements? This is how Serra proceeded, from rubber to lead and on to steel, and from sheet to rolled pole to plate, probing these materials as tectonic elements. Throughout this investigation a set of questions was posed: What is it to be upright—as a body, as a structure—in a world of gravity? What is it to be freestanding if we assume that verticality is not a given but a goal? As the basis of his sculpture shifted from a logic of materials to axiomatic principles of building, Serra activated our own "kinaesthetic apprehension" (as Dan Graham described it), an apprehension in which the body is engaged as a kind of architecture and vice versa.[11] This was already suggested in *To Lift*: Is our first association here to a figure or to a shelter, or somehow, given this surface that is at once an exterior and an interior, to both at the same time?

"If we were purely visual beings, we would always be denied an aesthetic judgment of the physical world," the art historian Heinrich Wölfflin wrote in the late nineteenth century. "But as human beings with a body that teaches us the nature of gravity, contraction, strength, and so on, we gather the experience that enables us to identify with the conditions of other forms."[12] Although Wölfflin is still identified with a disembodied formalism that privileges the eye alone, this statement is altogether relevant to Serra. In his dissertation, *Prolegomena to a Psychology of Architecture* (1886), Wölfflin considered the kinaesthetic apprehension of built form: "We read our own image into all phenomena," he argues there. "The expression intrinsic to horizontal and vertical articulations is presented according to human (organic) principles."[13] Not only do we project

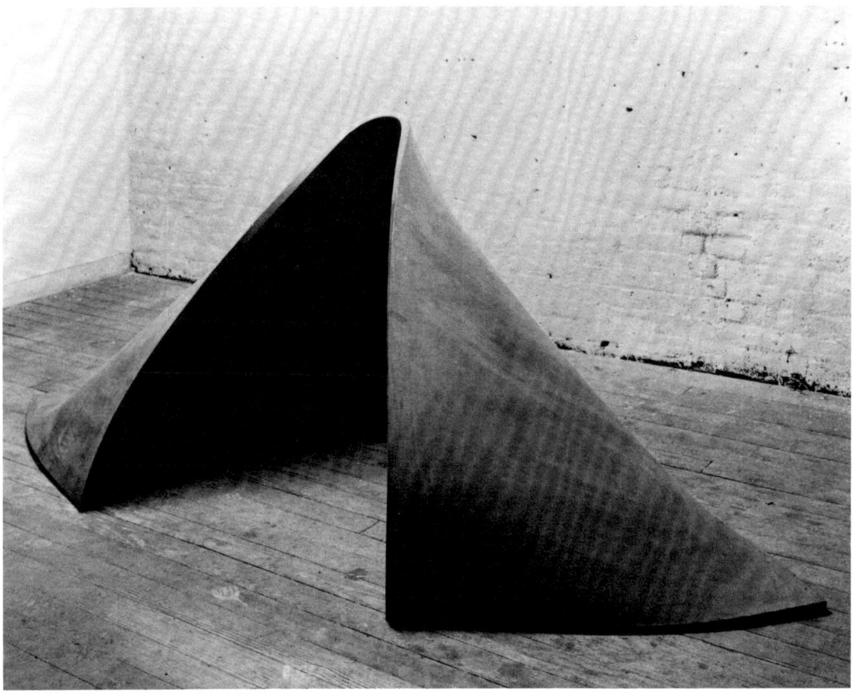

Richard Serra, *To Lift*, 1967. Vulcanized rubber, 36 × 80 × 60 inches. Museum of Modern Art. Photo: Peter Moore. © Richard Serra.

a head and a foot as well as a front and a back onto these forms, but we also perceive them in terms of other qualities that we share: "Briefly, there are degrees of heaviness, balance, hardness, etc., all of which have expressive value for us."[14] As with the young Wölfflin, so with the early Serra: an abstract mimesis exists between bodily subject and built object, one that involves what Wölfflin terms *Formkraft* ("form force"). "We assume that in everything there is a will that struggles to become form and has to overcome the resistance of a formless matter," Wölfflin asserts, and "the task of art is to present these antithetical ideas clearly. The load wants to fall to the ground; the supports, thanks to their rigidity, oppose this will."[15] To come to terms with these "antithetical ideas"—and with *Formkraft* in general—Serra looked to ancient types of building for inspiration. He traveled to Sardinia to see stone dolmens, to England to experience the stone circle at Stonehenge, and to other sites where ur-forms of post-and-lintel construction are found.[16] Especially in his early *Props* Serra reenacts this drama of primordial tectonics, of rising upward and remaining upright, as a struggle between verticality and horizontality, structure and gravity, undertaken according to the building principles of "pointload, balance, counter-balance, and leverage," again with the body as measure.[17]

This made a phenomenological reading of his work attractive, and certainly some Minimalists and Postminimalists were drawn to the writings of Maurice Merleau-Ponty when *The Phenomenology of Perception* appeared in English in 1962. That said, phenomenology was less appropriate to the early work than to the field pieces that Serra produced after 1971.[18] Moreover, whether early, middle, or late, there are two dimensions in his work that this approach doesn't adequately address: the architectural and the psychological. The empathy theory developed by Wölfflin can be brought to bear on the former dimension, but what about the latter? The Minimalist bias against the psychological is well known: reaction against the subjective orientation of Abstract Expressionism was strong in Donald Judd, Frank Stella, and others, and Rosalind Krauss argued early on that Postminimalists also advanced a model of meaning that was public and transparent, not private and hidden.[19] Again, this is mostly true of Serra too, yet he didn't subscribe completely to the suspicion of the psychological. "I came up with Smithson, [Bruce] Nauman, and [Eva] Hesse," he has remarked, "and we never bought into that part of the Minimalist dogma."[20]

There are a few intimations of this dimension in the early criticism. Robert Pincus-Witten hinted at a sadomasochistic implication in the *Belts*, for example, and Max Kozloff detected an aggressive "attack on the status of the object" in the early work in general (he wasn't alone here).[21] Yet these readings are too literal or too projective or both. It was assumed, often on the basis of a few

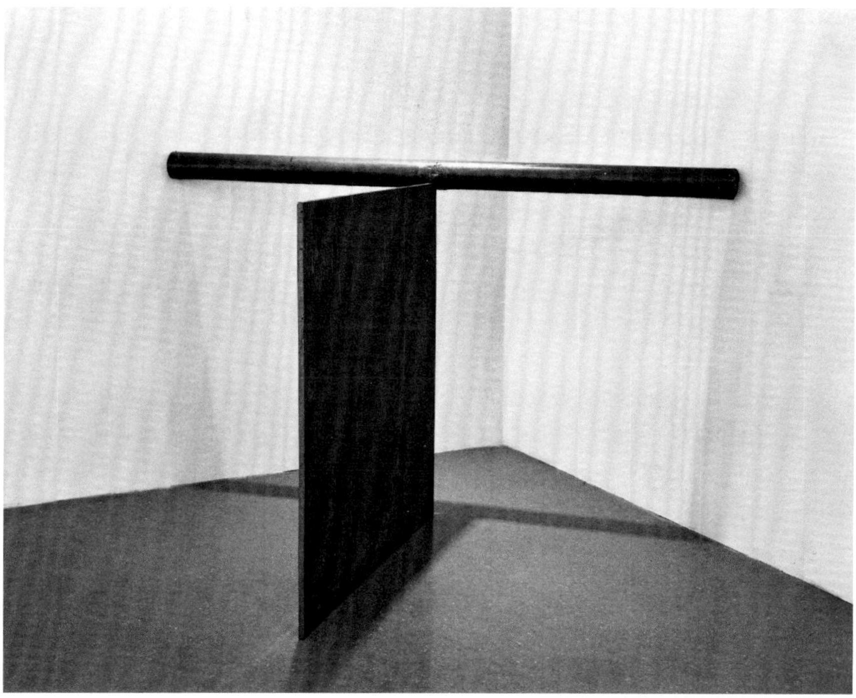

Richard Serra, *Equal (Corner Prop Piece)*, 1969–1970. Lead antinomy, plate 48 × 48 × ¾ inches, pole 7 feet. Museum of Modern Art. © Richard Serra.

photographs, that Serra splashing lead was like Pollock splashing paint, and that each displayed a macho mastery in the process. Although this easy reading has partly stuck, Serra was no more certain about his casting and propping than Pollock was about his dripping.[22] In fact, however declarative the early work was about its materials and methods, it was also provisional about its results; "precarious" is a term that cropped up in the initial reviews. Sometimes the status of the pieces as objects (not to mention as art) was in doubt, and often they appeared unstable in both substance and structure.

Another way into the psychological dimension of early Serra was offered by Lucy Lippard, who curated an important group show titled *Eccentric Abstraction* in October 1966 (it included Hesse among others, but not Serra, who moved to New York only later that year). In her text Lippard argued that artists such as Hesse posed an affective alternative to Minimalism, often doing so through a forthright confrontation of contrary attributes like hard and soft, rough and smooth, composed and aleatory, and so on. In the process, Lippard intimated, they sometimes evoked a "body ego," not by means of any overt image but in an abstract shaping of materials that resonated psychically, as though this shaping might register human drives, desires, or fantasies.[23] Although early Serra has nothing so fraught, some pieces do evoke a body ego as well, one that suggests a state of emergence (rather than of disturbance, say, as often with Hesse).[24] This drama of primordial structuring enacted in the work has implications for the subject too. Faced with a work like *House of Cards*, we compare its precarious status with our own tentative freestanding, and this is true of many other pieces as well.

In psychoanalysis there are two mythic stories about human emergence, the first involving the species as a whole, the second the individual alone. In *Civilization and Its Discontents* (1930) Freud offered a wild speculation about our becoming-human. When *Homo sapiens* stood erect, Freud proposed, our orientation to both our bodies and our world changed utterly, as the anal and the olfactory were suddenly subordinated to the genital and the visual. Not only did vision become the dominant sense, but vertical posture also reframed the environment completely. In "The Mirror Stage" (1936/49) Jacques Lacan offered a related story about the individual. In the first years of life, Lacan argued, there occurs a moment when the infant, usually propped before a mirror by his mother, sees his body as a coherent image for the first time. Since this upright form feels so different from the actual body, which is still experienced as a chaotic mess of disconnected parts and divergent drives, the infant takes great joy in this mirror image, and cathects it as the mold of its ego to come. In some early pieces Serra taps into primordial beginnings of this sort, of rising up and holding together, and of the difficulty and the delight of such experiences. Of course, the work doesn't repress the horizontal ground or the nonvisual senses, as in the Freudian myth, nor does it mirror an ideal image of our selves, as in the Lacanian story. On the contrary, in early Serra verticality and integrity are always tenuous, autonomy is partial, and all three states are attained, if at all, only with the support of others.

In this light, "precarious" is indeed a good term for the early work, but an even better one is "anaclitic," which I adapt from Freud. "Anaclisis" derives from the Greek "to lean on" (we might say "to prop"); it is a technical translation of *Anlehnung*, which is in everyday use in German. "A cornerstone of the first Freudian instinct theory," Jean Laplanche and Jean-Bertrand Pontalis write in *The Language of Psychoanalysis*, anaclisis "designates the early relationship of the sexual instincts to the self-preservative ones: the sexual instincts, which become autonomous only secondarily, depend at first on those vital functions which furnish them with an organic source, an orientation and an object."[25] In other words, the infant requires milk to survive, so sucks at the breast, and yet, in sucking, also experiences pleasure. The breast thus becomes an erotogenic zone, and desire becomes detached from need, as does satisfaction from survival. It is in this manner, according to Freud, that the sexual drives are propped on the self-preservative drives—both in touch with them and autonomous from them. Desire exceeds need, we might say, in the manner that the aesthetic exceeds the utilitarian.

The early work of Serra is anaclitic not only in relation to function, architecture, and other disciplines, but also in terms of both the subjectivity and the sociality that it models. Initial sculptures such as *Doors*, *Trough Pieces*, and *Candle Piece* are clearly in touch with function yet autonomous from it; here the aesthetic can be said to be propped on the utilitarian.[26] Then, too, some of the rubber works and all of the *Props* (to say nothing of the *Castings*) are supported by the ambient architecture literally, even as they are also defined against it ontologically, and this is precisely how Serra came to conceive of sculpture—in relation not only to the space around it but also to the disciplines adjacent to it. Unlike contemporaries like Morris, Serra retained the word "sculpture," yet he rethought it in terms that are not medium-specific so much as medium-differential. Even as he insisted on the status of sculpture as a language of its own, Serra also manipulated this language to partake of aspects of both painting and architecture—to partake of them in order to be differentiated from them. Thus, even as his sculpture opposes painting to the degree that it resists figure-ground conventions, it draws on the pictorial in the sense of its framing of sites. (This framing is parallactic, not fixed: we produce a variety of views as we move in, through, and/or around a given piece.) And even as his sculpture critiques architecture to the degree that it refuses the scenographic, it draws on the architectural in the sense that it privileges the structural.[27]

Again, the early work is anaclitic in relation to our corporeal images as well: it engages our bodies not only in form (which we never perceive, from within, as integral) and in substance (if we follow Wölfflin, we respond to the shapings of rubber and lead according to our own attributes of flaccidity, rigidity, and the like) but also in structure (our struggle to remain upright above all). Just as importantly, the early work suggests that our body egos are anaclitic in a social sense—that we rely on others for support. Consider *House of Cards* once more: it enacts a drama of (inter)dependence among the four plates of lead that constitute it, as well as among the riggers required to assemble it, and as experience attests (and photos indicate), this is true of many other pieces too. Recall what Serra said of Judson Church dance: "One figure would fall and another would catch and hold him or her." So it is with the plates in his works. Not only are the elements of a piece (inter)dependent, and hence equal in principle (this is all but proclaimed in *Equal (Corner Prop Piece)* [1969–1970]), but so too are its riggers. There is a politics intimated here as well, whereby, as in the Neoplasticism of Piet Mondrian, all elements are given full expression even as they are coordinated as a whole, in a sum that is more than the total of its parts. This is a model of self-reliance in which, paradoxically, the self relies on others. It is an ethos of mutuality that is Transcendentalist in spirit (Ralph Waldo Emerson is an important reference for Serra).

Freud used "anaclitic" in another sense, too, to describe a type of romantic choice. Some of us, he proposed, model our love objects on our own selves, an object choice he termed "narcissistic," while others of us seek out partners based on those on whom we have depended, an object choice he called "anaclitic." In analogy with this Freudian typology, much modernist art tends to the narcissistic, as it often cathects its own forms, materials, and media, and much postmodernist art tends to the anaclitic, as it is often propped on other disciplines and discourses. Along with other movements of the period, Minimalism signaled a shift from the first kind of object choice to the second. The early work of Serra programmatically deconstructs the modernist will to autonomy and develops the postmodernist interest in contingency. At the same time it suggests that this binary is far from absolute, that these paths aren't as divergent as they seem. As imagined in early Serra, the work of art, like the subject, develops by turning inward and outward at once.

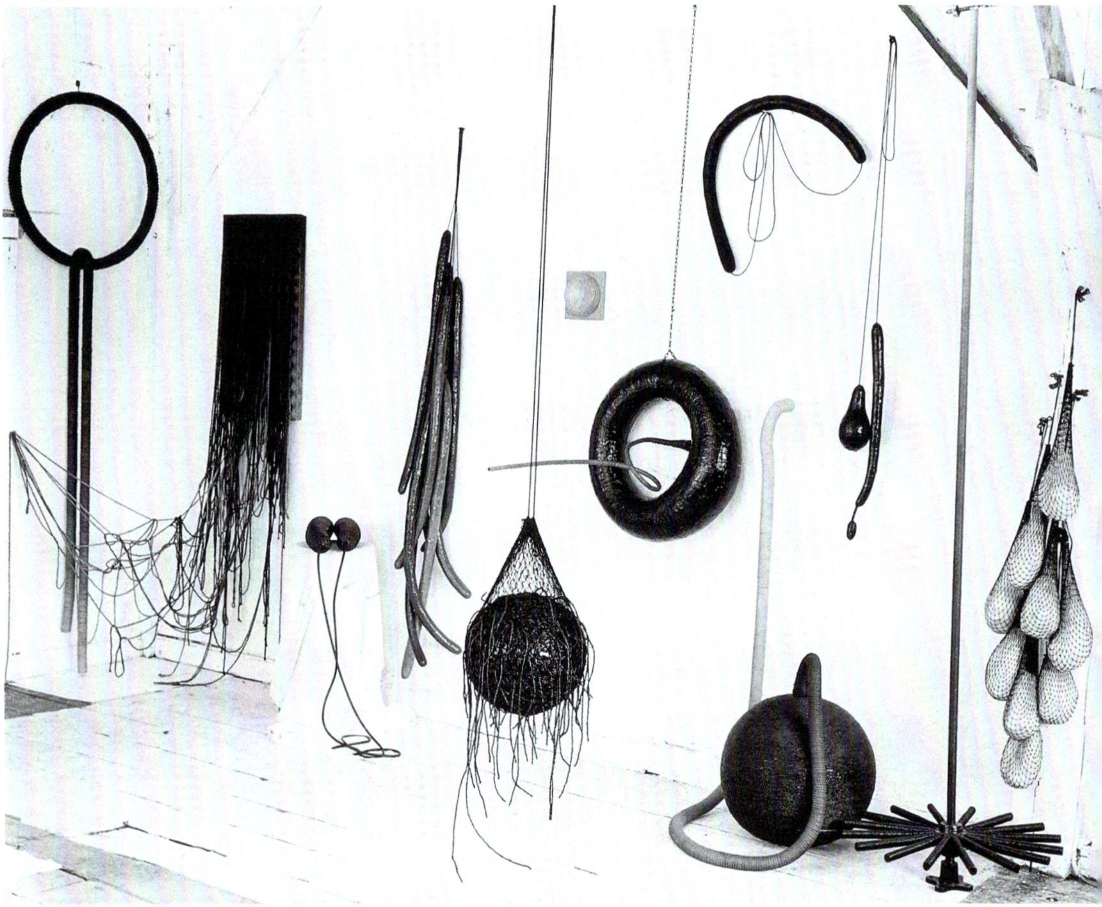

View of Eva Hesse studio with works from 1965–1966. Photo: Gretchen Lambert.

8 Serial and Fused

In May 1970 *Artforum* magazine published an extraordinary conversation between artist Eva Hesse and critic Cindy Nemser. Heavily edited (from ninety pages of transcript down to a five-page article), it proceeds by quick shifts and abrupt juxtapositions, and nowhere more so than in the first exchange. Asked about her affinity with "any particular school of painting," Hesse names Jackson Pollock and Claes Oldenburg, only to single out Andy Warhol in a way that suggests her own ambition: "He is the most as an artist that you could be. His art and his statements and his person are so equivalent."[1] And then Hesse drops this bombshell: "I feel very close to Carl Andre. I feel, let's say, emotionally connected to his work. It does something to my insides. His metal plates were the concentration camp for me." Although we can't know exactly what she intended, clearly Hesse favors art that is affectively intense, that somehow pierces the subject ("it does something to my insides"). And though no explanation is given for her association of Minimalism with Nazism, it isn't meant as a condemnation—on the contrary.[2] To her mind it isn't merely metaphorical either—the plates *were* the camp for her, not like it—and her use of the past tense suggests that they triggered an old trauma. Such a reading is supported by the fact that Hesse escaped Nazi Germany in 1938 as a Jewish girl of two and that she was terminally ill with cancer at the time of the interview. (She died at thirty-four, less than a month after its publication.) This framing prepared the psycho-biographical account of her work—of "Hesse as wound"—that pervaded the critical literature until Anne Wagner cautioned against it in 1994, and, though it's not wrong, it is partial. Among other problems, it doesn't do justice to the formal complexities of her art, let alone its sociopolitical implications.[3]

Elsewhere in the interview Hesse claims the true content of her work to be the "total absurdity of life," which she associates with extremity:

> There isn't a thing in my life that has happened that hasn't been extreme—personal health, family, economic situations. . . . Now art being the most important thing for me, other than existing and staying alive, became connected to this, now closer meshed than ever, and absurdity is the key word. . . . It has to do with contradictions and oppositions. . . . I was always aware that I should take order versus chaos, stringy versus mass, huge versus small, and I would try to find the most absurd opposites or extreme opposites.

Another term for this absurdity might be "antinomy." Certainly, Hesse proceeded by negation as she pursued "a non-anthropomorphic, non-geometric, non-non" basis for her art. Here she offers no mediation between her "extreme opposites"—her artwork *is* that mediation—and this accords with the extremity of the time, not only in her own life but also in the artistic debates that engaged her and the world events that impinged on everyone.[4] Relevant here is an anecdote told by her friend Mel Bochner involving a run-in with Andre at a restaurant-bar from a few years before:

> At Max's Kansas City, I was introduced, for the first time, to an artist I had written about very positively. He immediately attacked me for misunderstanding his work. When I asked what he objected to about my interpretation, he shouted, "My work is the cry of dying babies in Vietnam. Every unit represents a dead baby."[5]

Initial detractors called Minimalism "cold" and "inhuman," and subsequent opponents deemed it "masculinist" and "totalitarian." I see these responses as reactive or reductive or both, and, like other critics and historians, I have stressed the phenomenological dimension of Minimalism, its engagement with the body and the space of the viewer, in part to counter such readings. Nonetheless, they did represent the sentiments of many observers, and some of these accounts did point to the historical problem at stake here, even if they misconstrued it in doing so.[6] For what was seen as "inhuman" in Minimalism is better understood as "antihumanist," a position that was largely shared by Conceptual artists. This antihumanism was active, for example, when, in another well-known conversation from 1966, Donald Judd and Frank Stella claimed to jettison European "rationalism," or when Bochner insisted a year later that Conceptualists sought to bracket all considerations of style and metaphor.[7] Not only a local reaction against Abstract Expressionism, this rejection, widespread among artists, writers, and philosophers of the time, targeted a humanism that had had no answer for fascism, the Holocaust, and the Bomb, and that continued to fail in the face of American imperialism in Southeast Asia and elsewhere.[8]

So how are we to understand the blunt juxtaposition posed by Hesse between the Andre plates and the concentration camp? What if we were to see the relationship as one of "antinomy"? Fredric Jameson has defined dialectical thinking as "the unmasking of antinomy as contradiction" through which we come to recognize "the interpenetration of opposites" in any given situation.[9] Thus, for example, Brecht, in "Hollywood Elegies" (1942), his caustic poem about his Los Angeles exile, presents the same place as both heaven and hell—heaven for those who thrive in the culture industry, hell for those who don't. Often Jameson runs the dialectic in the other way so as to point to the utopian possibilities in the most dystopian of historical conditions. For instance, he has presented Walmart as a gigantic corporation that not only preys on local communities but also offers a new model of production and distribution that might be adapted to radically different ends.[10] What if we attempted a similar experiment with the Hesse juxtaposition? The dystopian trajectory is clear enough, but what utopian horizon might be limned, however tendentiously?

Sartre is helpful here. Hesse read his Existentialist writings such as *Nausea* (1938), which informed her sense of absurdity (she cites him in the interview), but the text I want to bring to bear is *Critique of Dialectical Reason* (1960). In the first volume Sartre takes up the problem of seriality, which he sees as fundamental to capitalist society, especially in its consumerist stage, given how its markets and media address us en masse but separate us in doing so. For Sartre seriality is "a plurality of separations," a multitude of alienations, which are internal as well as external; in a serial condition "everyone is the same as the Others in so far as he is Other than himself."[11] His famous example is a queue at a bus stop, a line of anonymous people, backs turned, silent, indifferent to one another. To this serial line Sartre opposed "the fused group," for which he offers the most celebrated instance of revolt, the storming of the Bastille in 1789. Significantly, Sartre positions seriality as primary; fused groups rise out of this state and fall back into it. If atomized, passive alienation sometimes flips into collective, active solidarity, it does so only for a time; soon these "groups die and then disintegrate."[12]

As Briony Fer and Mignon Nixon have underscored, seriality informs many pieces by Hesse; it is a structure she inherited from both Minimalism and Conceptualism. And, like her friend Sol LeWitt, she pushed its logic toward the illogical; this is one more antinomy crucial to her aesthetic.[13] "Series, serial, serial art is another way of repeating absurdity," Hesse stated, and, curious about words as she was, she would have known that "absurd" stems from the Latin for "out of tune," the regular tipped into the irregular.[14] More importantly, Hesse turned seriality back toward its Sartrean opposite of fusion. Several works illustrated in the interview perform her characteristic drama of composition and decomposition, material concentration and formal dispersion. To be sure, this tension between binding and unbinding has psychic resonances, which are well discussed by Fer and Nixon, but it also has sociopolitical implications, which are not much considered.[15]

That Hesse was concerned with the serial and the fused, the separate and the together, is intimated in the titles of some of her sculptures, such as *Ennead* (1966), named after a family of nine deities in Egyptian mythology, and *Vinculum I* and *II* (both 1969), named after the Latin for "bond." (Germane, too, is that "vinculum" is used in anatomy for connective tissue and in mathematics for the horizontal line placed over a group of terms to indicate that they are to be treated as a single entity.) *Ennead* consists of nine strands of dyed string that begin evenly spaced near the top of a dark rectangle on the wall, only to fall three feet into actual space where many of the strands tangle before they rise to the adjacent wall where they are again attached: "stringy versus mass," serial versus fused. A different interplay occurs in *Vinculum I*, a double ladder structure of metal screens covered with latex; the two vertical series of panels, which rise above human height, are both separated and sutured by the vinyl tubes that fall between them. *Repetition Nineteen* (1968) activates the serial-fused dynamic in another way. These nineteen fiberglass buckets are both like and unlike, and Hesse allowed them to be rearranged as though to underscore the relay between individual and group. Sometimes this dynamic is staged between works, as in *Schema* and *Sequel* (both 1967–1968). In *Schema* little latex hemispheres are neatly placed on a latex square in twelves rows of twelve each, while in *Sequel* little latex spheres are spread as through randomly on a cheesecloth rectangle. The title suggests that *Sequel* follows *Schema*, but seriality and fusion are in play variously in both, and they are presented as bound up with each other.[16]

Since seriality runs through Pop as well as Minimalism and Conceptualism, it was much on the minds of artists and critics at the time. *Artforum* alone published "The Serial Attitude" by Bochner in December 1967 and "Serial Imagery" by John Coplans in October 1968. For his part Bochner deemed seriality "self-exhausting and solipsistic"; as a result, its sociopolitical dimension goes unremarked, and no mention of Sartre is made.[17] This is true of other relevant texts as well, even though the problem of the serial and the fused was everywhere evident in contemporary politics. The fusion of civil rights, antiwar, and feminist movements, both internally and with each other, was a very vexed issue in a society that was ever more serial as well as spectacular.[18]

To return to my initial question: What possible utopia could be glimpsed in the linking of Minimalist object and concentration camp? The very possibility seems offensive, but dialectical thinking is often perverse in this way, an overturning (*per-version*) of the accepted framing of a problem. If Hesse was antinomic in her thinking, Andre aimed to be dialectical in his. "My work is part of the objective condition of capitalist American society in the 20th century," he wrote in 1975; nonetheless, "I would like to say that my work is socialist art."[19] Already in 1966 Andre had asserted that it is "communistic because the form is equally accessible to all."[20] This thinking might sound more magical than Marxist, yet what it suggests is that art, in order to be critical, must be immanent to the structures of its world—in this case, that it must work *with* the given forms of seriality, of serial objects, serial people, even serial death, in order to work *through* them, that is, to imagine a different life beyond them.[21] Perhaps in her juxtaposition of Andre plates and concentration camp Hesse means to signal not only the importance of affective intensity in art but also the necessity of an artistic figuration of serial absence transformed into fused presence.

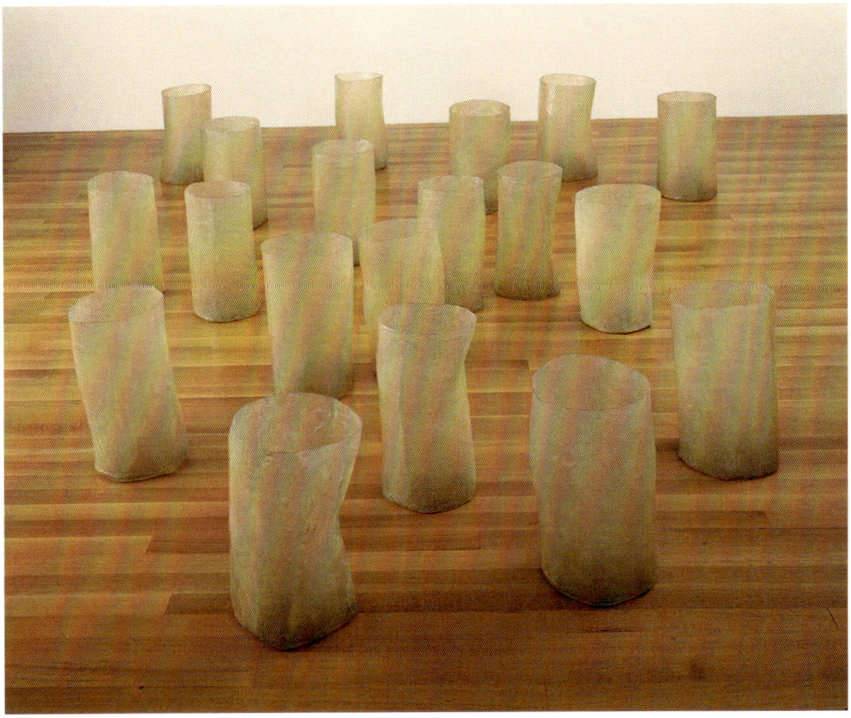

Eva Hesse, *Repetition Nineteen III*, 1968. Fiberglass and polyester resin, 19 units, each 19–20¼ × 11–12¾ inches. Museum of Modern Art. © Estate of Eva Hesse. Courtesy Hauser & Wirth.

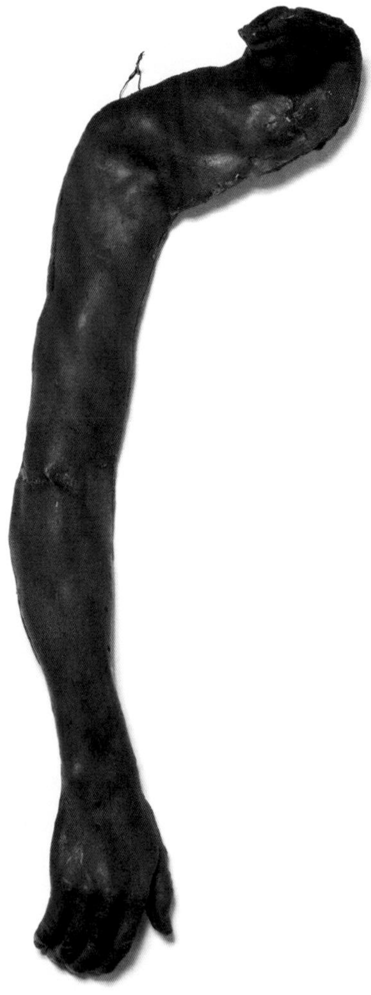

Bruce Nauman, *From Hand to Mouth*, 1967. Wax on cloth, 28 × 10⅛ × 4 inches. Hirshhorn Museum. © Bruce Nauman / Artists Rights Society (ARS). Courtesy Sperone Westwater.

9 The Underside of Things

When Bruce Nauman was in graduate school at the University of California, Davis in the mid 1960s, the traditional media of visual art were in trouble. The best new work, Donald Judd had asserted, was neither painting nor sculpture, and he was hardly alone in this judgment. So what might serve as a medium in default of the usual ones? What might count as art at all? In 1917 Duchamp had declared that art is whatever the artist names as such. Fifty years later Nauman believed that art is whatever an artist does in his studio—"pacing around," for example—and in lieu of painting or sculpture the body might be a place to start.[1] In this way Nauman turned a negative condition into a positive possibility. In 1949 John Cage wrote, "I have nothing to say and I am saying it"; two decades later Nauman said in effect, "I have nothing to do and I am doing it."[2] Although this formulation isn't as dire as "I can't go on, I'll go on," Nauman did share with Beckett (another early influence) a keen sense of stark humor. For instance, in a short film titled *Square Dance* (1967–1968) Nauman steps around a rectangle chalked on his studio floor in a deadpan manner that both parodies the modernist obsession with this form and opens it up to movement.

For Nauman "art became more of an activity and less of a product," a shift that aligned him with contemporaries such as Richard Serra and Eva Hesse as well as choreographers such as Simone Forti, Yvonne Rainer, and Trisha Brown, who refreshed dance with everyday gestures and basic tasks. At the same time, as Anne Wagner has argued, Nauman held on to historical sculpture as a "shadow antithesis" and undid "the outworn ethos of monolith and monument" from the inside.[3] The demythologizing of this art carried over to the figure of the artist; certainly, failure is a persistent theme in Nauman (as it was in his contemporary Vito Acconci). An early photograph titled *Failing to Levitate in the Studio* (1966) shows Nauman collapsed between two chairs—no transcendence there—and an early neon piece turns the lofty sentiment "The true artist helps the world by revealing mystic truths" into a kitschy curlicue.

Although Nauman relied on his own body, his presence was not guaranteed; long ago he declared his interest in "withdrawal as an art form."[4] Even when Nauman offers his own measurements, as he does in *Neon Templates of the Left Side of My Body, Taken in Ten-Inch Intervals* (1966), what is conveyed is absence more than presence. This is also the case with *Wax Impressions of the Knees of Five Famous Artists* (1966), only here the nonpresence is complicated further by deceit: this frieze punctuated by five indentations is fiberglass and resin, not wax, and the marks are his own, not the auratic relics of any great visionaries. At the same time, his corporeal substitutes often serve to evoke the body all the more—the chair is his favorite "stand-in for the figure"—and this is true, too, when Nauman shapes other voids, as in *The Cast of the Space under My Chair* (1965–1968). The concern with "the underside and backside of things" became central to his early work.[5]

Many artists were enamored of the Duchampian readymade, but not Nauman or, for that matter, Serra or Hesse. Again, they stressed process over product, which led them back to Jasper Johns, who not only foregrounded art as making but also used simple devices like stencils and rulers in this making. In addition, Johns pointed Nauman to the late Duchamp who cast different parts of the body, a cue that helped Nauman get around the precedent of the Minimalist object. In 1959 Duchamp made a plaster of the right side of his face, added a drawing of his profile, and called it *With My Tongue in My Cheek*. In other words, he took a phrase for saying one thing while meaning another and literalized this definition of irony. Nauman tried his hand at this impossible reducing out of linguistic ambiguity in several works. These include *Henry Moore Bound to Fail* (1967/70), an iron cast of two arms held behind a back; *From Hand to Mouth* (1967), a wax cast of just this length of the body (the model was not Nauman but his first wife, Judy Govan); and *Feet of Clay* (1967/70), a photograph of his extremities lightly modeled in this earthy material. "Sometimes it's necessary to state the obvious" is one moral that Nauman learned from Johns, but the actual lesson is that meaning is never simple—an idea that Johns gifted Nauman through his reading of Wittgenstein as well as Beckett.[6]

"There's a kind of restraint and morality in Johns" that Nauman also appreciated.[7] With an eye to his use of cast body parts such as blank faces, Leo Steinberg termed this Johnsian posture one of "sufferance" before the world, which appeared to press on his passive art almost directly.[8] Nauman transformed this sufferance into self-examination: "doing things you don't particularly want to do . . . to find out why you're resisting."[9] In this way his bodily actions took on an emotional charge, and his studio became a stage for a psyche turned inside out. "Anger and frustration are two very strong feelings of motivation for me," Nauman admitted, and in the 1970s his work did take on a violent edge. Aggression came to the fore—a 1973 lithograph declares (in reversed script) "Pay Attention Motherfuckers"—as did the relay between sadistic and masochistic impulses—"Help Me Hurt Me" reads a 1975 lithograph. His neon pieces flash binary warnings to the effect that we are all trapped in basic oppositions of domination and submission and life and death. His stick figures, also in neon, grind away at each other in mechanical acts of torturous sex, while his *Hanged Man* (1985) alternates between being garroted and erect and being dead and limp as though the relay between life and death was a simple on-off switch. Nauman locates this aggression in our humor and sexuality, but he also intimates that it is rampant in our media and politics as well. One neon sign from 1981–1982 flickers in sequence "violins violence silence." Another from 1984 conjugates different verbs like "speak" and "cry" with "live and die."

Nauman didn't restrict this theater of cruelty to the human realm. In 1979 he moved with his second wife, the painter Susan Rothenberg, to a ranch in New Mexico, where a new series of pieces soon emerged: carousels hung with animal dummies (made of polyurethane foam), often cut up with no fur, that slowly rotate in an endless circuit. At the same time Nauman suggested that this disassembly hell had ample slots for humans too. During this period, one of neoimperialist adventures under Reagan and Thatcher and authoritarian crackdowns by other regimes, he also conceived steel cages, claustrophobic corridors, and underground tunnels, some of which were equipped with video monitors. An oppressive sense of discipline and punishment, security and surveillance, pervades this body of work. *South America Triangle* (1981), which features a cast-iron chair suspended upside down within a large frame of steel beams, conveys more than a hint of political torture, while *Learned Helplessness in Rats (Rock and Roll Drummer)* (1988), which consists of both a maze and a live video of a rat in the maze made frantic by the percussive beating of a punk percussionist, suggests a form of scientific abuse that cuts across species. Here Nauman shows how thin the line is between perceptual experiment and behaviorist manipulation.[10]

How are these different registers of violence—psychic and political, technological and scientific—connected? For Nauman they are all rooted in a fundamental splitting of the self. Almost in a Lacanian way he intimates that our mirror image, however coherent and intimate it might appear, is actually divided and alien, and that narcissism easily flips into aggression.[11] When video art first emerged, Rosalind Krauss theorized it in terms of "an aesthetics of narcissism," but early adopters like Nauman discovered that the relay between camera and monitor, self and image, is often delayed and sometimes broken, and that the medium is suited to a sense of rupture more than repletion. As in Beckett soliloquies that disperse the self rather than declare it, Nauman explored this breaking up of body and ego alike ("Make Me Think Me," a 1993 drawing exhorts). As we walk down one of his corridors with a camera

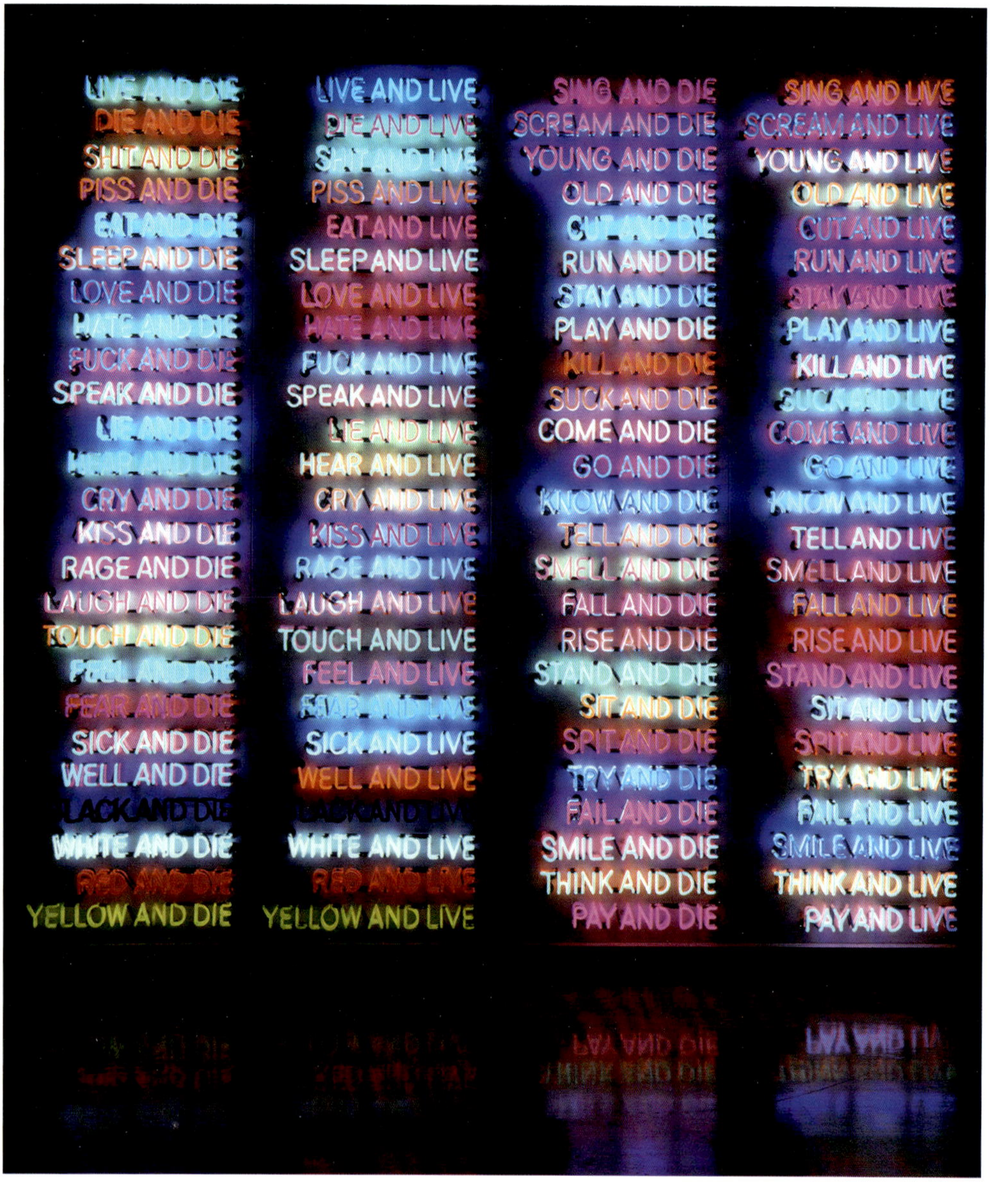

Bruce Nauman, *One Hundred Live and Die*, 1984. Neon tubing with clear glass tubing on metal, 8 feet 10 inches × 11 feet × 21 inches. Benesse House Museum, Naoshima. © Bruce Nauman / Artists Rights Society (ARS). Courtesy Sperone Westwater.

behind us and a monitor in front, our image gets bigger, not smaller, and we feel discombobulated by our own appearance. Nauman messes with his own image too. In a series of videos he takes the epochal animation of the body that the word "contrapposto" names—when the lively Greek kouros emerged from its static Egyptian precedent—and demonstrates how visual media confound the figure instead; Nauman is doubled, reversed, and fragmented, not enlivened, let alone made whole. Divided by our image as well as by our unconscious, we are never self-same, and Nauman suggests that this splitting is compounded technologically and politically: again, aggression and anomie are at once within us and all around us. In many ways this confusion of inside and outside is the great subject of his un-funhouse art.

This work hardly needs a silver lining—it is anti-redemptive after all—but an unexpected one can be extracted nonetheless. In 1995 the Museum of Modern Art staged a large Nauman show, and two moments in the exhibition stick in my memory. In the first instance I followed a young woman into a constrictive room flooded with yellow light in which a male voice repeated, in various tones of threat, "Get out of the room, get out of my mind.'" We listened together for several minutes, made uneasy by the tense scenario; then, as she left, she muttered under her breath, "I had a boyfriend like that once," and we both burst out laughing at the miserabilism of men. The second moment involved watching my two sons, young at the time, delight in a two-channel video titled *Good Boy Bad Boy* (1985), in which a black man and a white woman conjugate, at times sweetly, at other times furiously, such verbs as shit and fuck: "I shit, you shit, we shit, this is shitting . . ." The boys found it hilarious, scandalous, and scary all at once, and I like to think that they intuited a weird commonality there, one that we used to call the human condition. For Nauman our humanity is steeped in misunderstanding and cruelty, and he aims to humanize us through the bits of our being that often seem the most inhuman—base bodily acts and baser psychic rages.

Nauman calls some pieces "leftovers," and other pieces model spaces that seem more virtual than actual, so any presentation of his work can feel a little inert—so many things scattered in a field like the props of a performance that we missed or that never happened.[12] Then there is this paradox: not many of his works are true knockouts—Nauman is masterpiece-averse—yet he is very impactful nonetheless (his friend Serra deemed him the most influential artist of his American generation apart from Warhol). One sees many connections to younger figures, male and female, expected and unexpected, such as Cindy Sherman, who also stages a self that is not one; Jenny Holzer, who also delights in contradictory messages; Mike Kelley, who also probed the pathetic underside of men; Robert Gober, who also presents the body image as divided, even damaged; and Doris Salcedo and Mona Hatoum, who also excel at spaces evocative of political violence and social anomie. And the influence extends to others as well, such as Matthew Barney (art is what the artist does in the studio), Rachel Whiteread (casts of negative space), Claire Fontaine (neon alarms), Rachel Harrison (sculpture as pseudo-pathological contraption), Nicolás Guagnini (psychosexual contortions), and so on.

The Nauman oeuvre is thus anachronic in the sense that it anticipates the work of subsequent artists who reposition it in turn. He presaged the fascination with abject states and troubled masculinities in the 1990s, and he was concerned with surveillance long before 9/11. Then, too, there is no more autofictional artist than Nauman, and his theater of cruelty, in which impotence triggers violence in a nihilistic way, seems to play out daily in the news. Finally, there are his *Clown Torture* videos from 1987. In one piece a clown repeats (as if stuck) the opening of a ghost story, "It was a dark and stormy night." Could that be Trump behind the face paint? In another a clown on a toilet weeps and moans "No no no . . ." Is that us?

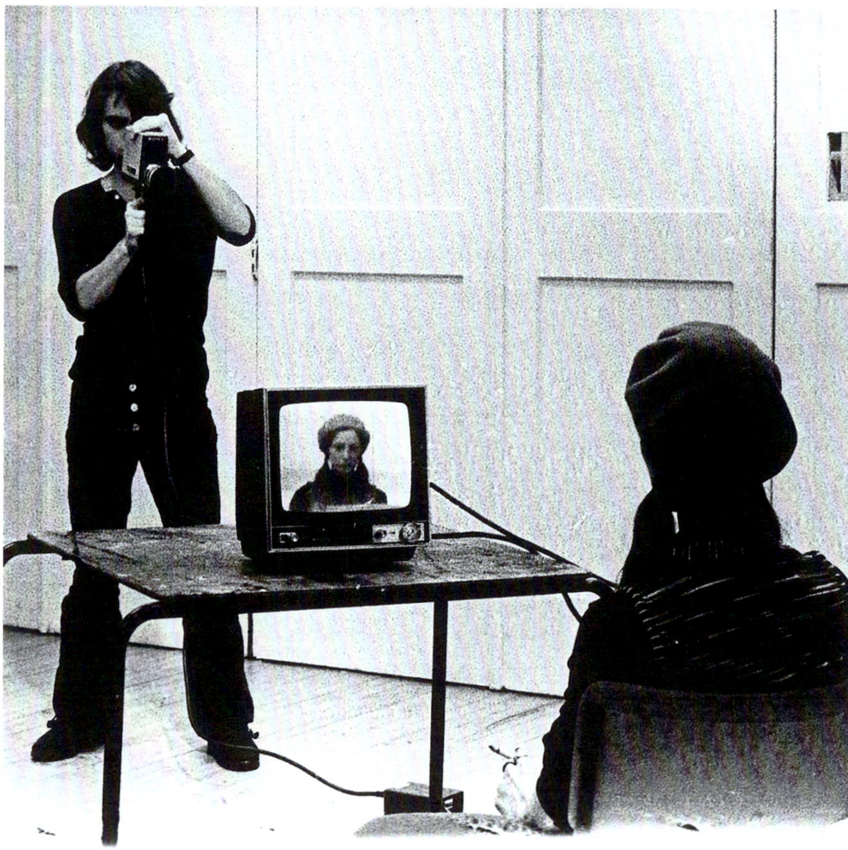

Dan Graham, *Two Consciousness Projection(s)*, 1972, performed at the Nova Scotia College of Art and Design, Halifax, Canada. © Estate of Dan Graham. Courtesy of the Estate of Dan Graham and Marian Goodman Gallery.

10 Cultural Studies

Although Dan Graham was never as celebrated as his contemporaries Robert Smithson, Richard Serra, Bruce Nauman, and Eva Hesse, he was, for many subsequent artists, the most important figure of his generation. What might explain this influence? Minimalism opened art to the involvement of actual bodies in social spaces, but this potential still had to be activated, and Graham did just that. "All my work is a critique of Minimal art," he commented. "It begins with Minimal art, but it's about spectators observing themselves as they're observed by other people."[1] Hence many of the strategies associated with his work, including interactions between two performers, performances by the artist that directly engage audiences, films and videos that reflect on the means and spaces of their own making, installations involving viewers with partitions, mirrors, and videos, and architectural models and glass pavilions.

First and foremost, Graham questioned the phenomenological presence to which Minimalism aspired. In various pieces he demonstrated how that presence is complicated by duration and movement, media and technology, the persistence of memory and the sheer fact of other people. Although Maurice Merleau-Ponty, the phenomenologist most important to the Minimalists, dwelled on the gaps between self and image and subject and object, as well as on the decentering produced by the presence of others, he also promised a wholeness of being in "the flesh of the world."[2] Graham took programmatic aim at this ideological soft spot.

As early as *Project for Slide Projector* (1966) Graham questioned the possibility of any direct relation to the object of perception. This piece is a coordinated sequence of projected photographs of nested glass boxes taken at different positions and focal lengths; given that its elements are continually in and out of focus, no sculptural object as such emerges. Then, in a one-minute double film projection titled *Roll* (1970), Graham played with the non-fit between subject and object. Here two films are projected on opposite walls, one of the artist rolling on the ground with a camera in his hands, the other of what he filmed while rolling, a landscape in slow tumble. Caught between the two projections, the viewer can't suture the two scenes.

Graham further questioned our transparency to both self and other in his performances and installations, which were and are often complicated by partitions, mirrors, and videos. A compelling instance is *Opposing Mirrors and Video Monitors on Time Delay* (1974). With its two wall mirrors, two video cameras, and two color monitors opposite one another, the viewer is thrown into a dueling mise-en-abîme of reflections and relays that renders any coherent sense of self in space nearly impossible to achieve. The architectural models and pavilions that emerged from such installations also complicate phenomenological experience. Produced in glass, often in the form of two-way mirrors, these pieces distort our body images, and sometimes the most basic of spatial distinctions are confused. Importantly, Graham didn't restrict these works to the preserves of the art world, proposing to locate them in everyday settings as well—a middle-class home (as in *Alteration to a Suburban House*, 1978), a city building (as in *Three Linked Cubes*, 1986), a public park (as in *Elliptical Pavilion*, 1995–1999).

Graham thus passed through the crucible of Minimalism into an expanded world of projects. Along with other artists he opened phenomenological experience to social and historical contexts, extending the possibilities of "medium" greatly. This rethinking had already prompted his early magazine pieces such as the influential *Homes for America* (1966–1967), a deadpan typology of suburban tract housing that, among other things, took over the publication page as an artistic site. Such reconsideration also led to his later essays on rock music, television comedy, garden history, corporate atria, and postmodern architecture. This concern with "the social-economic framework" of culture at large distinguished Graham not only from the tautologies of much Conceptual art (which he once dismissed as "academic bullshit") but also from the involutions of much Institution Critique (that is, its tendency to remain within the prescribed parameters of the gallery and the museum).[3] "Art is a social sign" was always his motto.

In American art after 1960 Minimalist and Pop genealogies often appear distinct. From the start, however, Graham crossed the two lines and short-circuited the opposition. Like Nauman, he presented situations that implicated the body as well as the image, space as well as media. Moreover, Graham suggested that these terms—body, space, image, media—are not sexually indifferent. In the performance *Two Consciousness Projection(s)* (1972), for example, a seated woman, focused on a television monitor of her own image, verbalizes the contents of her consciousness, as a standing man describes the woman as she appears in his camera. (A later version of the performance in the nude raised the gender stakes all the more.) And though Graham didn't

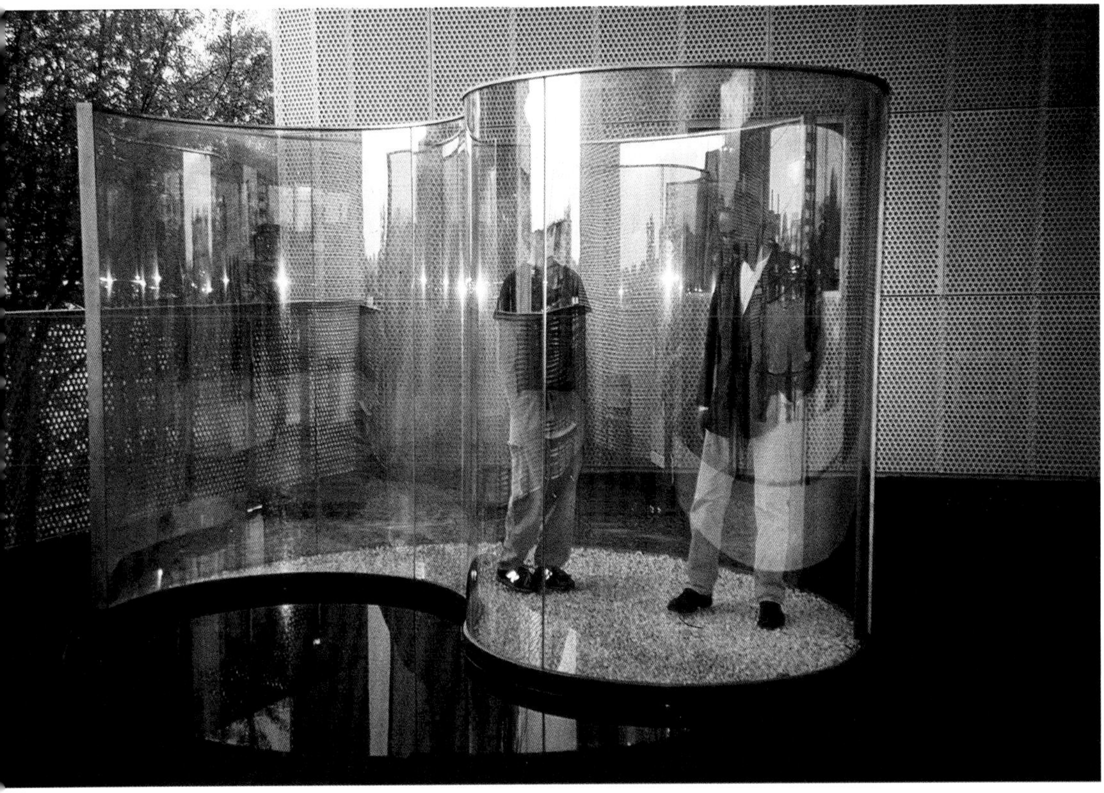

Dan Graham, *Yin/Yang Pavilion*, 2003. Tempered glass, steel, gravel, and water, 7 × 11 × 11 feet, installed at Simmons Hall, MIT, Cambridge, MA. © Estate of Dan Graham. Courtesy of the Estate of Dan Graham and Marian Goodman Gallery.

develop the psychological theater set up by such performances in the manner of Nauman, let alone Vito Acconci, he did anticipate some of what was to come in feminist art. "I was a feminist from the early '70s," he once claimed.[4]

Perhaps this is enough to suggest why Graham is highly regarded by many subsequent artists; in retrospect, though, his practice prompts some questions. At times his version of experiment suggests a laboratory where the viewer is positioned as scientist and test subject in one. For instance, in his initial pavilion, *Public Space/Two Audiences* (1976), a soundproofed structure is divided in two by a pane of glass, and the rear wall of one room is mirrored. Viewers must pick a room to enter (each has a door) where they are instructed to stay for thirty minutes (in our distracted age, the stipulated time is now ten minutes). One purpose of the piece is to see what kind of behavior might develop in each space—social, asocial, or in-between. There is more than a touch of the Skinner box here, and in fact Graham did intend "a combination of behaviorism and phenomenology."[5] This sense of manipulation might qualify the claims, made by both the artist and his advocates, about the egalitarian and democratic implications of his work.

More significant are the mixed ramifications of the opening to social and historical discourses that Graham helped to initiate. "Twenty years before 'Cultural Studies' became a 'discipline,' Dan Graham practiced it as a mode of artistic intervention," Benjamin Buchloh wrote in a blurb for *Rock My Religion* (1993), a collection of writings and projects by the artist. Certainly, along with Smithson and others, Graham initiated a reordering of the cultural sources of visual art as radical as that proposed by the Independent Group in the 1950s. Apart from *Homes for America*, the best example is his video *Rock My Religion* (1982–1984), a "documentary fiction" that traces a genealogy of ecstatic communion from the Shakers to rock 'n' roll and punk, arguing that, in its sexualization of ecstasy, rock turned religion upside down, but that, in its Oedipal rebellion, it marginalized women in doing so. For all its insights, though, *Rock My Religion* qualifies as art mostly by default, and, even as it exudes the enthusiasm of a super-smart autodidact, it also suffers from the idiosyncrasy of self-schooling.[6] At the same time, the piece demonstrates how Graham was able to stay in meaningful dialogue with a wide range of artists and musicians, some much younger than he.

"I always try to put together two things that shouldn't go together," Graham once commented.[7] In this regard *Rock My Religion* links Ann Lee, the founder of the Shakers, to Patti Smith, and the subjects of his essays range from Walter Benjamin to Dean Martin. Taken by the theory of estrangement presented by the Russian formalist Viktor Shklovsky, Graham aimed to defamiliarize through unexpected juxtapositions. Yet, for Shklovsky, to defamiliarize convention was to push art ahead—in his famous phrase, art proceeds "by knight's moves"—while Graham sometimes shifts into other worlds laterally in such a way as to almost disappear into them altogether. For all his opening to everyday subjects and settings, then, a question of legibility arises in his work. How objective is his matrix of references? Did its logic exist only in his head? Graham once referred to his art as "a passionate hobby," and clearly his commitments drove his art.[8] But does the DIY history of one artist extend to the rest of us, or might some of his "hybrids," however productive for Graham, be sterile for others?

But then the interdisciplinarity pioneered by Graham was not mere culture-surfing, and, again, it has proved fecund for many artists that followed him. What Warhol was to the mass-media fascinations of the Pictures artists, so Graham was to the subcultural investigations of Mike Kelley, Tony Oursler, John Miller, and Nicolás Guagnini (to name only a few), with the proviso that, in part because of artists like Graham, art history no longer seems to develop in that old dynastic way.

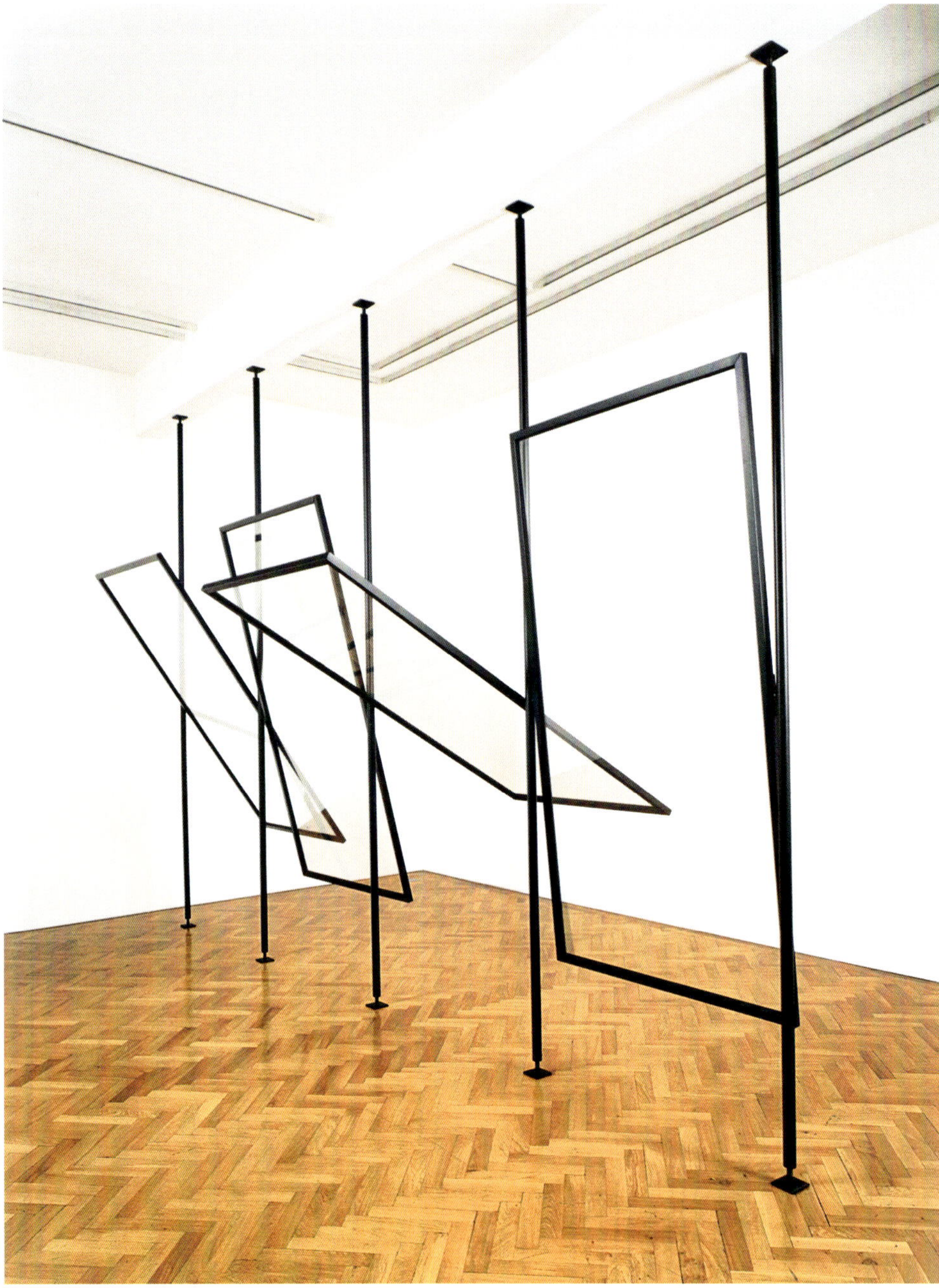

Gerhard Richter, *4 Panes of Glass,* 1967. Glass and steel, each unit 77¼ × 41¾ inches. Herbert Foundation, Ghent. © Gerhard Richter. Courtesy the artist.

11 In a Glass Darkly

Gerhard Richter isn't well known for his glass pieces, but they have played an important role in his work. Over the years he has expressed different ideas about them. In a note from 1971 he writes, "Perhaps the Doors, Curtains, Surface Pictures, Panes of Glass, etc. are metaphors of despair, prompted by the dilemma that our sense of sight causes us to apprehend things, but at the same time restricts and partly precludes our apprehension of reality."[1] One piece in question here, *4 Panes of Glass* (1967), his first one in glass, consists of the titular elements set vertically in iron frames and attached with iron rods from floor to ceiling in a way that (at least originally) allowed viewers to rotate them. The work appears very matter of fact; yet, as in related Minimalist objects, *4 Panes* sets up a double tension, first, between the transparency of the panes and the physicality of the frames and rods, and, second, between what we know—these are four identical rectangles in front of us—and what we perceive—different framings, reflections, and refractions caught in the angled glass. Through this double tension Richter stages an almost Cartesian doubt about "our apprehension of reality."

A year later, in 1972, Richter returned to this glass piece: "Illusionism has never interested me, with the exception of the *Large Curtain* painting, the *5 Doors* and the *4 Panes of Glass*. Those rather structured paintings are out of the frame, and in fact I rather disappointed myself, because I don't really want to think structurally in this way. I prefer to go through destruction to construction."[2] This dense statement speaks to a new caution about *4 Panes*—that it moved too quickly "out of the frame" of painting into the actual space of "structure"—which can be read, in turn, as an implicit critique of the Minimalist shift from painting to the "specific object" and the architecture around it, a shift associated, above all, with Donald Judd and Dan Flavin.[3] Richter is disappointed by this shift, or rather with the feeling that he followed it almost obediently (etymologically, a "disappointment" is a "loss of position"). It is as though it led him to stray from his preferred path "through destruction to construction," that is, with making painting by undoing it rather than obviating it, as the Minimalists had done.

Several years later, in 1977, in an important letter to Benjamin Buchloh, a close interlocutor, Richter again altered his view of the glass piece and its

Minimalist associations: "In the Grey Pictures it's lack of differentiation, nothing, nil, the Beginning and the End; in the Panes of Glass it's the analogy with attitudes and possibilities; in the Color Charts it's chance, anything is correct, or rather Form is Nonsense; in the new Abstract Pictures it's arbitrariness, almost anything is possible."[4] In this litany of negatives the relatively positive assessment of *4 Panes* stands out, elliptical though it is. With his doubt about perception and his skepticism about structure abated, Richter is intrigued by "the analogy with attitudes and possibilities" that *4 Panes* suggests, by the way that the framings, reflections, and refractions of the glass permit an experience of actual and virtual positions, not only of the works themselves but of their viewers as well. In short, he sees *4 Panes* as involved in the phenomenological dimension of Minimalism with its special attention to the interrelationship among artwork, perception, and environment.

A few years later still, in a telegraphic comment of 1981, Richter focuses on yet another aspect of glass, its mirroring, which he soon explored directly in his work. "Picture in itself," Richter writes, "cropped effect, likeness to photograph, readymade character."[5] This studio note is again cryptic, but it does point to the automatic illusionism of mirrored glass as well as its everyday quality as furniture. Richter then adds an abrupt "polemic" about such glass: "devaluing of all other pictures; provocation of the viewer, who sees himself instead of a picture."[6] On the one hand, a mirror is a "picture in itself" because it images whatever is placed before it, and, as Richter comments later, it is "the only picture that always looks different."[7] As such, it trumps and so "devalues" other kinds of representation. On the other hand, mirrored glass is "devalued" in turn because it confounds viewers, who can't get around their own reflection to see the glass properly. Traditional paintings, especially in the vertical format of the portrait, invite our bodily identification. (The ego is first and foremost an image, Freud tells us, a basic point that Lacan underscores in his famous account of the mirror stage in our development.) In fact, the felt analogy between a composed painting and a contemplative viewer is so fundamental that we are mostly unaware of it until it is interfered with. And this is precisely what the glass pieces do: our reflection, in the sense of our mirrored image, disrupts our reflection, in the sense of our contemplation. "I see the mirror as a metaphor of your work as a whole," Hans Ulrich Obrist commented to Richter. "The word 'reflect' has two planes of meaning, which bring the viewer into the picture, and thus the viewer is in two states at once."[8]

Finally, in 1991, at a time when Richter was at work on glass pieces coated with single colors, such as *Mirror, Blood Red*, he had this to say: "In the case of the colored mirrors, the result was a kind of cross between a monochrome painting and a mirror, a 'Neither/Nor'—which is what I like about it."[9] This is another rich statement, one that Richter repeats, so it deserves special attention. If some of the glass pieces like *4 Panes* evoke windows, others like *Blood Red* double as mirrors, and both allude to the monochrome as well. Of course, the window and the mirror were the primary paradigms of Western painting from the Renaissance onward, and they were often challenged but never overthrown, at least until the monochrome, a prized device of the twentieth-century avant-garde, canceled both.[10] Buchloh has situated the glass pieces brilliantly in this modernist context, so little more needs to be added on that score.[11] Still, the question remains: Why did Richter call up these old models of painting, not only after the postwar repetition of the monochrome by Rauschenberg, Piero Manzoni, and others, but also during the Minimalist and Postminimalist move from painting into ambient space? According to Buchloh, Richter effectively voids the old paradigms of window and mirror, and "the monochrome seems to have become an affectless record of loss" as well, no longer "mystical in its purity or critical in its self-reflexivity," as it was for Malevich and Rodchenko respectively.[12] Moreover, the glass pieces attest to "the extreme negation of the very promises of an emancipatory potential of perceptual and social experience with which monochromy and transparency were initially endowed."[13] Although I agree with this assessment, it doesn't fully account for the ambiguity of the "neither-nor" quality that Richter valued in these works.

In his epochal treatise *De pictura* (1435) Alberti proposed the window as the paragon of painting. According to Svetlana Alpers in *The Art of Describing*, this southern European model became so dominant in the early modern period that it occluded a paradigm favored in northern Europe, one based on the mirror.[14] For Alpers the window positions the viewer as primary (I see the world arrayed before me), while the mirror puts the world first (it is reflected in the image as though my presence isn't required). However, both Michel Foucault and Louis Marin challenged this north/south dichotomy, which runs deep in the discipline of art history, and argued that "classical representation" actually combines the two models of window and mirror. For Foucault the masterpiece of such representation is Velázquez's *Las Meninas* (1656), whereas for Marin it is Poussin's *Et in Arcadia Ego* (1639), but that matters little: the essence of both paintings is "reflecting transparence."[15] With great panache Velázquez depicts not only a window and a mirror but also the back of the very canvas that he seems to paint on, the subject of which is the king and the queen, who appear dimly in a distant mirror. Again, whereas Alpers sees *Las Meninas* as an anomaly, one caught between northern and southern orientations, Foucault regards it as an epitome of classical representation.[16]

In his glass pieces Richter literalizes the use of windows and mirrors and, in doing so, produces a very unclassical representation, one that we experience as neither "I see the world" nor "the world is seen." These works also defy the first purpose of traditional painting and photography, which is to fix an image, to arrest a figure.[17] ("The pleasant thing," Richter comments about glass, "is that it makes the pictorial space even more variable and more subject to chance than it is in photography.")[18] Often, even as the panes turn our bodily substance into virtual shadow, they also transform ambient light into actual illumination.[19] They thus destabilize not only the objects in front of them—again, no motif is captured once and for all—but also the viewers, whose images are reflected and refracted in protean ways. This effect directly counters the fundamental goal of classical representation, for both paradigms of traditional painting, the window and the mirror, were dedicated to the mastery of the subject as well as the control of the object. In fact, Foucault claimed *Las Meninas* as an epitome of classical representation precisely because it locates the viewer in "the place of the king," which allows us to feel that we are sovereign over a world given to us to behold and to possess. "I see the world"—I summon it into appearance—is a clear expression of such imaginary power, but so too is "the world is seen." On the one hand, the fiction that the world simply appears before us undergirds the empiricist belief that we can know the world objectively and manipulate it instrumentally. On the other hand, the same fiction allows us to look on the world as though in secret, from a position that combines unobserved command with voyeuristic pleasure.[20]

Richter collapses the models of the window and the mirror in his glass works. In the more transparent pieces we struggle to see or to be seen clearly at all, and in the more reflective ones we can't get out of our own way. Objects as well as subjects appear and disappear in a manner that can't be predicted, let alone controlled. They loom up and fade away; they look distorted, obscured, or otherwise lost in space. Lacan once argued that the primary function of traditional painting is not *trompe l'oeil*, to fool the eye, but *dompte-regard*, to tame the gaze.[21] Often the glass pieces do much the opposite: they render the gaze wild. Sometimes the effect approaches the schizophrenic sense of space evoked by the Surrealist associate Roger Caillois, who described the schizoid subject as one possessed by space, without boundaries, "not similar to something, but just *similar*."[22]

How does this dark view of the glass work jibe with the positive comment about its "analogy with attitudes and possibilities"? In part, Richter seems to stage his ambivalence about Minimalism in these pieces; certainly, they point to the changed valence of Minimalism over the years.[23] Initially, according to Judd, the Minimalists turned to specific objects in order to defeat the illusionism of painting once and for all, a mission that Richter first supported (again, "illusionism has never interested me," he wrote in 1972). Yet the reflective surfaces of many Judd boxes and shelves (not to mention the diffusive glow of all Flavin lights) belie this Minimalist rhetoric, and illusionism became rampant in work by Robert Irwin, James Turrell, and others who followed the example of Judd and Flavin. With these artists, the pictorial is not negated by objecthood so much as atomized in space. Initially, too, the Minimalists underscored the spatial parameters of the artwork in order to guide the phenomenological experience of the viewer. Yet the elaboration of Minimalism since then—from Turrell to Olafur Eliasson and beyond—has had much the opposite effect: it confounds rather than articulates both space and subject.[24] In short, Minimalist theory is largely contradicted by subsequent practice that purports to develop it, and the Richter glass pieces can be seen to have anticipated this problem.

Historically, interest in phenomenological experience returns during periods of technological transformation; it is as though a focus on the body might offer a respite from the distraction of new media. It's no surprise, then, that Minimalism emerged alongside Pop. But phenomenology can't save us from a world given over to the commodity image, especially in its digital forms. As Dan Graham suggested in his works and writings alike, both the subjects and the spaces posited by Minimalism are never as pure as the phenomenological account of this art suggested; they are always already social and mediated.[25] Seen from a contemporary perspective, Richter makes a similar point with his glass pieces; in this respect they are neither aligned with Minimalism nor opposed to it. Put positively, they allow for a kind of viewing that is both durational, of the sort associated with Minimalism, and punctual, of the sort that Michael Fried, the great antagonist of Minimalism, associated with abstract painting.[26]

Here again Richter revealed his penchant for a "neither-nor" stance, which also speaks to his discomfort with ideological oppositions. This neutrality is the aim of a good number of his key devices: the nonstyle of his snapshot paintings, the blandness of his encyclopedia portraits ("which neutralize everything and all ideology"), the evasive quality of his blurred images, the blasé indifference of his gray paintings, the arbitrary nature of his color charts, and so on.[27] Distinct from negativity, such neutrality serves as a protection against ideological confinement, and it aligns Richter with Roland Barthes, for whom the neutral doesn't cancel meaning so much as it "baffles" it. "I define the Neutral as that which outplays the paradigm," Barthes writes, with "paradigm" defined linguistically as "the opposition of two virtual terms from which, in speaking, I actualize one to produce meaning." "Or rather," he continues, "I call Neutral everything that baffles the paradigm. . . . Whence the idea of a

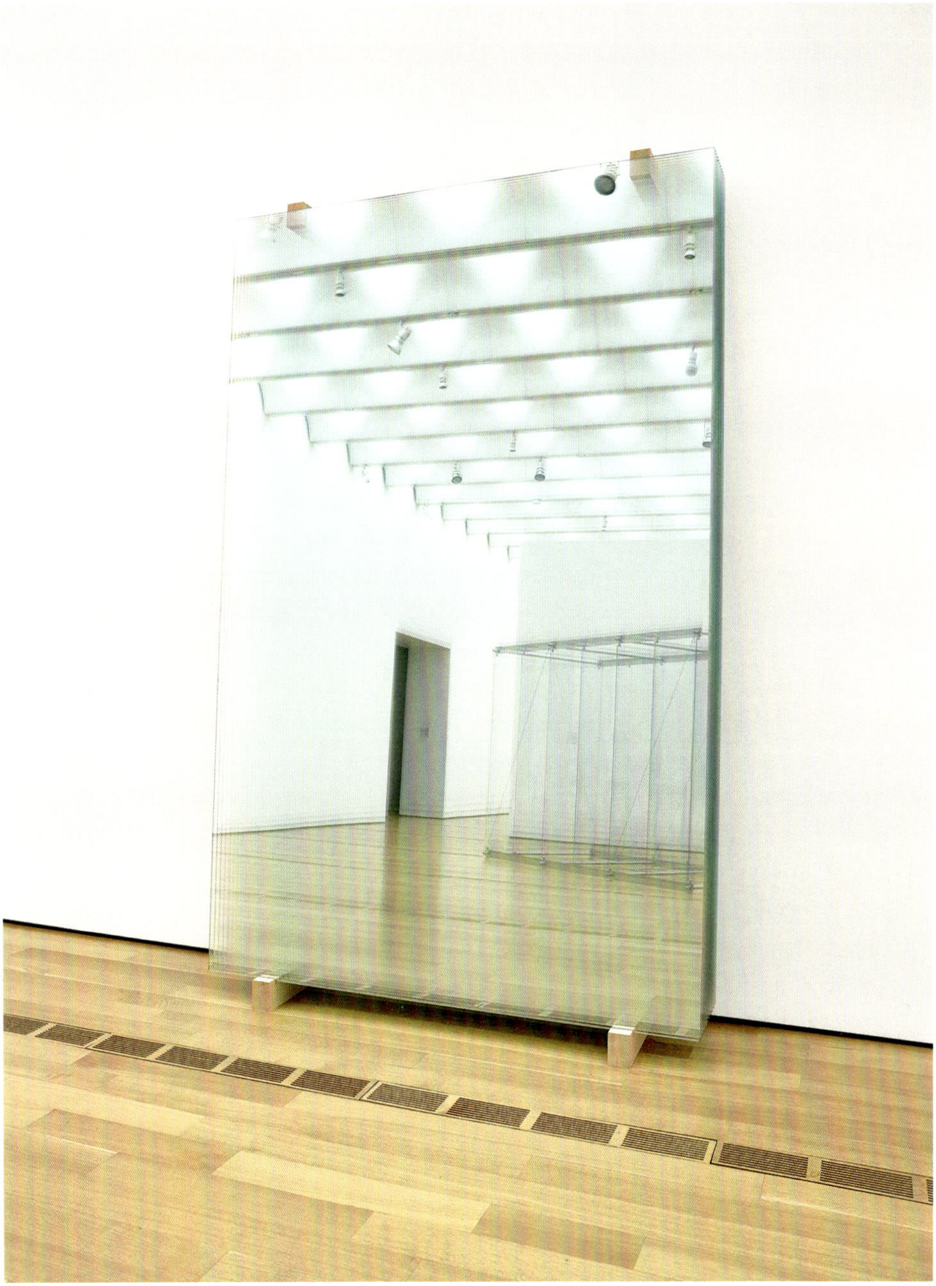

Gerhard Richter, *11 Panes*, 2004. Glass and wood, each unit 109½ × 83½ × ¼ inches. National Galleries of Scotland. © Gerhard Richter. Courtesy the artist.

structural creation that would defeat, annul, or contradict the implacable binarism of the paradigm by means of a third term."[28] It is this third term, this elusive way through restrictive oppositions, that Richter seeks: "Something has to be shown and simultaneously not shown," he believes, "in order perhaps to say something else again, a third thing."[29] That is precisely what the glass pieces attempt through an equal insistence both on window and mirror and on picture and object. In this same way they treat Minimalism as both "a new alphabet" and a problematic phenomenology, and they both activate and baffle viewers.[30]

Not only old paradigms of artistic representation, the window and the mirror are also familiar devices of commercial display, not to mention common instruments of security and surveillance. "Seeing oneself and watching oneself seeing have become the almost exclusive modus of being in the world," Buchloh has commented, and this is even more the case with the dominance of social media.[31] The window and the mirror are often reformatted, sometimes quite literally, by the digital screen, which has become a pervasive model of visuality, one that has already transformed film and television beyond recognition. "Windows" was trademarked long ago, and what is the selfie universe of Facebook and Instagram but an endless hall of mirrors? Several of the glass pieces—the multilayered *11 Panes* (2004) above all—challenge our narcissistic drive for mirroring, as our images are both multiplied and dispersed.

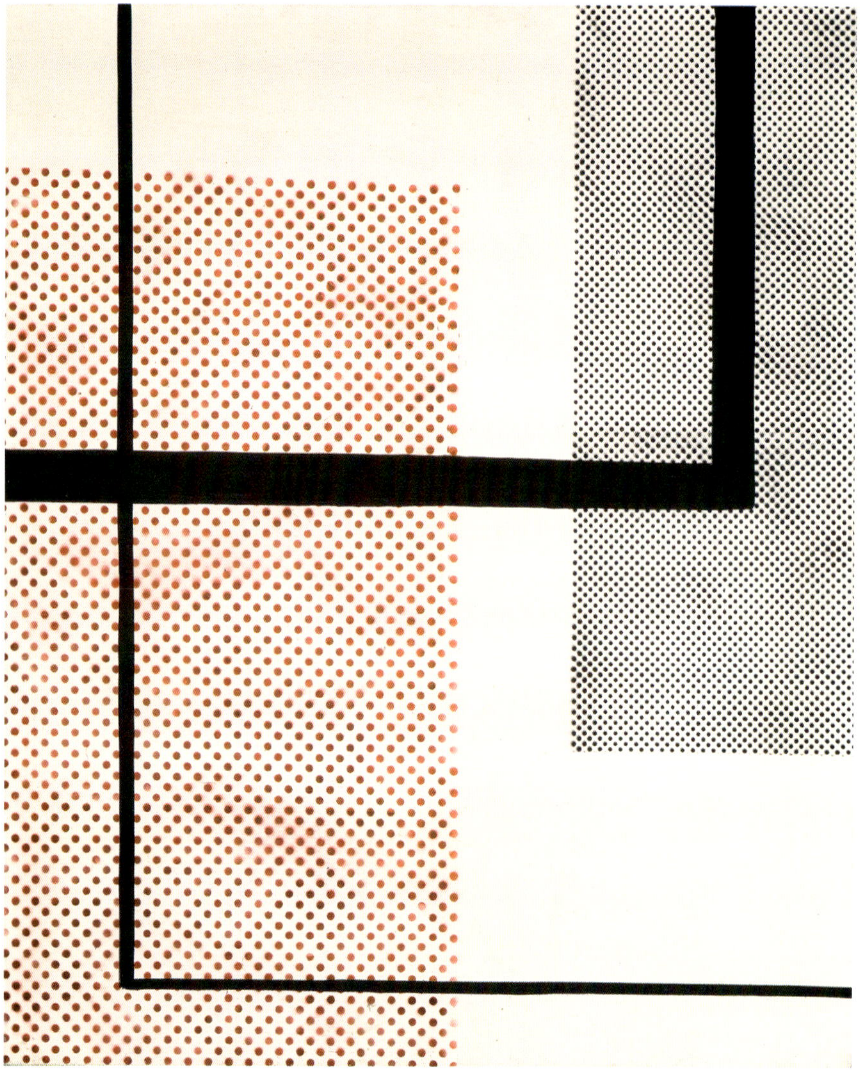

Sigmar Polke, *Constructivist*, 1968. Dispersion paint on canvas, 59 × 49 inches.

12 The Culture of the Raster

Born in Silesia in 1941, the German artist Sigmar Polke fled west with his family twice, first to Thuringia in 1945 and then to Düsseldorf in 1953, where he attended the art academy in the early 1960s. Among his fellow students was Gerhard Richter, another East German émigré, who was close to Polke during this time. In fact, the two are now bound together in art history in a way that resembles the pairing of Robert Rauschenberg and Jasper Johns, with Polke, like Rauschenberg, cast as the restless experimenter, and Richter, like Johns, as the recursive painter. In some ways the mercurial Polke was his own greatest work. Certainly, he learned the importance of persona from his charismatic teacher Joseph Beuys, and he passed this lesson on to subsequent artists who were also wayward performers, such as the German Martin Kippenberger and the American Mike Kelley. His 2014 retrospective was appropriately titled *Alibis*.[1]

If Rauschenberg and Johns prepared the way for Roy Lichtenstein and Andy Warhol, Polke and Richter quickly adapted the work of Lichtenstein and Warhol, which they first encountered in magazines, to their own ends. In 1963, along with Konrad Lueg (soon to metamorphose into the gallerist Konrad Fischer), Polke and Richter claimed the title "German Pop artists" and, with an ironic nod to both Pop in the West and Socialist Realism in the East, contrived the label "Capitalist Realism." Inspired by the early silkscreens of Warhol, Richter developed his famous blur technique to underscore the mediated nature of his source images. For his part Polke riffed on the faux Ben-Day dots devised by Lichtenstein. Although they are hand-painted, his raster spots (*raster* is German for "grid" or "screen") also indicate that his paintings derive from photographic images in newspapers and magazines. However, unlike their Pop predecessors (among whom Richard Hamilton must also be counted), the young Germans didn't much delight in mass media or commercial culture. Despite the fact that they fled East Germany, Polke and Richter were skeptical about the "economic miracle" of West Germany. In two deadpan paintings from 1963–1964, for example, Polke presents three support socks and three white shirts for men, crisply folded on blank grounds, in a serial manner that somehow suggests both the well-being of a white-collar job and the uniformity of a bureaucratic society. His immaculate images of mass-produced chocolates and cookies from the same years also depict new products of plenty as both perfect and empty, and his young man in a tennis sweater is beautiful and bland in a similar way: the good life of the postwar period as the banal pastime of leisure and sport. The doubt about a reconstructed West Germany raised in such paintings extended to its quick embrace of American imports like Pop art, and this makes German Pop cut critically against its own artistic source as well.

In his best works of the 1960s Polke is thus double-edged, equally biting about the vulgar lows and the arty highs of the consumer culture then new to West Germany. He is also scathing about the institutional fate of modernist abstraction during this period. Thus a 1963 watercolor reduces the pure abstraction of Mondrian, with the utopian ambition of its primary colors, to a decorative sheet of polka dots, and a 1969 painting turns the transcendental abstraction of Malevich into a mock-totalitarian order from on high: *Higher Beings Commanded: Paint the Upper-Right Corner Black!* His best jibe is a 1968 painting simply titled *Moderne Kunst*, an array of modernist tokens—Expressionist gestures, Suprematist geometries, Bauhausian angles—presented as so many inert signs in a one-painting résumé of early twentieth-century art history. These works debunk international modernism, to be sure, but they also question the West German celebration of this art as a show of distance from the Nazi condemnation of modernism in particular and from the Nazi past in general, as though one could believe, as Polke once put it (in a nasty twist on the infamous motto at Auschwitz), that "Kunst macht frei."[2] In this respect his most acerbic piece is another 1968 painting, *Constructivist*, which presents, in faux-Lichtenstein dots, a faux-Mondrian composition that resembles a backward swastika. In front of an overdetermined travesty like this, which is also a well-made artwork, one hasn't a leg to stand on.

Produced in the wake of Minimalism as well as Pop, these paintings from the late 1960s suggest that the abstract forms and the serial formats of twentieth-century art had been overcoded by the logic of the commodity image—all those advertisements for socks, shirts, and chocolate bars. Nothing escapes the "cliché quality" of "the Culture of the Raster," as Polke phrased it in 1966, so why not push it to the limit and see what happens?

> I like the impersonal, neutral, and manufactured quality of these images. The raster, to me, is a system, a principle, a method, a structure. It divides, disperses, arranges and makes everything the same. . . . [It is] the structure of our time, the structure of a social order, of a culture. Standardized, divided, fragmented, rationed, grouped, specialized.[3]

Early in this treatment of the cliché Polke and Richter shared mundane sources such as the family snapshot, but Richter soon made this banality his own, and Polke focused on the related subject of kitsch, that volatile compound of mass-produced decoration and petit bourgeois aspiration otherwise known as vulgar taste.[4] Often he used patterned fabrics as the supports of his paintings, to which he might screen or daub an image of a beach, a tropical palm, or a heron, all tokens in the middle-class imaginary of happy relaxation, exotic travel, or gemütlich décor. This anthropological expedition into the West German petite bourgeoisie is often hilarious, but it's also sometimes cruel, with more than a hint of class contempt.

Perhaps Polke sensed this problem, for in the 1970s he ditched his cool detachment, and, with Fluxus events rather than Pop paintings as his primary prompt, his work became more immersive, performative, and chaotic. Polke drew on popular forms like comics and caricature, deployed deskilled forms of amateur and outsider art, and relied on photography and film to document his antics in the studio and beyond. At this time, too, with the aid of projectors, Polke adapted a particular way of layered picturing from the Dadaist Francis Picabia, a device soon appropriated in turn by the Americans David Salle and Julian Schnabel. At its best this hallucinated mélange suggests not a dream space so much as a media overload, a kind of Surrealism without an unconscious in which subjectivity, no longer private, is scattered among images in the public domain.[5] At its worst it becomes a matter of random juxtaposition to which the artist often seems as indifferent as the viewer is likely to be. Drugs were involved here; that's part of the problem. Although psychedelia might feel like freedom, it often looks like conventionality (as any number of rock album covers from this period also attest). Sad to say, the stoned mind tends to be a little factory of readymade images.

In the later 1970s Polke went south, literally, as he traveled to Pakistan, Afghanistan, Indonesia, and Brazil, among other countries, and figuratively, as his work became uneven. His experiments with chemicals not only in his body but also on his paintings and photographs issued in mixed results. At times these images point to realms of occult experience that came to preoccupy Polke, while at other times they are simply hermetic; for the most part the process concerned him more than the product. Then in the 1980s his paintings went big, often too big, as if the point were to keep up with the painterly bluster of the Neo-Expressionists. In several instances the scale is effective, as it is in a 1984 series of concentration camp watchtowers grimly titled *Lager*. Yet even here opinion is divided. For some viewers these paintings are chilling reminders

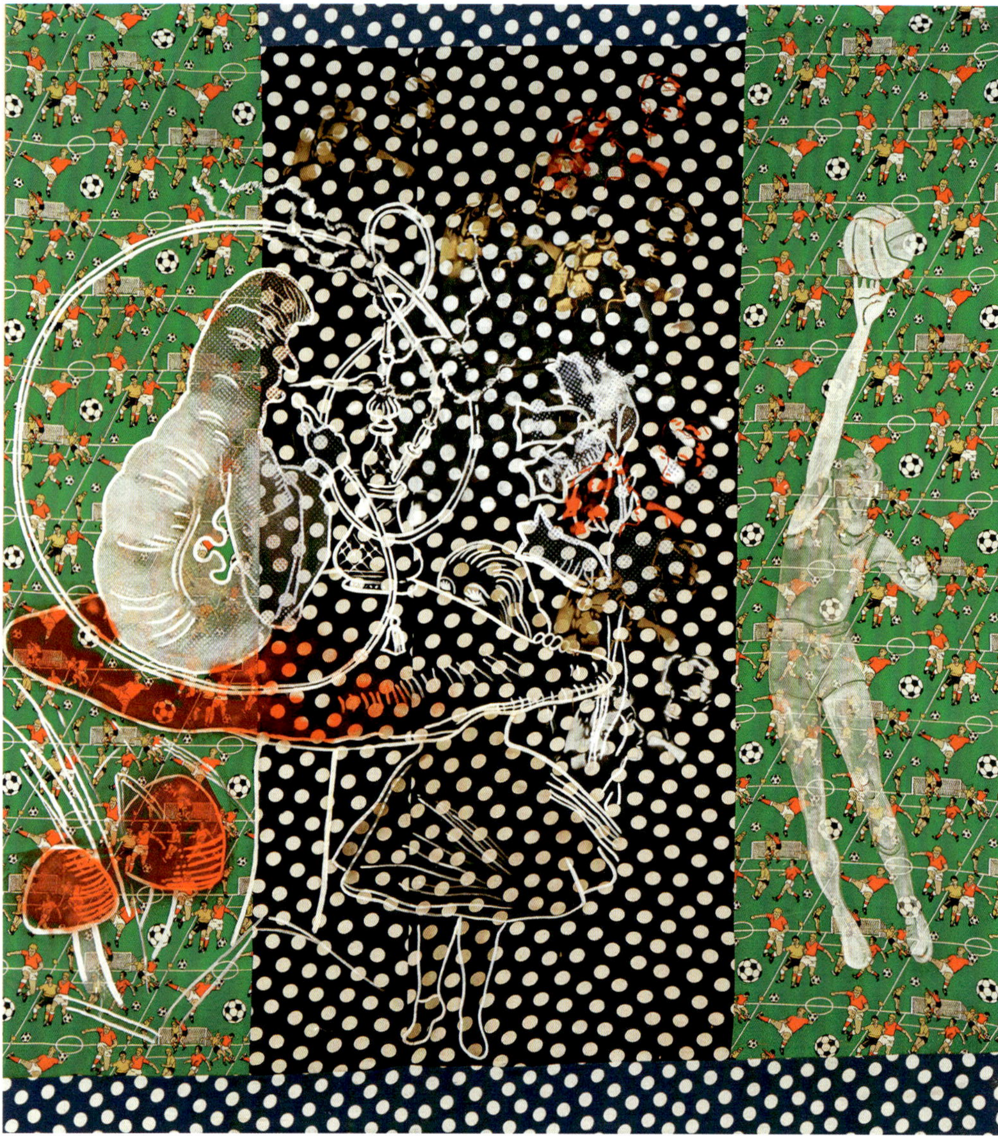

Sigmar Polke, *Alice in Wonderland*, 1972. Mixed media on decorative fabric, 118 × 114 inches. Sammlung Raschdorf, Düsseldorf. © Artists Rights Society (ARS).

of the Nazi past, while for others they threaten to turn Holocaust iconography into so much kitsch.[6]

An acclaimed artist of the same generation as Polke once remarked to me that Polke was "too creative," by which he implied that there wasn't enough concentration in the artist or enough constraint in his materials to produce a logic that sustained the work over time; in short, that Polke had too many "alibis." But it might also be that his prime devices, parody and pastiche—devices that are often associated with postmodernist art of which Polke is an important progenitor—refuse such expectations of stylistic consistency and subjective stability, and that the very point of his practice was to resist art-historical inscription and social recuperation, to show, as Benjamin Buchloh has put it, that any secure selfhood "rests on some type of oblivion or disavowal."[7] Yet there is a touch of the adolescent posture of the avant-garde-of-one in this position too, and isn't advanced-capitalist life an effective enough auto-da-fé of the subject in its own right?

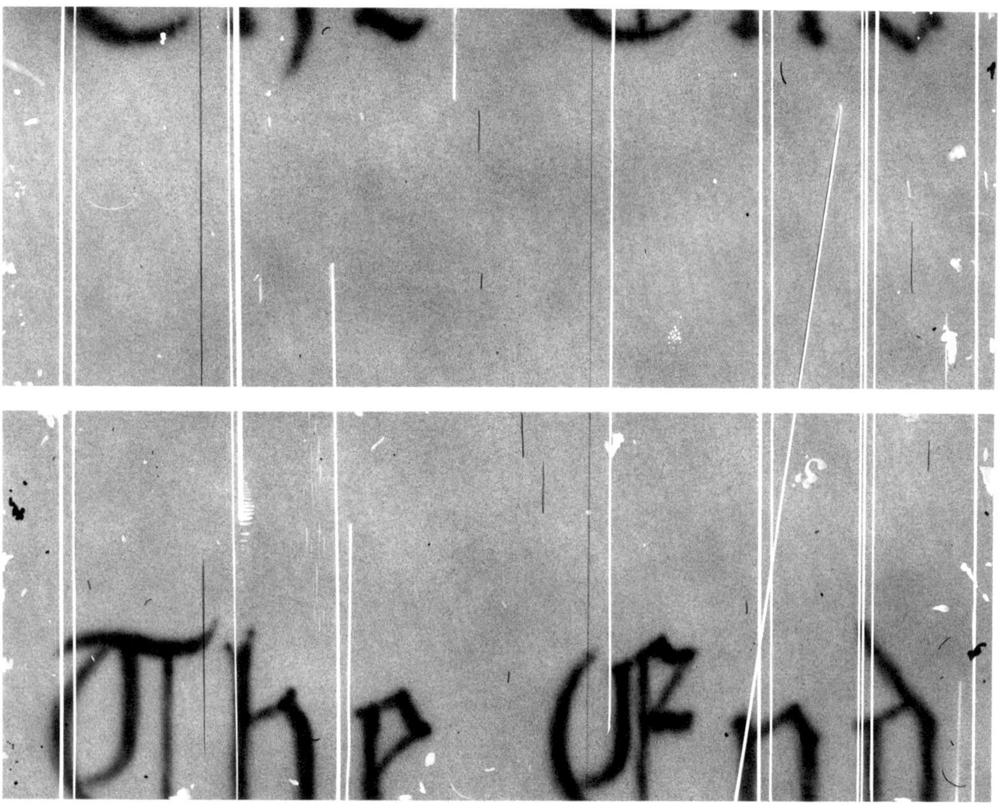

Ed Ruscha, *The End #1*, 1993. Acrylic paint and graphite on board, 20 × 26 inches. Tate.
© Ed Ruscha. Courtesy the artist and Gagosian Gallery.

13 Evening in America

"Whatever my work was made up of in the beginning," Ed Ruscha said in 1989, "is exactly what it is like today." Well, not exactly, but his art has remained largely consistent over its six decades. Ruscha was always intrigued by "paradox and absurdity," and his images usually emit a buzz of "visual noise," a glitch in communication that provokes "a kind of a 'Huh?'" This effect is central to his work, and often Ruscha produces it through various kinds of mischief with the relationship between words and pictures. On the one hand, he treats words as images in their own right; on the other, reading is never quite congruent with seeing in his work. "A flip-flop between those two things" is how Ruscha describes the relationship.[1] And this weird elasticity is even more evocative: "I like the idea of a word becoming a picture, almost leaving its body, then coming back and becoming a word again."[2] At the extreme, Ruscha has acknowledged, "I see myself working with two things that don't even ask to understand each other."[3]

For the most part the upshot of these visual-verbal miscues is not to undo meaning, as is sometimes argued, but to complicate it, to offer puzzles that look obvious but are impossible to solve. In the process Ruscha invites us to reflect on the workings of representation. For instance, though his images tend to be iconic—in the semiotic sense that they resemble what they signify—he is also interested in indexical forms of mark-making, as in his many drawings and paintings produced by staining the support with various non-art substances like gunpowder, tobacco, and rose petals. Ruscha also plays with the effects of illusion. For example, several paintings across his career play with the motif of grapes painted in near trompe-l'oeil, which calls up the ancient story about illusionism from Pliny the Elder, about how Zeuxis painted grapes that appeared so real that birds were tempted to peck them. Yet Ruscha rarely lures his viewers in this way; his work attracts us through ambiguity more than deception.

One version of undecidability in the work is the scale of words. Words "live in a world of no size," Ruscha has remarked, which makes it difficult to measure the space in which they appear. This space is ambiguous in other ways too. It is flat, of course (since 1986 he has often produced it with a spray gun), but it is also theatrical—"a stage [that] is nothing more than a backdrop for the drama that happens." And this space partakes of other media as well, such as the horizontal format of billboards and the projected light of cinema—media that are also sometimes evoked by the stretched proportions of his paintings.[4]

All these characteristics are familiar to Ruscha viewers. They appear in one guise, then reappear in another. This is how he tends to work, in multiple patterns of theme and variation, renewing old motifs and methods while introducing novel ones. Another of his persistent concerns is with "objects that become words" and vice versa.[5] If words are material, Ruscha suggests, they might be subject to entropic decay and other kinds of trouble. Thus in *US* (1993) this italicized term—short for "United States" or an unspecified group of "us" or both—is spelled out in six sticks of wood on sprayed linen: whoever or whatever "us" is here, it looks as though it could be broken up easily. Then in *Sic* (1993) this editorial term (Latin for "thus"), which calls attention to the original form of a quotation (especially when its spelling or syntax is incorrect), is spelled out in nine sticks on canvas, but the word is sprayed in blood-red, which suggests that this "sic" might also be sick, and this in turn summons the category of the "sick picture" or the "sick readymade" proposed long ago by Duchamp.[6] (Duchamp was a formative figure for Ruscha, who met the French artist at the opening of his 1963 retrospective at the Pasadena Museum of Art curated by Walter Hopps.)

In other paintings Ruscha depicts letters or words in various predicaments. In *The Sinking V* (1993), for example, we see this letter, painted large and black, sinking into a low murky horizon, while in *Ice* (1993) this word appears in bluish white on a diagonal that divides a cool black ground from a cold white sky. In such instances the image seems to reinforce the title, as with the poetic figure of the calligram, where the words of a poem are arranged on the page in such a way as to image its principal motif or meaning. As Michel Foucault explained in his 1968 essay on René Magritte, the calligram is designed "to trap things in a double cipher": "it lodges statements in the space of a shape, and makes the text *say* what the drawing *represents*." Nevertheless, the differences between the visual and verbal orders persist: "The calligram never speaks and represents at the same moment," Foucault continues. "The very thing that is both seen and read is hushed in the vision, hidden in the reading."[7] In such celebrated works as *The Treachery of Images (This Is Not a Pipe)* (1929), Magritte plays on tensions already at work in the calligram, and unravels its apparent redoubling of word by image from within: "Magritte reopens the trap the calligram has sprung on the thing it described," with the result that the object "escapes" and the text and the image are "redistributed" in space, with little common ground between them.[8] Again, Ruscha plays with the visual and the verbal in related ways: "I began to see the printed words," he once commented, "and it took over from there."[9] Thus he might give us a sinking V or a cold Ice, but not indicate why a letter should sink, or how a word could freeze, or, for that matter, why a term like "Hero" might break up before our eyes, as happens in several paintings in the early 1990s.

By the mid 1990s another category of distressed words came to predominate. These are paintings, on monochromatic fields, with censor strips, rectangular blocks of phrases that, like so many scratched-out messages or redacted letters, are effaced. In each case the title presents the putative message, from the jokey to the menacing, like so many lines from gang and prison movies of the 1940s and '50s, such as "Agree to Our Terms or Prepare Yourself for a Blast Furnace," and "I'll Be Getting Out Soon and I Haven't Forgotten Your Testimony Put Me in Here" (most boil down to the succinct "Your a Dead Man"). There are multiple ambiguities and ironies here. Some of the strips are ragged, as if done in an angry afterthought by the would-be perpetrator; others are neat, as though executed by a policing authority—newspaper, cop, court, or government. And as we match up phrases and strips we, too, are caught between these positions of expression and erasure, exposing and withholding. All of this is a fiction, and we don't have to believe any of it. Why trust that the messages correspond to the titles, or the strips to the messages? We could see them instead as slightly odd abstractions. But then it becomes apparent that what's in question is precisely belief and trust. This is made clear in a singular work, *In God We Trust* (1994), which can also be read as an abstract circle except for the censor strips placed where the title phrase appears on some American coins. What constitutes value, this painting asks, and by whose authority?

Two other two kinds of painting recur in the 1990s. These feature a common image—a coffee cup, a retriever, a famous leader, an old sailing ship, an antiquated clock—usually presented in blurry silhouette. "It's the icon/logo concept, I suppose," Ruscha commented in 1988 not long after these paintings first emerged. "Things that are immediately recognizable. The idea is that recognition and a silhouette go hand in hand."[10] We recognize these near-archetypal images, to be sure, but this knowing gets us only so far, for here, like "Will Rogers playing Pied Piper in Mr. Rogers's neighborhood" (as Lawrence Weiner nicely put), Ruscha makes the common odd, and frequently we are led astray.[11]

Some of these images are common in an everyday sense: along with the cup, there is a shoe, a table, a pair of pliers, and so forth. Others are common in an emblematic sense, and this category divides into three. First there are two historical figures loaded with symbolic value, George Washington and Thomas Jefferson, who appear in profile as they might in a cameo or on a coin, but the silhouettes appear abraded, even charred, as though these founding fathers were long since worn down or burned out. Then there are almost totemic figures with symbolic value of another kind. Some, like a dog or a rooster, are evocative of home or farm life, while others, like a crow or a coyote, are suggestive of lost wilderness. Finally, there are common images that summon the fantastic, such as the many paintings that feature a frigate, which appears as a ghost ship under full sail, or that recall a film noir scene, such as a lone cottage that suggests a gang hideout. Some of these paintings are almost surreal, such as the eerie images of clock faces, all at once enlarged and truncated, most without hands, and some otherwise distorted. However, the Surrealism here is less that of Salvador Dalí in *The Persistence of Memory* than that of Ingmar Bergman in *Wild Strawberries*.

This interest in the common runs deep in Ruscha, who draws it out from both folk and Pop elements. Biographically he was well positioned to do so: born and raised in the Midwest, often seen as the folk heart of the country, he has lived since 1956 in Los Angeles, often taken to be the capital of its popular culture. For example, some of his early photographs (especially the ones made on his European sojourn in 1961) focus on emblematic signs and structures that qualify as folk, and some of his early paintings also allude to folk signage (a few include the names of southern towns visited on a 1952 hitchhiking trip: Sweetwater, Dublin, Vicksburg). This relation to the folk isn't sardonic, for, again, Ruscha prizes the element of the common found in it. This common touch is evident in other ways, too, as in the font favored in his word images, which he calls "Boy Scouts Utilitarian."

From the start the concern with the common also informed his attraction to both Duchamp and Jasper Johns. "Duchamp discovered common objects" as artistic material, Ruscha once claimed, and, like Johns, Ruscha has made them "the foreground central subject" of his work.[12] He first did so at a time when, as in the moment of Duchamp, increased commodification altered the look not only of common objects but also of common words, images, colors, and spaces—in short, the very nature of appearance. In effect, Ruscha updated the device of the readymade in a way that addresses this condition, with particular attention to the reification of language, the branding of products, the artificiality of color, and the abstraction of place. Here his aim was not only to trouble our automatic perception of these things but also to wrest a common element from them. For every impulse to mock or even destroy "standards" and "norms" in his work (his representations of a Standard gas station or Norm's diner in flames—or, for that matter, the Los Angeles County Museum of Art on fire—are not simply gags), there is a counterimpulse to reclaim the degraded commonplace as a shared vernacular (this is already evident in some of his early photo-books, such as *Twentysix Gasoline Stations*).[13] Centrally, the found language of his jokes,

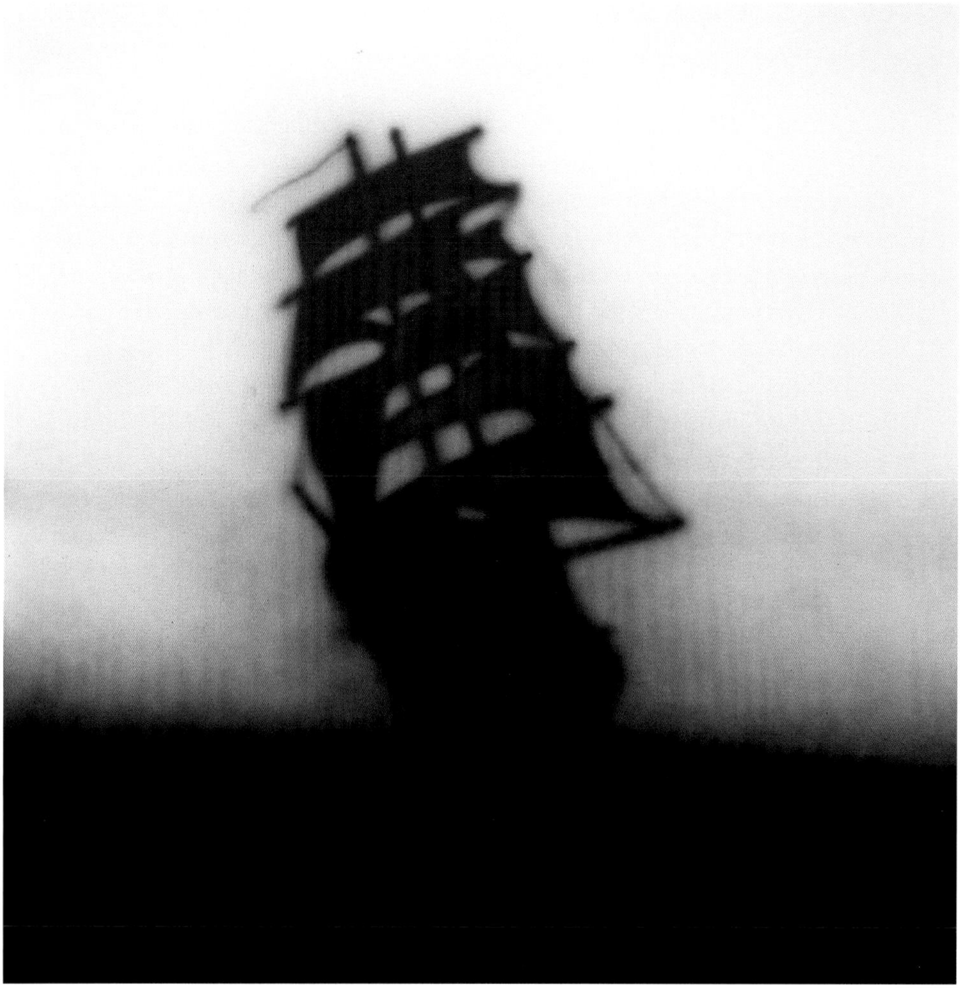

Ed Ruscha, Untitled, 1986. Oil and enamel on canvas, 64 × 64 inches.

sayings, and clichés is also a shared one. Since nobody possesses this kind of speech, everybody can partake of it, and Ruscha underscores this commonality as well.

A change in the weather of his work occurred in the late 1980s, however. Where once his words were liquid-hot and his skies toxic-brilliant, both took on a foggy chill, and almost everything turned nocturnal. The sense of time changed, too, as if his subjects had begun to recede into the past as well as into the dark. In large part this effect is due to the dominant technique of the silhouette, and here we might ask what kind of "recognition" goes "hand in hand" with the silhouette for Ruscha. As his subjects drift back in time (as in the allusions to old films and clock faces), this recognition takes on a mnemonic dimension (recall the semimythical life that these images evoke). In a way like the blur in Gerhard Richter, the silhouette in Ruscha suggests two opposite things at once: a powerful collective symbol and the fading away of such shared images. Thus the darkening also seems cultural, as though, not long after Ronald Reagan declared "morning again in America," Ruscha had countered with an evening world. In the paintings of the 1990s we sense not "a shining city on a hill" but the twilight of American gods.[14]

The exceptionalism of the United States—its democratic dream, its eternal future—was long staked on its Western frontier, that is, on its settler colonialism, but in his cycle of paintings for the Denver Public Library (1995) Ruscha displayed the old wagon train headed for darkness, with the implication, already in play in recent Westerns, that the West was one part myth and two parts genocide. (Related subjects that follow the Denver paintings, such as silhouetted teepees, buffalo, and trains, point to this same disastrous past.) Ruscha described the Denver commission as "a rolling historical landscape" of the West, with the stress on "historical," and this fading-to-black is not limited to his Western subjects.[15] Not only have everyday objects become dark or distorted (his coffee cup or his clocks), but American symbols have also lost their shape (his Shirley Temple is a blob, his Thomas Jefferson looks charred). Again, the word "Hero" falls apart in some paintings, and "In God We Trust" is put under erasure. This slow fade is also felt in a 1996 painting of a lone porch post in twilight. A staple shot in Westerns (it evokes *The Searchers* among other films), the painting appears in the midst of similar images of Ionic and Doric columns, as if to suggest that the porch has become less defiant outpost than fragile ruin.

Already in the 1970s Ruscha produced word paintings that declared shared qualities such as "Faith," "Duty," "Hope," and "Truth," as well as collective categories such as "We Humans," "Days of the Week," "America's Future," and "Anybody's Destiny." And this commonality applies to later paintings that name entities like decades, states, and countries and, even more, that depict formations like mountains, the earth, and the sky. Not only common, the latter subjects evoke the category of the commons, that is, an unregulated resource like air that in principle is open to use by all but is always subject to enclosure for private use and profit. (Of course, in our time of pervasive pollution, global warming, and systemic scarcity, the commons have become a renewed site of political contestation.) Often such things "common to all" (in Roman law *communis omnium*) are in fact "no one's things" (*res nullius*), and here too, in his evocation of the commons, there is a darkening in Ruscha.[16] Consider his paintings of the coyote and the crow, creatures that, in Native American lore, are tricksters, that is, in-between beings in their own right, at home everywhere and nowhere.[17] Consider, too, his many representations of the same ghost ship. This image calls to mind the Kafka story "The Hunter Gracchus" that tells of a German hunter who fell to his death from a precipice in the Black Forest ages ago. Only Gracchus didn't die. For reasons he can't fathom, he is neither dead nor alive, but doomed to lie on a ship that wanders from port to distant port, where again and again he stirs just enough to realize his purgatorial state: "Nobody knows of me, and if anyone knew he would not know where I could be found, and if he knew where I could be found, he would not how to deal with me, he would not know how to help me."[18]

Despite his continued affirmation of American vernaculars, then, Ruscha suggests that the American empire has run its course (a couple of paintings from 1997 are in fact titled *Bloated Empire*). Even in the years when he evoked a "deeply Californian version of infinity" in paintings of brilliant sunsets, this space appeared thin and fragile, and sometimes it contained a hint of catastrophe too.[19] Like Nathanael West, Ruscha intimated that Los Angeles might be a mirage and California a myth—a facade about to crumble into the desert or slip into the sea.

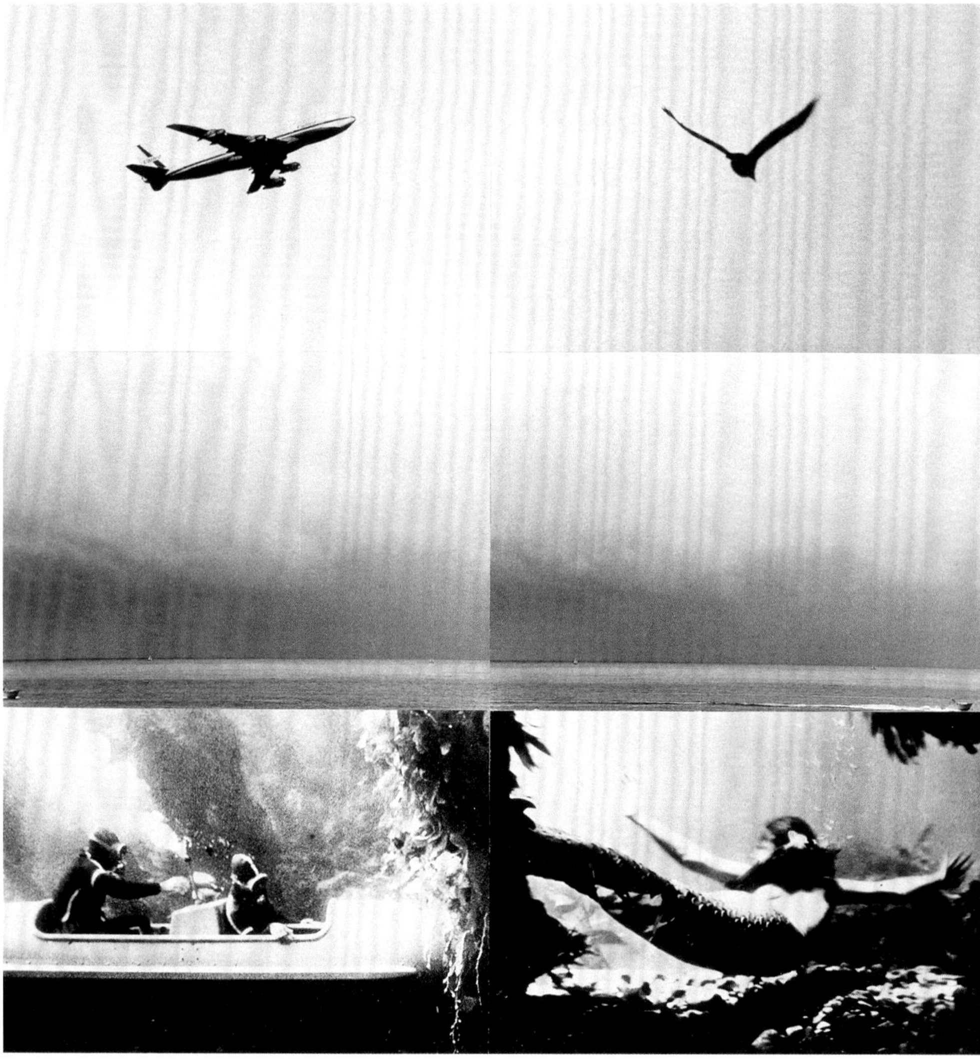

John Baldessari, *Concerning Diachronic/Synchronic Time: Above, On, Under (with Mermaid)*, 1976. Six black-and-white photographs, 28 × 27 inches overall. © John Baldessari. Courtesy Estate of John Baldessari, John Baldessari Family Foundation, and Sprüth Magers.

14 Blasted Allegories

"I am interested in when two images abut each other," John Baldessari once said. "It's like when two words collide and some new word in some new meaning comes out of it."[1] This concern with montage, both visual and verbal, is a through line of his work, and already in the 1970s he related it to his interest in art as a language. However, rather than use images and words to clarify one another, Baldessari highlighted the ambiguities that arise when they are juxtaposed. For this double investigation he drew on experimental filmmakers (especially the Godard of the 1960s) as well as on structuralist theorists (he read Lévi-Strauss at this time as well).[2] Yet his method was distinctive: out of an archive of images—staged photographs, random shots of television screens, old film stills found at a Hollywood store, and so on—Baldessari selected individual pictures, manipulated them according to set rules (usually with one-color filters and one-word overlays), then combined them in a way that suggests phrases or sentences, which sometimes function in terms of syntax but rarely work in terms of sense. "I think one of the fundamental issues of art is making a selection," Baldessari also remarked, and selection and combination are indeed the essential operations of his art.[3] They are, of course, fundamental to theories of montage and language as well.

First, montage. "In front of me lies a crumpled yellowed sheet of paper," Sergei Eisenstein wrote in *Film Form*, published in 1949, a year after his death. "On it is a mysterious note: 'Linkage—P' and 'Collision—E.' This is a substantial trace of a heated bout on the subject of montage between P (Pudovkin) and E (myself)." Eisenstein continued: "A graduate of the Kuleshov school, [Pudovkin] loudly defends an understanding of montage as a *linkage* of pieces. . . . Bricks arranged in series to *expound* an idea. I confronted him with my viewpoint on montage as a *collision*. A view that from the collision of two given factors *arises* a concept."[4] This note refers to a key debate among Soviet filmmakers in the 1920s about the proper use of montage: either to build a narrative through connected scenes or to propose a thesis through juxtaposed shots. Baldessari drew on both models of montage, especially in his important series *Blasted Allegories* (1977–1978). In fact, he sometimes played one method against the other, at times favoring thematic linkage, at times dialectical collision. More often than not, though, both montage methods are seen to fail, or, rather, Baldessari arranged it so that neither kind of meaning is secured.

Baldessari invented his own types of montage as well, at times building it through subtraction rather than addition. For example, he might excise a geometric form from a found image; in a well-known instance from the *Violent Space* series (1976), a white rectangle à la Malevich appears, like an alien from outer space, to captivate two men who otherwise exist in a very different scene. Or he might cut a given picture according to a template of his choosing, as in *Shape Derived from Subject (Snake): Used as Framing Device to Produce New Photographs* (1981). In some pieces Baldessari combined these two methods, as when his excisions from found images assume the form of silhouetted figures (a pelican is a favorite form). In other pieces these shaped pictures take in the space of the gallery wall, becoming installations in their own right (this is especially true of his *Fugitive Essays* of 1980, which are also keyed to particular creatures). His montage can appear simple too, a matter of two images set up as opposed terms, as in *Eagle and Rodent* (1984), in which predator and prey face off, or in *Man and Woman with Bridge* (also 1984), in which two attractive people gaze at each other, at once connected and separated by a dark plank across which a coyote steps warily.

Baldessari also practiced yet another form of montage, one that returns us to Eisenstein. "While the conventional film directs the *emotions*," Eisenstein wrote in another put-down of the Kuleshov-Pudovkin montage of thematic linkages, his own montage of dialectical collisions "suggests an opportunity to encourage and direct the whole *thought process* as well."[5] Here Eisenstein alludes to the famous "Kuleshov effect," an experiment that was central to the Soviet debate about montage, in which Kuleshov took a short clip of the tsarist movie star Ivan Mosjoukine—he simply gazes into the camera—and alternated it with a few other shots, first of a plate of soup, then of a girl in a coffin, and finally of a woman on a divan. When Kuleshov screened this test film, the audience believed that Mosjoukine looked hungry in the first instance, mournful in the second, and aroused in the third; that is, it projected its own response, as stimulated by each montage, onto the impassive actor. For Kuleshov this effect was crucial to the construction of cinematic narrative, and obviously it has played a crucial role in much filmmaking (Hitchcock used it often enough), yet Eisenstein always objected to its privileging of emotion over intellection.[6] Interested in affect as well as in signification, Baldessari didn't dismiss this type of montage in the same way. In fact, in several series he played on the Kuleshov effect, though it too fails more than often not.

Consider the *Action/Reaction* series (1975), which juxtaposes images of a young woman with images of a mundane action (the photos change only slightly, if at all, in each sequence). Is her vague expression altered by the attendant gesture (a light is switched on, a cup is put down), or is the action so banal as to resist any reading of a reaction at all? Baldessari also questioned our habit of projecting meaning in another 1975 series, *Pathetic Fallacy*, the title of which refers to the famous caution of John Ruskin against imposing human feelings on nonhuman things. Can a photo of a mottled sky be called "happy"?, Baldessari asks. Is an empty chair "wistful"? Is curly hair "glowering"? Is pink "suspicious" or "tremulous"? Is yellow "resigned" or "yearning"? Other experiments, more Kuleshovian in spirit, came later. For example, *Laughing Man/Architecture/Angry Man* (1984) presents, on either side of an everyday photo of a building site, two theatrical images, one of an older man "laughing," the other of a younger man "angry," and our response to "architecture" differs greatly depending on whom we identify with. "Can one match accurately a facial expression to a word?," Baldessari asked in relation to a piece in his *Prima Facie* series (2005), which juxtaposes a photo of a young woman, with eyes and mouth wide open, with an alphabetical list of related adjectives that runs from "aghast" to "upset." "When a person's facial expression appears angry," Baldessari continued, "can one link the word 'angry' to that expression? Perhaps 'troubled' would be more accurate if he were to inquire. Our judgment is prima facie or at first sight."[7] In his own way, then, Baldessari was as skeptical about affective projection as Eisenstein was; certainly, he interrupts snap judgments of the prima facie sort here. Given that this kind of projection is a chief form of ideology in our media world, this skepticism remains salutary. Indeed, this aspect of his work takes on new significance at a time of ever more intrusive technologies of face recognition and emotion detection.

For Eisenstein the montage of dialectical collision was essential to film as a language, which also obsessed Baldessari. "Why does the cinema follow the forms of theater and painting rather than the methodology of language," Eisenstein asked, when it is language that "allows wholly new concepts of ideas to arise from the combination of two concrete denotations of two concrete objects?"[8] Again, though Baldessari came to the model of language through structuralism as much as film, the question is much the same in each domain: Can a cultural construct—myth for Lévi-Strauss, film for Eisenstein, art for Baldessari—be seen as a system, one governed by the linguistic operations of selection and combination?

In 1976 Baldessari produced *Concerning Diachronic/Synchronic Time: Above, On, Under (with Mermaid)*, which he later called a "watershed work" because it revealed the "magical transformation" that can occur between images.[9] Three pairs of photos appear in two vertical rows: "above" we see a jet in the sky next to a bird in flight; in the middle is a speedboat "on" open water photographed twice seconds apart; and "under" are two divers in a submarine launch next to a mermaid. "Diachronic" and "synchronic" are linguistic terms for two kinds of temporality; a language or an art can be studied in its historical (diachronic) development or in its present (synchronic) usage.[10] However, this distinction doesn't help us much with this work. The primary category is spatial here, and what time does a mermaid occupy anyway? More pertinent is a related opposition in linguistics, which involves the operations of selection and combination that intrigued Baldessari. When we construct a sentence, we select a word from a set of related words—"jet" rather than "bird," say—and combine it with other words from other sets—like "above" rather than "below." The first axis of selection, often graphed as vertical, is called "paradigmatic," and the second axis of combination, often presented as horizontal, is termed "syntagmatic."[11] After this opposition was proposed by the linguist Ferdinand de Saussure, it proved to be very generative in semiotics at large. Roman Jakobson, a contemporary of Eisenstein, used it to demonstrate that prose, which is more metonymic in character, favors the syntagmatic axis, while poetry, which is more metaphorical, favors the paradigmatic. Yet it was Lévi-Strauss, influenced by both Saussure and Jakobson, who provided the most influential application of this binary analysis in his structuralist study of myth.[12] In his own orderings of images and words Baldessari seemed to follow this structuralist line in order to ask whether an art that draws on photography, film, and television can also be understood as a language, that is, as a process of paradigmatic selection and syntagmatic combination.

In some pieces Baldessari favored syntagmatic combination. This is implied in the title of *Car Color Series: By Color Wheel (First Instances Seen Walking from the Studio)* (1976), in which he photographed car doors as he encountered them on the street (the images are exhibited in this sequence too). "It is the syntax of colors that is important and not a well-composed photograph," Baldessari commented. "One might call them 'street sentences.'"[13] More often, however, he focused on paradigmatic selection. Many pieces—early, middle, and late—present various arrangements of swords, guns, teeth, feet, spectators, and shadows, among other images. Mental states like "stress situations" and physical conditions like "types of chaos" appear in such paradigmatic orderings too. Occasionally Baldessari turns one axis toward the other in a way that confuses them. For example, *From Antelope to Goose* (1976) is a figure made up of three postcards glued together such that the bottom is the body of an antelope and the top is the head of a goose, while the middle is an old tower with a folksy attendant; and *Lizards to Pianist (with Gold Sphere)* (1984) is a complicated chain of eight photographs that build, as if by free association, from two lizards at the bottom to a pianist at the top. What becomes clear is that neither selection nor combination can abolish the erroneous and the arbitrary. In fact, both *Antelope* and *Lizards* recall “the exquisite corpses” of different parts of the body drawn by Surrealist friends, each of whom didn’t know what the others had depicted. This suggests that such montage is less thematic, dialectical, or indeed structuralist in character than it is unconscious—or, rather, that it mimics unconscious connections.[14] Sometimes there is a compulsive dimension to this kind of montage too, as implied, for instance, by the deathly turn in such Baldessari pieces as *Horizontal Men* (1984), in which various cowboys, soldiers, and other males are stacked like corpses (most of them appear already dead), and *Inventory* (1987), which juxtaposes goods on supermarket shelves with bodies in an extermination camp railcar.

In short, what Baldessari reveals is how images and words resist the order provided by selection and combination as often as they conform to it. This is the Baldessari effect, and it can be, by turns, funny, painful, or bizarre. It is especially bizarre when he opens his arrangements to the complications of language, as he did fully in his *Blasted Allegories*. For these pieces he asked friends and assistants to caption his images as they saw fit (which they did mostly in a denotative manner); he then saw to the coloring and the arranging of the results (often in accordance with the place of the given color in the color spectrum). Baldessari experimented with different presentations—simple rows (horizontal and vertical), double rows, grids, crisscrosses, and so on—as well as with various designations. Most pieces are called “phrases” or “sentences,” some “equations,” and one or two are titled “poem” or “pun,” “rebus” or “puzzle.” We are invited to consider what qualifies as each category, and how arbitrary the designations might be.

The principal operation of the *Blasted Allegories* seems simple enough: the ordering of television shots with overlaid words in a way that suggests a grammatical unit. The primary incentive appears fairly clear as well: to test whether words can serve “as substitutes” for images and vice versa.[15] What counts as an effective combination? What works as a legible one? Yet the results rarely turn out to be straightforward. “I can never seem to figure out what one does and the other doesn’t do,” Baldessari said of his images and words, “so it propels me, this kind of bafflement.”[16] Consider *Burn Crossing: First Long Poem* (1976), which precedes the *Blasted Allegories* proper. It presents the possible orderings of four words in a simple grid, from which, as in a verbal puzzle, Baldessari selects the arrangement that appears on the diagonal—“angry clouds watch swim”—and matches only those words with appropriate photos. Why this choice? Clearly this ordering of the words comes close to a sentence (and perhaps closer to a poem), but just as clearly it falls short. *Three TV Sentences* (1976), another piece that anticipates the *Blasted Allegories,* offers these image-word combinations, “cowboys meeting mermaid” and “submarine stalking

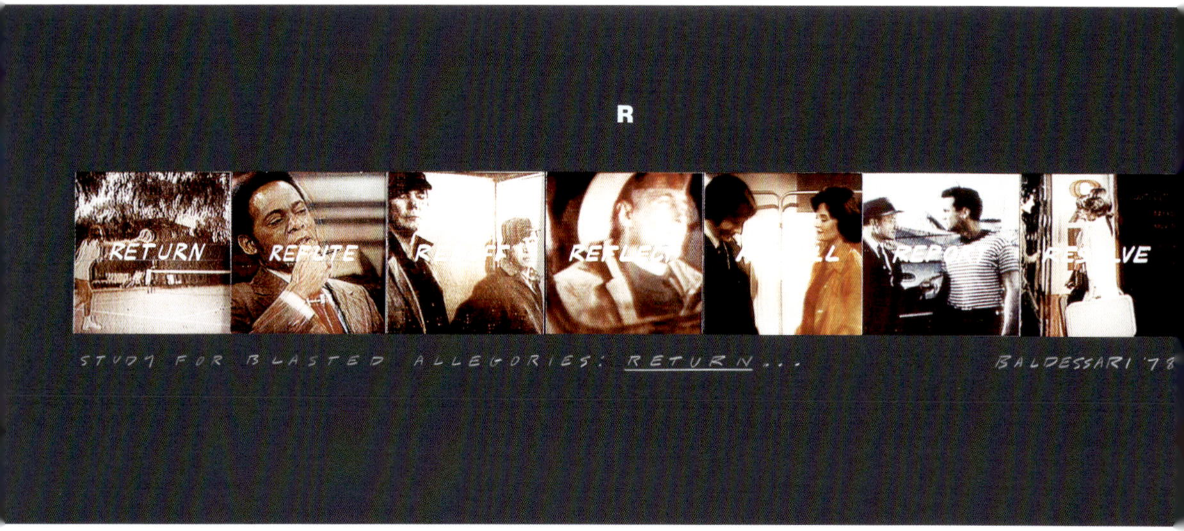

John Baldessari, *Study for Blasted Allegories: Return . . .* , 1978. Seven color photographs with paint marker and pencil on board, 16 × 40 inches overall. © John Baldessari. Courtesy Estate of John Baldessari, John Baldessari Family Foundation, and Sprüth Magers.

elderly orange." Both are exquisite corpses, thrown up by a televisual world. Such "allegories" are indeed "blasted," for often image and word don't fit, and syntax and sense come unglued.

"The goal of all structuralist activity," Roland Barthes wrote in 1965, "is to reconstruct an 'object' in such a way as to manifest thereby the rules of functioning (the 'functions') of this object." This analysis, "whether reflexive or poetic," relies on the operations of selection and combination; only in this way, Barthes concluded, can "homo significans" come "to know how meaning is possible."[17] Again, Baldessari appeared to be on board with this project. If Lévi-Strauss charted the elements of mythic narratives in his structuralist grids of selection and combination, Baldessari did much the same in his image-word allegories.[18] Yet in his very attempt to reconstruct his units in terms of language, he also revealed the limitations of the linguistic model for visual art. The result is a sly deconstruction, with parodic touches, that aligns Baldessari less with Lévi-Strauss, the hero of structuralism, than with Jacques Derrida, its scourge.[19]

In 1970, not long before Baldessari first deployed film stills and television shots in his art, Barthes wrote an influential essay titled "The Third Meaning: Research Notes on Some Eisenstein Stills." For Barthes, who had come to question structuralism by this time, these stills, mostly taken from *Ivan the Terrible I* (1944), point to an elusive sort of sense, one that is neither literal nor symbolic but obtuse. "The obtuse meaning is a signifier without a signified," Barthes explained, "hence the difficulty in naming it." At the same time "it seems to open the field of meaning totally" because "it shows its fissure and its suture."[20] Before an Eisenstein still, Barthes continued, our "reading remains suspended between the image and its description."[21] Often we experience a similar suspension before a Baldessari piece—in part because, as with a calligram, we both see the work as an image and read it as a text but we can't do both at the same time, and in part because, even after we sort out our seeing and reading, sense is difficult to come by.[22] "What the obtuse meaning disturbs," Barthes concluded, is "metalanguage," that is, what it resists is any system of knowledge that decides, definitively, on one truth. What Barthes calls the "impertinence of the signifier" can't be so easily contained.[23]

The *Blasted Allegories* are obtuse in this way, offering us both too much meaning and not enough. To apply a term deployed by Baldessari, they cause truth to "tergiversate," that is, to equivocate.[24] This equivocation might make for an analysis that is "interminable," as Freud once remarked of psychoanalysis. For the same reason, it might also point to a politics that is resistant to the ideological closure of any "metalanguage," any total system. That, too, is an important part of the Baldessari effect.

What is a "blasted allegory"? In traditional usage an allegory is a text or an image structured by different levels of meaning, and one interprets the allegory accordingly. For example, one might read a passage in the Bible literally (for the historical event), metaphorically (for the symbolic import), or anagogically (for the spiritual truth). Baldessari was interested in allegory in this old-school sense. In 1981 he produced fourteen images representing *Virtues and Vices* (which he dedicated to Giotto), as well as a *Vanitas* series involving photos of globes, bubbles, skulls, and other objects that speak of the transience of worldly things (they evoke allegorical Dutch still lives of the seventeenth century). "Allegory" is already present in a pair of pieces from 1976 titled *Repair/Retouch: An Allegory about Wholeness*. Here, in the first instance, we see a plate broken, then reassembled, along a top row of photos, and a hand first severed, then reattached, along a bottom row, and, in the second instance, a man with an amputated leg above a broken plate, and then the same man with his leg restored above an intact plate. "The act of healing is posited as synonymous with art," Baldessari commented of these pieces. But surely this deadpan statement is tongue-in-cheek, for modern allegory, like avant-garde art, favors the fragmentary over the unitary. This predilection is his own as well, as he acknowledged: "I could never have this feeling of totality, of wholeness."[25]

This "blasted" sense of allegory also became important to criticism in the early 1980s. In a brilliant text on postmodernist art Craig Owens theorized its "allegorical impulse" in terms that pertain directly to Baldessari, who had recently completed his *Blasted Allegories*.[26] "Allegory appears whenever one text is doubled by another," Owens writes, as when figures in the Old Testament are read through others in the New Testament.[27] This doubling involves the projection "of structure as sequence" in a way that complicates any fixed distinction between the spatial and the temporal or the visual and the verbal. "Identified as the domain of the arbitrary, the conventional, the unmotivated," Owens continues, allegory is also "the structural interference of two distinct levels or usages of language, literal and rhetorical (metaphoric), one of which denies precisely what the other affirms."[28] So it is with many of the *Blasted Allegories* that involve a doubling of image and word, a projecting of structure as sequence, and an interfering of modes of representation. What Paul de Man (who guided Owens in his account) remarked of allegorical narratives in general is true of the *Blasted Allegories* in particular: they "tell the story of the failure to read."[29] Baldessari derived the epithet "blasted" from Nathaniel Hawthorne, who, despite his mastery of the genre, deemed allegory "blasted" in the sense of "cursed," perhaps because he saw it as both too complex and too simple or, again, both too meaningful and not meaningful enough. Again, the

Baldessari allegories are "blasted" in the further sense that they deconstruct the very linguistic structure that they otherwise propose.

For de Man language is always blasted in this way, always riven, as Owens puts it, by the allegorical "distance which separates signifier from signified, sign from meaning."[30] However, another theory of allegory also emerged in the early 1980s, one that redirected this understanding. For Water Benjamin, whose writing on the tragic drama of the German Baroque and the poetry of Baudelaire became current in English only at this time, allegory is again about the fragmentary and the failed, yet he historicizes rather than essentializes this condition. For Benjamin modern allegory bears the stigmata of industrial capitalism, of its propensity to reify and to fragment objects, subjects, and representations alike, and he regarded Baudelaire as the first great allegorist of this creative destruction. "The allegorical mind arbitrarily selects from the vast and disordered material that its knowledge has to offer," Benjamin writes of Baudelaire. "It tries to match one piece with another to figure out whether they can be combined. This meaning with that image, or that image with this meaning. The result is never predictable since there is no organic mediation between the two."[31]

Given this description, we can place Baldessari squarely in the modern tradition of allegorical mixing and matching, of semi-arbitrary selection and combination. This intuition is supported by Benjamin Buchloh, who in 1981 adapted the Benjaminian reading of allegory to contemporary art in terms that are also relevant to Baldessari. "The allegorical mind sides with the object and protests against its devaluation to the status of a commodity by devaluing it a second time in allegorical practice," Buchloh writes. "In the splintering of signifier and signified, the allegorist subjects the sign to the same division of functions that the object has undergone in its transformation into a commodity [that is, its division into use value and exchange value]."[32] Again, for de Man and Owens this splintering is intrinsic to language, whereas for Benjamin and Buchloh it is determined historically: it is the commodity above all that is ruinous to representation.[33]

Baldessari was modest about the political implications of his art. He spoke of its effects in terms of defamiliarization—as so many ways to see things "askew," to keep us "off balance," to baffle prima facie responses.[34] Yet there is more here. Especially in his *Blasted Allegories* Baldessari protests against the "devaluation of the object"—the reification and the fragmentation of both image and word—even as he also puts this breakup of representation and language to his own creative use. He shows how the breakup of visual and verbal signs—in photography, film, and television—looks. He gives us, in short, a blasted grammar of the media environment of his time.

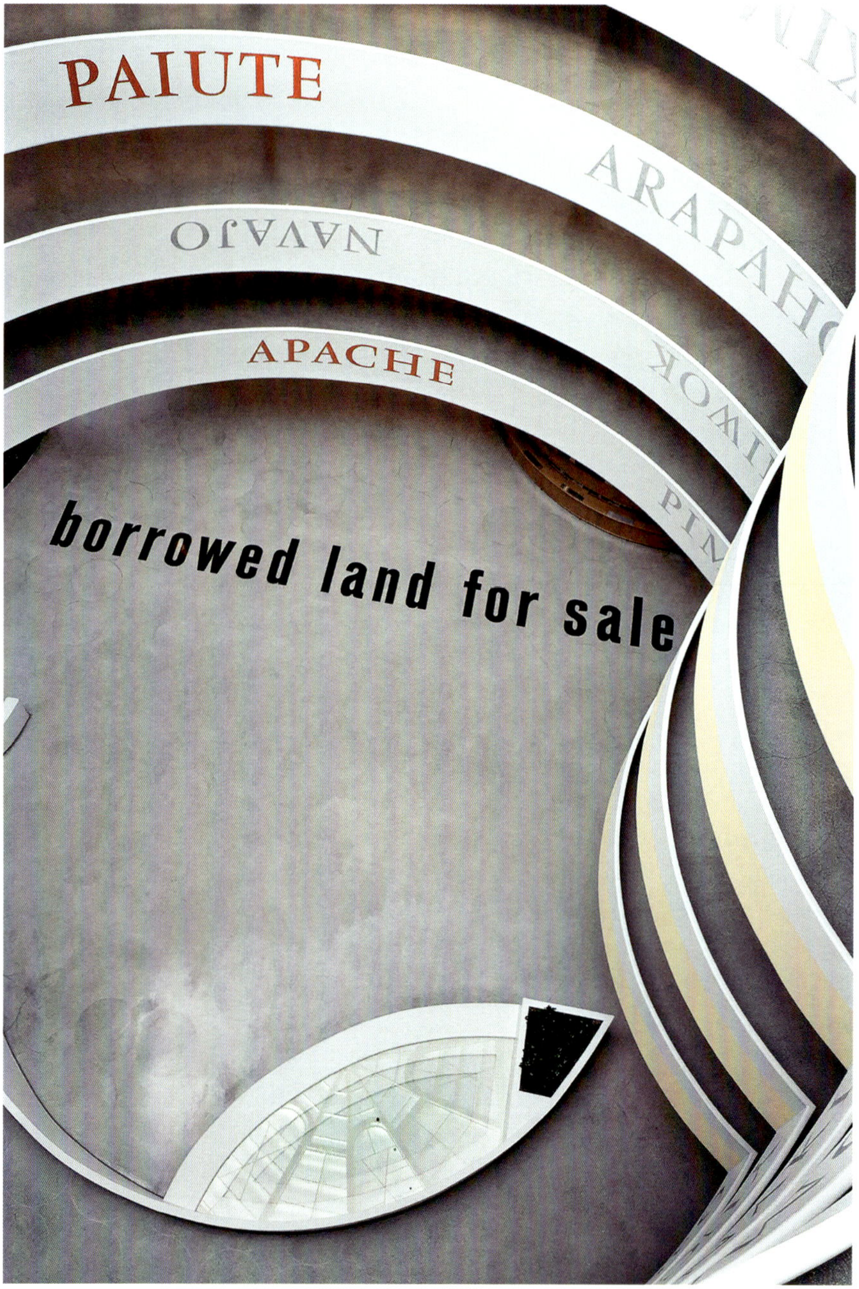

Lothar Baumgarten, *AMERICA Invention*, 1993. Painted wall drawing in the Solomon R. Guggenheim Museum. © Lothar Baumgarten Estate. Courtesy Marian Goodman Gallery.

15 The Writing on the Wall

The traditional art museum is a space-time machine that works to transform different locations (from specific objects to entire cultures) into moments in a narrative, and different temporalities (from individual biographies to whole histories) into places in a building. Never smooth in its operation, this machine is now broken down: today most museumgoers sense how exclusive and arbitrary it is, and how little justice it does to the little that it represents. Yet its ideological power can still be felt. “This collection of cultures, this array of history, is spread out for you,” it intones. “You are more than you think you are.” The imperialism in this solicitation is clear enough, but that doesn’t dispel its force.

This space-time machine is only one model of the art museum, of course, but it was the one long dominant in the West. In its strong form it emerged in early nineteenth-century Europe, when royal and aristocratic collections were first prised open in the name of a new bourgeois audience. Discursively it responded to such questions as these: How to make a private collection of objects into a public representation of cultures? How to reconcile the Romantic recognition of the diversity of people with the Enlightenment principle of the universality of history? Such questions were also foundational to art history, and the discipline long subtended the art museum as the art museum long supported the discipline. From Alois Riegl to Ernst Gombrich a primary concern of its discourse was to assimilate divergent forms of *Kunstwollen*, or “the will to art,” within a dominant narrative of history. However binary or cyclical the terms—with art seen to favor “the optical” or “the haptic,” for example, or “the linear” or “the painterly”—this narrative was mostly evolutionary in thrust: stories of technical, formal, conceptual, or spiritual progress toward verisimilitude, abstraction, truth, or beauty, in which specific cultures advanced the narrative, only to be subsumed within it. If they couldn’t be factored in, they were set aside or dropped out. Most often modernist art was seen to punctuate these stories by either rupturing them or completing them or both at once.[1]

In the postmodern collapse of “grand narratives,” this universal art history, at once assimilative and exclusive, was said to be dispersed too. But two of its assumptions are hard to put to rest. The first is that, just as world cultures can somehow be pulled within the museum, so the museum, its mapping of space and time, can somehow be projected onto the world. As Johannes Fabian argued in relation to anthropology, the sister discipline of art history, this projection operated according to two almost biblical principles:

> 1. Time is immanent to, hence coextensive with, the world (or nature, or the universe, depending on the argument); 2. Relationships between parts of the world (in the widest sense of both natural and sociocultural entities) can be understood as temporal relations. Dispersal in space reflects directly, which is not to say simply or in obvious ways, sequence in time.[2]

In effect, as space and time were read in terms of each other, "over there" became conflated with "back then," and the most remote (as measured from some Greenwich mean of European civilization) was marked as the most "primitive."

This mapping of primitivity was racist; in the Western white imagination the place of primitivity was dark. This mapping was also absurd, especially after the momentous diasporas and migrations of the last century when colonial "peripheries" and metropolitan "centers" could no longer be held apart. Nevertheless, the mapping remained tenacious because it was fundamental to conceptions of history as development and civilization as hierarchy. Indeed, "the primitive" operated as the necessary limit-term of too many discourses for it to be simply discarded. Defined as privative, "the primitive" was long seen to be without writing, before history, without proper religion, before the advent of the state, and so on. As such it was the ground against which the emergence of these institutions could be set, the ground that defined Western subject and society alike as progressive. Of course, this fantasy made "the primitive" an object of desire as well: hence the ambivalence so often inscribed in its construction. From this Romantic perspective, "the primitive" also represented the innocent body in an original state before all history and any division, a projection imaged most powerfully by Gauguin.[3]

As Fabian argued, a prime precondition of the mapping of primitivity was "the denial of coevalness": "The absence of the Other from our Time has been his mode of presence in our discourse—as an object and victim."[4] It is this denial of coevalness that Lothar Baumgarten consistently challenged in his work. Again and again, as a partial survey of his early work reveals, this German artist recalled the names of other cultures in the institutional spaces of his own, doing so through techniques of doubling and inverting, superimposing and displacing.[5]

In 1982, at Documenta 7 in Kassel, West Germany, Baumgarten painted the names of South American indigenous societies (Tupinamba, Bororo, Xavante, Toba, Arekuna . . .) within the neoclassical dome of the Museum Fridericianum. In lieu of the ancient motto, humanist sentiment, or illustrious pantheon of great white men typical of such idealist architecture, one was confronted with the names of others, written in two reds evocative of blood and body paint. Here, as if in a hallucinated return of the repressed, Old World enlightenment appeared as New World conquest, and the names appeared less elegiac than defiant, less preterite than present.

In 1984, at the German Pavilion of the Venice Biennale, Baumgarten again decentered a European space, here by means of marble stones inscribed with names of the seven great rivers of the Amazon and Orinoco systems and with pictographs of the four animals most emblematic of the South American rainforest—jaguar, eagle, caiman, and turtle.[6] This superimposition of Amazonian rivers on the Venetian lagoon also confounded conventional oppositions of worlds Old and New or First and Third. Also importantly, it countered the practice of renaming that long governed the relations between the two, the practice of renomination-as-possession whereby explorers, conquerors, and missionaries often claimed the "new" land in "old" languages, as Amerigo Vespucci claimed Venezuela when he named it "little Venice" in 1499.[7]

In 1987 Baumgarten defamiliarized another Western museum twice over—by reference not only to excluded others but also to a degraded space within the Western metropolis, the subway. In *Accès aux quais: tableaux parisiens* (1985–1986) at the Musée d'art moderne de la ville de Paris, he enlarged a diagram of the number 9 line of the Métro (replete with lights and sounds) on one wall, placing a row of station seats and billboard frames along the opposite wall. Traversed by many immigrants, the Pont de Sevres/Mairie de Montreuil line (which passes by the museum) includes several stations with Napoleonic names. Baumgarten replaced these imposed names with ones evocative of colonial rebellions and wars (for the station name "Nation," for example, he substituted "Dien-Bien Phu"). At least for a moment this act reversed the imperialist practice of renomination, turning official commemoration into disruptive remembering.

In two other works from the late 1980s Baumgarten turned to North American institutions. For *The Tongue of the Cherokee* (1985–1988) he reinscribed the glass ceiling of the Hall of Sculpture of the Carnegie Museum of Art in Pittsburgh, a neoclassical gallery with Greek and Roman casts (including a copy of the Panathenaic frieze from the Parthenon) situated between the museums of art and natural history. There, in the 189-pane ceiling, Baumgarten set the eighty-five-figure syllabary of the Cherokee Nation, devised by a man named Sequoyah in the early nineteenth century (the only alphabet to be created by one person). The critical ironies were multiple. First, the placement of the work between spaces devoted to art and natural histories pointed to the old racist classification of such cultures typical of traditional museology. Do they qualify

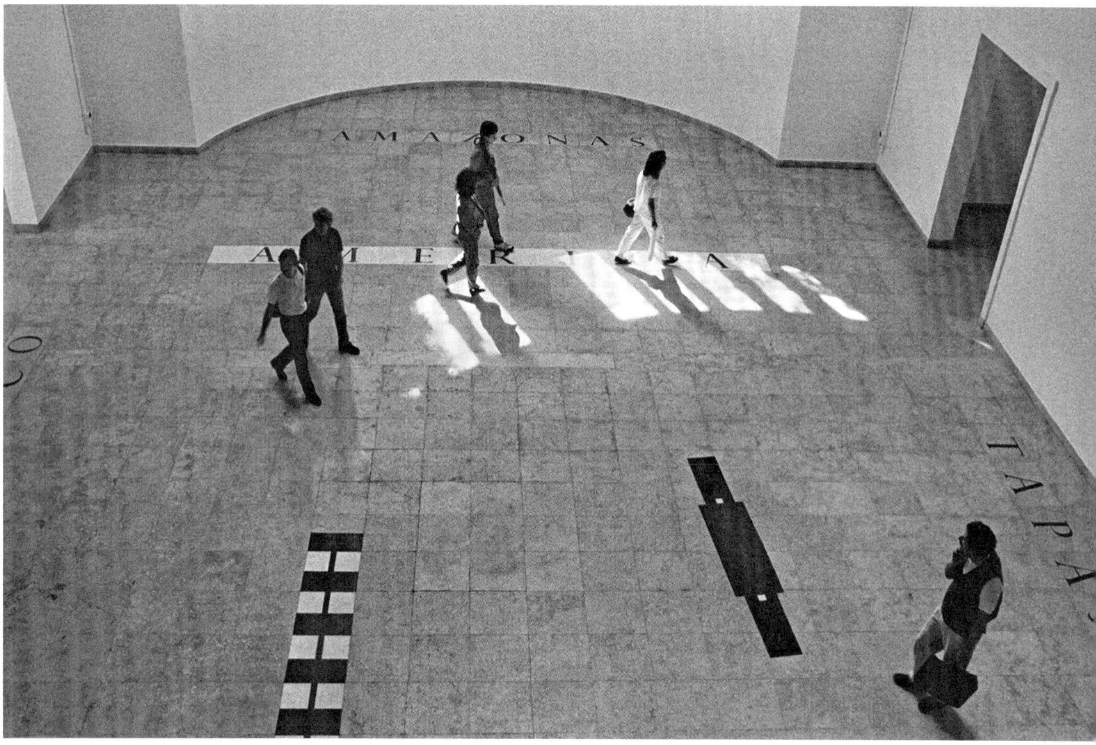

Lothar Baumgarten, *America Señores Naturales*, 1983–1984. Names of principal rivers of the Amazon Basin with four symbolic figures (Jaguar, Eagle, Caiman, and Turtle) inlaid in the floor of the Germany pavilion, Venice Biennale, 1984. © Lothar Baumgarten Estate. Courtesy Marian Goodman Gallery.

as autonomous art, or are they to be relegated to natural history? Second, the opposition of the foreign and the native was turned inside out. If the syllabary was alien to the neoclassical setting, were the Cherokee alien to America? The conflicted answer, no and yes, invoked a history of displacement and genocide but also one of contestation and countermemory. Third, the opposition of the old and the new was made ambiguous. This hall of antiquities was intended (by robber baron Andrew Carnegie) to ennoble the New World in its industrial age, to embellish "Dear Old Smoky Pittsburgh" with the signs of culture.[8] But the casts aren't ancient, nor was the New World new to the Cherokee. Partly adapted from the alphabet of the expropriators, the syllabary represented a third term that disrupted such space-time oppositions.

In order to become "An American Palace of Culture," the Carnegie had to forget other American cultures. Such forgetting, which Baumgarten countered in *The Tongue of the Cherokee*, is foundational to all such museums.[9] But there was another erasure at work here as well. The museum was founded on capital from the Carnegie Steel Company, which profited in turn from the railroad network, that is, from an abstract tracking of space that covered prior pathways. This reterritorialization of the railroad, later deterritorialized by still other trackings (telephone lines, airports, freeways, satellites, fiber optics), was the subject of *Carbon* (1987–1990), a work at the Los Angeles Museum of Contemporary Art. There, at the edge of the American West, after months of travel, Baumgarten inscribed the names of sixty-six Indian societies upside down on the walls along an east-west axis and in a scale relative to the population of each group. He also mounted colored bars, curves, and crosses evocative of modernist abstraction, a code that mapped the relation of the different railroads to the appropriated names of the displaced societies. Baumgarten glossed *Carbon* in this way:

> The subject and raw material of *Carbon* is the aroma of geography, as embodied in the names of the railroad lines covering this country. These names are polyphonic. They talk back to us about the confrontation of two multiple-shaped worlds: that of the continent's first inhabitants and that of the pioneer migrants to the West. On the one hand the names reflect the movement of a territorial expansion, the natural destination of which was the Pacific Ocean; on the other they testify to an older stratum, that of the Indian populations, their rivers and mountains, fords and trails. The linguistic blend of these names signifies the superimpositions of heterogeneous cultural strands.[10]

Baumgarten had no illusions about the violence of these superimpositions, and he invoked this violence again in *AMERICA Invention*, staged at the Guggenheim Museum in 1993. On the parapet of the Frank Lloyd Wright building Baumgarten wrote the names of North American indigenous societies in rough geographical order from Alaska above to Mexico below, and on the interior walls he inscribed the names of South American indigenous societies from Tierra del Fuego above to Guatemala below. These societies were divided into west and east by the bulge of the elevator, which, situated to the north, bisects the spiral of the museum like a longitudinal line. At each level of this bulge Baumgarten reestablished a horizon line painted in sandstone (the color first envisioned by Wright for the walls). When the northern names came to this meridian, they flipped in orientation—from right-side-up to upside-down and vice versa. Meanwhile the orientation of the southern names alternated in this way from bay to bay. Otherwise the continental helix of names was punctuated only by an alcove lined with words—past participles that evoked the violence visited on these societies ("abandoned . . . baptized . . . classified . . . decimated . . .").

AMERICA Invention refashioned the Guggenheim spiral into a globe turned outside in, one that, at first glance, maintained the usual opposition of North and South America with its hemispheric hierarchy of power and wealth. So, too, it seemed to position the viewer in a conventional way—as the sovereign surveyor of the world, the masterful collector of named cultures. Yet in fact Baumgarten defamiliarized such museological mappings. North and South were not opposed here; doubled back on each other, they were made to interpenetrate in a way that figured interdependence, not hierarchy. And rather than a detached gaze above the map, the viewer was plunged bodily into a labyrinth, interrogated by the names as so much "writing on the wall." Framed as we framed, with perspectives only partial, we were placed in a parallax that undid any simple binary of a we-here-now versus a they-there-then. The greatest displacement was the simplest: in lieu of official maps with names of nation-states, Baumgarten offered a map of "societies against the state," that is, societies under siege by colonial states abroad and neocolonial states at home.[11] Moreover, in lieu of famous figures in modernist art, Baumgarten invoked names representative of cultures sometimes appropriated in that same art. Implicitly he posed these alternative maps against the official ones, but again the relation between the two was one of imbrication rather than opposition. This imbrication, which counters "the denial of coexistence," is central to his art.[12]

At the Guggenheim Baumgarten imaged this imbrication through a reinscription of the spiral. A central figure for many writers and artists (James Joyce, W. B. Yeats, Vladimir Tatlin, Robert Smithson . . .), the spiral is also a common trope in Western historiography, where it has long functioned as a symbol of dialectical time. For the Italian Enlightenment philosopher

Giambattista Vico, who inaugurated this trope, history was human, not divine, that is, it was legible to its human makers, but only if they referred it not to biblical patterns but to cultural progressions of *corso* and *ricorso* as represented by the spiral.[13] This figure was put to related use, in the early years of the twentieth century, by art historians such as Riegl, Heinrich Wölfflin, Wilhelm Worringer, and Erwin Panofsky. Riegl saw the progression of art as a "screw of time" that extended in two directions at once, boring downward while turning upward, returning to the past while advancing into the future.[14] Clearly, this model of progress-toward-the-new via recovery-of-the-old was based on the example of the Renaissance, the paragon of periods in traditional art history, but it was also active in the historical conceptions of Romanticism, with its various medievalisms, as well as of modernism, with its various primitivisms. Of course, the lost original is never simply there to be recovered; it is always constructed in the present, out of the present, in exclusive terms. Additionally, as the stake of such historical returns is cultural identity, this temporal "inside" is often articulated against a spatial "outside," that is, against alien cultures perceived to threaten whatever is considered proper and pure. Thus in the Renaissance "the rediscovery" of the classical world was contemporaneous with "the discovery" of the New World—as though the cultural monism claimed in the former was needed to counter the cultural relativism posed by the latter. After all, 1492, the quincentenary of which *AMERICA Invention* commemorated in its own way, was not only the apogee of the Renaissance but also the year that Moors were expelled and Jews banished from Spain.[15]

If the spiral was a figure used to chart the development of a cultural history—that is, to maintain the trajectory of a proper identity vis-à-vis debased others—what exactly did Baumgarten do with the one inscribed in the Guggenheim? Again, he turned the official spiral of American history outside in, bringing back some of the names written out of its narrative. The spiral became a map that acknowledged many cultures rather than a sequence that privileged a single history. And rather than a list of current nation-states, it became a testimony of absented societies, some submerged forever, others that persist to this day. In a sense *AMERICA Invention* unraveled the usual victory columns, complicated the positions of the protagonists, and made the frieze speak other names. But might it have remained a kind of victory column nonetheless? Such was the rhetorical risk that Baumgarten ran in order to reveal the underside of monumental histories.

The first displacement in *AMERICA Invention* was that from "discovery" to "invention." By this simple shift in terms Baumgarten underscored that America was never a newfound land but one constructed with images, maps, legends, and names—especially names. This renomination began with Columbus, who rebaptized himself Cristóbal Colón (bearer of Christ) as well as all that he beheld according to a Christian-cum-royal hierarchy (thus in order of "discovery": San Salvador, Santa María de Concepción, Fernandina, Isabella . . .).[16] Columbus couldn't grant the status of language to those already in place; held to be without writing, these peoples could only be inscribed within his own language. According to Tzvetan Todorov, "discovery" depended on this refusal to read the native code, and "conquest" on its cynical manipulation.[17]

"One never names," Claude Lévi-Strauss once wrote. "One classes someone else . . . [or] oneself."[18] To which Jacques Derrida replied: "For writing, obliteration of the proper classed in the play of difference is the originary violence itself."[19] Baumgarten was sensitive to this violence; at the same time, his version of America didn't insist on the absolute authenticity of its names. On the contrary, Baumgarten knew them to be mostly imposed and often rejected. In some ways *AMERICA Invention* existed between the word as arbitrary, the name as what-others-call-others, and the word as referential, the name as truth of being. This ambiguity, this ambivalence, not only recalls old debates about language but also speaks to recent arguments about identity.

So what, finally, was this writing on the wall? For some viewers these names appeared too commemorative, even cenotaphic, and the passive, past verbs in *AMERICA Invention* ("abandoned," "decimated") seemed to replay the first move of the old humanist game: to be reanimated, the cultural object must first be declared dead, or, to be rescued, it must first be deemed ruined, incapable not only of self-understanding but also of self-protection.[20] That assumption seals the other in a past that is then seen to be its only true temporality, one removed from both the impure present and the complex future. Just as importantly, such a view also arrogates the place of memory—arrogates the right to commemorate in the first place. Yet Baumgarten didn't locate these names in any pure past. On the contrary, they were invoked precisely as present: "These names talk themselves," he insisted.[21] Neither were they simply appropriated or displaced in relation to his own. Indeed, rather than arrogate the names of others, Baumgarten used them to question the representational space-time of his own culture. This is not to suggest that the critique of ethnographic authority was no longer important; on the contrary. Yet this critique needed to be critiqued in turn, so rote had its crude versions then become. Does a representation displace its referent? Must one be an identity in order to represent it?

So, again, what was this writing? Perhaps its ambiguity was its salient characteristic. Ambivalence about writing is as old as writing. In his *Phaedrus* Plato presented writing less as a memory device than as a means of forgetting.

In a celebrated moment in *Of Grammatology* (1967) Derrida glossed this ambivalence in terms of writing as a *pharmakon*, a term used by Plato that means both poison and antidote. It was this ambiguity of writing as a tool of memory and a drug of oblivion, of writing as an instrument often of violence and sometimes of reparation, that *AMERICA Invention* foregrounded.

II Some Contemporaries

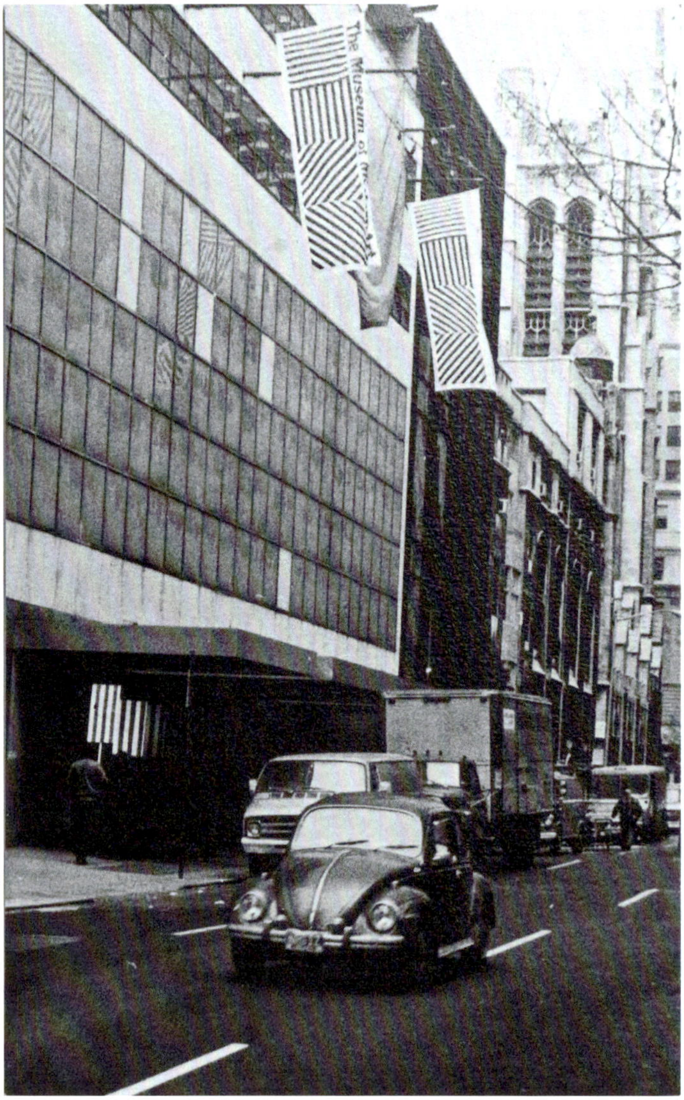

Louise Lawler, *Volkswagen Postcard*, 1978 (detail). © Louise Lawler.
Courtesy the artist and Sprüth Magers.

16 Oblique Looking

Among the early works of Louise Lawler are two black-and-white postcards titled *Volkswagen* and *Truck* (1978), the first oriented on the vertical, the second on the horizontal. Photographs of a dark VW and a generic truck, they appear so straightforward that we might not recognize at first that they were taken outside the Museum of Modern Art in New York on a wintry day (trees are bare, dirty snow lies on the pavement). On closer examination we see two striped banners hanging from the facade and a few striped posters being carried on the sidewalk. The banners announce a show by Sol LeWitt, and the posters are part of a demonstration by Daniel Buren, so the postcards also capture prime examples of Conceptual art and Institution Critique. Already at the time, Buren was known, through striped signs such as these, for his questioning of the parameters of art—precisely where and how it becomes legible as such. By these means Buren aimed to shift attention from the art object to its framing by the art institution. Here Lawler takes his displacement one step further. "Why not push the analysis of the institution further," she asks implicitly, "why not also deal with its outside?" Or, more innocently (if also more subversively), "How do this car and this truck—how do people and things in everyday life—matter to the machinations of art and vice versa, or do they?" In this way the postcards nudge the Institution Critique of Buren and his peers into other spaces, other discourses.[1]

In "From Work to Text" (1971) Roland Barthes also effected a critical displacement, in his case from the traditional concern with the literary work as a unitary artifact to the poststructuralist interest in the text as "a serial movement of disconnections, overlappings, variations."[2] And in "From Work to Frame" (1987) Craig Owens carried that displacement further in order to come to terms with artists like Buren who, as Robert Smithson once put it, focused on "the apparatus the artist is threaded through."[3] Sometimes this critique projected the art museum as a faceless institution of restrictive walls and oppressive discourses. Yet, as Lawler reveals in her pictures and objects, the art apparatus is also a diffuse network of routine protocols and throwaway things that, often in innocuous ways, structure not only the recognition of art but also its value—souvenirs like postcards and paperweights, publicity like announcements and matchbooks, information like wall labels and exhibition pamphlets, certification like object provenances and gallery contracts. Lawler reveals these apparent supplements to be central to any contemporary art that wants to qualify as such, and travesties of these devices make up a good part of her early practice.[4] In a sense, then, she moved from work to text as well as from work to frame, developing a distinctive model of picture-making that combined the two. This way of working has allowed her to catch these crucial supplements, which are often hidden in plain sight or just out of view. For once the frames of art are opened up, as when she takes us into storage rooms or office files, then the props that support them, that keep the institution up and running, come into focus. As captured by Lawler, this view is at once bemused and analytical—bemused because these props still appear trivial, analytical because we move to compensate for our initial oversight with a critical gaze.

Early on, then, Lawler questioned Institution Critique and, in so doing, extended it: she showed us an institution that isn't limited to a physical space or a single discourse. The problem is that this apparatus might then appear only ambiguous, never to be pinned down, as suggested in a caption that Lawler once printed on the mat of her *Sappho and Patriarch* (1984), a photograph of a statue of Sappho in the foreground and a bust of a patriarch in the background, both illuminated in an otherwise dim gallery: "Is it the work, the location or the stereotype that is the institution?"[5] This uncertainty is true to the situation of art today as much as it was then.

Frames include through exclusion, so that once they are prised open a little, various things appear that aren't usually seen. Through her oblique gaze into sundry settings—galleries, museums, elegant homes, corporate offices, auction houses, and other stations in the circulation of artworks—Lawler shows us different objects colliding and different spaces overlapping. Often we confront a juxtaposition of things and places that are typically held apart. A classic example is *Living Room Corner, Arranged by Mr. and Mrs. Burton Tremaine, New York City* (1984), a color photograph of a domestic interior of prominent collectors in which hangs *First Disk* (1913) by Robert Delaunay, a strong contender for the inaugural abstraction in twentieth-century art. Yet to the left of this modernist icon is an early bust by Roy Lichtenstein that seems to be part of a lamp, at the center is a television with Stevie Wonder on the screen, and to the right is an African mask on the wall. In short, this domestic corner is a mélange of cultural tokens—modernist, Pop, mass, and tribal. Or, conversely, we encounter an arrangement of things and places that fit together all too nicely, but in which the result doesn't add up to much more than high-class décor. A well-known example of this genre comes courtesy of the same collectors: *Pollock and Tureen,*

Arranged by Mr. and Mrs. Burton Tremaine (1984) presents a beautiful tureen with a floral design and a truncated drip painting by Jackson Pollock, the two framed as pseudomorphic doubles, a rhyme in color and line across the registers of decorative object and high art. Or, even better, there is *Monogram, Arranged by Mr. and Mrs. Burton Tremaine, New York City* (1984), where a lush off-white bed cover appears below a lush off-white *Flag* by Jasper Johns. Here the rhyme is not only between the personal monogram on the sheet and the signature work by Johns but also between the flag in the painting and the four pillows arrayed on the bed.

Perhaps in the end the two genres aren't so different: the things in *Living Room Corner* are cultural tokens of taste or social distinction as well as of exchange or financial worth (the prized *Disk* was later sold to other collectors), as are the objects in *Pollock and Tureen* and *Monogram*. They all are so many "arrangements" of sumptuary value, which is to say value that is produced through the display of exclusive possession. Periodically, Lawler has asked her audience to respond to a question, one that assumes the opposition, made by Walter Benjamin in "The Work of Art in the Age of Its Technical Reproducibility" (1936), between the archaic "ritual value" of art and its modern "exhibition value": "She [Lawler] makes no attempt to rescue art from ritual—yes/no." The question is semi-ironic, for, at least as seen in her pictures, there is no hope for a restoration of aesthetic autonomy, let alone of ritual value. The only autonomy here is that of capital, the only ritual that of conspicuous consumption. Such is the not-so-discreet charm of the bourgeoisie today, and while some of us might still shadowbox with its old ideology of autonomous art, that class has long since moved on.

In 1988 and 1992 Lawler collaborated with Allan McCollum on a series of dingbats, which they titled *Fixed Intervals* (dingbats are typographic devices that indicate divisions in texts). In effect, Lawler shows us the institutional dingbats that mark the intervals of art, the divisions between its spaces, and she unfixes them slightly in order to take us behind the official settings of gallery or museum into storage rooms, collector homes, and so on. This usually occurs in one of two ways. Either she takes "an arrangement of pictures" by a gallery, museum, collector, or corporation and frames it in her own way, or she opens up a given frame, enters the semiprivate spaces behind it, and records what she finds there. In this respect her pictures are both like and unlike collages of a Surrealist kind. Like those collages, they bring together disparate things on a single plane, but, unlike those collages, her pictures don't transform the mundane into the marvelous. This is not to say that chance, much less contingency, doesn't operate in her pictures; it's only to underscore that they come "arranged" in such a way that the juxtaposition of disparate things is already internal to the image. In this way Lawler suggests a new category: found montage.

We see the "making [of] meaning by juxtaposition and alignment," Lawler has said of her pictures.[6] Yet sometimes we witness the unmaking of meaning too, as in her images of the indifferent storing of artworks. Either these pictures reveal a syntax of things (a tureen next to a Pollock, a monogrammed cover next to a signature painting), or they present the lack of syntax, with things jumbled together (such as statues wrapped in plastic sheeting and stashed in a back room). If these objects were words, we might call this (non)order an example of parataxis, which the dictionary defines as "the placing of clauses or phrases one after the other, without words to indicate coordination or subordination, as in 'Tell me, how are you?'"[7] Rhetoric opposes parataxis (which literally means "side-arrangement") to hypotaxis (literally, "under-arrangement"), in which the parts of a sentence are hierarchically ordered. A similar opposition obtains in linguistics between metonymy and metaphor. Roman Jakobson defined metonymy as an operation of juxtaposition (one phrase positioned after another), which he associated with prose (e.g., "a rose is a beautiful thing"), while he defined metaphor as an operation of substitution (one phrase replaces another), which he related to poetry (e.g., "my love is a rose").[8] For the most part Lawler works with juxtaposition and against substitution; in fact, the title of an early project, produced with Sherrie Levine, proclaims "A Picture Is No Substitute for Anything." Like poetry, art tends to be on the side of metaphor, for its effect is also achieved through substitution or at least elevation (the Pollock over the tureen, the Johns over the pillows, in value as well as position). Often in her pictures, Lawler show us objects and spaces juxtaposed without much hierarchy, and the poetry of art is thereby returned to the prose of the world. Elevated hypotaxis or metaphor becomes everyday parataxis or metonymy in *Every Other Picture* (1990), which presents parts of a lush abstraction by Gerhard Richter and an electric-chair silkscreen by Andy Warhol simply slotted into storage cages, or in *Pictures That May or May Not Go Together* (1997–1998), which presents framed images merely laid out on wood shelves.

"A Picture Is No Substitute for Anything" is in keeping with the poststructuralist critique of representation, which was often associated with postmodernist art in the 1980s. The statement was taken as a caution against the authority arrogated in the very act of imaging. At the same time, it could also be understood as an assertion about the democracy of images—that pictures, like people, should be treated as equal. Today, however, any equivalence of images is the effect of the sheer fungibility of all things in our hyperfluid market, and the salient question to ask of Lawler is not "Does she attempt to rescue art from

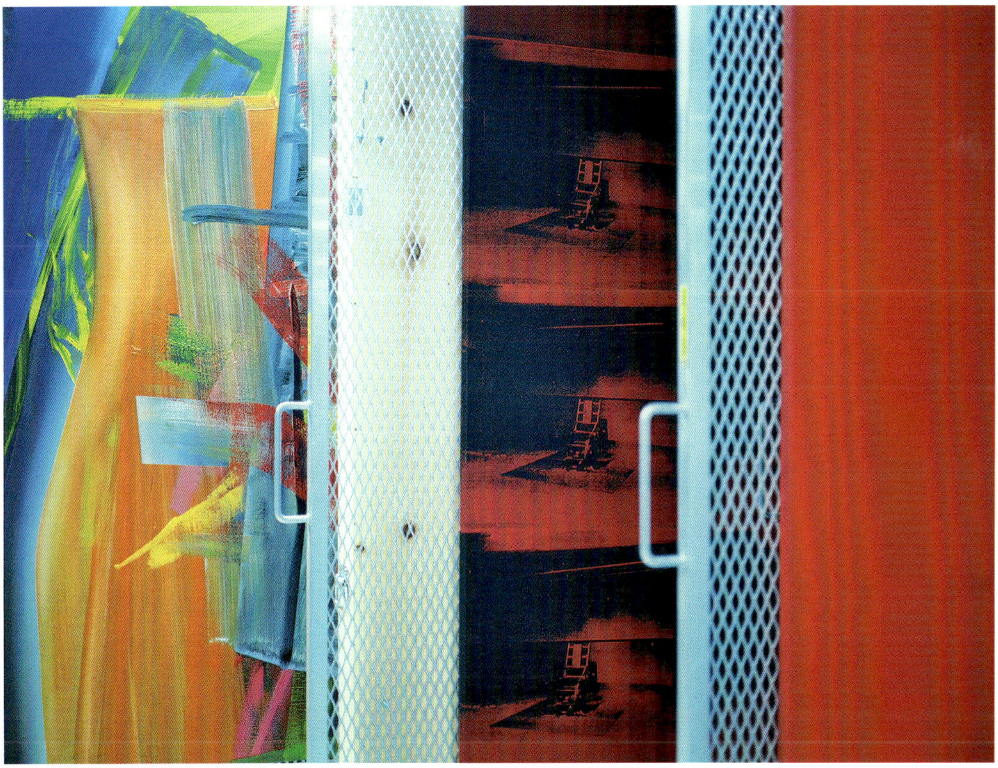

Louise Lawler, *Every Other Picture*, 1990. Cibachrome photograph, 40 × 53 inches. © Louise Lawler. Courtesy the artist and Sprüth Magers.

ritual value?" but "Does she attempt to rescue art from exchange value?" She never presents art in its autonomous glory; again, that fiction is long dispelled. In fact, what Lawler often shows us is not an ideal arrangement of pictures so much as the everyday *de*rangement of the same. This, too, is part of the not-so-discreet charm of the bourgeoisie today.

Avant-gardes such as Surrealism projected a bourgeois order that was fixed, with clear lines that could be transgressed. However, the filmmaker Luis Buñuel, a onetime Surrealist, understood that this order wasn't so obvious, even to its greatest adherents. Thus, in *The Discreet Charm of the Bourgeoisie* (1972), his bourgeois protagonists try to dine together but fail each time, and in *The Exterminating Angel* (1962), they manage to dine together but fail to leave. "Buñuel himself is not outside the world he criticizes, he is part of it, and so are his friends and family," the critic Michael Wood writes in a brilliant gloss on this predicament.

> Social arrangements are foolish and apparently fragile, because they are so arbitrary and groundless. Everything about them could be different, and is different in other times and places. "Everyone is a barbarian for someone," as a character says in *The Phantom of Liberty* [a 1974 Buñuel film]: "on est toujours le barbare de quelqu'un." And yet it is because these arrangements are arbitrary and groundless that we have so little purchase on them, and they seem so strangely unchangeable.[9]

So it often appears in the world revealed by Lawler: it is precisely because these arrangements are arbitrary and groundless that we have little purchase on them and that they seem strangely unchangeable. Today the art institution has no coherent ideology, so Lawler doesn't dress it down didactically; one can't reason with the contemporary bourgeoisie or hope to be more irrational than it already is. Again, Institution Critique tended to project an authority onto the art apparatus that it didn't always possess. For Lawler that power is partly a show, a pretense, that requires our projection; it's a matter of ceremonial performatives that often work but sometimes don't, like the Wizard of Oz operating his levers fitfully behind the curtain. But that doesn't make this power any easier to contest, let alone to change—on the contrary. Like Dorothy and Toto, Lawler pulls back the curtain, but that doesn't put an end to the Wizard. The emperor might not have any clothes, but that revelation hardly makes his empire collapse.

"Pulling back the curtain" suggests that Lawler demystifies the art institution, but hers isn't really an exposé of that sort (again, what she reveals is usually hidden in plain sight). Moreover, to call it demystification is to miss the humor of her subtle practice, its resistance to official authority, its proclivity for the oblique view (Lawler has a lighter touch than most of her peers in appropriation art). If her pictures have the structure of collage, they also have the logic of a joke, for all three—a collage, a joke, and a picture by Lawler—involve the "coupling of dissimilar things."[10] In his 1905 book on the joke Freud lists this characteristic as well as others—contrasting ideas, sense found in nonsense, looking at the overlooked, bewilderment followed by enlightenment, sharp wit, playful judgment—and most of these apply to Lawler as well.[11] "Joking is the disguised priest who weds every couple," the nineteen-century novelist Jean Paul wrote. "He likes best to wed couples whose union their relatives frown upon," the nineteenth-century philosopher Theodor Vischer added.[12] Lawler is that kind of mediator, one whose jibes often come at the expense of would-be superiors. For Freud jokes make "criticism possible against persons in exalted positions who claim to exercise authority"; as usual, he sees them in terms of an economy of (un)pleasure: "They make possible the satisfaction of an instinct . . . in the face of an obstacle that stands in its way."[13] The hitch in this analogy is that Lawler doesn't offer much relief. Often her pictures are jokes without a punch line or riddles without a solution, as in the title of her *Something about Time and Space but I'm Not Sure What It Is* (1988/1998). Or they are puzzles without a picture, or fairy tales without a narrative, as in the title of her *Once There Was a Little Boy and Everything Turned Out Alright. THE END* (1985). We are left to contemplate the vagaries of communication. This "Huh?" effect is strong in Ed Ruscha too, and Lawler shares his ability to make common images and words suddenly appear odd.[14]

"It's Something Like . . . Putting Words in Your Mouth" is another Lawler phrase from 1988. It can be read as a caution against ideological persuasion, but it's also an instance of blocked speech or failed signification, along the lines of Duchamp casting his right cheek in plaster and titling it *With My Tongue in My Cheek* (1959).[15] This is a familiar colloquialism for irony, for saying one thing and meaning another, and certainly there is irony in Lawler. Yet often this irony comes across as inadvertency, less tongue-in-cheek on the part of the artist than a slip-of-the-tongue somewhere in the photographed scene. At times, that is, the parataxis in the picture seems to point to a parapraxis, to a minor error that might indicate a repressed motive, as elaborated by Freud in *The Psychopathology of Everyday Life* (1901). Are there conflicted wishes to be detected in these photos of elegant homes and refined galleries? Might Lawler intimate a "psychopathology of everyday art"?

Of course, the art institution isn't a human subject, and it doesn't have an unconscious. For the most part it's a bureaucratic operation with its own rules. But it also comes with many quirks. In 1974 the Italian philologist Sebastiano Timpanaro presented a critique of the theory of the Freudian slip. According to

Timpanaro, many of our confusions of letters and words signal not repressed motives but cognitive mistakes, such as the substitution of a more familiar term for a less familiar one.[16] Timpanaro called this kind of substitution "banalization," and the psychoanalyst Ben Kafka has given us a nice example—a student writing "fantasy echo" instead of "fin-de-siècle" on an exam. Sometimes there are visual corollaries of this sort of slip in Lawler (as when that Lichtenstein bust suddenly looks like a lamp base). Kafka ascribes these errors to "the demon of writing" caused by the strain of institutional "paperwork." In a related way Lawler goes hunting for the demons of the art institution. She gives us not only its smooth running but also its glitches and gremlins.

However, recourse to language gets us only so far with Lawler. She produces images after all, very self-aware ones, and they make us aware of our looking as we look at them. Standing publicly in front of pictures of spaces that are often private, we too can feel a little exposed, almost as though we were caught looking. So what exactly is the mode of seeing solicited by a Lawler image? I called this gaze analytical, and in this respect it's close to the suspicion about seeing that the art historian Michael Leja has associated with a capitalist world of "frauds, hoaxes, swindles," and the like: "A modern self, knowing well the perils presented to modern vision, looked askance."[17] According to Leja, Duchamp played on this looking askance in art, and certainly Lawler falls within that lineage. Yet there's as much sympathy as suspicion in her point of view; she doesn't look askance so much as she sees on the oblique. In geometry the oblique is a line neither parallel nor perpendicular to a given line, and in rhetoric it's a mode of address that's indirect. Both definitions are pertinent to Lawler.[18]

Oblique can also be pointed, as it is in her sharp framing of *Perseus with the Head of Medusa* (1804–1806) by Antonio Canova.[19] Before its removal to the sculpture galleries in 2003, *Perseus* was the first artwork that visitors encountered at the Metropolitan Museum in New York; it stood in the center of the balcony above the Great Hall. In his left hand the Greek hero holds up the severed head of the Gorgon by her snaky hair, and in his right the sword that decapitated her. Although the beheading is fresh, he appears calm, even Apollonian. In fact, Canova modeled his sculpture on the Apollo Belvedere (120–140 CE), so that his Perseus evokes Apollo formally, just as his Medusa evokes Dionysus thematically, and we understand which power won: masculine reason vanquishes feminine unreason. In its old positioning the sculpture marked the primary axis of the museum in a dramaturgy that was ceremonial: to pass under the triumphal Perseus was to enter the museum under his aegis, that is, under the sign of the subdued Medusa. Beyond the statue lay the grand stairway that leads to the galleries devoted to European painting, which

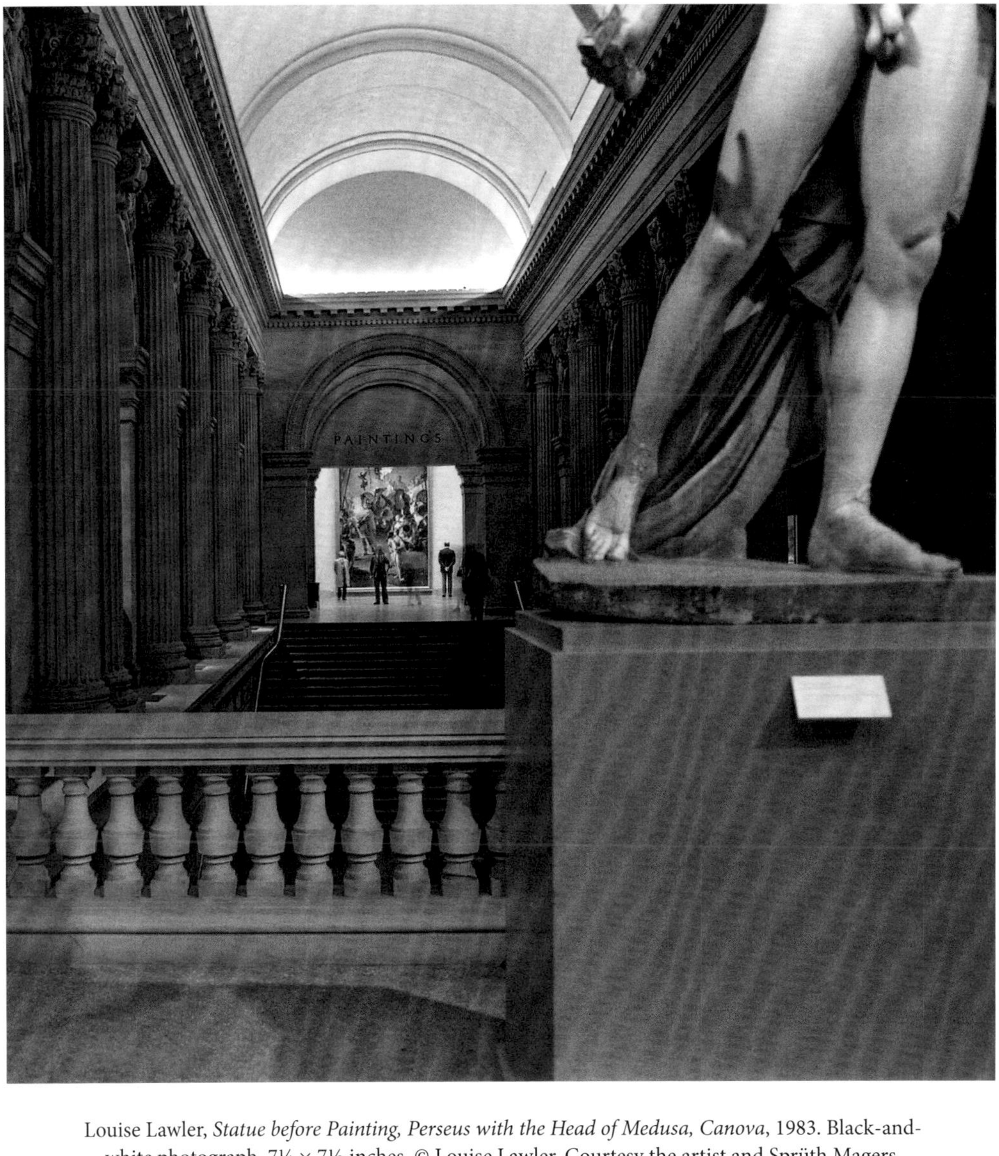

Louise Lawler, *Statue before Painting, Perseus with the Head of Medusa, Canova*, 1983. Black-and-white photograph, 7¼ × 7½ inches. © Louise Lawler. Courtesy the artist and Sprüth Magers.

was long inaugurated by *The Triumph of Marius* (1729) by Giovanni Battista Tiepolo. This massive canvas depicts the triumphal procession of the Roman general Marius on January 1, 104 BCE, following his capture of the African King Jugurtha, who, though still mighty, is shown bound in chains. The museum made its introduction, then, by way of two aesthetic-moral models, the mythical subjugation of a supernatural form of otherness, Medusa, and the historical subjugation of a cultural instance of otherness, Jugurtha. In the statue and in the painting, the taming of the monstrous and the barbarous is celebrated explicitly as a heroic event and implicitly as an artistic task—as the touchstone of this museum in particular and of Western civilization in general.

In *Statue before Painting, Perseus with the Head of Medusa, Canova* (1983), Lawler brings this stagecraft into view. Shot from below, Perseus is truncated—as though he were the one who is decapitated—and it seems as though his trunkless legs might topple. His penis, though visible, is no longer phallic, and his sword is cut off just above its hilt—a double castration. Deep in the background, we glimpse *The Triumph of Marius*, but, shrunk to the size of a postage stamp, it no longer appears triumphal either. Lawler thus frames the great theme of the sculpture and the painting—civilization as the taming of the wild (the Dionysian, the Medusan, the feminine, the other)—on the oblique. It is seen wryly, shown to be a myth, set up as a joke. Here the institution is indeed the work, the location, and the stereotype, all three at once, and all three are put into question.

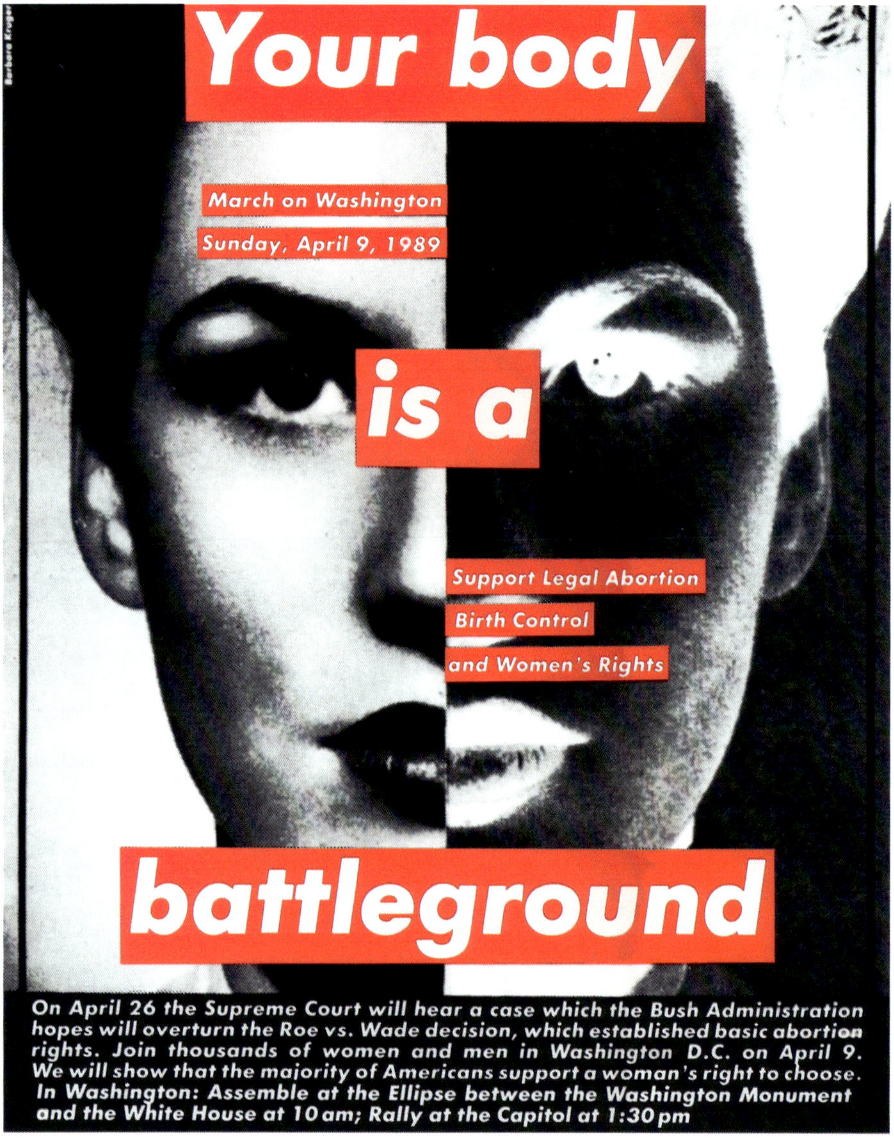

Barbara Kruger, *Untitled (Your body is a battleground)*, 1989, adapted for March on Washington, April 9, 1989. Photographic silkscreen on vinyl. © Barbara Kruger. Courtesy the artist and Sprüth Magers.

17 Direct Address

The most trenchant of feminist artists, Barbara Kruger cracks open appropriated images with invented slogans, hoisting everyday assumptions on their own petards. For decades now, she has done this critical work at every scale, from matchbook covers to giant billboards, and across many media, from simple photo-text montages to immersive installations of statements and screens. Ever alert to questions of address and audience, Kruger has always sought new ways to insert her practice in the public realm, drawing political debate into artistic discourse and vice versa. For some viewers this approach has made her work too political. We know her position, they say; it's feminist and anticapitalist in a way that advances little more than her own version of knowing better. For others Kruger is not political enough. From this perspective her work, informed by her early experience as a graphic designer (for *Mademoiselle* and other publications), is already bound up with the sexed-up consumerism that it claims to challenge, and so is not truly feminist or anticapitalist at all. Of course, both takes are only that—reflex reactions that let us off easy, that allow us not to look, read, and think further.

If Kruger has a consistent motive, it's to question any assumed authority, to suspect any univocal position. And if she has a consistent method, it's to proceed by implication in the strongest sense—to trace the ties to capital and power that bind us all, including Kruger, who never exempts herself. To be sure, she is critical, but hers is a critique that doesn't pretend to stand apart, outside of commerce or ideology, love or war. On the contrary, she has done more than any artist of her generation to alert us to the extended reach of these forces in our everyday lives. "Outside the market there is nothing," Kruger remarked in 1987, "not a piece of lint, a cardigan, a coffee table, a human being . . ."[1] "There's a politic in every conversation we have," she added in 1990, "every deal we make, every face we kiss."[2] This worldview isn't cynical, as is sometimes charged; it is realist. And the work that rises from it isn't aridly conceptual, as is often claimed; it is richly visual. Far from opposed to seduction, Kruger calls for new sorts of pleasure as well as new subjects to experience them.

"To question the seemingly natural appearance of images through the textual commentary which accompanies them": this is how Kruger described her practice already in 1981, and it has remained true over the years.[3] As Craig Owens demonstrated long ago, Kruger transforms stereotypes into "apotropes," that is to say, images that betray the purpose of the stereotype to arrest us, even to petrify us with its "Medusan gaze."[4] And she does much the same with language, where the cliché is turned against its own imperative to stun our thinking, to keep us obedient. Although her art is one of striking declarations—Kruger calls her method "direct address"—it is equally one of troubling paradoxes: she catches language out as it attempts to beguile us. Kruger fences with ideological words and images, highlighting what Barthes once called the "various kinds of music out of which active language is made"—"the desires, the fears, the appearances, the intimidations, the advances, the blandishments, the protests, the excuses, the aggressions . . ."[5]

That Kruger uses "active language" is central to the purpose of her art, which is to trouble common sense, especially regarding gender. Her talent for mimicry is key, and Kruger has made it as important for feminist art as Homi Bhabha did for postcolonial critique. "We are very good mimics," she wrote in 1982. "We replicate certain words and pictures and watch them stray from or coincide with your notions of fact and fiction." Her mimicry is undertaken not only to foil the conventional expectations of male viewers, but also "to welcome a female spectator into the audience of men."[6]

This program sounded too theoretical to her early detractors. Kruger emerged in a heady time for critical theory, and her criticism, like her art, attested to her involvement with different thinkers. When she wrote of history as "a univocal voice-over, an instructor of origin, power, and mastery," one heard echoes of both Walter Benjamin and Michel Foucault. And when she spoke of "a culture ruled by images" that places us "elsewhere, not in the real but in the represented," one was reminded of the Situationist critique of spectacle. Projected as abstractions, "power," "mastery," and "spectacle" can appear so total as to induce a sense of helplessness, and Kruger isn't immune to this effect ("we are clasped in a relentless tango of remote controllings," she once wrote of television). Yet she has also long insisted that we can "decline" the subject positions assigned to us, and that we can choose to be open to histories of discontinuity "and, one might add, difference."[7] (Kruger plays here on an additional meaning of the verb *to decline*, which is "to state the forms of a noun, pronoun, or adjective corresponding to case, number, and gender.") Most importantly, she has always given a feminist turn to these various strands of theory, most of which, however critical of mastery, were dominated by men. Her emphatic questioning of binary thinking evokes Derrida too, but his deconstruction is revised with a feminist eye to sexual difference. And all her

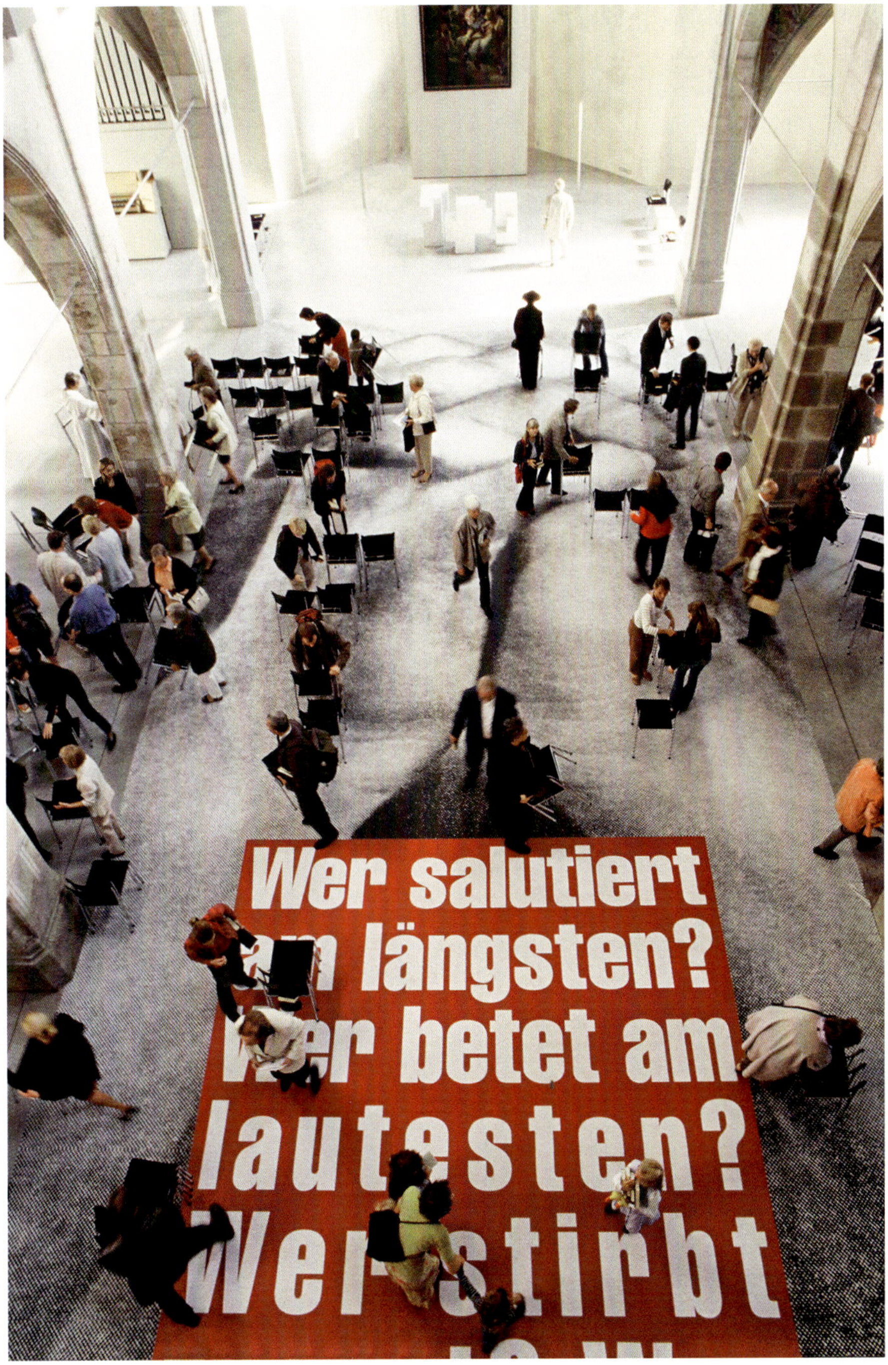

Barbara Kruger, installation in St. Peter Church, Cologne, 2003 ("Who salutes the longest? Who prays the loudest? Who dies first? Who laughs last?"). Photo: Bernhard Schaub. © Barbara Kruger. Courtesy the artist and Sprüth Magers.

points have a street-smart edge that these thinkers lacked. The upshot is that Kruger is as keen a critic of the language of contemporary patriarchy—in theory too—as we have had.

"The richness and complexity of theory should periodically break through the moats of academia," Kruger wrote in 1992, "and enter the public discourse via a kind of powerfully pleasurable language of pictures, words, sounds, and structures." She has acted on this mandate in her writing as well as in her work, pushing wide her range of references (including art, popular culture, movies, and television), subjects (including Yvonne Rainer, Chantal Akerman, Andy Warhol, Samuel Fuller, and Howard Stern), and venues (including *Artforum*, the *Village Voice*, *Esquire*, and the *New York Times*). And her ethic of pleasure is as strong as her commitment to discourse. In 1991 Kruger reframed "esthetic emotion" as "a showing and telling as it is," but she also retained its old sense as "a kind of 'felt' moment, a visual resonance," concluding: "I think I could go for that esthetic. I think I could second that emotion."[8] Here she both departs from the suspicion, in early feminist theory, of the image as a mere vehicle of male desire, and anticipates the concern, in recent critical discourse, with the political valence of affect. First and last Kruger has practiced the pleasure of interruption, combining "the muteness of picturing with a seriously playful display of language."[9]

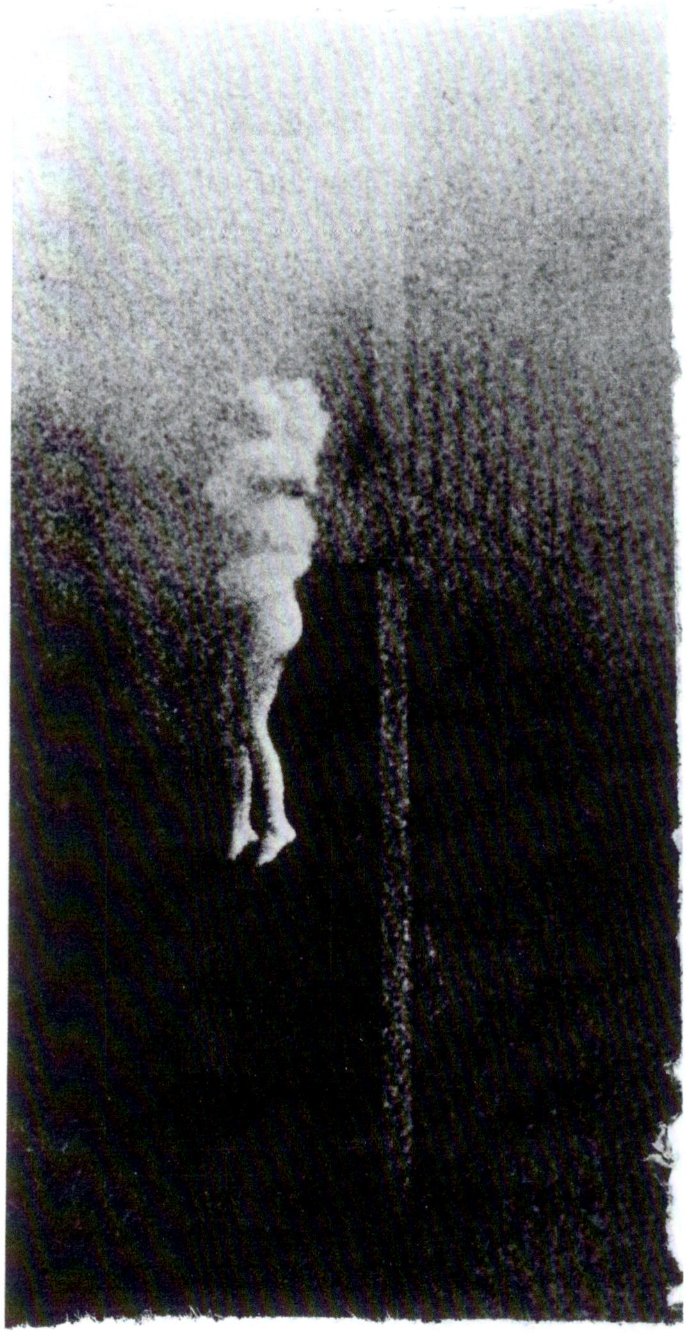

Sarah Charlesworth, *Unidentified Woman, Hotel Corona de Aragon, Madrid*, 1980. Gelatin silver print, 78 × 42 inches. © Estate of Sarah Charlesworth. Courtesy Paula Cooper Gallery.

18 The Sex Appeal of the Inorganic

Sarah Charlesworth liked to turn the received ideas of visual culture into productive paradoxes, questioning clichés in the process, such as the notion that critical art must be didactic. I count seven paradoxes that her work puts into play.

Paradox #1: I don't think of myself as a photographer. Charlesworth made this remark in 1990, and immediately clarified its relation to her practice: "it is an engagement with a problem rather than a medium."[1] Here she spoke for an entire group of Pictures artists, including Silvia Kolbowski, Barbara Kruger, Louise Lawler, Sherrie Levine, Cindy Sherman, and Laurie Simmons. Variously initiated into strategies of Conceptual art, performance, and Institution Critique of the 1960s and 1970s, these artists were also marked by new developments in the 1980s—on the one hand, by a complication of feminist theory that foregrounded the question of sexual difference in visual representation and, on the other, by an expansion of mass media that changed the terms of image production, distribution, and reception. Some of these artists also contended with the ambiguous model of Andy Warhol, who colluded with the media image-world that he also exposed. Certainly, Charlesworth engaged his precedent, and her critical elaboration of Pop art, reframed by both Conceptualism and feminism, is a key instance of postmodernist practice.

With images purloined from both ads and news, Charlesworth questioned photography in multiple ways. She was critical of media images designed to solicit our consent or trigger our desire, even as she was also opposed to art photography that assumed the values of the unique image associated with painting (art photography had begun to attract a strong market by the early 1980s). Her art was positioned, too, against Neo-Expressionist painting of the period with its forced reclamation of the cliché of the male artist as expressive genius.[2] Like some of her colleagues, Charlesworth tended to treat the photograph as both a serial multiple and a simulacral image (that is, one without any secure referent in the world). She regarded photos as coded constructions that produce real effects as well as artificial affects, and she dedicated her art to an exploration of this rhetoric of the image.[3]

Consider her early series *Tabula Rasa* (1981), four near-white silkscreens based on a faint image of a dinner table produced by Nicéphore Niépce in the 1820s, which is often claimed to be the first photograph. The original, a glass plate long lost, exists only as a faded paper version, which Charlesworth reworked with slight variations in each case. With this deft gesture she thus complicated any attempt to uphold a hierarchy of original and copy. Today the notion that the reproducibility of the photograph challenges the aura of the unique artwork is very familiar, but its implications were yet to be clarified in 1981.[4] Moreover, even as Charlesworth questioned the status of the original in *Tabula Rasa*, she didn't simply dispatch its aura. On the contrary, she showed how that aura is conjured, and how copies support the idea of the original as often they as subvert it. (Ontologically, of course, the very category of "original" depends on that of "copy.")

Paradox #2: To subtract is to add. The Surrealists defined collage as the meeting of two or more things on a plane that doesn't suit them. Yet what if collage were rethought as a process of subtraction, not addition, of cutting away, not gluing together?[5] Charlesworth proposed as much in her first series, *Modern History* (1977–1979). For one section of the work she photocopied the front pages of the *International Herald Tribune* for the month of September 1979, masking out everything except the masthead and the photographs. At first glance this deletion only produces arbitrary juxtapositions, but the ideological framing of the news becomes apparent once we notice the recurrence of male politicians. With the simple device of the newspaper as assisted readymade (deployed to different ends by Warhol and Dan Graham), Charlesworth underscored a first priority of official media: to maintain patriarchal authority in political power.

Modern History suppresses informational content in order to reveal ideological structure. Charlesworth performed a different sort of negative montage in her *Stills* (1980), a series in which news photos of people in free fall are enlarged even as the world around them is elided. In *Unidentified Woman, Hotel Corona de Aragon, Madrid*, a woman is "stilled" in midair, her lower half exposed, her upper obscured, an apparent suicide. Yet "neither the intention nor the outcome of the jump is apparent," Charlesworth claims, which suggests that her true subject here is the indeterminacy of signification, in particular the paradox that to subtract denotation is often to expand connotation: ambiguous meanings flow into the space that literal reference leaves behind.[6] At the same time, the *Stills* trouble this undecidability too, for they are also concerned with existential decision-making—on a fundamental level, the taking of a life, and on an ethical one, the taking (or selecting) of a photograph. In this respect they call up Warhol again, not only his silkscreens of falling bodies but also his obsession

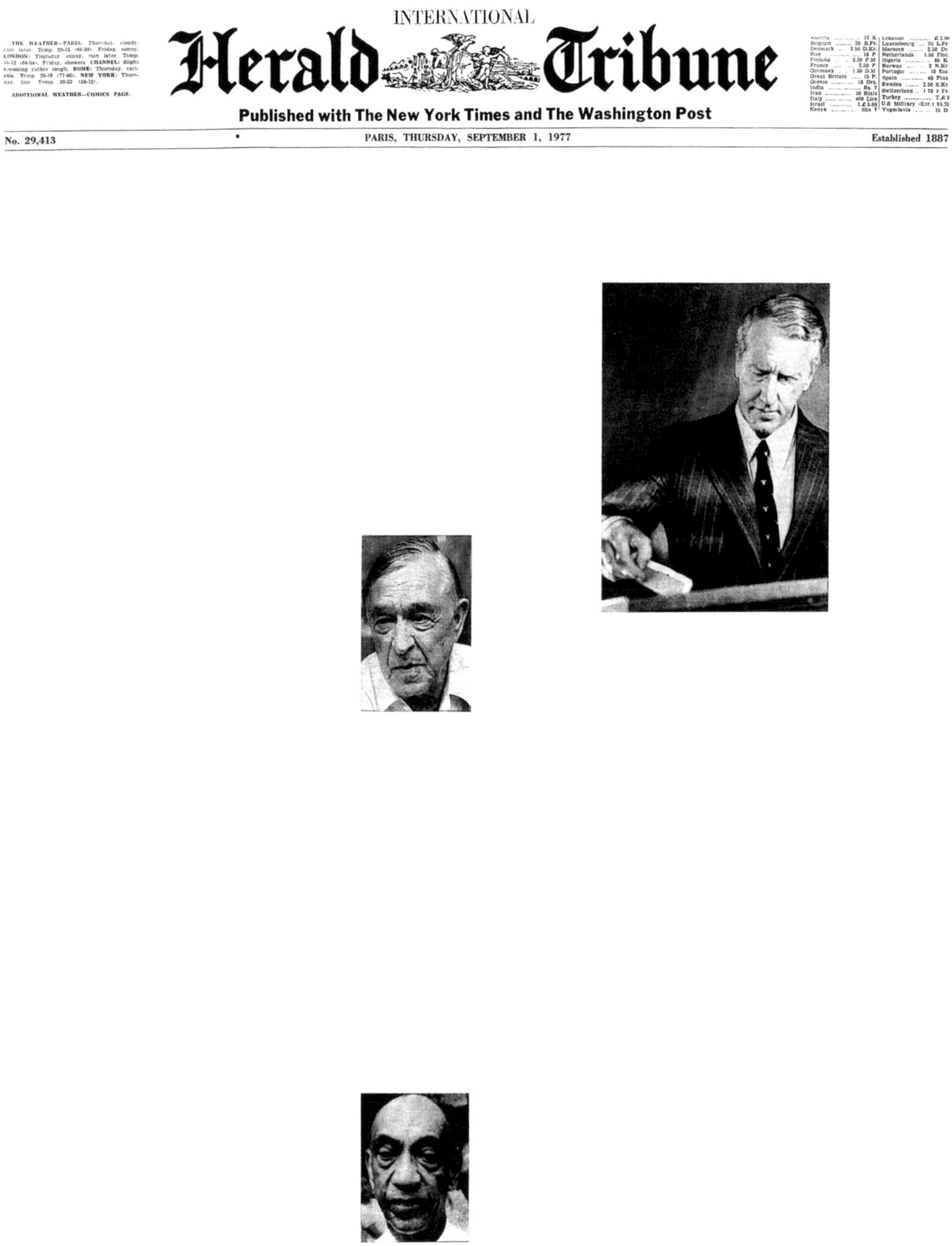

Sarah Charlesworth, *Herald Tribune, September 1977*, 1977. Black-and-white print, 23 × 16 inches. © Estate of Sarah Charlesworth. Courtesy Paula Cooper Gallery.

with "death in America," that is, with the anonymous victims of car crashes, state electrocutions, and food poisonings. Perhaps more than any contemporary except Richard Prince, Charlesworth developed this dark side of Warholian Pop. So, too, the *Stills* point to the old association between photography and death—the superstition that the photo steals the soul as well as the idea (advanced by Barthes and others) that the camera not only arrests its human subjects but also mortifies them.[7]

Paradox #3: Aura loswaura regained. For Benjamin, of course, photographic reproduction stripped the artwork of context as well as aura. André Malraux saw this decontextualization in a different light. In his famous account of "the museum without walls," first sketched under the partial influence of Benjamin, Malraux argued that, even as the reproduced artwork loses some of its properties as an object, it gains others as an image, such as "the utmost significance as to style."[8] It is this dialectic between de-auraticization and re-aestheticization that Charlesworth stages in her best-known series, *Objects of Desire* (1983–1988). Here the rephotography of solitary objects on lush grounds of color—an African mask on a black field in *Black Mask* (1983) or a Byzantine crucifixion on a red field in *Cross* (1986)—both evokes the aura of the precious artwork and suggests that its charismatic style is largely a special effect. We see how an emblem, an icon, or indeed a cliché is produced. In this way Charlesworth played both sides of the Benjamin-Malraux debate, pitting one against the other. She was provoked by a paradox that became the central operation of her work: to subtract meaning and value is often to augment them, and to reduce effect and affect is often to increase them. In a sense, Charlesworth put the Lacanian formula, "desire is born of lack," into aesthetic practice.

Paradox # 4: The sex appeal of the inorganic. In most of the *Objects of Desire* Charlesworth appropriated images from glossy magazines, cropped them, then rephotographed them on fields of saturated color. These fragments of models and accessories suggest a language of fetishistic desire, which Charlesworth underscored with the shiny allure of her Cibachrome prints and lacquered frames. Some of these works present solitary accoutrements of the female body such as a chic scarf, while others juxtapose two or more images for our reflection. *Figures* (1983) sets a headless female figure in a silver evening gown on a black ground next to a covered female body bound and tied in silver fabric on a red ground. Here, as the critic Abigail Solomon-Godeau argued, "the (desirable) female body is bound not only by the gown, but by the cultural conventions of desirability, and the delimiting and defining convention of representation itself."[9]

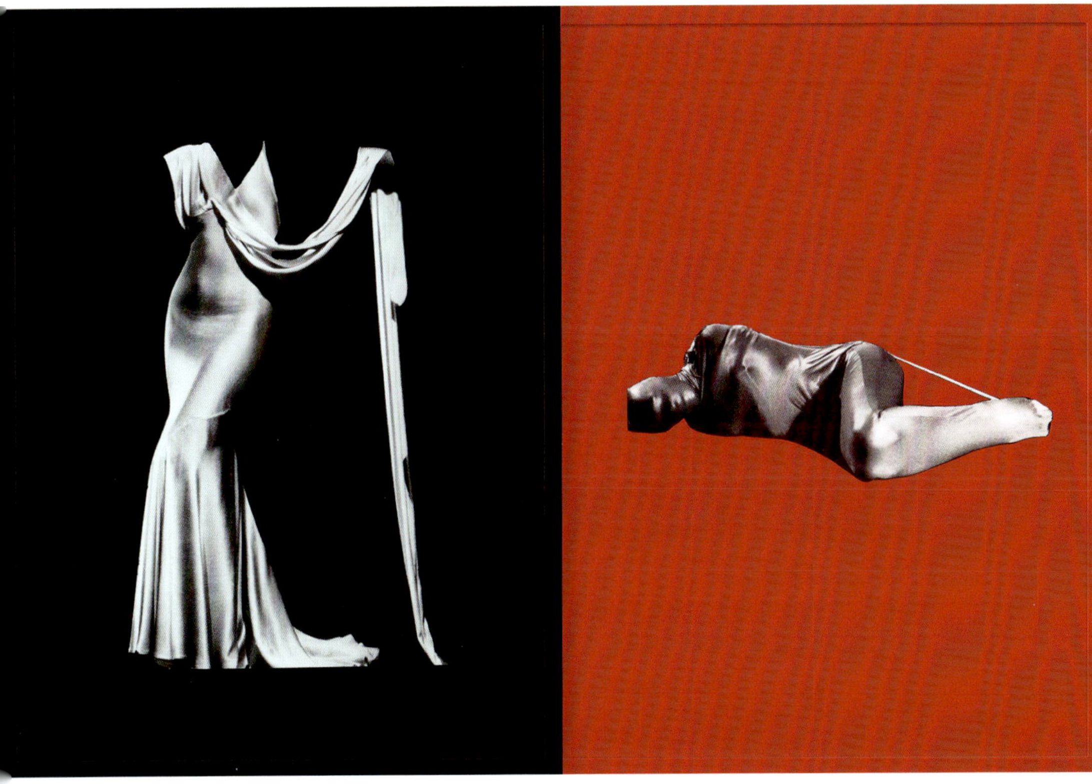

Sarah Charlesworth, *Figures*, 1983–1984. Cibachrome prints with lacquered wood frames, 42 × 62 inches overall. © Estate of Sarah Charlesworth. Courtesy Paula Cooper Gallery.

Fetishism stems from a confusion about how products are made, as in commodity fetishism, or about which objects are to be desired, as in sexual fetishism. In both cases it involves a displacement in value from a person to a thing, as when a chic dress is preferred to a human being. Benjamin once defined fetishism as "the sex appeal of the inorganic"; it is a common way that we forfeit a part of our humanity in our everyday interactions with the world.[10] In Freud fetishism is crystallized at moments of a charged sight—moments of seeing and not seeing at once, which are even more active in consumerism than they are in art. All of this is highlighted in *Objects of Desire*, some of which reflect on the conflation of the commodity fetish with the sexual fetish to the extent that products and bodies exchange properties as well as parts. This conflation of fetishisms was still novel at the time of Pop art (the key figure here is Richard Hamilton), a function of a consumerist economy in which the production of commodities became ever more obscure and our libidinal investment in them ever more intense.[11] In *Objects of Desire* Charlesworth points to how this super-fetishism developed from the moment of Pop to that of postmodernism, in particular how it came to be focused on the typical treatment of the media image—its saturated color and bright light, its luscious surface and brilliant shine.

Paradox #5: Can alienation be desired? Series like *Objects of Desire* are not simply antifetishistic. Like Freud (if not Marx), Charlesworth understood that fetishism will always play a part in our lives, and she was hardly opposed to visual pleasure. For Charlesworth the watchword of 1970s feminism—that men possess the gaze while women are positioned as its objects—was a political caution, not an ontological truth. For example, the blonde youth in a buff suit in *Golden Boy* (1983–1984), his arms wrapped in a narcissistic self-embrace, is offered up for admiration from various subject positions, straight, gay, and other. Charlesworth understood, too, that objectification is fundamental to art-making. For instance, her *Renaissance Paintings and Drawings* (1991) reflect on the stereotypical language of bodily postures and gestures developed in that celebrated era of art.

In fact, far from only antifetishistic, her work often makes fetishism look good, almost too good. At the conclusion of his famous essay on art and reproducibility, Benjamin wondered, with respect to Futurism, whether technology hadn't changed the human sensorium to the point where mankind might regard its own alienation, even its own annihilation, as a source of aesthetic pleasure. If desire is alienated, can alienation also be desired? In *Objects of Desire* Charlesworth posed that difficult question for her time.

Paradox #6: Critique and complicity at once. Perhaps no one conveyed the ambivalence of the Pictures artists regarding media images—how we can be both seduced by them and suspicious of them—as directly as Charlesworth. While many of us talked about the ambiguous zone between complicity and critique, she actively explored it. Always as elegant as it is precise, her art stages our entanglements in images in ways that suggest that pleasure and critique aren't mutually exclusive.

Again, like some of her contemporaries, Charlesworth said she was an artist who "used" photography. Yet this rhetorical posture obscured her deep involvement in the medium, not only in its commercial applications and media manipulations but also in its traditional genres and historical variants. Her series *Doubleworld* (1995) is an extended essay on matters of perspective, stereoscopy, illusionism, and still life. One feels that the title is also reflexive, a term for her own paradoxical practice (or practice of paradox), in which beauty and rigor, affect and analysis, and ambivalence and conviction are more complementary than contradictory.

Paradox #7: Para-doxa. "Doxa" are ideologies that are so accepted as to be taken for truths; "para" means to stand alongside. This is where the paradoxical art of Sarah Charlesworth is located, and what it does: rather than simply oppose received ideas, it rubs up against them, making them shine and chafe at the same time. It's an art that looks great and hurts a little.

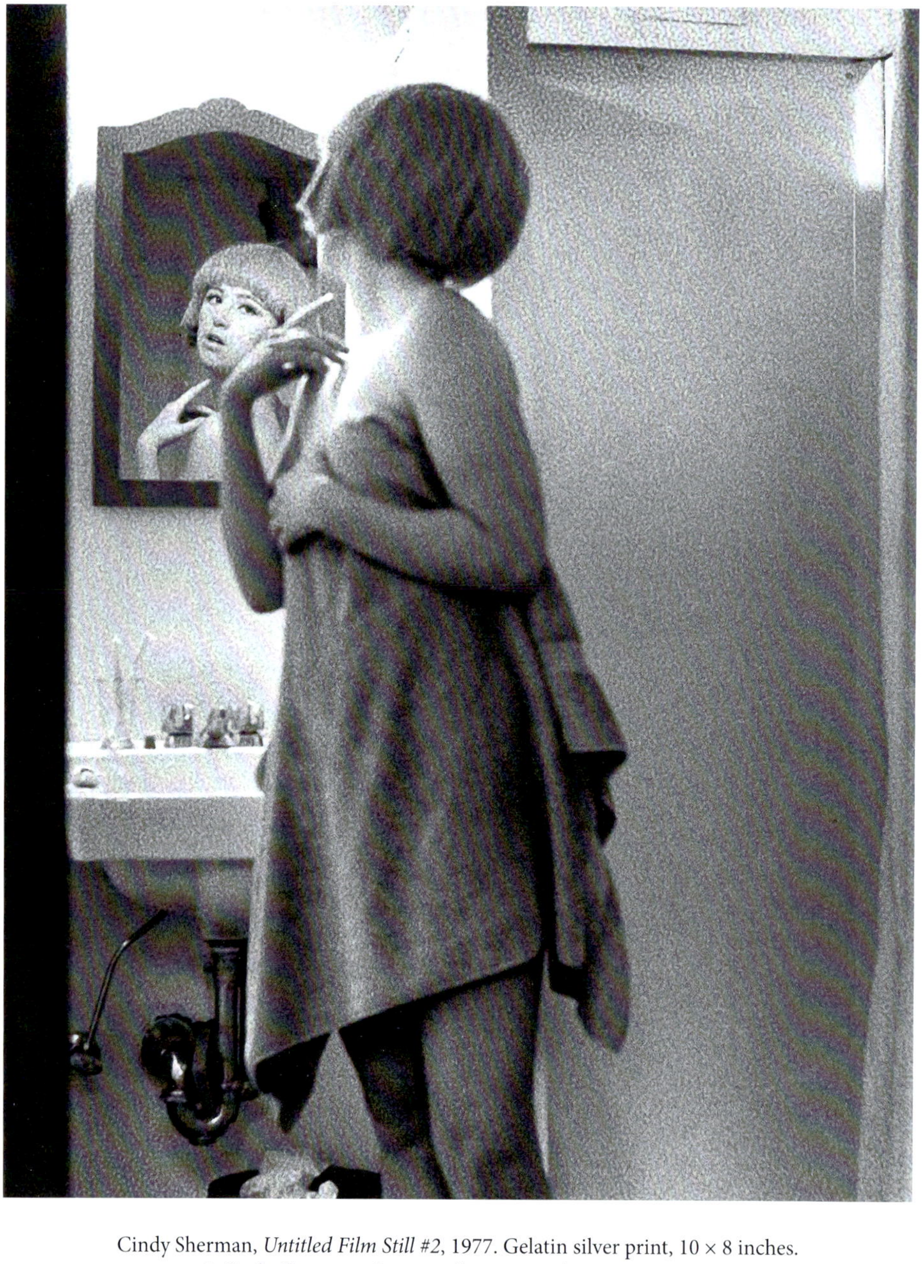

Cindy Sherman, *Untitled Film Still #2*, 1977. Gelatin silver print, 10 × 8 inches.

19 I Could Be Me

A virtuoso of impersonation, Cindy Sherman has served as the model in her photographs since 1975, playing with familiar roles of female identity in series after series of inventive work. Almost from the beginning her art appeared almost too good to be true. It was popular, first with other artists, gradually with the art world at large, and eventually with a broad public.[1] At the same time Sherman became a key figure in the postmodernist vanguard, for, along with her peers in appropriation art like Louise Lawler, Barbara Kruger, and Sherrie Levine, she advanced the then-novel idea of the picture as a text of other pictures, in her case of various allusions to B-movie types and stock television characters. Just as importantly, her art seemed to fit neatly with catalytic ideas in the critical theory of the period. In her catalogue of women feminists saw an exposé of stereotypes of femininity, and in her performance of roles poststructuralists found an exemplum of the constructed nature of identity.

Even before her well-known "untitled film stills" (none of which derived directly from actual movies), Sherman investigated the effects of gender expectations and fashion fantasies on young women. In one early sequence of images her made-up subject passes from male to super-femme. In another series Sherman donned different clothes so rapidly as to become her own protean Barbie doll (mostly of the "weird" type). In this initial phase of work (1975–1982), which evokes generic formats like the magazine centerfold as well as the film still, Sherman presented the female subject under the gaze, the woman *as* a picture, which was also a principal topic of feminist work in appropriation art. Her subjects see, of course, but they are much more seen, and how they react to this capture by the gaze provides the drama of each image. Often this gaze seems to come from a subject off-camera, with whom the viewer might be implicated. Sometimes it seems to come simply from the world at large. Yet sometimes, too, it seems to come from within. Here Sherman showed her subjects to be self-surveyed, but in a mode less of narcissistic absorption than of psychological estrangement. Thus, in the distance between made-up woman and her mirrored face in *Untitled Film Still #2* (1977), Sherman points to the gap between imagined and actual body images that yawns within each of us, the gap that most of us attempt to fill with hopeful identifications with movie stars, athletes, and other idols of the day.

In her next phase of photos (1983–1990), now in color, Sherman drew on associations with fashion, art history, fairy tales, and horror movies. The first two image repertoires have long influenced self-fashionings, which Sherman parodies mercilessly. In her hands vanguard design produces so many fashion victims, and grand portraiture is given over to ugly aristocrats with scarred sacks for breasts and funky carbuncles for noses (she riffs on celebrated paintings by Raphael, Caravaggio, and Ingres, among others). This play turns perverse when, in some fashion photos, the subjects seem all but psychotic, with no ego awareness at all, and when, in some art history photos, the figures are little more than patchworks of broken-down prostheses.

The turn to the grotesque was even more emphatic in the fairy tale and horror pictures that followed, many of which show imagined freaks of nature (a young women with a pig snout, a doll with the head of a dirty old man). Here horror means, first and foremost, horror of the maternal body, which is the primary site of “the abject” as well, a liminal category of (non)being defined by Julia Kristeva as neither subject nor object and thus charged with disgust.[2] Sherman evokes this extreme state in scenes suffused with signifiers of menstrual blood and sexual discharge, vomit and shit. The domain of her so-called civil war and sex pictures of the 1990s is also abject, punctuated as they are by close-ups of simulated damaged or dead bodies and sexual or excretory organs respectively. Lou Andreas-Salomé (who is often called the first female psychoanalyst) opined that the vagina is “taken on lease” from the rectum, and in some pictures Sherman conflates these orifices in obscene ways, adding the odd penis as well. In other images the subject is so disarranged, so overwhelmed by her awful surroundings, as to disappear altogether.

“Abject art” arose during a grim period in the United States. Ravaged by the AIDS epidemic, the art world in the 1990s was indeed steeped in a “civil war” with political leaders over “sex” (Sherman gave these titles to two series of work during this time). There was also the neoliberal attack on the social contract at large, which Bill Clinton waged with only slightly less relish than Ronald Reagan and the first George Bush. Who could have imagined that life would get worse under the second Bush and drastically worse under Donald Trump? During the latter Bush regime, however, Sherman pulled back from horrific images and, in her fourth decade of work, focused on portraits of middle age, a period of relative neglect in mass-cultural representations of femininity. At first Sherman showed lower-income women struggling to meet the cultural demands of sex appeal, with expressions ranging from the desperate to the defiant. Then she moved on to nouveau-riche ladies decked out in ostentatious gowns and jewels. More burned than tan, with skin stretched to the limit, these wealthy women

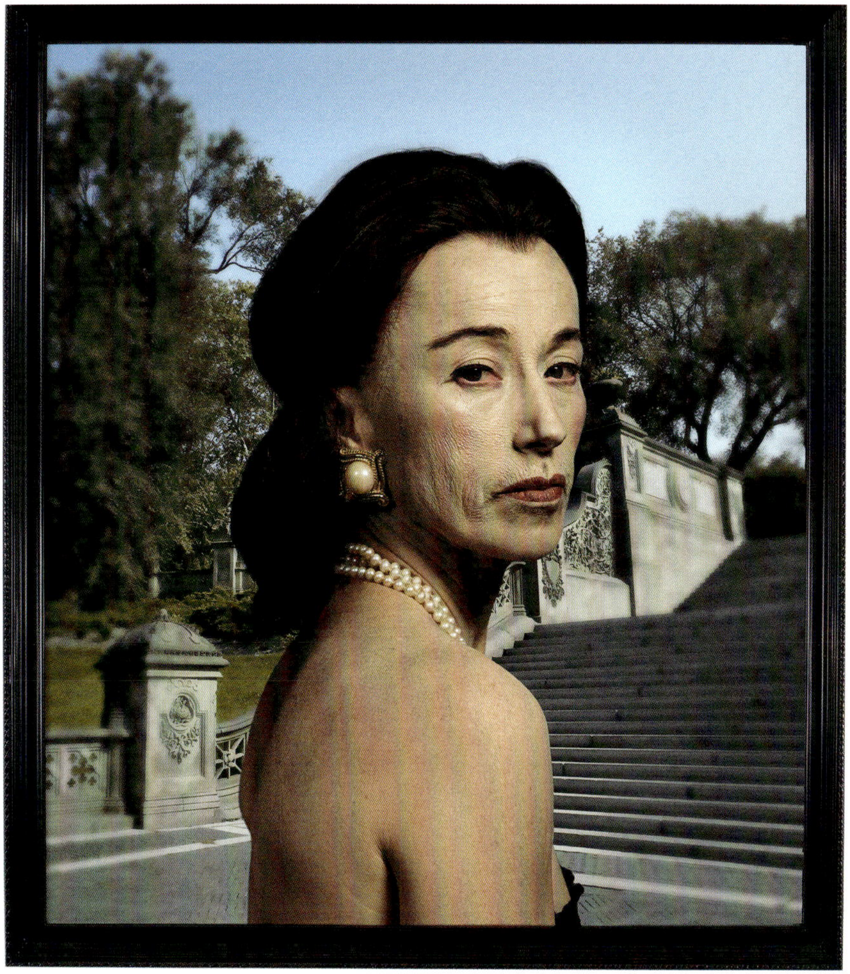

Cindy Sherman, *Untitled #465*, 2008. Chromogenic color print, 70 × 63½ inches.

look as though they have scratched their way to the top, only to confront there the inevitable fall into gravity, age, and mortality.

These pictures, which came to be known informally as "the Hollywood/Hamptons," preoccupied Sherman during the 2000s, but she also produced a complementary body of work, a group of clowns made up so excessively as to appear more crazy-scary than funny-sad. In the conservative art of the 1920s, after the radical experiments of Expressionism, Cubism, and Dada, clowns, harlequins, and the like cropped up, in the work of Picasso, Max Beckmann, and others, as so many guises of the melancholic artist resigned to the status of court jester to the rich and the reactionary. In another time of Right dominance Sherman put on a clownish face too, but her clowns have bite. They are not simply "ciphers of regression."[3]

As I look back over this signal body of work, its implications seem different from what I initially thought. First, the ingénues in the early pictures aren't simply the victims of imposed types, as some of us wrote during those years. These are scenes not only of ideological interpellation from outside but also of aspirational identification from within: even as some of the young women strive to escape their scripted roles, others struggle to approximate them. In some ways this makes the work even more feminist than feminist critics believed at the time, because it suggests how we import alien identities into our intimate selves, as if to say, "If only I could style my hair in that way, buy the right makeup, get that special blouse, I could be me."[4]

Second, Sherman doesn't negate biography as much as we thought. As the series roll on, we glimpse the artist aging behind all the makeup, and the arc of her subjects from ingénue to dame isn't unlike that of her own life—from the young artist new to the city to a cultural figure in her own right. The images trace this trajectory in their production as well—from small black-and-white faux film stills (most galleries were more modest then too) to large color pictures produced digitally at the scale of paintings (Sherman has spoken of her wish to compete with the grand installations of some of her male peers). In this social story there's also a political allegory: those of us who started out as the postmodernist generation, eager to build on the advances of the 1960s and 1970s in art, theory, and other domains, had that future hijacked by a reactionary turn in almost all arenas. That painful narrative can also be read in the trajectory of this influential art.

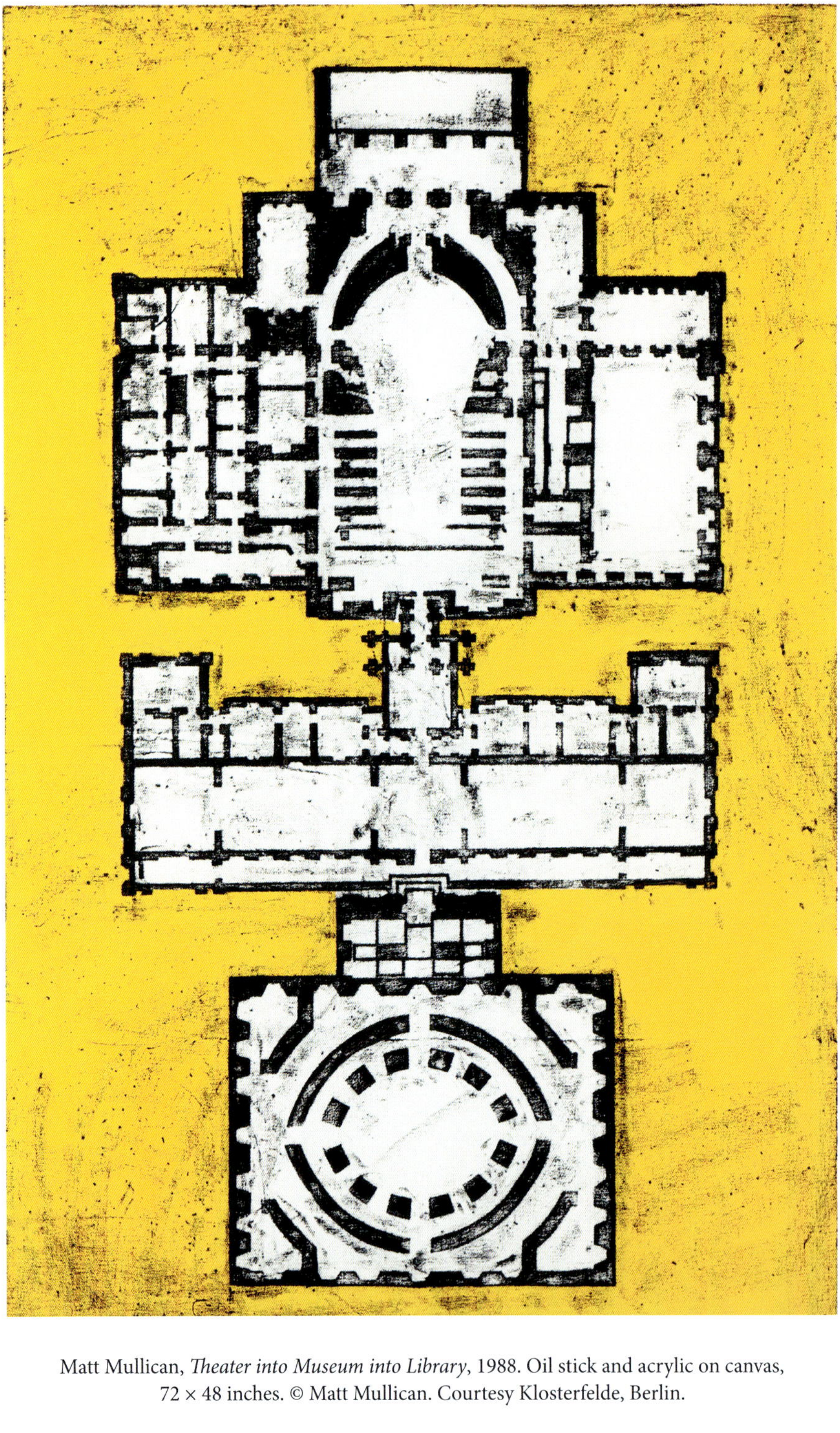

Matt Mullican, *Theater into Museum into Library*, 1988. Oil stick and acrylic on canvas, 72 × 48 inches. © Matt Mullican. Courtesy Klosterfelde, Berlin.

20 A Passenger in My Own Psyche

Matt Mullican operates across many media—drawings, paintings, found images and objects, banners, rubbings, performances, videos, and computer simulations. At the same time his work has a consistency that is distinctive. Although Mullican can be aligned with various figures in Pop, Minimalist, Conceptual, and Postminimalist art (above all Bruce Nauman and John Baldessari, his mentor at Cal Arts), he often inverts the positions taken by those predecessors. Whereas most Minimalists and Postminimalists worked to get rid of metaphor and allegory, Mullican invites them back in. And whereas most of those artists sought to banish the image—largely because it seemed to encode an old space of illusionism or model of consciousness—Mullican believes that images are inescapable and that we always project a subject or a story onto them.

Neither does Mullican fit neatly into his own Pictures generation, and often he seems the odd man out even in his Cal Arts cohort, which included David Salle, Jack Goldstein, and James Welling, among others. Like them, Mullican declares, "I am a post-modern, post-conceptual artist. I will have distance on everything I do."[1] At the same time, he is relatively free of irony, let alone cynicism, and his art isn't much concerned with the critiques of representation and subjectivity that were central to other postmodernist artists. Far from suspicious of language, Mullican has devised a sign system, a symbolic order, of his own; and far from skeptical about the self, he is preoccupied with subjectivity. That Mullican is drawn to the "psyche of the situation" more than its material conditions also marks him as unusual in his cohort.[2]

For all his post-studio credentials, Mullican returns art to the studio in the etymological sense of this word; his work is a form of inquiry into both subjective and objective worlds. In this respect he evokes the hermetic traditions of the Renaissance as well as the encyclopedic projects of the Enlightenment: "My idea of knowledge is more affiliated with the eighteenth than it is with the twentieth or the twenty-first century; at least one had the idea that one could actually list all knowledge."[3] More unexpected still is that his work calls up aspects of premodern cultures (classical, Christian, and Tantric, among others) in which art, in its aim to understand the world and to order the universe, wasn't yet separate from religion and philosophy. In fact, the elaboration of cosmologies is fundamental to his practice.[4] Mullican also suggests a mode of making that recalls ritual magic and spiritual exercise as much as the disenchanted operations that dominated most twentieth-century art. "The tradition of the artist-priest-doctor exists in every culture," he has said. "In a way, I fulfill a very traditional idea about what an artist could be."[5] His work is so traditional, we might say, as to be original all over again.

Most of the questions posed by Mullican concern either the life of the self or the nature of the world. "One cosmology describes the passage of the individual soul, my soul," he tells us. "The other does not describe a passage of anything to anywhere. It simply breaks down the world as I see it."[6] This second cosmology has governed most of his production since 1983. It consists of five orders, each represented by a color and a symbol. The first order is that of the material world; inert as yet, without meaning, it is green, the conventional color of nature. The second order presents the world as quickened with life but still unframed by culture; it is blue, like the sky. In the third order the world is framed by cultural forms like art; it is yellow, which Mullican associates with the gold of traditional picture frames. The fourth order is "the area of the sign, the area of language," and it appears in the black-and-white of script.[7] Finally, the fifth order, the most important, is that of subjective experience; it is red, the most vital of colors, and its sign is an outline of a head with either a schematic brain or an abstract circle inscribed within it.

With its five levels that ascend from the material to the spiritual, the Mullican universe is almost classical (or at least Platonic). An ancient Greek might be at home in it, and a nineteenth-century Hegelian would recognize it. And yet, as Mullican gives pride of place to subjective experience, his cosmology is also Romantic. In fact, it resembles any number of mythological systems proposed by Romantic poets from William Blake through William Butler Yeats. (Like Mullican, Yeats devised his own complicated cosmology, which he called *A Vision*, in order to reconcile objective and subjective principles, classical and Romantic world views.) Like such systems, the Mullican cosmology might be a representation of the universe, but its primary purpose is to support, even to generate, visionary art.

As Mullican developed the cartography for this cosmology, he saw its resemblance to city plans, and he has elaborated its five worlds largely through quasi-architectural representations. Although he associates his city with theaters of memory—"my city allows me to place everything there is inside of it so that I can recall it"—it appears less mnemonic than futuristic or even utopian in character: "it represents my model of everything."[8] Utopia, then, is another traditional mode of inquiry reclaimed by Mullican, who looks back to Enlightenment schemes by Ledoux and Boullée as well as ahead to virtual realities like Sim City and Second Life. (Mullican explored cyberspace as early as the late 1980s, in a project undertaken with Digital Editions in Los Angeles.) The utopian city often produced more contradictions than it solved, and the Mullican version is no different.[9] Its strict geometries establish a distance from us, even as its panoramic views invite our immersion. Moreover, even though, like most utopias, this world is designed for us, no people appear in it (but then "utopia" does mean "no place"). This contradiction points to a greater one, which is that utopia can flip into its dystopian opposite: the planned city can quickly devolve into the gulag or the camp. Mullican is alert to the ambiguities of his utopia; "it might appear rational," he warns us, "but it is absolutely not."[10] This combination of reason and unreason calls to mind the representational fantasies of Borges, such as his vision of a map as large as the territory it charts. Mullican, too, elaborates on "the city as a map and the map as a city."[11]

Why create such a vision? More than once Mullican has called his cosmology "paranoid," and the term is more appropriate than it appears at first. The paranoiac projects his complex system onto the universe precisely because it appears to be without any order at all: his elaborate meaning is intended to fill in for a cosmic significance that has gone missing. The founders of the great religions, Freud opined, tended to paranoia; so too does the Mullican cosmology.

This leads us to the other fundamental concern of his art, the nature of subjective experience. His first cosmology, devised as early as 1973, takes up the basic riddles of our lives: "What happened before I was born? Why do things happen in the way they do? What happens after I die?"[12] According to Freud, children ponder such riddles through "primal fantasies," that is, real or imagined scenarios that help them to tease out the origins of identity, gender, sexuality, and so on. However, interested though Mullican is in the unconscious, his conception isn't a Freudian one; for him, for example, fate is far more formative than trauma. Moreover, his performances take up the very technique—hypnosis—that Freud abandoned on his way to psychoanalysis.

What, then, is the nature of the unconscious according to Mullican? Not an unknown zone where events are repressed, it is, he says, an "outside self" that is "deep inside," and its principal avatar is the alter ego that emerges in his performances when he is placed under hypnosis. Mullican designates this persona simply as *that person*, a term that underscores its alien impersonality.[13] "I am totally in the middle between *that person*—the person I am when I am hypnotized—and me," Mullican tells us. "I am always floating between the two." When he is in a trance it's as though he were on a drug: "I am like a passenger in my own psyche" or "a bug inside my own skull."[14] This is a kind of subjectivity

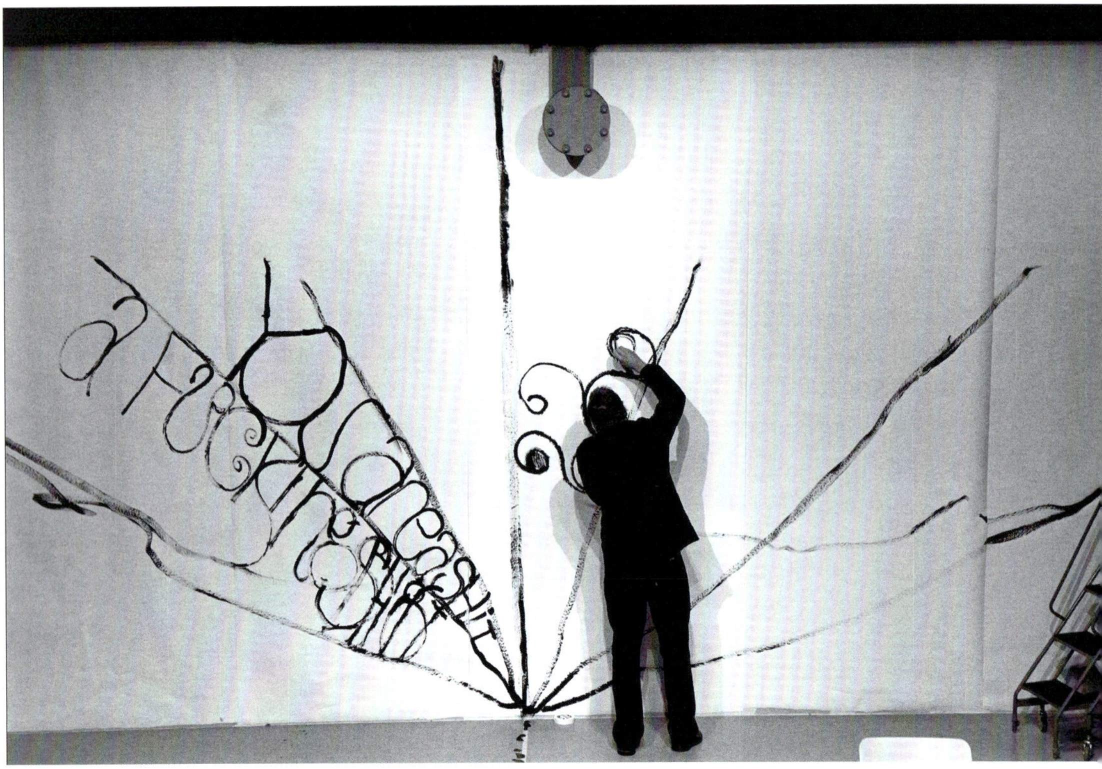

Matt Mullican, *Under Hypnosis*, as performed at Tate Modern, 2007. Photo: Sheila Burnett. Courtesy Peter Freeman, Inc.

without an ego to pilot it, and a kind of an unconscious where one finds not hidden truths so much as "all the conventions of life."[15] "In a way I am miming *that person* like a found object," Mullican says.[16] The unconscious according to Mullican, then, is "the iconic brain," which he sees as almost automatic in its operations.[17] Is this iconic brain irreducibly human, or is it a machinic double installed within us, or is it somehow both at once? This question becomes more pertinent every day.

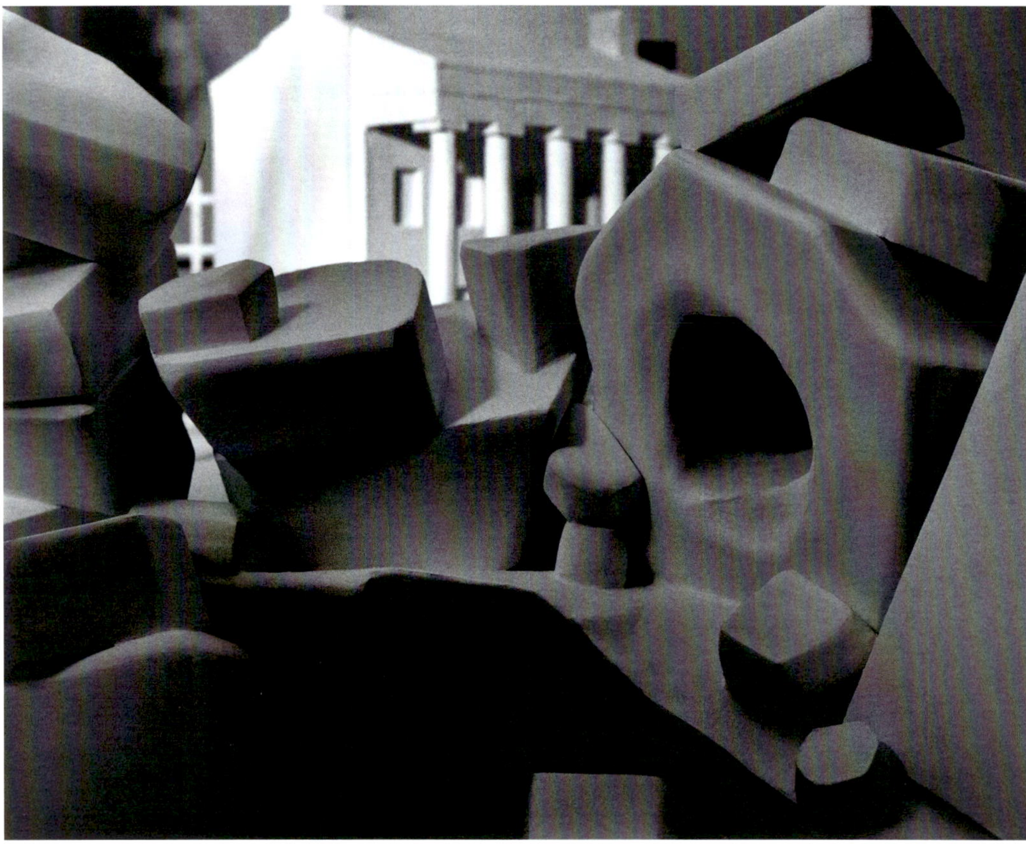

James Casebere, *Sutpen's Cave*, 1982. Gelatin silver print, 16 × 20 inches.

21 Imaginary Tableaux

For five decades James Casebere has created photographic tableaux of various architectures that evoke different periods and cultures—some American-vernacular, some international-modern, others more distant in time and place—to the point where today his oeuvre stands as a capacious archive of imaginary buildings and sites. At the same time, Casebere has also reflected on what images tell us about the operations of the mind, both conscious and unconscious, in particular how structures and spaces serve as settings for stories of identity (socioeconomic, ethnic, religious, political, regional, national). The imaginary, then, defines his project in terms of both what it is, an image repertoire of architecture, and what it does, which is to explore the relations between images, identifications, and ideologies.

Born in Lansing, Michigan, in 1953, Casebere is a Midwesterner of the television generation. "This shaped our whole archive of available images and image devices," he told Okwui Enwezor in a 2011 conversation.[1] Although this generation was marked by movies, its primary screen was TV, which informed its understanding of images in general. Black-and-white television of the late 1950s and early 1960s looked flimsy, a matter of simple props on bare sets, as in all those soundstages for sit-coms that were no more than makeshift ensembles of a sofa, a coffee table, and a window to nowhere. Clearly, TV suggested "image devices" to Casebere, for his early photographs deploy the most basic of fabricated models for his tableaux (his materials are simple too: plaster, Styrofoam, Foamcore, museum board, and plaster).[2] This generic quality allowed him to lay bare his devices, to show reality precisely as constructed. In his conversation with Enwezor he calls this approach both "constructivist" and "Godardian."

The mixing of the fictive and the real also occurred in the content of television, for the daily diet of an American child in the 1960s was a combination of the happy fictions of middle-class family life and the grim realities of national and international conflict (we flipped from *The Dick van Dyke Show* to political assassinations and the Vietnam War). This unstable combination soon became volatile as we were asked to believe in anodyne stories even as we were exposed to violent scenes. When this blatant contradiction couldn't be sustained, the happy fictions were pushed back in time; they became "the 1950s" or "the Eisenhower era." In his photographs of the mid to late 1970s, in which schematic models of suburban rooms and domestic appliances predominate, Casebere focused on the middle-class vernacular of this recent past. But he didn't mock this America, as did many postmodern performers who emerged at this time (like the Talking Heads). As Casebere acknowledges, "alienation" was his fundamental response to this world.

An alienated atmosphere permeates his early images. The models in these tableaux are especially schematic, as though they were distorted traces of memories or dreams. The scale is often inconsistent and the space sometimes claustrophobic, as if we were trapped in that fictive world. At times, too, some element disrupts, even deranges, the image. This element can be obvious, like the huge utensil that spears the fridge in the otherwise tidy kitchen of *Fork in the Refrigerator* (1975), perhaps the phantasmatic act of a distressed homemaker who turned on her appliance instead of her kids. But it can also be subtle, as in *Three Freezers* (1976), in which the different units with open doors appear, through repetition alone, to be three coffins. Critics called such images "uncanny," and sometimes they are.[3] But the uncanny involves the return of a familiar thing or event made strange by repression, and what is imaged here is more like a psychopathology of everyday life, a vision of the American middle class in which neurosis (if not psychosis) has become the norm.

Perhaps this is why Casebere was drawn to construct his scenes of the past, for embedded there are myths that his modeling can work to expose. Here the imaginary becomes a productive way to probe the ideological as well. His early exploration of the middle-class home soon led him to the development of the suburb, as in *Subdivision with Spotlight* (1982). It also directed him to signal moments in the history of American architecture, domestic and otherwise, such as the Shingle Style, which Casebere also viewed with ambivalence; this is intimated in the ghostly *Winterhouse* (1984), which is more haunted ruin than stately home. Images of structures associated with different regional histories appeared too, such as *Cotton Mill* (1983), evocative of a South bedeviled by slavery, or *Lighthouse* (1983), suggestive of a Northeast whittled down by asceticism, or a *Street with Pots* (1983–1984), redolent of a Southwest marked by a Spanish colonial idiom. These images include stereotypical cues familiar from movies and television, signs of authenticity that Casebere heightens to the point of artificiality. This is most evident in his pictures of the folkloric West, such as *Covered Wagons* (1985), with the wagons overturned and spiked with arrows, and *Western Street* (1985–1986), which recalls a model film set replete with saloon, dry goods store, and jail.

At the time, this incursion into Western kitsch seemed to be an ironic comment on the cowboy president Ronald Reagan, but by the late 1980s the Reagan-Bush regime had proved so disastrous that Casebere began to question the imagery of power directly. He turned to models that evoke general types of control, both economic and political, as in *Industry* and *Capitol Façade* (both 1990), as well as specific kinds of oppression, both distant and near, as in *Venice Ghetto* (1991) and *Tenement/Market Place* (1992). In effect, Casebere looked through the Reaganite vision of the United States as a "shining city on a hill" to the dark realities of its history, and in this way deepened his exploration of the split personality of American society as inscribed in its everyday architectures. This doubleness is palpable, for example, in the regularity of the factory windows in *Industry*, where one can read both progressive rationality and oppressive discipline, and in the austere classicism of *Capitol Façade*, where one confronts the ambiguity of a style that has served authoritarian governments as well as democratic ones. As Enwezor comments, Casebere traces a dialectic of enlightenment and myth, freedom and unfreedom, in his imaginary tableaux of past and present. On this point Casebere notes that, even as Thomas Jefferson designed Monticello in Virginia, his monument to Enlightenment values, this slave-owning president also worked on prison designs.

In the early 1990s Casebere turned his attention to the history of a society become carceral, especially with respect to young African American men, an outrageous number of whom were then, as now, in jail. These images refer to particular institutions, but they also represent general types of prison design, including the panoptical model, as in *Panopticon Prison #3* (1993), the radial model, as in *Prison at Cherry Hill* (1993), and the reformist Auburn model based on shared spaces of work, as in *Sing Sing* (1992).[4] These initial prison pictures are exterior views. Casebere then moved inside, with images of cells that invite the viewer to identify with the implied prisoner; an imaginary sharing is set up with an incarcerated subject at the mercy of the state. Meditative shafts of light, intense openings to an outside, are common in these photos of cells (which run into the late 1990s). At times, then, a spirituality in solitude is suggested to offset the degradation of imprisonment. During the same period, however, images of abandoned hallways and empty tunnels undercut this intimation of hope. Although some of these spaces are bathed in light, they are literally underground, and, though there are some apertures, there is little chance of escape. The implied subject has become almost feral, and the suggestion is that the same condition has befallen the society above ground too.

At this point Casebere introduced water into these tableaux, and the floods seem almost biblical. He also deluged more elaborate models of traditional

American interiors—rooms at Monticello, for example, and at Phillips Academy in Andover, Massachusetts—and of such foreign sites as the royal palace at Versailles and various ports of the slave trade. These are exquisite pictures, full of brilliant reflections, but, in another variation on the theme of the double, this beauty often accompanies destruction; the flood images read almost as imagined acts of retribution.[5] Casebere continued them through most of the George W. Bush years, and they moved well beyond American shores in much the way that American power did, especially in its dead-end wars in the Middle East.

In a 2007 show titled *The Levant* Casebere expanded his range of subjects, both secular and religious, from a Greek theater and a Roman arena to a slave dormitory in the Topkapi Palace in Istanbul and the now-destroyed Golden Mosque in Samarra. This range advanced a political point about the possibilities of coexistence, past and future (Casebere sees medieval Andalusia as one example of such cohabitation). At the same time, he also pointed to a dark turn in the dialectic of freedom and unfreedom, a partial reversal of the "clash of civilizations" in which, stereotypically, the Islamic East is taken to represent fundamentalist violence and the Judeo-Christian West enlightened tolerance. On the one hand, Casebere has produced beautiful images inspired by the exalted mosques of Mimar Sinan (c. 1490–1588), the celebrated architect who worked under Suleiman the Magnificent at the peak of the Ottoman Empire. On the other hand, he has created stark spaces based on accounts of rendition sites where the CIA has taken alleged terror suspects for interrogation and torture. In the latter pictures the prison returns in the present, and the implication is that the logic of the carceral is hardly restricted to one architectural type, social space, or national territory.

As Casebere plays on our cultural imaginary of different architectures, he also investigates the operations of the imaginary as such—our imagining of settings for the making and unmaking of identity and world. Here he connects with a line of philosophy obscured by recent theories, poststructuralist and psychoanalytical in character, that privileged the registers of the symbolic and the real over that of the imaginary.[6] This other kind of thought, which Sartre termed "the phenomenology of the image," is associated primarily with Gaston Bachelard, especially his *Poetics of Space* (1958), which is concerned above all with the imaginary places of the house—a point of obvious relevance to Casebere. But, as much as he recalls the Bachelardian project, Casebere differs from it in two important ways. First, he doesn't subscribe to the phenomenological bracketing of the historical that led Bachelard to remark that "the poetic image . . . is not an echo of the past."[7] Again, Casebere works to historicize our imaginary of space, and, as he does so, he brings out its shadows. This is the second point of divergence from Bachelard, who focused on "images of felicitous space . . . the space we love."[8] Yet Casebere accords with Bachelard in this respect: he, too, suggests a "psychological study of the sites of our intimate lives," a phenomenology of the image that has psychoanalytical import. And he, too, asks, "How can an image, at times very unusual, appear to be a concentration of the entire psyche?" Often, as with Bachelard, his answer depends on the "quality of origin" in the image, that is, on what it might evoke about our imagined beginnings, our primal scenes of identity.[9]

How does Casebere open up the space of the imaginary? Though often based on actual sites, his photographs of fabricated models have no direct referents in the world, and in this unfounding of the image there is a subverting of the viewer as well: our access to the world is complicated, as is our mastery of representation. Not quite referential or indexical, his images are akin to phantasms in which representation has revised, even usurped, reality. At times we feel drawn within these simulacra too, and they in turn appear distorted by our imagined presence in them.[10]

In *Boats* (1980), for example, we seem to be positioned inside the picture, in the bow of the truncated rowboat in the foreground, whose stern tilts up as if on account of our weight. From that perspective, though, the space is wrong; in fact, the picture is a mishmash of scales, and the sizes of the ocean-liner, tug, sailboat, and barge in the middle ground (let alone the buildings in the background) are impossible to gauge. It's like a dream in which we are simultaneously too big and too small for the world, as if we were both in a bathtub stuffed with toys and adrift on a congested Hudson River. Sometimes it's not our imagined presence that disturbs the space, but an object with which we might be associated. One instance is *The Golden Apple* (1986), a shadowy scene in which, from within a kitchen, we look out an open window onto the object of the title. Once more the scale is off; the apple, like the leafy branch from which it hangs, is too large, as though it were charmed somehow, invested with a special power. One thinks immediately of myths: the golden apple of the Brothers Grimm tale, with all its ambiguous force, as well as the fateful apple that precipitated the Fall of Adam and Eve, the jealous-making apple that led to the Trojan War, and so on (the tree that rises up beyond the frame evokes the magic beanstalk that lured the intrepid Jack as well). These effects can't be referred to childhood stories alone; despite the artificiality of the apple, there's a strange actuality to this object (Casebere is close to David Lynch here). Again and again he hints at trouble in our everyday paradises, or casts us back to primal scenes of our own, to the threshold of a traumatic event that has marked us.[11] This anxious temporality—of foreboding that feels like remembering and vice versa—is palpable in many of his tableaux.

Sometimes Casebere intimates a kind of metaphysics, one that is also double. On the one hand, the consistency of his model material and photographic surface implies that his world is all made up of the same substance. On the other, this world remains Manichean, as in the cell pictures where the lofty and the abject coexist, or the flood pictures where the beautiful and the destructive coincide. Often, too, this world appears to be dark at its core, and light must struggle to appear in it. Similarly, whatever counts as civilization sometimes seems wrested, literally carved, out of a wilderness that threatens it on all sides. My favorite example, an early one, is *Sutpen's Cave* (1982), in which the viewer is positioned low in the dim space of high boulders, beyond which appears a mansion with a classical colonnade bathed in light. We are on the outside, like an outcast or an animal that has only the cave of the title for shelter, with little chance for the civilized realm in the distance, and a bitter mix of longing and resentment for this house stirs as a result. The title alludes to Thomas Sutpen, a character in the great Faulkner novel *Absalom, Absalom!* (1936); a shady character, he emerged from the wilderness to establish a powerful plantation by obscure means. This cave, then, is his, but so is the mansion, and neither can be easily assigned to wilderness or civilization.

This double position of the viewer, within the picture and without, continues in subsequent images. We are alone in front of these abandoned spaces but sometimes inside them as well, as though we were the last survivors in a world left to ruin. Sometimes, then, the viewer is made to feel as spectral as the space, as if we were asked to adopt the impossible perspective not only of the lost, as in some of the tunnel pictures, but almost of the dead, as in *Needles* (1985), where we confront a row of shadowy figures that resemble the sentinels of some afterworld. Yet not everything is bleak in the Casebere universe. As Bachelard writes, "Our soul is an abode," for good as well as for bad.[12] Even in the cell pictures, such as *A Barrel Vaulted Room* (1994), where the barred circle of an aperture at the end of the barren room glows like a small rose window, there are intimations of grace.

In a group of large color photographs called *Landscape with Houses* (2009–2011) Casebere reprises his old theme of the middle-class home. However, these homes evoke not a postwar childhood in a renewed America but a post-2008 present of economic distress, and rather than placed inside these spaces, sheltered like children, we are above them, as though surveying real estate online. Moreover, these images are not of single houses in vernacular styles but of a planned community with limited variety (what we see is not one development but a few, from different angles, with some elements reused). In part inspired by subdivisions in Dutchess County in upstate New York, the world of these

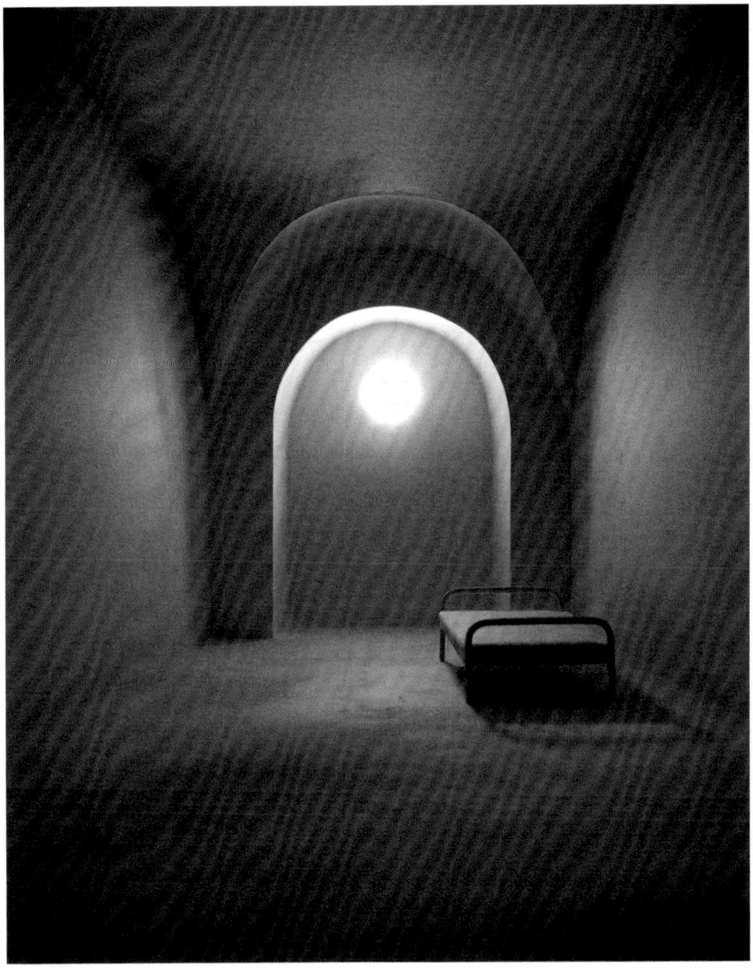

James Casebere, *A Barrel Vaulted Room*, 1994. Dye destruction print, 30 × 24 inches.

pictures seems more real than in earlier photos, and, though the time of day is sometimes ambiguous, they are often brighter in feeling, without a trace of American Gothic or any association of tenement or prison. Still, all is not well under these sunny skies. A rainbow is too perfect to be true; the pastel light seems a little druggy, too drowsy or too cheery; and, though there are far more details, some things go missing: no driveway or sidewalk, a staircase without steps, a house with no entrance. At the same time, these scenes are almost illusionistic enough to pass for the real thing, so that, even more than usual with Casebere, we are cast in an ontological twilight zone, as though we were viewers of a miniature *Truman Show*, but with no protagonist to be seen (unless we are the ones trapped on this stage).

The houses are at once specific and generic, with allusions to historical styles too faint to trace. In this respect, too, they are like the real thing, that is, like developments such as Celebration, Florida, a planned town designed by the Disney Corporation near Disney World, with contributions by postmodern architects Philip Johnson, Michael Graves, and Robert A. M. Stern. The "new urbanism" of these communities was new only in an oxymoronic sense, for they traded on nostalgia for the old—the small town or the friendly suburb—that, like most nostalgia, is a longing for a past that never existed. In a way *Landscape with Houses* updates *Homes for America* (1966–1967), a photo-text sequence in which Dan Graham documented the superficial stylistic variety laid over the deep structural sameness of postwar American suburbia. However, Casebere locates his community in semirural exurbia, and there are more signs of a do-it-yourself individualism (even if this is kept to a Home Depot palette). That said, the homogeneity of taste, status, condition—in a word, class—is very strong, and this class doesn't seem confident.

With its plastic pools and satellite dishes the Casebere community is actually a poor cousin of Celebration. There's still house pride, and for the most part the grounds are kept up, but one senses that a man's house is not his castle so much as the bank's. In short, not only is autumn in the air, but the mortgage crisis is too, and the malaise is less a psychological one of uncanny threat than a social one of economic decline. The absent details take on an allegorical significance—of houses unfinished, unsold, or simply abandoned. At the dawn of the neoliberal era, Reagan claimed that it was "morning again in America," and in his final address he borrowed the old trope of America as a shining city on a hill, as an example for all the world to see. Yet when John Winthrop, the initial governor of Massachusetts Bay Colony, first used this metaphor in 1630 on the decks of the *Arbella* that brought the Pilgrims to the shores of the New World, he meant it as a warning about "Christian charity": "For we must consider that we shall

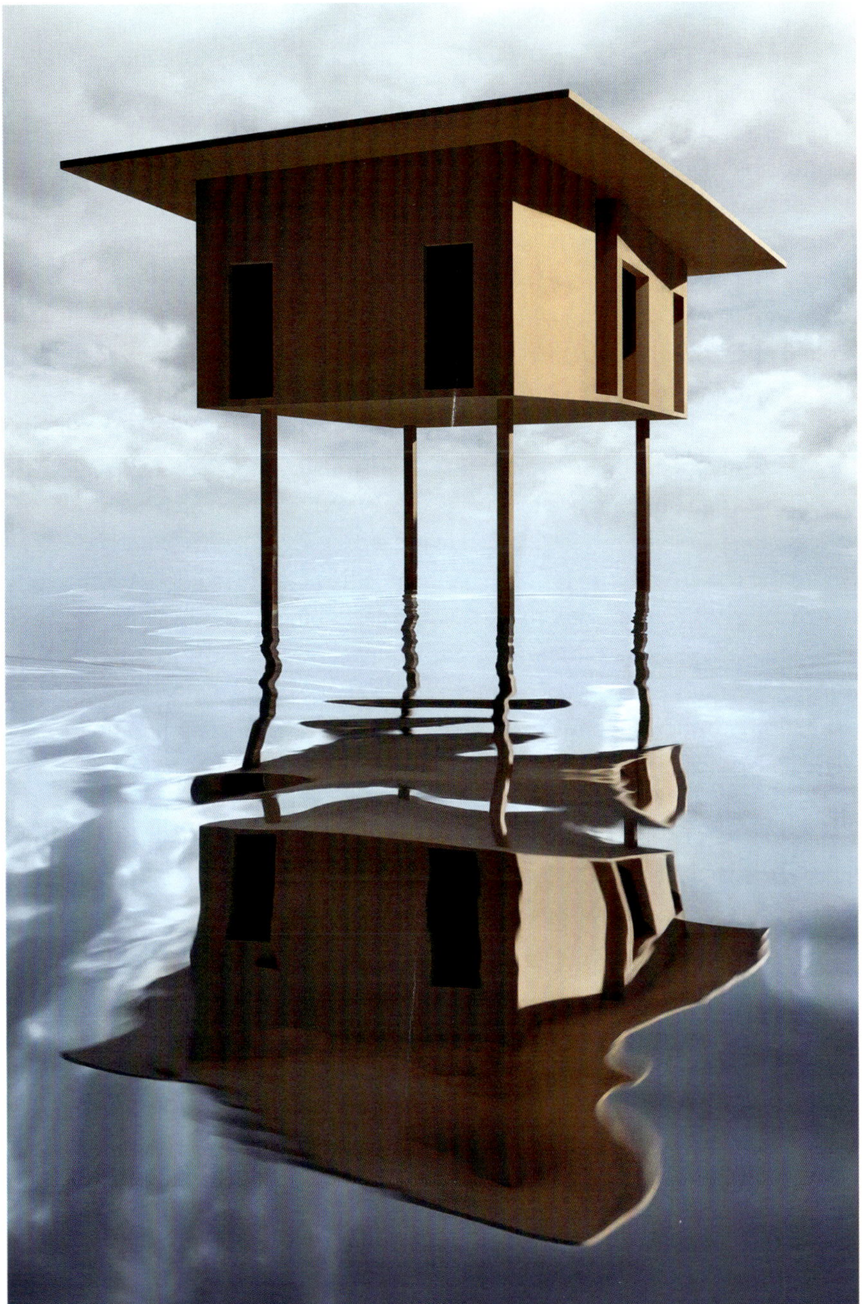

James Casebere, *Tan House on Stilts*, 2019. Archival pigment print, 69½ × 47 inches.

be as a City upon a hill. The eyes of all people are upon us. So that if we shall deal falsely with our God in this work we have undertaken, and so cause him to withdraw his present help from us, we shall be made a story and a byword throughout the world."

In the 2010s Casebere returned to scenes of disaster, but the destruction appears manmade, so many results of climate change, and only rarely, as in a redo of the famous Caspar David Friedrich painting *Sea of Ice*, is the catastrophe allegorical. We are taken to a flooded underground tunnel in Bologna, for example, and to two colonial houses incongruously sited on Ninety-Second Street in New York City, which somehow remain standing amidst the ruination around them. Some modeling is more hopeful, though, including a sequence of luminous images based on the colorful houses of the Mexican architect Luis Barragán, but then a few of these are also flooded. By the time of the series *On the Water's Edge* (2018–2019) the deluge has spread. Even the most rigorous of modernist elements, such as platforms and *pilotis*, are no match for the rising waters of climate change. These schematic structures on stilts look unfinished before the cataclysm or stripped bared by it; either way they attest to the vanity of private architectural projects in the midst of global environmental collapse. As often with Casebere there is great beauty here—colorful outposts above calm waters with brilliant reflections under varied skies—but no sign of actual habitation or indeed of any life. It is a beauty for a time without us, after us.[13]

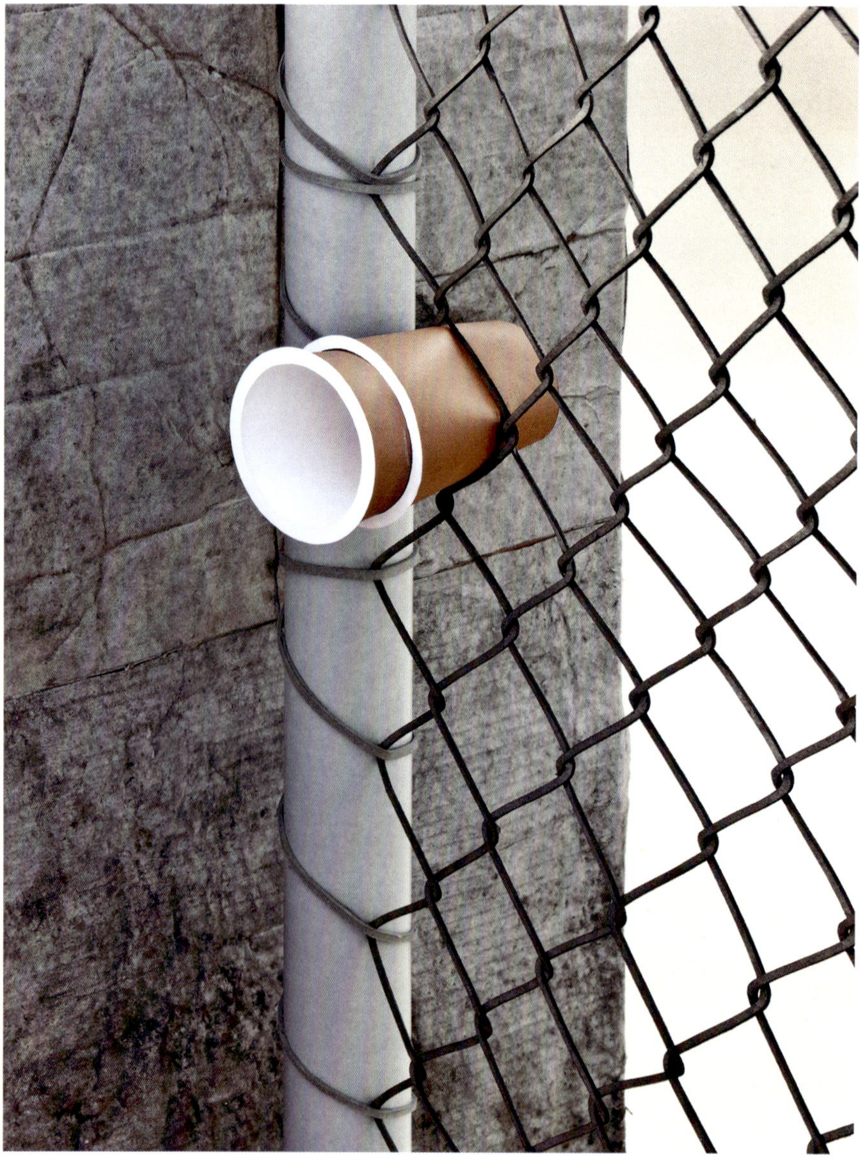

Thomas Demand, *Daily #15*, 2011. Dye print, 23¼ × 29 inches.

22 Third Nature

Thomas Demand produced the thirty-six photographs that make up *The Dailies* (2008–2022) from iPhone snapshots of everyday things in ordinary settings, such as cigarette butts snuffed out in a bowl or plastic cups stuck in a fence. Newspapers were once called "dailies," as was movie footage shot on the previous day, and together these references evoke the ephemeral and the fast. Yet *The Dailies* are hardly transient or rapid. Even though the initial snaps were taken quickly, Demand mulled them over slowly and selected them stringently, and a great deal of effort was put into the construction of each picture, which involved his usual making and photographing of paper and cardboard models as well as a special dye-transfer process chosen for this particular series. ("It takes forty hours for each print," Demand tells us.)[1] Different orders of time and attention are thus in play in *The Dailies*, and in this respect they raise the question of whether art can be made of our smartphone image-world. That phrasing might sound too grand for such modest subjects, but then the modest and the grand often converge in ambitious work. Consider *Daily #18*, a picture of a drink cover and straw without the cup. So much garbage on the sidewalk, it lies on its side like an abandoned top, yet with the rotation it suggests and the semi-elliptical shadows it casts, this little top might be taken to sketch a planetary system. As we will see, these pictures of the mundane also revisit momentous debates about what constitutes photography as an art.

For Demand *The Dailies* marked a turn from his images based on media stories about important events, such as the death of a German politician or a British princess, images that we might call "The Histories." Whereas "The Histories" are often freighted with obscure significance—each discernible detail looks as though it might be a clue to a mystery, in part because most details are suppressed—*The Dailies* aren't so laden with hidden meanings. "It's still the same author," Demand says simply, "it's just a different form."[2] We might think of this shift as one from a high genre—"The Histories" as a kind of "history painting"—to the low genres of picture-making: most of *The Dailies* are interiors, and nearly all qualify as still lifes. This genre reference is only one way that Demand positions photography in relation to painting.

As in most still lifes, the focus is on things at hand, such as the comb under a bathroom mirror in *Daily #3* or the two coffee saucers on a breakfast table in *Daily #13*. These are images of near space into which we want to reach. Of course we can't, not simply because the pictures are two-dimensional artworks, but because there's nothing real to touch in the first place: the model has displaced the referent, and the model disappears after the image is made. Frequently still lifes set up a double tension between haptic proximity and optical distance, and between a sociable offering (of food, say) and a cool withholding (the food can't be eaten).[3] Both kinds of ambiguity are active in *The Dailies*, and they are heightened by the ontological ambiguity of the constructed motifs.

In many still lifes the objects are centered or seen straight on. Not so here: often caught at an angle, they appear as if glimpsed, sometimes from above, as though they had caught the eye of the artist in passing. Yet the objects are usually set indoors; the days of *The Dailies* pass mostly in apartments, offices, and hotels. In fact, not only is the natural world largely absent, but the quotidian environment of *The Dailies* is highly administered. It's made up, almost entirely, of the "second nature" of man-made things and denatured spaces.[4] In these pictures abstraction often implies alienation; in this regard the blank red DON'T DISTURB sign on the anonymous hotel latch in *Daily #12* is a little chilling, as is the obscured EXIT light in *Daily #29*. If windows are pictured at all, they are frosted, as in *Daily #14*, covered with a blind, as in *Daily #16*, or grated as well as blinded, as in *Daily #19*. The thing seen prevails over the view out.[5]

Window and Mirror. In her classic book, *The Art of Describing* (1983), Svetlana Alpers considers still lifes and interiors in seventeenth-century Dutch painting and presents a strong opposition between two models of Western European representation during that period. The first is the dominant, Southern type, the picture as a perspectival window onto the world, which she attributes to Alberti. The second is the subordinate, Northern type, the picture as a mirrored reflection of the world, which she associates with Kepler.[6] In her account the first kind of representation privileges the viewing subject ("I see the world"), whereas the second focuses on the observed thing ("the world is seen"). In addition, the first type proposes that the world exists for the viewing subject to command, whereas the second imagines that the representation, even the subject, might not exist at all: it's as though the world simply appears as an image of its own accord.[7]

Demand plays with both modalities in *The Dailies*. Not only do windows and mirrors appear here, but the two dispositions underwritten by these two models—"I see the world" and "the world is seen"—are placed in tension, with each other and internally. Windows aren't transparent, as in *Daily #14*, and mirrors reflect little, as in *Daily #3*.[8] Demand also introduces presentational surfaces that are neither window nor mirror, such as the bulletin board in *Daily #8*, which recalls the use of similar devices in the trompe l'oeil painting of William Harnett, John Peto, and others—another genre that brings together the painterly and the photographic. Alpers associates photography with the Northern type of picturing, and the common understanding of the photograph as a direct imprint of the world supports this art-historical filiation, yet Demand has long worked to complicate the indexical understanding of the medium.[9] Even as the objects in *The Dailies* seem simply to appear, we know that the images are constructed several times over. They imply not only a viewing subject but also a very deliberate artist, taking shots, selecting images, building models, determining views, lighting scenes, arranging compositions, and deciding on prints. If people are nowhere in his photographs explicitly, Demand is everywhere implicitly. Indeed, for Michael Fried these works are artifacts of "sheer artistic intention."[10]

Accident and Inadvertence. Demand puts this strong formulation of Fried's under pressure in *The Dailies*. Certainly, they test the sense of "sheer artistic intention" with scenes that appear incidental or accidental. An outlet sags from a wall in *Daily #1*, four panels have fallen from a cheap ceiling in *Daily #5*, a green tissue is caught in a gray grate in *Daily #7*, and so on. The root of both "incident" and "accident" is *cadere*, Latin for "to fall," and gravity is foregrounded in images such as *Daily #11*, which looks down on green maple seeds that have landed on a brown wood deck, and *Daily #27*, in which various envelopes are scattered on a dark floor beneath a door slot. Also featured is the contrary state of suspension: *Daily #17* shows five pins on a clothesline strung across a blue sky, and in *Daily #24* old photographic slides, already discarded and darkened, appear to be stuck in a forgotten place. Other images thematize a precarious balance between the two conditions: a plastic glass with a bilious liquid sits uneasily on a window ledge in *Daily #20*, as does an orange bar of soap on the edge of a white bathtub in *Daily #21*.[11] When an accident isn't staged, then, an inadvertence is suggested, again in a way that pressures the intentionality that otherwise suffuses the work. In this series Demand seems to turn his gaze to these scenes and away from them at the same time (the *advertere* in "inadvertence" means "to turn to"). Perhaps the world pictured here isn't as administered as it initially appears.

Demand pressures the ultracomposed nature of his photographs in other ways as well. There is disorder in the cigarette butts in *Daily #2* and abstraction in the bulletin board in *Daily #8*. The aleatory strategies of the historical avant-garde are also evoked by the dropped panels in *Daily #5* and the fallen seeds in *Daily #11*, which call up famous experiments by Duchamp and Arp in such works as *3 Standard Stoppages* (1913–1914) and *Collage with Squares Arranged According to the Laws of Chance* (1917) respectively. In short, Demand plays the appearance of noncomposition against the actuality of composition, and the result is a set of paradoxical images that seem both very calculated and almost random. Twentieth-century strategies of chance look a little different in light of *The Dailies*: they appear more arbitrary than aleatory (an arbiter, after all, is a person who decides), and intentionality and indeterminacy no longer make for a stable opposition.

In this way *The Dailies* disturb conventional assumptions about both photography and painting. Central to the discourse of nineteenth-century photography was the conflict between art and automatism; in its claim to be an art, photography was thought to be compromised by its reliance on mechanism as well as its susceptibility to chance. In *The Dailies*, however, that double relation to automatism is both staged and suspended.[12] No less crucial to the discourse of modernist painting was the opposition between abstraction and representation. Given that *The Dailies* fit both categories at the same time, they trouble that old binary too.

Details and Dummies. Roland Barthes, in his influential essay "The Reality Effect" (1968), considers the function of the detail in narrative, both fictional and historical (his test cases are Flaubert and Michelet respectively). In a traditional narrative, Barthes argues, everything is expected to signify, and incidental details that seem not to signify do so nonetheless, for what they signify is insignificance—the insignificance of the mere facts of the contingent world—which helps the author build an impression of reality.[13] When a photograph is bound to the world indexically—a condition once understood to be necessary, even natural, to the medium—it refers to the world intrinsically; in a sense it is nothing but details and so can only produce effects of the real. With his schematic models Demand stretches this assumed connection between photography and reality, but he doesn't sever it entirely. Like his other images, *The Dailies* give us only schematic illusions, as the discrepancies between the constructions in the pictures and the things in the world soon become apparent. For Fried this is essential: the images are thereby able to register "sheer artistic intention" because they contain only the details that Demand mandates, that he literally makes. This is true, but it doesn't explain why he includes some details and excludes others.

Demand likens *The Dailies* to haiku, which suggests a degree of descriptive detail, and many of his images do possess a poetic concision.[14] For example, the green seeds on the brown wood in *Daily #11* might call up Imagist poems inspired by the haiku, such as the famous lines of Ezra Pound—"The apparition of these faces in the crowd / Petals on a wet, black bough"—and William Carlos Williams—"so much depends / upon / a red wheel barrow / glazed with rain / water / beside the white / chickens."[15] Some *Dailies* are apparitional in this way;

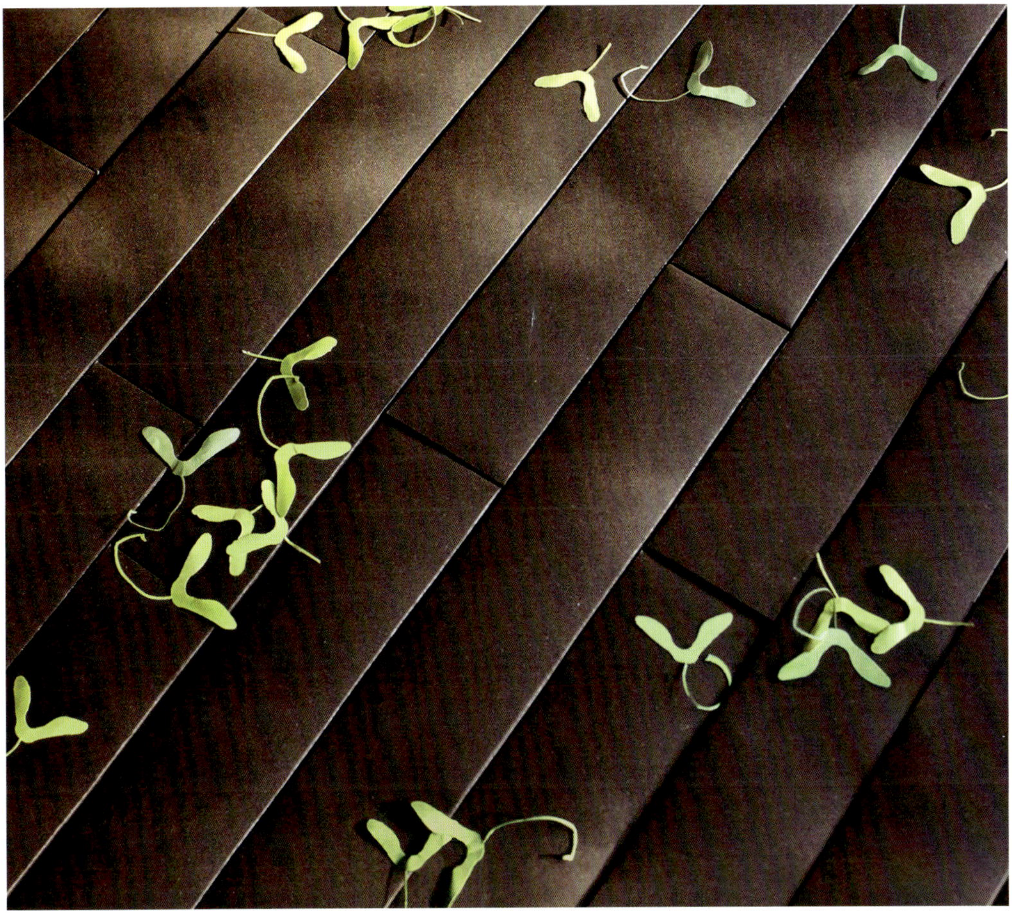

Thomas Demand, *Daily #11*, 2009. Dye print, 32½ × 29 inches.
© Thomas Demand. Courtesy the artist.

the dance of the colored pins on the clothesline in *Daily #16* is so for me, as is the curl of the yellow notes on the brown pole in *Daily #34*. And this quality invites us to reflect on the status of little epiphanies today. Can the ephemeral still touch the eternal, as Baudelaire proposed 150 years ago in his inaugural charge to modern artists? ("By 'modernity,'" runs his celebrated line, "I mean the ephemeral, the fugitive, the contingent, the half of art whose other half is the eternal and the immutable.")[16] More modestly, can everyday things still prompt thoughtful insights into an administered world? Imagist poetry arose in the second decade of the twentieth century during a time of technological transformation (often called the Second Industrial Revolution); it stressed perception in part because perception was threatened by increased mediation. Like its contemporaries, Russian formalism and European phenomenology, Imagism sought to refresh the human sensorium against a "second nature" on the rise. So, too, does Demand a century later in *The Dailies*. The great difference is that he accepts his mediated world as given and proceeds from there.

For Demand his photographs are also about recognition. "My sculptures are only imitations," he says, "dummies made of things that bear precisely the right number of symbols to be recognized as such."[17] His play with detail, then, doesn't merely underscore that his images are fabrications; more importantly, it activates them as tests of our looking, understanding, and remembering. ("Dummies" is suggestive in this respect: it's as though we are invited to ventriloquize his photographs.) Distraction is "the actual state of what we absorb as news," Demand once remarked. "What is decisive" are "the blurred traces left in the media by the incidents" that they relay. On the one hand, distraction produces "a very diffuse sense of dullness." On the other, it allows the "blurred traces" of incidents to "lodge in the memory," a memory that Demand understands to be collective as well as individual. Could these blurred traces somehow be evoked in the blunted details of his photographs? Certainly our shared media memory is a deep subject of his work, and *The Dailies* point to a mnemonic dimension that also lies buried in the trivia of our lives.

"Blurred traces" is almost an oxymoron, but it's useful here as such. In order to be potent, a detail, a *punctum* in the Barthesian sense, need not be precise; for example, there are blurred traces with traumatic force in Andy Warhol and Gerhard Richter, and so there are in Demand too.[18] Not only is the symptom lodged in the detail but, often enough, death is as well; frequently it's the little things that kill us. In *The Death of Ivan Ilyich* (1886), Tolstoy leads his protagonist to this recognition, as Ilyich watches with anguish as an innocuous bump become a relentless cancer that slowly stalks him and finally takes him away. He calls this mundane-mortal object *It*, and one might scan *The Dailies* for similar signs of things with potentially deadly force. Might *It* be there, for instance, in the slightly bilious water in the glass in *Daily #20*, or the overly orange splotch on the pavement in *Daily #33*?

Gaze and Punctum. The artist has a gaze, we viewers do as well, but other looks are implicated in *The Dailies* too. Sometimes it's as though a detail, an object, or the photograph as a whole gazes back at us.[19] Not only does "I see the world" vie with "the world is seen," but "I see it" is also troubled by "it sees me." What do we mean when we say "it caught my eye," as the elliptical rubber band in the concentric coffee saucers in *Daily #13* catches mine? What gives a particular detail its special power, and where exactly does this power reside—in the detail, in the viewer, or somehow in both at once? This seizing of vision by things is thematized by the green tissue trapped in the steel grate in *Daily #7* and the brown cups wedged in the wire fence in *Daily #15*: captured in mesh, they capture our gaze in turn.

In *Looking at the Overlooked* (1990), an essay on still life, Norman Bryson plays on the double meaning of "overlooked." The objects in this genre tend to be minor, overlooked things, but often they are depicted in a way that elicits an excessive looking; we "overlook" them in this sense, too, sometimes with an almost Medusan intensity.[20] Again, our gaze gets stuck in details, and this is one way they seem to possess power. This power might come with a hint of threat as well, a threat precisely to our vision. The English "detail" derives from the French verb *détailler*, which can mean "to cut from," and psychoanalysts since Freud have noted a psychic connection between the fear of blindness and the threat of castration.[21] For Lacan, moreover, there is a gaze at large in the world, one that preexists us as subjects and that we feel as a threat, and so it is, in his account, that the gaze "comes to symbolize this central lack expressed in the phenomenon of castration."[22] This notion of a traumatic gaze influenced Barthes when he theorized the *punctum* in *Camera Lucida* (1980), the unexpected detail in a photograph that catches our eye and, in doing so, pierces our psyche.

According to Barthes, the *punctum* isn't intended by the photographer; it's an accident experienced only by the viewer. But in Demand we confront the paradox of a *punctum* that, if not always intended, isn't accidental.[23] Certainly in *The Dailies* there are details that qualify as "punctal" for me (I mentioned the rubber band in *Daily #13*), just as there are views that approach the Medusan (the cigarette butts in the sand bowl in *Daily #2* have some of this force). At the same time, the smooth facture of the models softens our looking; as the critic Ralph Rugoff remarked, Demand images "seem to welcome our gaze with a pacifying order and stillness."[24] If some pictures effect a *trompe-l'oeil*, a tricking of the eye, almost all pictures, Lacan argues, aim for a *dompte-regard*, a taming of the gaze. At different moments *The Dailies* activate all three kinds of looking: a tricking of our vision, a wilding, and a taming.[25]

Artifice and Obstinacy. *The Dailies* are visual aperçus, yet often they trigger a sense of déjà vu, and this paradoxical combination of the fresh and the familiar is typical of Demand. "The images that come to me," he tells Alexander Kluge, "some are very banal, others greatly laden with meaning, but actually they are all things I know." And we know them too, or we think we do. In part this is because Demand builds his images from prior representations, such as news photos, postcards, and iPhone snaps. But this doubling isn't performed in the interest of a postmodernist critique of reality as a construction. Again, Demand treats the photographic mediation of the world as given, and he assumes that we do as well. His project is less to demystify the real than literally to remodel and to reimage it. In this way his art is indicative of a cultural shift in the perceived relation between representations and referents, one in which the old opposition between the indexical and the constructed becomes much less relevant. In a world where almost every image is both photographic and manipulated, the indexical aspect of the medium doesn't automatically trump its other aspects. We no longer assume the truth value of the photographic image, and we are alert to its capacity for deception. In this condition a new realism becomes necessary, one that uses artifice to make reality real again—that is, sensible, credible, or otherwise effective as such. Demand is an important figure in this new art of artifice in the service of reality.[26]

This artifice makes his photographs appear to precede us or anticipate us somehow, and this imbues them in turn with an "obstinacy" in the sense of the term developed by Alexander Kluge and Oskar Negt in *History and Obstinacy* (2008)—the obstinacy of things that persist, things that belong to the "the underside of history."[27] "Your images," Kluge says elsewhere to Demand, "are suffused with the absence of humans." Kluge doesn't mean simply that people don't appear in the photos; rather, he's concerned with the paradoxical presence of others who are absent but whose traces remain. "There is no vacuum that is empty," Kluge continues. "To my mind that vortex is a key medium in your images." Though cryptic, this remark points to the presence-absence not only of prior representations but also of prior people whose activities live on, again obstinately, in the everyday furniture of our existences. This is precisely the material of *The Dailies*, "the residues of dead labor," as Kluge puts it. Might this be another way to think of the "blurred traces" in this work, and another way in which its making isn't a matter of "sheer artistic intention" alone?

"Your images unfold," Kluge continues, in a second nature where all things are man-made and where "human abilities appear outside us and confront us" as alien. The "medium" of a Demand image, then, might be understood as one that

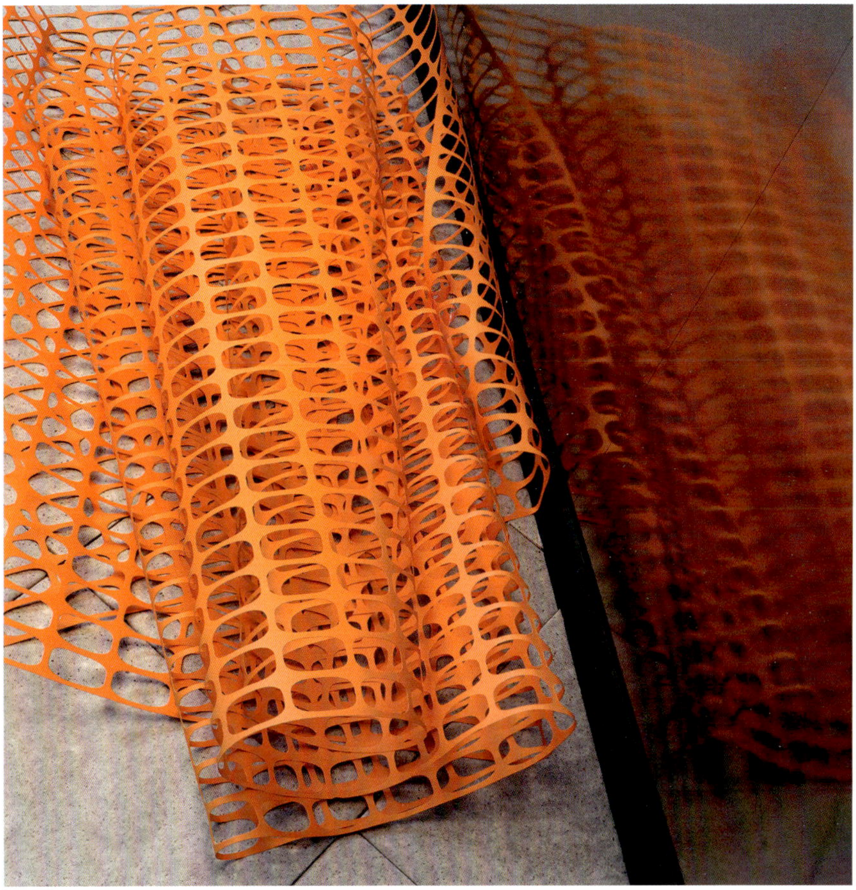

Thomas Demand, *Daily #9*, 2009. Dye print, 33½ × 33¼ inches.

aims to reanimate the "residues of dead labor," to open up this second nature, to reclaim the "human abilities" that are alienated there, or at least to point to such a project. This isn't easy—in fact, it's utopian—but it is in this way that his images function as both "vacuum" and "vortex." Here "medium" touches on its old meaning as a form of contact with the dead.

Kluge and Demand also speculate about a "third nature," by which they mean a world that's not merely man-made and machine-produced but also driven by structures, systems, and networks that are largely beyond human control. "If the public sphere, the arts, the relationship to people no longer grows with the complexity of society as a whole," Kluge warns, "then third nature arises." This is where Kluge believes artists such as Demand can intervene: "the core of your entire oeuvre," Kluge asserts, is focused on "the way people oscillate between first, second, and third nature."[28] But what does this intervention entail at the level of artistic practice?

Consider the kinds of objects pictured in some of *The Dailies*, such as the loose roll of orange fencing in *Daily #9*, the tacky stool in the changing room in *Daily #10*, or the exposed box of electrical wiring in *Daily #30*. They are the very stuff of capitalist junk space; they appear so artificial and so alien as to be almost posthuman.[29] Not many people understand how such things are produced, yet they are used, every day, by many of us. And in *The Dailies* they appear more than used; they are broken, like the outlet in *Daily #1*, or discarded, like the drink in *Daily #18*, or gashed, like the surface in *Daily #31*. Paradoxically, however, this use, this breakage, this trashing renders them human again; at least they show the signs of our consumption, if not of our production. And this is where Demand intervenes with his "organized tinkering," which is how he describes his selecting, modeling, and photographing of the banal things that stock our daily lives. "Things must be slowed down," he says, if the mediation of our world is to be understood and the second and third natures that weigh on us are to be resisted.

"We see what the specters of history left behind," Kluge remarks to Demand. "It looks ghostly and yet realistic." But the traces of past representations and the residues of dead labor that Demand offers us are not only uncanny. Again, he aims to trigger a recognition that has a mnemonic dimension: "A bell rings in your long-term memory." And, paradoxically, this mnemonic dimension can have a projective force, a future vector, as well, one with an ethical component. This is the material of our lives, *The Dailies* say to us. It's often tacky, trivial, and tiresome; it's sometimes a little deadly. But there's beauty here too. This beauty isn't redemptive, but it's real. It deserves our attention.

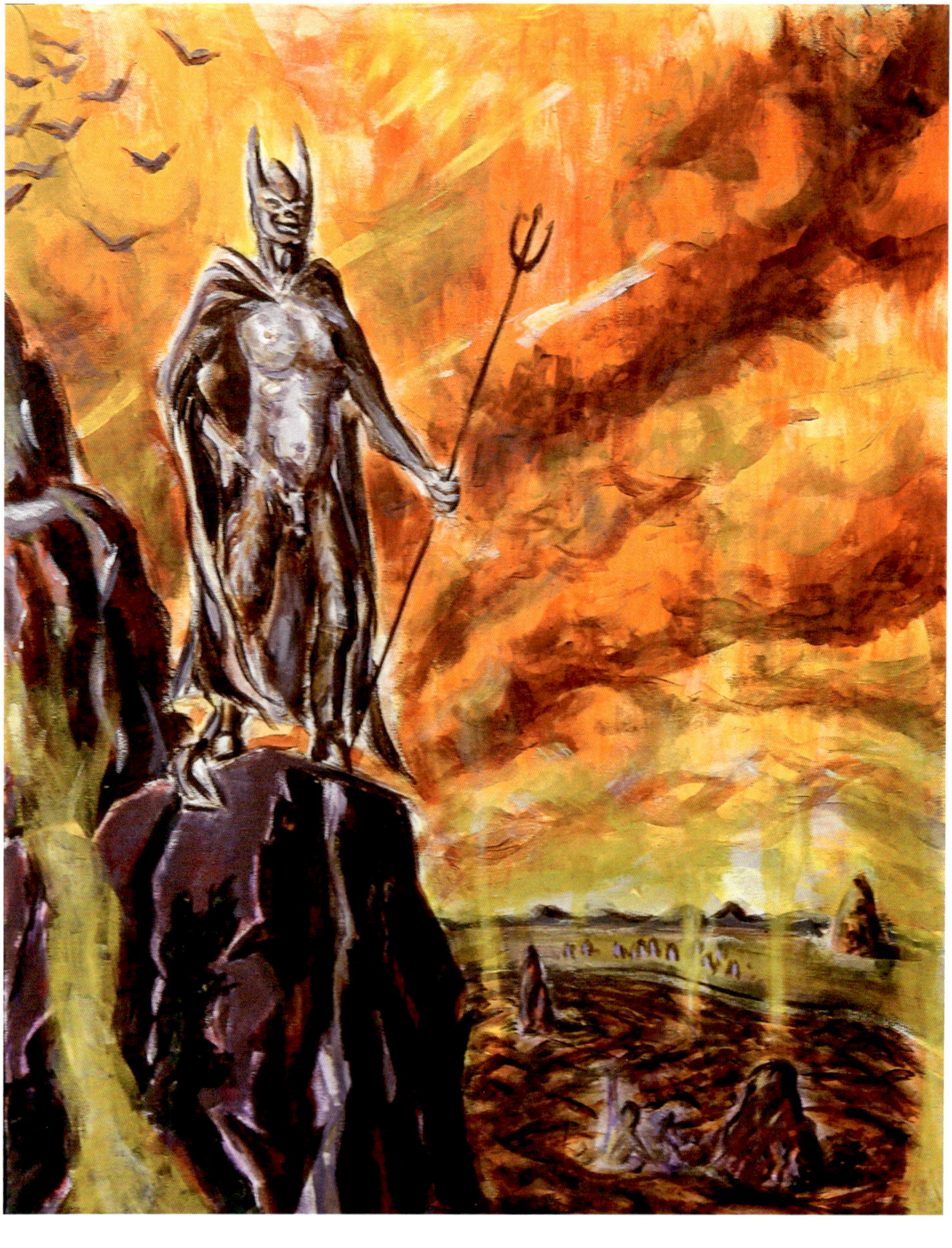

John Miller, Untitled, 1983. Acrylic on canvas, 30 × 24 inches. © John Miller. Courtesy the artist.

23 Perverse Pantomime

In the mid 1970s John Miller was a student at both the Rhode Island School of Design and the California Institute of the Arts, where he studied with pioneers of Conceptual art and Institution Critique, such as Douglas Huebler, John Baldessari, and Michael Asher, experimenting primarily with video. On coming to New York in 1978, though, Miller felt that video "lacked clout" with the public and the market alike, and he decided to test whether "the political agenda of alternative media" could be advanced in traditional forms like painting.[1] Support for this move came from Tom Lawson in "Last Exit: Painting," an influential essay published in *Artforum* in 1981. Although painting was seen by some critics as the last refuge of artistic aura (this was the moment of Neo-Expressionism), Lawson argued that it could be used as a Trojan horse. Precisely because it was embraced by collectors, painting offered a way behind the walls of the class enemy where artists could release small strikes of subversion. Whether viewed as clever strategy or simple opportunism, this argument made painting relevant again to young artists like Miller who had run the gauntlet of Conceptualism and Institution Critique.

Some who took this "last exit" filled painting with a pastiche of styles, high, low, and in-between (David Salle was exemplary for Lawson). Miller developed a different strategy that he called "mummery": he would mimic a given style in an exaggerated way, prompting the viewer to reflect on the style less as a manner of representation than as a marker of aesthetic value and social distinction (or lack thereof).[2] For Miller such mimicry allowed viewers enough distance to make this sociological analysis. At the same time, it also pointed to "how mimesis operates as a form of 'real life,'" that is, how everyday people often adopt styles and use media in semi-magical fashion, as though they had special powers of their own.[3] As Miller developed this way of working, he came to see photography not as a neutral instrument of representation but as a programmed apparatus that scripts particular attitudes and postures for people on both sides of the camera (he acknowledges the early influence of Dan Graham here).[4] Soon Miller adapted this idea to traditional media as well; henceforth any painting or sculpture by the artist would also be a comment on how such forms signify socially and operate subjectively.

This approach was aligned with that of the Pictures artists, who used photography to reframe media images in order to reflect on our habits of looking. Yet figures like Barbara Kruger and Sarah Charlesworth were the conflicted children of Andy Warhol, at once seduced by the mass-cultural image and affronted by its pervasive sexism, while Miller had affinities with different predecessors, such as Martha Rosler, who were attuned to working-class vernaculars as well as feminist concerns. "I didn't have the same love/hate relationship with mass media that the Pictures artists did," Miller states simply, and that was true for his Cal Arts classmates Mike Kelley, Tony Oursler, and Jim Shaw as well.[5] They acted as ethnographers of specific subcultures more than as critics of mass culture at large.

Since Miller likes to twist given styles and codes, he could be called a perverse artist both literally (in Latin *perversus* means "turned around") and figuratively: his *père*-verse work turns styles and codes against normal usage, that is, against "the law of the father." One approach to his work, then, is to consider how it transforms accepted categories of art such as painting, sculpture, relief, installation, and photography.

Painting is a picture of a picture. In 1981 Miller initiated a project that brought his old commitment to Conceptual art into line with his new orientation to painting: he attempted to make one picture every day. He started with sketchy drawings, then shifted to illustrational paintings in a style that is nondescript, brushy, and dominated by blues and browns. ("I meant to avoid Pop's authoritarian slickness, its machine-made look," he commented.)[6] The subject matter is also generic, with scenes that evoke a cheesy movie or television show, a trashy magazine or comic book. We encounter a cemetery vault whose doors are flung open, a poor wretch hanging high in a Western town, a giant octopus wreaking havoc on a fishing boat, a devilish Batman who is naked beneath his cape, or a Ku Klux Klan gathering around a burning cross. Even though, as with much appropriation art, no original is directly quoted, these pieces seem to be "pictures of pictures" nonetheless.[7]

This kind of painting is performed in the paradoxical style of the self-conscious amateur, reminiscent of the thrift store pictures emulated by Jim Shaw, a style with no pretension to high art that Miller admired for its "non-authoritarian" quality: "I could do them," he remarked, "but so could anyone else."[8] Miller viewed these images, then, as demotic in form as well as in content, as though they had emerged from a common repertoire of cultural clichés (what is a cliché if not "a picture of a picture"?), and in fact he presented them almost as if they were collectively imagined. At the same time, as pictures of pictures, they are also reflexive, inviting us to think about picturing as an ideological program. "I wanted these paintings to deflect viewers rather than draw them in," Miller commented. "You could see these paintings quickly, too quickly."[9] But then one was often called back to look again, to search out what was truly at stake here.

In the mid 1980s Miller added abstract paintings to this series of pictures. Mostly done in reds and browns, these abstractions are surrogates of another sort, intended to evoke the "idea of fine art" held by "the proverbial man (or woman) on the street."[10] Like his imitations of pulp fiction, these pantomimes of high art prompt us to consider the picture "as an ideological construct—or, dialectically, as a construct of ideology."[11] By this point, then, Miller had established his distinctive practice as a participant-observer in popular culture and art world alike, whose images, taken as tokens and executed in series, explored the terms of legitimation in both realms—what is embraced, what is rejected, and who benefits from the hierarchies that result.[12]

Miller makes his figurative and abstract works generic in a way that seems normal, even normative; at the same time, most of the paintings are a little discordant.[13] It is as if, born of a quasi-collective unconscious, they were subject to a dreamwork that distorted them, or as though they weren't sufficiently sublimated in the first place—the products of an imagination, part proletarian, part adolescent, that, however colonized by mass culture, was still eager to twist its imagery, that was at once resistant to control and open to fantasy. Consider his version of Batman. Like a kid entranced by goth games, Miller messes with this icon of DC Comics, turning the Dark Knight into the Prince of Darkness. Yet, perched atop an infernal world with his penis exposed, this devil is more ludicrous than subversive, like a porn star popping up in a superhero movie.

Sculpture is a partially buried penis. By the mid 1980s Miller had adopted brown as his signature color, which he called "a trademark no one wanted, a repugnant trademark," for the obvious reason that it evokes both dirt and shit, the two things most alien to order and art alike (shit is even more "matter out of place" than dirt).[14] Along with the low orders of culture, then, Miller called up the low orders of the body, in a materialism that crossed the socially degraded with the physically base. "My questions about aesthetic sublimation," Miller states concisely, "led to sociological critique."[15]

In 1988 Miller laid down a brown brushstroke on a mirror. On the one hand, this act recapitulated the Pop travesty of painterly gesture—gesture as a reified sign of subjective expression—performed by Roy Lichtenstein. On the other hand, it returned that gesture to the primordial smear that, at least according to Freud and followers, is the first artwork that any of us makes, our messing with our own feces. A student of psychoanalysis, Miller knew that the anal stage is regarded as one of symbolic exchangeability: in the infantile imagination a turd, a baby, and a penis are thought to be analogues, or, as Miller glossed this idea, "feces appear as a detachable phallus, in other words, as the first artificial signifier."[16] From prehistoric grave markers onward, the dominant verticality of sculptural figures has mirrored our upright posture, set above the horizontality of earth and animal alike; this proud form, this ideal body-ego, is the subliminal message of every statue.[17] Miller overturns this model, brings it low; his sculptural figures rarely appear intact, and sometimes they lie on the floor. Just as Bruce Nauman literalized a saying like *Feet of Clay* (1966–1970), photographing his feet covered in that substance, so Miller painted the clothes on his first mannequin, *My Friend* (1989), shit brown. Despite his good looks, this model can't escape the crap of the world; like our big toes according to Georges Bataille, he is steeped in mud.[18]

In one way or another, for Miller sculpture stems from "the first artificial signifier," the turd penis. Certainly this is what he gives us in *Untitled (small totem)* (1985), a tall brown figure on a pedestal that is fecal stick and big dick in one.[19] And if all sculptures emerge from this primordial matter, they might return to it as well. In *Partially Buried Woodshed* (1970) Robert Smithson presented a construction given over to destruction (it is all but decayed today). With this paradigmatic work in mind, Miller offers "Partially Buried Penis" as his paradigm of sculpture: the figure as fecal phallus threatened with entropic collapse.[20]

Relief is the ruin of exchange. In 1989 Miller began to focus on monochromatic works. He complemented brown, his "repugnant trademark," with gold, which, given the Freudian equation between shit and money, carries some of the same associations. In its origins over a century ago, the modernist monochrome could be either transcendental or immanent in orientation; for every idealist like Malevich there was a materialist like Rodchenko. In the postwar period, however, the monochrome became a worldly thing. At times it was as though this purest of painterly forms had even been passed through the interior of the body, with Rauschenberg, or through the crucible of kitsch, with Yves Klein, or through both, with Manzoni. Miller is a self-aware member of this party of desublimation.

Just as Rauschenberg pushed his paintings out into space with his Combines, so Miller extruded his monochromes into his reliefs. Traditionally a medium that partakes equally of the pictorial and the sculptural, the relief was the privileged format for stately representations of myth and history, most often in the form of heroic narratives of ideal male bodies. Of course, that logic broke down long ago. Early in the last century Duchamp signaled how the commodity might displace the body as the principal object type in modern sculpture, and by the 1980s, in the accelerated consumerism registered in the readymades of Jeff Koons, Haim Steinbach, and others, the product had come to dominate all other references. Miller also viewed everyday life as swamped by consumption ("utopia is a space outside the market" is one of his aphorisms), but unlike his contemporaries he understood this condition to implicate the body as well.[21]

As Miller developed his reliefs, they became clotted with objects. He literalized consumption twice over, presenting foodstuffs and products, and figuring our relation to these things directly as one of ingestion in a way that recalled the *Store* objects of Oldenburg.[22] Sometimes his reliefs resemble nothing so much as congealed latrines mounted on the wall, which is a far cry from the noble scenes of traditional reliefs. Miller thus evokes that glorious past only to bring it low. Strewn with broken body and commodity parts, his reliefs rework heroic battles as consumer binges, while his titles, such as *Work Hard, Play Hard* (1992) and *We Drank Some Cokes and Beat Our Toys into Ploughshares* (1991), point to a delirious economy in which overproduction struggles to match overconsumption, no matter the cost to our health or environment. If the "Death and Disaster" silkscreens of Warhol count as history paintings of "America" in the early 1960s, perhaps the brown and gold reliefs of Miller will someday qualify as the same for the early 1990s.

"We drank some Cokes and beat our toys into ploughshares" is a twist on Isaiah 2:4, the Old Testament command to exchange swords for plows, war for peace, strife for civilization, to redirect destructive libidinal energies to proper cultural ends; in short, to sublimate. By the early 1990s, Miller suggested, consumer capitalism was at odds with this civilizing process; it needed us hyped up on Cokes and consumed with toys. If fascism was psychoanalysis in reverse, as Adorno once claimed, so capitalism had become sublimation in reverse. Certainly, in his reliefs sublimation flips into desublimation, as shit brown covers everything. Recall that the anal zone is one of symbolic exchangeability; Miller presents contemporary capitalism as a world of dedifferentiation as well.[23] Just as Rauschenberg Combines are dense with images appropriated and collaged, so too are these reliefs thick with objects exchanged and consumed. To this extent they depict "the ruin of exchange"; at the same time they also show how exchange can ruin representation.[24] For Miller "polymorphous perversity" no longer threatens capitalism, concerned as it now is to stoke libidinal energies rather than to sublimate them. "Polymorphous perversity holds out the promise of unaccountability, devaluation," he writes. "Everything is as good—or as bad—as everything else."[25] His reliefs stage that equivalence as so much mess.

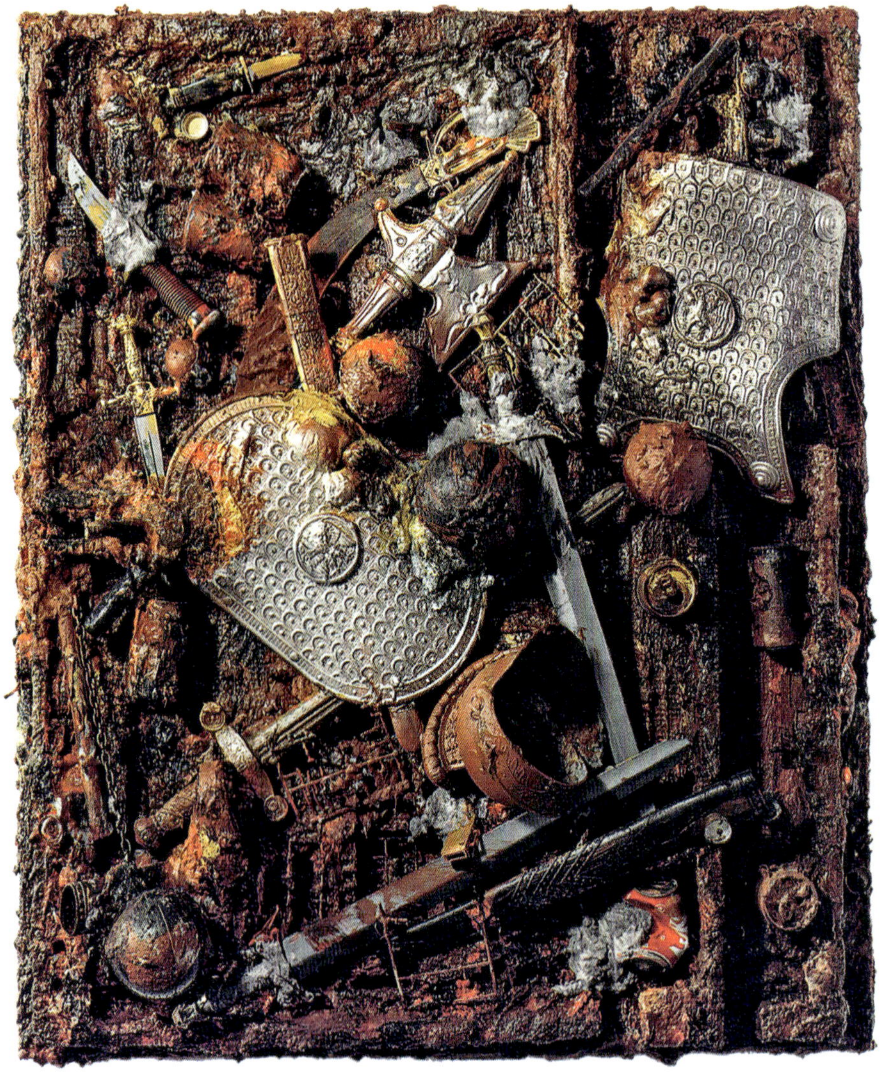

John Miller, *We Drank Some Cokes and Beat our Toys into Ploughshares*, 1991. Plastic objects, aluminum cans, insulation foam, plaster, papier-mâché, modeling paste, Styrofoam, and acrylic on Masonite panel, 47¼ × 39½ × 11 inches. © John Miller. Courtesy the artist.

The cultural politics of (de)sublimation is thus central to Miller, and here his critical thinking tracks his historical moment closely. In the late 1980s he held that patriarchal power and social hierarchy still "demand sublimation"; hence the assault on the aesthetic, as performed by Miller, Kelley, and others, remained pertinent.[26] He also still viewed desublimation as liberatory, at least potentially (the Marquis de Sade was important to him at this time). Yet, after the political controversies surrounding Robert Mapplethorpe and Andres Serrano in 1989–1991, Miller began to reconsider this position. And with the advent of abject art in the early 1990s (in which he figured prominently), Miller wondered whether "the slightest allusion to the body or to sexuality" could be "held up as a kind of critical intervention."[27] In short, as a student of Herbert Marcuse as well as Freud, Miller cautioned against "repressive desublimation" in popular culture and art world alike. In fact, as early as 1992 he doubted "whether sublimation continues to be the process through which civilization is made."[28] "The global economic system," Miller continued, "appears to militate against it. And . . . the threat of the unchecked libido (that was subordinated to the primal father) begins to look increasingly melodramatic."

Installations (of affect) and photographs (of anyone). How to respond to this state of affairs? One way was to point to how "unchecked libido" is exploited precisely as melodrama on television, in movies, on the internet, and in everyday life. This is the subject of many paintings and several installations that Miller has produced since the late 1990s. "In the late 1970s, the dominant mode of installation art was to treat the gallery as a large canvas," he comments; "I was part of a tendency that rejected that [pictorial space] in favor of installation as rhetorical space," that is, as a space for reflection about space, in particular about how spaces of both work and leisure have become sites for the training and testing of capitalist subjects.[29] For Miller one paradigm of such space is the television game show, which he mimics in such installations as *The Lugubrious Game* (1998).[30] "The quiz show or game show allows for the symbolic circulation of goods within a family that is not a family," he writes; "it creates a surrogate 'family' out of an arbitrary set of contestants."[31] As we watch this made-up family, we identify with its members, especially with the manic highs and lows that befall them.

A century ago Siegfried Kracauer noted that urban crowds were often arranged, in political parades, sports events, and the like, into "mass ornaments," that is, into vast spectacles designed to be consumed as images by those same crowds. The equivalent today might be the rapid mediation of "mass affects," sentimental feelings and impassioned opinions that sweep over us, even take us over, despite the fact that they don't originate in us (in fact, they can be quite alien).

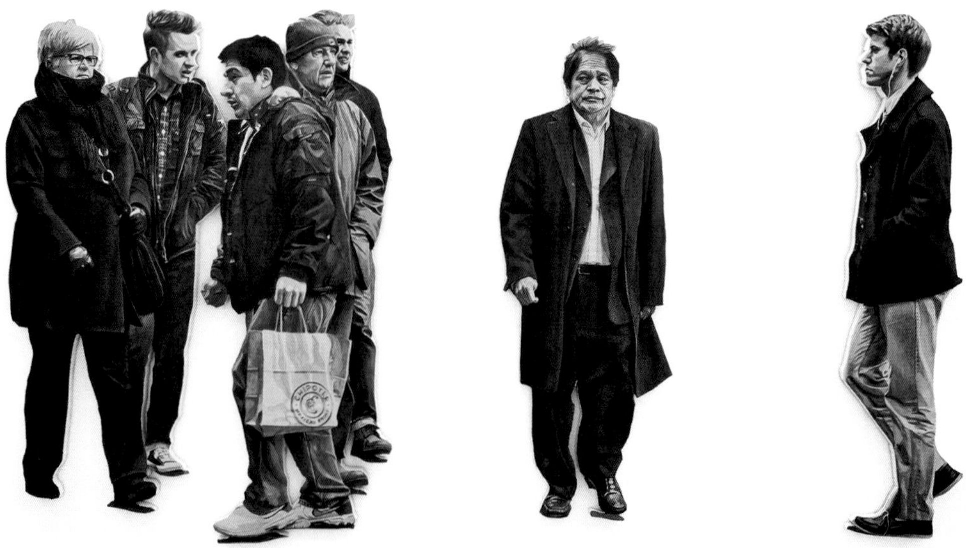

John Miller, *Chipotle*, 2013. Acrylic on wood and Styrofoam, three panels, 38 × 14 inches, 41 × 11 inches, 34 × 42 inches. © John Miller. Courtesy the artist.

In a nice phrase Miller calls this common phenomenon “a potlatch of emotions,” and in a series of paintings titled *Everything Is Said* (2009–), which depict young women and men on reality TV shows in moments of extreme distress, he presents some of the characteristic expressions of this mass affectivity.[32]

More than a century ago, when Hugo Ball opened the headquarters of Zurich Dada and named it Cabaret Voltaire after the French satirist, he declared it to be both a “playground for crazy emotions” and “our *Candide* against the times.”[33] At the same moment Ball defined the Dadaist as one who “suffers from the dissonances [of the age] to the point of self-disintegration.”[34] Again, Miller is part of this lineage of critical mummery, of perverse pantomime. However, he also knows that the acting out of “crazy emotions” doesn't automatically count as Dadaist subversion, that often it is the stuff of mass entertainment. To indulge in the psychopathology of everyday capitalist life is to take “a cheap holiday in other people's misery” (a line from a Sex Pistols song that Miller adapted for a 2009 show). He had to adjust his practice once again.

Miller did so through a dialectical turn in his thinking. He argued that we can “learn to feel again” through such displays of affect, “even though the whole setup is artificial.”[35] At the same time, this turn is in keeping with his old understanding of mass culture as a vernacular commons and not only a capitalist spectacle. In his *Middle of the Day* photographs (1994–2009), which Miller took from noon to 2 p.m. on the streets of New York and Berlin, he offers us images of everyday life, a life that, however dominated by consumption, remains open to chance, distraction, and daydream. The same is true of his *Social Portraits* (begun in 2013), which are photographic friezes of random groups of people—friends and strangers, tourists and shoppers—also on city streets. Most evoke anomie, but some suggest unexpected connection.

In *Variable Piece #70* (1971), a Conceptualist touchstone for Miller, Douglas Huebler proposed to photograph everyone in the world. In his photos and friezes, Miller intimates a similar project—to represent anyone in the world—and points to a political solidarity that might be found in this anonymous “anyoneness.”[36] “The work quixotically aspires, for better or worse, to be an utterly democratic representation,” he writes of *Variable Piece #70*; the same can be said of his own recent images.[37] Not only does Miller aim to reveal the repressive values imposed on the vernacular, but he also strives to reclaim the vernacular as a legitimate form of culture and experience.

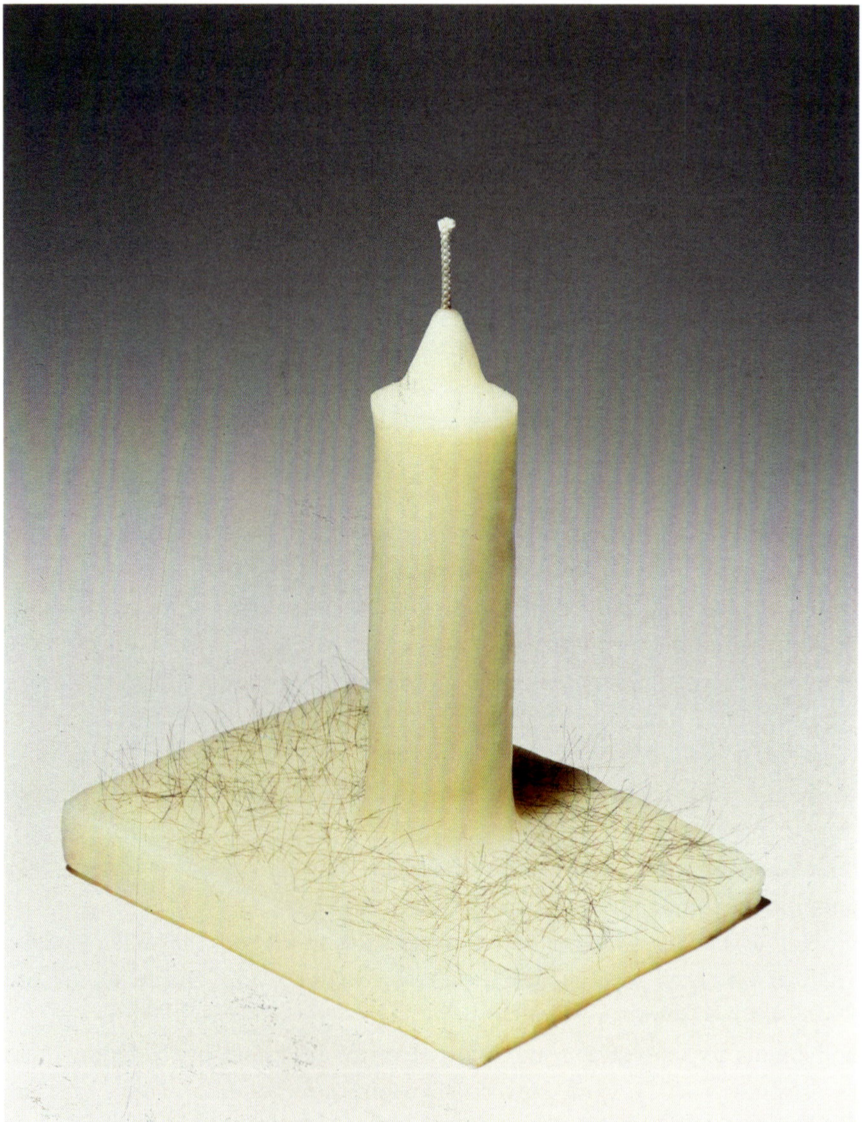

Robert Gober, *Untitled Candle*, 1991. Beeswax, string, and human hair, 8 × 4⅞ × 6½ inches. Photo: Geoffrey Clements. © Robert Gober. Courtesy of the artist and Matthew Marks Gallery.

24 Inexplicable Things

Metamorphosis has always driven the art of Robert Gober. An early work, *Slides of a Changing Painting* (1982–1983), consists of a slide show of eighty-nine photographs of a single painting of a male torso that the artist altered again and again, and it has served as a source for many pieces since. In time his work became a matter of transformation not only from one image to another but from one medium to another, above all from pictures to sculptures and sculptures to installations. This double transfer, in which a trace of the initial image persists in the final object, is essential to the characteristic ambiguity of his art.

Gober is best known for inexplicable things such as unplumbed sinks, unusable cribs, and male legs planted with candles or fitted with drains. Although they appear to be porcelain or flesh, they are in fact plaster or beeswax, and this material substitution moves them away from the politics of the readymade, with its aesthetics of indifference and its association with the commodity, toward the poetics of the found object, with its aesthetics of affect and its evocation of the body. Gober also works between conventional forms like cast figures and applied ones like theater props (as a student at Middlebury College in the 1970s, he was involved in dramatic productions).[1] These shifts often leave his objects in an ontological no-man's-land, in the vicinity of categories like replica, relic, and refuse, but not quite at rest in any one.

Above all it is the illusionism of his materials that estranges his sculptures, and this mixing of the real and the imaginary contributes to other confusions that Gober puts into play: confusions between the utilitarian and the aesthetic, as with his chairs and beds; between the public and the private, as with his urinals and sinks; and between the lived and the dreamed, as with his crazy cribs and hairy candles. No less crucial to the oddity of his objects is the meticulous craft that goes into them. Among other qualities, this manufacture separates Gober from artists of fabricated facsimiles like Jeff Koons, who makes a shiny fetish of production value. Gober builds his miniature houses with a hands-on, can-do pragmatism of the sort that led his father to build the family home on his own in Connecticut. These objects are literally painstaking, and just as pain is often evoked at the level of subject matter (all the broken body parts), so is care often intimated at the level of process, where physical work sometimes takes on the resonance of a psychological working-through. Damage and melancholy are inscribed in this art, then, but also reparation and mourning. In some pieces, such as the legs planted with candles or the butts printed with music, these different states are evoked at the same time.

Reparation, not redemption. Redemption is too final a state for Gober, given his commitment to the shapeshifting of natural things, human bodies, selves, and communities. (The Catholic church, which was central to his childhood, was hardly redemptive for Gober, along with countless others, during the darkest years of the AIDS epidemic.) Gober titled his 2014 retrospective at the Museum of Modern Art *The Heart Is Not a Metaphor*, a line drawn from the 1979 novel *Sleepless Nights* by Elizabeth Hardwick: "Alas, the heart is not a metaphor or at least not always a metaphor." Repositioned by Gober, this statement echoes the proclamation of feminist artists Louise Lawler and Sherrie Levine from 1982, "A Picture Is No Substitute for Anything," which stood as a caution against representation as a form of displacement, of speaking for others.[2] Yet the "not" in the Hardwick statement is more ambiguous, not a full negation, for the heart is also, ineluctably, a metaphor, and though, like a rose, it remains a thing, it's never only literal. In Gober, too, the real and the symbolic interrupt one another, as when an actual hair disturbs his allegorical candles. Perhaps his art proceeds less by metaphor than by simile, that is, by way of likenesses that suggest a logic (or illogic) of transformation, whereby a torso can become a sink and a sink can become a grave marker.

Sometimes this metamorphic quality is almost Ovidian, as when a human leg seems to be covered in tree bark, a change that can be read as traumatic or transcendent or both (as it was for the transformed Daphne of the ancient myth). More often, though, the shapeshifting is Surrealist, as when Gober divides a torso between male and female breasts à la Magritte. Georges Bataille once dismissed this Surrealist operation as a simple "play of transpositions"; he preferred his desire fixed, like that of a fetishist erotically attached to his shoe.[3] And there are times when Gober agrees. These are times, that is, when one is so damaged, as countless gay men were during the AIDS crisis, or so abjected, as countless people of color are every day, that metaphor becomes impossible—times, that is, when nothing can serve as a substitute, when no one can take your place, when your heart is broken, when you die.

Gober stages his play between metaphorical transposition and its ethical refusal most dramatically in his installations, which he once called "natural history dioramas about contemporary human beings."[4] Like dioramas, they are scenes where, again, reality and illusion mix; they are in our world yet not quite of it, at once actual and oneiric. Scalar disorientation is part of the psychological theater here; rather than site-specific, they seem almost psyche-specific, particular to Gober yet usually available to the rest of us too. This is so because, even as they emerge from his memories, dreams, and fantasies, they treat of objects and spaces known to all—habitats of home, school, religion, and so on. They also tap into phenomenological symbols that are general, like fire and water. This quality can lend his model of a burned house or a tidal pool the force of a folk tale. In such storytelling, as Walter Benjamin once remarked, we often warm our souls over a dead body.[5] That is true here as well, though sometimes with the uncanny twist that the dead body somehow seems to be our own.

Crucially, Gober also engages history in his installations, weaving traces of his life, community, and country into enigmatic narratives about persistent racism, homophobic bigotry, and terroristic wars on terror. An acclaimed installation from 1989 presented a sleeping white man and a lynched black man depicted on the same wallpaper, as well as a bridal gown and bags of cat litter positioned in the same space—so many figures tensed between repose and murder, purity and pollution. Another celebrated diorama, this one from 1992, included wallpaper of a lush wood mottled with sunlight and punctuated by sinks in which actual water flowed, but this evocation of a Transcendentalist landscape à la Thoreau was contradicted by bundles of old newspapers and packages of rat poison, and its barred windows suggested that it was also a prison. Finally, a chilling installation from 2005 revisited the events of 9/11 in the form of a display of objects and images that hovered between a chapel and a morgue. The politics of these spaces was never polemical; the agitation that they stirred seemed to build from within us, with a sobriety that allowed for both mournful reflection and political engagement.

All is not perfect in this art. There are moments when Gober is too gothic (a fireplace stacked with legs?), and some pieces that enlarge, distort, or combine different objects seem a little calculated for effect. Sometimes, too, the installations appear scripted in their unfolding; it seems contradictory for work so committed to enigma to be so resolved in presentation. Yet this self-curation can also be seen as a strength, and certainly curating is a form of care that Gober extends to others. He is acclaimed for his exhibitions of Charles Burchfield (at the Hammer Museum in 2009–2010) and Forrest Bess (at the Whitney Museum Biennial in 2012), among other instances, and in his MoMA retrospective in 2014 he included artists such as Anni Albers, Joan Semmel, Robert Beck, Nancy Shaver, and Cady Noland, whose work speaks to different aspects of his own.[6]

Gober resists interpretation in order to keep the meaning of his art open—a long-time stance that one must respect. Yet this can forestall interpretation, or

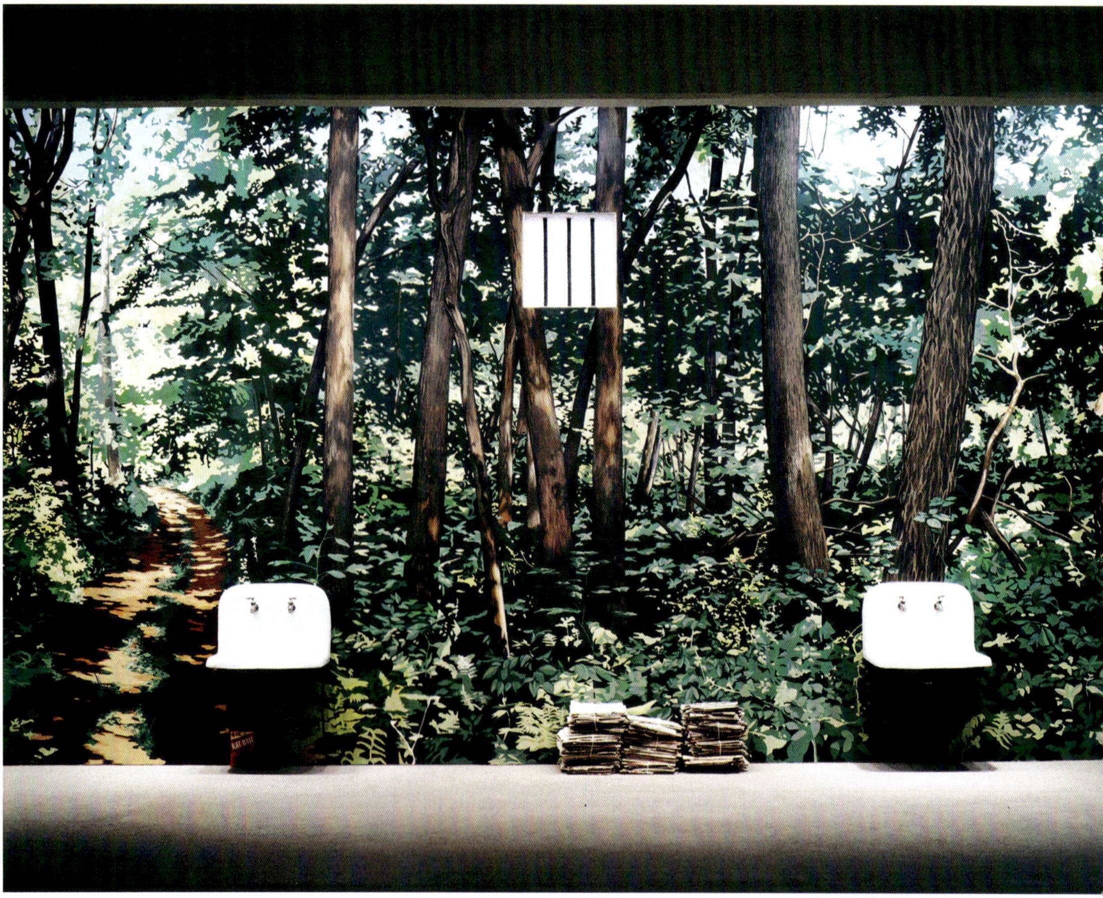

Robert Gober, installation at Dia Center for the Arts, New York, 1992–1993.
Photo: Bill Jacobson. © Robert Gober. Courtesy of the artist and Matthew Marks Gallery.

at least run the risk of a reticence that can seem withholding.[7] Gober offers bits of stories that we can only take to be his, but sometimes he is oddly absent or at least difficult to locate in his work. In short, this art is intimate to the point of private, but then, given that it treats some material that isn't conscious, it might not be entirely accessible to Gober either. Finally, the great interest of this enigmatic art might lie in the fact that no one, not even the artist, can claim to know it, to possess it in any final sense.

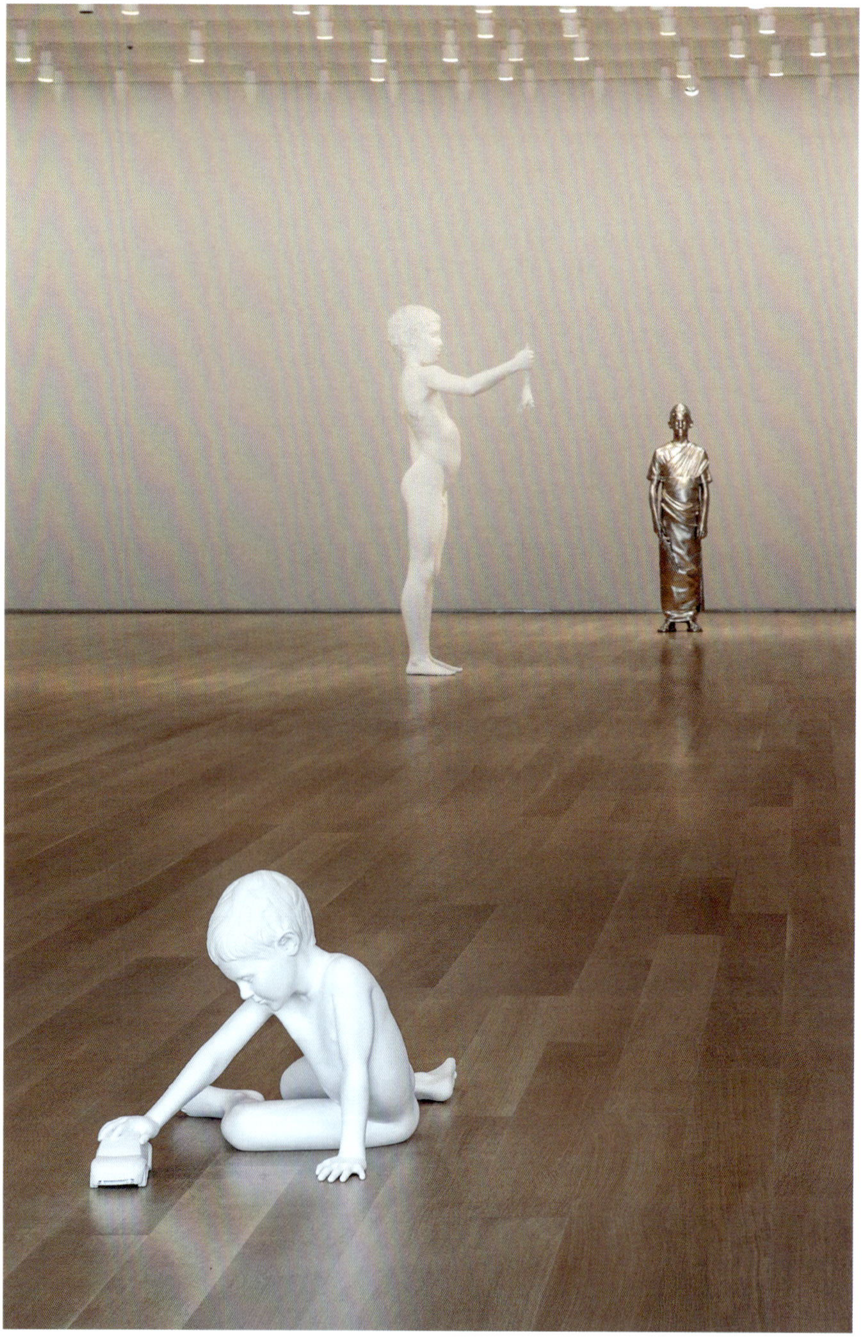

View of *Charles Ray: Sculpture 1997–2014* at the Art Institute of Chicago, 2015. From left to right: *The New Beetle*, 2006, *Boy with Frog*, 2009, *School Play*, 2014; stainless steel.

25 Philosophical Objects

The tree, the crashed car, the big lady—for me, these works are not images. They're fundamentally sculptural, and that's where my interest lies. . . . I'm using these images, things from my life, from our world, as a way to think. I'm not thinking about mannequins, or fire trucks, or trees. I'm thinking about sculpture. I have to wonder what it would be like to be free of those external images. But I don't know if it's possible for me, and they do bring a richness. The abstract notion of an intrinsic space is what allows me to look at both ancient and contemporary sculpture as working on the same problems.

—Charles Ray

Charles Ray has good reasons to deflect our attention from the imagery of his work; so striking is it that we might simply stop there. Yet more is involved in this redirection, for Ray places the image not only in tension with sculpture but almost in opposition to it. First and foremost, sculpture is "a way to think," to think "about sculpture"; whereas the image is "external," sculpture is concerned with "the abstract notion of an intrinsic space." It is this quality that makes sculpture sculptural for Ray and that connects his work to ancient prototypes as well as modernist precedents. He hesitates only when he comes to the "richness" of the image, by which he means its associative power. Although this is difficult to do without, clearly part of Ray would like to be so "free," and certainly most of the time he sees his sculpture as essentially abstract.[1]

Many of the critics attracted to Ray, including excellent art historians such as Michael Fried, Anne Wagner, and Richard Neer, share this suspicion about the image. They are happy that Ray has moved away from the "psychodrama" of mannequin figures like *Family Romance* (1993), relieved that he has left behind the "sensationalism" of such pieces.[2] Often these critics connect the psychological and the sensational with Surrealism and Pop respectively, which are a little disparaged by the association. And sometimes they fear that these characteristics will bring Ray too close to two peers, Robert Gober and Jeff Koons, who also make highly finished figures (implicitly, they see Gober as suspect because he is too Surrealist, and Koons because he is too Pop). But, above all, reading-for-the-image is dismissed as overly literal (art historians take pride in not reducing the meaning of art in this way). Here, however, they allow a problematic gap to open up with the public, for most viewers of Ray do read his work, at least initially, for the image—"Wow, that's a smashed car!," "Woah, that's a crushed truck!"—even if this image recognition soon prompts more complicated questions about material, process, and effect: How is the car remade in fiberglass, and why? How is the truck refashioned in solid stainless steel, and why? With Ray viewing begins with the image, and it's a mistake to bracket it altogether.[3]

Another reason not to dismiss the images is that they speak to the concerns that have driven Ray throughout his career, concerns with family, gender, and childhood. The first two topics are already raised by *Family Romance* and "the big lady," and Ray often plays with both familial fantasies and gender stereotypes. As for childhood, consider his sequence of three figures, *The New Beetle* (2006), *Boy with Frog* (2009), and *School Play* (2014), all of which feature the same model (the son of the fabricator of these pieces at different ages). Ray has suggested that together they "chart a course" through childhood, one that proceeds from an absorption in private play, through a curiosity about the otherness of the world, to a bored performing of cultural roles.[4] These sources can also be personal. For example, Ray has said that *Tractor* (2005) stemmed from a memory of playing on a broken-down machine like the one he meticulously reconstructs. As often with the artist, this memory became an idée fixe, one that prompted him to seek out a stand-in for his long-lost tractor, and then to have it taken apart, modeled piece by piece in clay, cast in aluminum, and assembled. In the process Ray also acted out, hyperbolically, the typical investigations of a child. In "The Philosophy of Toys" (1853) Baudelaire pondered why children endow inert things with special life, speculating that toys represent not only "the first concrete example of art" but also "the first metaphysical stirring." Yet this stirring can turn aggressive, even sadistic, Baudelaire believed, as the child strives "to get at and see the soul" of the toy, shaking it, banging it, finally prying it open, only to be devastated by the discovery of its soullessness.[5] This epistemophilic drive (as Freud might put it) is active in Ray too, and it has both destructive and reparative aspects (as Melanie Klein might add). In any case we impede these rich lines of inquiry if we overlook the imagistic and dismiss the psychological.

Of course, subject matter is also central to the big questions that Ray asks—questions not only about the politics of public sculpture, the status of the classical tradition, and the continuity of art history, but also about the nature of time, life, and death—questions that twentieth-century art, like modern philosophy, has sometimes broached but usually bracketed.

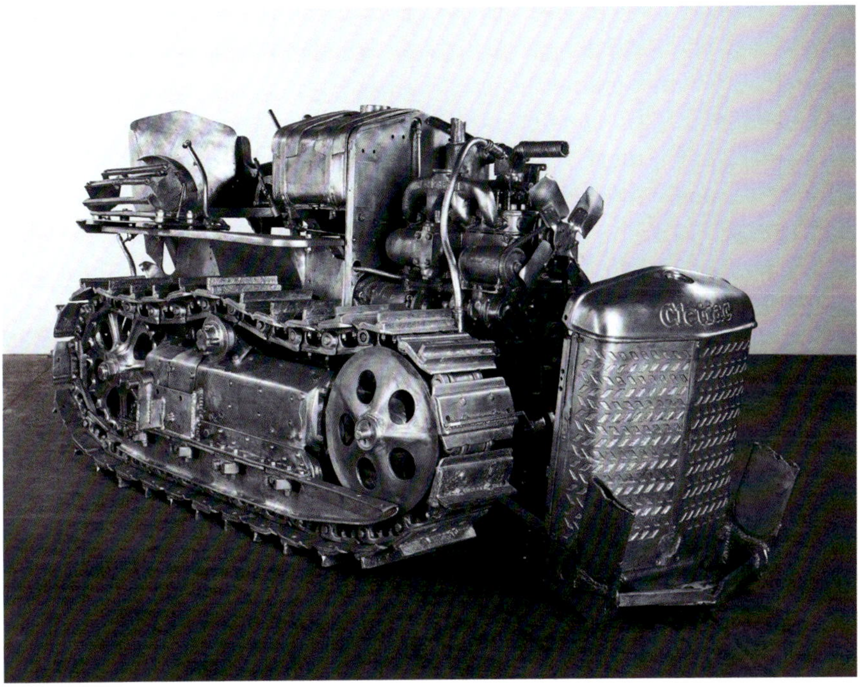

Charles Ray, *Tractor*, 2005. Aluminum, 56⅝ × 120 × 61 inches. © Charles Ray. Courtesy the artist and Matthew Marks Gallery.

If not "image," then, what are the terms Ray proposes and his critics elaborate on? Two are essential, and they have become almost magical words for all concerned with his work: "armature" and "embedment." "Everything has an armature," Ray has written, "every idea, every object. Once you locate the structure of something, you can start to think about it."[6] Here armature isn't simply the internal support of a sculpture, which is the common meaning of the term; it has to do with the structure of a work understood as the very source of its meaning. Counterintuitively, it can be a property of the surface of a sculpture; for Ray the skin of *Aluminum Girl* (2003) is "where sculptural events react and interrelate."[7] More often, however, armature involves the structure produced within a sculpture, the syntax (to use a term Fried has applied to the work of David Smith and Anthony Caro) that generates significance abstractly through an exact arrangement of formal elements. In his own writing on Smith, Ray credits this achievement to "a philosophical eye for a relationship of parts," which allows space to be "brought into the equation in an active way."[8] This aspect of armature is evident, for instance, in *Boy with Frog*, "the meaning" of which, for Ray, "resides in the space between the boy and the frog," or more exactly in the triangle carved out by the frog, the bellybutton of the boy, and his nipple.[9] (So focused was Ray on this virtual volume that he deemed the left nipple a distraction and so removed it.) Finally, armature can also be a matter of the space beyond the sculpture, the ambient space that it articulates. For Ray this is another legacy of constructed sculpture as developed by Smith and Caro. "Space as a container or empty field is lost forever," he has written incisively about this line of work. And of Smith in particular he offers this beautiful insight: his "sculpture is an armature for space, not clay. Turn the sculpture, and the world turns with it."[10]

Here we pass from "armature" to "embedment," the second privileged term in the Ray lexicon. For Ray embedment isn't the same as site-specificity; in fact, it can be "disconnected from location," and so it is less about the "placement in a room" than about the "geometry" produced by the sculpture.[11] How, then, does it differ from armature in the extended sense of that term? For Fried it doesn't differ much; this is so in part because he wants to align Ray with "the high modernist sculptural syntax" of Smith and Caro, and for the most part Ray is happy to be so affiliated.[12] Certainly he falls in this lineage by training: at the University of Iowa in the early 1970s he was a student of Roland Brenner, who was in turn a student of Caro, and Ray has acknowledged that he took Caro as "a template": "This way of working taught me to think sculpturally rather than to think about sculpture."[13] In this spirit, too, Ray is content to declare, "I am a late modernist," and, in fact, just as Caro abstractions sometimes recall figures, so Ray figures sometimes read as abstractions (again, he sees them mostly in this way).

However, it's difficult to think this embedment outside of the opening onto actual space made by Minimalism—by Donald Judd, Dan Flavin, Carl Andre, and others. For these artists the part-to-part composition of Smith and Caro was precisely a limitation of late modernist sculpture to overcome, a task they accomplished, at least initially, with unitary elements—Judd with his boxes and shelves, Flavin with his light fixtures, Andre with his plates and bricks—gestalt forms that activate spaces and viewers in direct ways. As we know, this move was contested by critics like Fried, who deemed it mere "literalism"; it's no wonder, then, that he wants to pull Ray back toward his favorites and away from his antagonists. At stake here are complicated issues—rival readings of the implications of phenomenology in art and opposed views about intentionality and indeterminacy in its meaning.[14] But the aim is clear enough: to perform an end-run around Minimalism both as a historical fact and as an aesthetic break. This is fair enough in art-historical debate, but to do so in relation to Ray is problematic on two counts. Not only does it diminish a key moment in his formation as an artist—his earliest work stemmed from Postminimalist principles of process and performance learned from Richard Serra and Bruce Nauman—but, more importantly, it reduces his achievement, for if this were all that Ray had accomplished in his sculpture it would be more a reversal than an advance. Does Ray only reissue the old Friedian ultimatum of art versus objecthood, "high modernist sculptural syntax" versus postmodernist involvement in space?[15] No. To put it technically, Ray challenges the unitary gestalt of Minimalism with the formal syntax of Caro, even as he embeds Caroesque syntax in Minimalist space.[16] In simpler terms, Ray presents formal object and spatial articulation at once, with the two in tension, to be sure, but necessarily bound up with each other. He also presents them as bound up with imagistic "richness," also necessarily, in both the making and the viewing of the work. In this respect Ray depends on Pop almost as much as he does on Caro or Minimalism, as he all but admits here: "Not that everything is Pop, but it changed the way we look at things."[17] This is also to suggest that Ray is as much postmodernist as he is late modernist; he is a member of the Pictures generation after all, and, again, he shares its concerns with gender, sexuality, and identity.

Thus we must think all three together—image, armature, and embedment; a Pictures involvement with popular culture, a high modernist syntax of form, and a postmodernist articulation of space—for this is how Ray delivers them to us. If we detach one from the others, we will end up with a partial reading. Certainly, this inextricability is central to my own experiences of his recent work, the most powerful of which occurred in three installations in the 2010s.[18]

In 2007 Ray presented three sculptures: *Chicken*, *The New Beetle*, and *Father Figure*. The egg (in stainless steel and porcelain) is only two inches long, the boy (in stainless steel) rises just two feet or so, while the man-machine (in painted steel) stretches eleven feet, and yet, though very different in subject and size, the three were positioned, with great care in a large space, as one ensemble. To use the Ray terminology, armature is foregrounded in *The New Beetle*: as with *Boy with Frog*, we follow the gaze of the boy to the object that he controls with his hand, but the arc described by his supporting arm, bent knee, and trailing leg is also essential to the geometry here. This geometry extends beyond the sculpture, as we project another arc described by the car as he pushes it, and it is this extended geometry that embeds the sculpture in a world that it creates, a world that is both actual and imagined. Such play between inside and outside is then thematized in *Chicken*, which Ray describes as "a sculpture that pits two forces against each other. The curiosity of the viewer peering in is met by the energy of the chicken birthing out."[19] Here, too, there is no opposition between object and space, artwork and viewer: like the chicken and the egg, neither comes first, both are in play at once. For its part *Father Figure* caps the imagistic narrative that the other sculptures set up. If *The New Beetle*, *Boy with Frog*, and *School Play* chart a course through childhood, these three pieces suggest an allegory of the "ages of man." We pass from birth, through boyhood, to patriarchal masculinity (at least as imagined for a boy: the source of *Father Figure* is a small toy); or, more precisely, from a first encounter with an outside world, to a playful investigation of subject-object relations, to an initial acceptance of the world of manly work (that the father and the tractor comprise one huge machine suggests how rigid this order might appear to a boy). Finally, this "ages of man" is also an "ages of sculpture." As others have noted, the father has a hieratic quality, the boy evokes classical models (such as *The Dying Gaul*), and the egg calls up the modernist objects of Brancusi.

In 2012 Ray again presented three pieces—*Young Man*, *Shoe Tie*, and *Sleeping Woman*—all produced in solid stainless steel and positioned in a precise arrangement. Once more armature was foregrounded in the postures, and embedment in the triangulation, of the pieces. An imagistic narrative was suggested too, here not about ages of man or sculpture but about types of classical figures. *Young Man* is a slacker version of a heroic nude, the *Doryphoros* of Polykleitos, say; *Shoe Tie* updates the *Spinario* (aka *Boy with Thorn*), a Roman copy of a lost Hellenistic original; and *Sleeping Woman* is a twenty-first-century sort of sarcophagus.[20] Even more explicitly than the 2007 exhibition, then, did this show juxtapose classical types and contemporary subjects—a young LA artist as a Greek nude, a middle-aged man as a Hellenistic-Roman boy (Ray was his own model), and an African-American woman asleep on a bus bench as a tomb sculpture.

Finally, in 2015 Ray continued this collision of the classical and the contemporary with *Baled Truck* (in solid stainless steel) and *Girl on Pony* (in solid aluminum). Gender stereotypes were again in play ("boys like trucks, girls like ponies"), but so too were two sculptural types, the sarcophagus and the relief, as well as two fundamental dispositions of this art: sculpture as a horizontal mass and sculpture as a vertical plane. While *Girl on Pony* was hung in a small gallery as though it were a picture, *Baled Truck* lay flat in a large space, which it commanded less with its size (nearly ten feet long) or even its weight (thirteen tons) than with its compression: it drew one into its internal complexities like a giant Transformer toy stuck in closed position. Once more Ray put image, armature, and embedment into play together to great effect.

What are we to make of these allusions to classical forms of the heroic nude, the relief, and the sarcophagus (not to mention the grave stele and the equestrian statue)? Ray invokes classical art in other ways as well. Stylistically his sculpture also stretches between realism and idealism: *Young Man* is "both a portrait and an abstraction," Ray comments, and the same is true of *Aluminum Girl*.[21] So, too, both works speak to the so-called miracle of classical art, the invention of contrapposto, that hip-swivel counterpoise that first imparted a sense of quickening to the figure, which Ray updates with his own hipster models. Other pieces call up other classical postures (such as the concentration of *Spinario* in *Shoe Tie*); clearly Ray is concerned to discover what makes a gesture eloquent or a pose iconic. This is a matter less of overt citation than of indirect allusion, and it might be related to the "mnemotechny of the beautiful" that Baudelaire detected in the modern painting that he most admired, or to the *Pathosformeln* (or formulas of pathos) that Aby Warburg traced from the classical period to Renaissance art and beyond.[22] In any case, the classical is no simple origin here (most models are Roman copies of Hellenistic copies anyway). As Richard Neer puts it nicely, "Ray discovers in historical mimesis a mode of repetition."[23]

Ray recovers two classical types in particular, the relief and the sarcophagus. The relief is the most pictorial of sculptural forms. Modern aesthetics long privileged painting; in fact, the traditional critique of sculpture—at least from Diderot through Baudelaire to Clement Greenberg—was that it is not enough like painting: it presents too many viewpoints, and so involves the viewer too much in movement and bodiliness, time and worldliness (of course, these are the very reasons that many artists since the 1960s have preferred it). Thus, at the end of the nineteenth century, the German artist and aesthetician Adolf von Hildebrand advanced the relief as a model for all sculpture in the hope

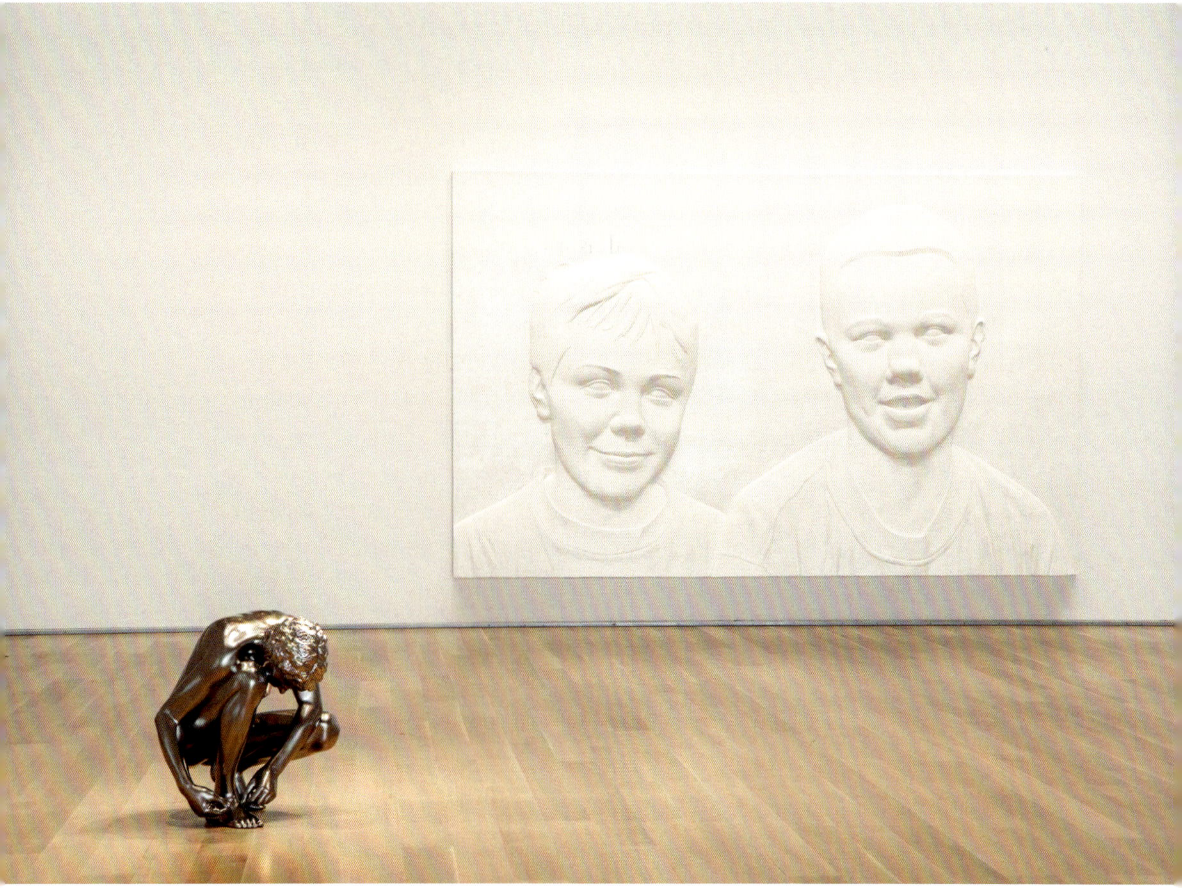

Charles Ray, *Shoe Tie*, 2012. Stainless steel, 28⅞ × 29¼ × 23½ inches. *Two Boys*, 2009. Fiberglass, 110 × 178 × 10½ inches. © Charles Ray. Courtesy the artist and Matthew Marks Gallery.

that the medium might thereby be made more pictorial, and so more unified, in its effects. Ray works to pull relief back toward sculptural complexity. "The conventions inherent in a relief are both interesting and useful to me," he writes of his fiberglass relief *Two Boys* (2010).

> Modeling form and its surrounding space necessitates a relationship between the work and the position of the viewer with respect to the work. An illusion is maintained by careful orchestration of both pictorial and sculptural elements. When approaching a relief tangentially or viewing it up close, distortions in the surface of the form arise. The pictorial experience disintegrates.[24]

Here Ray offers an initial illusion, which he calls the "story of two boys," and, viewed frontally, the relief is as pictorial as a family portrait on the wall, one that suggests the similarities and the dissimilarities between the two brothers (for that is what they are). However, looked at up close or from the side, the relief becomes more like an object and "the pictorial experience disintegrates." In its place come "distortion," Ray says elliptically, that "speaks to the nature of the landscape of childhood," by which I take him to mean that, viewed as an object—that is, as sculptural art—the relief opens up a philosophical space beyond the family picture.[25] Into this space flows a different sense of time, perhaps one touched by mortality (at least since the Romantics childhood has presented an "intimation of immortality" that summons its opposite as well). And drained of color and deprived of pupils as the boys are, the relief is as much a grave stele as it is a family picture. To view from the side is also to view anamorphically, and here *Two Boys* calls up the most celebrated example of anamorphosis in Western art, *The Ambassadors* (1553) by Hans Holbein, which shows two French diplomats at the English court, surrounded by rich tokens of art and science, as vital as life can be. Yet from an oblique viewpoint we see a distorted skull, a *memento mori*, which intrudes from below as if from a hallucinated grave. Jacques Lacan read this skull as a phallus, the symbol of castration, the lack that, in his account, a child must accept as he or she enters language and society. Perhaps that "distortion" cuts across the landscape of these boys too. At any rate, there is a mortal, even fatal dimension here.

This dimension is also strong in *Girl on Pony*, another relief that evokes both a family picture and a grave stele. Greek stelae and sarcaphogi commemorated the dead as though they were still alive, with their spirit or *pneuma* intact. *Pneuma* is one more term adapted by Ray; he defines it as "the Greek word for breath, wind, or life," and points to a beautiful instance at the Metropolitan Museum, a Cycladic grave stele of a young girl (c. 450 BCE). "She has a bird in her hand that she's about to kiss," Ray comments. "I find it so touching, and fundamentally sculptural—this bird and girl and kiss and breath. Everything is in relief, and the only space that flows through and around is between her mouth and the bird in her hand."[26] Ray calls such pneumatic passages philosophical as well as sculptural—it's where art quickens into knowledge for him—and there are touches of this quickening in his *Girl on Pony* too. It's there in her bashful smile, in her proud posture, in her clenched hands. At the same time a touch of death is felt too; perhaps it's the same touch.

This chiasmus of life and death is at work in the sarcophagus, which is evoked in *Sleeping Woman*, *Mime* (2012), and even *Baled Truck*. In *Tomb Sculpture* (1957) Erwin Panofsky distinguished between a Greek type of sarcophagus, which commemorates a past life, and so presents the figure as if alive, full of *pneuma*, and an Egyptian type, which anticipates an afterlife, and so locates the figure beyond this world, as an immortal soul or *ka*. If there is *pneuma* in *Girl on Pony* as well as in *Two Boys*, then in *Sleeping Woman* Ray "tried to sculpt the kinesthetic aspect of her *ka*."[27] Panofsky pointed to a third type of ancient sarcophagus too, the Etruscan, which often presents the dead as though asleep, and so falls between the Greek and the Egyptian types. Perhaps *Sleeping Woman* is in this Etruscan lineage, but her sleep, like her body, is heavy, as though it could last for an Egyptian eternity. The sleep evoked in *Mime* is lighter, more ambiguous. "Is his sleep a form of miming," Ray asks, "or is he miming sleep?"[28]

The miming of life in death is the sculptural task of the sarcophagus across its variations; it's a kind of "haunting" that Ray often grapples with. Maybe this is one reason that he moved away from the "creepy" psychology of his mannequins; maybe he came to see figurative sculpture as uncanny in its own right, in the sense that it can't help but confuse the appearance of the animate with the reality of the inanimate, pneumatic life with compressive death. In any case, Ray explored "haunting" as early as *Unpainted Sculpture* (1997), which he describes as an attempt to contain "the ghost" of the driver killed in the original car: "I studied many automobiles that were involved in fatal crashes. Eventually I chose a car that I felt held the presence of its dead driver."[29] *Baled Truck* also suggests a kind of sarcophagus, one that is body, coffin, and instrument of death all in one.[30]

Ray thus reaches back to very ancient forms: after all, the vertical relief is a kind of first picture, and the horizontal sarcophagus a kind of first sculpture. But, again, he also cuts these classical references with contemporary allusions. In a way this is to follow the celebrated project of "the art of modern life" proposed by Baudelaire: "By modernity I mean the ephemeral, the fugitive, the contingent," the poet wrote in 1863, "the half of art whose other half is the eternal and the immutable."[31] This imperative—"to distill the eternal from the transitory"—appears intermittently in twentieth-century art (it is one complement to the drive to abstraction), passing through Pop (especially Richard Hamilton) and on to artists like Ray, who can't do without the "richness" of contemporary images.

His intercutting of the ephemeral and the immutable isn't always a success. For me *Future Fragment on a Solid Base* (2011), in solid aluminum, is too much *Game of Thrones* and not enough Roman fragment, and *Light from the Left* (2007), in painted fiberglass, is too much Hallmark greeting card and not enough pagan frieze or Christian Annunciation. Most often, though, Ray hits the right note, a double one in which the classical is updated and the contemporary is deepened. This combination occurs, for example, in *Boy with Frog*: though the dangled frog is far from the severed head of Goliath, one thinks of the Donatello *David* (c. 1440) nonetheless. It is also achieved in *School Play*, where the plastic sword held by the boy undermines the phallic blades grasped by the father in the *Oath of the Horatii* (1784) by Jacques-Louis David (one is reminded about the painful inscription into patriarchy all the same). So, too, *Horse and Rider* (2014), where once again Ray served as his own model, is a critical sendup of the noble function of the equestrian statue. Not only is the Roman emperor Marcus Aurelius long gone, but the heroic ideals of a Donatello or a David are also dispatched, and the machismo of Wild West statues à la John Wayne is mocked as well.[32]

There is more here than a joke or two. At question in such pieces is what might count today as a public sculpture in a civic space. When classical art was not about the gods (and even when it was), it was about the *polis*, and Ray has aimed there as well, only to be deflected (at least for the most part). For example, *Boy with Frog* was offered to Venice, only to be rejected by the good people of that city: "I wanted him to become a citizen," Ray has said, "but politics removed him."[33] A public commission, *Huck and Jim*, was displaced even before it could be installed at the Whitney Museum in New York. These cases prompt the question of whether the classical tradition, with all its political implications, can be recovered in the present, after a long history of ideological degradation, the nadir of which was the Nazi propaganda of sculptors like Arno Breker and Josef Thorak.[34] Perhaps there is no authentic use of this language after such speech, but Ray believes otherwise. Well before the Nazis, Rainer Maria Rilke felt a moral imperative as he gazed at the Miletus torso (c. 480 BCE) in the Louvre. In his view, the poet wrote in "Archaic Torso of Apollo" (1908), this figure was "still suffused with brilliance from inside": "For here there is no place / that does not see you. You must change your life." It's likely that this famous charge mostly falls on deaf ears (or blind eyes) today, yet Ray wants us to believe otherwise.

There is a complex temporality embedded in these sculptures. One dimension of time is registered in the complex production of each piece—the long search for the right motif, the labored shaping of the exact mold, the intensive production of the perfect facsimile—which can take the artist, the studio, and the foundry several years to complete. Another dimension involves the different historical periods that are evoked. Again, for Ray, if we view sculpture in terms of "the abstract notion of an intrinsic space," then "both ancient and contemporary" practitioners can be seen to work "on the same problems." It's this continuum that allows many of his pieces to "tumble into time" as though they had no one date of origin.[35] Some works are literally "preposterous" in the sense that they montage a *pre* and a *post*, a time before and a time after; other works are more "anachronic" in that they suggest a more ambiguous time, one that, as Ray puts it, is "like space fluid and dynamic."[36] Then there are pieces that stretch beyond the preposterous and the anachronic toward "the ancestral," a term that the philosopher Quentin Meillassoux uses to describe the object world in the era before the human—and perhaps after it as well.[37] *Hinoki* (2007), a great hulk of a dead tree, points toward this superlong *durée*: it took a decade to complete, and Ray calculates its lifespan, as the cypress wood slowly breaks down, to be at least a millennium. This is a space-time that moves beyond cultural history toward natural history, where ancient ruins and philosopher rocks are found, and Ray aspires to this quasi-Platonic status for some of his works. Of *Tractor* he writes, "I think of this sculpture as a tractor in heaven. I would like to rename it *Philosophical Object*."[38]

Ray calls this space-time "the great outdoors," and defines it, with a nod to Meillassoux, "as what is here when we are not."[39] Although some of us might see this as a posthuman sublime, for Ray it's a projection that serves as a limit test for art. "How do certain works enter time while others die when we forget the purposes they originally served?" he asks. Why do certain sculptures "find a way to remain as objects when other artifacts are long lost or have disintegrated?" In this realm authorship becomes deeply paradoxical. On the one hand, "with time," Ray argues, "sculpture sheds its ideas, and what is left is what the artist made." On the other, if given enough time, "the sculpture makes itself."[40] On the one hand, in this scenario, the artist is the last man standing. On the other, the sculpture is freed of his limited being as well.

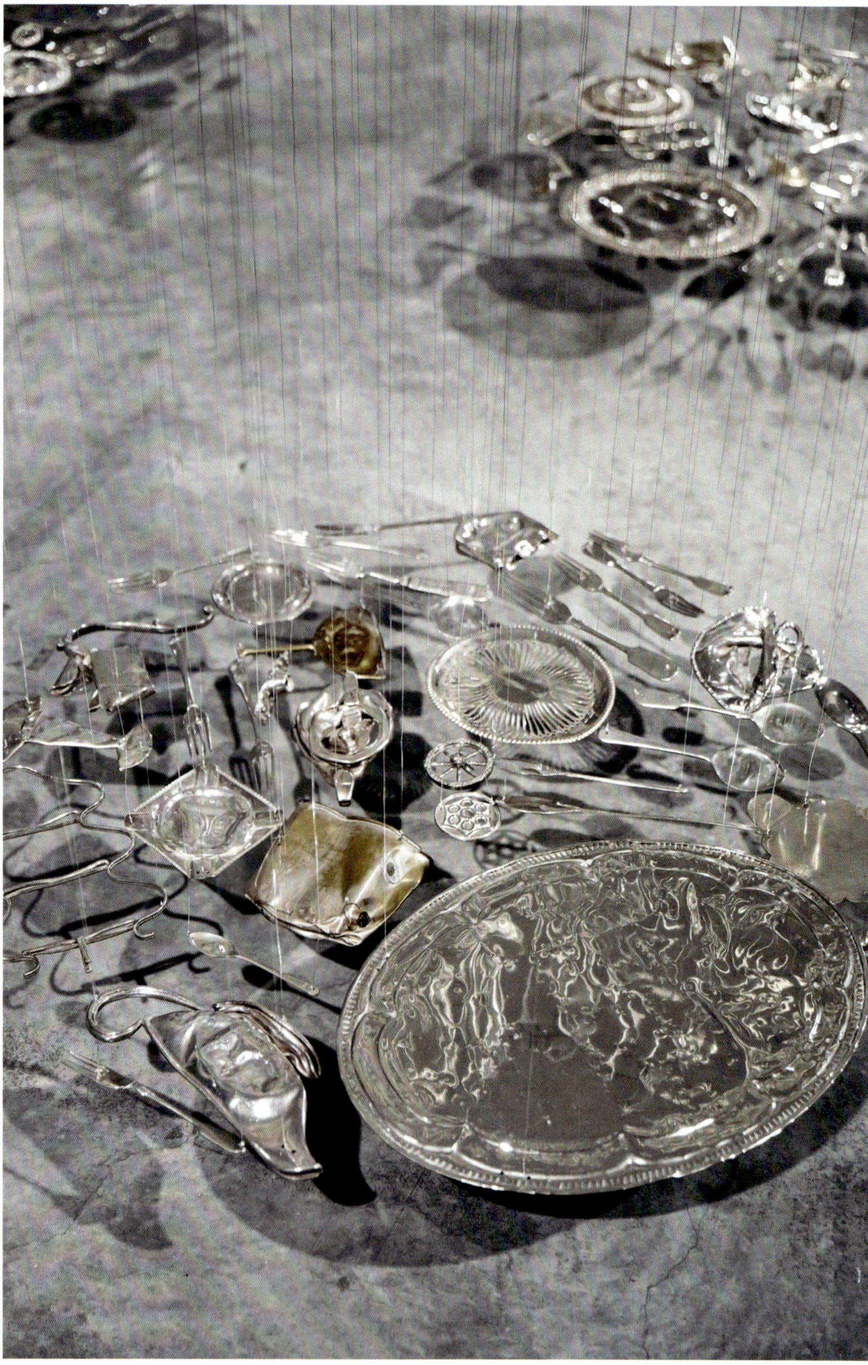

Cornelia Parker, *Thirty Pieces of Silver*, 1988–1989 (detail). Silver, copper wire. Tate.

26 Lost and Found

Although the Dadaist readymade and the Surrealist found object have long been drained by overuse, there are still ways to recharge them. Since the 1980s Cornelia Parker has passed these familiar devices through unexpected crucibles of her own devising. In the process she has also reanimated various strategies of Postminimalist art, upping the ante of the famous *Verb List* of Richard Serra ("to roll, to crease, to fold, to store . . .") with violent actions like shooting, burning, steamrolling, and exploding. Much of the frisson of her work stems from the tension between her extreme procedures and her clinical presentations, a tension heightened by the white-cube orderliness of most galleries and museums. All this would be only of art-historical interest, however, if Parker didn't also reflect on the social world around her, illuminating different aspects of institutional and political life in Britain both past and present.

Gerhard Richter once commented that Minimalism set a "new alphabet for the art of the future," one that is abstract, modular, and serial, and already by the late 1960s Eva Hesse and her peers had made this abstraction "eccentric," that is, emphatically material, corporeal, and erotic.[1] In the late 1980s these affective cues were picked up by a new generation of artists such as Robert Gober, Zoe Leonard, and Félix Gónzalez-Torres in the United States, who often used them to evoke queer experience, as well as Mona Hatoum in Britain, who, like Parker, sometimes staged situations of danger or threat. Occasionally, to get her desired effects, it was enough for Parker simply to photograph her selected objects, as with the rosary beads worried by Napoleon, the pin cushion that Charlotte Brontë liked to stab, or the couch, blanket, and pillow provided by Freud to his analysands, so freighted were these things already. But often she resorted to more drastic measures, as in the two early pieces that first brought her to attention.

For *Thirty Pieces of Silver* (1988–1989) Parker scavenged cutlery, candlesticks, and other objects made of silver plate, steamrolled them all on a dusty road (at the time her East London home was slated for demolition to make way for a new motorway), and then suspended the flattened shapes in groups of thirty a few inches above the floor. And for *Cold Dark Matter: An Exploded View* (1991) she convinced the British Army to help her blow up a garden shed, the blackened fragments of which Parker fastidiously gathered and hung up piece by piece from the ceiling, illuminating them with a single interior light that casts shadows worthy of a Halloween haunted house. These objects are both lost and found, or, better, they are both destroyed and resurrected—not brought back to use value, of course, or readily given over to exchange or exhibition value (these works are obviously difficult to display), but placed in a state of suspended (in)animation.

As Parker mines the eccentric vein of Postminimalism, she also exposes the sadistic side of the found object. Already latent when Man Ray added little tacks to an everyday iron in *Gift* (1921), this dimension is manifest in the "disagreeable objects" of Giacometti, one of which is a spiked fetish, and the high heels of Meret Oppenheim, which are bound with twine like a chicken ready to roast. Parker might agree with Georges Bataille that any representation betrays a destructive impulse; in fact, she makes this disturbing point in comical ways.[2] Sometimes there is a bit of sadism in humor (as a child Parker loved the *Roadrunner* cartoons), and often there is a note of pleasure in destruction (pleasure defined by Freud as a release of tension both physical and psychological). There may be a touch of guilt as well. Who, after all, is the Judas implicated in the title of *Thirty Pieces of Silver*? Parker targets unused things, like the family silverware that we stash away in embarrassment, or the old stuff that we forget in a garden shed, and so taps into our ambivalence about unloved presents and other stranded objects. Guilt and pleasure can also mix, as in the nasty thrill we take in explosions, whether benign as in fireworks, or barbaric as in "shock and awe" military bombings, or somewhere in between, as in anarchistic fantasies of attacks on the powers that be. Parker triggers these volatile feelings too.

Does Parker aestheticize trauma? If so, that's a vice pervasive in a culture like ours addicted to tell-all memoirs and troubling autofictions. But when she extracts lead from bullets and turns it into wiry script, for instance, she doesn't aestheticize trauma so much as she ritualizes violence, transforming it, controlling it, framing it, and there's nothing personal in the outcome (in my view we need more such sublimation, not less). As Chris Burden showed long ago, the residues of performances can become relics, and, as Parker suggests, these relics can also function as cautions. *Mass (Colder Darker Matter)* (1997) recalls its garden shed predecessor, only here are suspended the charred fragments of a Baptist church hit by lightning. This was the first Parker installation I saw in person, and it struck me then as a memorial of church bombings during the civil rights years—and ever since as a warning about shootings in mosques, synagogues, and other places of worship. There is also a forensic character to such work: the *Cold Dark Matter* pieces are like "cold cases" whose dormant clues point to violent events. Although for Parker these events needn't be crimes, they must prompt stories, and most of her pieces do tell strange tales.

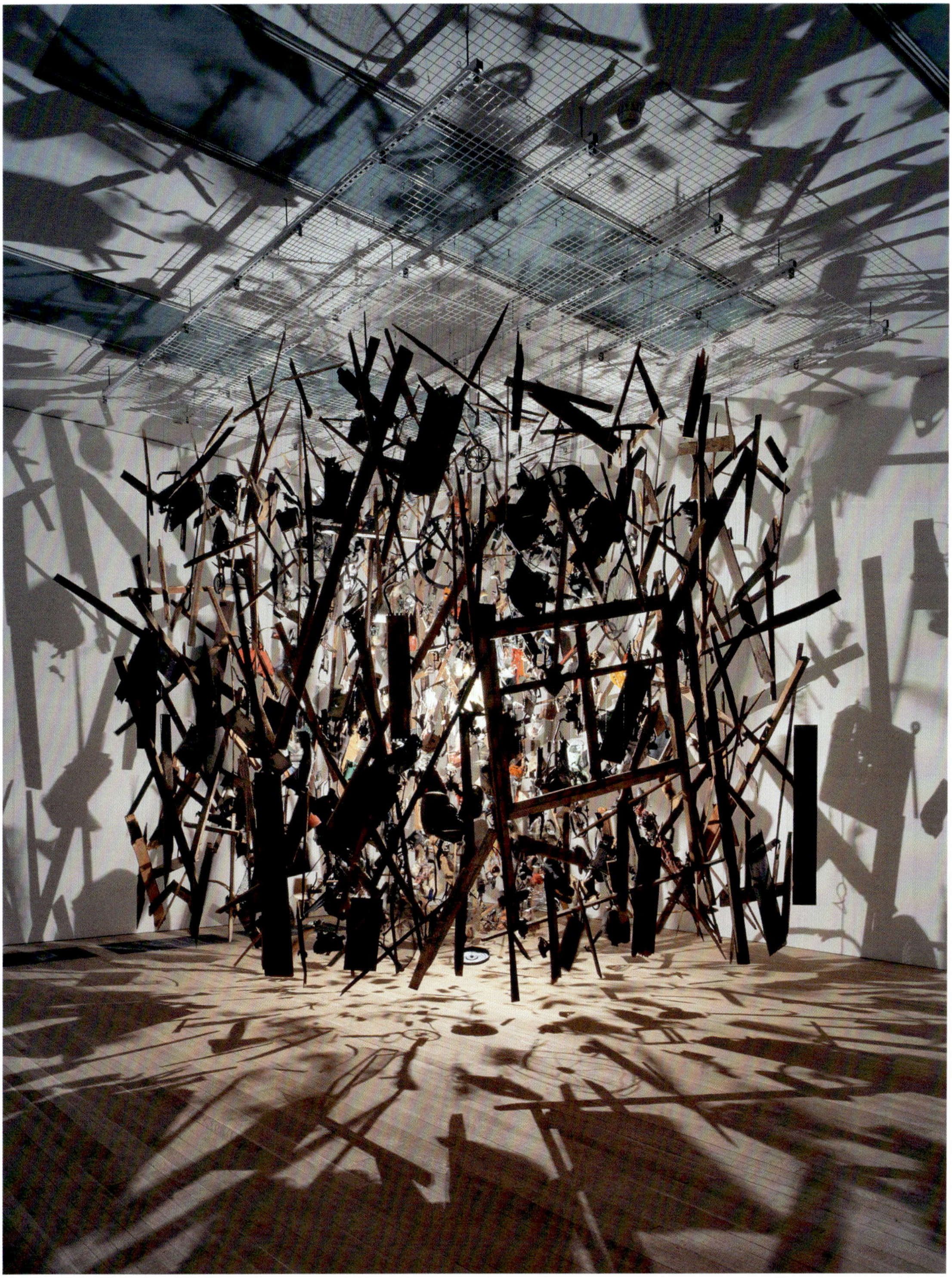

Cornelia Parker, *Cold Dark Matter: An Exploded View*, 1991. Wood, metal, plastic, ceramic, paper, textile, and wire. Tate. © Cornelia Parker. Courtesy the artist and Frith Street Gallery.

In an important essay from 2000 Mignon Nixon detected a turn, in Anglo-American feminist art, from a focus on desire in the 1970s and 1980s to a plumbing of drives in the 1990s; in theoretical shorthand, this was a shift from the world of Lacan to that of Melanie Klein.[3] Parker is part of this generational reorientation, yet while Klein opposed two drives, the destructive and the reparative, Parker holds them together. Put otherwise, her work suspends the opposition between ruination and preservation, and this result might make it relevant to current debates about monuments. As we know, many monuments commemorate acts of violence (war, conquest, empire), but they do so in ways that often cover them up. Parker began her career with little acts of "demonumentalizing": she cast souvenirs of iconic structures like Big Ben in lead, and then hung them upside down or flooded them with bathwater. Her inaugural move was thus one of antimonumental counterviolence. In a stretch this might be related to the ancient Roman practice known as *damnatio memoriae* (literally, "condemnation of memory") whereby the image of a leader, once honored on a coin or a column but later deemed an enemy of the people, was struck out in such a way that both acts, the commemoration and the cancellation, were retained (subsequent iconoclasts carried on this practice in their own ways). Updated, such an approach might split the difference between the unsatisfactory alternatives of simply retaining an offensive monument and removing it altogether. Parker points us to such a third way. How many disputed monuments might be given her treatment—blown up, in order to answer demands for social justice, and then strung up, for purposes of historical reflection? That sentence would be fitting for the likes of Cecil Rhodes and Theodore Roosevelt.

Given this antimonumental aspect of her work, how does Parker convince British soldiers and customs officers, let alone museum curators, to collaborate with her? Do they believe they are just on an arty lark, or does Parker tap into anti-institutional sentiments that institutional agents also harbor? In either case, she always delivers a pill of critical suspicion inside her sugar-coated pranks. For example, one of her prime subjects is national identity, which was vexed long before the onset of Brexit. *Island* (2022) is a glass structure modeled on a family greenhouse whose panes Parker dabbed in brushstrokes of chalk taken from the Dover cliffs, which she calls a "patriotic feature of our coastline—it literally marks the edge of England." With a floor made from old tiles from the House of Parliament and an interior light pulsing on and off, the white marks turn to black and back again. In this way *Island* evokes a lighthouse (for migrants and refugees) one moment and a shuttered shelter the next.

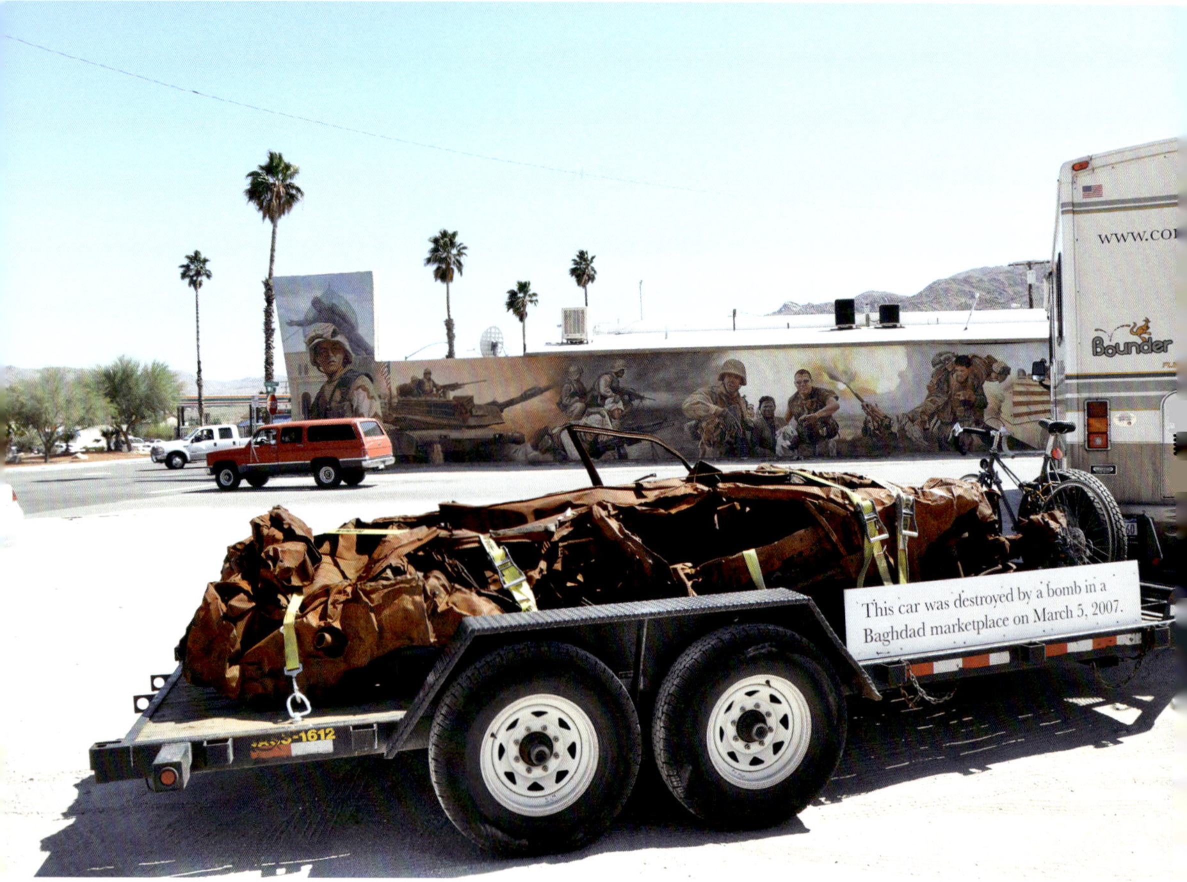

Jeremy Deller, *It Is What It Is: Conversations about Iraq*, 2009. Near the Marine Corps Air Ground Combat Center at Twentynine Palms, California. © Jeremy Deller. Courtesy the artist.

27 Civil Wars and Pop Utopias

> We sit starving amidst our gold.
> —William Morris, "The Socialist Ideal" (1891)

Since the early 1990s several ideas have guided the art of Jeremy Deller, and some have appeared in his titles.[1] The first notion is *open bedroom*, named after a show of his early work that Deller staged in his family home in London in 1993 (his parents, who were away at the time, didn't find out until ten years later). Although this arrangement speaks to the exigencies of a young artist without a studio, much less a gallery, it also suggests that he was already alert to the ways in which the contemporary home had become an extended workplace. If the public often penetrates the private in our neoliberal economy, so too is the private sometimes offered up to the public for its entertainment, as Deller implied with T-shirts, also produced in 1993, emblazoned with lines like "My Drug Shame" and "My Booze Hell"—a parody of tabloid headlines in which celebrity disgrace is sold as voyeuristic titillation.[2]

At the same time, against the dominance of mass culture, Deller has insisted on the power of vernacular forms, which we might call *joy in people*, after the title of his 2012 retrospective at the Hayward Gallery in London. Deller finds his artistic materials and media in common things and events, such as posters, street signs, bumper stickers, parade banners, bathroom graffiti, historical reenactments, brass bands, rock fan clubs, and city festivals. In a sense, this repertoire is a cultural version of the commons—that is, resources that, at least in principle, are available to all—and, like prior British artists and critics involved in Mass Observation, the Independent Group, and Birmingham School cultural studies, Deller aims to repurpose these shared materials in such a way that, as Stuart Hall once put it, "egalitarianism" might be given "artistic form."[3] Sometimes Deller crosses subcultural expressions that are foreign to one another, as in *Acid Brass* (1997), in which he commissioned a brass band to perform acid house music for rave enthusiasts. "I realized I didn't have to make objects anymore," he commented of this project. "I had been liberated by a brass band."[4] In this way Deller not only works on the public but also collaborates with it, and in this respect he is close in spirit to slightly older artists such as

Mike Kelley and Thomas Hirschhorn. Like Kelley, Deller finds rich materials in musical subcultures, and, like Hirschhorn, he taps the vernacular energies of everyday fans. In fact, like both artists, Deller sees popular affect as an important resource for contemporary art. (One of his favorite sayings comes from Ché: "The true revolutionary is guided by great feelings of love.")

For some critics Deller projects a *pop utopia*.[5] Yet he is hardly blind to the darker implications of the collapse of private and public or to the weirder aspects of the psychologies of fans and cults. For instance, Deller has spoken of the emotional outpouring over the death of Princess Diana as "collective insanity," and in a characteristic work titled *Our Hobby Is Depeche Mode* (2006) he explores the strange (over)identifications with this band by its followers in Eastern Europe.[6] Such expressions are examples of *social surrealism*, another key notion of his practice. Like the Surrealists, Deller takes up found objects, most dramatically in the case of the bomb-mangled car featured in *It Is What It Is: Conversations about Iraq* (2009), his mobile exhibit about the Iraq war that toured the United States, but he revises the Surrealist device radically in the process. For the Surrealists the found object pointed to an unconscious desire that the *trouvaille* might somehow ease, if not altogether satisfy. For Deller, on the contrary, the found object catalyzes a social contradiction or a political conflict that isn't readily resolved. Again and again he connects disparate developments in cultural and political histories; for example, in his diagram *History of the World* (1997) Deller charts the links between brass bands and acid house by way of deindustrialization and civil unrest (among many other things). At the same time, he is well aware that such connections can be forced and that tensions between those worlds remain.

This awareness leads to a related idea that is also crucial to Deller, *civil war*, which is explicit in *The Battle of Orgreave* (2001), his mass restaging of a violent confrontation between police and miners during the 1984 strike (some 200 miners from the original conflict participated in the filmed performance, along with some 800 veterans of historical reenactments). This interest in civil war aligns Deller with that dimension of Marxist thought advanced by Antonio Gramsci, who regarded the forms of civil society as political sites of counterhegemonic struggle. For Deller any *polis* hinges on the actual antagonism of different groups as much as any potential solidarity among them. Like the latter-day Gramscians Ernesto Laclau and Chantal Mouffe, he sees democracy as a matter of *dissensus*, with irreducible conflict always at its core. Yet this dissension can have a light side too, as captured in such projects as *A Social Parade* (2004) and *Procession* (2009), in which Deller arranged for various communities, in San Sebastián and Manchester respectively, to march with special banners displaying their sundry commitments (one group identified as proudly unrepentant smokers).

"I've always described it as digging up a corpse," Deller remarked of *The Battle of Orgreave*, "and giving it a proper post-mortem."[7] This is another important motive of his practice, but what exactly is *a proper post-mortem*? An autopsy of a troubled past that is also its laying to rest? That would imply a working-through or a coming-to-terms that is at odds with his other principles of *social surrealism* and *civil war* where the point is to sustain such tensions, not to resolve them. By "digging up the corpse" Deller suggests that it might be premature to announce the disappearance of the Left, that its many funerals might be (as the Mekons once put it) for the wrong body. Although as a child Deller was fascinated by historical reenactments, as an adult he recognizes that these restagings usually drop out the politics of the very events that they otherwise strive to reanimate. His version of historical reenactment is modeled instead on the song cover, which Deller describes as "a social adaptation."[8] To restage a past event like a miner strike, then, is less to memorialize than to reactivate it.

In 2013 Deller created a show called *English Magic* for the British pavilion at the Venice Biennale. "Magic," the dictionary tells us, is "the ability to influence the course of events through the use of mysterious or supernatural forces." To qualify it with "English" is to point to native traditions of expert conjurers, from the druids of Stonehenge to sorcerers like Merlin and Gandalf. Deller also intended the term to evoke "the mythical qualities of popular culture and its abilities to weave spells, especially in music."[9] The notion of "English magic" might also be extended to his summoning of an unexpected array of figures and events, both past and future, in order to comment on "the beginning and the end of socialism/communism as we know it." For example, his semifantastic history staged in Venice involved other tricksters, such as Tony Blair, who helped to contrive the story of the so-called weapons of mass destruction that prepared the Iraq War, Prince Harry, who escaped from every scandal as if by magic (until family and media finally got the better of him), and Roman Abramovich, who, along with other Russian Midases, turned the collapse of the Soviet Union into a mountain of gold. In the age of neoliberalism, Deller suggests, the real magic is the ability to transform public resources into private gains, and the question becomes what countermagic can contest such diabolical sorcery. Can the ghost of William Morris be summoned to wreak vengeance on the likes of Blair, Harry, and Abramovich? One mural in the British pavilion pictured Morris as a colossal Poseidon about to plunge the prized yacht of Abramovich into the Venice lagoon (the 115-meter *Luna* dominated the Giardini quai during several Biennales). Here the socialist past returns to smite the capitalist present, and civil war looks ahead to popular utopia.

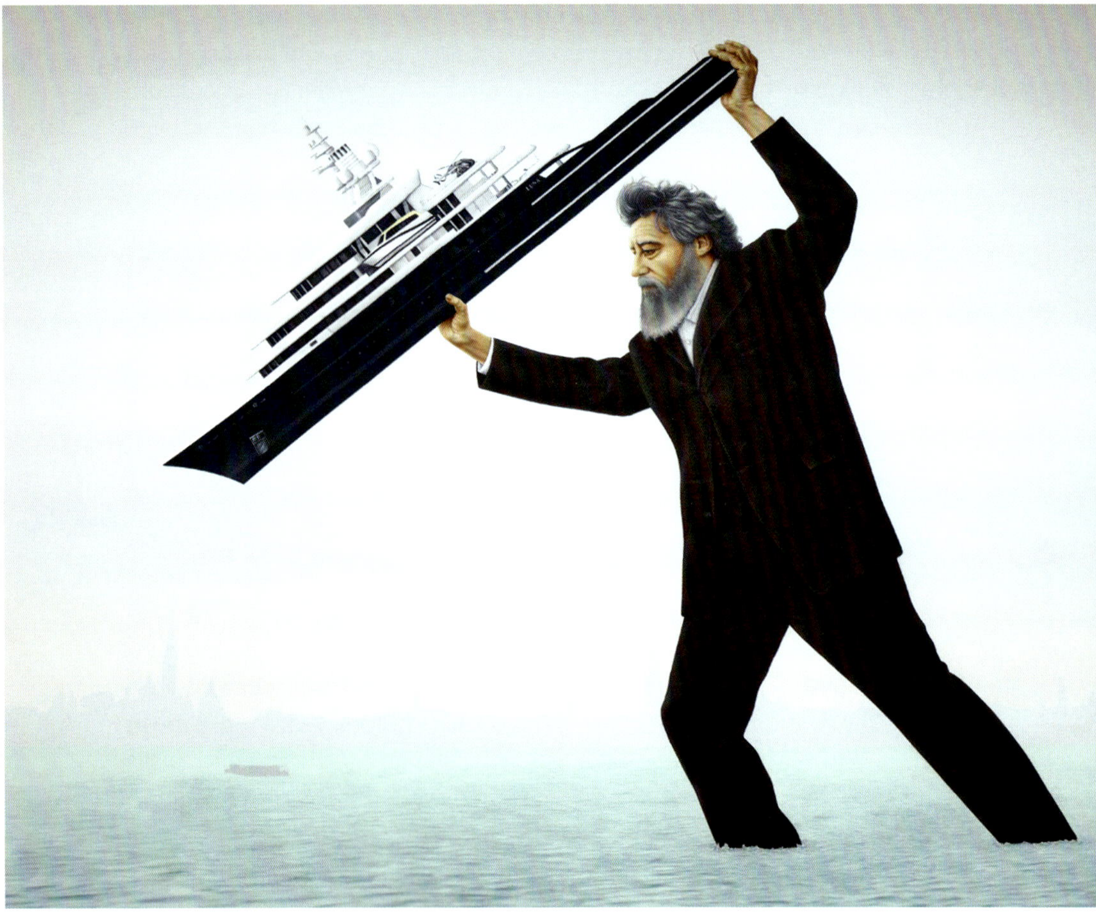

Jeremy Deller, *We Sit Starving Amidst Our Gold*, mural painted by Stuart Sam Hughes for *English Magic*, British pavilion, Venice Biennale, 2013. © Jeremy Deller. Courtesy the artist.

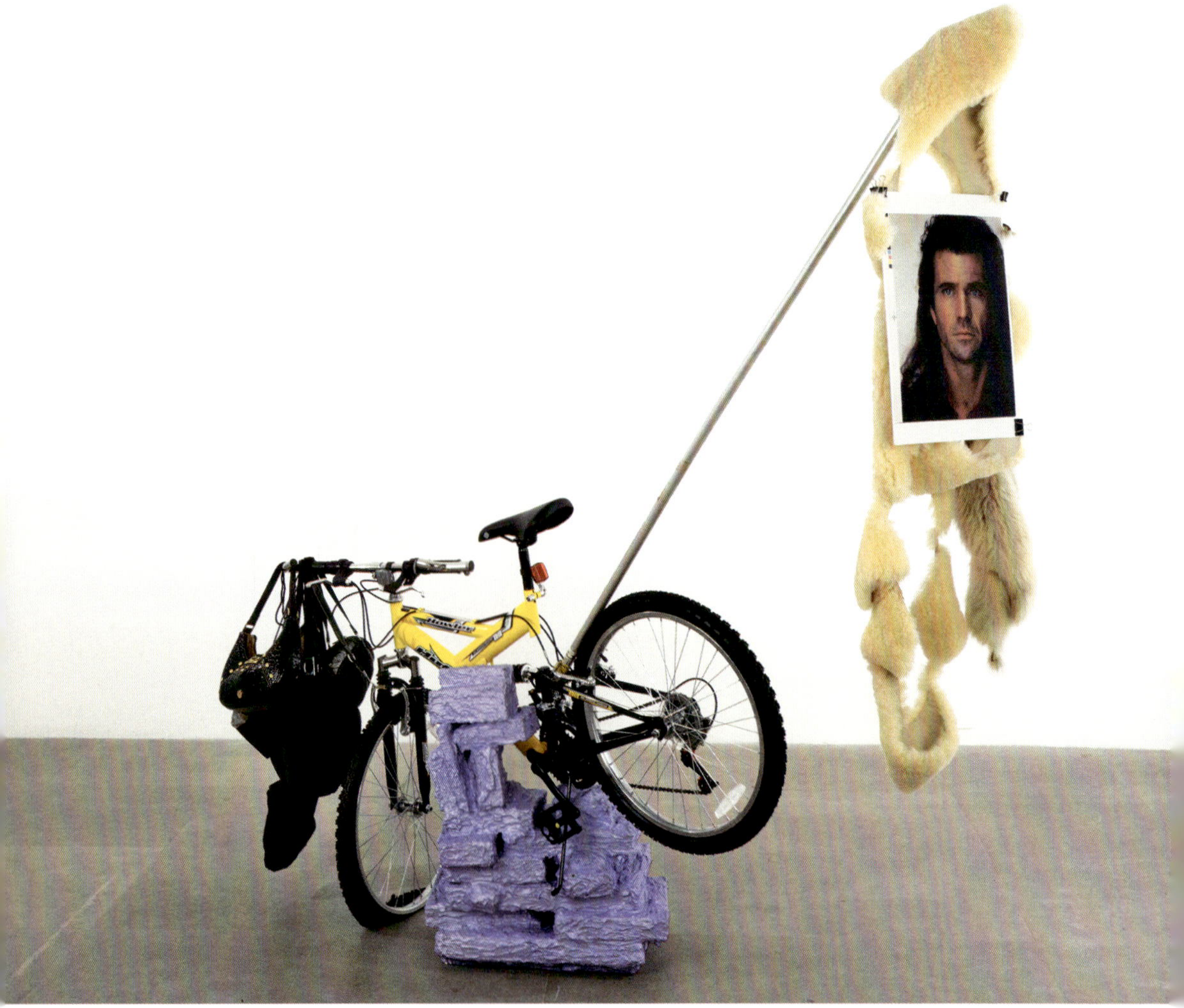

Rachel Harrison, *Huffy Howler*, 2004. Wood, polystyrene, cement, acrylic, Huffy Howler bicycle, handbags, rocks, stones, gravel, brick, one sheepskin, two fox tails, metal pole, wire, pigmented inkjet print, and binder clips. Walker Art Center. © Rachel Harrison.
Courtesy the artist and Greene Naftali Gallery.

28 Happy Days

Rachel Harrison was born in 1966, a moment when Pop art was in full force and Postminimalism had just emerged. With her canny use of mass-cultural signs à la Andy Warhol and funky industrial materials à la Eva Hesse, her rambunctious art points to an unlikely combination of these two idioms. Although Harrison is often taken to be a devil-may-care assemblagist, her image-object hybrids ask to be considered as sculptures, and doing so allows us to reflect on the contemporary status of that medium vis-à-vis the other media that she samples. Early on Harrison compressed her dispersive installations into composite objects, thereby heightening the cultural contradictions called out by her pointed riffs on postwar art, mass media, and American politics.

For David Joselit the key term for this practice is "remediation," by which he means how Harrison transfers the effects of painting to the format of sculpture and interrupts the mixed results with photos and videos—in other words, how disparate materials, colors, textures, pictures, and texts combine, conflict, and conspire with one another in her work.[1] This remediation reaches beyond the appropriated forms to the structures that support them: Harrison has used scrap sheetrock, cardboard containers, and packing crates as (anti)aesthetic material too. Here the traditional hierarchy between sculpture and base, knocked over by the Minimalists, is undone, as palettes and boxes are stacked up to shape the sculptural object or simply appear as such in a travesty of plinths and pedestals. Even though Harrison sometimes inscribes the site into her sculpture through installation photos and debris, she also occasionally puts her objects on dollies, which underscores how site-specificity is now undercut by site-provisionality—that is, how sculpture, like almost everything in a world given over to rapid exchange, is on the move, and how brute labor, so rarely acknowledged in the art world, must provide the motive force.

Harrison is the opposite of Richard Serra on the question of site, as she is in another respect. Her go-to materials like cement and polystyrene aren't disclosed as such, as materials in a postindustrial world seldom are, and it's difficult to know whether her sculptures, painted in garish colors, are heavy or light, solid or hollow. Both boxy and blobby, they often make the formless funny and the abject everyday, not at all as those states were once imagined by

Georges Bataille and Julia Kristeva.[2] Imagine a Costco stack of Adult Depends, wetted and hardened, then paint-bombed in acid yellows, greens, and purples, or a giant banana split with all-over sprinkles left outside, then sealed with a roughened resin. (The best description of her work might be the lyrics of "MacArthur Park," more than once voted the worst song of all time: "Someone left the cake out in the rain . . .") The effect is an almost oxymoronic one of rigid fragility or arrested entropy, as though Harrison had updated the science fictions of Robert Smithson, Thomas Pynchon, and J. G. Ballard in the 1960s with the science facts of product glut, junk space, and climate destruction today.

In such a world distinctions between natural and artificial are overrun. Harrison remediates her sculpture not only with other art forms but also across the linked spaces of commodity display and digital information, and it picks up bits and pieces from both realms along the way. However, to count as sculpture at all, she insists that it must confront us physically in our space. Although "remediation" suggests a smooth transfer between image worlds, her objects seem more physically stuck than smoothly networked.[3] Dysfunctionality, not interconnectivity, is the watchword here. As in a scene from a David Cronenberg film like *Videodrome* (1983), Harrison jams a USB flash drive loaded with Harun Farocki films into the purple blob of a body in *Bears Ears* (2017), and an Apple AirPort crashes into the pink and yellow tower of *Vampire Wannabes* (2010). Like our bodies, these objects appear resistant on account of their materiality as well as their proclivity for breakdown. In fact, some sculptures look as though they had passed *through* our bodies, as though they had endured an intestinal acid bath. Harrison imagines consumption, both aesthetic and commercial, in literal terms. Oldenburg is the predecessor to name-check now; his great *Cash Register* (1961), which also appears semidigested, comes first to mind. Harrison collapses product display and art exhibition even more than Oldenburg did in *The Store* (1961). Her use of mannequins signals this conflation too (as it does in the work of her contemporaries Isa Genzken, Thomas Hirschhorn, and John Miller), and she confuses public realm and private space even more than Oldenburg did in his *Bedroom Ensemble* (1963).[4]

The psychoanalyst Ernest Jones declared our first painting to be our fecal smearing as infants. Harrison claims this dubious honor for sculpture, yet her work is anything but a mess. She wrests construction out of destruction, and while her image-object juxtapositions can be abrupt, even brutal, they are also highly calculated, delivered with Flintstonean ingenuity more than Luddite aggressivity. Early on Harrison liked to spell out puns, as in *John Davidson with Mop* (1992), which shows a 1970s poster of the mop-head heartthrob with an actual mop attached to his head, or *Circle Jerk* (1989), where a fluorescent light punctures a metal chair at the angle of erection. (This work anticipated by a year "Minimalism and the Rhetoric of Power," the essay by Anna Chave that chastised Dan Flavin and others, also in literal terms, for phallic geometries.) From the concision of the joke Harrison moved to a compositional mode somewhere between a stalled Rube Goldberg machine and a dream-rebus of images and objects, as in *Huffy Howler* (2004), where a publicity photo of Mel Gibson in *Braveheart* (1995) is clipped to a sheepskin hung lankly on a metal pole, which is attached in turn to a yellow Huffy Howler bike loaded down with cheap handbags stuffed with rocks (its front tire is flat). This arrested seesaw is its own proof that most dreams aren't about wish fulfillment. As Fredric Jameson once remarked of video art, it suggests a blank Surrealism, with the unconscious reimagined as a suburban garage or attic piled up with crappy stuff. At the extreme in this vein, Harrison evokes an Amazon warehouse where guerrilla gremlins have seized the algorithms, or an IKEA storeroom where the poor souls represented in the famous Prinzhorn Collection of "The Artistry of the Mentally Ill" are let loose to assemble the kits.

With Harrison references are no more random than compositions. Mostly American, her image appropriations often locate us in terms of age and class and sometimes in terms of gender too. At times she also deploys the textures of everyday life, such as the paneling in a den, to suggest an economic position or a historical period. Harrison is especially drawn to social media before the regime of Facebook and Instagram, such as paparazzi photos and publicity shots that register lost styles of celebrity and old rituals of fandom. *2 a.m., 2nd Ave.* (1996), a yellow globe set atop a black tripod dotted with photos of Johnny Carson and Carroll O'Connor in tuxedos, looks like a disinterred time capsule or a wayward alien probe from *Lost in Space*. Yet three decades later it seems weirdly prophetic. Even if we don't recognize the late-night TV host and the Archie Bunker actor, we realize that a cross between an omnipresent showman and a bigoted uncle from Queens occupied the White House.

If celebrity sometimes carries over from one era to the next, fandom is often stranded in time. In *1:1 (Wonton: John)* (1996) Harrison offers thirty-eight pictures of personages named John on a wall, along with an equal number of ceramic wontons on a pedestal, for us to consume (though we can't eat either). Most of these Johns are entertainers, and though some are stars, others are flash-in-the-pan teen idols. It's like a shrine to pop crushes past, one that the young Albrecht Dürer, in a reproduction of a self-portrait deposed to the floor, seems to look upon with disapproval. Here Harrison mimics the attachments of young people as shown in bedroom pictures. In more recent reflections on stardom she seems to tap her own investments. In a suite of bravura drawings of Amy Winehouse (2011–2012) Harrison limns the tragic singer in the idioms of Picasso, de Kooning, and others, as though to hold on to her, manically and melancholically, by repeated imaging alone. The drawings collect and combine styles, a bit like pastiches by Richard Prince and David Salle, but the effect is to vivify Winehouse, not to vivisect her.

In a move mediated by Warhol, Harrison deploys canned vegetables as found signs. In the decade when she was born, many families turned to industrial food (first canned, then frozen) as a testament to technological progress as well as social standing. (For the Marxist economist Ernst Mandel, the industrialization of produce was a signal achievement of late capitalism; fresh vegetables pointed to the relative poverty of farm life.)[5] At that time canned stuff represented a (lower) middle class on the rise; today many art world denizens associate it instead with food drives for the urban poor or emergency provisions for the next catastrophe. Like Warhol with his *Tunafish Disasters* (1963), Harrison signals a threat with her packages. An early work, *Untitled (Poles for a Dangerous Art World)* (1992), features substances such as bread, beeswax, tuna, and hair extensions stuck in Ziploc bags and suspended from different sticks, some innocuous, such as old brooms, others less so, such as billy clubs. Everyday life in America is still, is ever more, a matter of not-so-accidental death and disaster.

The cans point to expiration dates in another way as well. Harrison is interested in the shelf life of culture, especially celebrity culture, which in her reckoning is time-coded to more than the Warholian fifteen minutes but not much more. A hundred years ago Max Ernst updated the adage *Fiat ars, vita pereat* (let there be art, let life perish) to *Fiat modes* (let there be fashion); today "fame" is the more likely substitute. Yet Harrison highlights the vicissitudes of celebrity instead—John Davidson mopped off the stage, Mel Gibson hung up like a pelt, many of the Johns pulled after a single hit song or TV show.[6] The dimming of a star is also surveyed in *Teaching Bo to Count Backwards* (1996–1997), a shelf arrayed with thirty cans of olives punctuated by three paparazzi shots of Bo Derek, a sexy beauty of the 1980s, shepherded by her husband, the actor-director John Derek. The work conveys a canned life lived under the heat of the camera and destined to spoil soon. Like the Winehouse drawings, the Derek tableau encapsulates an entire miniseries of abuse by men—boyfriends, spouses, fathers, agents, and fans. Whereas Mike Kelley and Cady Noland stage a toxic masculinity in terms of the weird things that boys of all ages make and do in basements and backyards, Harrison reflects on a distressed femininity in the media world at large. Maybe Bo and Amy are to her what Liz and Marilyn were to Warhol.

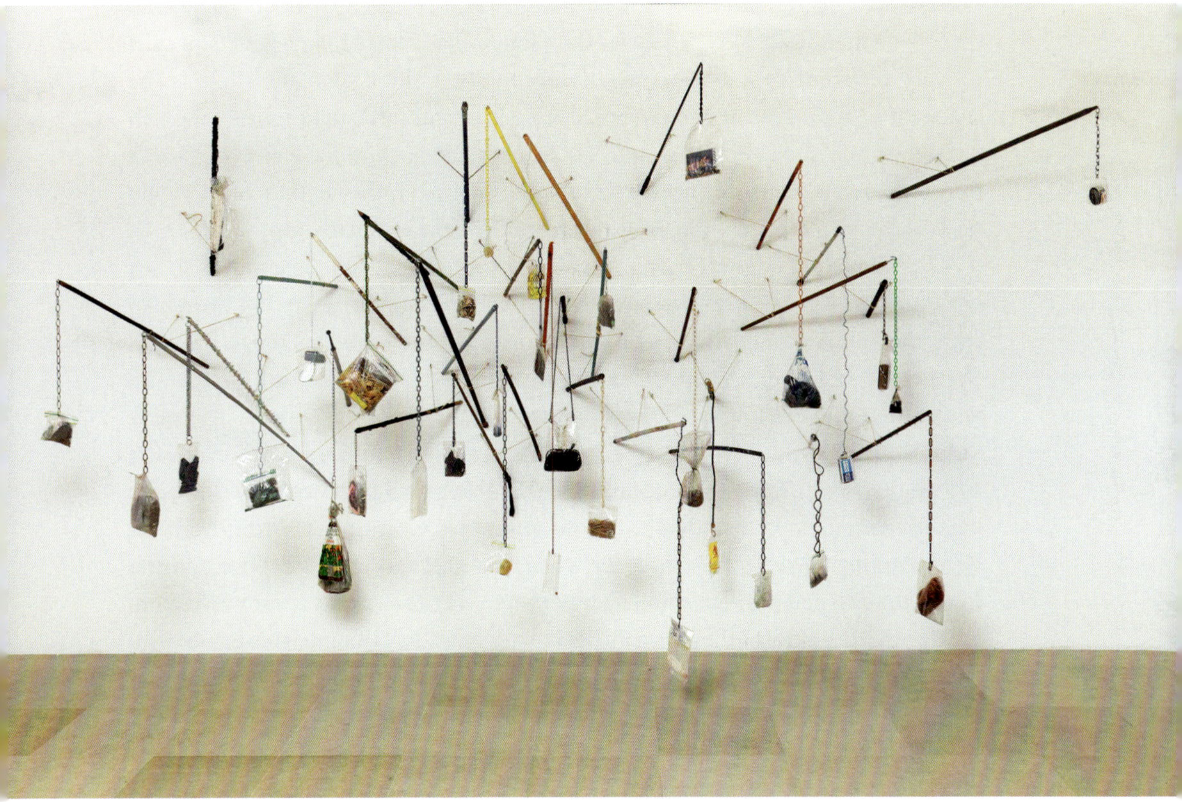

Rachel Harrison, *Untitled (Poles for a Dangerous Art World)*, 1992. Broomsticks, paint roller extension poles, pool cues, billy club, ski pole, chains, ring-pull tabs, Ziploc bags, potting compound, hair extensions, matches, denim, bread, beeswax, Bible, tuna can, vacuum lint, foam, tape, wire, mixed media, 12 × 15½ × 5 feet. © Rachel Harrison. Courtesy the artist and Greene Naftali Gallery.

The stars influence us (etymologically, the word concerns light that flows down from the night sky), but they do so at a great distance. In *1:1 (Wonton: John)* Harrison summons the space of a mostly teen passion that seems so close to its love object (right there on the bedroom wall) yet remains so remote from it (hidden in a gated estate somewhere). She uses stanchions in a related way, as signs less of the detachment of artworks than of the restriction of desired places—from Studio 54 to whatever the exclusive clubs are today. Harrison calls up very different spaces too, ones that are still gendered female, such as the spaces of shopping, as in *Nice Rack* (2006), a greeting card stand refitted with an old phone and cheap barrettes, and of cleaning, as in *All in the Family* (2012), a purple vise that clamps down on an orange Hoover. (If the shelf in *Teaching Bo* nods to Haim Steinbach, the vacuum cleaner smirks at Jeff Koons.)[7]

To what ends does Harrison put all these allusions? One is tempted to see her sculpture as a performance of ideology critique, a neo-Brechtian theater of appropriation, estrangement, and repurposing. "Myth robs language," Roland Barthes wrote in 1957, so "why not rob myth?" "Art is what we do," Carl Andre added in 1967, "culture is what is done to us," so why not use the first to push back on the second?[8] Yet these associations don't quite work. In fact, Harrison is intrigued by the mythical thinking that fuels popular culture (in 2001 she devoted an entire installation to a rumored apparition of the Virgin Mary in Perth Amboy, New Jersey), and her work is concerned less to expose cultural myths than to retell them, often in a perverse way that twists their patriarchal meanings.[9] Like most jokes, many of hers have brunts, and some viewers do find condescension in her art. Certainly there are notes of anger, even violence, but they originate in the culture at large. Her attitude is like that of an ethnographer whose reports from the field mix analysis and appreciation with an occasional touch of derision. At the same time, Harrison doesn't route the cultural circuits traced in the work through her own biography (as does Tracey Emin, say, and many others). As the title of her 2019 survey at the Whitney Museum had it, this is "life hack," not autofiction.

What's in play, then, is not ideology critique so much as mimetic exacerbation: Harrison takes a bad thing and makes it worse, and then combines it with another bad thing to make it worse still. Historically this strategy runs back through the Zurich Dadaists, who, as Hugo Ball once wrote, embodied the "dissonances" of the time "to the point of self-disintegration," and on to the young Marx, who urged his readers "to make petrified conditions dance by singing them their own song."[10] Adapted by artists like Isa Genzken as well as writers like George Saunders, this means, among other things, to travesty whatever counts as the lingua franca of the moment. Art is not immune from this travesty. In a 2017 press release presented as a burlesque of a roundtable, Harrison has a character named "Judith Beheading Holofernes" say simply, "Make art history scream."[11]

In her work the primary target is the old typology of sculpture, not only the figure but also the models that displaced it, such as the construction, the readymade, and the found object. Harrison mocks the structural integrity of constructed sculpture; she knocks over a bottle rack in a 2016 piece; and she takes the piss out of *The Enigma of Isidore Ducasse* (1920), a proto-Surrealist object by Man Ray, in her *Warren Beatty* (2007), which consists of blankets used for moving thrown over an amorphous mass. Harrison gives Postminimalism more mixed reviews. Though her early painted things like socks look back to Hesse, and her recent installations of suspended cords call up Fred Sandback, both appreciatively, the papered doors of *Mind the Gap* (1996) poke fun at the prop pieces of Serra. Harrison also shifts his associations of material, process, and labor away from the industrial arena long identified with men to the domestic realm still associated with women. Nods are made to Institution Critique as well. *Nice Rack* cites Hans Haacke, other works remember Michael Asher, and Harrison drags her sculpture through the behind-the-scenes spaces of the art world that Louise Lawler has pictured.[12] But her heart isn't really in such analysis. For Harrison images and discourses cut across and coalesce with one another in ways that can't be easily parsed in critical terms. Sometimes, when she flies her Rauschenberg flag too fervidly, the work exudes a carefree attitude, and this allows the viewer to pass by too quickly.

Psychoanalytically speaking, Mignon Nixon has argued, feminist art of the 1980s focused on questions of desire, whereas abject art of the 1990s tapped the energy of the drives; in doing so, the former featured the commodity image, while the latter favored the part object.[13] These are separate, even opposed models of art-making, the first associated with Dada and its followers, the second with Surrealism and its descendants, but Harrison partakes of both (her crossing them is another way of combining Warhol and Hesse). In this respect she doesn't trash the Dadaist readymade and the Surrealist found object so much as she refashions them. In the process Harrison also adapts vernacular forms such as everyday containers—small, like baggies, jars, and cans, as well as large, like the pantry shelf in *Teaching Bo*, the tchotchke stand in *Nice Rack*, and the teen shrine in *1:1*—which evoke a range of activities from shopping and storing to wishing and hoping. Some of her objects go so far as to reimagine the human figure, but it returns sea-changed, either as a precarious assemblage, like *Cindy* (2004), a green stack of rickety tables topped by a blonde wig and set behind a drywall, or as an entropic blob, like *Al Gore* (2007), a lime and pink mess of a menhir with a thermostat attached. Such works suggest an individual shot through with the social and discombobulated by the assault, with front, sides, and backs that don't much cohere. Nonetheless, some figures do seem animated, but less as human fetishes than as contemporary totems. It's as if they could speak to us, and to walk among them is a bit like the natural procession through "the forests of symbols" imagined by Baudelaire in "Correspondences," only restaged in an abandoned shopping mall. Although "to travesty" once signified "to dress so as to appear ridiculous" ("transvestite" long carried this negative connotation too), Harrison aims to reclaim as much as to ridicule. She even intimates that a collective good might be "wrested from commodities in their decline" (as Giorgio Agamben puts it), that there might be a glimmer of utopia in our morass of reification.[14] This is another valence of "life hack."

This work thus reveals a social dimension that runs counter to its nihilistic bent. Historically, artists turned to collage and assemblage—to juxtapositions of disparate images and objects—in order to open up the traditional work of art. Harrison repurposes these old devices in order to include, through such proxies, diverse *subjects*—different perceptions and disparate perspectives. Oldenburg once described his *Store* objects as "birth flesh-fragments" torn from the Lower East Side of Manhattan; Harrison extends this range of perspectives radically.[15] This is why her sculpture is often not only funny but also egalitarian: it convokes a chorus, however cacophonous, of many voices. The objects tell tall tales, crack jokes that even they don't get, and argue contradictory points of view all at the same time. The roundtable imagined in her 2017 press release includes artists from the classical Greeks through Caravaggio, Marinetti, and Duchamp, to Nam June Paik, Lee Lozano, and Lynda Benglis, and on to Kara Walker, Andrea Fraser, and Hito Steyerl. This is art history travestied and made utopian at once, and it points to the conflict at the core of any democracy worth the name, an antagonism that, per Ernesto Laclau, Chantal Mouffe, and other political theorists, democracy requires: we need generative *dissensus*, not *e pluribus unum* kumbaya. Harrison looks to this space of conflict and negotiation despite all the crap and noise around us. Like Winnie in the Beckett play, she talks about happy days even as she stands half-buried in very bad ones.

Harrison concluded her 2019 survey with a colorful group of fourteen discrete works set on white pedestals, brought together in a circle surrounded by a ring of gray folding chairs that face outward. *Al Gore* was the central totem here, and among others was a figure painted salmon and called *Travis Gregory* (2016), with an Antonin Scalia mouse pad at his feet. Leaders like Gore and Scalia are patriarchal, to be sure, and in good Dadaist fashion Harrison took a whack at the most Père Ubu of contemporary politicians too—her piñata

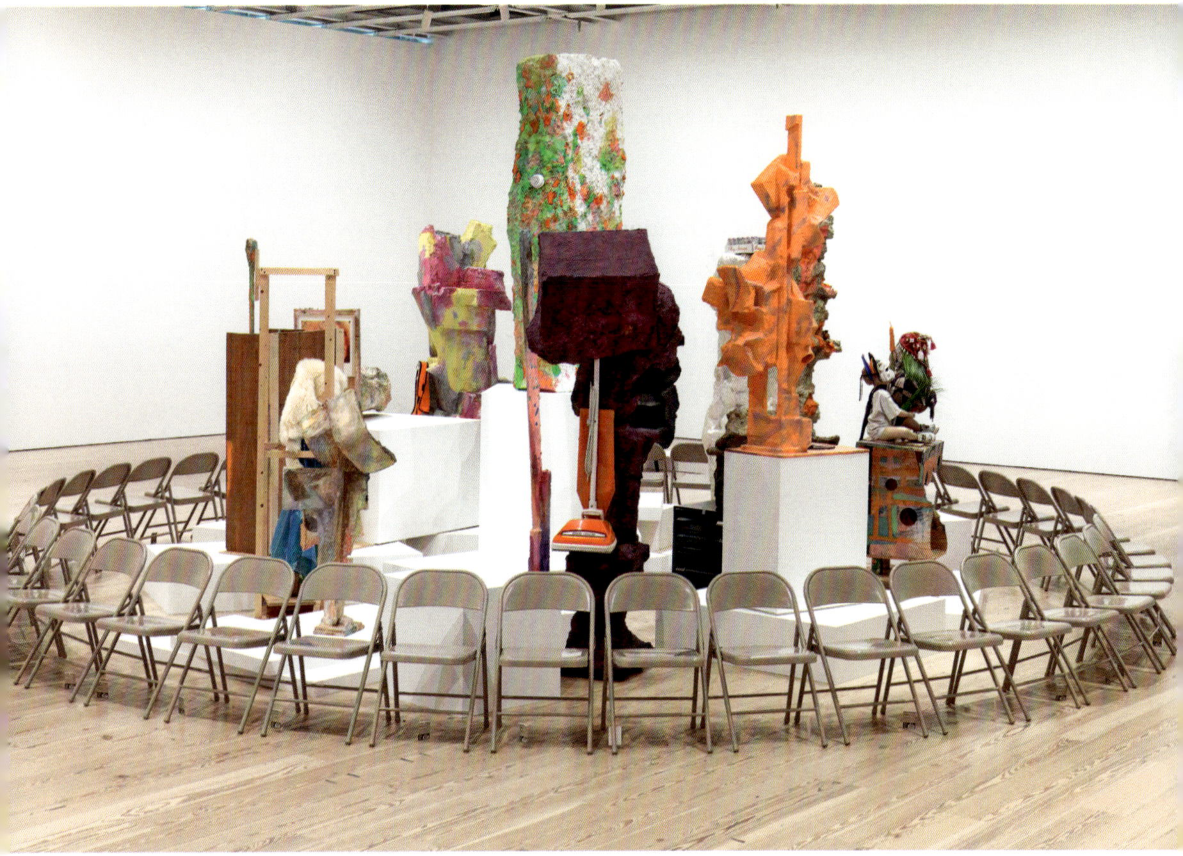

View of *Rachel Harrison Life Hack* at the Whitney Museum of American, 2019, with *Vampire Wannabes*, 2010, *Al Gore*, 2007, *All in the Family*, 2012, *Travis Gregory*, 2016, and other works. © Rachel Harrison. Courtesy the artist and Greene Naftali Gallery.

versions of Trump were a spring 2016 hit. These are pathetic men, "life hacks" in yet another sense, but not all are utterly craven. (Gore looks very much like that cake left out in the rain, which, as he has long warned us, only gets warmer by the minute.) In fact, if we squinted a little, the circle of figures resembled an assembly of Day-Glo totem poles, a political *ding* on drugs, a funky parliament designed by George Clinton or Sun Ra. Yet the ring of chairs was ambiguous. Did these placeholders pen these figures in, lock them up, or did "we the people" protect them? Was it both? Was the suggestion that we should turn our backs on them and look to each other for ways forward?

In a 2002 video titled *Edmund's Base* (that trope again of sculptural hierarchy that stands in for sociopolitical hierarchy), Harrison quotes the upstart Edmund from *King Lear*: "Edmund the base / Shall top the legitimate. I grow; I prosper: / Now, gods, stand up for bastards." Harrison is certainly on the side of bastards, but she also knows that Edmund is a psycho, that bastards can be just bastards, and that some are hell-bent on wrecking state and society alike.

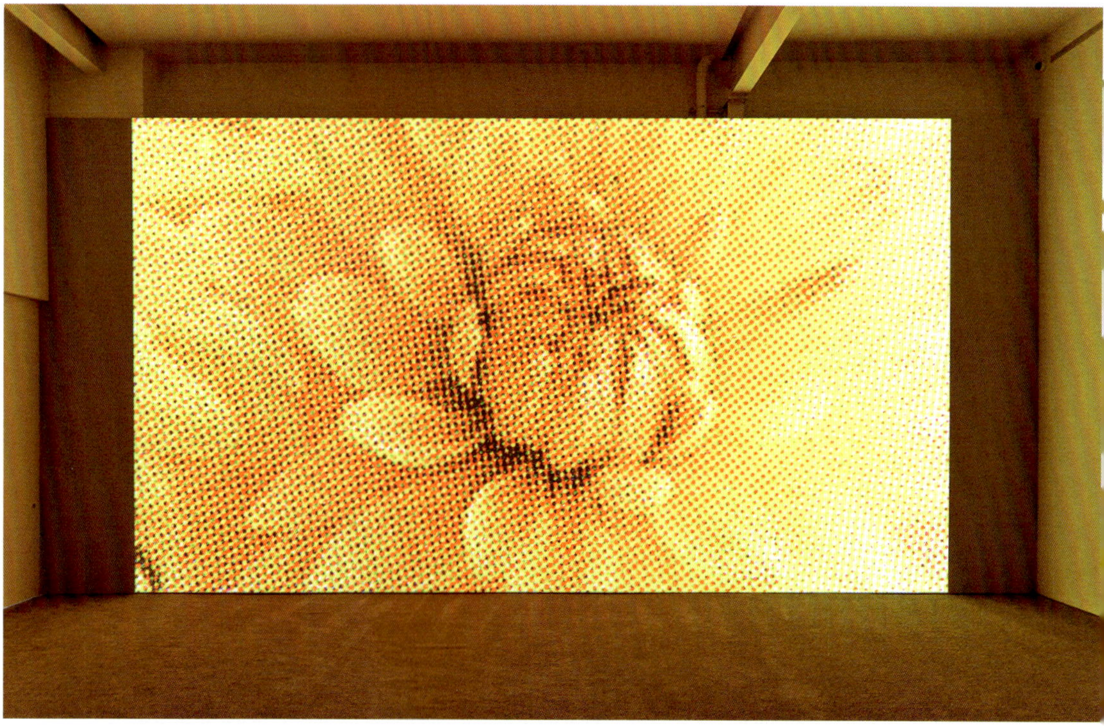

Mungo Thomson, *Volume 3: Flowers (Nahbild)*, 2015–2022 (detail). 4K video with music by Sven-Åke Johansson, 10:08 minutes. © Mungo Thomson. Courtesy the artist and Karma.

29 How Not To

A "volume" is either a single book of printed sheets or a book that is part of a series. The word, which stems from the late Middle English for a parchment of writing, is rooted in the Latin *volvere*, "to roll." In *Time Life* (2022) Mungo Thomson plays on a few meanings of the term. Long in the making, this work consists of seven high-resolution stop-motion videos, roughly two to twelve minutes in length, that Thomson calls "volumes," and each rolls through a great number of images and texts, all taken from books that the artist photographed, painstakingly, page by page.[1] To produce each volume Thomson mounted a Canon 5D camera on a copy stand (its white bars on a black ground sometimes appear) and attached it to a Macintosh computer loaded with Dragonframe stop-motion software. The resulting animations are played at breakneck speed (five at eight frames per second and two even faster), accompanied by mostly percussive music, both curated and commissioned, that underscores the jerky rapidity of the editing (of course, "volume" also means level of sound). In five of the videos Thomson synced the images to the music, while in the other two a score was composed for a finished cut.

For the first four volumes—*Foods of the World*, *Animal Locomotion*, *Flowers (Nahbild)*, and *1000 Questions*—Thomson selected from the *Time-Life* series of books published from 1961 to 2003. These popular publications drew from the vast archives of the two eponymous magazines to construct instructional guides to a host of topics from cooking and craft to technology, science, and history. According to Thomson, one tagline for these books was "Become an Instant Expert"; today they are often used in homeschooling; and the series as a whole suggests an "analog prototype for the internet" (the series declined in popularity as use of the web expanded).[2] With his format established, Thomson turned to other sources and subjects for his final three volumes—*Sideways Thought*, *The Working End*, and *Color Guide*.

Foods of the World draws on four cookbooks from the *Time-Life* series, some of which explore international cuisine. Countless pages of cooking and baking flash by, switching between image and text and vertical and horizontal orientations, all set to a soundtrack involving chimes, castanets, drums, and bells. Ironically, given the rampant appropriation at work, Thomson centers the copyright symbol for the first half-minute, but it's not clear what might count as pirated information since the sequences taken from the books are too interrupted, too many pages are cropped, and the images and texts pass by too quickly for any instruction to occur. This holds for the other volumes as well. Although some are based on teaching guides, they are almost the opposite of how-to videos: we couldn't learn from these animations no matter how hard we tried.

Flowers (Nahbild) is a flurry of floral images, both photographed and painted, some with text, most on the horizontal, and all accompanied by a drumroll that varies in speed and volume; this video might qualify as a still life if it weren't the opposite of still. Here the subject of the source books is gardening, but again little knowledge of this activity is conveyed, and even less of botany. Close-up shots alternate with framed ones, abstract images with hyperrealist ones (*Nahbild*, the title of the soundtrack and the subtitle of this volume, literally means "near image"), and as petals and pistils turn into pixels and vice versa, the lines between the organic and the electronic, the analogue and the digital, are literally blurred. What is color in nature and what is color in culture, or has the difference between the two—which the genre of the still life long reflected on—become all but impossible to determine?

While *Flowers* evokes all-over painting, *Color Guide* calls up the old avant-garde paradigm of the monochrome. This volume was made from a single 2021 Pantone Color Formula Guide photographed at eight swatches of color per second and sequenced from front to back as in the source book. Matched with synthesizer music of a high tone combined with a low pulse like a heartbeat, no fewer than 2,161 colors appear in its four and a half minutes of running time. Each page of the guide has seven swatches of one color ranging in value from dark to light, and "the pulsing in the video is the rhythm as each page reaches its brightest color."[3] Otherwise there's no evident order to the mostly yellow, red, green, and blue screens that pass by. The soundtrack is the most visceral of all the volumes, even though the images are the most retinal. This is one tension created by the volume; another is the tension between the chroma on the printed page and the color in the digital video. At times we confuse the craquelure of the paper (which also evokes that of canvas and skin) with the pixilation of the screen. What exactly is the fundamental ground or support here—paper, photograph, video, or a combination of all three—or is the question of distinct media rendered entirely moot?[4]

With *Sideways Thought* Thomson turns from monochromes to sculptures, Rodin's in particular. In this fifth volume he also moves on from his *Time-Life* source materials, pulling some 4,000 pages from over fifty books on the artist. Thomson organized his images in stacks so that, once videoed, they produce a

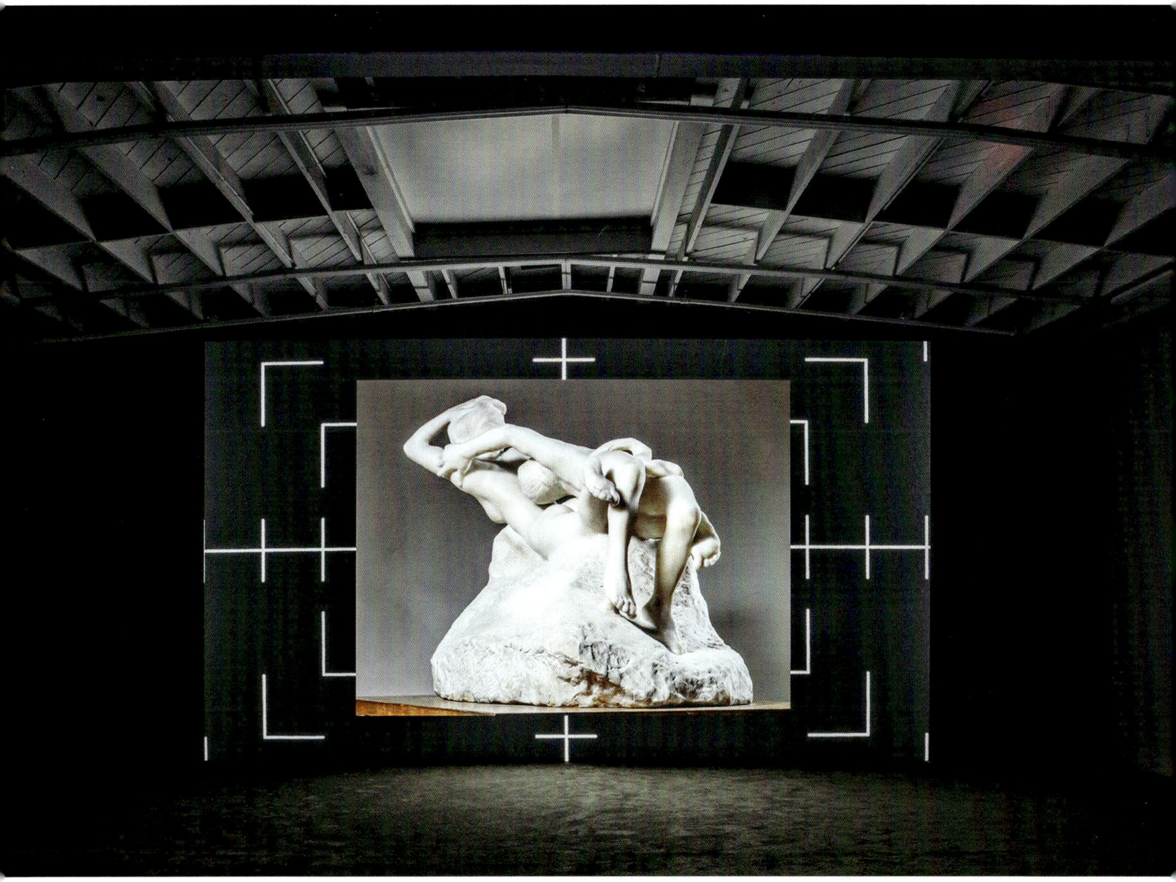

Mungo Thomson, *Volume 5: Sideways Thought*, 2020–2022 (detail). 4K video with music by Ernst Karel, 8:09 minutes. Photo: Joshua White. © Mungo Thomson. Courtesy the artist and Karma.

clockwise rotation of each sculpture, a circling that seems driven by the pulsating score (the "roll" in this volume is especially intense). In modern aesthetics from Diderot to Greenberg, sculpture was deemed subordinate to painting because it requires time to circumambulate and so is not as immediate. In *Sideways Thought* sculpture pushes back against this old bias by means of photography and video. At the same time, this volume produces a tension of its own between the immateriality of the images and the materiality of the sculptures. More than any predecessor, Rodin stressed both the tactility of the medium and the touch of the artist as inscribed in clay, plaster, and bronze; in fact, the way that his expressive fragments register his own subjectivity came to be taken as one source of his great originality. However, this modernist value of uniqueness is undercut by how often his sculptural elements are repeated in different ensembles, an operation that this volume also underscores. Thus in his work the singular artwork confronts its historical antagonist, the industrial copy, and this artisanal-industrial tension in Rodin is doubled by the photographic-digital tension in *Sideways Thought*.[5]

Animal Locomotion also juxtaposes a postindustrial present with an industrial past. Here the source materials are *Time-Life* books devoted to exercise and sport—from stretching and massaging to jogging and running, from calisthenics, weightlifting, and martial arts to swimming, rowing, and biking—and the images are set to a computer score that mimics chimes and pipes. The title calls up the first experiments in time-motion studies undertaken in the late nineteenth century by Eadweard Muybridge and Étienne-Jules Marey, who devised distinct versions of chronophotography that were then adapted not only by artists such as the Futurists and Duchamp but also, and more importantly, by engineers who developed "the scientific management" of labor, first in the factory (Frederick Taylor) and then in the home (Frank and Lillian Gilbreth). With the consumerist stage of postwar capitalism, this technical disciplining of the productive body penetrated leisure activities as well: hence the fitness and sports industries represented in the images. "Animal Locomotion," this volume suggests, remains a booming business in which we perform the roles of producer, product, and consumer in one.[6]

The Working End also features instructional manuals, here for the tying of knots ("the working end" is the end of the rope advanced through a knot). Once an essential skill in maritime labor, knot-tying is now mostly a hobby. In fact, about half of the knots in this volume are ornamental, made for their own sake. Again, as though driven by the rapid drumroll of the score, the images of *The Working End* come too fast, and too many steps are dropped out, for any instruction to occur. Thomson invokes the transmission of technique only to

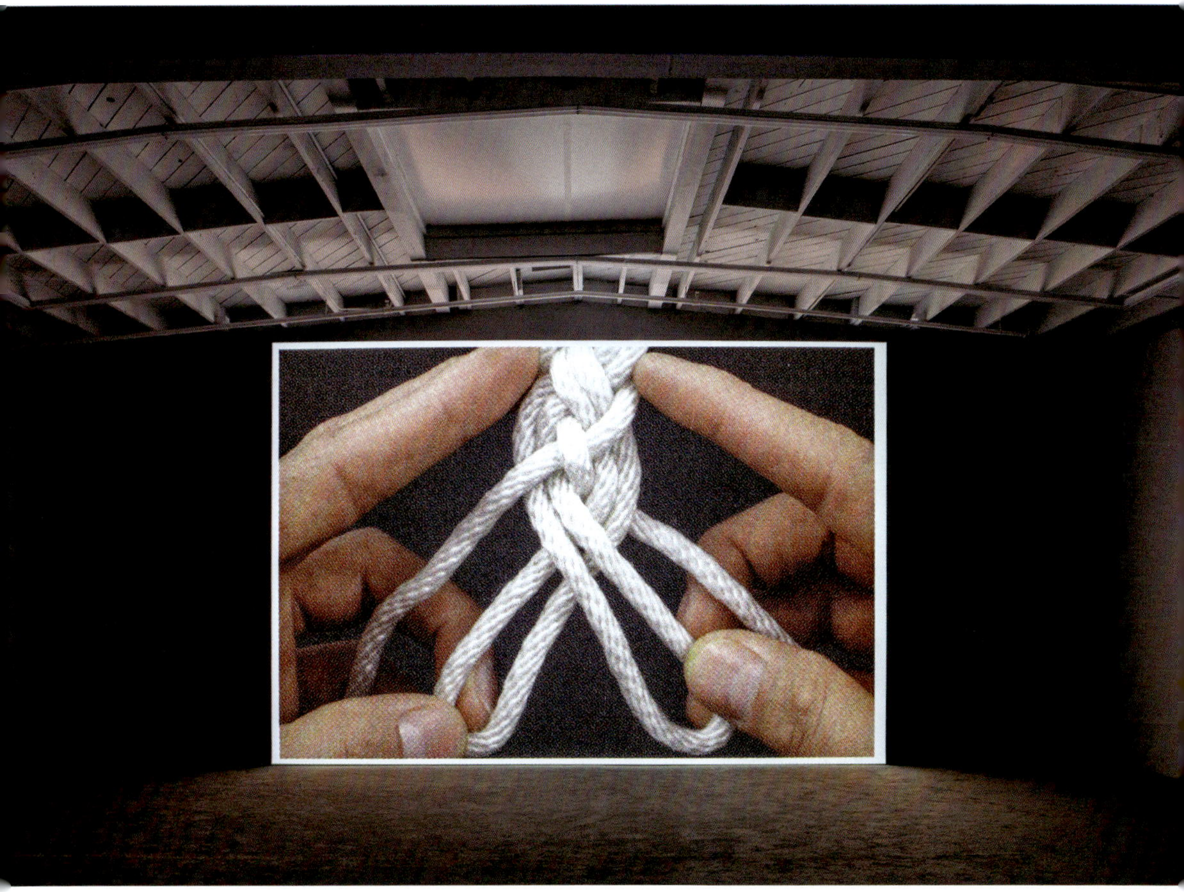

Mungo Thomson, *Volume 6: The Working End*, 2021–2022 (detail). 4K video with music by Pauline Oliveros, 4:51 minutes. Photo: Joshua White. © Mungo Thomson. Courtesy the artist and Karma.

thwart it, and many knots end up untied or tangled. In this volume "the working end" doesn't work.

While *The Working End* promises skill only to foil it, *1000 Questions*, drawn from another *Time-Life* multivolume set, does the same with knowledge. Myriad whys, whats, and hows roll by in just over two minutes, too rapidly for us to offer any answers (even if we had them), and the music, which recalls a wind tunnel, only adds to the sense of frantic rush. This volume occupies a middle ground between the epistemophilic inquiries of the child ("Where do butterflies go when it rains?") and the countless searches that occur on the internet every day and night. The *Time-Life* books assumed a relatively stable nature and a mostly progressive culture: the series believed that the universe can be known, and that mankind will continue to know more and better. But this is in tension with the vicissitudes of technology (which figures prominently in *1000 Questions*) and the fact that the world will never be transparent to us. (This volume could be titled after the 2020 novel by Benjamin Labatut, *When We Cease to Understand the World*.) If put in a loop, *1000 Questions* might be experienced as more torture than test.

As I watch the seven volumes of *Time Life*, my own questions revolve around matters of medium, instruction, process, and archive. There are several media in play—books, photographs, video, software programs, and music. Thomson displays most of these openly, as though to answer, almost incidentally, the old modernist call "to bare the device"; we see fluttering pages, wire bindings, copy stands, levels, tape, Post-it notes, and so on. Yet what emerges is not any medium-specificity grounded in a single practice, but rather an intermedial condition that allows us to consider the hybridity of our media ecology at large. "This is not a just image," Jean-Luc Godard remarks in his 1970 film *Vent d'est*, "this is just an image," but this comment was made at a time when the critique of the truth value of representation was still urgent. Now, for good and bad, such suspicion is almost automatic, and Thomson presents such a surfeit of images that the question of a "just" representation doesn't occur in any case. Moreover, the very surplus of images exceeds the usual categories of how they come to us—as singular, sequential, or serial—and in fact the volumes manifest neither the montage of cinema nor the flow of television.[7] During the media explosion of the postwar period Marshall McLuhan held that each new medium aims to absorb the previous one (his prime example was television vis-à-vis radio), and during the media explosion at the turn of the millennium Lev Manovich argued that the computer and internet did much the same with television and film.[8] McLuhan and Manovich were more techno-optimistic than Thomson is now: at times the implication of the volumes is that each new medium all but destroys the ones before it. Certainly, the making of the videos necessitated the destruction of most of the source books.[9]

For Thomson the old *Time-Life* books were also optimistic insofar as they were pledged to self-improvement.[10] But then instructional guides are never simple, let alone innocent; they work to discipline bodies and minds as well.[11] Recall how time-motion studies led to the regimentation of labor, and how, in our own time, training in exercise, say, easily slips into a regime of drilling (not to mention consuming). In this way the volumes underscore the world of rampant testing in which we live. The copy stand sometimes looks like a target, and the rapid-fire images and texts often make for a barrage.[12] At the same time, the volumes subvert both instruction and discipline. Again, like flash cards that go by too fast, the images and texts can't be processed, and the given sequences are broken up in such a way that we can't learn the very activities that the source books are made to inculcate. For Walter Benjamin the prime function of cinematic montage was to teach us how to absorb the shocks of modern industrial life. In a related way the volumes might help us to weather the informational storm of contemporary internet existence. Yet they also push back against its drives to dematerialize and disembody. Along with the percussive music, the frenetic editing makes the volumes physical—corporeal—in a way that resensitizes us more than the opposite.[13]

One way to understand the volumes is to relate them to what film scholar Salomé Aguilera Skvirsky calls "the process genre," or "processual representation in which the important steps in a process are shown in chronological order."[14] The landmarks of this genre include some of the formats already mentioned: chronophotography and time-motion studies, industrial and ethnographic films, educational and tutorial programs on television, and countless how-to videos on YouTube. For Skvirsky processual representation is best served by film because of its "constitutive capacity to visually and analytically decompose movement and to curate its recomposition." This is where Thomson intervenes in the genre. He decomposes and recomposes movement, but hardly so as "to display the successive steps or phases of a process." In this way the main purpose of process demonstrations—to "bring out the skilled character of technical processes"—is undercut.[15] If the process genre comprises an "aesthetic of labor" for Skvirsky, we might see the volumes in terms of an aesthetic of antidiscipline. And if the process genre is concerned above all to provide knowledge and to effect fascination, as Skvirsky also argues, the volumes interrupt both. There's no continuous process to enlighten and absorb us, no completed product to delight and reward us. If we are instructed, it is, paradoxically, in how-not-to.[16]

This how-not-to aspect is also a function of the outdated status of the source materials. The *Time-Life* books are artifacts of the second half of the twentieth century. The Thomson volumes thus register changes not only in techniques but also in styles: clothing, equipment, even people appear outmoded. What were these activities? Who were these people? The 1,001st question might be: Where do image, text, and information go—where do humans go—when they are superseded or otherwise lost in time? Where but that amorphous nonplace we call, too loosely, "the archive"? This is how Thomson sees his project: as a mimesis of how "reference encyclopedias, photo books, how-to guides and production manuals" are "scanned by a high-speed robotic book scanner, the type used by universities and tech companies to archive libraries."[17] In this automated process, even as the books are "saved," they are also often destroyed, "literally dematerialized in order to become data for the internet."[18] Even more problematically, they are less preserved than put in deep freeze (literally so: at great cost servers must be kept at extremely low temperatures). It is as though to record today is also to stash away forever, that is, to forget (Plato already feared as much about writing). For whom or what is all this information on the various iterations of the internet to be "saved"? Might it be archived less for us than for whomever or whatever comes after us? Here the title *Time Life* takes on an uncanny valence: human knowledge and activity contained in a vast time capsule-cum-trash bin lost in space.[19]

Yet Thomson intervenes crucially at this point too. In his mimicking of the automated operations of scanners and servers, he also parodies them with the old-fashioned human actions of framing, shooting, and editing. He even returns the digital to its original sense of the finger, redeploying ancient skills of eye-hand-and-mind coordination along with new forms of technical composition, and so interrupts machine vision even as it becomes more and more the rule.[20] His art allows us to reflect on techniques of the human body and psyche at the point of their historical eclipse.

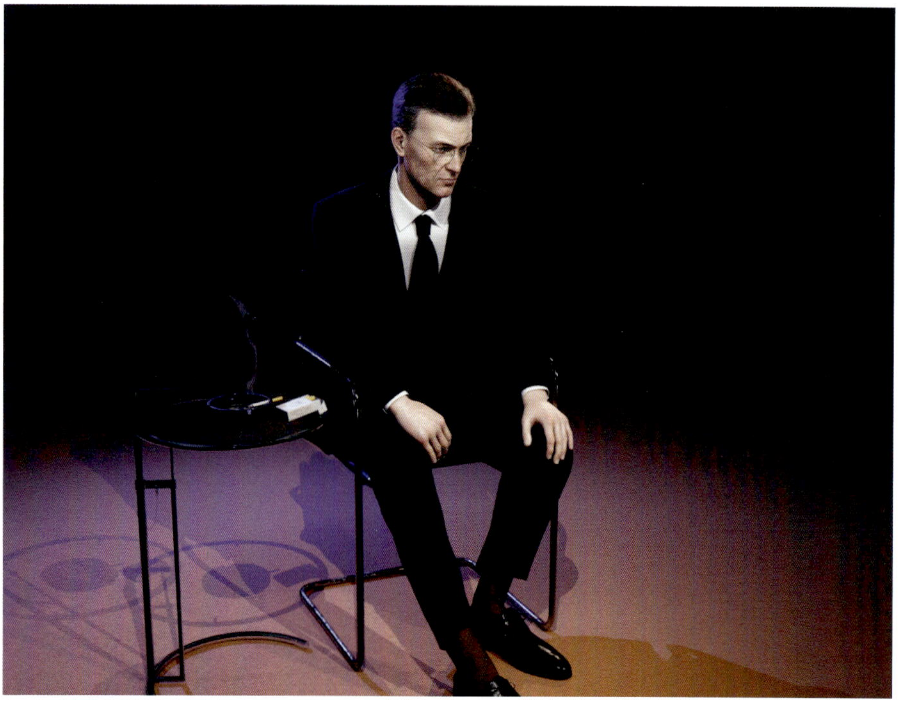

Ed Atkins, *The Worm*, 2021 (still). Digital video projection, color, sound, 12 minutes 40 seconds.

30 Media Corpsing

How many of us, when we speak with our parents, feel like stock characters, as though we had become our own simulations? In *The Worm* (2021) the English artist Ed Atkins presents a telephone call with his mother in this very manner.[1] In the roughly thirteen-minute animation his mum is heard but not seen, while Atkins is rendered, by way of performance capture technology, as a digital avatar who listens attentively, mumbling sympathy or surprise, asking a question only when her narrative falters. Aurally close, the mother is spatially distant (*The Worm* was made during the Covid-19 lockdown), while the son is almost too present on the large screen—there are extreme closeups, odd angles, abrupt cuts, awkward gestures, and unconscious tics—even though we know what we see is not truly Atkins.[2] His double, a three-dimensional model purchased online, is no double at all. The usually scruffy artist appears as a natty television host in a dark windowpane suit with wire-rim glasses, who diverges from the often-abject characters featured in his previous videos. And the setup, with its sound stage, blue light, stylish chair, small table, whiskey glass, Silk Cut cigarettes, and ashtray, is indeed that of a studio interview, a genre that conflates reality and artifice in its own way. One inspiration for *The Worm* was the final TV appearance of the English writer Dennis Potter, who, at the point of death from cancer in 1994, talks, bluntly yet poignantly, about the immediacy of sensuous experience (a plum flower outside his window strikes him as the "blossomest blossom"), his commitment to writing till the end, his faith in human community over "the rumor" that is God, and the corruption of journalism and politics by Rupert Murdoch (already then!).[3]

The mum talks about her family—some about her insensitive father, more about her depressive mother—and how she took on the worries of the latter, especially about "lovability," but to little avail, mostly because such cares couldn't be expressed openly (depression was euphemized as "weekend letdown"). The theme of her reminiscences is emotional inheritance, in particular how people pass on everyday unhappiness, and we watch the avatar struggle to metabolize this misery even though (or precisely because) he's not altogether human. "The way she talks of her mother, Nanny Bea, is how I could talk about my mother," Atkins writes. "Thwarted artists, manic depressives, chronic dysmorphics through and through. All of which is contagious, hereditary poison." This "empathy-mirroring" was arduous for both parties, a self-conscious performance, but it was "also love," Atkins insists. "Love! Tenderness!"

This point brings into focus the import of his titles. Consider *Get Life/Love's Work*, the title of the 2021 show at the New Museum where Atkins debuted *The Worm*. To "get life" is an ethical imperative, in this case to address the repressions in nuclear families and to resist the predations of media technologies. Yet to "get life" is also a prison sentence, and both these struggles can go on forever. "The worm" is multivalent too. A worm is base, like the spider that represents the formless for Georges Bataille, lowly like a daughter burdened with the pain of her mother, squirmy like a son who can't settle the debts of the past. "The worm of time" comes to mind as well, the turns of fortune through the generations, as does "The Sick Rose," the Blake "song of experience" in which a worm threads together eros and disease: "O Rose thou art sick. / The invisible worm, / That flies in the night / In the howling storm: / Has found out thy bed / Of crimson joy: / And his dark secret love / Does thy life destroy." This allusion calls up another source cited by Atkins, *Love's Work*, the 1995 memoir of the English philosopher Gillian Rose, who, like Potter, was brought to an early "reckoning with life" (the subtitle of her book) by a death sentence of cancer. This sick Rose, who writes magnificently about eros and disease, argues that the near-oxymoronic work of love is to convert melancholy into mourning—a Freudian labor also important to Atkins—and then, somehow, into delight: "I want to sob and sob and sob," Rose tells us, "until the prolonged skrieking becomes a shout of joy."[4] Atkins desires this transformation too. Even as *The Worm* foregrounds the difficulties of his mother, the death of his father, also from cancer, looms in the background, as it does in other of his videos (Atkins calls his characters "dead men, surrogates, auto cadavers").[5]

At times the maternal monologue verges on confession, yet there is no priest here, only a son, one who, rather than talk about his mother, listens to her talk about her mother. The expected analysand becomes the unexpected analyst, and this also makes the Atkins avatar squirm. The fact that he processes private matters in a public setting (fictively in a television studio, actually in an art gallery) makes us squirm too, especially as we are reminded how personal exposure has become the obscene norm in social media. Atkins adapts the Lacanian term "extimacy" for this everyday confusion of the intimate and the alien. "Everything's become involutional," he writes in a free association typical of his hyperbolic prose. "Think family, heredity, history, antecedents. Think of history as a movement inward maybe." Yet, rather than see this involution as a limitation only, Atkins wants to run with it, to revalue it. "Going inward in memory, in body, in heredity, in technology, and, of course, in psychology. That we might pursue this psychical memory . . . bliss."

The sound of *The Worm* is as penetrative as the image is immersive. The avatar appears as "a country of pores, wrinkles, and, I hope, the tiny inflections and winces of a detailed, silent response." So what kind of realism is at stake here? The video is hardly realist in the old sense of referential; its setup is entirely artifactual. Yet Atkins seeks not to reiterate the technological derealization of the world so much as to resist it. His aesthetic goal is to "model those parts of life that steadfastly elude representation." "That's my utopianism: a faith in the eternal singularity of materiality," which he locates above all in "the irreducibility of IRL/mortal experience." This realism is rooted in the body and the psyche, especially in extreme states of abjection and trauma (Atkins is interested in Kristeva and Lacan as well as Bataille).[6] It is the real as remainder, understood as that which resists the symbolic order—a task made all the more difficult given that this order is now suffused with technologies of computer generation, artificial intelligence, and algorithmic scripting.[7]

The original wager made by Atkins is that, if reality can be derealized by such technologies, it might also be rediscovered there, and this in a few ways. First, he believes that, once outmoded, a given technology passes over to the side of "base materiality"; its very clunkiness becomes a sort of reality effect. Atkins adapts the term "corpsing"—which indicates the moment when an actor breaks character and so dispels the illusion of the performance—"to describe a kind of structural revelation more generally"; his examples are when a vinyl record skips or a streaming movie buffers.[8] To corpse a medium, then, is to expose its materiality, even to intimate its mortality, and in this moment the real might poke through all the mediation. Second, punctuated by the gestural tics of the Atkins avatar, *The Worm* is also rife with manufactured glitches—sudden blurs, flares, beeps, and crackles—and these apparent cracks in the artifice might provide another opening to the real. Although these reality effects are also artificial, "they baffle the signs of reality by parodying them, engendering a new kind of realism."[9] Third, if the real might be felt when an illusion fails, so too might it be sensed when that illusion is "glazed with effects to italicize the artifice," that is, when illusionism is pushed to a hyperreal point. In this register Atkins conforms to the criterion of fidelity in technological reproduction but excessively so, and in this way he claims such fidelity for the side of "revelatory materialism rather than techno magic." Fourth, Atkins exploits a central feature of high-definition video inherited from photography and film, at least when they were experienced by early viewers—that the inanimate appears to be alive. This confusion is a telltale attribute of the uncanny (in his account Freud was inspired by those avatars known as doppelgängers), and this uncanniness is another "mortal experience" that evokes the real.[10] Finally, if photography and film opened up an "optical unconscious" for Benjamin, a reality not perceived by the naked eye, high-definition video expands this realm for Atkins.[11] His surrogate dead men make visible the psychopathology of everyday technological life.

"Unlike with movies, my CG stuff is deliberately janky," Atkins states. "Enough to underscore it, draw attention to it. Which is a perversion of its aim to disappear." This is a contemporary version of the modernist call to reveal the medium, "to bare the device" (as the Russian formalists put it), but Atkins goes much further. His formalism is dedicated to realism, one of "bleak histrionics" that he calls "Bruegelian."[12] "[I] want to realign the tech in the service of life's *beggared*—'love's work'—rather than as a tool of captivity." For Atkins, then, to bare the device is also to "impoverish" the medium, and thus to point to other impoverishments—in his life, in his family, in society at large. At the extreme, the bared device stands in for "bare life," or life defined by Giorgio Agamben as utterly subject to power, life that is indeed beggared.[13] Here Atkins proceeds by way of analogies: "Analog error feels as if it is to the reality of a CG image what impoverishment is to representation at large—what tragedy is to depictions of life; what misery is to experience." He knows that this string of allegories is a stretch, but he's not afraid of bathos, which he sees as the other side of pathos. Atkins risks these states because he sees affect as an essential dimension of life that must be both rediscovered in media technologies and wrested from them. This is why he aims to find an "emo, cybernetic surrogacy" in computer-generated avatars and to graft his "sentimental self to the tech, rather than the other way around."[14] This is not to deny that life is steeped in loss but, on the contrary, to acknowledge that reality, and to produce work that addresses it, that assists in "affective recognition." It is to contribute to "love's work."

Here his notion of art confronts his theory of media, which Atkins sketched in a 2018 lecture titled "Losslessness." "Losslessness," he tells us, "refers to a category of data-compression algorithm that allows original data to be perfectly reproduced." To achieve this fidelity, digital media, even more than analog media, aim to disappear; "technology constantly seeks to be lost." The magic of technology wants not only to cover up our existential lack—this is what makes it the ultimate fetish—but also to distract us from its inevitable failure. Its myth of losslessness serves "ideological ends," among them our fantasies of "coherency," "holism," even "immortality." However, it never quite succeeds. Loss is still felt, and since this loss can't be acknowledged, our relationship to technology is rendered "neurotic," marked by "aimless melancholy or shame." In response, Atkins argues, "the artist first must set out to *find* the technology,"

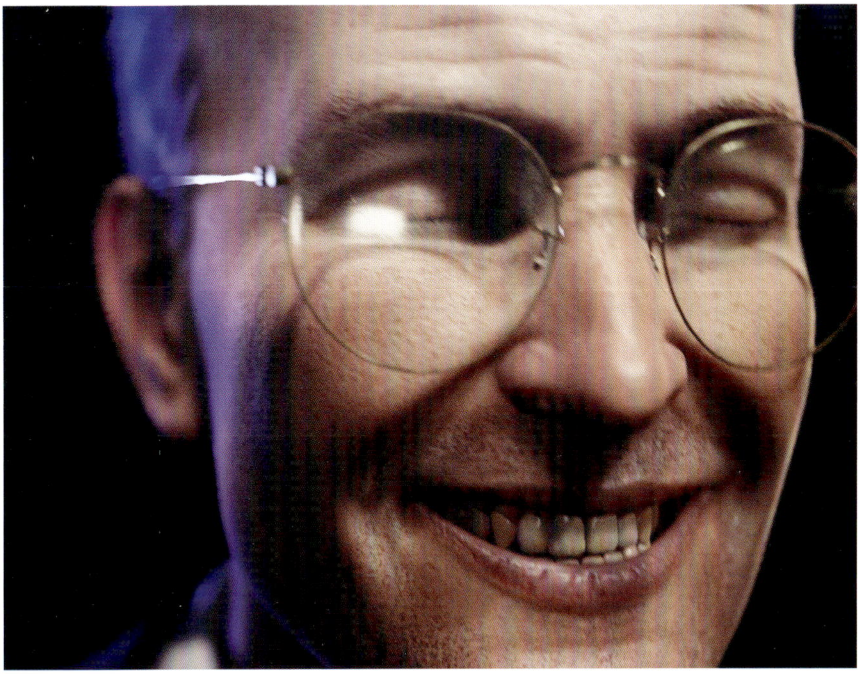

Ed Atkins, *The Worm*, 2021 (still). Digital video projection, color, sound, 12 minutes 40 seconds. © Ed Atkins. Courtesy the artist and Barbara Gladstone Gallery.

and the initial step is to make the technology "corporeal, analog, mortal." This "movement toward the literal" is not simply "a rebuttal of the desires of the tech"; it also points to the "uncovering of other realities," which in turn promotes the "freedom of the subject."[15] Here we are back on the familiar ground of modernist defamiliarization, a project that is vastly complicated now that the human seems almost fused with the technological and the world often appears to be media all the way down. Moreover, for Atkins it's not enough to defetishize technology, to demystify its magic. For his work to be effective, illusion must be allowed "sufficient function" not only "to sustain critique" but also to promote affective recognition—to express loss, to "set in motion a shift from melancholy to purposive mourning," to find in media technology an interpersonal connection that it always promises but rarely delivers.

Atkins signals a shift among artists steeped in new media. Just as the Pictures artists once assumed the society of the spectacle so that they could engage its image repertoire, so Atkins takes computer-generated technology as a given but attempts to "misuse" it critically. Here he differs from the practice of immediate predecessors such as Harun Farocki, Hito Steyerl, and Trevor Paglen. Rather than reiterate how the human is given over to technology, Atkins seeks, perhaps impossibly, to bend technology back toward the human. His utopian gambit is to believe that technology might aid the human to become human again—to become emotive and empathic on our own terms. His art is not a lament for humanism or a celebration of posthumanism but a snatching of the human from the belly of the beast.[16]

Again, Atkins subscribes to a philosophy of the remainder—of the recalcitrant detail, the personal *punctum*, the traumatic real. Yet, as with Barthes on photography, this fascination can lead Atkins, notwithstanding his Bruegelian (or Brechtian) concern with the beggared, to occlude another reality: social reality.[17] His interest in the "arts of impoverishment" (a title taken from Leo Bersani, who, in his account of such arts, features another Atkins favorite, Beckett) is also in tension with his commitment to an aesthetic of reparation (Bersani is critical of any "culture of redemption" that frames experience as always already damaged).[18] Finally, can media technologies truly be turned so as to enrich our affective lives rather than strip them like so many assets? Alongside the old "ideological state apparatuses" such as the church and the military, there has arisen a whole slew of social media leviathans that produce, circulate, and monetize all kinds of intense affects in ways that disorient us politically as well as psychologically. But then, when it comes to art, one shouldn't complain about contradictions. Contradiction is what drives a practice like Atkins's; it might also be a condition that keeps us human.

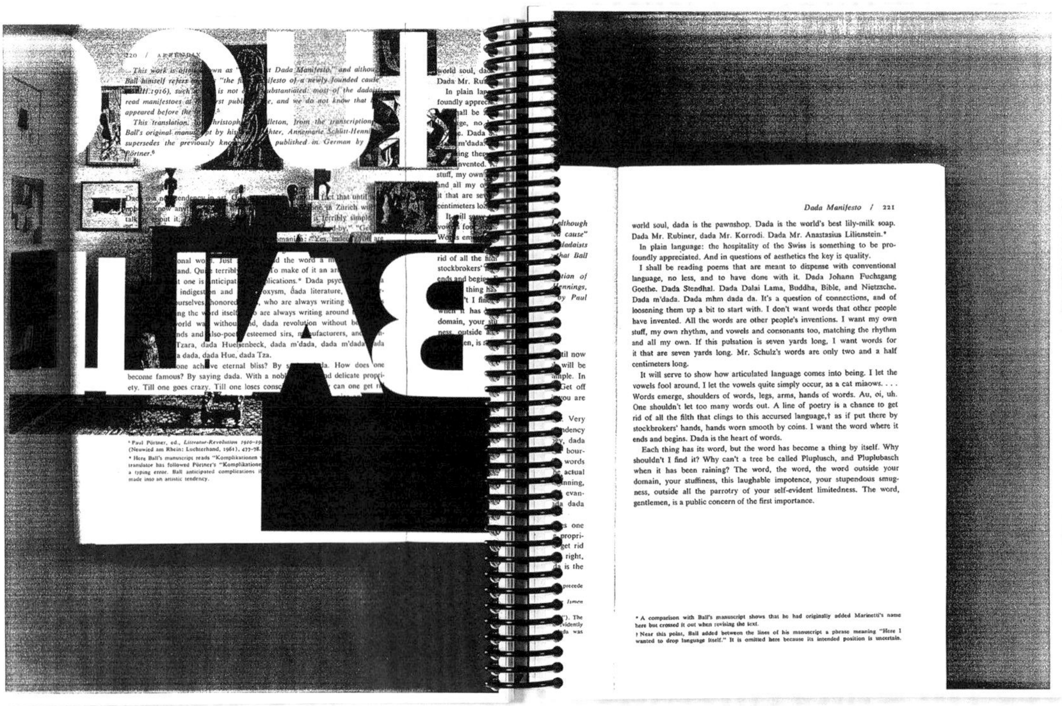

Adam Pendleton, *Black Dada Reader*, 2017 (detail). © Adam Pendleton. Courtesy the artist.

31 The Artist as Anthologist

Anthology-making is central to the art practice of Adam Pendleton, who has produced three generous compilations of texts and images to date: *Black Dada Reader* (2017), *Pasts, Futures, and Aftermaths: Revisiting the Black Dada Reader* (2021), and *Who Is Queen? A Reader* (2021). In the virtual space of these books diverse artists, activists, and authors—Black, brown, and white, feminist, queer, and straight, dead, alive, and overlooked—encounter one another in ways that they never could in life.

In the first instance the readers have served Pendleton as manuals for his art, which involves the active montage of artistic and political materials—"active" in the sense that it is intended to activate readers and viewers, not to exist as an inert object to consume. His anthologies are also offerings to others, which is in keeping with the etymology of the term: derived from the Greek *anthos*, or flower, and *logia*, or gathering, "anthology" originally denoted a collection of poems and epigrams by sundry authors for purpose of pleasure as well as instruction. Pendleton means his anthologies, then, as gifts, as resources to help others not only survive but flourish, even as gestures of love (he is interested in "the politics of love").[1] Of course, his anthologies are readers in the more prosaic sense too: packets for an imagined gathering of interlocutors, as in a seminar, say, or a symposium.[2] Equally, like any gift—or any seminar or symposium—they invite, almost obligate, whoever receives them to become participants, even collaborators, in his project. (While the phrase "what can black dada do for me" appears on the cover of the first anthology, "What can Black Dada do for you?" is a recurrent question in the second.) In short, these readers read us in turn, and that is part of their activation.

The three anthologies draw on materials that range across the last century and into the near present (for the most part, the texts proceed chronologically), and they cut across many disciplines with aplomb (politics, philosophy, art, poetry, literary criticism, music, dance, performance, film, and video). What consistency emerges in their tables of contents? Or is the point, rather, to produce a feeling of inconsistency, a testing of expectations of sense and order, of conventions of inclusion and exclusion? The project of Black Dada is "diametrically opposed" to classification, one commentator has argued, and others tend to agree.[3] For his part Pendleton is drawn to ambiguous terms like "creative stammering."[4] In my view he splits the difference between order and disorder: apparently arbitrary arrays of texts and images are gradually revealed to be concerted assemblies of different voices. It is left to us to provide the connections, make the introductions, facilitate the dialogues. This, too, is part of their activation.

Pendleton opens *Black Dada Reader* with a section titled "Foundations," and any education in art today would do well to include the writings here. It begins with three expressions of radical alienation. First comes the famous statement of W. E. B. Du Bois, from *The Souls of Black Folk* (1903), about the "double consciousness" that haunts African Americans ("One ever feels his two-ness,—an American, a Negro. . . ."), an account of Black lives lived under white gazes that looks ahead a half century to Frantz Fanon. This is followed by *Dada Manifesto* (1916) by Hugo Ball, in which, in the midst of World War I, the first ringleader of Zurich Dada positioned his sound poetry as the negation of all discourse corrupted by power ("a line of poetry is a chance to get rid of all the filth that clings to this accursed language"). This idea of Dada was then repurposed fifty years later by the poet-critic Leroi Jones (soon to become Amiri Baraka) in *Black Dada Nihilismus* (1964), his revenge fantasy about systemic racism, which is the crux of the *détournement* of Dada that Pendleton performs in this reader. Significantly, these three critiques are followed by four texts that caution against forms of accommodation. In a 1969 statement the Black Panther Stokely Carmichael warns that the liberal is often a duplicitous "arbitrator" between "the oppressor and the oppressed." In a 1976 interview the French philosopher Gilles Deleuze salutes Jean-Luc Godard for his refashioning of montage as a means of inclusive conjunction rather than dialectical resolution ("The AND is diversity, multiplicity, the destruction of identities"). In a 1990 essay the Conceptual artist Adrian Piper insists on "the joy of marginality" over and above the comfort of institutional recognition. And in a 2003 dialogue the Language poet Joan Retallack discusses her notion of "the poethical wager" whereby poetics and ethics implicate one another.

Many of these figures become touchstones in the readers, and they call up related artists and activists along the way. Jones/Baraka is joined by other radical poet-critics such as June Jordan and Harryette Mullen. Carmichael is connected to other political revolutionaries like Malcolm X and Angela Davis. Godard is accompanied by other innovative filmmakers such as Toni Cade Bambara and Stan Douglas. Piper is affined with other Conceptualists of color like Lorraine O'Grady and William Pope.L. And Retallack is associated with other language and concrete poets such as Leslie Scalapino and Augusto de Campos. Various voices from different disciplines are heard as well—choreographers like Ishmael Houston-Jones, Trajal Harrell, and Ralph Lemon, and composers such as Sun Ra, Julius Eastman, and Anthony Braxton. Pendleton allows the pertinence of all these figures to his own practice to emerge slowly and silently. For instance, we come to realize that, just as his work extends Conceptual art and language poetry, so, too, does it elaborate on the intermedial performances of Joan Jonas and the collaborative monuments of Thomas Hirschhorn, both of whom reappear in the readers.[5]

Already in *Black Dada Reader* Pendleton foregrounds radical work on language. The second section, simply titled "Language," includes "Fourteen Anonymous Portraits" by Gertrude Stein, which is a distant model for his video portraits of artists and activists (the latter project is anthological in its own way); Ron Silliman on "The New Sentence," which argues that philosophy, linguistic theory, and literary criticism have failed to address the prose poem adequately; and June Jordan on Black English, which Pendleton draws on in his manipulation of phrases and words in his art. He probes language and concrete poetry further in *Pasts, Futures, and Aftermaths*, which also deepens the connections between writing and politics—for example, with an excerpted chapter from the poet Juliana Spahr that examines "movement literatures" (with a telling emphasis on the role of anthologies). Emphasized here, too, are the affinities between avant-garde art and music via texts by jazz legends Charles Mingus and Cecil Taylor as well as premier abstractionist Piet Mondrian, for whom jazz served as an essential analogue for the "dynamic equilibrium" that he sought in his own compositions. Pendleton throws a theoretical odd couple into the mix too: the Soviet literary critic Mikhail Bakhtin, whose idea of the novel as a form of "social heteroglossia" is highlighted, and the German art historian Aby Warburg, whose deep interest in the mnemonic dimension of art Pendleton shares.

Finally, *Who Is Queen?* pulls these intertwined lines of activism, art, poetry, dance, and music toward recent uprisings, above all Occupy and Black Lives Matter, with texts that connect BLM to the civil rights movements of the 1960s and that speak to the political occupation of time as well as space. Pendleton also includes reflections on poetic and musical practice that resonate with his own anthological work, as in the call of the poet Simone White for "recollection" over "rejection": "We make culture this way, entirely in retrospect."[6] The occasion of this reader was the installation that Pendleton staged at the Museum of Modern Art in autumn 2021, which, among other concerns, surveyed select moments in "the aesthetics of protest" in the United States over the last half century.[7] On an immense scaffold set up in the vast MoMA atrium Pendleton hung his paintings and drawings—black-and-white abstractions, many of which incorporate words or phrases—and played a sound collage that combined dozens of sources, including Baraka speaking in 1980, the musician Hahn Rowe playing in 1994, and BLM demonstrators chanting in 2014. The scaffold also supported a large projection screen for three videos: a portrait of the gender theorist Jack Halberstam, an interrogation of a defaced Confederate monument, and a documentary about Resurrection City, a protest camp constructed on the National Mall in Washington, DC, in 1968 a few months after the assassination of Martin Luther King Jr. The *Who Is Queen?* reader is intercut with photos of Resurrection City as well.

Although Pendleton includes a few manifestos in the anthologies, including his "Black Dada" text from 2008, he is leery of the grandstanding that often attends the genre.[8] At the same time, he is fascinated by how artists self-present; *Black Dada Reader* devotes a section to "Artists' Positions," and the other anthologies include multiple interviews and dialogues with a diverse array of practitioners. In this way Pendleton intends his compilations both to convene authors and to disperse authorship.

Why does Pendleton anthologize? Again, one reason is pragmatic: to prepare the foundations of his own work. Another is pedagogical: to offer these materials to others. There are many partial precedents for such collections, from the great store of materials involving the African diaspora assembled by Arturo Schomburg with Alain Locke and Langston Hughes a century ago, through anthologies of African American literature published since the time of the Harlem Renaissance, to more recent compilations of writings by slaves and others produced by scholars like Henry Louis Gates Jr.[9] Yet these examples have museological and academic qualities that the Pendleton readers resist: his photocopied texts and images come rough and ready, without introductions or notes. Here we are, they say, use us as you see fit. As Deleuze once remarked of theory in general, these books are toolkits.

"Archive" is a term that often appears in discussions of the anthologies, and *Pasts, Futures, and Aftermaths* includes an incisive essay titled "The Power of the Archive and Its Limits" by the Cameroonian philosopher Achille Mbembe. Ironically, his account suggests why "archive" isn't such a good fit for the Pendleton project. Mbembe argues that archives tend to create "an illusion of totality and continuity" in a way that these anthologies reject. Akin to the temple and the cemetery, the typical archive performs "a kind of interment" that these readers also resist (they are "resurrection cities" in their own right). Finally, the archive effects "an instituting imaginary" that can serve, intentionally or not, the interests of the state. No anthology featuring Malcolm X, Stokely Carmichael, Angela Davis, and Amiri Baraka could be accused of that accommodation.

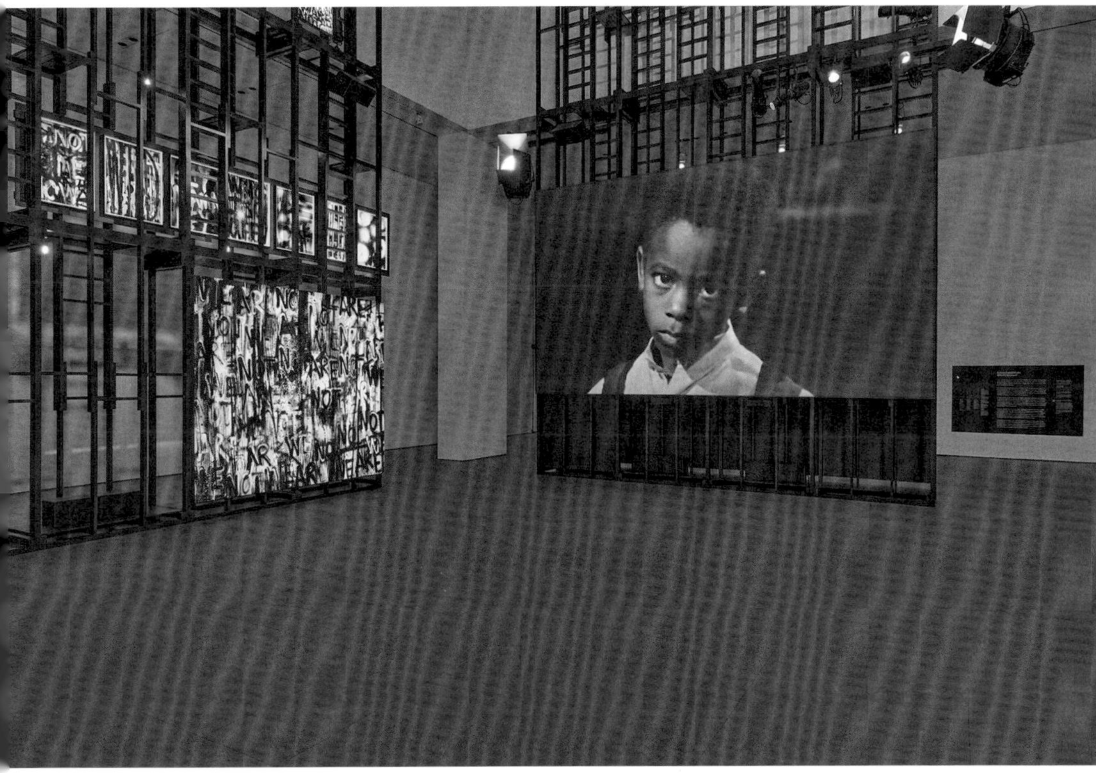

View of Adam Pendleton, *Who Is Queen?* at the Museum of Modern Art, 2021–2022.
Photo: Andy Romer. © Adam Pendleton. Courtesy the artist.

"Genealogy" is another term that crops up in the reception of the readers. First proposed by Nietzsche in *On the Genealogy of Morals* (1887), the concept was developed in a 1971 essay by Michel Foucault, who opposed the "effective history" of genealogy to "the metahistorical deployment of ideal significations and indefinite teleologies" in official history. According to Foucault, genealogy is a type of "knowledge not made for understanding" but "for cutting"; it bores down into the past in a way that supports a "vertical projection" of a position in the present.[10] Clearly, this approach is pertinent to the Pendleton project, except for the stubborn fact that no official history of art and activism focused on questions of race and sexuality already exists to counter. (As the literary critic Hortense Spillers argued long ago, the brute dislocation caused by centuries of slavery has made any historical narrative, genealogical or other, problematic in the extreme.)[11] Of course, the readers are chock full of documents; "critical fabulation," which the historian Saidiya Hartman has proposed as a workaround when abominations like slavery obliterate the very possibility of an archive, isn't necessary here.[12] Instead, the anthologies are, in equal parts, missions of construction and recovery, and at times this double operation is intimated by the contributors as part of their own practices. For instance, in *Black Dada Reader* choreographer Trajal Harrell notes his attraction to "movement that hasn't been recorded or hasn't been historicized," while in *Who Is Queen?* the experimental writer Alexis Pauline Gumbs insists on "the act of choosing, of choosing each other again," alluding, even more suggestively, to "ones that steal themselves and donate each other, back to the collective."[13] For his part Pendleton underscores how Black Dada aims to activate "incomplete postulates and beginnings"; it's "a way to talk about the future while talking about the past; it is our present moment."[14] In his view history is "an incomplete cube shirking linearity": there's no origin or end, no narrative or telos—and no "moral arc" to the universe or benighted path to "a greater union"—only the continued struggle for progressive transformation.[15]

In the mid nineteenth century Baudelaire defined recent French painting as a "mnemotechny of the beautiful," while in the early twentieth century Aby Warburg detected a mnemotechny of the traumatic in much postclassical art, as registered in repeated expressions of heightened emotion that he called *Pathosformeln*.[16] In an analogous manner Pendleton suggests that art can serve as a mnemonic reserve of gestures of political action, as a dynamic image repertoire of the aesthetics of protest.[17] Again, *Who Is Queen?* is punctuated by documentary photographs of Resurrection City like so many reminders-cum-prompts. In the same reader the critic Jason Adams argues, appositely, that "events of the past that are narrated as failures can be renarrated from the standpoint of the *possible* success they have left behind, which remain to be actualized."[18]

From the Paris Commune to Resurrection City and beyond (WTO protests, Occupy, Black Lives Matter), political movements have produced provisional architectures; the barricade is only the best known. In exhibitions like *Who Is Queen?* Pendleton draws on such structures for both content and form. (Here he is influenced by another important predecessor, Thomas Hirschhorn, who has adapted the ad hoc signs and banners of demonstrations in his own work.) The scaffold that dominated *Who Is Queen?* suggests that Black Dada remains a site under construction—under deconstruction, too, lest it become too rigid—and the anthologies can be seen as scaffolds in their own right, as supports for language that might serve as triggers for action. (In his artwork Pendleton treats words almost as architectural elements as well.)[19] In a sense the readers actualize the influential definition of the text, presented over a half century ago by Roland Barthes, as "a multi-dimensional space in which a variety of writings, none of them original, blend and clash."[20]

Also relevant here is the notion, proposed by the curator and critic Adrienne Edwards, that art-making for Pendleton is a form of gathering in which "freedom of assembly" is paramount: "His convocation of these writers and artists is a speculative and conceptual manifestation of this right."[21] This version of the *polis* explicitly admits the heretofore excluded and overlooked (the original *polis* of ancient Greece ignored the very people it depended on—slaves and women). In this respect it is a counter public sphere updated for the contemporary conditions of a racist and sexist America. Again, Pendleton is interested in the politics of love, but his assemblies hardly ignore the politics of contestation.

Like his art, his anthologies have two temporal dimensions: a synchronic axis that cuts across a heterogeneous present and a diachronic axis that summons different pasts. A primary purpose of the readers is to point to connections in a given moment that couldn't be made at the time—that describe an epistemic space shared by actors most of whom were unknown to one another.[22] These links are both artistic and political; in fact, they work to (re)connect art and politics, to put these two aspects of the avant-garde (back) into conversation. "Did our conceptual artists join hands with our freedom fighters?" Pendleton asks in his "Black Dada" text. If they didn't in the 1960s, can their legatees do so today? In a subsequent interview he offers another example of a hypothetical encounter: John Cage and Malcolm X arriving in New York at the same time in the early 1950s. We can speculate as to what kept them apart then, but why not imagine them—or, again, their legatees—together now?[23] In this semicounterfactual history Pendleton is inspired by artists like Harrell, who has created a dance that unites Black queer voguing in Harlem with downtown Judson Church choreography: "The whole thing is an imaginative possibility," Harrell has said of his performance. "I'm interested in the impossibility, that history that could not come together."[24] Historical impossibility prompts a utopian revision that ambitious art can limn.

The diachronic dimension of the anthologies is even more pronounced than the synchronic. As expected, this dimension begins with Dada. If a general mission of the humanities today is "to provincialize" European culture, Pendleton has taken on the specific task of provincializing this movement. "White dada remains within the framework of european weakness," he states matter-of-factly in his "Black Dada" text, and *Black Dada Reader* works to reposition and reactivate it. (That entire line, aside from the word "white," is a quotation from Tristan Tzara.)[25] More radically still, prompted by Baraka, Pendleton suggests that, with its critical mimesis of reified life under capitalism, Dada was, in some sense, already in league with Black experience.[26] Just as important to his own practice is Conceptualism, which, in his view, is also ripe for refashioning: "The history of conceptual art as (is) an intimately constructed narrative deserving of aggressive deconstructive interpretation."[27] In this project Pendleton is affined with Piper, O'Grady, and Félix González-Torres, whose work he has engaged directly. As others have noted, Pendleton also attempts further diachronic *détournements* in his art, which repositions such key modernist paradigms as the grid and the monochrome, as well as such essential avant-garde operations as montage and appropriation. In his hands these become devices of counterappropriation.[28]

For all his desire to make connections that are both synchronic and diachronic, Pendleton is concerned to interrupt as much as to transmit; at times opacity is as significant as transparency to him. Some terms for his project are intentionally ambiguous: he speaks of Black Dada as a "filter," a "mask," and a "labyrinth."[29] In part this (il)legibility is manifest in his emphasis on the materiality of print and paint, a point of resistance to a culture dominated by digital virtuality. In fact, with his photocopied essays Pendleton suggests a notion of "the poor text" that has affinities with "the poor image" advocated by Hito Steyerl.[30] At the same time, and perhaps counterintuitively, this materialism is also a way for Pendleton to convey the "texture of things from the past."[31] He shares his interest in opacity with the philosopher Édouard Glissant, and his involvement in (il)legibility with the artist Glenn Ligon; Pendleton sees both strategies as ways to resist the fixing of identity as well as meaning. This "refusal to mean" is largely why he considers abstraction to be "a political imperative," even "a mode and mechanism of survival."[32]

Adrienne Edwards has pointed to "the radical love between blackness and abstraction" that runs from Jack Whitten to Pendleton, who invites us to think about this rapport in new ways.[33] After Jackson Pollock released black lines from the age-old task of description, Ad Reinhardt deployed black rectangles to eradicate representation altogether. *Black Dada Reader* includes a text by Reinhardt on abstraction as an act of negation, which Pendleton extends beyond painting in his "Afterward" to the anthology: "Is there a role for abstraction in the abolition of alienated labor?"[34] While Kerry James Marshall has underscored not only the scarcity of Black figures in Western painting but also the difficulty that the color black poses for figuration (black has served as "ground" far more than as "figure"), Pendleton exploits an ambiguity between blackness as figure and blackness as ground. Indeed, this is central to his play with (il)legibility.[35]

In his "Afterward" Pendleton points to another ambiguity, an even more important one within abstraction at large: a tension between "two modes or two experiences."

> The first is the experience of abstraction as a *force*, which happens when the body is subject to violence. . . . The belly of the slave ship, sexual violence, and the fourteen-hour day on the assembly line are all examples of this kind of abstraction. Abstraction is a force whenever and wherever the subject is misrecognized as an object. . . . It is in the service of this demand for recognition that the second experience of abstraction arrives: the *practice* of abstraction, or abstraction as a relationship. . . . For it is precisely by practicing abstraction—by poetry or painting or *whatever*—that the subject confirms itself as other-than-object.[36]

In his articulation of abstraction as practice, Pendleton draws on Piper, whose "Flying" (1987) he quotes here:

> Abstraction is also flight. It is freedom from the immediate spatiotemporal constraints of the moment; freedom to plan the future, recall the past, comprehend the present from a reflective perspective that incorporates all three; freedom from the immediate boundaries of concrete subjectivity, freedom to imagine the possible and transport oneself into it; freedom to survey the real as a resource for embodying the possible.[37]

In this account there is love between blackness and abstraction, to be sure, but there is also violence. The Hegelian inflection of his language ("the demand for recognition") suggests that Pendleton sees this relation as a dialectical one, at once dystopian and utopian in the extreme: abstraction as reification wrought by enslavement and commodification on the one hand, and abstraction as negation, transcendence, freedom, and autonomy on the other. At the same

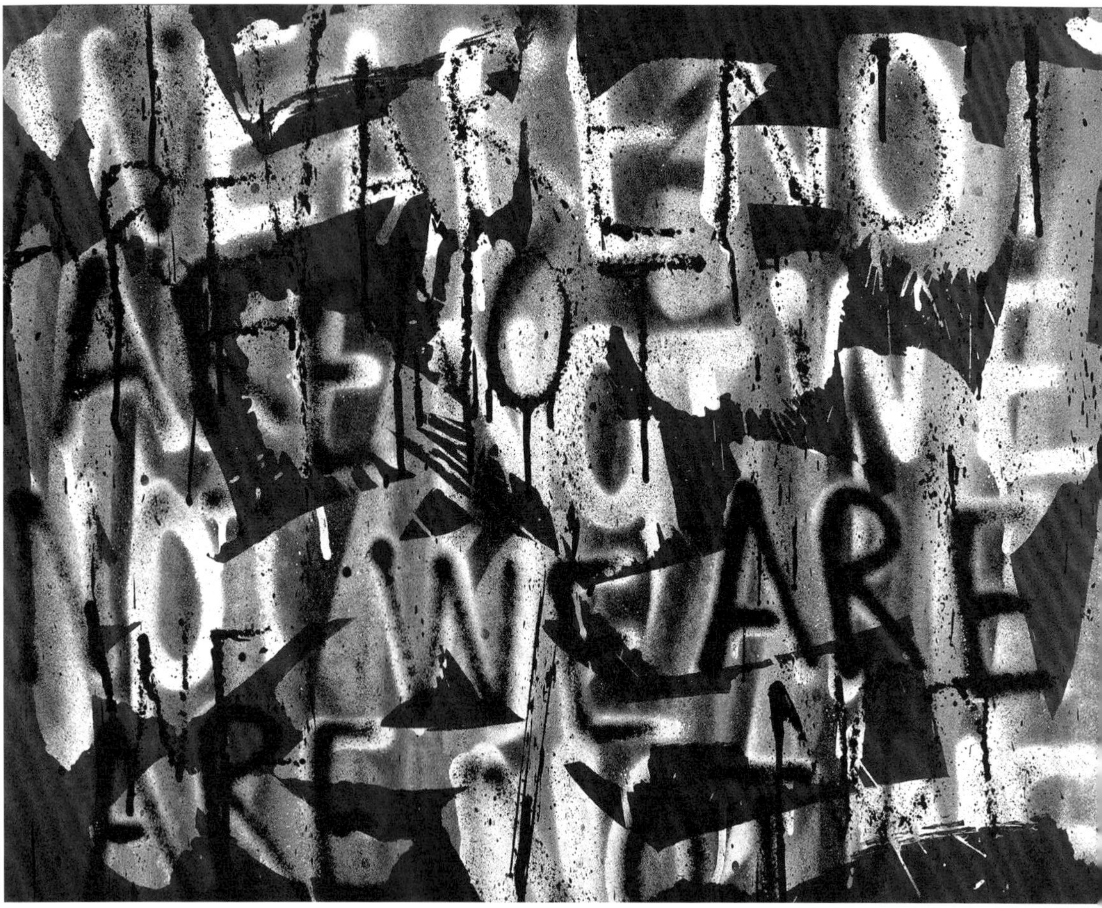

Adam Pendleton, *Untitled (WE ARE NOT)*, 2023. Silkscreen ink on canvas, 8 × 10 feet.

time, in *Who Is Queen?* he includes a brilliant critique of Hegel by the literary critic James A. Snead, who argues against the Hegelian dialectic (notoriously, Hegel placed Africa in a time before history) and for "repetition as a figure of Black culture."

Is the Pendleton project a dialectical one? The question hinges on the matter of reconciliation. The Hegelian dialectic looks to resolve contradictions, whereas the Marxist dialectic aims to exploit them: for Marxists dialectical thinking is "the unmasking of antinomy as contradiction" through which we come to recognize "the interpenetration of opposites" in any given situation.[38] Pendleton is an antinomic artist and a dialectical thinker in these ways. Certainly he draws equally on Afro-futurism and Afro-pessimism, on Sun Ra and Frank B. Wilderson III (both appear in his anthologies), on the euphoric gospel of the Black church and the nihilistic despair of Jones/Baraka, on love and violence. And there is nothing more antinomic than his paired slogans "We Are Not" and "But Now I Am." His assemblies—anthologies and artworks alike—are animated by contradictions, which activate us in turn.

III Some Critics

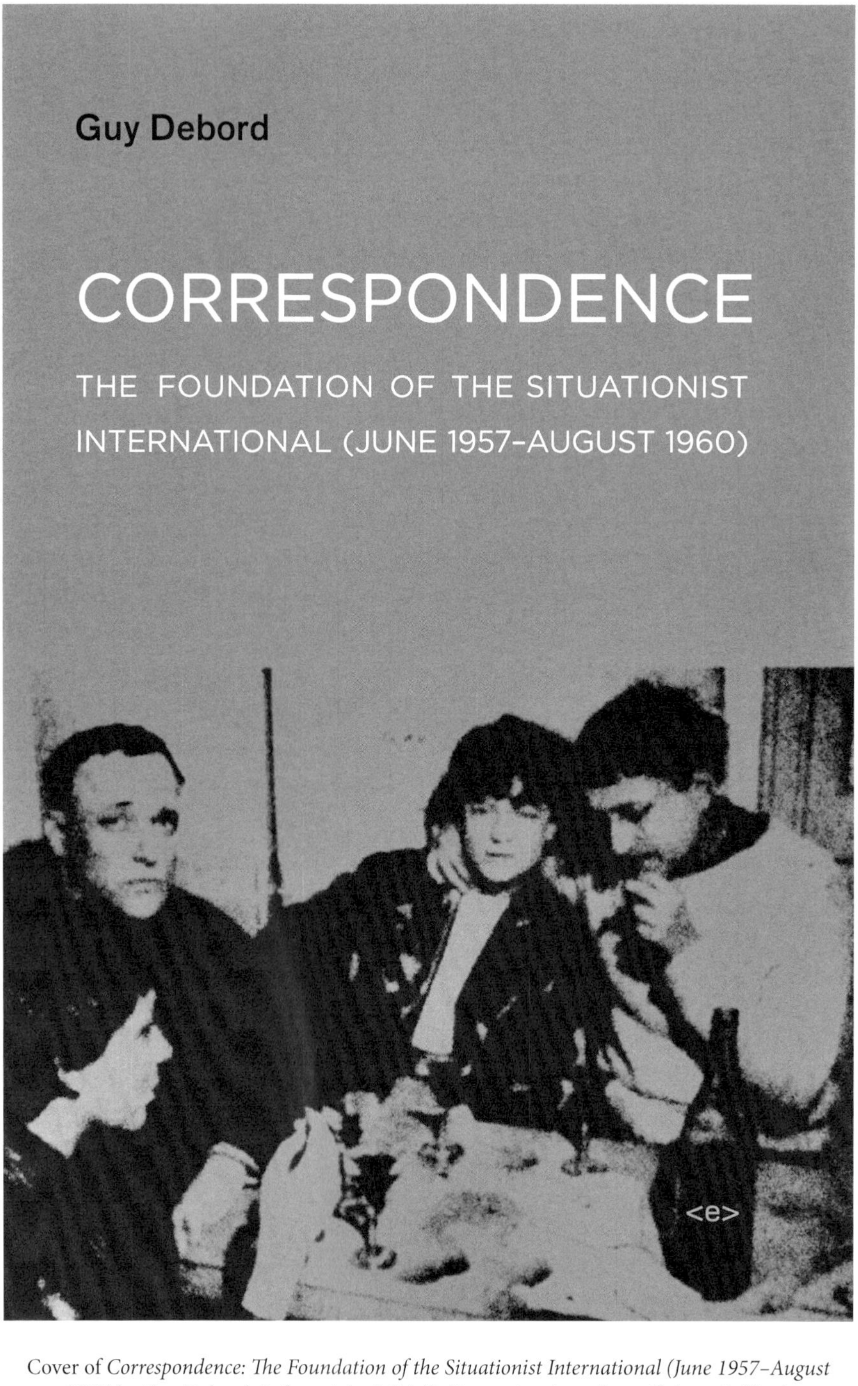

Cover of *Correspondence: The Foundation of the Situationist International (June 1957–August 1960)* by Guy Debord. Left to right: Michèle Bernstein, Asger Jorn, Colette Caillard, and Guy Debord in Paris, 1959. Design: Hedi El Kholti.

32 A Certain Practice of Life

The Situationists are legendary, in large part because they constituted an avant-garde, very rare in the postwar period, that held radical art and radical politics together, until they decided, in dramatic fashion, that this project was no longer feasible or even desirable. But the Situationists were also the stuff of legend from the start, as the early letters of Guy Debord, the leader of the group, make clear. In late July 1957, in the little town of Cosio d'Arroscia nestled in the Ligurian Alps, the young Frenchman met with a motley crew of seven other alienated souls—including two artists, the Dane Asger Jorn and the Italian Giuseppe Gallizio (aka Pinot), the core of a momentary movement called the Imaginist Bauhaus—in order to found the Situationist International (SI), a grand name for a small gathering in a remote place. Even the vote to initiate the group wasn't overwhelming; a surviving scrap of paper shows a tally of five in favor—Debord, Michèle Bernstein (an astute writer who was his first wife), Jorn, Ralph Rumney (an English "psychogeographer" who was soon excused from the group), and Walter Olmo (an experimental composer whose name is followed by a question mark on the sheet)—with one opposed and two abstaining (including Pinot). Yet, schooled in the history of avant-gardes, Debord seized on this occasion as the requisite origin myth: "We should present the 'Cosio conference' as a point of departure," he wrote to Jorn a month later, "and, from now on, move quickly (a new legend must be created immediately around us)."[1]

Like Constant Nieuwenhuys, the Dutch painter turned visionary urbanist who soon joined the group, Jorn was also a central figure in Cobra (1948–1951), a collective of artists from Copenhagen, Brussels, and Amsterdam that was another key predecessor of Situationism. Although Debord later referred to the early stage of the SI as "the supersession of art"—it concluded in 1962 with the purging of all such practitioners—his chief interlocutors at the time were three artists: Pinot, Constant, and Jorn. Affectively, intellectually, and financially, Debord was closest to Jorn. With a market established for his paintings by the late 1950s, Jorn was able to bankroll many Situationist projects, including the two short films made by Debord during these years (*On the Passage of a Few Persons Through a Rather Brief Moment in Time*, 1959, and *Critique of Separation*, 1961). It is with real regret that Debord watched him recede from SI activities (Jorn withdrew in April 1961), whereas Pinot was purged for art world opportunism on May 31, 1960 (after copious letters in which Debord addressed him as "grande e nobile amico"), and Constant resigned a day later (though Debord entreated him to return to the fold several times). For a stage dedicated to its supersession, then, art was a persistent subject. There was much ado about how to stage a first exhibition of "industrial paintings" by Pinot in Paris—he "has found an excellent formula," Debord wrote as the show approached, "to cover the entire gallery (the walls, the ceiling, the floor) with 200 meters of painting"—as well as a survey of Cobra and Situationist manifestations at the Stedelijk Museum in Amsterdam (after long and testy negotiations, it was finally abandoned). There was much ado, too, about how to attract artist-collaborators (such as the Spur Group in Germany), how to keep them in line, and ultimately how to ditch them.

Amazingly, Debord was only twenty-five years old when this period began. And yet, already a veteran of the Lettrist movement, another predecessor of the SI, his voice was almost preternaturally cool and in control, except when he was provoked by the cerebral Constant, struggled to track down the peripatetic Jorn (who drifted between Denmark, Alba, and Paris), or flamed the odd enemy or tiresome bureaucrat. At the same time, as Debord pulled together, among myriad other projects, additional SI conferences in Paris (January 1958) and Munich (April 1959), with a fourth meeting in London on the horizon (September 1960), his letters were often animated by impassioned appeals, directives, and calls to action. Although some served as sketches for later texts, and a few are intimate in tone, most of his missives were launched like missiles.

Debord served as "secretary" of the SI in the sense of both party head and general assistant: philosopher and disciplinarian, he was also publicist and agent, debating with collaborators and tracking strays, promoting events and arranging rendezvous, sometimes at a clip of a couple of letters a day.[2] However, his own preferred designation, "strategist," is also appropriate: the letters are laced with the rhetoric of battle. (Debord was a devoted reader of Clausewitz, and with Alice Becker-Ho, his second wife, he later devised a board game called *Game of War*.) "Strategist" has the right ambiguity too, for the lines between actual politics, group positioning, and individual posturing aren't always clear—were they, one wonders, to Debord then? What is clear is his keen sense of how to forge a movement that had aims that were more than artistic. Again, the SI might be the last avant-garde in Europe with a genuine claim to be a proper avant-garde at all, that is, again, one that articulated artistic and political revolt together, the one whetting the other, at least for a while.

At the same time, the SI emerged in a crowded field of artistic groups, and Debord wasn't above art world tricks. "The paintings must be the most *stunning*, the most *shocking* possible," he told Pinot in January 1958 in the long run-up to his Paris première. Only "show the paintings in which the search for *new materials* has been pushed farthest," and ensure they are "very different from each other." So, too, he wasn't reluctant to pit Situationism against other avant-gardes. First in this order came the historical precedents of Dada and Surrealism, to which the SI had a split Oedipal relationship. As Bernstein once remarked: "There was the father we hated, Surrealism. And there was the father we loved, Dada."[3] For Debord both progenitors, which were ideological complements, had failed, and Situationism was born to overcome them dialectically. As he put it later in *The Society of the Spectacle* (1967): "Dadaism sought to *abolish art without realizing it*; Surrealism sought to *realize art without abolishing it*. The critical position since developed by the Situationists demonstrates that the abolition and the realization of art are inseparable aspects of a single *transcendence of art*."[4]

Less distant from the Situationists, given the presence of Jorn and Constant among them, was "Saint Cobra," as Debord called it in one letter. Debord valued Cobra for its commitment to "experimental research," and its journal was animated by the exploration of many things—prehistoric art, folk motifs, universal forms like the spiral, and so on. Yet he also questioned it for this tendency to formalist "neoprimitivism"; like prior avant-gardes, Cobra emulated the impulsive picture-making of children and naïfs. In the end Debord positioned Saint Cobra as the artistic prophet to the political SI, a pivot to launch Situationism proper, which should be presented, he wrote early on to Jorn, as "the necessary transcendence of that era."

Always keep in mind, Debord warned in late summer 1957, that "Situationism, as a body of doctrine, does not exist and must not exist." In part this occlusion was protective: "Yesterday, the police questioned me at length," he wrote a year later. They "want to regard the SI *as an association in order to set about its dissolution in France*. I protested then and there. . . . Not being declared, the SI cannot be officially dissolved." Not only pragmatic, this stance was also philosophical, in keeping with the Situationist desire to be alert to the radical possibilities in any conjuncture. "Of course, never any *doctrine*," Debord reiterated in late autumn 1958. Only "perspectives. A solidarity around these perspectives." This is inspiring, but solidarity is difficult to achieve with points of view that often shift and rarely intersect. Centrifugal in spirit, the SI was centripetal in design, and his early letters show Debord struggling to inhabit—to embody—that center. Only eight months into the SI he had begun to insist, "We should emphasize the centralized aspect of the movement," and by the time Constant resigned in summer 1960 Debord was defensive (albeit defiantly so) about his treatment of comrades (he had just expelled two Dutch architects for designing, of all things, a church): "I am with the SI and, as long as I am in it, I will keep a minimum of discipline that precludes all collaboration with uncontrollable elements." And yet, if there was no doctrine, why were there so many apostates?

In these moments Debord moves center-stage, and his early letters become a fine study in the art of enmity. With an almost aristocratic touch he sprinkled ridicule on his pages, but at times he went low and nasty, as though scenting them with pee as well. "Small-time hoodlum," he addressed one miscreant, and telegrammed another, a journal editor who had sent him a token fee for an article: "save your nine florins imbecile it was a gift!" For pseudo avant-gardists and rogue associates alike, Debord insisted on "a clear attitude of insult and contempt," and as the letters piled up, so did the bodies. At one point or another he deemed critics and artists such as Michel Tapié, Georges Mathieu, Yves Klein, and Simon Hantaï, not to mention all the Angry Young Men (John Osborne et al.), "apolitical and fascistic," and even the once-recruited Spur artists were soon dismissed as "ridiculous." Sentiments like this one—"we already have among us too many young artistic elderly who have missed out on their own 19th century"—also anticipated the purge of artists to come. Even a close ally like Jorn could feel the heat. "The economic surplus that my social situation as a painter offers me finds its best place in the situationist movement," Jorn wrote in a self-critique of masochistic generosity, "even if the same movement is obliged to attack me so as to attack a situation from which I cannot escape, but which disrupts the movement."

Yet Debord was hardly the show-trialing tyrant that his detractors make him out to be. Nearly all the ruptures remarked in his letters served to clarify what was at stake in the SI. This is true, for example, when Debord responded to Constant after his resignation, which followed hard on the purging of Pinot and the Dutch architects. "Let's clearly distinguish the manner of the break," Debord wrote.

> I am sure that, here, we had reached the point where the SI had to make an instant choice (or had to be abandoned). Because you know well that I have always thought that "there are moments at which it is necessary to know how to choose"; that you don't have to teach me this; and that, if there has been a certain opportunism in the SI, I have been among those (you, too) who have counterbalanced it.

"What primarily constitutes the SI," Debord concluded, "is this group control, expressed by expulsion—or, more rarely, resignation." Sadly, he might be right here: "What is revolutionary organization?" is an implicit question throughout his early letters. But Constant was also correct in his reply: "In what presently remains of the SI, it would be too ridiculous to speak of expulsion or of resignation." In its fifteen years of life—the SI dissolved in 1972—it had a grand total of seventy-two members.

The pathos of these early letters is that they show Situationism falling apart even while coming together, and that, in the complicated machinations of his scattered group, Debord was able to perform as many acts of friendship as he did of malice. To borrow the title of his 1959 film about his Lettrist friends, the letters trace a "passage of a few people through a rather brief moment in time," a tracing triangulated by three comrades above all, Pinot, Jorn, and Constant. Along with his essay-films, in which Debord montaged found images and hidden citations with home movies and pithy aphorisms, these three figures represent the prime art practices of the SI in this period.

Both the "industrial paintings" of Pinot and the "modifications" of found paintings by Jorn came to a head when the two opened shows in Paris in May 1959. Pinot covered the Galerie René Drouin with rolls of canvas painted in lurid colors as though automatically. He then added lights, mirrors, sounds, and smells to create a total environment. A "shrewd mixture of chance and mechanics," as Bernstein once described it, "industrial painting" was intended to prefigure a world of play that automation, once detached from capitalism, would allow.[5] At the same time, it parodied the current world of capitalist production and consumption, for not only were the canvases made on a mock assembly line with paint machines and spray-guns, but they could also be cut up and sold by the meter. The Jorn "modifications" bear the stigmata of capitalism in another way. The source pictures were kitschy landscapes and city views, produced for petit bourgeois decoration, that he scavenged in flea markets and painted over with primitivistic figures and abstract gestures à la Cobra. "Painting is over," Jorn wrote in a statement for the 1959 show. "You might as well finish it off. Détourne. Long live painting." Like kingship, Jorn suggested, painting is dead, but it might live again—cultural-political authority might live again—in a very different guise. "Our past is full of becoming," he concluded. "One needs only to crack open the shells."[6]

Finally, the "unitary urbanism" advanced by Constant developed two practices dear to the Lettrists and the Situationists alike: the *dérive*, defined in the SI journal as "a transient passage through varied ambiances," and "psychogeography," defined as "the study of the specific effects of the geographical environment."[7] In effect, "universal urbanism" was a radical proposal for new modes of collective experience in metropolitan space, as exemplified by *New Babylon* (1959–1974), a project in which Constant modeled the future city of automation as an arena for nomadic movement and mass play, with high-tech elements refitted by residents like so many giant toys. Ultimately, all these practices were specific variations on the Situationist theme of *détournement*, or "the integration of present or past artistic production into a superior construction of a milieu."[8] Derived from the old avant-garde models of collage and montage, *détournement* extended from the refashioning of individual words and images to the reimagining of entire cities. It was a general theory of radical culture that anyone might practice, one in keeping with the old Surrealist insistence (via Lautréamont) that poetry must be made by all.

These techniques were never ultimate ends for Debord. "If we fail to *effectively use* the new experimental conceptions that we have already defined," he warned one comrade in early summer 1958, "we will always fall back into the art market, yet another pseudo-school of the same outdated artistic kind." In the same vein he wrote to Constant in early autumn of the same year, "if the artistic present does manage to make some of its values prevail within the SI, the true cultural experiences of the period will be undertaken elsewhere." So it is that Debord cast the SI as "a total project," not in the modernist sense of a *Gesamtkunstwerk*, but as a movement that applies the tactical lessons of art so as to intervene in the social world at large. "Our necessary activity is dominated by the question of the *totality*," he cautioned Constant in spring 1959. "Take note of it." A Hegelian Marxist in the lineage of Lukács, Debord looked for art to be superseded not by philosophy but by action. "Nothing has ever interested me beyond a certain practice of life," he commented more than once in his early letters, and he didn't mean at the level of individual or group alone. "When one feels powerless about other things," Debord wrote in an implicit critique of existentialism and phenomenology, "there is a tendency to remain on a level of a *discourse on experience*." Clearly this discourse was insufficient to him: first and last, "a certain practice of life" meant political engagement. "What can intellectuals do without ties to an enterprise that brings comprehensive change to social relations?" he asked Constant.

"The SI," Debord wrote in 1960, "possesses nothing—except its demand for totality." Philosophically as well as politically, Debord answered this call, but he did so in a way that attracted the criticism of others on the Left both then and since (orthodox Marxists, Gramscians, Althusserians, Foucauldians, feminists). Especially in question is his theory of spectacle, which extends Lukács on "the riddle of the commodity-structure" in *History and Class Consciousness* (1923), first translated into French in full in 1960. "The problem of commodities," Lukács wrote early in this influential essay, is "the central, structural problem of capitalist society in all its aspects. Only in this case can the structure of commodity-relations be made to yield a model of all the objective forms of bourgeois society together with all the subjective forms corresponding to them."[9] Debord agreed, but he also understood that in consumer capitalism "the phantom objectivity" of the commodity had grown exponentially, and that it had merged with mass media in such a way as to produce a world of spectacle, which he famously defined in his 1967 text as "capital accumulated to the point where it becomes image."[10] This commodity-image had proliferated like mad, colonizing once protected areas of social life, and the SI took up the fight there—in "the battle for leisure" above all—using strategies that Debord first sketched in his early letters. The Situationists, he underlined in June 1958, must indicate "*the transition between the artistic commodity-object of today and the free experimental activity in a new dimension of culture.*" But how exactly to do so? How to détourne the commodity at the scale of the spectacle? Here as elsewhere Debord tended to swing between calls for immediate action—"a direct construction of a liberated, affective and practical existence," as he puts it in his film *On the Passage of a Few People*—and hopes for dialectical magic: "the alienating satisfactions of the spectacle can at the same time be outlined, in negative, for a planned development of affective life."

Sometimes in his letters Debord seems overwhelmed by the very totalization that he sought to achieve, blaming its blockage on the "non-achievement" of the age at large. Here his critics on the Left have what salience they do. A note of resignation sounds at these moments, and it is heard intermittently from *On the Passage of a Few People* (described as a "realistic description of a way of life devoid of coherence and importance") through his "anti-memoir" *Panegyric* (1989), until his suicide, after a difficult illness, on November 30, 1994. A telling scene in *All the King's Horses*, a roman à clef about this period written by Bernstein in 1960 to make money for the SI, captures this feeling of futility, leavened a little by a sense of absurdity. In the scene the mistress Carole enters the lair of Gilles, the protagonist modeled on Debord, for the first time. The narrator, based on Bernstein, is also present. Carole begins the conversation:

> "What are you working on, exactly? I have no idea."
>
> "Reification," he answered.
>
> "It's an important job," I added.
>
> "Yes, it is," he said.
>
> "I see," Carole observed with admiration. "Serious work, at a huge desk cluttered with thick books and papers."
>
> "No," said Gilles. "I walk. Mainly I walk."[11]

The early days of the SI were free from such resignation, though the saturnine Debord hinted at it all the same. "Neither Paradise, nor the end of history," he wrote in December 1958. "We will have *other misfortunes* (and other pleasures), that's all." And again in June 1959: "Life in France is still heading in a very unpleasant direction. But we have our fun too." At one point in May 1960 Debord had to rebut a charge leveled by Henri Lefebvre that the SI indulged in "revolutionary romanticism." This was tough to take from the theorist of "everyday life," who was otherwise an important predecessor for the Situs, especially so because Lefebvre wasn't wrong. There was romance here, and in part it was one of failure, yet it wasn't defeatist. Early in *Lipstick Traces* (1989), "a secret history of the 20th century," in which the Situationists figure centrally, Greil Marcus limns a phantom community in the shadows: "Is history simply a matter of events that leave behind those things that can be weighed and measured—new institutions, new maps, new rulers, new winners and losers—or is it also the result of moments that seem to leave nothing behind, nothing but the mystery of spectral connections between people long separated by place and time, but somehow speaking the same language?"[12] In this sense the SI isn't finished.

Then, too, there was the move, sometimes made by Debord and associates, whereby failure was recouped as success, as, for example, in "Theses on the Paris Commune," published in 1962: "Theoreticians who examine the history of this movement from a divinely omniscient viewpoint (like that found in classical novels) can easily prove that the Commune was objectively doomed to failure and could not have been successfully consummated. They forget that for those who really lived it, the consummation was *already there*."[13] This seems to hold for Debord and company too. Yet even here there's a fatalism that contradicts the Situ language of "situation" and "construction." This fatalism is voiced most vividly in a scene from the movie *Mr. Arkadin* (1955), which Debord used to conclude his film version of *The Society of the Spectacle* (1973). Played by Orson Welles, the lordly Arkadin tells his guests at a ball in his castle the parable of the scorpion that asks a frog to carry him across a river. "Why should I risk it?" the frog replies. "You'll sting me." The scorpion responds that logic would prevent this outcome, for he too would then perish with his partner. Reassured, the frog agrees to assist the scorpion, but midway across he feels a deadly sting. Arkadin takes over from here: "'Logic?' cried the dying frog as he started pulling the scorpion down with him. 'Where is the logic in this?' 'I know,' said the scorpion, 'but I can't help it, it's my character.'" "Let's drink to character!" Arkadin cries, while on the screen Debord shows us found footage of a doomed cavalry charge. Debord was sometimes the scorpion, sometimes the frog, and always the cavalry charge.

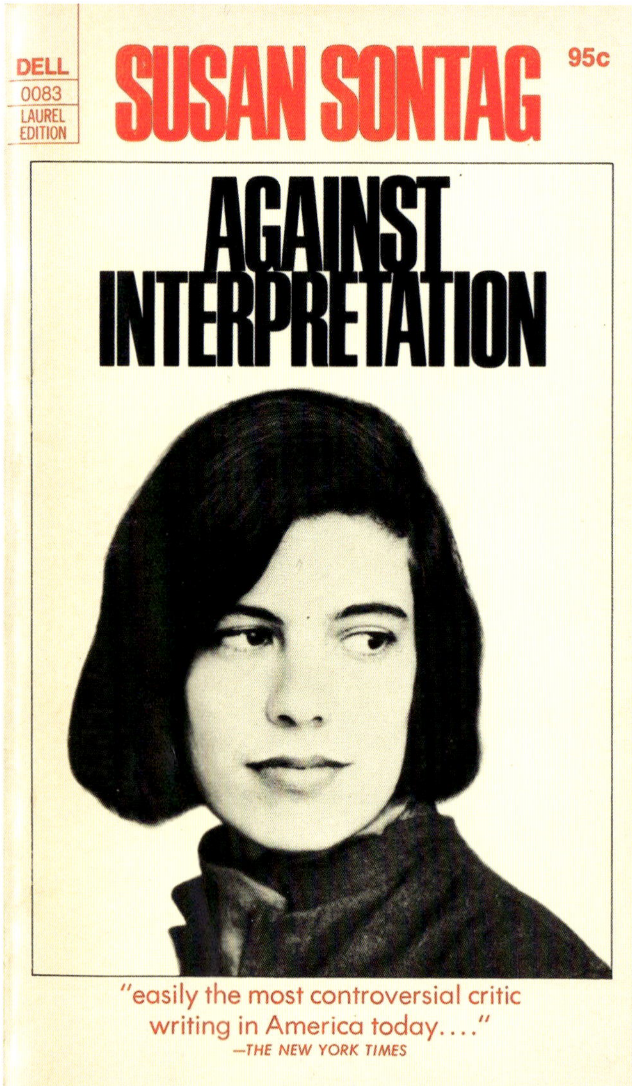

Cover of *Against Interpretation* by Susan Sontag. Photo: Peter Hujar.

33 Radical Style

In the late 1960s very few critics penetrated American middle-class homes like mine, maybe Edmund Wilson, Malcolm Cowley, Lionel Trilling, one or two others, but Susan Sontag managed to be among them. Through a forceful combination of intellect and style, her books found a way into suburban dens where young rebels were in hiding, longing for an artistic culture that might somehow match the political upheaval of the time. Like other restless kids born in the Eisenhower years, I first encountered Sontag through her photograph on *Against Interpretation* (1966) showing a striking woman with short hair swept aside and intense gaze directed elsewhere (it was taken by her friend Peter Hujar). *So this*, I thought, *is what a New York intellectual looks like*. Austere like her prose and engaged like her subjects, Sontag was my first inkling of avant-garde culture, my initial point of access to an edgy alternative to the Anglophonic modernism—Yeats, Eliot, Pound, Joyce—that represented high literature. Her European protagonists—Lukács, Sartre, Camus, Leiris, Artaud, Weil, Sarraute, Pavese, Cioran, Ionesco, Godard, Bresson, Resnais, Bergman—were exotic to me, and the notion that philosophers, writers, and filmmakers could be political was even more so. I didn't understand the many differences among these figures, but I sensed a shared posture, one that pointed to a way around the given terms of American culture, mass versus elite, and American politics, liberal versus conservative. I too wanted to be *against*. If Sontag could cross over to my living room, maybe I could cross over to her New York downtown (which even then I took to be the name of an elective affinity as much as an actual place), and I was hardly alone in wanting to do so.

It was her combination of lucidity and ambition that made Sontag so attractive; hers was a "style of radical will," and we didn't understand then that her emphasis on style might also be her limitation. Certainly it prepared her critical success, which left Sontag, like other prominent women of her generation, somewhat unmoved by feminist critiques: smart and "serious" (her preferred term of approval) knew no gender for her. As is often remarked, Sontag was a popularizer, but only in part, and if she invented terms that later became clichés, isn't that what significant critics often do? (Two phrases that qualify in this respect are her plea for "an erotics of art" and her definition of camp as dandyism "in the age of mass culture.")[1] A more fitting appellation for Sontag is guide, which she was from beginning to end. Again, she introduced many of us to the figures discussed in *Against Interpretation* and *Styles of Radical Will* (1969), and later she insisted that her *New Yorker* readers should at least be acquainted with authors like W. G. Sebald and Alexander Kluge. However, by the time of *On Photography* (1977), *Illness as Metaphor* (1978), and *Under the Sign of Saturn* (1980) we had gained on her. We had read the same authors, often differently, studied others, and worked alternative lines of thought: the Frankfurt School, the different Marxisms of Althusser and Debord, Lacanian psychoanalysis, feminist film theory, deconstruction, discourse analysis, reception theory, and cultural studies. And we had received our reports from other sources as well—journals like *New Left Review*, *New German Critique*, *October*, and *Screen*—not from venues like her *Commentary*, *Partisan Review*, and the *New York Review of Books*, which remained mostly indifferent if not hostile to such critical work.[2]

Yet this flourishing of theory also made us more sectarian than Sontag was. From first to last, she was a committed generalist, a "master synthesist," as the *New York Times* obituary put it.[3] Although she was "against interpretation" in principle, Sontag was always for it in this sense: she believed deeply in her mission to report to interested laypeople about difficult avant-gardes. Today both sides of this relationship are less clear than they were then, and this difference makes the time of her rise appear distant. But then that very distance might challenge us to renew the vocation of mediator that she served for so long.

Sontag worked to bridge that gap on her own terms. At the same time, in "Notes on 'Camp'" (1964) and "One Culture and the New Sensibility" (1965), the two texts that made her name, she insisted that other notorious divides—between avant-garde and kitsch and between high and low culture—had narrowed. It wasn't easy to explain such matters, and sometimes Sontag showed the strain. Some of her arguments are more declared than demonstrated, with an authority claimed through assertion, though this is true of other commentary as well. (Clement Greenberg was expert at this apodictic sort of address, and many critics in the 1960s and '70s followed suit.)[4] Here, chosen more or less at random, are the first lines of a few essays from *Against Interpretation* and *Styles of Radical Will*: "The earliest experience of art must have been that it was incantatory." "Most serious thought in our time struggles with the feeling of homelessness." "A new mode of didacticism has conquered the arts, is indeed the 'modern' element in art." "Every era has to reinvent the project of 'spirituality' for itself." "Ours is a time in which every intellectual or artistic or moral event is absorbed by a predatory embrace of consciousness: historicizing." These are large claims, and sometimes they float away or pop like balloons, but in a way that is what they are, test balloons, and often enough they brought back accurate readings of the weather of the time.

Another vaunted term in the Sontag lexicon is "position." The rush to position, which sometimes seems endemic to criticism, can end up as a posture unless it's politically grounded. This isn't to question her commitment, which was evidenced by her controversial trips to Hanoi in 1968 and Sarajevo in 1993, her consistent support of oppressed writers through PEN, her courageous statements about AIDS, 9/11, and Abu Ghraib, but it is to query how much it transformed her own production, which was the crucial test for at least one of her favorites, Walter Benjamin. A common charge is that her seriousness was a matter of aesthetics or ethics more than politics, precisely a *style* of radical will. And her most engaged piece, "Trip to Hanoi" (1968), is about her own consciousness more than Vietnam, which becomes the scene of a personal disorientation, even though Sontag is also torturously aware of the Orientalism in play in her text. Sometimes she turned the treatment of a problem, political or aesthetic, into an explanation of herself. Moreover, some of her essays on fellow critics contain worries that sound autobiographical: Am I, like Cioran, not original enough? Like Benjamin, too saturnine? Like Barthes, too seduced by sensibility? In "Remembering Barthes," her moving homage to the great French critic on his death in 1980, Sontag touches on his "self-absorption" and comments that "his interest in you tended to be your interest in him."[5] One can't help but wonder the same about her.

But then "self-absorption" was central to her work, to its interest, even to its strength. Her essential method was to replay her thoughts while reading, to dramatize her struggle toward interpretation, and sometimes her shifts in perspective did lead Sontag to rethink and to write again. She could turn her political ambivalence into critical insight (at least since Baudelaire many important critics, especially when caught between class identifications, have done as much), and so Sontag made good on what Adorno (a critic she didn't much engage) once called "a flagrant contradiction"—that "the cultural critic is not happy with civilization, to which alone he owes his discontent."[6] Beyond critical insight, however, Sontag attempted to push her ambivalence into "passionate partiality," as she wrote (echoing Baudelaire on criticism) in her preface to *Against Interpretation*.[7] As she also implies there, criticism remained a literary offshoot for her, and sometimes her writing suggests an updated version of the *Bildungsroman*. This self-absorption could be excessive (when her book of short stories *I, Etcetera* came out in 1978, one heard the plea "less I, more others"), and sometimes Sontag advanced it in default of other grounds on which to work, as she does here in her 1967 essay on Cioran: "The time of new collective visions may well be over. . . . But the need for individual spiritual counsel has never seemed more acute. *Sauve qui peut*."[8] No collective vision, everyone for himself, in 1967?

For these reasons I balked when the *New York Times* obituary claimed that Sontag made "a radical break" with the postwar criticism of New York intellectuals, especially those around *Partisan Review*. Early on, her fondest dream was to write for that journal. Like most of its contributors, she occupied a cosmopolitan territory associated with the academy but not restricted to it (no university presses for her), and she made a living as an independent critic—not easy then and almost impossible now. More important, though she might challenge particular judgments of *Partisan Review* writers, her language of evaluation was largely consistent with theirs. Against interpretation, Sontag remained an interpreter; dismissive of the opposition of form and content, she didn't deconstruct it but valued style where they had valued "substance." And her other central terms are all old-school: "condition," "sensibility," "temperament," "taste." "Taste," she states in "Notes on 'Camp,'" "governs every free—as opposed to rote—human response."[9] For good or bad, no one who has passed through Adorno, Althusser, Lacan, Derrida, or Foucault, let alone Bourdieu, could easily write such a sentence. However opposed in principle to "the Matthew Arnold apparatus," Sontag also argued for "the best that has been thought and known" in culture, as well as for a necessary connection between the aesthetic and the moral—and what could be more Arnoldian than her "seriousness"?[10] Certainly, her embrace of popular culture irritated some New York intellectuals, for it seemed to undercut their faith in modernism as high culture. Hence, in part, their enormous resentment of the counterculture of the 1960s, which also derided this belief, and their marked shift from liberalism to neoconservatism over that period.[11] Yet for Sontag the embrace of popular culture was a testing of high/low divides, a testing that was avant-gardist, not populist. Seriousness was always the criterion, even when it was mocked, as in camp; and sophistication was still the goal, even when it concerned the products of entertainment.

Strong signs of her good standing as a New York intellectual (perhaps Sontag was the last of the kind) were the encomia delivered by the *New York Times* on her death in December 2004 (no less than four articles), in stark contrast, say, to the smear given Derrida when he died three months before her. Charles McGrath, former editor of the *New York Times Book Review*, proclaimed her "the preeminent intellectual of our time," a valuation that depends, of course, on the definition of "intellectual," let alone of "our time."[12] The preeminent *critic*? On this score she was overshadowed by Barthes, to name just one. The preeminent *theorist*? That's not her category. One test of intellectual preeminence is whether young critics continue to engage the work, and Sontag isn't high on reading lists today. Perhaps she's too New York or "American," neither "French" or systematic enough in her thought, nor "German" or philosophical enough, nor "British" or social-historical enough. She didn't participate in the great rereadings of Marx, Nietzsche, and Freud, which did in fact produce a "radical break with traditional postwar criticism."[13] She also didn't write much about the great adventures of the sign, the psyche, and sexuality that were so formative to "the preeminent intellectuals of our time." Nor was identity her thing. Perhaps the strength of her work—the focus on European avant-gardes—now appears as its restriction, but she's not alone there.

In every cultural interregnum there are a few figures on whom old and new generations can agree. Mahler was one such composer in fin-de-siècle Vienna. Sontag was one such critic in the latter decades of the last century, indulged by old New York intellectuals as a willful prodigy, yet valued by post-1968 intellectuals as a countercultural voice. As such she also served as a buffer between the two generations, and she was celebrated in part for this compromise position. In this light Sontag was less a new model of the intellectual than a transitional figure between the critic and the theorist: between the critic, liberal in culture and politics, with one foot in (memories of) the Old Left and one foot in the studio, and the theorist, radical at least in philosophy, with one foot in (memories of) the New Left and one foot in the academy.

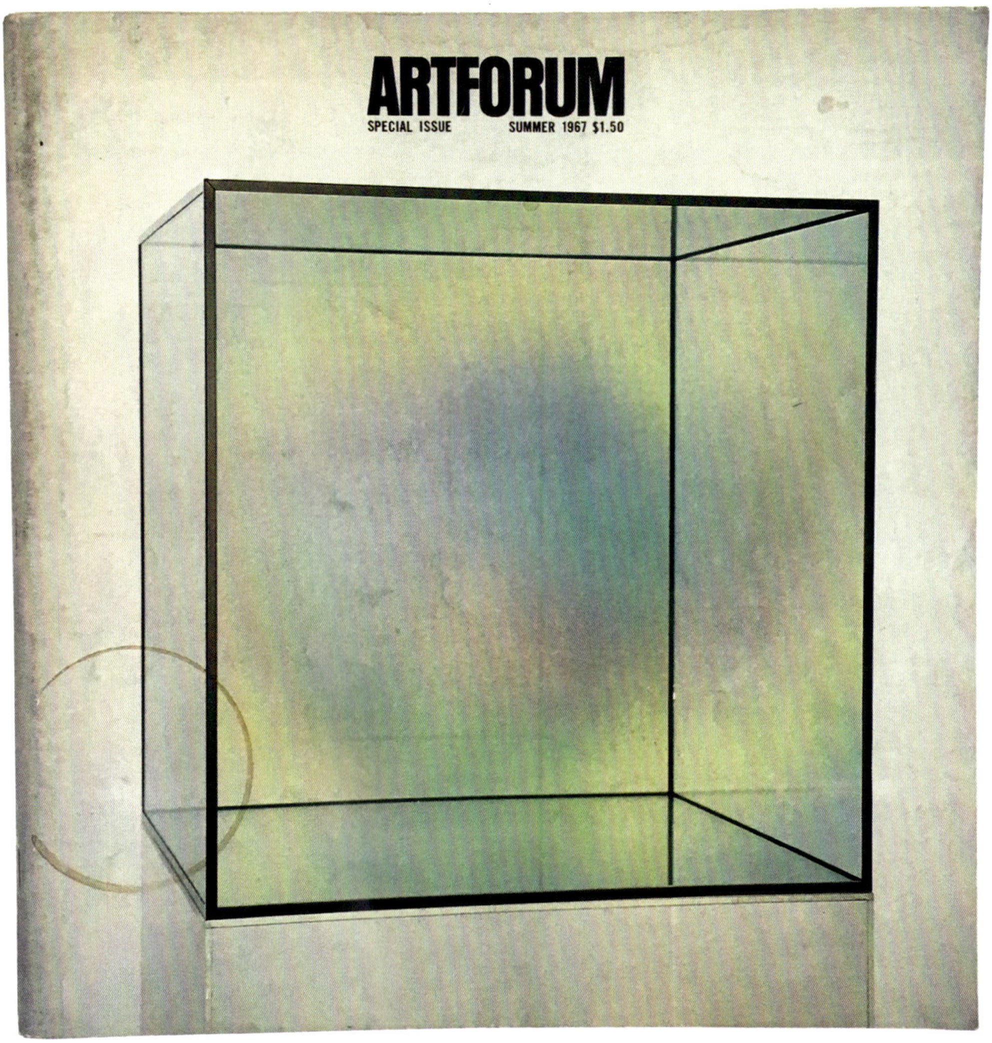

Cover of Summer 1967 issue of *Artforum*, with Larry Bell's *Memories of Mike* (1966–1967).

34 Hyperbolic Criticism

How can we account for the rhetorical intensity of the art criticism published in *Artforum* in its initial heyday, from the mid 1960s to the early 1970s? That era of the magazine saw Michael Fried prosecuting Minimalism in his brief against "objecthood," Robert Morris deconstructing sculpture in his series of essays on the subject, and Rosalind Krauss parsing the "sense and sensibility" of Postminimalist practice, to name only a few examples.[1] This writing was so incisive about the art of its moment in part because it was produced by its makers or their interlocutors. *Artforum* took full advantage of the new phenomenon of the artist-critic, which included Robert Smithson and Mel Bochner, among others.

Sometimes, though, the criticism overreached in its claims. In retrospect, Krauss designated hyperbole as the "very form of speech" of the magazine under the editorship of Philip Leider, and Fried admitted to the "tremendous stress on the writing" during the same period.[2] For Fried this strain was born of the struggle "to get the intensity of the response into the right register," to match the power of the relevant art rhetorically.[3] Yet some skeptics argued the converse. In a notorious instance Tom Wolfe declared late modernist art to be little more than an illustration of late modernist criticism, a "painted word."[4] *Pace* Fried, the writing was more than a response to the art, and, *pace* Wolfe, it was less than a conspiracy of critics. Rather, it was a system of support that was semiautonomous, and it was driven by anxiety as much as by ambition. "The verbal part, the theoretical part, sustained me through my doubts," Leider remarked. "Every time I began to doubt the way things looked, the value, the quality, the plain quality of the work as it looked to me, I was able to fall back on this *structure* of thought."[5]

Sometimes late modernist critics made fine distinctions on which the fate of art was thought to depend—the difference, say, between the "deductive structure" in a Frank Stella, which asked to be seen as a painting, and the "specific object" in a Donald Judd, which did not—and often they presented these distinctions as absolute.[6] Hyperbole was doubtless in play here, but so, too, was hypostatization, an awkward term for a common move in criticism, which is the inflating of a particular characteristic of art into a general criterion of aesthetics. As Clement Greenberg wrote first of the “flatness” of late modernist painting, and later of its “opticality,” adjectives became nouns, and attributes became values.[7] Why this drive to hypostatize? These terms clarified important aspects of the art of the time, to be sure, but they also served as bulwarks for an aesthetic field that was under enormous pressure (it wasn't only criticism that was strained). In fact, this field was already breached from without and eroded from within. The external enemy was variously labeled “kitsch” (Greenberg), “theatricality” (Fried), or simply “mass culture” (Pop art was targeted as the great traitor here), while the internal enemy was the extended arena of artistic activities, often performative in nature, opened up by Happenings, Fluxus, Nouveau réalisme, Minimalism, Conceptualism, Process art, and so on. For late modernist critics these activities were problematic because they exceeded the proper parameters of painting and sculpture, but even more so because they threatened to push art into an arbitrary realm beyond aesthetic judgment. One could always evaluate painting and sculpture in relation to their storied pasts; this wasn't possible with novel forms and media.

The arbitrary was an acute problem for artists too. If some resisted it through a refinement of late modernist painting in the form of an ever more reflexive abstraction, others undertook a “search for the motivated” in the physicality of new materials and processes or in the actuality of the body of the artist and the site of the work.[8] Ironically, even as the latter project aimed to remotivate art and to reground it—that is, to render its making and its meaning more transparent to its audience—the result was often the opposite: it made art appear more arbitrary, rarefied, illegible. Ironically, too, the former project wasn't so different in its implications, for the refinement of late modernist painting didn't disclose the definitive essence of this art (as Greenberg hoped it would), or even its necessary conventionality (the correction offered by Fried), so much as it revealed the fragility of its conventions as the basis of shared meanings—shared, that is, by a public that was broader than the assiduous readership of *Artforum*. That's why, at a time when the operations of art became both more varied and less legible, “compelling conviction” (a phrase often used by Fried) became so urgent—and, again, so strained. “It was an enterprise,” Fried wrote in his 1971 essay on Morris Louis, “which unless inspired by moral and intellectual passion was fated to triviality and unless informed by uncommon powers of moral and intellectual discrimination was doomed to failure.”[9] A decade and a half later Thomas Crow glossed this statement succinctly: “Modernist criticism brought into the 1960s a surplus of moral commitment that was the relic of an earlier dream of art as the focus of an ideal public sphere.”[10]

What was involved in the hypostatization of aesthetic attributes into critical values, then, was the displacement of commitments that were moral, intellectual, and—yes—political. Already in his 1965 essay "Three American Painters: Kenneth Noland, Jules Olitski, Frank Stella," Fried pointed to this displacement but didn't name it as such. There he wrote of a "dialectic of modernism" that was consonant with the Hegelian-Marxist "conception of historical progression," according to which, through "radical criticism" of each new conjuncture, the Trotskyite hope of "perpetual revolution" was kept alive. "It is no wonder such an ideal has not been realized in the realm of politics," Fried concluded, "but it seems to me that the development of modernist painting over the past century has led to a situation that may be described in these terms."[11] Today, with the 1960s long behind us, this statement might elicit astonishment at its ambition or admiration for its faith, or merely a rueful sigh. But what must also strike us is how positive Fried was in his understanding of modernist painting as a continuation of the dialectic by other means—or, more precisely, a partial compensation for its apparent breakdown in the political realm—whereby permanent revolution in social life might be somehow sublimated into permanent innovation in artistic form.

However, if we simply decry this displacement as a retreat or even a ruse, we overlook what it aimed to retain, such as the basic expectation that artists and critics alike work through the central problems posed by their ambitious predecessors ("work through" in a sense that is Freudian as well as Hegelian-Marxist). Even more fundamental was the idea that art and criticism might still serve, if not as agents of history, then at least as indices of historical change, and hence as forms of critical consciousness with respect to the cultural significance of such change. (Here again it becomes clear why the arbitrary posed such a threat.) Today the notion that art and criticism might be a means of purchase on a past that opens onto both a present and a future seems farfetched, almost bizarre. We can call this idea whatever we like—naive, parochial, chimerical—and we can dismiss it as a petty expression of a will to power whereby art history is read forward into contemporary practice in such a way that an elect few are scripted in and everyone else is dropped out. But we should also acknowledge what was lost when it was junked.

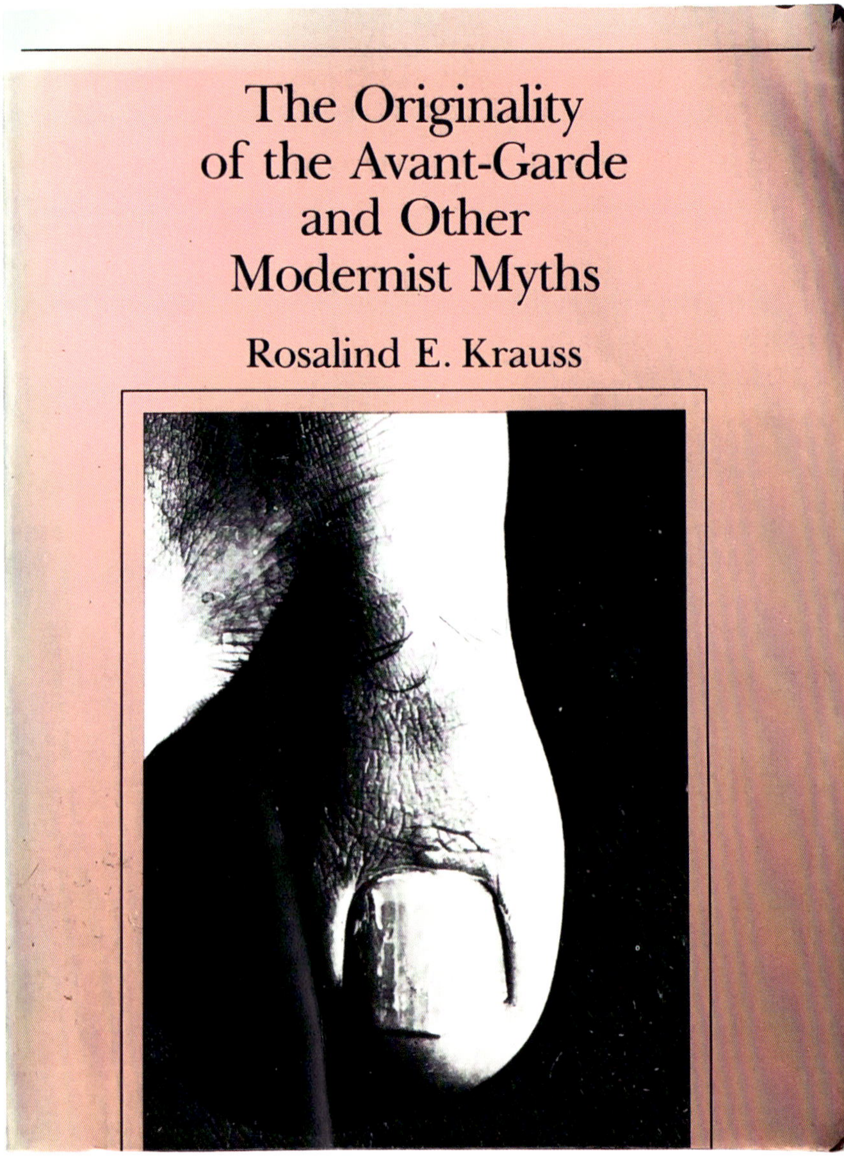

Cover of *The Originality of the Avant-Garde and Other Modernist Myths* by Rosalind E. Krauss, with Jacques-André Boiffard's *Big Toe* (1929).

35 Made for Cutting

In September 1972, in the tenth anniversary issue of *Artforum*, Rosalind Krauss published an essay titled "A View of Modernism." Though only thirty at the time, she had already written for the magazine for several years, commuting to New York from Harvard, where she was at work on a PhD, to review exhibitions. During this period Krauss was a follower of Clement Greenberg, to the point where Donald Judd had dubbed her, along with Michael Fried, a "Greenberger." "A View of Modernism" was her declaration of apostasy.[1]

First, though, Krauss detailed her attraction to the Greenbergian account of modernist art, which lay primarily in its method. It "demanded lucidity," and it asked that its language be subject to "testing," that its claims be verified by direct reference to the work under discussion (this was not always true of Greenberg, it must be said). Above all, it stipulated that "perceptions about art in the present" be tied back to "the art of the past," that there be a "historical logic" to any argument. These demands encouraged a "curiously dissociated tone," Krauss admitted, one that "I could hide behind," and that is "why I wrote like a forty-year-old." This last comment referred to a remark, made by *Artforum* editor Philip Leider at their first meeting, that had stung the young critic.

The historical logic of the Greenbergian account aimed for "the clear provability of an 'if x then y.'" It was "progressive," moving "only in one direction," from Manet through Cézanne and Picasso, to Pollock, Helen Frankenthaler, Kenneth Noland, and others.[2] Modernist art thus appeared to Krauss "like a series of rooms *en filade*":

> Within each room the individual artist explored, to the limits of his experience and his formal intelligence, the separate constituents of his medium. The effect of his pictorial act was to open simultaneously the door to the next space and close out access to the one behind him. The shape and dimensions of the new space were discovered by the next pictorial act; the only thing about that unstable position that was clearly determined beforehand was its point of entrance.
>
> This historical logic seemed to be based on two familiar assumptions. First, each medium has a specific nature, and the distinctive element of painting is its flatness, which pre-modernist art had occluded in the pursuit of spatial illusionism. Second, the task of the modernist artist is to reveal another aspect of that essential nature, usually as prompted by the aspect revealed just before.[3]

"I never doubted the absoluteness of that history," Krauss commented about her younger self. "It was out there, manifest in a whole progression of works of art, an objective fact to be analyzed."[4] But then she did begin to doubt it, and gradually she lost "the sense of historical necessity" in the contemporary practices advocated by Greenberg and Fried. At the same time, she was compelled by other kinds of art, including work that demanded to be experienced over time, which violated the additional Greenbergian criterion that visual art be present to the viewer all at once, that it involve no "theatrical" duration, as Fried put it famously in "Art and Objecthood" (1967). As one such artist Krauss named Richard Serra, whose sculpture neither Greenberg nor Fried could support. She also mentioned structuralism, which suggested that she was already on the lookout for an alternative methodology.

Although Krauss doesn't delve into structuralism in "A View of Modernism," she does cite Alain Robbe-Grillet, who, a decade before, had launched a critique of the bourgeois novel. Its omniscient narrators and linear plots "tended to impose the image of a stable, coherent, continuous, unequivocal, entirely decipherable universe," the *nouveau romancier* argued, and this "innocence" had to be put aside.[5] Krauss detected a related innocence in the Greenbergian account of modernism: like traditional narrative, it too aimed to appear "stable, coherent, continuous, unequivocal." Ironically, insofar as it arranged its historical artists in an orderly sequence (those rooms *en filade*), it also assumed a "perspectival armature." "The flatness that modernist criticism reveres may have expunged spatial perspective," Krauss charged, "but it has substituted a temporal one—i.e., history."[6] So, too, though it insisted on self-criticism on the part of artists, it wasn't reflexive enough about its own tenets, and it had become prescriptive to boot.

The Greenbergian account of modernism also had blind spots, which now appeared as such to Krauss. It couldn't locate a specific nature in sculpture (Greenberg tried out "opticality," but the transfer of this painterly quality appeared to contradict his own principle of medium-specificity), and it questioned whether film could qualify as a modernist endeavor at all (it was too bound up with the world, it unspooled in time, etc.). In response Krauss turned to movements scanted by Greenberg, above all to Surrealism, which he had dismissed as "literary," not medium-specific enough.[7] Already in 1971 Krauss co-curated an exhibition of Joan Miró at the Guggenheim Museum, and over the next few decades she undertook a rereading of Surrealism through the writings of the dissident Surrealist Georges Bataille (heretofore André Breton had dominated most accounts of the movement). This research led Krauss first to an interpretation of Alberto Giacometti (for the 1984 *Primitivism* exhibition at Museum of Modern Art) that redirected attention to his pre-Existentialist concern with Bataillean *bassesse*, as well as to a theory of Surrealist photography (for her 1985 show *L'Amour fou: Photography and Surrealism* at the National Gallery in Washington, DC) that conceived it as a subversive enterprise dedicated to Bataillean formlessness.[8]

In 1971 Krauss transformed her dissertation on David Smith into her first book, *Terminal Iron Works*, which Greenberg endorsed.[9] However, her next volume, *Passages in Modern Sculpture* (1977), followed through on the apostasy announced in "A View of Modernism" in 1972. Rather than a historicist narrative of twentieth-century sculpture, the "passages" of the title concerns the actual movement of the viewer around and through the work that Krauss had come to value. In effect, *Passages* is an account of sculpture from Rodin to Serra read through the Minimalist and Postminimalist preoccupations with structure, embodiment, and space. This framing worked to relocate the meaning of the artwork in its material surface and public setting rather than in any hidden interior or private intention that might transcend its time and place.[10] For this argument Krauss drew on phenomenology as well as structural linguistics; coeval with the mature sculpture of Rodin, both philosophies became current again in the aesthetic debates of the 1960s and 1970s sparked by Minimalism and Postminimalism. This reorientation signaled the key features of her post-Greenbergian criticism: to opt for structural analysis over historical explanation, to look for epistemic connections between art and philosophy (or what Foucault termed the "historical *a priori*" that underwrites both), and to be guided by the example of contemporary practice and theory in the process.[11]

Another rupture occurred in 1976 when Krauss resigned from *Artforum* along with fellow editor Annette Michelson. In their view the new editor-in-chief, John Coplans, was focused on art as "social statement" and was thus "hostile to the aesthetic concerns" that most engaged them.[12] To pursue these interests they launched *October* magazine (the painter-critic Jeremy Gilbert-Rolfe coedited the first three issues); they also wanted a venue to develop the new French theory that informed their recent thinking. This was not a project for *Artforum* or, for that matter, literary journals like *Partisan Review* and the *New York Review of Books*. In fact, at a 1980 symposium organized by *Partisan Review*, Krauss targeted such publications as retrograde for that reason. In her talk, published as "Poststructuralism and the Paraliterary" in *October* a year later, Krauss argued that poststructuralism challenged the principles of humanist literary criticism as well as formalist art criticism. Although publications like *Partisan Review* had once championed modernist experiments in writing, they had either ignored or denigrated the very theory that now constituted the "paraliterary" avant-garde. "Barthes and Derrida are *the* writers, not the critics, that students now read," Krauss concluded. This polemic made official what was already obvious: a divide had opened up between "downtown" and "uptown" in criticism as well as in art.

If a first project of *October* was to advance poststructuralist theory in the United States, a second was to come to terms with postmodernist art—which was only recently understood as such—with the aid of this theory. Whereas *October* looked to Paris for the theory, it still focused on New York for the art. Krauss took the lead here, but she was supported by her students at the CUNY Graduate Center (where she had taught since 1977), above all Douglas Crimp and Craig Owens, who had begun to write for *October* by the late 1970s. A third project of the magazine was to disarticulate "the discourse of modernism" received from Greenberg and others, and to do so through the double lens of poststructuralist theory and postmodernist art; here her declared apostasy became active deconstruction. Krauss published most of her texts along these lines in *October*, and in 1985 she collected them under the title *The Originality of the Avant-Garde and Other Modernist Myths*.[13]

As announced in the title, the central myth in question was the vaunted originality of modernist art. Since modernist critics were steeped in the same discourse as the artists, they couldn't analyze its assumptions effectively. Poststructuralist theory and postmodernist art provided the necessary perspective, for both revealed how "originality" often "emerges from a ground of repetition and recurrence."[14] Mindful of Benjamin as well as Barthes and Derrida, Krauss found repetition and recurrence both revealed and repressed in the work of central figures such as Rodin and Monet. Despite "the autographic character" of his sculpture, Rodin liked to assemble his work out of repeated elements; he also permitted posthumous casts and so opened his oeuvre "to an afterlife of mechanical reproduction." Monet also participated in an "aesthetic economy of the pairing of singularity and multiplicity"; the effects of spontaneity and uniqueness in his paintings of the Rouen Cathedral facade, say, were produced through the continual reworking and serial formatting of his canvases. Krauss found repetition and recurrence at work in paradigmatic forms such as the grid and the monochrome as well. When modernist painters like Mondrian crossed over into abstraction, they arrived at an ur-form of painting, the grid, whose pure presence appeared self-evident, only to discover that under each iteration there was always "another, prior system of grids . . . a system of reproductions without an original."[15]

The Originality of the Avant-Garde remains a brilliant demonstration of deconstructive art history: Krauss shows how, in practice as well as in theory, the discredited term in binaries such as copy/original and multiple/unique often underwrites the privileged term. Although such deconstruction might appear rote today, that was hardly the case four decades ago. Already then, too, Krauss was alert to how the discourse of originality served the museum and the market, not to mention academic art history. As she acknowledged in her introduction, this awareness prompted "the often combative posture" of her writing.[16] Shuttered from the events of the 1960s, academic art history in the 1970s was still an erratic patriarch clothed in a threadbare tweed of connoisseurship and iconography, dismissive of contemporary art and critical theory alike, and Krauss had the *chutzpa* to take on this old guard—though social and feminist art historians such as T. J. Clark, Thomas Crow, Linda Nochlin, and Griselda Pollock were forceful combatants in this war too.

Then as now Krauss is an agonistic thinker by design: a characteristic strategy of her texts is to set up a given account, undercut it, and then pivot to her own reading. Nevertheless, the motive of her criticism was less to pass judgment than to reflect on that very operation. "The interest of critical writing lies almost entirely in its method," Krauss asserted in *The Originality of the Avant-Garde*; in "constituting the object of criticism, [it] exposes to view those choices that precede and predetermine any act of judgment."[17] Like other essential thinkers in the history of the discipline, Krauss demonstrated that art is "good to think with," and in a way that takes little away from its affective dimension.[18] In fact, she insisted on the primacy of aesthetic experience almost as much as Greenberg did.

Again, even as Krauss launched a poststructuralist critique of modernism, her first precept was a structuralist one: to consider art on the model of language as understood by Saussure, a model that understood signification to be "a function of the system at a given moment in time—the system synchronically displayed—rather than the outcome of a specific development or history."[19] Thus her focus was less on what a work means, and even less on what might have caused it in the first place, than on how it signifies. This emphasis led Krauss to diagram the structural relationship among different types of work. The most influential example is her use of "the Klein Group" in "Sculpture in the Expanded Field" (1979), which repositioned sculpture as just one site in "the quaternary field" defined by the oppositions of architecture and landscape and not-architecture and not-landscape.[20] Yet the most sustained application is her deployment of the "L Schema" of Lacan in *The Optical Unconscious* (1993), which uncovered various versions of visuality repressed by the formalist account of modernism. More importantly, this approach drew Krauss to concepts that cut across disparate practices synchronically, connecting them in surprising ways.

"Notes on the Index" (1976–1977) offers an early instance of this kind of concept at work. After the rapid-fire positions of the 1960s, a fatigue with art movements set in during the 1970s, and no stylistic designation could comprehend the wide range of production in any case. However, for Krauss this pluralism, which was both celebrated and lamented at the time, was only apparent, for a good part of the aesthetic field was actually informed by the operations of a single type of sign: the index. "As distinct from symbols, indexes establish their meaning along the axis of a physical relationship to their referents," Krauss explained with reference to the semiotics of Charles Peirce. "They are the marks or traces of a particular cause, and that cause is the thing to which they refer, the object they signify."[21] A footprint is a classic example, but a photograph is an index too (at least in its analog modes, which were still dominant then), and it was this direct registering of physical presence that Krauss detected in diverse work of the 1970s—from body, performance, and video art to site-specific installations, earthworks, and related documentation. Krauss believed that much abstract painting was also reconceived in indexical terms as "the mute presence of an uncoded event."[22]

Although this framing of artwork was primarily synchronic, it opened up a diachronic perspective that allowed Krauss to detect an indexical operation in Duchamp too. This is evident in his later objects such as *Female Fig Leaf* (1950) and *With My Tongue in My Cheek* (1954), which seem to involve direct impressions of body parts. But Krauss also revealed his early painting *Tu m'* (1918), which was not much discussed until this point, to be "a panorama of the index," with its depicted index finger and distended shadows of readymades as well as its actual tear in the canvas. More provocatively, she reinterpreted the readymade as an indexical event in its own right—as "the physical transposition of an object from the continuum of reality into the fixed condition of the art-image by a moment of isolation, or selection."[23] This definition revealed an unexpected connection between the readymade and the photograph in Duchamp and other artists.

The strategy of "Notes on the Index" became a modus operandi for Krauss: a particular practice, contemporary or historical, suggests a model of art, such as indexical mark-making, which is then found to operate in other practices that aren't otherwise related to it stylistically or formally. The impetus can also be theoretical in origin. For example, in "Bachelors" (1989) Krauss detected a type of sculpture that combines aspects of the psychoanalytic concept of "the part object" with aspects of the Duchampian device of "the bachelor machine," a type that she then revealed to be active, intermittently, from Duchamp and Brancusi through Eva Hesse to Sherrie Levine, with different implications depending on which term (part object or bachelor machine) is more pronounced in a given work. In this way Krauss sketched out a diachronic series of structural effects, not a historicist line of stylistic influences.[24] Due to her fierce critique of historicism, and her repeated appeal to structure over history as a mode of explanation, Krauss has tended to underplay the diachronic dimension of such arguments. Nevertheless, this genealogical perspective is one of her primary contributions to modernist studies in particular and to art history in general.

This counterintuitive claim requires some explanation. One undertaking common to both structuralism and poststructuralism was a critical return to key thinkers of modernity. Initially these rereadings were focused on three figures—Marx, Freud, and Nietzsche—as advanced by Althusser, Lacan, and Foucault and Deleuze respectively. Although these returns weren't as objective as they purported to be, they did aim to strip away extraneous interpretations in order to recover the conceptual radicality of the historical theorists. The first proposition of these revisions was that the work of each thinker constituted a rupture with the relevant discourse that preceded him, "an epistemological break," to use the phrase that Althusser adopted from Gaston Bachelard. (In his case Althusser meant to underscore the leap from the young, "pre-scientific" Marx, steeped in the humanist ideology of the Hegelian tradition, which was still privileged by Sartre, Guy Debord, and others, to the mature, "scientific" Marx, founder of dialectical materialism, on which Althusser aimed to build.)[25] Such breaks were thought to reconfigure the given discourse almost entirely. At the same time, even as the rereading recovered this rupture for the present, it also opened up the historical field to its own epistemological complexity.

This was the second implication of such revisions, one made explicit by Lacan, who described the methodological "wager" of his return to Freud as an attempt "to promulgate as necessary to any articulation of [psycho]analytic phenomena the notion of the signifier, as opposed to that of the signified, in modern linguistic analysis."

> Freud could not take this notion, which postdates him, into account, but I would claim that [his] discovery stands out precisely because, although it set out from a domain in which one could not expect to recognize [structural linguistics], it could not fail to anticipate its formulas. Conversely, it is Freud's discovery that gives to the signifier/signified opposition the full extent of its implications.[26]

Lacan followed this statement with his famous formulation: "It is not only man who speaks, but . . . in man and through man it speaks [*ça parle*—i.e., the id speaks, the unconscious speaks]. . . . His nature is woven by effects in which is to be found the structure of language, of which he becomes the language."

Hence his influential understanding of the unconscious as "structured like a language," of the signifier as primary to the signifier, of desire as a "metonymic" displacement from one object to another, and of the symptom as a "metaphorical" condensation of a psychic conflict onto the physical plane of the body. In short, Lacan reread Freudian psychoanalysis through Saussurean linguistics, and in the recovery of the extensive implications of both discourses he also sketched the epistemological field that they share—an interdisciplinary exchange that couldn't occur then because, though almost exact contemporaries, Freud and Saussure weren't aware of one another.

In the late 1980s, partnered with Yve-Alain Bois, Krauss undertook a related return to a fundamental figure of modernist art. They revisited Picasso, in particular his Cubist collages, *papiers collés*, and constructions circa 1912, and reread him, as Lacan did Freud, through Saussure. In doing so they not only recovered the aesthetic radicality of this aspect of his art (against interpretations that read it in formalist terms of flatness or in social-iconographic terms of popular culture), but also opened it up to its own epistemological field, and thus demonstrated how Cubism is semiotic in its own way.[27] Again, this strategy was already incipient in *Passages in Modern Sculpture* where Krauss reinterpreted twentieth-century sculpture in terms of both phenomenology and structuralism. Both revisions involved a tracing of conceptual affinities across diverse fields, whereby contemporaries were read in terms of each other and related retrospectively in a way that couldn't be done at the time.[28]

A third implication emerged in such revisions, especially in the return to Nietzsche led by Foucault and Deleuze, and that was the urgency of the project of genealogy or "effective history." Here a few lines from Foucault became talismanic. "History becomes 'effective' to the degree that it introduces discontinuity into our very being," Foucault wrote in his 1971 essay on Nietzsche. "Effective history studies what is closest, but in an abrupt dispossession, so as to seize it at a distance. . . . Through this historical sense, knowledge is allowed to create its own genealogy in the act of cognition; and [effective history] composes a genealogy as the vertical projection of its position."[29] From such tenets—above all, that knowledge is "made for cutting"—Foucault developed his own "history of the present" through his various analyses of madness, clinics, prisons, and other discourses and institutions. This isn't a history in the service of the present, one that serves to monumentalize it in relation to the past, but, on the contrary, a genealogy that seeks to problematize the present through history read "against the grain."[30] It is a double intervention that aims to defamiliarize both the present and the past, the one through the other.[31]

This leads to a basic principle that Krauss has long put into practice: rather than apply theory mechanically to art, art should be shown to be theoretical in its own terms and with its own ramifications. Theory and art can be tested against each other, in large part so as to elucidate the concepts embedded in practice and to point to the parallels with concepts in other disciplines, both in its moment and thereafter. Krauss won over readers not only with the lucidity of this demonstration (a criterion of criticism retained from Greenberg) but also with the charisma of its insights. This was an identification less with a person than with a position: she showed that one can be an art historian *and* an intellectual, and be so with commitment; more, that one can be an art historian, a critic, *and* a theorist, and be so without contradiction.

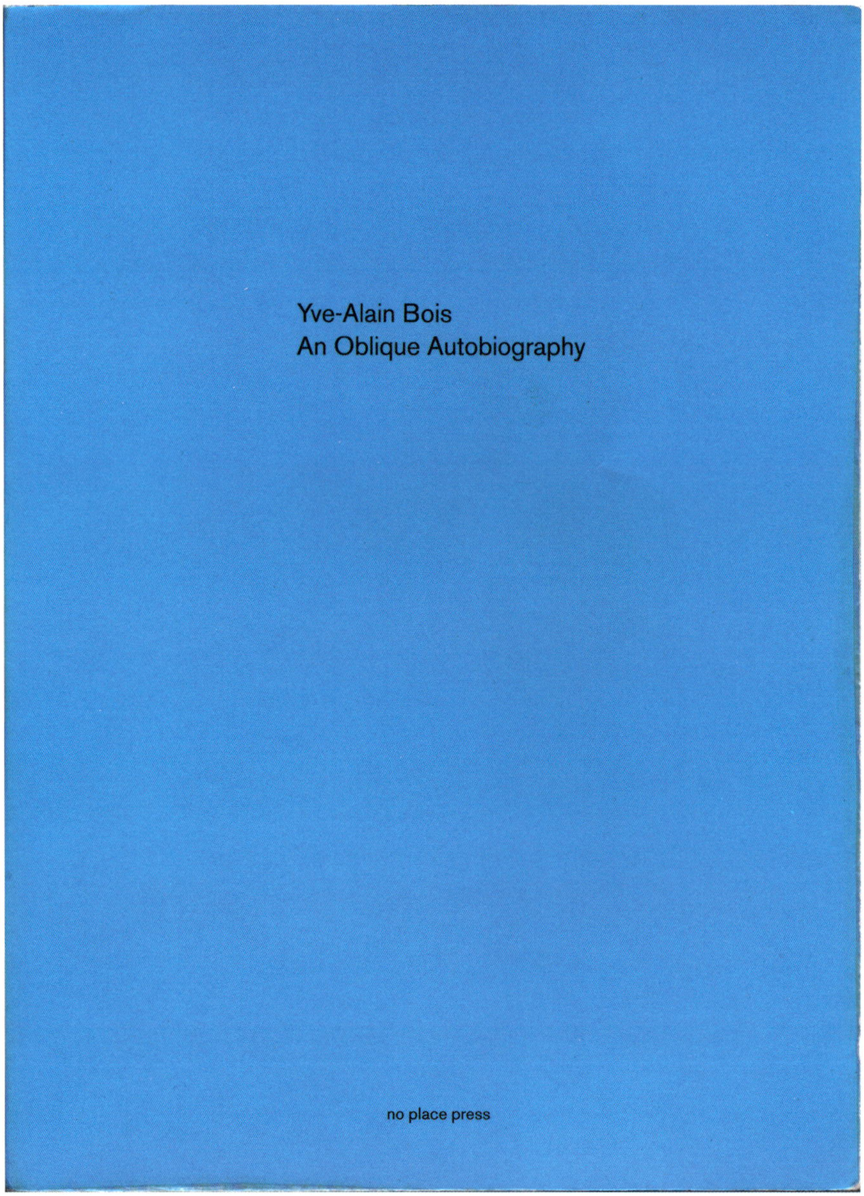

Cover of *An Oblique Autobiography* by Yve-Alain Bois. Design: Geoff Kaplan.

36 An Inventory of Encounters

Origin stories of artists are familiar, but not those of art historians. Yve-Alain Bois, the preeminent modernist among French scholars of his generation, narrates his beginnings in *An Oblique Autobiography*. One day he travels with his mother and little brother to Paris from a small town near Bordeaux. (Born in 1952, Bois thinks he was nine, though she puts him at five.) They head to the maritime museum, but it is closed, so on the spur of the moment his mother takes her boys to the nearby Musée National d'Art Moderne. For Bois the experience is almost Proustian, the art vivid to this day. There is the Brancusi studio donated to the French state by the Romanian sculptor, a room of Léger paintings, a huge allover canvas by the Canadian Jean-Paul Riopelle, a great Matisse cutout. Return visits confirm Bois in his desire to be an artist, and soon he knows exactly what kind: "a geometric abstract painter."[1]

As a teenager Bois writes blind letters to well-known figures and works odd jobs to fund solo trips to Paris, where he haunts galleries and museums chaperoned by a family friend, the critic Jean Clay, who teaches him how to look at painting. Though still in high school, Bois is swept up by the events of May 1968, which prompt him to connect radical art with radical politics whenever he can, an avant-garde commitment that is confirmed when he meets the Brazilian artist Lygia Clark later that summer. In 1969, age seventeen, Bois is offered an exhibition of his paintings in Paris, but he turns it down as premature. His interests then take a theoretical turn. On a tip from another family acquaintance, the philosopher Paul Ricoeur, Bois reads his first book on aesthetics, *The Open Work* (1962) by Umberto Eco, and buys his first book of art history, *Form and Meaning: Writings on the Renaissance and Modern Art* (1970) by Robert Klein. The latter includes an essay on "the eclipse of the work of art" that especially intrigues him. Soon Bois is obsessed with the transformations in American art glimpsed in the pages of *Artforum* magazine, and he contrives to come to the United States as an exchange student in 1970. Though isolated in rural Pennsylvania, he manages a few trips to New York, including momentous visits to the Museum of Modern Art, where he catches a Frank Stella exhibition, and the Guggenheim Museum, where he sees a Moholy-Nagy retrospective.

On his return to France Bois gives up his art-making, and after a tedious course in Pau, a small city in the southwest, he decides against art history too. The siren call now comes from critical theory, which has taken on the status of an avant-garde. To his surprise Roland Barthes accepts him into his seminar on semiology at the École Pratique des Hautes Études, which Bois begins in fall 1971. Barthes urges him to study also with Hubert Damisch, who becomes his other great mentor, steering him back toward art history. At this point Bois is all of nineteen. He calls his youth "immodest," but in fact it is precocious, and his writing has retained its verve for over fifty years—intellectually curious, conceptually brilliant, often witty, sometimes petulant.

Bois sees Barthes and Damisch in almost structural terms as "two perfectly complementary guides." Philosophically they have much in common: "the same enemies, the same structuralist past . . . the same capacity to actualize their inquiry, to make it relevant *hic et nunc*." Affectively, though, they are very different: Barthes plays the "seductive pied piper," Damisch the "tough love" father. Pedagogically, too, they take opposite approaches. Barthes teaches his students how to pare a project down to "a couple of essential issues," while Damisch shows them "how independent fields of knowledge can rub against one another, and how new ideas emerges from such friction." Damisch is also alert to how an apparent flaw in a mode of thought or practice might serve as its actual foundation, how "a structural system can only be 'proven' through a central exception—that it is what cannot be taken into account by a system, framed by it, that explains it and at the same time makes it possible for it to survive." Bois extracts this methodological lesson from *A Theory of /Cloud/* (1972), where Damisch demonstrates how clouds, precisely because they can't be drawn in one-point perspective, played an essential role in the development of this epochal technique. If this sounds like deconstruction, it is (by this time structuralism had given way to its poststructuralist critique), and in his own work Bois will often look for the deconstructive "cloud" in whatever artistic system is in question.

For his part Barthes demonstrates "how to write by writing in front of us." "Let us show ourselves in the speech-act," he says. "Let us write in the present." What Barthes passes on, then, is not a method per se but "a thousand practical recipes" that each student is left to adapt in his own way (most seminar participants were male). Barthes draws these critical tips from different phases of his work, which Bois glosses in his own terms. "Always look, behind Nature, for History" recalls the early Brechtian criticism in *Mythologies* (1957), while "Nothing that seems trivial is meaningless" echoes the 1968 exposé of "the reality effect" in realist fiction. Another lesson stems from *S/Z* (1970), where Barthes articulates the many codes in play in a single Balzac story. Bois understands it in this way: "We have to look at things very closely, *at the end of our nose*, as materially as possible, because only this slight nearsightedness frees us at the outset from the myth of Depth." For the poststructuralist Barthes, meaning dances on the surface of a text; it's "in the grain of things," Bois learns, that "the real flavor is found."

My favorite piece of direct advice from Barthes runs in a different direction: "It's when you lift your head that you're really reading." Perhaps the greatest gift a work can bestow is the semi-free association it inspires. "Barthes applied this floating quality to the entire sphere of language, to reading, to every utterance, to all conversation," and Bois turns this saying into a tip of his own. Wait for "the click" in your response to a given piece, "that sudden, insouciant turning of the key" that releases a rush of ideas. "Let a swarm of thoughts bounce off a snap; let the signs proliferate over and around an opposition, an analogy, before putting them in order." Finally, Barthes conveys to Bois "the Principle of Unbelief," a skepticism about method in the very practice of it. "Beware of Theory," Barthes says, "it is a great castrator." Bois draws three corollaries from this warning: retain "the right to abjure" (admit when you're wrong about a work), "the right to bypass" (not everything that seems urgent needs to be taken up), and "the right to safeguard" (keep historical authors handy since you never know when you might need them). If "no theory remains true forever," Bois concludes, it's also the case that "critical ideas should not be let go of prematurely."

Even in his early essays Barthes had an inkling of deconstruction, about how concepts are often put together out of opposed terms that can be picked apart. This is "how one begins," Bois understood him to suggest; "posit a paradigm in order to produce a meaning and then be able to divert, to alter it." Bois also learned this approach directly from Jacques Derrida, whom he read in high school and met during his studies in Paris: "first overturn a hierarchical opposition, then dispel its binarism by the introduction of a new concept." Derrida commissioned the twenty-one-year-old Bois to write an essay on Matisse, his first of several about the artist, for the illustrious journal *Critique*, which he took as a rite de passage: "I knew, after passing this test, that I could, if I wanted to, become an art historian." Bois later returned the favor when he asked Derrida to turn his notes concerning Martin Heidegger on van Gogh into an influential article that Bois published in the journal called *Macula*, which he launched with Jean Clay in 1976.[2] *An Oblique Autobiography* includes a stirring eulogy for Derrida and a scathing rebuttal of the stupid obituary published by the *New York Times*.

Like Derrida, Bois was born in Algeria, and his early years, spent in a mountain village, coincided with the Algerian war (the family returned to France in 1959). During the war his father, a scholarly Huguenot minister, was suspicious to both sides—to the Algerians because he was French, and to the French because he was sympathetic to the Algerians. This ambiguous, even deconstructive position may have left its mark on his son. Certainly, Bois sees a benefit in such "foreignness," which he defines as "the freedom with which the stranger can look at a complex cultural system without having to fully know or understand the rules of its game, a freedom that often enables the foreigner to pick and choose what is most vibrant (and most controversial) in a given culture." Above all he ascribes this lesson to Lygia Clark, who in her Paris exile "creatively misread" the European tradition of abstraction as she developed her own Neo-Concrete practice. "My first artistic epiphany was the discovery of the work of Mondrian," Bois tells us, but "my adolescent reading of his art, standard at the time," took it to be a "Neo-Platonic paean to pure form." "'*Au contraire*,' Clark told me, 'Mondrian is all about destruction.'" Mondrian also hinted at this understanding ("I think the destructive element is too much neglected in art"), and it prompted Bois to discover in his Neo-Plastic painting a perpetual deconstruction of the fundamental conventions of the medium—a relentless undoing of the oppositions of figure and ground, line and plane, and color and noncolor.[3] This lucid account of Mondrian was laid out beautifully in the 1994 retrospective that Bois curated with Angelica Rudenstine and Joop Joosten.

Mondrian grew up in a Calvinist family, a background that may have predisposed him to his iconoclastic version of abstraction. Might his Huguenot formation have had a similar effect on Bois? He would object to this psychobiographical angle, but his deconstructive understanding of abstraction is a through line of his writing. Bois sees it at work in austere painters like Martin Barré as well as expansive artists like Clark: "Her goal was to undo the empty/full, inside/outside oppositions upon which planar geometry and rationalism are based." It has also led Bois to highlight "noncompositional" strategies wherever he can find them. In abstract painting these devices include the monochrome, as initiated by Malevich and reiterated by many postwar artists; the grid, as proposed and then overcome by Mondrian; and various chance operations and found forms, as deployed by Ellsworth Kelly among others. Kelly is another painter who has inspired a deep commitment from Bois.[4]

Bois wrote his dissertation for Barthes and Damisch on conceptions of space in Malevich and El Lissitzky, and not long thereafter he delved into Russian and Polish Constructivism as well as Dutch de Stijl. No less than his methods did these interests make Bois foreign to the dominant concerns of art history and criticism in France as well as the United States. His primary targets in both countries were the same: a reductive use of iconography, which "mistakes the meaning of a work of art for its referent," and a superficial application of formalism, which attends more to how artworks appear morphologically than to how they signify structurally. Perversely for Bois, iconographers look for hidden themes even in abstract artworks, and formalists simply delight in "the pure visibility" there. Hence the two complaints that recur in *An Oblique Autobiography*, the first about the intellectual poverty of postwar French art writing and curating, the second about the dogma of modernist art promulgated by the American critic Clement Greenberg and his followers.

Greenberg positioned modernist art as part of the Enlightenment project that sought to ground every discipline in its own "area of competence." To pursue its proper mission painting had to highlight its medium-specific properties, "flatness and the delimitation of flatness" above all; what appeared extraneous must be rejected.[5] For Bois this version of modernism boiled down to two operations: essentialism and historicism. While the first posited an essence to painting, the second tasked artists with the gradual revelation of that essence. For a good stretch this mix of Kantian and Hegelian ideas helped to shore up modernist art history and to pilot contemporary art criticism. Curators also liked it since it offered a fairly straightforward story to tell from, say, Manet to Stella. And so "modernist painting" sailed along, skirting such reefs as Dada and Surrealism, until it ran into the sand in the 1960s.

Many others objected to this model of modernism as well. By the late 1960s Leo Steinberg had proposed "other criteria" to the ones marshaled by Greenberg, and by the early 1970s Rosalind Krauss had become a vocal apostate of his formalism.[6] Bois embraced both thinkers; in fact, Krauss counts as his third great intellectual encounter after Barthes and Damisch. Bois met Krauss in summer 1977 soon after she had founded *October* with the film theorist Annette Michelson and after he had launched *Macula* with Clay. The two journals had the same opponents: iconographic art history and formalist art criticism, not to mention all belletristic writing. And Krauss and Bois had similar projects: they wanted to use the tools of structuralism and poststructuralism to probe modernist art history and contemporary art criticism, fields that the leading French theorists had mostly overlooked. Along with other *October* authors, Krauss parsed postmodernist practices, which had fully emerged only then, with poststructuralist concepts. Bois, who was skeptical of the rubric of postmodernism, did much the same with modernist practices, collecting many such essays in *Painting as Model* (1990).

This double unpacking became the principal mission of *October* in its first decade (*Macula* folded after four issues, and eventually Bois became an editor of *October*). Krauss published her landmark book in this vein, *The Originality of the Avant-Garde and Other Modernist Myths*, in 1985; in a review Bois made the salient point about its Nietzschean credo: "that to be a real historian, one has to be a critic; that one cannot give an historical account unless one has a critical theory." This triangulation of history, criticism, and theory was a primary point of affinity between Bois and Krauss, and it led to important collaborations, such as, in the early 1980s, a semiotic rewriting of the Cubist collages of Picasso and Braque through structural linguistics, as well as, in the mid 1990s, an exhibition-cum-book titled *L'Informe* that highlighted the attacks on aesthetic form that had erupted intermittently in twentieth-century art (here the theoretical guide was Georges Bataille).[7]

Already in his 1971 seminar on semiology Barthes had pointed Bois to "the historical link between modernism and the awareness that language is a structure of signs." This link was the work of very different formalists, the Russians Roman Jakobson and Yuri Tynianov, who were not only close to modernist artists and writers like Malevich and Mayakovsky but also crucial to the subsequent development of structuralism by Claude Lévi-Strauss and others. (Lévi-Strauss, alas, didn't share their modernist commitments.) In effect, Bois used Russian formalism to break the hold of the American variety; it also launched him on one of his central lines of inquiry. No less than modernist art did Russian formalism respond to a fundamental predicament in modern culture at large: if neither Nature (aka the worldly referent) nor God (aka the transcendental signified) anchored representation any longer, what did? And if representation had become wobbly, what grounded art?

This is the dread problem—or the wonderful opportunity—of "the arbitrariness of the sign," as Saussure famously called it, which modernist art worked variously to contain, as in "the delimitation of flatness" in painting, or to exploit, as Cubism did with its multivalent signifiers and as Dada did with its chance experiments. How to remotivate an art that had become arbitrary? This is the imperative behind key catchwords in modernist discourse, such as "the inner necessity" proclaimed by the idealist Kandinsky and "the truth to materials" demanded by the materialist Tatlin. Nothing, not even the simple idea of composition as a hierarchical division of a canvas, was immune from the threat of arbitrariness. For Bois one modernist solution was "to abolish composition by suppressing division per se (the monochrome) or by adjusting this division so that it became an index of the surface in question (modular grid; symmetry; deductive structure; adequation of figure and field)." By the 1960s another solution was to move out of painting altogether into object-making in space, as long as that object was simple and so could be seen as motivated, at least in part, by its physical surroundings. This was the path opened up by Minimalist art.

In this light an attention to form is not at all a turn away from history. "It's remarkable how often one hears it stubbornly repeated that formalism is congenitally antipathetic to history," Barthes once complained. "I myself have always tried to state the historical responsibility of forms."[8] This last phrase is a prized motto for Bois, who reads it in a double sense: not only is form responsive to history, not only are historical situations inscribed in artistic transformations, but any such transformation is also accountable to its present, and only thus is it historically responsive in the first place. In short, there is an ethics as well as a historicity in all art-making, even of the most abstract kind. One senses here the mandate, which Bois took from the events of 1968, to hold together the two halves of the avant-garde, the artistic and the political. To frame art in this way is also to ease the stark opposition between semiotic and social-historical approaches that divided modernist art history in the 1980s and 1990s. Bois was a central voice in this debate, first at Johns Hopkins (1983–1991), then at Harvard (1991–2005), and finally at the Institute for Advanced Study in Princeton, but that story is mostly beyond the scope of *An Oblique Autobiography*.

How can an autobiography be oblique? One way is to present its parts in reverse chronology as Bois does with his essays in this volume. This allows us to see how his concerns persist rather than how they develop; he is opposed to any historicist narrative of necessary evolution even when it comes to his own thinking. But this embargo also prompts a question. More than once Bois mentions his ban on the word "influence" in his writing and that of his students. "Precursor" is also forbidden. "No one ever considered himself or herself as someone else's precursor; indeed, no one could," the philosopher of science Alexandre Koyré once remarked. "And to envisage someone as such is the best way to preclude the possibility of understanding his or her work."[9] Yet how can an autobiography ignore influences and precursors? Bois gets around the first prohibition with an unexpected reference to Harold Bloom, who argued in *The Anxiety of Influence* (1973) that influence flows both ways, that the latecomer can affect the predecessor too; "a spark between poles" is how Bois phrases it. He sees the "creative misreading" that Clark visits on European abstraction in these terms. As for precursors, he prefers to think in terms of elective affinities—of "declensions" of artists and "constellations" of critics (this last echoes Walter Benjamin). "This book is an inventory of encounters," Bois tells us at the outset. "It takes two to tango." Often, though, more people are involved. He begins with an intimate account of a discursive throuple that he enjoyed with the English critic Guy Brett and the Filipino artist David Medalla, detailing how the three friends inflected each other, mostly at a distance, over the years.

Still, how can a person indoctrinated in "the death of the author" write an autobiography? Here "oblique" takes on another meaning. Bois tells his story through encounters in a manner that almost inverts, say, *Roland Barthes by Roland Barthes* (1975). Whereas Barthes looked for his image mirrored in that of others, here we mostly glimpse Bois to one side of his reflections on mentors, collaborators, and friends. "Oblique" also alludes to his persistent interest in different kinds of perspective. He has written on the parallactic viewing that the sculptures of Richard Serra often require of us, and he has worked for years on an account of axonometric projection in art and architecture (it appears often in Lissitzky and De Stijl). Such projection dictates no vanishing point within the picture and no viewing point in front of it, and this book is oblique in that sense too. It recalls a passage in *A Berlin Chronicle* (1932) where Benjamin narrates his attempts to diagram his life. His first try is "a series of family trees," and, though he is devastated when he loses this drawing, the scheme is a conventional one. He then hits on the idea of a life imaged as a labyrinth. "I am concerned here not with what is installed in the chamber at its enigmatic center, ego or fate," Benjamin tells us, "but all the more with the many entrances leading into the interior. These entrances I call 'primal acquaintances'; each of them is a graphic symbol of my acquaintance with a person whom I met . . . through neighborhood, family relationships, school comradeship, mistaken identity, companionship on travels, or other such—hardly numerous—situations. So many primal relationships, so many entrances to the maze."[10]

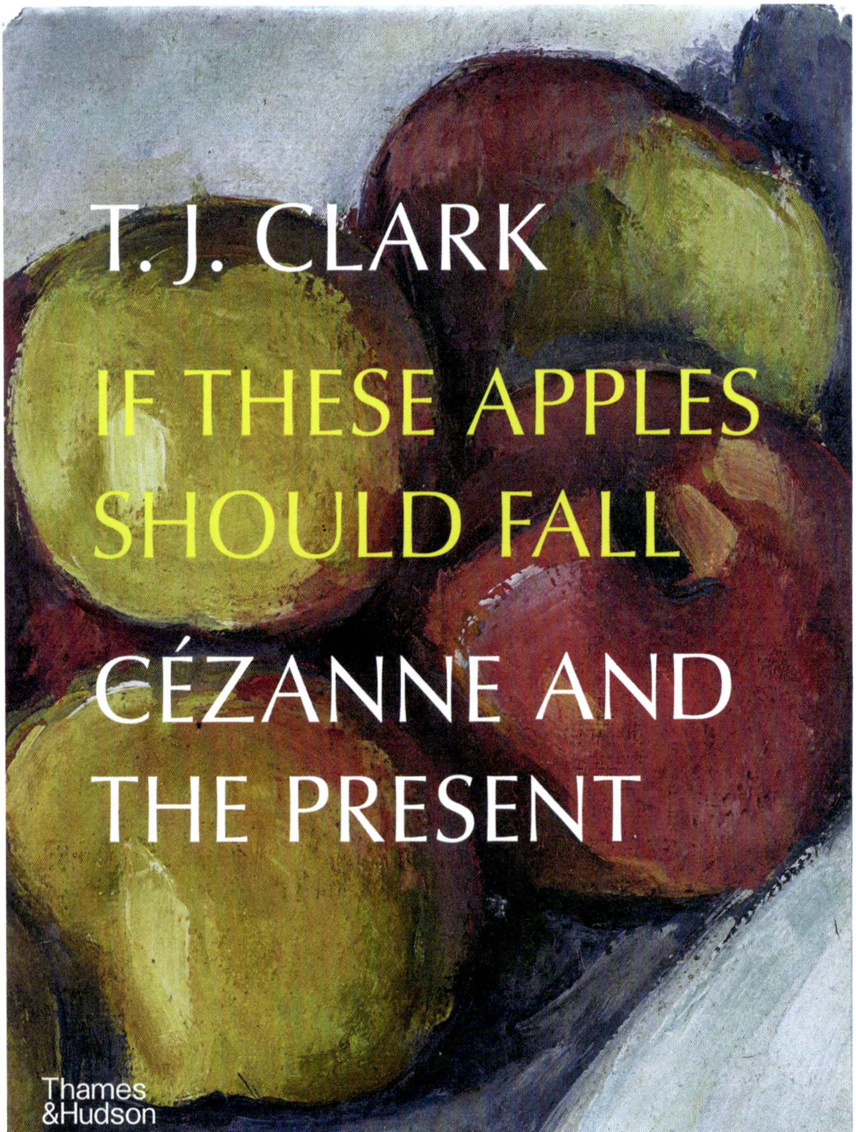

Cover of *If These Apples Should Fall* by T. J. Clark, with detail of Paul Cézanne's *Still Life with Apples* (c. 1893–1895).

37 Antinomic Modernism

T. J. Clark begins *If These Apples Should Fall: Cézanne and the Present* (2022) with a restaging of his initial encounter with the great painter. A reproduction of *The Basket of Apples* (c. 1893) amazed him as a fifteen-year-old in 1958, and it amazes him still: "I think I can retrieve the feeling even sixty years later."[1] This is one version of "the present" in the subtitle of his book, the summoning of a *then* of Cézanne painting and Clark looking into the *now* of his writing and our reading. It is a fiction of immediacy that Clark deploys, very effectively, to different ends. First and foremost, it conjures up the celebrated struggle of the artist to capture the "sensation" of his motifs, including the still lifes, landscapes, and portraits of peasants that Clark focuses on and frames with chapters on what Cézanne learned from Pissarro and what Matisse learned from Cézanne. "Putting aspects of the world into the same surface is, for Cézanne, putting them into the eye," yet "being in the eye" is also "its being over there in space." This is the crux of "the Cézanne effect": it is how he makes a world "happen," Clark argues, and another sense of "the present" is his own vigorous account of this painstaking process. In turn this present opens onto a further meaning of the word that qualifies the others, the present of our time, which is hardly one with Cézanne's. "The world I saw there was so entirely familiar and yet so distant," Clark writes of *The Basket of Apples*, and "that basic uncanny"—the word recurs often in this book—is one of his deep subjects.

The primary focus of *If These Apples Should Fall* is on perception—Cézanne's, Clark's, our own—and its distinct translations into paint and prose, but any phenomenological bracketing of society and history is only intermittent. Even if it were desirable for Clark, our distance from Cézanne makes it impossible, and into this space Clark pours a near lifetime of research and reflection. The book is very dialogical as well, with various interlocutors called up as needed. Some voices are expected, such as contemporaneous commentators on the artist (testimony of this sort is a staple of social art history). We hear, too, from Cézanne exegetes like Roger Fry and Clement Greenberg, whose formalist approach Clark has become more patient with over the years. Clark also cites key figures in the Hegelian-Marxist line of critique, such as Georg Lukács, who have informed his thought since his days as a young Situationist (he was quickly purged from the group). More surprising are powerful statements from Ernst Bloch, who gives Clark his minatory title, and Samuel Beckett, who underscores the alien aspect in Cézanne that most intrigues him. Above all, as Clark debates these others, he argues with himself, and though he often assumes his readers in the "we" of his thinking, he sometimes positions them as potential skeptics as well. The conversation is orchestrated in this complex way because under no circumstances does Clark want his perspective to resolve or indeed any account to settle: "The kind of writing that I find best gets me not to have a 'view' of Cézanne, thus moving me closer to that first incomprehension [in 1958], is a narrative of repeated looking." Such resistance to resolution is what he values most in Cézanne, and in this respect his prose is true to the painting, even mimetic of it. As Cézanne confronts his motif again and again, so Clark confronts Cézanne.

This art history also appears entirely familiar and yet so distant: familiar because it partakes of the social art history that Clark did so much to reanimate in the 1970s and 1980s, and distant because his approach has undergone a sea-change since then. In 1973 (more than a half century ago!) he published two companion volumes, *Image of the People: Gustave Courbet and the 1848 Revolution* and *The Absolute Bourgeois: Artists and Politics in France, 1848–1851*, that soon became essential references in nineteenth-century art history. These were followed by his equally influential *The Painting of Modern Life: Paris in the Art of Manet and His Followers* (1985), a recasting of Impressionism and Postimpressionism in Situationist terms as ambivalent responses to the becoming-spectacle of Paris and environs during the Second Empire and the Third Republic. While the first two texts were written "in ignominious but unavoidable retreat from the events" of 1968, as Clark later remarked, the third could be read as an indirect attack on the neoliberalism spearheaded by Thatcher and Reagan in the 1980s.[2] In all three books, then, he worked to keep modernist art in critical parallax with contemporary politics. As announced by the title, this tense connection was given a different twist in his next volume, *Farewell to an Idea: Episodes from a History of Modernism* (1999), which claimed that, though modernism and socialism had often belonged together as co-antagonists of capitalism, this uneasy rapport was rubbished by "the new world order" after 1989. In fact, *Farewell to an Idea* argued that the very modernity that modernism had engaged critically in an early stage had ruined that modernism in a subsequent stage, with the result that modernism had become "our antiquity."

Clark shifted his approach dramatically in *The Sight of Death: An Experiment in Art Writing* (2006), which recorded his multifarious responses to two paintings by Poussin, *Landscape with a Man Killed by a Snake* (c. 1648) and *Landscape with a Calm* (1650–1651), over the course of a few months in 2000 while they appeared together at the Getty Art Museum. Although Clark has always hewn closely to the work of art, his attention became almost obsessive here. In effect, he placed his own reactions to Poussin ahead of the comments of contemporaries that had long provided the source material of his social-historical accounts. Many of his followers were dismayed by his apparent apostasy, but Clark was forthright about what drove him to it. Social art history had reemerged in reaction to the dominance of iconographic and formalist protocols; at the time it was almost scandalous to relate the artwork to its cultural conditions. By the 2000s, Clark averred, this procedure had become accepted, almost rote. Who didn't believe that art was part and parcel of the world? If Clark lost some supporters with this phenomenological turn, he gained others for whom his experiment became a template: *The Sight of Death* launched a thousand seminar papers.

While *If These Apples Should Fall* follows on *Farewell to an Idea* in its essayistic structure, and on *Picasso and Truth: From Cubism to Guernica* (2013) in its monographic focus, it returns to *The Sight of Death* in its rhetorical style, for the Cézanne book is also sometimes diaristic and often discursive. Here again Clark crafts an informal address in order to keep his thought as lively and unfixed as possible. However, social-historical forces and art-historical precedents are hardly ignored; rather, they are treated as "inherences" in the work more than as "surroundings" of it. At moments Clark declares his approach directly: "The deeper the thinking involved in an artwork's way with its sources, the more imperative it is that interpretation stay on the surface"—a statement that many formalists and semioticians, with whom Clark once sparred, would happily affirm. Or again: "We have no choice . . . but to move between two sorts of concern," what Cézanne does with his material and "other accounts of the world"; "framing a better answer to questions of the second type will not displace those of the first . . . but rather, will sharpen the questions, refocus them, letting the critic see the material . . . more precisely—because the intentionality of the material has become clearer." This is an exacting procedure but not a controversial one, and at times *If These Apples Should Fall* is almost traditional in its concern with influences and techniques, often juxtaposing artworks to adduce both. "Cézanne came to Pissarro to unlearn his first style, and, seemingly, to change his mind about Courbet, Manet and Delacroix" is not an atypical sentence.

Or, rather, *If These Apples Should Fall* might seem traditional if Clark weren't such an active protagonist in his own argument. In part this self-staging comes with a phenomenological perspective (Clark counts "Cézanne's Doubt," a 1945 essay by Maurice Merleau-Ponty, as one inspiration), and it is accentuated by psychoanalytical probes as well. This isn't new to Clark—his social art history often read its sources symptomatically too—yet in this case he's the analysand as much as Cézanne. This self-staging is engaging, and certainly Clark has earned it, but at times it comes close to cajoling. Like a passionate friend at a museum tugging at your sleeve, he constantly enjoins us to see, to compare, to reconsider, and the very intensity of this viewing-and-reviewing can wear a little. Ditto all the rhetorical questions and Socratic teases: "Is it the case," "Can we agree," and so on. Yet *If These Apples Should Fall* is also a very generous text. Clark invites us in on his reflexive meditations, and this comes as a welcome relief from academic texts that are almost paranoically designed to be bullet-proof from first sentence to final footnote.

"The fundamental wordlessness of painting" is precious to Clark, all the more so in a world that seems subsumed by image technologies (an updating of the Situationist complaint about spectacle) but that, in his view, remains driven by verbal commands and brand logos (agree here, buy this, post that, just do it). The materiality of painting is also a prime ground of his own materialism, and here as elsewhere Clark regards both the difference of the visual and the difficulty of picturing as almost intrinsically resistant. At the same time, like all art historians, he is tasked with translating pictures into words, and he embraces, even exacerbates, this difficulty as well. For Clark ekphrastic description is at once necessary and doomed to failure, a verdict he passes on his own poems too, which, often based on the paintings under discussion, first appeared in *The Sight of Death* and return here: "I think the two poems make an appropriate start to the book, above all because they try to suggest—almost to perform—the bewilderment of seeing a Cézanne for the first time." Clark worries his terminology throughout *If These Apples Should Fall*: "The balance of oddity and accuracy" in Cézanne is "hard to hold onto in words." "What kind of language is appropriate" for Matisse? And so on. That "language is under strain" is underscored by the proliferation of italicized phrases and scare quotes, as well as ventriloquized eruptions when the pictures, as though frustrated with all this talk, speak their intentions directly. All this is so disarming because Clark is such an artful writer, with a lexicon as demotic as it is expert.

Clark is most keen on moments when meaning, both in the painting and in his prose, breaks down or refuses to come together. This interest had led him to an affinity for deconstruction, that of Paul de Man in particular. This is a strange fellowship, especially given the onetime fascist sympathies of de Man, and Clark almost begrudges it: "The term 'deconstruction' might really be technically appropriate for once," he writes at one point. But no other term accounts as well for another crucial aspect of the Cézanne effect, which is that "notions as seemingly basic as foreground and background may no longer apply. . . . Maybe not even inside and outside. Nor experience and representation. Nor 'now' and 'then.'" Clark has commented on this de Manian dimension in his work; here is fellow art historian Christopher Wood on the same subject: "A de Manian reading would reveal the mismatch between meaning and image—both the failure of the image to say what it means, and the way that image generates inadvertent and unexpected meanings in the very process of trying and failing to signify."[3] For Clark "this is the anxiety, and also the utopian horizon, that drives the fanatic process on" in Cézanne. Much the same came be said of Clark: "Over-interpretation is just the name we give to the moment when criticism admits—gives a gasp at—the gap between form and content." Clark turns to deconstruction as a further defense against any fetishization of the paintings or any reification of his thinking.

Perhaps this is also why Clark resorts to the term "uncanny" as often as he does; it is his way to signal the many moments in Cézanne when his "strangeness of vision . . . refuses to take anything for granted." Although the repetition of the word sometimes renders it a floating signifier, connoting "disquiet" here and "unreality" there, that may be just as Clark intends. For many of us the uncanny is overshadowed by Freud, who defined it as the return of a familiar event made strange by repression. For Clark, however, the uncanniness in Cézanne is a matter less of the psyche (there is no shortage of such readings of the artist) than of the world around him. The effect of estrangement might be psychological, but the cause is social, a concomitant of the "uncertainty" that modernity brings with it. (The famous line about capitalism from *The Communist Manifesto*, "all that is solid melts into air," comes to mind.) In short, Clark pushes uncanniness in Freud toward estrangement in Marx to get at the particular weirdness of the Cézanne world: a piece of fruit that is a "non-pear [and] non-apple," a surface in one of *The Card Players* that is a "non-wall and non-window," folds of cloth that are "liable to take on a life of their own," landscapes that somehow get "familiarity and unfamiliarity, nearness and apartness" to coexist. It's a world of "deathly animation," Clark insists, "and isn't this the basic scandal—the aliveness and deadness entwined—that gives a Cézanne its power?" As we might guess, what Clark detects in Cézanne is a world touched with the black magic of the commodity, a world in which (to cite another famous line, now from *Capital*) "the fantastic form of a relation between things" has begun to displace the "definite social relation between men." "Vividness"—a term Clark offers for this uncanny (in)animation of objects produced for exchange value—"is one thing, availability—humanness, use value—another." Although a Cézanne still life, landscape, or portrait might appear to be "autarkic," his "view of matter and space" is thoroughly "social." His art is directed at a culture in which "an entirely necessary, but utterly foreign, language for a new form of apprehension had come into being."

"If a piece of writing stays true to that basic uncanny," Clark proposes as his own test, "it passes muster." In this respect it's fair to say that Clark not only emulates Cézanne but also identifies with him, even (or especially) in his willfulness. Certainly, the prose of *If These Apples Should Fall* "tips" and "tilts" as much as any Cézanne still life, and its argument is punctuated by striking comparisons and stretched connections. Clark likes to jump from sensation to significance, and from specific painting to general point, and back again. Often considered a theoretical flaw, this lack of mediation is, for Clark, true to looking at and thinking about Cézanne. "Je vois. Par taches," Cézanne remarked, which Clark translates freely as "Seeing is patchwork." Saying what the art is "about," he states in this same spirit, "I flinch from doing this." Clark is thus most mimetic in his desire to tarry in the antinomies of a Cézanne painting in a way analogous to how Cézanne tarries in the antinomies of modern perception. "No painter, I reckon, has ever risked conjuring space out of such a standoff between opposed realities," Clark claims of the truly bizarre landscape titled *The Red Rock* (1895–1900). And of a peculiar rendering of a favorite motif, Mont Sainte Victoire, that is both "most like a body" and "least like an organism," Clark writes, "we are treated . . . to the spectacle of two kinds of understanding of the material world confronting each other nakedly, with no other mediation than the painter's will."

Clark also values this tolerance—or talent—for antinomy in Pissarro, who is less extreme than Cézanne, as well as in Matisse, who at times is more so. For instance, he describes "the Matisse effect" as "the coexistence of hedonism and anxiety, or blandness and blackness" in one and the same painting. In fact, for Clark modernism as such is antinomic, necessarily so because the modernity that it addresses is antinomic to begin with. After contrasting Matisse with artists as different as John Heartfield and Andy Warhol, Clark concludes, "The choice, however, is a false one. For it seems to be the very nature of the twentieth century that it invites, in a sense prescribes, entirely opposite and contradictory art tactics in face of its enormities." For Clark modernity is not simply the condition of the best modernist work; rather, it is "*the question the picture exists to put*": "the argument—the absolutism of the alternatives, the beauty of the either/or, the complete conviction that here, in the picture, at last one alternative or the other will be proven—*is* modernity."

In this way "modernism" and "modernity" do a lot of labor in *If These Apples Should Fall*, and sometimes they border on *mana* words, signifying at once too much and too little. This is an occupational hazard for anyone who strives to relate modern art to its social conditions, and it can't be avoided with Cézanne. "His painting was his knowing what modernity felt like. And he understood that a very great deal—almost everything—about painting would have to be reconstructed if that knowledge was to be given form." To give artistic form to modern formlessness: Clark has offered this thumbnail definition of modernism before, and he doubles down on it here. It draws on an old-school idea of modernity whose hallmarks are largely German—Max Weber on "the disenchantment" of a rationalized world, Georg Simmel on the "indifference" of a money economy, and Lukács on the "homelessness" of the modern novel. Clark sees a "no-whereness" in Cézanne too: "Modernity is loss of world. Cézanne is the painter who makes that cliché draw blood." Yet Cézanne expresses "elation" as well as "horror" at this state of affairs. Clark carries over this formula for modernist ambivalence about modernity from *Farewell to an Idea*; it is how his preferred artists respond to the creative-destructive energies of capitalism (shades of *The Communist Manifesto* once more). Clark sees these effects translated into pictorial terms in a typical Cézanne: "groundlessness, airlessness, absence of contact, lack of distance but also of proximity, lack of the sense of a palpable shared world, uncertainty and a strange false vividness" (that synonym for uncanniness again). "Modern experience just *is* this evenness and disequilibrium in high tension," and Cézanne delivers it. At the same time Cézanne was no Marxist; in fact, he was far more conservative than the anarchist Pissarro. Yet this very conservativism, when embedded in the paintings, may make them critical in another, romantic anticapitalist way, even if this resistance necessarily fails: "*The Basket of Apples hates* the object called modernity. It sets up a whole impossible anti-modernity to stave it off . . .—a peasant world, a natural world, a world of endurances and irremovables. . . . But not for a moment does the painting asks us to believe that its set-up will stave off the reality of the 1890s."

Clark wants art history to match the philosophical ambitions of artists like Cézanne, Pissarro, and Matisse, a determination that prompts exquisite insights in his case. For example, of *Landscape near Pontoise* (1872) Clark writes: "Space is not distance, says Pissarro, not a journey to a horizon: it is here where we are, an immense proximity, a total intuition of place and extent. And Time is not becoming, not endless contingency: it is a Now that goes on being Now as we live it, a unique kind of permanence." "Every instant deserves to be monumentalized," Clark adds, dissolving in a sentence the old cliché about

Impressionism. "It isn't a 'moment' fizzing by." Other claims might come across as excessive: "Greek philosophy and French painting (meaning the line from Corot to Matisse . . .) may be seen as events of equal weight," since both "speak to a fundamental change in the conditions of representation in the cultures that gave rise to them." Clark isn't shy about comparing his favorite painters with the mightiest philosophers—Cézanne with Plato and Kant, Picasso with Nietzsche, and Jackson Pollock with Hegel—if that is what it takes to make the art count. Although he admits that such analogies might make other art historians squirm, he believes that such embarrassment often "functions as an alibi . . . for not exposing oneself to what painting is capable of, and not pushing language to follow in painting's wake." (Clark launched a similar critique of the discipline in the *Times Literary Supplement* already in 1974.)[4] Sometimes, however, his own drive to equal the ambition of the art leads him to hyperbolize and hypostatize. This is a risk Clark is willing to take ("outlandish" is a compliment in this text), and he isn't the first (or, hopefully, the last) art historian to do so.

Not long ago, Clark avers, "the very nature of modern art, and the nature of writing *about* art, ancient and modern, had seemed to turn on the Cézanne problem." This is hardly self-evident today (if it ever was); so "remote from the temper of our times" is Cézanne that it is unclear whether he can even be "written about anymore." This, finally, is why Clark works so hard to make Cézanne matter; his value across time and culture can no longer be assumed. Of course, both extremes—everything turns on Cézanne, nothing does—are overstated. Here Clark seems charged by the urgent warning issued by Bloch in *The Spirit of Utopia* (1916) that serves as the epigraph of *If These Apples Should Fall*: "The apples of Cézanne are not fruit any longer; nor fruit made over into paint; instead all imaginable life is in them, and if they should fall, a universal conflagration would ensue." This threat to "all imaginable life" speaks to the catastrophe of World War I, which many Europeans—not only the Oswald Spenglers of the time but also art historians such as Heinrich Wölfflin and Aby Warburg—did imagine to be the end of civilization. Clark asks where we are now in relation to this fall (again, another sense of "the present" in his subtitle), with the implication that it might be more disastrous if we don't feel any loss at all, if we are past caring about those odd old apples.

"We are no longer part of a world" in which the Bloch line holds, Clark states. "Some will consider this a pity, some a relief." Several questions are mooted here, most of which he anticipates. First, is ours still a modernity of disenchantment and homelessness, or are we not, as Clark suggests in *If These Apples Should Fall* as well as in *Heaven on Earth: Painting and the Life to Come* (2018), deep into a massive reenchantment of the world, at least for people who, consumed with consumerism or religion or both, don't feel so estranged? Second, does the modernism of a Cézanne speak to that vast constituency now, if it did ever? Third, who is this "we?"—a question that today is almost reflex and often accusatory but can't be bracketed. For whom is the projected loss a "pity"? This seems clear enough; aficionados of modernism like Clark and me are only first among that number. Who might feel "relief" at this loss isn't so obvious. "What would it be like (here is the question) *not* to have a view of Cézanne? Not to have a sense of his meaning for us, in other words, his lesson, his largeness—not to have his art 'fit' anywhere, least of all in a history of modern art?" This is a scary notion for us modernists, for it broaches not only the historical obsolescence of modernism and its study but also the relative irrelevance of both pursuits. These "viewless" others aren't only the philistines of old whom the avant-garde required as its foil, or the pragmatic students of today whose parents shoo them away from art as though it were tantamount to economic suicide. They are also people who are as deeply committed to innovative culture as any modernist, but who come with questions and commitments that simply do not (or no longer) pass through the modernist gate.

In short, modernism might not be the central event, the quasi-universal, that many of us have long believed it to be, and perhaps modernity has to be rethought too. For many people modernism is just a distracting sideshow in the outrageous spectacle that is modernity—modernity understood above all as the history of colonialism and imperialism, of the primitive accumulation, labor exploitation, and wealth inequality that are still inscribed in the collections in which all these Cézannes hang, among countless other places. If the demise of socialism put paid to a particular idea of modernism, the contemporary politics of decolonization might call in a far greater debt, one that modernists are in no position to pay. Some will see this notion as a form of blackmail, if not of barbarism, yet Clark knows that most of these questions are serious and most of these claims are legitimate. Palliatives that come to mind, such as "art history is not a zero-sum game" or "seeing well, thinking hard, painting intensely is the best revenge," don't cut it.

"Everything in the painting is falling and where it falls to is where we are," Clark writes of *The Basket of Apples* at the outset. Is this book, then, a truly final farewell to an idea of modernism? It arrives three decades after the tome of that title and at a time of disaster that exceeds that of the 1990s. Yet the tone of *If These Apples Should Fall* is not "melancholic," as Clark admitted *Farewell to an Idea* might be taken to be, nor is it a collection of fragments shored against his ruin, as the prior book could also be understood. Clark once bestowed the paradoxical tag an "Eliotic Trotskyite" on the young Greenberg, and Malcolm Bull labeled the Clark of *Farewell to an Idea*, also oxymoronically, as a "Greenbergian Situationist."[5] Neither term applies to this book, but an equally contradictory formulation is needed. *If These Apples Should Fall* follows *Farewell to an Idea* literally, but it seems to come before it in the sense that the fate of Cézanne, of modernism, isn't sealed here yet. Perhaps Clark never did bid farewell to modernism, or maybe the "falling" in this book qualifies the end in *Farewell to an Idea*. Clark gives us a clue to this complicated, somewhat inchoate thought when he cites a line, attributed to Nietzsche, about late nineteenth-century art being "the last metaphysical activity within European nihilism," and comments that now that this "assumption is a thing of the past"—he means the phrase in its original Hegelian sense that an activity must be completely concluded before it can be fully understood—writing on Cézanne exists "in a strange, maybe fruitful, limbo." "Fruitful limbo" signals that "the Cézanne problem," the modernist question, isn't over and done with but waiting to be—what exactly? Not solved, let alone surpassed, but maybe kicked around and tripped over à la Beckett. We can't go on, we go on.

These reflections give the finale of *If These Apples Should Fall* a burst of intensity, which suggests an ultimate point of affinity between Clark and Cézanne. Clark deals mostly with late Cézanne, and taken together these willful pictures might qualify as a "late style" (at one point Clark analogizes them to the last quartets of Beethoven, the locus classicus of the notion).[6] Some of the paintings possess the contradictory mix of asperity and excess that is characteristic of this style. Also typical is how others of the pictures return to first principles in a way that renders the devil-may-care attitude of old age difficult to distinguish from the rashness of youth. And much the same might be said of this book. It is "late" not only in its embrace of the nonhuman in Cézanne (Clark relishes Beckett describing a Mont Sainte Victoire painting as "incommensurable with all human expressions whatsoever"), but also in its refusal to resolve contradictions. Less melancholic than *Farewell to an Idea* about the loss of the past, still contemptuous of any faith in posterity (Clark is the author of a blistering text, "For a Left with No Future," that calls for a renouncing of all technological pipe dreams), and very alert to "the present" as both riven by antinomy and shot through with possibility.[7] All this too is distinctive of late style at its most bracing.

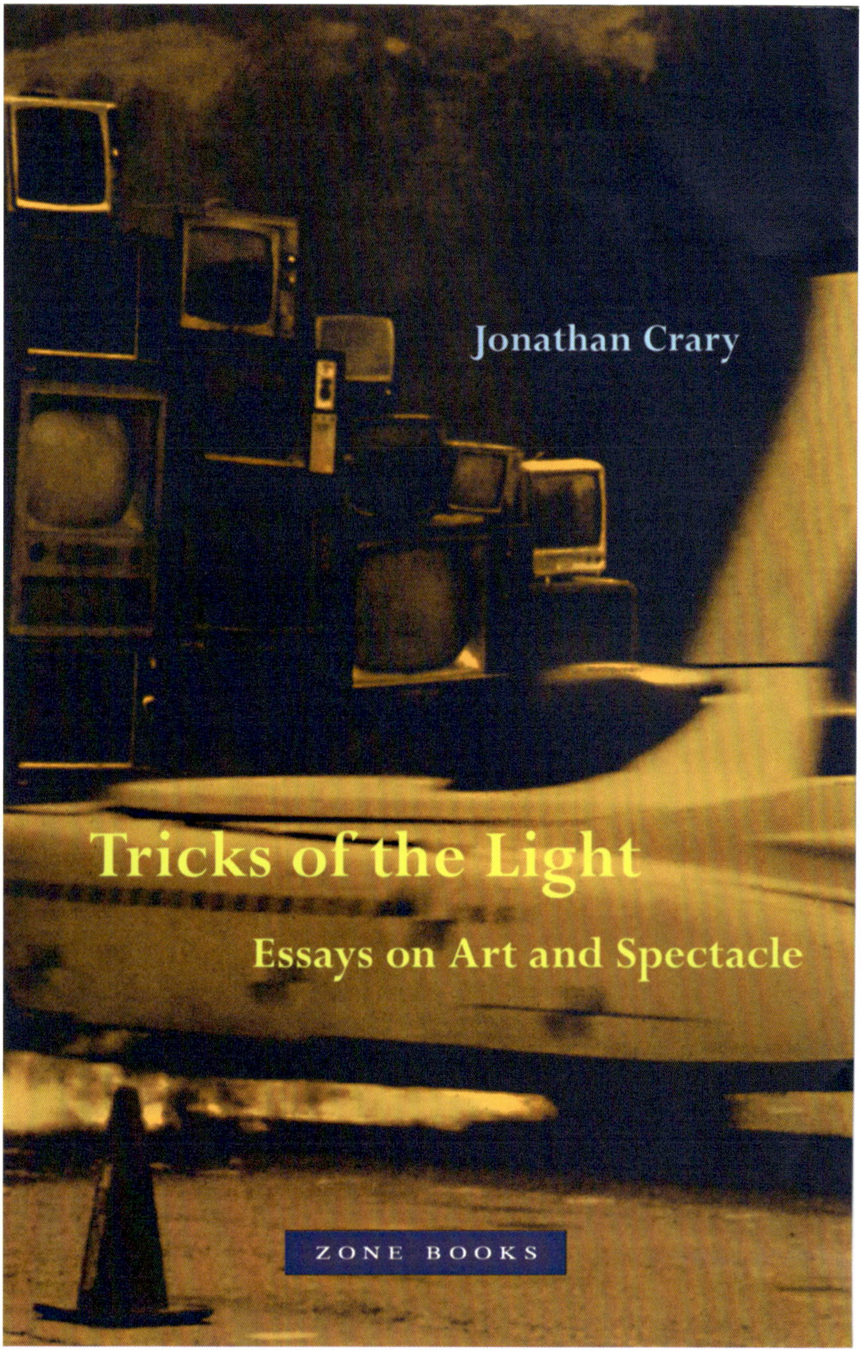

Cover of *Tricks of the Light* by Jonathan Crary, with detail of Ant Farm's *Media Burn* (1975).

38 The Ruins of Spectacle

Art history was shaken in the 1970s and '80s, and the epicenter was nineteenth-century art. Emboldened by the resurgent Marxism and feminism of the 1960s, engaged scholars such as T. J. Clark, Thomas Crow, Linda Nochlin, and Griselda Pollock asked difficult questions about class, audience, gender, and sexuality, questions that soon rumbled through other fields as well. Yet, disruptive though those inquiries were, they mostly retained the centrality of the French avant-garde. Even as social and psychological readings were extended and deepened, the modern transformation of pictorial representation was still credited to a celebrated line of male painters from Courbet to Cézanne, with a few female names like Mary Cassatt added to the list. A partial decentering of these artists had to await *Techniques of the Observer: On Vision and Modernity in the Nineteenth Century* (1990), the first book by Jonathan Crary, now Meyer Schapiro Professor of Modern Art and Theory at Columbia. The pressure still came from the present, but here the impetus was the forced move to digital modes of image production and distribution, which prompted Crary to reflect on past revolutions in visuality.

Techniques of the Observer first confronts the "bifurcated model of vision" in the nineteenth century, the familiar story that, while photography perfected representation, painters like Manet broke heroically with that mimetic mode of picturing.[1] As Crary points out, these opposed narratives are in fact complementary, the first one of continuity setting up the second one of rupture. More problematically, this break is ascribed to avant-garde artists alone, as though they operated autonomously, apart from the "massive reorganization" of scientific knowledge, technological invention, and social practice that "modified in myriad ways the productive, cognitive, and desiring capacities of the human subject."[2] It is this reorganization of seeing that *Techniques of the Observer* articulates with great historical detail and theoretical sophistication.

Crary repositions both early photography and modernist painting as almost epiphenomenal consequences of a more fundamental change that preceded them. This was the shift from the geometrical optics dominant in the seventeenth and eighteenth centuries, which, modeled on the camera obscura, proposed a clear, Cartesian separation of subject and object, of viewer and scene, to the physiological optics of the nineteenth century, in which visual experience was loosened from worldly referents and relocated in the physical density of the human body, with its binocularity, peripheral vision, saccadic eye movements, and production of afterimages and other nonveridical effects. According to Crary, vision came to be understood as both abstracted and embodied, a double development that permitted "an unprecedented mobility and exchangeability" of visual activities.[3] As his language suggests, the prime mover of this new visuality was capitalist modernization.

With photography and painting decentered, *Techniques of the Observer* turns to visual culture at large, where Crary delves into optical devices, such as the stereoscope, thaumatrope, phenakistiscope, stroboscope, and zootrope, which exploited binocular vision and retinal persistence in order to create illusions of imagistic verisimilitude and movement. Rather than fold these devices into a prehistory of film, as is common in cinema studies, he asks what they can tell us about the construction of the nineteenth-century subject. Crary means the "techniques" in his title to comprehend both technologies imposed on viewers and practices performed by them, and he opts for "observer" because the word carries the sense of "to comply with" as well as "to look at." *Techniques of the Observer* is not usual art history, then, but neither is it visual studies, which often projects subversive potential onto popular forms, nor is it media archaeology, which sometimes assumes a consistency of technology across a given moment. For Crary visuality is always a matter of unstable assemblages of techniques and temporary arrangements of observers; his is an anti-ontological account that ascribes no essence or even specificity to objects or subjects. Consider, as just one example, how many different materials, techniques, attributes, and effects the term "photography" has covered over the last two centuries.

Crary dwells on stereoscopic images because they encapsulate a basic contradiction in nineteenth-century culture. Even as they conflate the real with the optical almost completely, they also "disclose a fundamentally disunified and aggregate field of disjunct elements." The stereoscope thus disrupted "the theatrical setup of the camera obscura" more radically than advanced painting did at least until Cézanne. Crary then adds another twist to his argument. Not only was the "pure perception" pursued by modernists like Cézanne "lodged in the newly discovered territory of a fully embodied viewer," but so too was the emergent spectacle of capitalist culture—in the sense given the word by the Situationist Guy Debord of a world made over into representation for our consumption. Yet "the eventual triumph of both [modernism and spectacle] depended on the denial of the body, its pulsings and phantasms, as the ground of vision." The body had to be suppressed, on the one hand, for modernist art to assert the "autonomy of vision" and, on the other, for capitalist spectacle to manage the "regulation of the observer." Key for Crary is "how these paths continually intersect and often overlap on the same social terrain," sometimes in support of each other but often at odds, "amid the countless localities in which the diversity of concrete acts of vision occur."[4] Importantly, these concrete acts can't always be governed; sometimes, then as now, the observer escapes oversight.

Nearly a decade after *Techniques of the Observer* came *Suspensions of Perception: Attention, Spectacle, and Modern Culture* (1999), which examines some of the consequences of the shift to physiological optics. Here Crary seems to return artists to the foreground—there are chapters devoted to one painting each by Manet, Seurat, and Cézanne—but they are focal points only, for once again he embeds art in a complex field of popular practice, scientific research, and philosophical reflection. In the process Crary questions the need of art historians to isolate purely aesthetic categories like contemplation, as well as the tendency of gender theorists to privilege "exclusively visual concepts such as 'the gaze.'"[5] Significantly, he undoes any binary of distraction and attention, departing from Walter Benjamin and many others on this score. For Crary there is always an uneasy relay between the two states, with new demands for attention prompted by new forms of distraction and vice versa.

Manet, Seurat, and Cézanne are most useful to Crary because they demonstrate, in different ways, both the effort to bind attention in painting and the difficulty of doing so amid the manifold diversions of modern life. Sometimes the extreme attentiveness of these painters "annihilates the seeming 'naturalness' of the world"; sometimes it crosses over into an "intensive re-creation of a subjective interface with the world"; and sometimes it does both. In all cases, though, "there arises an irresolvable contradiction between the aim of stabilizing the world to look at it analytically and the experience of a physiological apparatus incapable of such stability."[6] This failing had an upside, however, for it also expanded the running room for viewers in a culture that was more and more controlled.

Taken together, *Techniques of the Observer* and *Suspensions of Perception* trace an extraordinary genealogy of visuality in the nineteenth century, one in which the traditional concerns of art history—descriptions of style, analyses of form, interpretations of meaning, accounts of context—are largely absent. Methodologically, its primary guide is Michel Foucault, whom Crary cites early in the first book: "One has to dispense with the constituent subject"—that is, the notion that the individual is an autonomous agent—in order "to arrive at an analysis which can account for the constitution of the subject within a historical framework."[7] Paradoxically, though, this historically specific subject sometimes comes across as generally representative: we are given a portrait of *the* observer in nineteenth-century Europe, who, however complicated in physiology and behavior, is not much differentiated in terms of class and gender (not to mention race). On this point Crary is open to pushback from the Marxist and feminist art historians whose accounts he otherwise moves beyond.

Techniques of the Observer and *Suspensions of Perception* are genealogical in another way as well. Crary describes them as "prehistories"—of twentieth-century spectacle in the first book, and of our own "techno-institutional worlds" in the second. It is these regimes that he confronts directly in his two broadsides, *24/7: Capitalism and the Ends of Sleep* (2013) and *Scorched Earth: Beyond the Digital Age to a Post-Capitalist World* (2022). Although Crary aligns these jeremiads with the tradition of social pamphleteering that stretches back to the Levelers and Diggers, the diatribes of Situationists like Debord are the precedent closer in spirit as well as time.

"The ends of sleep" has a double meaning. The first, clear enough, is that sleep is threatened; a century ago most adults slept ten hours a day, while the average now is six and a half. Neoliberalism has colonized our nightly respite as part of its general operation of "bioderegulation." As with many other military initiatives, "the creation of the sleepless soldier" has moved into civilian life with online producers and consumers attached, 24/7, to global workplaces and markets. Once a kind of torture, sleeplessness is today a boastful lifestyle for a select few ("sleeping is for losers") and an economic necessity for countless others. Less asleep than in sleep mode, many of us live in "low-power readiness" where "nothing is ever fundamentally 'off' and there is never an actual state of rest." More and more we are our apps: "an individual is made into an *application* of new control systems," "a jumble of identities that exist only as effects of temporary technological arrangements," systems and arrangements that, passively or actively, we help to administer, thus collaborating in our own disciplining, surveillance, and data mining. For Crary "24/7 denotes the wreckage of the day as much as it concerns the extinguishing of darkness." As shared in-person experience gives way to serial keyboard solitude, "activities that do not have an online correlate begin to atrophy." Quotidian life becomes a "hollowed-out simulation," and the passage of time a "disabled and derelict diachrony."[8]

For philosophers of reason like Descartes, Hume, and Locke sleep was a potentially dangerous time of unconsciousness, if not derangement: "the sleep of reason produces monsters." For Crary that Enlightenment argument loses its validity in a 24/7 regime; he is also critical of Freud for both rationalizing and privatizing the dream. In a world that never sleeps, the old revolutionary call "to awaken" is misbegotten as well: "Worker-consumers of the world, log off!

You have only your screens to lose!" is more like it. This is the second sense of "the ends of sleep," its purposes today. For Crary sleep has a newfound role as a last ditch of resistance; it is "a natural condition" that can serve as a final barrier against "the theft of time from us by capitalism." Although he puts the phrase in scare quotes, this critical recourse to a "natural condition" is a new note in Crary. Also new is his ethical appeal to the care of others: "As the most private, most vulnerable state common to all, sleep is crucially dependent on society in order to be sustained." Since we require others to protect us while we sleep, sleep figures the necessary "durability of the social."[9]

The anarchistic language of mutual aid—*24/7* was written in the wake of Occupy—is more pronounced in *Scorched Earth*, which extends the critique of capitalism "in its terminal, scorched earth phase." Crary intends his title in the military sense, as in "the destruction of life-essential resources to deny them to a defeated population," and he sees "the internet complex" as a "techno-colonization" dedicated to this "dissolution of society." Obviously, the utopian dream of web interconnectivity has turned dystopic. In *Scorched Earth* even more than in *24/7*, it is our near-total identification with "our data, our search history, our passwords" that divides us, eroding whatever "democratic or communitarian values" might linger among people. Crary points to a further undermining of our intersubjective world as well: the voice, the face, and the gaze, all crucial to our being with others, are disrupted and distorted by chatbots, artificial emotional intelligence, eye tracking, iris scanning, facial coding, and all the rest. "Pathways to a different world will not be found by internet search engines," Crary states matter-of-factly. If there is to be a future, it will be offline.[10]

The outlook of *Scorched Earth* is explicitly anarcho-socialist (not to mention anti-identitarian). In his appeals for collective support Crary refers to worker councils from the Paris Commune onward, even though many of those experiments ended in disaster. He also calls, in vague terms, for "an active prefiguration of new communities and formations capable of egalitarian governance." "The threshold of a post-capitalist world is not far off, a few decades at most," Crary concludes, but this note of hope is quickly qualified: without prefiguration "post-capitalism will be a new field of barbarism." Based on the present situation, his prognosis is thus as stark as his diagnosis, which some readers might consider "scorched earth" in its own way. As often with left-wing critics since the Frankfurt School, Crary sees modernity as a near-total catastrophe, and a strong streak of romantic anticapitalism runs through his recent thought. *24/7* already warned, in a Heideggerian tone, of "worldlessness," which *Scorched Earth* now counters with a vision of "a life-world whose social rhythms were originally shaped by the alternations of the seasons, the phases of the moon, migration of birds, the oscillation of days and night, of sleep and waking, the sequence of festivals . . ."[11] Maybe the extreme predations of neoliberalism do call out for an extreme faith in nature in this manner, but such a prefiguration is not yet a politics. It is also at odds with the Foucauldian assumption, which informs both *Techniques of the Observer* and *Suspensions of Perception*, that almost everything is constructed.

Over the last five decades, then, Crary has sustained a double project: a history of the ceaseless remaking of the modern observer and a critique of contemporary technologies of image and information that discipline us in ever new ways. These two lines of his argument are present *in nuce* in *Tricks of the Light* (published by Zone Books, an important imprint that Crary co-founded in 1985). The volume gathers his "essays on art and spectacle," the earliest of which date from the mid to late 1970s.

Crary arrived at Columbia University in the wake of the student occupation of 1968. After graduation he studied photography and film at the San Francisco Art Institute, then returned to Columbia in the late 1970s to do a PhD in art history (*Techniques of the Observer* began life as his dissertation). This was during the heyday of critical theory on the campus. On one side was Edward Said, who taught Gramsci, the Frankfurt School, and poststructuralism (this was the moment of his *Orientalism*), and on another side was Sylvère Lotringer, who advocated Foucault, Deleuze and Guattari, Jean-François Lyotard, Jean Baudrillard, and Paul Virilio (through his journal *Semiotext(e)* Lotringer brought most of these theorists to lecture). Even as Crary learned from the first group, he gravitated toward the second; he was interested less in the deconstruction of language and representation à la Derrida than in the registering of revolutionary affects and the tracing of power networks à la Deleuze and Guattari, and he was attracted to artists and filmmakers concerned with these operations as well. Thus Crary considered practitioners not readily caught in the poststructuralist net cast by most postmodernist critics (myself included): Dennis Oppenheim rather than Richard Serra, say, Gretchen Bender rather than Cindy Sherman, and so on. Though written by a critic in formation, these early texts anticipate many of his later concerns, especially when it comes to artists focused on perception and technology, from Blake and Turner to Bridget Riley and Cerith Wyn Evans. ("The discipline of art history, born on the European continent," Crary remarks of the first two, "has never quite known what to do with these immense, idiosyncratic figures from the British Isles.")[12]

During his California sojourn Crary taught at the University of California San Diego, where he met performance artists Allan Kaprow and Eleanor Antin, whose work he discussed already in terms derived from Henri Lefebvre, the first theorist of "everyday life," and Deleuze and Guattari, who celebrated "nomadic" ways of being. Thus Kaprow was said to trouble "the differences between labor and recreation," while Antin was described as an "autobiographer of a subject-in-process."[13] Crary also befriended the French filmmaker Jean-Pierre Gorin, who had collaborated with Godard on Dziga Vertov Group productions like *Wind from the East* (1970). Godard remains a touchstone for Crary (*Tricks of the Light* includes the best essay I know on *Histoire(s) du cinéma*), and film is a through line of his criticism. His canon is an unusual one, though, at least from the perspective of cinema studies, including figures, not strictly experimental or popular but both, like Fritz Lang, Alfred Hitchcock, Stanley Kubrick, Roman Polanski, and David Cronenberg. Also distinctive is his selection of novelists; his deeply suspicious view of our techno-institutional worlds leads Crary to turn often to Thomas Pynchon, Philip K. Dick, and J. G. Ballard.

In 1982 Crary published a brilliant essay on horror movies, which he reads through Deleuze and Guattari (*Anti-Oedipus* appeared in English in 1977) and against Freud (psychoanalysis pervaded film theory in the 1970s and '80s). "How often we still hear the same restricted vocabulary to pinpoint the source of horror: the unconscious, the dark side, the return of the repressed," Crary argues, when films like *Psycho*, *The Shining*, and *Videodrome* are far more concerned with "the networks of images and institutions that 'normalize' individuals." Both our terror and our pleasure, he insists, are a matter of "sociopathic zones, of detours off main flows, of deviant patterns of circulation." A text on Ballard from 1986 is also explicitly Deleuzian and anti-Freudian. A novel such as *Crash*, Crary maintains, takes deterritorialization to the point where "anything can conjoin with anything," but this "promiscuity of forms" has little to do with perversion. The city diagrammed by Ballard is "not so much a text to be read and interpreted as a delirium of conjugations to be named and enumerated."[14]

The pivotal essays in *Tricks of the Light* are the two devoted to the development of spectacle; published in the charged years of 1984 and 1989, they are the critical counterpoint to the two books on nineteenth-century visuality. In *Comments on the Society of Spectacle* (1988) Debord wrote, elliptically, that spectacle was scarcely forty years old when his famous treatise on the subject appeared in 1967. He offered no further dates or clues, even though, as Crary notes in "Spectacle, Attention, Counter-Memory" (1989), spectacle assumes "quite different meanings depending on how it is situated historically." Another prompt to periodize spectacle came from T. J. Clark, whose *The Painting of Modern Life: Manet and His Followers* (1986) proposed the Paris of the Second Empire and Third Republic as its birthplace, given how the city was transformed by Baron Haussmann into so many scenes to be sketched, painted, and photographed, that is to say, consumed as images. Cued by Debord, Crary looks instead to the late 1920s as the historical threshold of this new phase of capitalism, for it was then that "the vast interlocking control of corporate, military, and state control of radio and television was effectively in place." These years also witnessed the coming of synchronized sound to movies, which not only captivated audiences all the more effectively, but also "accelerated the complete vertical integration of production, distribution, and exhibition within the film industry and its amalgamation with the corporate conglomerates that owned the sound patents and provided the capital for the costly move to the new technology."[15] So, too, Fascist and Stalinist spectacles were under way by the late 1920s, with the Nazis soon to perfect the staging of mesmeric mass events. Of course, all three regimes made dictatorial use of radio and film as well.

In *Society of the Spectacle* Debord pointed to the Cold War contest between two types of spectacle, which he termed "diffuse" and "concentrated," the first associated with a United States awash in commodity images, the second with a Soviet Union directed by top-down propaganda. But, in his *Comments* of 1988, a year before the fall of the Wall, he pointed to an "integrated" version. It is this compound spectacle that Crary already explores in "Eclipse of the Spectacle" (1984), which focuses on the place of television in postwar life. Characteristically, he frames TV in terms not of representation but of distribution and regulation, and not as a medium in its own right but as "an aggregate of bodies, institutions, and transmissions." In the 1950s and '60s televisions combined with automobiles both to expand the terrain of the market vastly and to fill this postnatural landscape with a cornucopia of commodity images. However, by the 1970s, Crary argues, this televisual-vehicular space had started to crack, and television had begun "to be grafted onto other networks." Soon enough the computer, an even more "coercive apparatus" than the TV or the car, became the core product of the postrecession economy. "Telecommunications is the new arterial network," Crary understood already in 1984, "analogous in part to what railroads were to capitalist accumulation in the nineteenth century." He also believed that this new "social machinery" might replace our old "'contemplative' relation to objects" with "different kinds of investments." However, unlike Baudrillard, who declared the total implosion of spectacle as a result, Crary forecasted only its partial eclipse. Here he sided with Virilio, for whom new telecommunicational speeds and old highway spaces were bound to "coexist side by side in all their radical incompatibility," "a planetary data-communications network physically implanted into the decaying, digressive terrain of the automobile-based city." What Baudrillard excluded, Crary argued in an early critique of that apocalyptic thinker, was "any sense of breakdown, of faulty circuits, of systemic malfunction; or of a body that cannot be completely colonized or pacified, of disease, and of the colossal dilapidation of everything that claims infallibility or sleekness."[16] Once again Crary looked to Dick, Ballard, and Cronenberg as the best guides to this strange world.

Crary has long drawn on Debord and Foucault equally, even though the two theorists conflict on many points. "Our society is not one of spectacle, but of surveillance," Foucault stated in *Discipline and Punish: The Birth of the Prison* (1975) with Debord in mind; "under the surface of images one invests bodies in depth."[17] However, as Crary has amply shown, these two regimes can readily combine, not least because "spectacle is also a set of techniques for the management of bodies." Nevertheless, Debord and Foucault are still difficult to reconcile philosophically, as Debord came out of the Hegelian line of Marxism that Foucault questioned sharply (as did his teacher, Louis Althusser, who produced his own anti-Hegelian reading of Marx). If the Marxist conceptions of ideology and class are bracketed, as Foucault sometimes urged, there is little of Marx left. Yet Foucault wasn't as distant from Marx as he often claimed to be. Both believed, as does Crary, that "the terrain and tools of invention, freedom, and creation are always intertwined with those of domination and control."[18] And all three view the human subject as a "social product," as the late Marx wrote, one fated to be remade again and again. Especially important for Crary is a line from the *Grundrisse*, the notes that Marx assembled for *Capital* in 1857–1861, where he muses on the perpetual "discovery, creation, and satisfaction of new needs" under capitalism.[19]

If everyone and everything are fungible, though, what persists for Crary? Maybe the physiological basis of vision, but certainly not any social construction of visuality—these arrangements come and go. Just as importantly, what can resist our continuous refashioning under capitalism? Although Crary allows for the unconscious, he seems to view it as mostly colonized, so not much recalcitrance will be found there. These questions became vexed by the time of *24/7* and *Scorched Earth*, for there Crary ditches the antihumanist constructionism of the late Marx (and all of Foucault), which pervades *Techniques of the Observer* and *Suspensions of Perception*, for the humanist naturalism of the early Marx, who, in his 1844 manuscripts, posited a human nature to be reclaimed against the capitalist "estrangement of the senses."

Crary emerged at a time when dialectical thinking had fallen into bad repute. It was one of the grand narratives of modernity that Lyotard dustbinned in *The Postmodern Condition* (1979), and Foucault and Deleuze were almost contemptuous of it. Yet this rejection produced a dilemma for them, and it might for Crary as well. Despite his genealogical accounts of clinics, prisons, and the like, Foucault remained largely archaeological in his approach, examining subjects in synchronic slices of time. This method produced stunning insights, but it also made it difficult for him to explain historical change except as sudden disruption. With the categories of subject and class bracketed, discourses and institutions appeared to break down almost of their own accord or to be overthrown almost apart from any human action. Crary is also a thinker of ruptures (though, again, he locates them differently from other art historians), and agency is somewhat mysterious in his work too. In Deleuze the problem is nearly the opposite: everything is a matter of ceaseless change, of endless flow, and if there is any dialectic left, it is internal to capitalism, the "schizophrenic" intensities of which its opponents are asked somehow to exceed. This perspective, once called "capitalogical" and lately termed "accelerationist," is rejected by Crary, but like Deleuze he thinks in terms of flux, and he too sees capitalism as riven by its own crises. Today, however, capitalism appears to thrive on these very crises, or, rather, to recoup the disasters that it wreaks on the rest of us to its own benefit, privatizing the gains while socializing the losses, somehow retooling as it careens along. We can't simply wait for it to fall apart; falling apart is often how its moves ahead.

Previously Crary looked for internal rifts in capitalism to find political openings outside it, which sometimes suggested a default dialectic of its own, however directionless it might be. Thus, for example, in "Eclipse of the Spectacle" he saw this "circuit of power" as "uniform and seamless as a macro-phenomenon," but "broken, diversified, and never fully controllable in its local usage."[20] And at the end of *Suspensions of Perception* he described spectacle as "a patchwork of fluctuating effects in which individuals and groups continually reconstitute themselves—either creatively or reactively."[21] Crary crafts a rich and restless prose to capture this dynamic mimetically; his writing is a wonderful "patchwork of fluctuating effects" in its own right. But sometimes the very attempt to match our techno-institutional worlds rhetorically lends a semiparanoid tenor to his critical points. (I mean this remark as praise, as in the definition offered by Dick in *Valis* [1981]: "A paranoiac, my friend, is a person who has gone crazy in the most intelligent, well-informed way, the world being what it is.") On the one hand, Crary warns against totalizing this system, imploring us to retire the pseudo-radical cliché that "it is easier to imagine an end to the world than an end to capitalism." On the other hand, *24/7* and *Scorched Earth* evoke its derelictions so powerfully that resistance, let alone prefiguration, seems all but impossible.[22] Crary scoffs at anyone who believes that "the internet could simply 'change hands.'" He is right, of course, but maybe a shot of dialectical thinking, even a desperate leap into the utopian unknown (Lenin proposing a Communist transformation of the postal system, Fredric Jameson imagining a Communist takeover of Walmart), might help. At least it couldn't hurt.

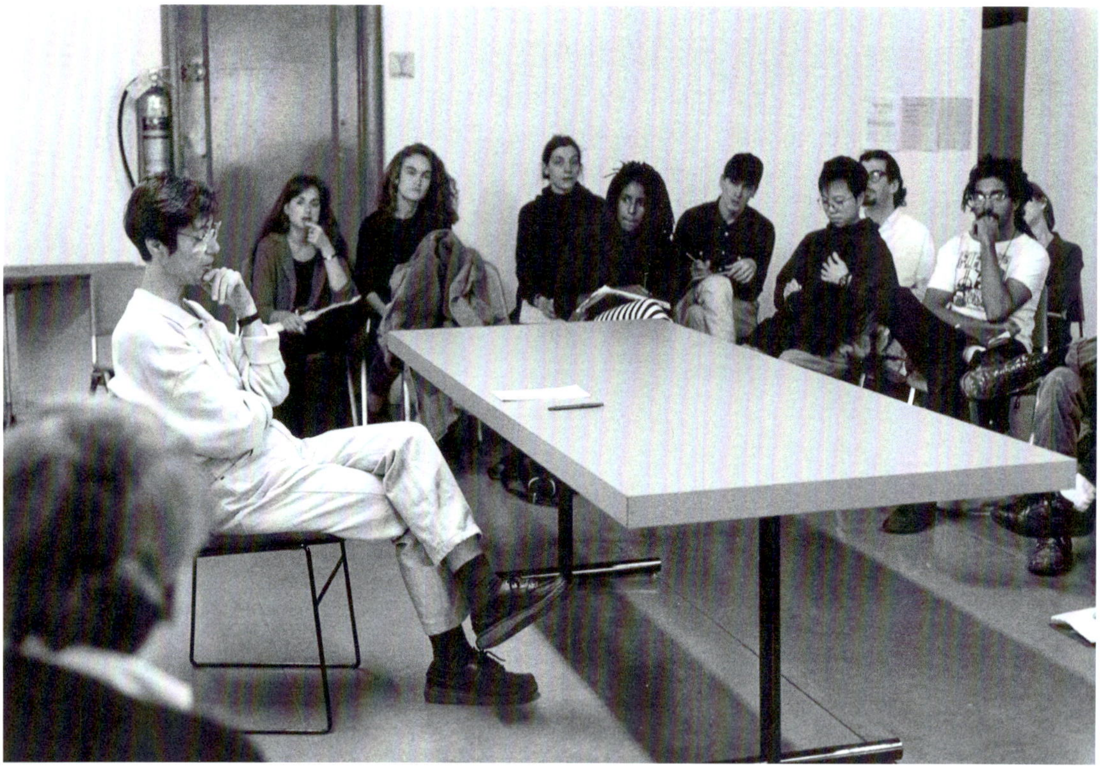

Yvonne Rainer leading a seminar at the Whitney Independent Study Program in 1992, with Ron Clark in the foreground. © Whitney Museum of American Art.

39 Interdependent Study

The Trump years were so awful that we might forget how bad the early 1980s were. Reagan and Thatcher had consolidated power, the welfare state was under relentless attack, large pieces of the public sphere were auctioned off, the AIDS epidemic had begun to rage, and the internet was about to be strung up with utopian promises that would later harden into dystopic realities. In short, neoliberalism was already rampant, and, to make matters worse, it was also the heyday of neoconservatism, of its curriculum hysteria in colleges and its culture wars in society. There were multiple fronts to fight on, then, and yet, perhaps paradoxically, this made it a relatively dynamic time for the Left. Long before the Trump Resistance there was a Reagan-Bush version, and for some of us the Whitney Museum Independent Study Program (ISP) was a small bunker in this large battle.[1]

When I first visited the ISP in 1984, I wasn't much older than the participants, so the Program was a testing ground from the start, a place to sort out my thinking and try out my writing. At the time I was a senior editor, alongside Craig Owens, at *Art in America* magazine, where we did our best to mediate postmodernist practice and poststructuralist theory, appropriation art and feminist politics, Institution Critique and Frankfurt School philosophy. My anthology of texts, *The Anti-Aesthetic: Essays on Postmodern Culture*, appeared in 1983, and my first collection of essays, *Recodings: Art, Spectacle, Cultural Politics*, in 1985. Then, too, I was involved with *Zone* as a founding editor and with *October* as a fledgling contributor. This, roughly, was what I had to offer Ron Clark, the longtime director of the ISP. My own situation was strained further by the fact that, with the deregulation of Wall Street, money had begun to flood the art world, which is one reason I left *Art in America* to join the ISP full-time in 1987. I was also at work on a PhD at the CUNY Graduate Center. For me art history and art criticism were bound up with each other dialectically, and the same was true for many students at the Graduate Center.[2]

From the beginning of the ISP in 1968, the writings of Gramsci and Brecht were primary references for Clark, and they were soon joined by the cultural studies of Raymond Williams and Stuart Hall. Through *Screen* magazine Clark also assimilated the essential ideas of Althusser and Lacan as well as the challenges to both schools of thought from French feminism and film theory. I learned a lot at the Program in those heady days. Above all it was a setting where, under political pressure, theory questioned practice and vice versa, and where criticism and history catalyzed each other. That said, the Program had its tensions. First, there was a gap between its two sections—studio practice and museum studies—that reflected the distance between artists and curators in the 1980s. In response Clark and I simply forced the two parts together in seminars and renamed the museum track "critical and curatorial studies." The latter move helped to attract many of the young minds that have done so much to transform contemporary curating ever since. Second, there was a related divide between uptown and downtown worlds, and the Whitney Museum was uptown ideologically as well as geographically (it still occupied its great Marcel Breuer building on Madison Avenue). I remember mostly futile attempts to explain ISP show topics, such as "The Desire of the Museum," to Whitney administrators. But then the ISP was foreign not just to the museum world but to the art world at large. In his 2004 overview of the Program Howard Singerman called this distance the gap between "critique and career."[3] At the time, it seemed, one couldn't have both, and the great majority of ISPers chose critique.

There was a third tension at the ISP, one between theory and activism. This was heightened by the AIDS crisis, or rather the murderous indifference of the Reagan-Bush administrations to the epidemic, which impacted Program participants and friends directly. I was seen primarily as a theorist, so at times this frustration was aimed at me. At one point I somehow thought it was a good idea to consider the role of *ressentiment* in critique, and so asked everyone to read Nietzsche, especially *The Genealogy of Morals*. That was just one of several grenades that blew up in my hand in those years. ("Why force us to read anything by that syphilitic proto-fascist?") Sometimes the productive encounter between theory and practice, so essential to the ISP, was difficult to maintain, but maybe that wasn't always a bad thing. Certainly it put theory to the test.

There were many critical positions to sort out, and partisanship in New York intellectual circles was intense: Gramsci or Adorno? Debord or Althusser? Lacan or Foucault? Luce Irigaray or Juliet Mitchell? And so on. No doubt from a distance this looked like so much "narcissism of small differences," but the stakes never seemed trivial to us. Yet rarely did the debates become tribal at the Program, and this was largely due to two shared commitments: to the seminar as a place of genuine discussion, and to the tripartite structure of the ISP. To borrow a neologism from Asger Jorn, this structure was "triolectical," a dialectics of three. Programmatically, there were three sections—studio art (which often meant post-studio art), critical studies, and curatorial work—with an engagement in theory across all three. Politically, our conversations were informed by three concerns above all—class, gender, and race (the ISP aimed to be intersectional *avant la lettre*). And, pedagogically, there was the triangulation of Clark, Silvia Kolbowski (later replaced by Mary Kelly), and me (later replaced by Benjamin Buchloh). Our orientations were different, to be sure, but our approaches were complementary.[4] Finally, there was the further triangulation of criticism, theory, and history, or at least that was our goal.

In many ways that triangulation became my modus operandi. For instance, questions of representation, subjectivity, and sexuality in contemporary art resonated with historical practices, in the first instance for me with Surrealism, the subject of my dissertation, which was written during my time at the ISP (I left in 1991 to teach at Cornell). Like many others, I was influenced by the returns to Marx, Freud, and Nietzsche, especially the rereadings by Althusser, Lacan, and Foucault and Deleuze respectively. As a reminder, Lacan reread Freudian psychoanalysis through Saussurean linguistics—an overlay that not only reanimated both discourses but also illuminated the conceptual world that they occupied.[5] So, too, I thought, might Freud share a psychological episteme with the Surrealists. Although they were certainly aware of Freud, they only knew early writings such as *The Interpretation of Dreams* (1900). I reread the Surrealists, then, against texts that they didn't know, *Beyond the Pleasure Principle* (1920) above all. In my account they misrecognized their own connection to the unconscious: whereas Breton and company presented Surrealism as a celebration of desire, a self-understanding that was passed on to generations of artists, critics, and historians, I saw Surrealism as directed, against its own program of erotic love, by the uncanniness of the death drive.[6]

This approach led me to an article of methodological faith that I tried to practice at the ISP. One develops theory in order to elucidate the concepts embedded in art, and in turn these concepts can be used to test the claims of theory; in the process parallels with developments in other disciplines might also come to light. What drove this approach was the perceived necessity of what Nietzsche called "effective history," or what Foucault termed a "history of the present," a genealogy that reframed the present through the past read "against the grain."[7] This last phrase is a familiar one from Benjamin. "The true picture of the past flits by," he wrote in "On the Concept of History" (1940). "The past can be seized only as an image that flashes up at its moment of recognizability, and is never seen again."[8] Many of us were taken by the powerful ethos of history written in emergency. I still am, especially now that emergency is often the norm.

Over the years the Program has received its fair share of criticisms. A common one is that theory overwhelms practice at the ISP, that it serves to paralyze artists. This figure of the artist struck dumb by thought is a caricature, a piece of condescension that artists would do well to reject. The critic Grant Kester once called it "the empty studio syndrome," but then noted that this emptiness can flip into an openness, that a pause in individual work (if such did occur) can be an invitation to collaborative practice, and several important groups have indeed emerged from the ISP.[9] Then there is the related complaint that the curriculum is somehow dogmatic, which, if my account of its triolectical structure is accurate, is also overstated: the Program is pulled in different directions by structural design. What the ISP did do is to refuse the anything-goes pluralism, incited by an expanded market, of a lax art world.

However, a related charge might hit closer to home. Sometime in the mid 1980s I overheard a comment that the ISP reading list was "prophylactic." Why assign secondary texts by Raymond Williams and not primary ones by Marx? Why Laclau and Mouffe and not Gramsci? And so on. (Remember that this was the time of critical returns to foundational figures.) Clark answered, directly, that he did so because those thinkers were also primary for him, and so they have now become, productively, for generations of ISPers. Then, too, there is the complaint that the Program is exclusive. Certainly it is small (about twenty-five participants each year), with a skeletal staff, but no art institute that is at all similar was as committed to diversity as early as the ISP (for Clark this was a matter of principle, both political and pedagogical). Finally, there is the charge that the problem is less critique *versus* career than critique *as* career, that the Program is a finishing school in criticality that sets one up nicely in the art world. That critique carries such prestige is my favorite fantasy of all. (A related accusation—that the ISP is a permitted enclave or safety valve within the New York art world—might have more purchase.)

I take other criticisms more seriously, mostly because they involve autocritique more than ISP-bashing. First, I believed in the politics of theory—that discourse can alter institutions, if not transform them—to a fault. Like others I tended to treat the critical theory of the 1970s and '80s as the continuation of the politics of the 1960s by other means. In part this was a deflection, and sometimes it supported the belief that the right theory could count as the right politics, that a correct critical line was a good-enough commitment. This deflection of politics into theory followed the displacement of politics into art for a previous generation. "Some day it will have to be told," Clement Greenberg once intoned, "how 'anti-Stalinism,' which started out more or less as 'Trotskyism,' turned into art for art's sake, and thereby cleared the way, heroically, for what was to come," that is, for Abstract Expressionism.[10] And Michael Fried argued similarly that the "perpetual revolution" advocated by Trotsky, though rooted in politics, was carried forward in modernism.[11] This was seductive to me as a young critic as a way to hold on to the idea of a progressive telos or goal in history. And, again, I participated in a related displacement of failed politics into fierce theory, which was, at least in part, a compensatory move as well.[12] At the extreme this was manifested in an ultraleftism of theory (Lenin might have called it an "infantile disorder") whereby the one who tacks hardest to the Left rhetorically gains the upper hand politically.[13] God knows we questioned authority—the death of the author and the critique of originality were our bread and butter—but, secretly or not, some of us also wanted authority, the authority of critique.[14] And here the charge of critique as career might have a point. At the same time, "authoritative" is not the same thing as "authoritarian," even though, in the trashing of theory, this slippage was common enough. I too wanted to question authority, but I also believe in expertise, and today many kinds of knowledge, cultural as well as political, are too quickly attacked as elitist—in Left-identified circles as well as Right-rabid networks. Of course, it is also crucial to ask who gets to speak—who is present to speak at all—and certainly there are times when people like me should fall silent.

On this score I wasn't attentive enough to questions of race. (This wasn't the case with Clark, who was quick to delve into Black British Cinema, for example, especially the work of Isaac Julien, in part through his involvement in Birmingham cultural studies.) I was drawn to two other interests: like many others, I was absorbed first by the intricacies of sexual difference, and then by the complexities of postcolonial discourse. (I studied with Edward Said, who presented his *Orientalism* in a seminar at Columbia in the late 1970s.) Despite its many insights postcolonial discourse, at least as developed in the United States, tended to project race away—either into historical periods, as with modernist primitivism (the *Primitivism* show at the Museum of Modern Art in 1984 was an important provocation), or into neocolonial territories, in any case into a space-time that was not, for us, here and now. This allowed people like me to fail to address the white confines not only of the art world but also of critical theory, that is, to fail to see the privileged conditions of our own vaunted criticality.

Third, as a young critic I sometimes collapsed the aesthetic into the ideological *tout court*. How Kant defined aesthetic experience, as the potential reconciliation of opposed faculties, didn't seem so different, structurally, from how Althusser defined ideological misrecognition, as an imaginary resolution of real contradictions. And so, too proudly, I titled that 1983 volume of essays *The Anti-Aesthetic*.[15] Four decades later I hear too much disdain for art in this title, a disdain that was born, paradoxically, of a disappointment in art, that is, of an excessive hope that wasn't met, perhaps couldn't be met.[16] Again, this was 1983, the time of a reactionary antimodernism that flew under the cover of postmodernism, which was really a forced return to market-friendly painting and sculpture in a macho key after the deconstructions of all these things in the 1970s. If that was what counted as aesthetic, I was happy to be anti.

Fourth, from an anti-aesthetic excess I tacked back to the neo-Adornian position that I had once abjured, that is, I came to argue for a critical dimension within the aesthetic. This shift chagrined Clark, who had long dismissed the Kantian framing of the aesthetic as the fantasy that art could somehow be disinterested, removed not only from politics but from life at large. Weirdly, I sometimes had to defend art against artists at the Program, at least against those who held that the ultimate point of artistic practice is to erase its difference from political activity. I tried to point out that historically this "sublation" had often proved to be problematic for both sides.[17] In a way this debate was a return of the antagonism between theory and activism, only now with art as the bad object. Here again I was frustrated by the opposition, and so, after Godard (and along with Thomas Hirschhorn), I wanted to ask, "Rather than make political art, why not make art politically?" That's too glib by half; the point is simply that I didn't want to see art sacrificed (once again) at the altar of politics.

There was another factor in play here. The pressure for commitment is intense at the ISP, which is what has made it the great crucible that it is, but sometimes it encourages a presentism that can be amnesiac, and often at the Program I insisted on the resources to be found in past art. This has a defensive dimension, to be sure: I don't want to give up on historical artists whom I deeply admire, and so, like Said (who was more of a high modernist than I), I have attempted a "contrapuntal reading" of the canon, one that attempts to see the seamy underside of great works. In *Culture and Imperialism* (1993) Said queried the English novel along these lines: Where in the British Empire does dark Heathcliff go to make his fortune in *Wuthering Heights* and how exactly is it made? What is the real story of Bertha Mason, the Caribbean wife in *Jane Eyre*, who, driven mad by her imprisonment in the attic, sets the Rochester mansion on fire? What are the unknown shares in the African rubber plantation that support the otherwise progressive Schlegel sisters in *Howards End*?[18] For Said such contrapuntal reading was a way to enrich our understanding of these novels beyond a rhetoric of blame. For me it remains an important aspect of any critical study of modernism.

Another key aspect of such study is to see modernist art as an archive that artists, critics, and curators can still develop. This leads to a final observation.

Again, when I first came to the ISP in 1984, art criticism and art history were in productive tension, and a parallactic view of contemporary practice and modernist art seemed essential to critical work in both fields. Twenty years later in 2004, when Singerman wrote his short history of the Program, he sensed my concern about a new disconnect between the two domains. He then quoted Clark, "My purpose is to strike a balance between critical cultural studies and what Hal refers to as critical modernist studies. There are very important historical precedents that need to be honored and represented." At this point Singerman interjected astutely: "Clark's response isn't quite written in the same tense as Foster's worry; his language works to memorialize an art (and a situation for art) that Foster wants to take as active and present."[19] I still want to take it as active and present, but a few decades down the line I'm less sure that this is possible. In short, critical modernism may well be "a thing of the past" in the Hegelian sense. This isn't my own version of "farewell to an idea," but it isn't "good riddance" either. A part of me keeps the faith.[20]

Lastly, another part of me keeps the faith about the old politics of representation—though, like the ultraleftism of theory, it looks different today. To put it crudely, some of us were so focused on cultural politics that we lost sight of political economy, so concerned with the critique of the subject that we didn't attend adequately to the demolition of the social. After Fredric Jameson I understood postmodernism as a way to periodize culture in relation to capital, but too often I thought that simply to connect the two, with updated examples of fragmentation and reification, might work a kind of critical magic. It didn't, of course.

The ultimate value of the ISP stems from the seminar as a micro-utopia (this is often a retroactive feeling—the actual event can be painful), that is, the seminar as a place of both affinity and agonism, where the discursive intensity of downtown art and criticism from decades past is developed in terms pertinent to the present, a space of analysis and invention alike, in short, a haven for critique in a postcritical world. It is this critical sociality that is the most important offering of the Program. Not only does it put interlocutors together who might not otherwise find each other so readily, but it also promotes an intergenerational through line that makes for a supportive dialogue across time. It is this elective community that the ISP has granted many of us over the years.

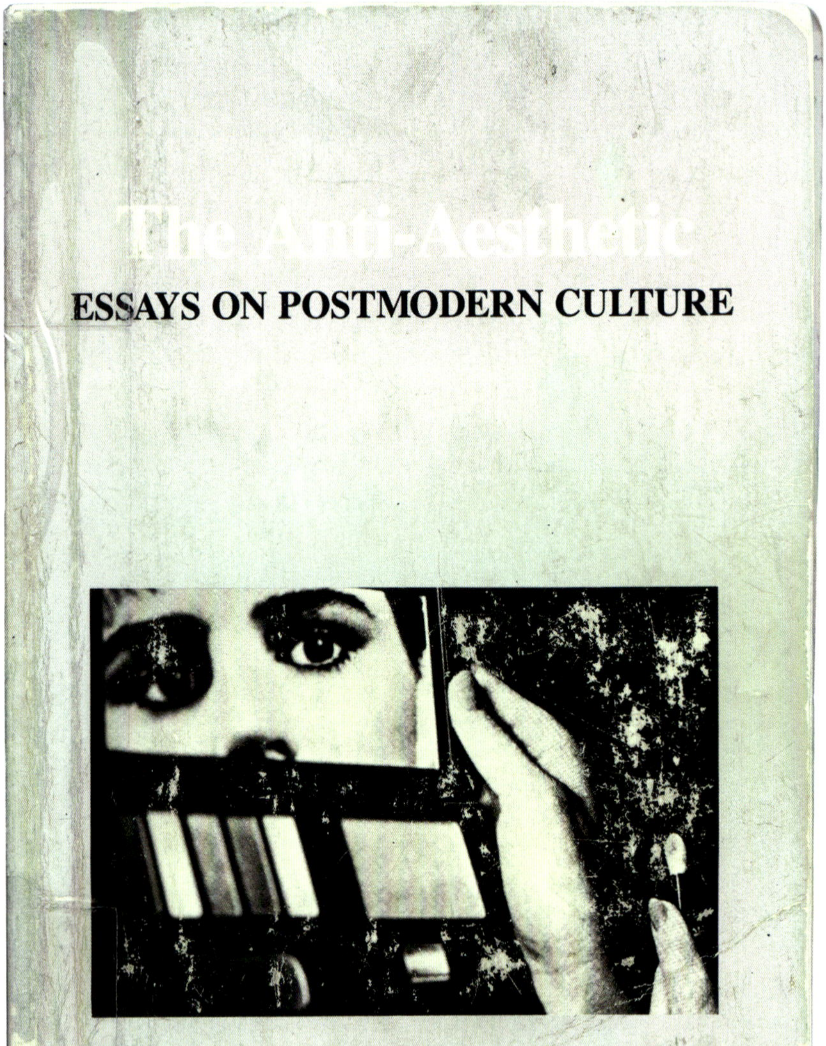

Cover of *The Anti-Aesthetic*, with Richard Prince's *Untitled (Make-up)* (1982).
Design: Thatcher Bailey.

40 *The Anti-Aesthetic* Then and Now

The notion of postmodernism was once a great stimulant to art and thought; today it feels like another anti-aphrodisiac of the just past. In some ways, postmodernism seems more historical than modernism, reanimated as modernism partially is by questions of diaspora and decoloniality. On the other hand, this untimeliness makes the present a good moment to look back at postmodernism, if only to measure our distance from it.

The Anti-Aesthetic: Essays on Postmodern Culture, which I edited, was published over forty years ago; it was quickly followed by *Art after Modernism: Rethinking Representation* (1984), assembled by Brian Wallis. Although academic presses produced related anthologies in turn, these initial entries were issued by an independent publisher (Bay Press) and a contemporary museum (New Museum) respectively. In other words, the discourse of postmodernism wasn't hatched in the academy, even if it came to roost there, and it wasn't conjured up by journalists and publicists, even if it came to serve the culture industry.

Although not as nihilistic as our libertarian present, the early 1980s were a time of deep reaction. With Thatcher, Reagan, and Kohl, neoliberalism had captured the levers of political power, and neoconservatives like Daniel Bell were ascendent ideologically. What motivated the neocons above all was revenge against "the 1960s." The problems of contemporary society, they claimed, were due to militant students, Black activists, and strident feminists, not, say, the ravages of advanced capitalism, and the necessary cure was a return to tradition, family, and moral values. Yet, even as the Left was in political retreat, it had advanced on cultural fronts. There was real vitality in these multifarious debates, not least in matters of critical theory, which was heterogeneous, especially in the Anglophone context. To come to terms with these ideas new and old, a bevy of reviews appeared, including *Camera Obscura*, *Critical Inquiry*, *Diacritics*, *differences*, *New German Critique*, *October*, *Representations*, *Screen*, *Semiotext(e)*, *Social Text*, *Telos*, *Third Text*, *Wedge*, and *Zone*. In retrospect, though, the drift from politics to criticism was a bad trade, however limited the options then were. When a *Social Text* editor said to me that critical journals were the political parties of our time, I didn't know whether to laugh or cry.

Due in part to the vagaries of translation, young intellectuals in the United States encountered the Frankfurt School about the same time as structuralism and poststructuralism. Gramsci came via British cultural studies along with Althusser and Debord, who represented very different lines in Marxist thought. French feminism and film theory, which drew on Saussure, Freud, and Lacan, arrived with Foucault, who was skeptical about all three of these thinkers. A main motive of *The Anti-Aesthetic* was to parse how these various models might bear on contemporary art and architecture. Yet this also set up the ambiguous posture of the book, which was vanguard in its commitment to theory but defensive in its opposition to the neoconservative-neoliberal order. *The Anti-Aesthetic* was unambiguous, however, in its rejection of any postmodernism associated with neofigurative art and neosymbolic architecture. Stylistic in orientation, that postmodernism was more antimodernist than anything else, and it appeared to support the cultural politics of the reactionary alliance in power.

The Anti-Aesthetic also appeared in the wake of *The Postmodern Condition: A Report on Knowledge* (1979), in which Jean-François Lyotard argued that "the grand narratives" of modernity—the dialectic of Spirit, the accumulation of wealth, the emancipation of the worker, the achievement of a classless society—had run into the sand. I wanted to begin, then, with a contrary voice, that of Jürgen Habermas, the central figure of the late Frankfurt School. As luck would have it, he had delivered his Theodor W. Adorno Prize lecture, "Modernity—An Incomplete Project," at New York University in 1981, and *New German Critique* published it later that year. The title of the essay carried its thrust, which insisted, against both Lyotard in *The Postmodern Condition* and Adorno and Horkheimer in *Dialectic of Enlightenment* (1947), that the modern commitment to "communicative rationality" must be recovered. Habermas acknowledged that the Enlightenment mission—to separate knowledge into the three spheres of science, morality, and art and to develop their "inner logic" professionally—had had mixed results at best, one of which was to distance such activities from the public. He also understood that "the 20th century has shattered this optimism" about "the rational organization of everyday social life." On the other hand, Habermas averred that "efforts to 'negate' the culture of expertise" à la Dada and Surrealism were mostly "nonsense experiments": "nothing remains from a desublimated meaning or a destructured form; an emancipatory effect does not follow." Hence his ultimatum cast in the form of a question: "Should we try to hold on to the *intentions* of the Enlightenment, feeble as they may be, or should we declare the entire project of modernity a lost cause?"[1]

Habermas wasn't sanguine about this holding on. "Modernism is dominant but dead," he admitted, "the disillusionment with the very failures of those programs that called for the negation of art and philosophy has come to serve as a pretense for conservative positions," and communicative reason was outmatched by capitalist (ir)rationality. Nevertheless, he urged that the good fight be fought, as did Kenneth Frampton in "Towards a Critical Regionalism: Six Points for an Architecture of Resistance." For Frampton architecture was a central arena in which "local culture" confronted "universal civilization." This shifted the question, which Frampton posed via the philosopher Paul Ricoeur: "How to become modern and to return to sources, how to revive an old, dormant civilization and take part in universal civilization?" Postmodern architects like Robert Venturi and Denise Scott Brown, Robert A. M. Stern, and Michael Graves promised a populist "return to history" but "merely fed the media-society with gratuitous, quietistic images."[2] Against this cynical program, Frampton pressed architects to "build the site" according to the principles of critical regionalism, which he saw exemplified in the work of Alvar Aalto and Jørn Utzon. With a similar emphasis on the tactile and the tectonic over the imagistic and the scenographic, architects might promote a sensuous kind of place-making that would support the realm of "human appearance" (an allusion to Hannah Arendt, for whom this was a *sine qua non* of all politics) and thus resist the predations of advanced capitalism. It soon turned out, however, that a greater threat than pop-historical postmodernism came from architecture refashioned as a sculptural media-logo à la the Guggenheim Bilbao, which suited the interests of a now-global capitalism even better.

Again, *The Anti-Aesthetic* advocated practices that were not merely antimodernist. At the same time, in essays first published in *October* magazine, Rosalind Krauss and Douglas Crimp demonstrated how modernist conceptions of both medium and museum had fallen into crisis. Concerned that the category of sculpture was stretched to the point of meaninglessness after Minimalism, Krauss, in "Sculpture in the Expanded Field," reasserted its old definition as a commemorative monument in order to trace the breakdown of that logic in the late nineteenth and early twentieth centuries, first in the work of Rodin, where sculpture entered "its negative condition—a kind of sitelessness," and then in that of Brancusi, where it became a "pure marker" that, through a reflection on its materials and processes, "depicts its own autonomy." For several decades, Krauss argued, modernists explored this "idealist space" productively, but in time it was "experienced more and more as pure negativity," with sculpture understood mostly as that which was not-architecture or not-landscape. However, in a deft structuralist move, Krauss argued that this negative binary could be expanded "into a quaternary field" in which sculpture was revealed to be "only one term on the periphery" along with "site-constructions," "marked sites," and "axiomatic structures." "Within the situation of postmodernism," she concluded, "practice is not defined in relation to a given medium—sculpture—but rather in relation to the logical operations on a set of cultural terms, for which any medium—photography, books, lines on walls, mirrors, or sculpture itself—might be used."

This renowned text remains a brilliant demonstration of method, one that openly privileges structure over history as a mode of explanation, yet that very emphasis also rendered it silent on socioeconomic factors, such as the dominance of the commodity form and the rise of spectacular society, which have impacted sculpture far more than any logical operation.[3] So, too, other critics have used the quaternary field deployed by Krauss to map not artistic expansion but ideological closure, and, though earthworks and other such constructions did extend sculpture spatially, for the most part they have proved to be a dead end aesthetically.[4]

Another ruse of history has operated on the art institution as analyzed by Crimp in "On the Museum's Ruins." According to Foucault, it was Manet who underscored the reflexivity of modernist art whereby "every painting now belongs within the squared and massive surface of painting."[5] So what happens, Crimp asked, when photography is let loose on that surface, not as a discrete medium of art but as an anti-auratic operation of image reproduction and proliferation as suggested by Rauschenberg? Can the disciplinary boundaries of the institution hold up, or does such postmodernist art demonstrate once and for all that, as the theorist Eugenio Donato put it, "the set of objects the museum displays is sustained only by the fiction that they somehow constitute a coherent representational universe"? Important at the time, this epistemological crisis of the museum seems a minor problem today compared to its complicities with colonialism and imperialism, not to mention its histories of expropriation and exclusion.

In "The Discourse of Others: Feminists and Postmodernism," one of the most influential texts in *The Anti-Aesthetic*, Craig Owens redescribed the postmodern crackup of the "grand narratives" of modernity as a "loss of mastery." Although "the representational systems of the West admit only one vision—that of the constitutive male subject," feminist artists had come to challenge that dominance. Long "excluded from representation by its very structure," the female subject was its most incisive critic, one dedicated to its "ruin." The prime move of feminist postmodernism was thus to "expropriate the appropriators," an operation that Owens described, in terms that are now canonical, in the work of Dara Birnbaum, Jenny Holzer, Barbara Kruger, Louise Lawler, Sherrie Levine, Martha Rosler, and Cindy Sherman. "Here," he concluded, "we arrive at an apparent crossing of the feminist critique of patriarchy and the postmodernist critique of representation." After Rosler, Owens warned that women should not be "a token for all markers of difference"; at the same time, he insisted, "sexual inequality cannot be reduced to an instance of economic exploitation." This tension between difference and totality has returned with force in contemporary debates about race and class.[6]

For the Marxist Fredric Jameson, however, it is only through such totalizing that any difference can be understood. A year after the publication of *The Political Unconscious* (1981) Jameson lectured at the Whitney Museum on "Postmodernism and Consumer Society," his first text on the subject. For Jameson the passage from modernism to postmodernism was a matter less of a rupture than of "a restructuration of a certain number of elements already given," of which he offered several telling instances. Whereas intellectual inquiry was once undertaken in discrete discourses like philosophy, history, political theory, and literary criticism, the new species of critical theory roamed across these disciplines, poaching from them freely. Jameson next pointed to a shift in the typical relations between high and low art. Whereas modernists tended to oppose the two, postmodernists liked to intermingle them. More precisely, whereas modernists alluded to classic texts for parodic effect (as with Joyce), postmodernists tended to incorporate them in a pastiche that undercut their normativity (as with Kathy Acker).[7] Most important, Jameson refused any stylistic understanding of the notion of postmodernism. Its purpose, rather, was "to correlate the emergence of new formal features in culture with the emergence of a new type of social life and a new economic order," those of advanced capitalism. If modernists stressed the originality of their oeuvres, postmodernists enacted "the death of the author," and their practice of pastiche took the modernist fragmentation of language to a new level, one that Jameson likened to the effects of schizophrenia in which "meaning is lost," "the materiality of words becomes obsessive," and the world is "transformed into an image." Through this staging of "unreality" that feels like "intensity," Jameson concluded, postmodernism expresses "the inner truth" of advanced capitalism, which is to erode any "sense of history." "Our entire contemporary social system has little by little begun to lose its capacity to retain its own past, has begun to live in a perpetual present and in a perpetual change that obliterates traditions of the kind which all earlier social formations have had in one way or another to preserve." Jameson ended with an ultimatum of his own: "Postmodernism replicates or reproduces—reinforces—the logic of consumer capitalism; the more significant question is whether there is also a way in which it resists that logic."

In "The Ecstasy of Communication" Jean Baudrillard also associated the postmodern subject with a schizophrenic who, no longer able to "produce the limits of his own being," "is now only a pure screen, a switching center for all the networks of influence." Of course, as with Jameson, such pathological diagnoses of an entire society are problematic, and Baudrillard was indeed prone to extreme statements, which were sometimes parroted in 1980s art talk. Yet he also produced important insights, some of which anticipate "the hyperrealism of simulation" all around us. Here are several examples: "Advertising in its new dimension invades everything, as public space (the street, monument, market, scene) disappears." "Bodily movements" are displaced into "electronic commands." "The instantaneity of communication has miniaturized our exchanges into a succession of instants." "In place of the reflexive transcendence of mirror and scene, there is a nonreflecting surface, an immanent surface where operations unfold—the smooth operational surface of communication." The opposition between private and public is "effaced in a sort of obscenity where the most intimate processes of our life become the virtual feeding ground of the media."

Finally, in "Opponents, Audiences, Constituencies and Community," Edward Said closed *The Anti-Aesthetic* with a critical reflection on "the politics of interpretation." This phrase performs a discursive twist typical of the time: rather than represent or interpret politics, the charge was to politicize representation, to politicize interpretation. Yet Said was already alert to the problem that such criticism, however interdisciplinary, hardly translated into more direct communication with a wider audience. On the contrary, "critics read each other and cared about little else." If "technical language" remained the criterion and "self-policing" remained the protocol, "the particular mission of the humanities" would be only "to represent noninterference in the affairs of the everyday world," and its primary function would be merely "to represent humane marginality, which is also to preserve and if possible to conceal the hierarchy of powers that occupy the center, define the social terrain, and fix the limits of use, functions, fields, marginality, and so on." Guided by figures like Said, the humanities have improved dramatically on these fronts, but representing "humane marginality" remains their primary purpose.

Most anthologies worth a damn are products of urgency and contingency, and *The Anti-Aesthetic* was no different. A twenty-eight-year-old editor and critic at *Art in America* at the time of its publication, I was almost too eager to trace the connections among art, theory, and politics that the contributors pointed toward.[8] Urgency and contingency bring oversights, then, some of which remain especially galling to me. Although the premier artists of postmodernism were women, only one woman appears as an author in the book, and there is only one text on feminist art, and that was written by a man.[9] And though I participated in a seminar on Orientalism given by Said, the book includes no text on postcolonial discourse. There are excuses—Said was focused on literature and music, not art, and critics like Geeta Kapur were not widely known and journals like *Third Text* not yet founded—but these are excuses. It took the autocritique of anthropology, along with the provocation of the notorious *Primitivism* show at the Museum of Modern Art in 1984, to foreground the many implications of postcolonial critique for art. Difference, as understood by both poststructuralism and feminism, was still "difference within" more than "alterity without."

I have already noted some shifts in the subjects taken up in *The Anti-Aesthetic* since its publication; here, to conclude, are several more. First, the valence of appropriation has obviously undergone a sea-change. Once central to postmodernist practice, which was often called "appropriation art," this operation was taken to challenge unexamined assumptions about authorship as authority and art as property. Now the notion is fraught with ethical peril, and the term often functions as an accusation. Second, though it was always trivial to treat postmodernism as a stylistic term, its use value as a period marker has become uncertain. Simply put, we overstated the break with modernism, if not with modernity (whose grand narratives appear more defunct than ever). Certainly, the modernism that provided a foil for postmodernism was a reductive one, often too focused on a straw man or an easy target (such as Greenberg or Color Field painting). Perhaps what Lyotard, Habermas, and others counted as modernity is also due for revision—and postmodernity along with it. Third, in my introduction to the book I opposed "a postmodernism of resistance" to "a postmodernism of reaction," and associated the former with poststructuralist critique and the latter with neoconservative politics. Already a year later I questioned this binary, for both appropriation art and postmodern architecture can be taken to promote a fragmentation of cultural signs that might speak to the corrosive action of capital more than anything else.[10]

Fourth, rejection of the aesthetic has eased. Suspicious of the lazy aestheticism all around us (Neo-Expressionist painting, bronze sculpture, art photography), my cohort of artists and critics was skeptical about the aesthetic as a category, and in an early moment of the digital revolution we were more dismissive of artistic aura than even Walter Benjamin (who influenced us enormously). As a site of reconciliation between different faculties (as Kant had defined it), the aesthetic seemed to be aligned with the ideological. This led me to draw, within the postmodernism of resistance, a distinction between two positions, one affined with Gramsci, the other with Adorno, and to offer an ultimatum of my own:

> The adventures of the aesthetic make up one of the great narratives of modernity: from the time of its autonomy through art-for-art's sake to its status as necessary negative category, a critique of the world as it is. It is this last moment (figured brilliantly in the writings of Theodor Adorno) that is hard to relinquish: the notion of the aesthetic as subversive, a critical interstice in an otherwise instrumental world. Now, however, we have to consider that this aesthetic space too is eclipsed—or rather, that its criticality is now largely illusory (and so instrumental). In such an event, the strategy of an Adorno, of negative commitment, might have to be revised or rejected, and a new strategy of interference (associated with Gramsci) devised.

In his account of the politics of interpretation Said had also advocated Gramsci; there was a counterhegemonic thrust in the texts by Frampton, Owens, and Jameson; and a Gramscian position was the one to take up in the face of the neoconservative-neoliberal order. Yet I have come to doubt the necessity of the Gramsci-Adorno opposition. They are not as mutually exclusive as I made them out to be in the exigencies of the moment. And today there is a new insistence on the aesthetic, even a return to the beautiful, especially among Black artists and critics, in large part because it offers some respite from an otherwise necessary focus on traumatic histories, some promise of "a transfiguration of the given."[11]

Fifth and finally, there is a shift in the valence of the critical, which is no longer the undisputed good or inviolate criterion that my cohort often took it to be. That said, I remain committed to the kind of critical intervention that *The Anti-Aesthetic* attempted to make; the postcritical is not for me. Nor is the insistence that criticism be reparative; in my view that notion edges toward a redemptive idea of culture that much of the most important art, modernist and postmodernist alike, rejects.[12] Criticism and culture are not therapy, not then, not now.

Acknowledgments

If my first debt is to the artists and critics discussed in this book, my second is to the editors for whom many of the texts were originally written, especially Mary-Kay Wilmers, Alice Spawls, and Paul Myerscough at the *London Review of Books*, and Tim Griffin, Michelle Kuo, and David Velasco at *Artforum*. I am grateful for the editorial guidance of Tom Weaver, Victoria Hindley, and Gabriela Bueno Gibbs at MIT Press. My thanks also go to Yasuyo Iguchi for her smart design, Matthew Abbate for his careful copyediting, and Michele Mazeris for her assiduous image research. I am grateful as well to my department at Princeton University for timely leaves and to the American Academy in Rome for a productive stay in spring 2023.

A few triangulations have guided my intellectual life. For several decades I have argued, in serious ways only sympathetic friends can, with Michel Feher and Jonathan Crary, Benjamin Buchloh and Yve-Alain Bois, and T. J. Clark and Greil Marcus. I make up a newer trio with Ben Lerner and Jeff Dolven, whose insights on our art sorties I crib shamelessly. For spirited conversations at the Scratcher I thank Alex Kitnick and Robert Slifkin, and for festive gatherings at Cabinet I thank Sina Najafi and Nina Katchadourian. I continue to learn from my Princeton colleagues and my *October* comrades, especially Leah Dickerman, Devin Fore, David Joselit, and Pamela Lee. Novelists steeped in art and criticism have inspired me too, in particular Rivka Galchen, Katie Kitamura, Hari Kunzru, Rachel Kushner, Tom McCarthy, Joseph O'Neill, and Zadie Smith. My graduate students, too many to name, have influenced me as much as I have them.

Closer to home, my daughters-in-law, Jackie and Gaby, and granddaughters, Georgia and Agnes (both named after extraordinary artists), are a pure delight. My oldest friends remain my closest companions, and my heartfelt thanks go once again to Charlie Wright, Thatcher Bailey, Bob Strong, and Rolfe Watson. Although I owe every book to Sandy Tait, this one is dedicated to our beloved sons, Tait and Thatcher.

Notes

Introduction

1. See Samuel Beckett, *Worstward Ho* (1983), his penultimate published piece.

2. In *Recodings* I wrote in advocacy of contemporary artists. As the art market expanded in the neoliberal 1990s, I stepped back from critical writing and into academic scholarship. Over the last twenty years, when art critics have had minimal effect on market values, I have returned to criticism intermittently.

3. Both "Antecedents" and "Contemporaries" conclude with practices that take up questions of cultural difference and appropriation.

4. See "Antinomic Modernism" in this volume.

5. There are many omissions, even of artists in my cohort. I address some in other books, I have done interviews with others (which I opted not to include here), and I have lacked the occasion to write about still others. This goes for critics as well, though figures like Benjamin Buchloh, Michael Fried, and Craig Owens appear often in the texts and the notes. (Also see Benjamin Buchloh and Hal Foster, *Exit Interview* [New York: no place press, 2024].) Some media are also scanted, especially painting, yet again other critic-historians have addressed its contemporary manifestations better than I. Although I have developed a few of these essays at length elsewhere, I present them in their initial form here, in the hope that first impressions really are the freshest.

6. Roland Barthes, "On *The Fashion System* and the Structural Analysis of Narrative" (1967), in Barthes, *The Grain of the Voice: Interviews 1962–1980*, trans. Linda Coverdale (New York: Hill & Wang, 1985), 50. Also see "Made for Cutting," "An Inventory of Encounters," and "Interdependent Study" in this volume.

7. See Terry Smith, "Introduction: The Contemporaneity Question," in Terry Smith, Okwui Enwezor, and Nancy Condee, eds., *Antinomies of Art and Culture: Modernity, Postmodernity, Contemporaneity* (Durham: Duke University Press, 2008).

8. See "*The Anti-Aesthetic* Then and Now" in this volume.

9. On diasporic interconnections see Leah Dickerman, "Diaspora Modern," *October* 186 (Fall 2023); on archipelagic thought see, among other texts, Édouard Glissant, *Poetics of Relation*, trans. Betsy Wing (Ann Arbor: University of Michigan Press, 1997); on global transfers see Daniel Spaulding, "A Scheme Transfer for Global Modernism," *October* 186 (Fall 2023). In *Bad New Days: Art, Criticism, Emergency* (2015) I point to such paradigms as the abject, the archival, the mimetic, and the precarious.

10. For more on these genealogies, see my "Tales of Twentieth-Century Art," in Elizabeth Cropper, ed., *Dialogues in Art History, from Mesopotamian to Modern* (Washington: CASVA, 2009).

11. Gerhard Richter, *Text: Writings, Interviews and Letters 1961–2007*, ed. Dietmar Elger and Hans Ulrich Obrist (London: Thames & Hudson, 2009), 129; Charles Ray in conversation. Also see "In a Glass Darkly" and "Philosophical Objects" in this volume.

12. Unexpected crossings of Minimalism and Pop have occurred from Dan Graham to Rachel Harrison and beyond. See "Cultural Studies" and "Happy Days" in this volume. Although Duchamp was a central reference for both Minimalism and Pop, resistance to his influence was already pronounced in the early work of Serra, Nauman, and Graham.

13. See "Made for Cutting" and "*The Anti-Aesthetic* Then and Now."

14. Again, my list is partial, and as with the other sections I hardly mean it to signal closure—just the opposite.

15. See Howard Singerman, "The Myth of Criticism in the 1980s," *X-TRA: Contemporary Art Quarterly* (Fall 2005), 4. His writing on the academicization of the art critic follows his study of the academicization of the artist, *Art Subjects: Making Artists in the American University* (Berkeley: University of California Press, 1999).

16. Singerman cites the testimony of Scott Rothkopf, then senior editor at *Artforum*, who recalled his undergraduate experience in the mid 1990s in this way: "We swallowed whole an official 'history' of the '80s that wasn't actually history at all, but rather a selective corpus of mostly primary criticism canonized in anthologies" (Singerman, "The Myth of Criticism in the 1980s," 9).

17. Ibid., 5. "Critical" was a term of approbation for modernist critics that postmodernist critics carried forward even as they redefined it. Like others, Singerman believes that it carried prescriptive implications in the latter case too. On the move to the academy as a (mistaken) sanctuary, see "Interdependent Study."

18. Cohen quoted in Singerman, "The Myth of Criticism in the 1980s," 9. The flurry of scare quotes and italics suggests a rhetorical strain.

19. See Buchloh and Foster, *Exit Interview*. Singerman splits the difference: "Criticism, precisely when it is serious, when it takes its object to be cultural or artistic practice, plots itself out as history. Its project is to generalize and situate, and to enclose" (Singerman, "The Myth of Criticism in the 1980s," 15). Again, much of the art discussed in this book isn't historical for me, though I grant it is for many others (witness the numerous publications and exhibitions already devoted to "the 1980s").

20. See David Joselit, *Art's Properties* (Princeton: Princeton University Press, 2023). Joselit considers the political and economic ramifications of this understanding in *Heritage and Debt: Art in Globalization* (Cambridge, MA: MIT Press, 2020). Also see "*The Anti-Aesthetic* Then and Now."

21. For the first shift see the title essay of my *The Return of the Real: Art and Theory at the End of the Century* (Cambridge, MA: MIT Press, 1996); for the second see "Third Nature" in this volume. There are other transformations over this period, of course, as well as different through lines in this book not evident to me before. I do attempt a partial self-historicization in "Interdependent Study."

22. On this last notion see "*The Anti-Aesthetic* Then and Now."

23. See "Antinomic Modernism."

24. See Claude Lévi-Strauss, “The Structural Study of Myth,” in *Structural Anthropology*, trans. Claire Jakobson and Brooke Grundfest Schoepf (New York: Basic Books, 1963).

25. On this double temporality see “The Artist as Anthologist” and “A Certain Practice of Life” in this volume. Benjamin Buchloh sketches a notion of failure as success in “Michael Asher and the Conclusion of Modernist Sculpture” (1980), in *Neo-Avantgarde and Culture Industry: Essays on European and American Art from 1955 to 1975* (Cambridge, MA: 2000). The Left has experienced this negative dialectic at least since the Paris Commune. For a recent articulation see Sara Marcus, *Political Disappointment: A Cultural History from Reconstruction to the AIDS Crisis* (Cambridge, MA: Harvard University Press, 2023). Traditionally, of course, the ultimate success of the great artwork was taken to be its ability, by virtue of its perfection, to transcend its time, or at least to persist across generations. In *The Painter of Modern Life* (1863) Baudelaire offered a twist on this formula with his proposal that modern art had two aspects, one transitory, the other eternal. His paradoxical implication was that the modern artwork might transcend its moment (only) if it delved deeply into it. Again, this was a revision of the traditional understanding, which valued the completion of the artwork as a symbolic totality, an aesthetic model that remained dominant from Romanticism through modernism. As Craig Owens argued, postmodernist art advanced a counter model to symbolic totality, that of allegorical fragmentation, which highlights the gaps between signifier and signified. This holds true of much of the art discussed here, some of which treats contradiction as a matter of political intent as well as aesthetic preference. See Craig Owens, “The Allegorical Impulse: Toward a Theory of Postmodernism, Parts I and II,” *October* 12 and 13 (Spring and Summer 1980).

Chapter 1

1. Unless otherwise noted, all quotations are from Phillip Spectre, *Introspective: Richard Hamilton* (Cologne: Walther König, 2019). The initial version of the present chapter appeared in the *London Review of Books* (October 24, 2019). For an extended reflection on Hamilton, see my *The First Pop Age: Painting and Subjectivity in the Art of Hamilton, Lichtenstein, Warhol, Richter, and Ruscha* (Princeton: Princeton University Press, 2011).

2. See Kevin Lotery, *The Long Front of Culture: The Independent Group and Exhibition Design* (Cambridge, MA: MIT Press, 2020).

3. Reyner Banham, *The New Brutalism: Ethic or Aesthetic?* (London: Architectural Press, 1966), 65.

4. Charles Baudelaire, “The Painter of Modern Life” (1863), in *The Painter of Modern Life and Other Essays*, trans. and ed. Jonathan Mayne (London: Phaidon, 1964), 12.

5. Marcel Duchamp, *The Green Box*, a typographic version by Richard Hamilton, trans. George Heard Hamilton (New York: Japp Rietman, 1976), 82; Richard Hamilton, *Collected Words, 1953–1982* (London: Thames and Hudson, 1982), 78.

6. See Roland Barthes, *Image Music Text*, trans. Stephen Heath (New York: Hill & Wang, 1977).

Chapter 2

1. Johns had retrospectives every twenty years or so, at the Whitney Museum in 1977, the Museum of Modern Art in 1996, and, after major shows at the Royal Academy in 2017 and the Broad Museum in Los Angeles in 2018, a double exhibition at the Whitney Museum and the Philadelphia Museum of Art in 2021 titled *Jasper Johns: Mind/Mirror*, curated by Carlos Basualdo and Scott Rothkopf. The initial version of the present chapter appeared in the *London Review of Books* (December 2, 2021) as a review of this last show. Unless otherwise noted, all Johns quotations are from *Jasper Johns: Writings, Sketchbooks, Notes, Interviews*, ed. Kirk Varnedoe (New York: Museum of Modern Art, 1996).

2. Leo Steinberg, "Jasper Johns: The First Seven Years" (1962), in Steinberg, *Other Criteria: Confrontations with Twentieth-Century Art* (Oxford: Oxford University Press, 1972), 26.

3. Robert Rauschenberg quoted in Dorothy Miller, ed., *Sixteen Americans* (New York: Museum of Modern Art, 1959), n.p. John Cage uses the same line in "On Robert Rauschenberg, Artist, and His Work," in Cage, *Silence: Lectures and Writings* (Middletown, CT: Wesleyan University Press, 1961), 105.

4. See Scott Rothkopf with Carlos Basualdo et al., *Jasper Johns: Mind/Mirror* (New Haven: Yale University Press, 2021), 30.

5. Marcel Duchamp, "The Green Box" (1934), in *The Essential Writings of Marcel Duchamp*, ed. Michel Sanouillet and Elmer Peterson (London: Thames & Hudson, 1975), 26. Johns bought his copy of *The Green Box* in 1960, and it prompted him to start his own books of notes and sketches.

6. See Roland Barthes, *Writing Degree Zero*, trans. Annette Lavers and Colin Smith (New York: Hill & Wang, 1968). The French original was published in 1953.

7. See Roland Barthes, *The Neutral*, trans. Rosalind Krauss and Denis Hollier (New York: Columbia University Press, 2007). Also see "In a Glass Darkly" in this volume.

8. *Dancing Around the Bride*, a 2012 show at the Philadelphia Museum of Art curated by Carlos Basualdo, explored the Duchampian code that Cage, Cunningham, Rauschenberg, and Johns shared. Also see Jonathan Katz, "The Art of the Code: Jasper Johns and Robert Rauschenberg," in Whitney Chadwick and Isabelle de Courtivron, eds., *Significant Others: Creativity and Intimate Partnership* (London: Thames and Hudson, 1993).

9. Duchamp dedicated a copy of *The Green Box* to Johns in this fashion.

10. Rothkopf et al., *Jasper Johns: Mind/Mirror*, 145.

11. See Sigmund Freud, "A Note on the 'Mystic Writing-Pad'" (1924).

12. André Breton, *Manifestoes of Surrealism*, trans. Richard Seaver and Helen R. Lane (Ann Arbor, 1972), 21. Also see my *Compulsive Beauty* (Cambridge, MA: MIT Press, 1993).

13. Rothkopf et al., *Jasper Johns: Mind/Mirror*, 145.

Chapter 3

1. Claes Oldenburg, *Store Days* (New York: Something Else Press, 1967), 54. The initial version of the present chapter appeared in *Artforum* (December 2012) as a review of *Claes Oldenburg: The Sixties*, curated by Achim Hochdörfer for Museum moderner Kunst in Vienna and Ann Temkin for the Museum of Modern Art in New York. For an extended reflection on Oldenburg, see my *Brutal Aesthetics: Dubuffet, Bataille, Jorn, Paolozzi, Oldenburg* (Princeton: Princeton University Press, 2020).

2. Oldenburg, *Store Days*, 14.

3. On the Lower East Side at this time, see Joshua Shannon, *The Disappearance of the Object: New York Art and the Rise of the Postmodern City* (New Haven: Yale University Press, 2009).

4. Oldenburg, *Store Days*, 26, 80. Throughout the 1960s Oldenburg also clipped and saved advertisements from a range of mass-market magazines. For all the humor and humanity in his work, there is also an undertone of violence.

5. Ibid., 62.

6. Julia E. Robinson, "Fetish or Foil: The Caprices of Claes Oldenburg," in *Claes Oldenburg: Early Work* (New York: Zwirner & Wirth, 2005), 21.

7. Oldenburg, *Store Days*, 62, 60.

8. Ibid., 51.

9. Ibid., 142. Also see "Perverse Pantomime" in this volume.

10. Ibid., 41.

11. Claes Oldenburg, "DRAFT A: The Collection" (n.d.) in Oldenburg van Bruggen Studio Archives, New York, as quoted in Benjamin Buchloh, "Annihilate/Illuminate: Claes Oldenburg's Ray Gun and Mouse Museum," in Achim Hochdörfer with Barbara Schröder, eds., *Claes Oldenburg: The Sixties* (Munich: Prestel, 2012), 267.

12. Claes Oldenburg in conversation with Richard Kostelanetz, in *The Theater of Mixed Means* (New York: Dial Press, 1968), 156; Claes Oldenburg, "Collecting Ray Guns in Nug Yar; or, The Use of a Useless Activity" (n.d.) in Oldenburg van Bruggen Studio Archives, New York, as quoted in Buchloh, "Annihilate/Illuminate," 252.

13. Oldenburg, *Store Days*, 51. In a way the slippage here is reminiscent of *Story of the Eye* (1928), in which Georges Bataille narrates the metamorphoses of an ovoid form from eye to egg to testicle to breast and so on.

14. Claude Lévi-Strauss, *Introduction to the Work of Marcel Mauss*, trans. Felicity Baker (London: Routledge & Kegan Paul, 1987), 59–60.

15. Ibid., 64.

Chapter 4

1. See in particular Fredric Jameson, "Postmodernism, or the Cultural Logic of Late Capitalism," *New Left Review* (July/August 1984). The initial version of the present chapter appeared in the *London Review of Books* (March 21, 2002) as a review of Wayne Koestenbaum, *Andy Warhol: A Biography* (New York: Penguin Press, 2001). Unless otherwise noted, all quotations are from this biography. For an extended reflection on Warhol, see my *The First Pop Age: Painting and Subjectivity in the Art of Hamilton, Lichtenstein, Warhol, Richter, and Ruscha* (Princeton: Princeton University Press, 2011).

2. See the title chapter of my *The Return of the Real: Art and Theory at the End of the Century* (Cambridge, MA: MIT Press, 1996).

3. Andy Warhol quoted in Gretchen Berg, "Andy: My True Story," in Kenneth Goldsmith, ed., *I'll Be Your Mirror: The Selected Andy Warhol Interviews, 1962–1987* (New York: Carroll and Graf, 2004), 90.

4. Andy Warhol and Pat Hackett, *POPism: The Warhol '60s* (New York: Harcourt Brace Jovanovich, 1980), 50.

5. Susan Sontag, "Notes on Camp," in Sontag, *Against Interpretation* (New York: Farrar Straus & Giroux, 1966), 288. Also see "Radical Style" in this volume.

6. Benjamin H. D. Buchloh, "Andy Warhol's One-Dimensional Art: 1956–1966," in Kynaston McShine, ed., *Andy Warhol: A Retrospective* (New York: Museum of Modern Art, 1989), 42–43.

7. Marcel Duchamp, "The Richard Mutt Case," *The Blind Man*, no. 2 (May 1917).

8. Warhol certainly produced "piss paintings" in the late 1970s; whether he did so already in the early 1960s is now disputed.

9. See Richard Meyer, "Warhol's Clones," *Yale Journal of Criticism* (January 1994).

10. Annette Michelson, "'Where Is Your Rupture?' Mass Culture and the *Gesamtkunstwerk*," *October* 56 (Spring 1991): 56.

11. Andy Warhol, *The Andy Warhol Diaries*, ed. Pat Hackett (New York: Warner Books, 1989), 325.

12. Roland Barthes, "That Old Thing, Art" (1980), in Barthes, *The Responsibility of Forms*, trans. Richard Howard (Berkeley: University of California Press, 1991), 200.

13. Michael Warner, "The Mass Public and the Mass Subject," in Bruce Robbins, ed., *The Phantom Public Sphere* (Minneapolis: University of Minnesota Press, 1993), 250.

14. Gilles Deleuze, *Difference and Repetition*, trans. Paul Patton (New York: Columbia University Press, 1994), 293.

Chapter 5

1. Unless otherwise noted, all Judd quotations are from his *Collected Writings*, ed. Flavin Judd and Caitlin Murray (New York: Judd Foundation/David Zwirner Books, 2016). The initial version of the present chapter appeared in *Artforum* (May/June 2020) as a review of

the retrospective *Judd*, curated by Ann Temkin, Yasmil Raymond, Tamar Margalit, and Erica Cooke for the Museum of Modern Art.

2. Judd also advanced this notion in a 1966 conversation with Frank Stella: "The qualities of European art so far . . . are linked up with a philosophy—rationalism. . . . All that art is based on systems built beforehand, a priori systems; they express a certain type of thinking and logic that is pretty much discredited now as a way of finding out what the world's like." Bruce Glaser, "Questions to Stella and Judd," in Gregory Battcock, ed., *Minimal Art: A Critical Anthology* (New York: E. P. Dutton, 1968), 151. Incidentally, Judd was resistant to conventional composition in his writing too. His prose often has a paratactic (non)quality, with statements that are at once specific and serial, one sentence after another, a bit like Hemingway or even Stein.

3. Karl Beveridge and Ian Burn, "Don Judd," *Fox* 2 (1975): 131.

4. Glaser, "Questions to Stella and Judd," 158.

5. Beveridge and Burn, "Don Judd," 132. Judd wasn't immune to this sense of "alienability." In one unpublished note dated January 3, 1976, it prompted a kind of nihilism: "For a long time I've considered time to be nothing. Any time that you think of is only the relation or sequence of events, how long a person lives, human biology, or how many times the earth goes around the sun. There is no other time than this. If you remove all of the events there is nothing. Space, also, is nothing. There are things in it, variously related. If you remove these and the means of measurement between them, their phenomena, most importantly light-years, there is nothing." On how the phenomenological plenitude of Minimalist installations can flip into the opposite—a voiding of the viewer—see Robert Slifkin, *The New Monuments and the End of Man* (Princeton: Princeton University Press, 2019).

6. Thierry de Duve makes this argument in *Kant after Duchamp* (Cambridge, MA: MIT Press, 1993) and other books.

7. Clement Greenberg, "Recentness of Sculpture" (1967), in Battcock, *Minimal Art*, 183; Michael Fried, "Art and Objecthood" (1967), in Battcock, *Minimal Art*, 116–147.

8. Michel Foucault, *The Order of Things: An Archaeology of the Human Sciences* (New York: Random House, 1970), 318. Foucault was concerned with Comtean positivism and Marxist eschatology in particular, but his point is more capacious than this one example.

9. See "Blank Magic" in this volume.

10. Also, unlike Morris and Serra, Judd didn't appear much impacted, at least in his art, by dance, even that of Judson Church, despite the fact that he was married to choreographer and dancer Julie Finch from 1964 to 1976.

11. See Richard Serra and Hal Foster, *Conversations about Sculpture* (New Haven: Yale University Press, 2018), 19–38.

12. I borrow this phrase from Charles Ray.

13. Beveridge and Burn, "Don Judd," 132. On this problem also see "Cultural Studies" in this volume.

14. Judd claimed that he was also "late" to De Stijl, though, given his primary colors, clean geometries, and scalar experiments, that too seems doubtful.

15. The more salient precursor is Josef Albers, whom Judd did acknowledge. They shared an interest in the ambiguity of appearances, the interaction of colors, and the variations that can be wrung from one theme. Like Albers, Judd also delved into illusionism more than his official literalism might suggest. On this point see my *The Art-Architecture Complex* (London and New York: Verso, 2011), 182–214.

16. See Leo Steinberg, *Other Criteria: Confrontations with Twentieth-Century Art* (London: Oxford University Press, 1972), 79.

17. See "Blank Magic" in this volume.

Chapter 6

1. Judd presented his case against illusionism most directly in "Specific Objects" (*Arts Yearbook 8*, 1965); see "Object Lessons" in this volume. Rosalind Krauss pointed to the persistence of illusionism in his work already in "Allusion and Illusion in Donald Judd" (*Artforum*, May 1966). The initial version of the present chapter appeared in *Artforum* (February 2005); it derived from a talk given on October 23, 2004, at the National Gallery of Art, Washington, DC, on the occasion of *Dan Flavin: A Retrospective*, curated by Tiffany Bell, Michael Govan, and Jeffrey Weiss. For an extended reflection on Flavin, see my *The Art-Architecture Complex* (London and New York: Verso, 2011).

2. Donald Judd, *Complete Writings 1959–1975* (Halifax: Press of the Nova Scotia College of Art and Design, 1975), 200.

3. "Please do not refer to my effort as sculpture and to me as sculptor. I do not handle and fashion three-dimensioned still works, even as to Barbara Rose's Juddianed 'specific objects.' I feel apart from problems of sculpture and painting." Dan Flavin, letter of June 17, 1967, to Jan van der Marck, in *Dan Flavin: three installations in fluorescent light* (Cologne: Kunsthalle Köln, 1973), 95.

4. Dan Flavin, "'some remarks . . . ,'" *Artforum* (December 1966), in ibid., 91.

5. Dan Flavin, "'. . . in daylight or cool white,'" *Artforum* (December 1965), in ibid., 87.

6. Ibid., 86.

7. Dan Flavin, "'The Artists say'" (*art voices*, Summer 1965), in ibid., 84.

8. "Dan Flavin Interviewed by Phyllis Tuchman" (1972), in Michael Govan and Tiffany Bell, *Dan Flavin: A Retrospective* (New York: Dia Art Foundation; Washington, DC: National Gallery of Art, 2004), 194. I am indebted here to Tiffany Bell.

9. Ibid.

10. *Dan Flavin: three installations in fluorescent light*, 94. "Pepsi denigration" is a good example of his wit.

11. Flavin sometime referred to such tension as a form of irony: "The radiant tube and the shadow cast by its supporting pan seemed ironic enough to hold alone" (ibid., 87). This suggests that each aspect "ironizes" the other in a way that resists our deciding for one as first or fundamental. In this respect Flavin is an ironist more than a literalist, or rather he finds in literalism an ambiguity that "holds" both work and viewer in tension. In contradistinction to the positivist motto of Frank Stella, here what you see is never quite what you see.

12. Ibid., 91.

13. Ibid., 87.

14. Perhaps this is what Robert Smithson had in mind when he wrote in 1966, "Flavin's destruction of classical time and space is based on an entirely new notion of the structure of matter" (*Robert Smithson: The Collected Writings*, ed. Jack Flam [Berkeley: University of California Press, 1996], 10).

15. Dan Graham called the effect a "reversed illusionism" in "Art as Design/Design as Art," *Rock My Religion: Writings and Projects 1965–1990* (Cambridge, MA: MIT Press, 1993), 211.

16. Rosalind Krauss, untitled review, *Artforum* (January 1969), 53–54.

17. *Dan Flavin: three installations in fluorescent light*, 89.

18. Ibid., 83.

19. Ibid., 82 and 89.

20. Ibid., 95.

21. Ibid.

22. Ibid., 87.

23. "Catastrophe" signals a revision of my initial reading of Minimalism as a "crux" between modernist and postmodernist art. See "The Crux of Minimalism" (1987), in my *The Return of the Real: Art and Theory at the End of the Century* (Cambridge, MA: MIT Press, 1996).

Chapter 7

1. In short, the *Newsweek* photo offers a good overview of his early work, that is, before the steel pieces of the1970s that jut dramatically into space. The initial version of the present chapter appeared in *Richard Serra: Early Work*, ed. David Frankel (New York: David Zwirner Gallery, 2013).

2. Serra designates a few early pieces "prime objects" because they "present each problem in its greatest simplicity." Richard Serra and Hal Foster, *Conversations about Sculpture* (New Haven: Yale University Press, 2018), 117. One of the works, *To Lift* (1967), a thick sheet of vulcanized rubber that, raised at the midpoint of one edge, holds its curved shape, doesn't appear in the *Newsweek* photo, while the other two, *One Ton Prop (House of Cards)*, the first of several *Props* made in 1969, and *Strike*, the first of the steel plates that open onto space, weren't yet produced. George Kubler defines prime objects as "principal inventions . . . not explained by their antecedents," in *The Shape of Time: Remarks on the History of Things* (New Haven: Yale University Press, 1962), 39. This was a talismanic text for Serra, Robert Smithson, and others in their milieu.

3. "A Conversation about Work with Richard Serra," in Kynaston McShine, Lynne Cooke, et al., *Richard Serra Sculpture: Forty Years* (New York: Museum of Modern Art, 2007), 37. Serra continues, "The verb list allowed me to experiment without any preconceived idea about what I was going to make and not worry about the history of sculpture."

4. Ibid. With these actions Serra reclaims an industrial material for manual work, or, as Dan Graham put it, "For Serra, all in-forming, technological or otherwise, begins with the hand." See Dan Graham, *End Moments* (New York, 1969), 21.

5. "A Conversation about Work with Richard Serra," 27.

6. Serra, in Serra and Foster, *Conversations about Sculpture*, 28. "A lot of people downtown were involved with making and doing, only everybody was making and doing different things. People didn't call themselves filmmakers or composers or musicians or painters or sculptors. You didn't want to identify. Everybody was just making something, and everybody was everybody else's audience." Ibid., 33.

7. "Exhibitions: Please Don't Feed the Sculpture," *Time* (July 10, 1966), 70, reprinted in *Richard Serra: Early Work*. Made while Serra was on a Fulbright fellowship in Italy, the *Habitats* were shown in 1966 in Rome, where they might have influenced some of the Arte Povera artists.

8. "A Conversation about Work with Richard Serra," 24–25. Serra questions other strategies associated with Duchamp. For example: "Chance gave poetic license to arbitrary juxtapositions and it still does. . . . [It produces] nothing other than extended-field collage." Ibid., 23.

9. See Robert Morris, "Anti Form," *Artforum* 6 (April 1968), reprinted in Morris, *Continuous Project Altered Daily* (Cambridge, MA: MIT Press, 1993). In such pieces Morris aimed to dedifferentiate vision. This mode of work emerged from a critique of Minimalism (his own included), in which "any order for multiple units is an imposed one" with "no inherent relation to the physicality of the units." This critique in turn led Morris back to Pollock, who appeared to retain process "as part of the end form" through a "profound rethinking" of tools and materials. Paradoxically, this model of procedural unity then incited Morris to develop a practice of informal dispersal, in which the materiality of the work is resistant to ordering and bound to entropy: "chance is allowed and indeterminacy is implied" as "random piling, loose stacking, hanging, give passing form to the material" (ibid., 41–46). This was not the path taken by Serra.

10. Richard Serra, "Play It Again, Sam," *Arts Magazine* (February 1970), reprinted in Serra, *Writings Interviews* (Chicago: University of Chicago Press, 1994), 7. "A recent problem with the lateral spread of materials, elements on the floor, in the visual field is the inability of this landscape mode to avoid arrangement *qua* figure-ground: the pictorial convention."

11. Graham, *End Moments*, 22. After *House of Cards* Serra felt that he could no longer bracket the term "sculpture." See Serra and Foster, *Conversations about Sculpture*, 38.

12. Heinrich Wölfflin, "Prolegomena to a Psychology of Architecture," in Harry Francis Mallgrave and Eleftherios Ikonomou, eds., *Empathy, Form, and Space: Problems in German Aesthetics* (Los Angeles: Getty Center, 1994), 151.

13. Ibid, 152, 158.

14. Ibid., 152.

15. Ibid., 159. Wölfflin, who was influenced by Arthur Schopenhauer here, adds: "The greater the resistance to overcome, the greater the pleasure" (161).

16. Serra referred to Stonehenge in his 1968 proposal to the Los Angeles County Museum of Art for the "Skullcracker" series of works. Produced at Kaiser Steel in Fontana, California, some of these steel slabs are vertical stacks that remain upright under the compression of their weight alone. The apposition of mass and frame, load and support, so fundamental to architecture, is central to Serra too. On this point see my "Sculpture Remade" in *The Art-Architecture Complex* (London and New York: Verso, 2011). In architecture the crucial point in this apposition is the joint. The joint is also key in Serra: left bare, not welded, the intersection of his steel plates is where his structure reveals its production most clearly, demystifying old modes of sculpture in doing so.

17. Serra, "Interview with Liza Béar," in *Writings Interviews*, 45.

18. In "Richard Serra: Sculpture," written for the 1986 retrospective of that title at the Museum of Modern Art, Rosalind Krauss presents a brilliant account of the phenomenological subject that Serra puts into play in his field pieces. This essay is reprinted in Hal Foster and Gordon Hughes, eds., *Richard Serra* (Cambridge, MA: MIT Press, 2000).

19. See Rosalind Krauss, "Sense and Sensibility," *Artforum* (November 1973). This statement from Steve Reich is characteristic: "His works and mine are both more about materials and process than they are about psychology." In Emily Wasserman, "An Interview with Steve Reich," *Artforum* (May 1972), 48.

20. Serra and Foster, *Conversations about Sculpture*, 115.

21. See Robert Pincus-Witten, "Slow Information: Richard Serra," *Artforum* (September 1969), 34–39, and Max Kozloff, "9 in a Warehouse: An 'Attack on the Status of the Object,'" *Artforum* (February 1969), 38–42. Both are reprinted in *Richard Serra: Early Work*.

22. There is also the macho association, again made through photos, of the artist as industrial worker à la David Smith. More revealing are the short films Serra made at the time, such as *Hands Catching Lead, Hands Tied*, and *Hands Scraping* (all 1968). Certainly they record the tasks performed (a hand catching, or not catching, falling pieces of lead; the wiggling free of two hands twined together; the removing of a pile of waste by four hands working together), but, like much body art of the time, they also open on to a psychological theater (repetition compulsion, bondage, obsessive behavior).

23. Lucy Lippard, "Eccentric Abstraction," in Lippard, *Changing: Essays in Art Criticism* (New York: E. P. Dutton, 1971), 102.

24. One might argue, however, that the "template" of the body in some early rubber pieces by Serra ranges, as it does in Hesse, from "intact" to "in pieces." See "Serial and Fused" in this volume.

25. Jean Laplanche and Jean-Bertrand Pontalis, *The Language of Psychoanalysis*, trans. Donald Nicholson-Smith (New York: W. W. Norton, 1973), 30, 29.

26. Benjamin Buchloh also finds "a memory of utilitarian function" in such pieces. See his "Richard Serra's Early Work: Sculpture between Labor and Spectacle," in McShine and Cooke, *Richard Serra Sculpture*, 48.

27. For more on this medium-differential dynamic, see my "Sculpture Remade," from which I adapt the last three sentences.

Chapter 8

1. Cindy Nemser, "An Interview with Eva Hesse," *Artforum* (May 1970), 59–63; unless otherwise specified, all Hesse quotations are from this source. The initial version of the present chapter was published in *Artforum* (September 2022).

2. For many readers today this statement will be colored by the charge brought against Andre in the death of his wife Ana Mendieta in 1985. There were other provocations like Hesse's, some prior, as when Frank Stella gave two of his "Black Paintings" (1959) titles with Nazi associations (*Arbeit Macht Frei* and *Die Fahne Hoch*); this was duly acknowledged but not much discussed at the time. See Caroline A. Jones, *Machine in the Studio: Constructing the Postwar American Artist* (Chicago: University of Chicago Press, 1996); James Meyer, *Minimalism: Art and Polemics in the Sixties* (New Haven: Yale University Press, 2001); and Mark Godfrey, *Abstraction and the Holocaust* (New Haven: Yale University Press, 2006).

3. See Anne M. Wagner, "Another Hesse," *October* 69 (Summer 1994), reprinted in *Three Artists (Three Women): Modernism and the Art of Hesse, Krasner, and O'Keeffe* (Berkeley: University of California Press, 1996).

4. This isn't to say that the extremity of the time explains her antinomies, or that they are only rhetorical. On the contrary, the stark juxtaposition offered by Hesse points us to dialectical readings of the art that most concerned her.

5. Mel Bochner, *Solar System & Rest Rooms: Writings and Interviews 1965–2007* (Cambridge, MA: MIT Press, 2008), xvii. In an oral history for the Archives of American Art, Bochner names the artist as Andre. My thanks to Samuel Shapiro for this reference.

6. See, above all, Anna C. Chave, "Minimalism and the Rhetoric of Power," *Arts* (January 1990).

7. Bruce Glaser, "Questions to Stella and Judd," *Art News* (September 1966), reprinted in Gregory Battcock, ed., *Minimal Art: A Critical Anthology* (New York: E. P. Dutton, 1968), 151; and Mel Bochner, "Serial Art, Systems, Solipsism," *Arts* (Summer 1967), reprinted in Battcock, 93. The Stella-Judd conversation was also heavily edited in *Art News* (a third participant, Dan Flavin, disappeared altogether).

8. This antihumanist position was programmatic in the *nouveau roman*, the literary movement most often cited by both Minimalists and Conceptualists, which was also received as "cold" and "inhuman." See Alain Robbe-Grillet, *For a New Novel: Essays on Fiction*, trans. Richard Howard (New York: Grove Press, 1966).

9. Fredric Jameson, *Valences of the Dialectic* (London and New York: Verso, 2009), 43, 13.

10. Ibid., 416–425. Jameson on Walmart follows Lenin on the big banks of his time, which, like other institutions of monopoly capitalism, he hoped to transform under Communism. Also see Fredric Jameson et al., *An American Utopia: Dual Power and the Universal Army* (London and New York: Verso, 2016).

11. Jean-Paul Sartre, *Critique of Dialectical Reason*, vol. 1, trans. Alan Sheridan-Smith (London and New York: Verso, 2004), 257, 260.

12. Ibid., 254. In this respect Sartre offers an important corrective to the usual narrative in critical theory about modernity as a tragic fall from a past state of integration—subjective as

well as social—into a present state of atomization. I explore the serial-fused dynamic in the present in "Seriality, Sociability, Silence," *Artforum* (December 2020).

13. On Hesse see Briony Fer, "Bordering on Blank: Eva Hesse and Minimalism," *Art History* 3 (September 1994), and Mignon Nixon, "o + x," *October* 119 (Winter 2007). On LeWitt see Rosalind Krauss, "LeWitt in Progress," *October* 6 (Autumn 1978).

14. Hesse quoted in Lucy Lippard, *Eva Hesse* (New York: Da Capo Press, 1976), 96.

15. On binding and unbinding see Sigmund Freud, *The Ego and the Id*, trans. James Strachey (New York: W. W. Norton, 1960).

16. There is also an individual-group dynamic in the collaborative making of her work then and in the conservational care for it now.

17. Bochner had earlier broached this subject in "Serial Art, Systems, Solipsism." There were important exceptions to solipsistic seriality in practice. For example, in *Homes for America* (1966–1967) Dan Graham demonstrated that seriality structured suburban tract housing. See "Cultural Studies" in this volume.

18. "The notion of seriality developed here," Jameson writes in his 2004 foreword to the first volume of Sartre's *Critique of Dialectical Reason*, "is the only philosophically satisfactory theory of public opinion, the only genuine philosophy of the media, that anyone has proposed to date" (xxviii). One might object that Debord offered such a theory in *The Society of the Spectacle*, but then spectacle for Debord is largely seriality for Sartre rethought through the commodity image. "Seriality" was one missed encounter between artistic practice and political theory during the 1960s. Another—even more pertinent to my concerns but too complex to develop here—revolved around "banality." Not long after *Artforum* was launched in San Francisco in June 1962, two controversies broke out in New York, both of which hinged on the charge of banality. One debate was political, provoked by Hannah Arendt with her notorious analysis of the Adolf Eichmann trial in Jerusalem, which ran in the *New Yorker* in February and March 1963. The other debate was aesthetic, sparked by the sudden emergence of Pop art, which was the subject of a symposium at the Museum of Modern Art in December 1962 (published in *Arts* magazine in April 1963). Arendt intended her infamous phrase "the banality of evil" as a neutral description, which enraged her critics all the more. Far from neutral, opponents of Pop used the term "banal" in order to condemn the new art. It appears that, for both groups of opponents, the word signaled a new lack of "depth"—historical, moral, psychological, artistic, critical—that each found intolerable.

19. Carl Andre, *Cuts: Texts 1959–2004*, ed. James Meyer (Cambridge, MA: MIT Press, 2005), 38. Here is another instance of his dialectical thinking framed almost as a Conceptualist proposition. Asked in 1969 by Lucy Lippard, "What is the relationship between politics and art?" Andre responds (ibid., 55):

A. Art is a political weapon.
B. Art has nothing to do with politics.
C. Art serves imperialism.
D. Art serves revolution.
E. The relationship between politics and art is none of these things, some of these things, all of these things.

20. Ibid., 291.

21. This remark from Giorgio Agamben is pertinent here: "In Auschwitz, people did not die; rather, corpses were produced. Corpses without death, non-humans whose decease is debased into a matter of serial production. . . . Precisely this degradation of death constitutes the specific offense of Auschwitz, the proper name of its horror." In *Remnants of Auschwitz: The Witness and the Archive*, trans. Daniel Heller-Roazen (New York: Zone Books, 2002), 71–72.

Chapter 9

1. Willoughby Sharp, "Nauman Interview" (1970), in *Please Pay Attention Please: Bruce Nauman's Words: Writings and Interviews*, ed. Janet Kraynak (Cambridge MA: MIT Press, 2005), 111. Duchamp made his comment in defense of his readymade *Fountain* (1917): "Whether Mr. Mutt with his own hands made the fountain or not has no importance," Duchamp wrote anonymously. "He CHOSE it." See "The Richard Mutt Case," *The Blind Man*, no. 2 (May 1917). The initial version of the present chapter appeared in the *London Review of Books* (December 20, 2018) as a review of the retrospective *Bruce Nauman: Disappearing Acts*, curated primarily by Kathy Halbreich for the Museum of Modern Art in New York and Heidi Naef for the Schaulager in Basel.

2. John Cage, "Lecture on Nothing" (1949), in Cage, *Silence: Lectures and Writings* (Middletown, CT: Wesleyan University Press), 109.

3. Anne M. Wagner, "Nauman's Body of Sculpture," in Constance M. Lewallen et al., *A Rose Has No Teeth: Bruce Nauman in the 1960s* (Berkeley: University of California Press, 2007), 122.

4. See the note of that title (c. 1970) in Nauman, *Please Pay Attention Please*, 60.

5. Joan Simon, "Breaking the Silence: An Interview with Bruce Nauman" (1988), in Nauman, *Please Pay Attention Please*, 330, 324.

6. Ibid., 319. Ed Ruscha took this point too. See "Evening in America" in this volume.

7. Ibid., 321.

8. Leo Steinberg, "Jasper Johns: The First Seven Years" (1962), in Steinberg, *Other Criteria: Confrontations with Twentieth-Century Art* (Oxford: Oxford University Press, 1972), 26. Also see "Watchman and Spy" in this volume.

9. Sharp, "Nauman Interview," 129.

10. Like Dan Graham, Nauman questioned the phenomenological plenitude sometimes suggested in Minimalism. At the same time, he also questioned the behaviorism sometimes implied by Graham. See "Cultural Studies" in this volume.

11. Thus in the English volume of his essays Lacan followed "The Mirror Stage" with "Aggressivity in Psychoanalysis." See Jacques Lacan, "The Mirror Stage," in *Écrits*, trans. Alan Sheridan (New York: W. W. Norton, 1977).

12. Simon, "Breaking the Silence," 397.

Chapter 10

1. "Interview with Dan Graham by Rodney Graham," in Bennett Simpson et al., *Dan Graham: Beyond* (Los Angeles: Museum of Contemporary Art, 2009), 96. The initial version of the present chapter appeared in *Artforum* (October 2009) as a review of the retrospective *Dan Graham: Beyond*, curated by Bennett Simpson for the Museum of Modern Art in Los Angeles and Chrissie Iles for the Whitney Museum of American Art.

2. See Maurice Merleau-Ponty, *The Visible and the Invisible*, trans. Alphonso Lingis (Evanston: Northwestern University Press, 1968).

3. "Dan Graham Interviewed by Kim Gordon" (2008), in Simpson et al., *Dan Graham: Beyond*, 171.

4. Ibid., 174.

5. Dan Graham, "Interview from *The Early Show: Video from 1969 to 1979*," in Simpson et al., *Dan Graham: Beyond*, 57. He repeats this formula in "Dan Graham Interviewed by Kim Gordon," 169.

6. Sometimes, too, in the quirky versions of cultural history pioneered by Graham and Smithson, there is a touch of adolescent provocation, as in this 2006 comment: "I'm sorry, we hated Duchamp. . . . We loved Speer at that time." In "A Conversation between Dan Graham and Nicolás Guagnini" (2006), in Simpson et al., *Dan Graham: Beyond*, 278.

7. "Interview with Dan Graham by Rodney Graham," 96.

8. Ibid.

Chapter 11

1. Gerhard Richter, *Text: Writings, Interviews and Letters 1961–2007*, ed. Dietmar Elger and Hans Ulrich Obrist (London: Thames & Hudson, 2009), 57. The initial version of the present chapter appeared in Sheena Wagstaff, Benjamin H. D. Buchloh, et al., *Gerhard Richter: Painting After All* (New York: Metropolitan Museum of Art, 2020). For an extended reflection on his painting, see my *The First Pop Age: Painting and Subjectivity in the Art of Hamilton, Lichtenstein, Warhol, Richter, and Ruscha* (Princeton: Princeton University Press, 2012). I am indebted here, as is anyone who writes on Richter, to Benjamin Buchloh.

2. Richter, *Text*, 67.

3. See Donald Judd, "Specific Objects," *Arts Yearbook 8* (1965), reprinted in Judd, *Complete Writings 1959–1975* (Halifax: Press of the Nova Scotia College of Art and Design, 1975), 181–189. Also see "Object Lessons" in this volume.

4. Richter, *Text*, 93.

5. Ibid., 120. Richter adds immediately, "Berges furnishing store," a reference to the store where, in 1963, Richter and Konrad Lueg staged a performance in the context of the show *Living with Pop—A Demonstration for Capitalist Realism*. Not incidentally, for Richter the glass pieces allude to Duchamp only negatively, if at all. Richter is opposed in particular to the "pseudo-complexity" and "manufactured mystery" of *The Large Glass* (ibid., 272).

6. Ibid., 120.

7. Ibid., 305.

8. Ibid.

9. Ibid., 272.

10. The monochrome, it can be argued, didn't void these paradigms so much as it sublated them—negated them in a way that also preserved them. See my contribution to "Abstraction, 1910–1925: Eight Statements," *October* 143 (Winter 2013).

11. See Benjamin H. D. Buchloh, "Gerhard Richter's Glass: Painting's Double," in *Gerhard Richter* (London: Marian Goodman Gallery, 2014).

12. Benjamin H. D. Buchloh, "Gerhard Richter's *Eight Gray*: Between *Vorschein* and *Glanz*," in *Gerhard Richter: Eight Gray* (New York: Guggenheim Museum, 2002), 15.

13. Buchloh, "Gerhard Richter's Glass," 87, 92.

14. Svetlana Alpers, *The Art of Describing: Dutch Art in the Seventeenth Century* (Chicago: University of Chicago Press, 1983).

15. See Michel Foucault, *The Order of Things: An Archaeology of the Human Sciences* (New York: Vintage, 1973), 3–16; and Louis Marin, "Toward a Theory of Reading in the Visual Arts: Poussin's *The Arcadian Shepherds*," in Susan Rubin Suleiman and Inge Crosman, eds., *The Reader in the Text: Essays on Audience and Interpretation* (Princeton: Princeton University Press, 1980), 310. I return to these paradigms in "Third Nature" in this volume.

16. See Craig Owens, "Representation, Appropriation, and Power," *Art in America* 70 (May 1982): 9–21.

17. Pliny the Elder regarded it as long established that the tracing of the outline of a human shadow initiated the art of painting and that this image was monochromatic. See David Summers, *Vision, Reflection, and Desire in Western Painting* (Chapel Hill: University of North Carolina Press, 2007).

18. Richter, *Text*, 305. Until recently, these models lingered on in photo discourse, as in the 1978 exhibition *Mirrors and Windows*, curated by John Szarkowski at the Museum of Modern Art.

19. Even the aleatory takes on a somewhat sinister cast, very different from the delight in "the airports for the lights, shadows, and particles" that John Cage experienced before the *White Paintings* (1951) of Rauschenberg. See his "On Robert Rauschenberg, Artist, and His Work" (1961), in Cage, *Silence: Lectures and Writings* (Middletown, CT: Wesleyan University Press), 102–103.

20. See "Third Nature."

21. Jacques Lacan, *The Four Fundamental Concepts of Psychoanalysis*, trans. Alan Sheridan (New York: W. W. Norton, 1978), 101.

22. Roger Caillois, "Mimicry and Legendary Psychasthenia" (1935), *October* 31 (Winter 1984): 30.

23. Richter expressed this ambivalence, or doubt mixed with disappointment, in a statement from January 26, 1983: "Minimal art: I saw this as an attempt to develop a new alphabet for the art of the future. And although it doesn't look as if it is being used in that way, my hopes

still go in that direction. But then perhaps that is a completely wrong way of looking at it" (*Text*, 129).

24. See "Blank Magic" in this volume.

25. See "Cultural Studies" in this volume.

26. See Michael Fried, "Art and Objecthood," *Artforum* 5 (Summer 1967). Perhaps this is the place to note a possible connection to Richard Serra, whom Richter admires. Richter gave *7 Panes of Glass* (2013) the subtitle *House of Cards*, an allusion to the key work in lead by Serra, *One Ton Prop (House of Cards)* (1969). Yet, apart from the precarious propping of the elements, I see little in common between the works. Serra is concerned with the tectonic properties of lead, Richter with the imagistic effects of glass. See "To Support" in this volume.

27. Richter, *Text*, 421.

28. Roland Barthes, *The Neutral*, trans. Rosalind Krauss and Denis Hollier (New York: Columbia University Press, 2007), 6–7. The *Oxford English Dictionary* defines "baffle" as a plate that regulates passage in and out, and "to baffle" as "to reduce to perplexity." See "Watchman and Spy" in this volume.

29. Richter, *Text*, 272. In Barthesian terms "the third meaning"—defined, saliently here, as an "obtuse meaning" ("*obtusus* means *that which is blunted, rounded in form*")—allows for both "a certain emotion" and a certain "drifting" of sense. See Roland Barthes, "The Third Meaning" (1970), in Barthes, *Image Music Text*, trans. Stephen Heath (New York: Hill & Wang, 1977).

30. Richter, *Text*, 129.

31. Buchloh, "Gerhard Richter's Glass," 89. Also see "The Ruins of Spectacle" in this volume.

Chapter 12

1. The initial version of the present chapter appeared in the *London Review of Books* (June 19, 2014) as a review of *Alibis: Sigmar Polke, 1963–2010*, curated by Kathy Halbreich and Lanka Tattersall for the Museum of Modern Art and Mark Godfrey for Tate Modern.

2. See Benjamin H. D. Buchloh and Hal Foster, *Exit Interview* (New York: no place press, 2024).

3. Sigmar Polke in Dieter Hülsmanns, "Kultur des Rasters: Ateliergespräch mit dem Maler Sigmar Polke," *Rheinische Post*, May 10, 1966. Here Polke accepts as given a condition of capitalist seriality that Sartre described only several years before, in his *Critique of Dialectical Reason* (1960)—accepts it in order to explore its effects on art and subjectivity alike. See "Serial and Fused" in this volume.

4. On banality in this sense, see my *The First Pop Age: Painting and Subjectivity in the Art of Hamilton, Lichtenstein, Warhol, Richter, and Ruscha* (Princeton: Princeton University Press, 2012). On vulgarity in this sense, see T. J. Clark, "In Defense of Abstract Expressionism," *October* 69 (Summer 1994).

5. I borrow this term from Fredric Jameson, *Postmodernism, or the Cultural Logic of Late Capitalism* (Durham: Duke University Press, 1991). Also see "Happy Days" in this volume.

6. The classic account of this problem is Saul Friedländer, *Reflections of Nazism: An Essay on Kitsch and Death* (New York: Harper & Row, 1982).

7. Benjamin H. D. Buchloh, "c. 1976," in *Alibis: Sigmar Polke, 1963–2010*, ed. Kathy Halbreich with Mark Godfrey, Lanka Tattersall, and Magnus Schaefer (New York: Museum of Modern Art, 2014), 196.

Chapter 13

1. Ed Ruscha, *Leave Any Information at the Signal* (Cambridge, MA: MIT Press, 2002), 297, 301, 65, 282. The initial version of the present chapter appeared in *Ed Ruscha, Catalogue Raisonné of the Paintings*, vol. 4, *1988–1992* (New York: Gagosian Gallery, 2009). For an extended reflection on Ruscha, see my *The First Pop Age: Painting and Subjectivity in the Art of Hamilton, Lichtenstein, Warhol, Richter, and Ruscha* (Princeton: Princeton University Press, 2011).

2. Ruscha quoted in Lisa Turvey, "Ed Ruscha and the Language That He Used," *October* 111 (Winter 2005): 96.

3. Ruscha, *Leave Any Information*, 302. Here Ruscha is close to Jasper Johns, who, in a sketchbook note c. 1963–1964, wrote, "One thing working one way/Another thing working another way/One thing working different ways *at different times*." See *Jasper Johns: Writings, Sketchbooks, Notes, Interviews*, ed. Kirk Varnedoe (New York: Museum of Modern Art, 1996), 54. Also see "Watchman and Spy" in this volume. Ruscha disturbs the image-word conjunction fundamental to the smooth operation of captioned photographs, advertisements, and the like.

4. Ruscha, *Leave Any Information*, 231, 265.

5. Ibid., 289.

6. Marcel Duchamp, "The Green Box" (1943), in *The Essential Writings of Marcel Duchamp*, ed. Michel Sanouillet and Elmer Peterson (London: Thames and Hudson, 1975), 32. Another painting, *Merfeldt Schmertz* (1993), in which four long parallel sticks, two above and two below, frame a smaller rectangle, alludes to the Merz collages and assemblages of Kurt Schwitters, whom Ruscha acknowledged as another important reference. Here Merz becomes a homely name, Merfeldt Schmertz, that in German suggests a "field of pain."

7. Michel Foucault, *This Is Not a Pipe* (1973), trans. James Harkness (Berkeley: University of California Press, 1983), 19–31, here 20, 21, 25.

8. Ibid., 28, 25. *The Treachery of Images* is in the collection of the Los Angeles County Museum of Art, a hometown institution for Ruscha.

9. Ruscha, *Leave Any Information*, 231, 265.

10. Ruscha, *Leave Any Information*, 275.

11. Lawrence Weiner, "Signage for an Exhibition of Ed Ruscha Paintings 1983–1987," in *Ed Ruscha, Catalogue Raisonné of the Paintings*, vol. 3, *1983–1987* (New York: Gagosian Gallery, 2007).

12. Ruscha, *Leave Any Information*, 330, 289. His first group show, also curated by Walter Hopps at the Pasadena Museum of Art, was called *New Painting of Common Objects*(1962),

and it included other connoisseurs of the common such as his friend Joe Goode, as well as Warhol, Lichtenstein, and Jim Dine, among others. In the same year Warhol proposed the term "Commonist" for Pop; Ruscha might have seconded the motion.

13. As Dave Hickey wrote of these works, "It wasn't a standardized station but a station which dispensed standards, like a restaurant which serves norms, or a museum which did both." Hickey, "Available Light," in Peter Plagens et al., *The Works of Edward Ruscha* (San Francisco: San Francisco Museum of Modern Art, 1982), 24.

14. See "Imaginary Architecture" in this volume.

15. Ruscha, *Leave Any Information*, 336.

16. See Daniel Heller-Roazen, *The Enemy of All: Piracy and the Law of Nations* (New York: Zone Books, 2009).

17. In his classic essay "The Structural Study of Myth" (1955), Claude Lévi-Strauss argues that the raven and the coyote are deemed tricksters in part because they lie outside or between the given oppositions of agriculture and hunting, "herbivorous animals" and "beasts of prey" (*Structural Anthropology*, trans. Claire Jacobson [New York: Basic Books, 1963], 224). Much in Ruscha is similarly tricksterish, both-and or neither-nor.

18. Franz Kafka, *The Complete Stories* (New York: Schocken Books, 1971), 228, 230.

19. Dietrich Dietrichsen in Marika Magers, ed., *Ed Ruscha: Gunpowder and Stains* (Cologne: Walther König, 2000), 12.

Chapter 14

1. John Baldessari, Ann Goldstein, and Christopher Williams, "The Things We Sweep under the Rug," in *John Baldessari: Life's Balance, Works 1984–2004*, ed. Peter Pakesch (Cologne: Walther König, 2005), 88. The initial version of the present chapter appeared in *John Baldessari Catalogue Raisonné*, vol. 2: *1975–1986* (New Haven: Yale University Press, 2014).

2. Baldessari attests to his interest in Lévi-Strauss in Coosje van Bruggen, *John Baldessari* (New York: Rizzoli International, 1990), 57. In "The *Petit Cinéma* of John Baldessari," David Salle suggests that Baldessari was also taken by "the syntactical visual poetry of Godard's great 1960s films, with their emphasis on montage over story." In Jessica Morgan, ed., *Pure Beauty* (Los Angeles: Los Angeles County Museum of Art, 2009), 145.

3. Pascale Cassagnau, "Interview with John Baldessari," in *Entretien/Intervista/Interview: Acconci, Baldessari, Fabro, Sarkis* (Turin: Lindau, 1999), 140. Salle adds: "The most primal act of selection is to point, and pointing/selecting is one of John's most powerful and often-invoked metaphors for making art" ("The *Petit Cinéma* of John Baldessari," 158).

4. Sergei Eisenstein, *Film Form*, excerpted in Gerald Mast and Marshall Cohen, eds., *Film Theory and Criticism* (New York: Oxford University Press, 1974), 76. Vsevolod Pudovkin (1893–1953) developed his theory of montage in such classics as *Mother* (1926). Also a prominent director, Lev Kuleshov (1899–1970) served as academic rector of the Gerasimov Institute of Cinematography in Moscow.

5. Eisenstein, *Film Form*, 87.

6. I mention Hitchcock because his world is closer to that of the images deployed by Baldessari, who know his filmography well.

7. John Baldessari, "An Overview of the Prima Facie Series," in *John Baldessari: The Prima Facie Series* (Deurie, Belgium: Museum Dhondt-Dhaenens, 2006), n.p.

8. Eisenstein, *Film Form*, 85.

9. Christopher Knight, "The Early Years: An Interview with John Baldessari," in *John Baldessari Catalogue Raisonné*, vol. 1: *1956–1974* (New Haven: Yale University Press, 2012), 364.

10. See "Made for Cutting" in this volume.

11. The paradigmatic axis is synchronic in the sense that words of one set exist, notionally, in the same time, while the syntagmatic axis is diachronic in the sense that words are linked in sequence.

12. There are other signal applications as well, such as the analysis of fashion proposed by Roland Barthes. A similar distinction is already implicit in the Eisenstein opposition of a montage of "linkages" and a montage of "collisions."

13. See his statement on the "Car Color Series" in *John Baldessari Catalogue Raisonné*, vol. 2. This series plays on *Every Building on Sunset Strip*, which Ed Ruscha produced a decade before.

14. One *Blasted Allegory* is subtitled "dereistic," which means to stray from reality into fantasy. Baldessari is interested in psychoanalysis, and fundamental to the Lacanian rereading of Freud is to consider the unconscious in terms of language—in particular, to see the operations of displacement and condensation at work in dreams in terms of syntagmatic combination and paradigmatic selection.

15. Meg Cranston, "John Baldessari: Many Worthwhile Aspects," in *Baldessari: While Something Is Happening Here, Something Else Is Happening There: Works 1965–2001* (Reykjavik: Reykjavik Art Museum, 2001), 55.

16. Ibid.

17. Roland Barthes, "The Structuralist Activity" (1964), *Partisan Review* (Winter 1967), 83, 87. Here Barthes calls selection and combination "dissection" and "articulation." He also picks out Mondrian, Boulez, and Butor as involved in similar activities.

18. In a sense, Baldessari combines the opposites made famous by Lévi-Strauss: he is *bricoleur* and engineer in one. His father was in the "salvage business" (Knight, "The Early Years," 353).

19. In the end the *Blasted Allegories* might be more aphasic than linguistic. In a classic essay, "Two Aspects of Language and Two Types of Aphasic Disturbances" (1956), Jakobson understands such speech disorders as a disturbance in the selection or the combination of words—as a disturbance, that is, in paradigmatic or syntagmatic operations. Baldessari often performs this kind of disorder.

20. Roland Barthes, "The Third Meaning: Research Notes on Some Eisenstein Stills," in Barthes, *Image Music Text*, trans. Stephen Heath (New York: Hill & Wang, 1977), 61, 55, 58. This book of essays, some of which rethink photographic representation, was catalytic for many artists and critics.

21. Ibid., 61.

22. In this regard the *Blasted Allegories* might recall "the unraveled calligrams" of René Magritte as understood by Michel Foucault in *This Is Not a Pipe*, trans. Richard Howard (Berkeley: University of California Press, 1968). See "Evening in America" in this volume.

23. Barthes, "The Third Meaning," 61.

24. This is the title of a 1978 "Blasted Allegory": *Tergiversate. Eat One's Words.*

25. Cranston, "John Baldessari: Many Worthwhile Aspects," 54.

26. Craig Owens, "The Allegorical Impulse: Toward a Theory of Postmodernism," *October* 12 and 13 (Spring and Summer, 1980), reprinted in Brian Wallis, ed., *Art after Modernism: Rethinking Representation* (New York: New Museum of Art, 1984). Owens reviewed the 1981–1982 Baldessari retrospective at the New Museum in "Telling Stories," *Art in America* (May 1981). I first wrote about the *Blasted Allegories* in *Artforum* (October 1979).

27. Owens, "The Allegorical Impulse," 204

28. Ibid., 214, 221. De Man: "The two readings have to engage each other in direct confrontation, for the one reading is precisely the error denounced by the other and has to be undone by it. Nor can we in any way make a valid decision as to which of the readings can be given priority over the other . . ." (quoted in ibid., 222).

29. De Man quoted in ibid., 221.

30. Ibid., 222.

31. Benjamin quoted in Benjamin H. D. Buchloh, "Allegorical Procedures: Appropriation and Montage in Contemporary Art," *Artforum* (September 1982), 46.

32. Ibid., 44.

33. Allegorical and postmodernist: these are terms associated with the Pictures artists who emerged in the late 1970s and early '80s, and the Baldessari influence on this generation (which is my own generation as well) is clear, especially on artists such as David Salle, Matt Mullican, Barbara Bloom, and James Welling, all of whom were his students at Cal Arts during this period (Salle picks out the "cool, uninflected look" of his art in particular ["The *Petit Cinéma* of John Baldessari," 147]). Not so familiar is his importance to the New York contingent of the Pictures group; the adaptation of film stills and photo-text montage by such figures as Cindy Sherman and Barbara Kruger was supported by his example. Also influential was his combination of Conceptual and performative approaches, his use of found images, and his tendency to work in series. This influence could be reciprocal as well: Baldessari came to treat the central concern of feminist art, the gaze, and, like the Pictures artists, he turned to film and television as the prime media of our postwar subject formation.

34. Quoted in Yve-Alain Bois, "Is It Impossible to Underline in a Telegram?," in *John Baldessari Catalogue Raisonné*, vol. 1, 1.

Chapter 15

1. The turn to "the primitive" in modernist art was very important in this narrative. In some accounts it was the crucial moment of the modernist break, while in other accounts this step outside the West was recouped as the next step within its dialectic. See my "The 'Primitive' Unconscious of Modern Art," in *Recodings: Art, Spectacle, Cultural Politics* (Seattle: Bay Press, 1985). The initial version of the present chapter appeared in Michael Govan et al., *AMERICA Invention* (New York: Guggenheim Museum, 1992).

2. Johannes Fabian, *Time and the Other: How Anthropology Makes Its Object* (New York: Columbia University Press, 1983), 11–12.

3. "Without writing" was the fundamental designation of "the primitive"; all the other privations followed from it. In the Romantic version of this designation, "the primitive" was violated by writing, which was taken to deceive, indeed to enslave—a view held from Rousseau to Lévi-Strauss (at least in his *Tristes Tropiques* of 1955).

4. Fabian, *Time and the Other*, 154. The "his" is Fabian's.

5. The best accounts of the early work in English are Denis Zacharopoulous, "The World and Its Traditions, or the Tradition of the World," in *Artforum* (October 1985), and Craig Owens, "Improper Names," in *Art in America* (October 1986).

6. Baumgarten designed these pictographs with the drainage slits in the marble of Venetian streets and piazzas in mind.

7. Tzvetan Todorov discusses such renomination in the first part of *The Conquest of America: The Question of the Other*, trans. Richard Howard (New York: Harper & Row, 1982). Owens raises it in relation to Baumgarten in "Improper Names."

8. Andrew Carnegie quoted in Anne Rorimer, "Lothar Baumgarten in Pittsburgh," *Parachute* 58 (Spring 1990): 5.

9. Ibid.

10. Lothar Baumgarten, "Carbon," in *Carbon* (Los Angeles: Los Angeles Museum of Contemporary Art, 1990).

11. See Pierre Clastres, *Society against the State* (1974), trans. Robert Hurley (New York: Zone Books, 1989).

12. This is a tricky operation, for even as Baumgarten insisted that these societies exist in the same time, he didn't mean to imply that they don't possess different histories.

13. See *The New Science of Giambattista Vico* (3rd ed., 1744), trans. T. G. Bergin and M. H. Fisch (Ithaca: Cornell University Pres, 1970).

14. Riegl wrote of the opticality of late Roman art: "Thus we find everywhere the same phenomenon: a regression, so it would appear, back to most ancient forms, to the haptic objectivity of the ancient Orientals, in fact, however, an extreme contrast, a radical optical objectivism. The screw of time has seemingly turned all the way back to its old position, yet in reality it has ended up one full turn higher, and it is now removed by a deep furrow from that point at which it seemed once again to have arrived." Alois Riegl, "Late Roman or Oriental?" (1902), in *German Essays on Art History*, ed. Gert Schiff (New York: Continuum,

1988), 187. Panofsky uses a similar trope in relation to medieval and Renaissance art: "When work on certain artistic problems has advanced so far that further work in the same direction, proceeding from the same premises, appears unlikely to bear fruit, the result is often a great recoil, or perhaps better, a reversal of direction. Such reversals, which are often associated with a transfer of artistic 'leadership' to a new country or a new genre, create the possibility of erecting a new edifice out of the rubble of the old; they do this precisely by abandoning what has already been achieved, that is, by turning back to apparently more 'primitive' modes of representation." Erwin Panofsky, *Perspective as Symbolic Form* (1924–1925), trans. Christopher S. Wood (New York: Zone Books, 1991), 47. Finally, here is Wölfflin on neoclassicism: "A closer inspection certainly shows that art even here did not return to the point at which it once stood, but that only a spiral movement would meet the facts." Heinrich Wölfflin, *Principles of Art History* (1915), trans. M. D. Hottinger (New York: Dover, 1950), 234.

15. This (non)coincidence is discussed by Todorov, who also notes that this was the moment of the (re)invention of the museum (i.e., the papal collection of antiquities), of cultural history (i.e., generic accounts of "life and manners"), and of modern grammar books. See Todorov, *The Conquest of America*, 50, 109.

16. Ibid., 26–27.

17. There is no monopoly when it comes to linguistic violence. Consider the Yanomámi, with whom Baumgarten lived for eighteen months in the late 1970s. This was the appellation long given them on maps; in Ye'kuana it means "monkey." Meanwhile, the Yanomámi, whose name for themselves means "human being" or "people," call other tribes "napë," a term less respectful than "stranger."

18. Claude Lévi-Strauss, *The Savage Mind* (Chicago: University of Chicago Press, 1966), 181.

19. Jacques Derrida, *Of Grammatology*, trans. Gayatri Chakravorty Spivak (Baltimore: Johns Hopkins University Press, 1976), 110.

20. On this point see James Clifford, "The Salvage Paradigm," in Hal Foster, ed., *Discussions in Contemporary Culture* (Seattle: Bay Press, 1987).

21. Baumgarten, "Project Description," in Govan, *AMERICA Invention*.

Chapter 16

1. The initial version of the present chapter appeared in Philipp Kaiser, ed., *Louise Lawler: Adjusted* (Cologne: Museum Ludwig, 2013).

2. Roland Barthes, "From Work to Text," in Barthes, *Image Music Text*, trans. Stephen Heath (New York: Hill & Wang, 1977), 158.

3. Smithson quoted by Craig Owens, "From Work to Frame, or, Is There Life after 'The Death of the Author'?," in *Beyond Recognition: Representation, Power, and Culture* (Berkeley: University of California Press, 1992), 122.

4. The literature on Lawler is excellent, led by Andrea Fraser, "In and Out of Place" (1985). See Helen Molesworth, ed., *Louise Lawler* (Cambridge, MA: MIT Press, 2013).

5. Perhaps this isn't as ambiguous as I make it out to be. George Baker opts for "the stereotype," which is to suggest that patriarchy trumps both the artwork and its institutional setting. See George Baker and Andrea Fraser, "Displacement and Condensation: A Conversation on the Work of Louise Lawler" (2004), in Molesworth, *Louise Lawler*, 92.

6. Lawler in conversation with Douglas Crimp, "Prominence Given, Authority Taken Away" (2001), in Molesworth, *Louise Lawler*, 35.

7. One can almost imagine this question printed on a Lawler matchbook or glass.

8. See "Blasted Allegories" in this volume.

9. Michael Wood, "That Wooden Leg," *London Review of Books* (September 7, 2000).

10. Sigmund Freud, *Jokes and Their Relation to the Unconscious*, trans. James Strachey (New York: W. W. Norton, 1960), 14.

11. Ibid.

12. Both are quoted in ibid., 11. Theodor Lipps: "A joke says what it has to say, not only in a few words, but in *too* few words. . . . It may even actually say what it has to say by not saying it" (ibid., 13). Sometimes this is applicable to Lawler as well.

13. Ibid., 105, 101.

14. See "Evening in America" in this volume.

15. See "The Underside of Things" in this volume.

16. See Sebastiano Timpanaro, *The Freudian Slip: Psychoanalysis and Textual Criticism*, trans. Kate Soper (London: New Left Books, 1975). My account relies on Ben Kafka, *The Demon of Writing: Powers and Failures of Paperwork* (New York: Zone Books, 2012), 126–129.

17. Michel Leja, *Looking Askance: Skepticism and American Art from Eakins to Duchamp* (Berkeley: University of California Press, 2004), 12. Rosalind Krauss offers "looking askew" as a way to come to terms with this aspect of Lawler. See her "Louise Lawler: Souvenir Memories" (1996) in Molesworth, *Louise Lawler*, 96.

18. In 2011 Lawler began an open series of works under the rubric "adjusted to fit," in which she stretches the parameters of her images to suit those of their exhibition. This distortion sometimes evokes anamorphosis, or the condition of pictures that appear distorted from a frontal point of view but not when they are seen on the oblique. Lawler has influenced other artists with her oblique looking (Rebecca Quaytman and Cameron Rowland come first to mind), who learned from her to be critical on the slant, so to speak—a critical angle that can be more pointed than blunt opposition. On oblique looking also see "An Inventory of Encounters" in this volume.

19. Rosalyn Deutsche gives an excellent account of this work in her "Louise Lawler's Rude Museum" (2006) in Molesworth, *Louise Lawler*. Also see my reading in *Prosthetic Gods* (Cambridge, MA: MIT Press, 2002), which I draw on here.

Chapter 17

1. Barbara Kruger quoted in Carol Squiers, "Diversionary (Syn) Tactics: Barbara Kruger Has Her Way with Words," *ARTnews* 86 (February 1987): 84. The initial version of the present chapter appeared in Alexander Alberro et al., *Barbara Kruger* (New York: Rizzoli, 2010).

2. Barbara Kruger, *Remote Control: Power, Culture, and the World of Appearances* (Cambridge, MA: MIT Press, 1993), 6.

3. Ibid., 218.

4. See Craig Owens, "The Medusa Effect, or, The Specular Ruse," in Owens, *Beyond Recognition: Representation, Power, and Culture* (Berkeley: University of California Press, 1992).

5. Roland Barthes, "Lecture," *October* 11 (Spring 1979): 7, 11. Also see "Subversive Signs" in my *Recodings: Art, Spectacle, Cultural Politics* (Seattle: Bay Press, 1985).

6. Kruger, *Remote Control*, 216, 220. See Homi Bhabha, "Of Mimicry and Man: The Ambivalence of Colonial Discourse," *October* 28 (Spring 1984).

7. Kruger, *Remote Control*, 12, 97, 5, 47, 13.

8. Ibid., 223, 9.

9. Ibid., 97. For example, early on Kruger was alert to the way that, in the electronic age, "narrative has leaped from the page to the screen," and that "truth has been splintered into an aerosol of demi-articulate self-interest which recomposes not into language, but into picture" (7, 229).

Chapter 18

1. Betsy Sussler, "Sarah Charlesworth," *Bomb* 30 (Winter 1990). The initial version of the present chapter appeared in Margot Norton and Massimiliano Gioni, eds., *Sarah Charlesworth: Doubleworld* (New York: New Museum, 2015).

2. In *Samurai* (1981) Charlesworth reworked a photograph of a samurai warrior wielding his sword such that he seems to slash this image (which is also *his* image)—a witty parody of the macho aggression of the Neo-Expressionist gesture.

3. Roland Barthes was a crucial guide here, as were Jean Baudrillard, Michel Foucault, and Gilles Deleuze for their accounts of the simulacrum, a notion that Baudrillard used to understand recent transformations in the commodity, and Foucault and Deleuze used to question traditional hierarchies of representation. Today these points seem obvious (who believes in the transparency of the photograph?) or outdated (our problem might be less the concentration of the image in spectacle than its circulation in a system of networks). But Charlesworth asked questions—about the manufacture of consent and the effect of fetishism, among others—that remain pertinent.

4. See Walter Benjamin, "The Work of Art in the Age of Its Technological Reproducibility" (1936), in Benjamin, *Selected Writings*, vol. 3: *1935–1938*, ed. Howard Eiland and Michael W. Jennings (Cambridge, MA: Harvard University Press, 2002). In *After Art* (Princeton: Princeton University Press, 2012). David Joselit argues that this immensely influential essay constrains our thinking about the contemporary lives of images.

5. See "Blasted Allegories" in this volume.

6. Interest in semiotic ambiguity was central to postmodernist art—Douglas Crimp referred it to the Symbolist poetics of Mallarmé, Craig Owens to the theory of allegory in Paul de Man, and others to "the third meaning" that Roland Barthes detected in the film still. See Douglas Crimp, "Pictures," *October* 8 (Spring 1979); Craig Owens, "The Allegorical Impulse:

Toward a Theory of Postmodernism, I and II," *October* 12 and 13 (Spring and Summer 1980); and Roland Barthes, "The Third Meaning: Research Notes on Some Eisenstein Stills," in Barthes, *Image Music Text*, trans. Stephen Heath (New York: Hill & Wang, 1977). This ambiguity has made the *Stills* open to resignification over time; for example, they were revised anachronically, reanimated uncannily, by the victims who leapt from the World Trade Towers on 9/11. See Peter Eleey, *September 11* (New York: Museum of Modern Art PS 1, 2011), and Matthew S. Witkovsky, *Sarah Charlesworth Stills* (Chicago: Art Institute of Chicago, 2014).

7. See the title essay of my *The Return of the Real: Art and Theory at the End of the Century* (Cambridge, MA: MIT Press, 1996).

8. André Malraux, *The Voices of Silence*, trans. Stuart Gilbert (Princeton: Princeton University Press, 1978), 112. Also see my "Archives of Modern Art" in *Design and Crime (and Other Diatribes)* (London and New York: Verso, 2002).

9 Abigail Solomon-Godeau, *In Plato's Cave* (New York: Marlborough Gallery, 1983).

10 Walter Benjamin, "Paris, the Capital of the Nineteenth Century" (1935), in *The Arcades Project*, trans. Howard Eiland and Kevin McLaughlin (Cambridge, MA: Harvard University Press, 1999), 8. Freud published his classic text "Fetishism" in 1927, but the subject appeared as early as his "Three Essays on the Theory of Sexuality" (1905).

11. See "A Painter of Pop Life" in this volume.

Chapter 19

1. The initial version of the present chapter appeared in the *London Review of Books* (May 10, 2012) as a review of the retrospective *Cindy Sherman* curated by Eva Respini for the Museum of Modern Art.

2. See Julia Kristeva, *Powers of Horror: An Essay on Abjection*, trans. Leon Roudiez (New York: Columbia University Press, 1980). Also see "Abject" in my *Bad New Days: Art, Criticism, Emergency* (London and New York: Verso, 2015).

3. See Benjamin H. D. Buchloh, "Figures of Authority, Ciphers of Regression: Notes on the Return of Representation in European Painting," *October* 16 (Spring 1981).

4. One measure of the standing of Sherman is how generative her work has proved to be, first for other artists and then for the culture at large. On the one hand, she prompted subsequent artists to experiment with self-staging, avatar-making, and the like (she, in turn, was preceded by figures like Eleanor Antin). On the other, Sherman made selfies long before the advent of Instagram, with the difference that, again, she emphasized the gap between aspirational and actual body images.

Chapter 20

1. Matt Mullican in Ulrich Wilmes, ed., *Matt Mullican: Conversations with Koen Brams and Dirk Pültau* (Cologne: DuMont Buchverlag, 2011), 175. The initial version of the present chapter appeared in Lynne Cooke et al., *Matt Mullican: Subject Element Sign Frame World* (New York: Rizzoli, 2013).

2. Matt Mullican in conversation with João Ribas, in *A Drawing Translates the Way of Thinking* (New York: Drawing Center, 2008), 10.

3. Mullican in Wilmes, *Matt Mullican*, 203.

4. His parents, Lee Mullican and Luchita Hurtado, were both artists, and they collected broadly. "Every single piece in their collection," Mullican comments, "had to do with cosmology in relationship to medicine" (ibid., 152).

5. Ibid., 174. Mullican has his demons too. Of course, other artists have played the shaman, Joseph Beuys above all. But there is little self-mythologizing in the guises assumed by Mullican; on the contrary, his rituals tend to scatter the self.

6. Ibid., 152.

7. Ibid., 162.

8. Ibid., 194, 203. The allusion to theaters of memory suggests another connection to the hermetic traditions of the Renaissance. See Frances A. Yates, *The Art of Memory* (Chicago: University of Chicago Press, 1966).

9. See Louis Marin, *Utopics: Spatial Play*, trans. Robert A. Vollrath (Atlantic Highlands: Humanities Press, 1984).

10. Wilmes, *Matt Mullican*, 192.

11. Ibid., 194. The irrationality of reason is a leitmotif in Sol LeWitt too.

12. Wilmes, *Matt Mullican*, 159. Of course, such queries are hardly new to art: "Where do we come from? What are we? Where are we going?," Gauguin asked in his 1897 summa of that title.

13. The complement of *that person* in early Mullican drawings is a stick figure named "Glen."

14. Wilmes, *Matt Mullican*, 169, 174, 178.

15. Mullican, *A Drawing Translates the Way of Thinking*, 170. Here he is close to those Surrealists who also dabbled in hypnosis and saw the unconscious as an automatist mechanism. See Rosalind E. Krauss, *The Optical Unconscious* (Cambridge, MA: MIT Press, 1993).

16. Wilmes, *Matt Mullican*, 176.

17. Ibid., 170.

Chapter 21

1. James Casebere in "Photography and the Illusion of History: Conversation with James Casebere and Okwui Enwezor," in Okwui Enwezor at al., *James Casebere: Works 1975–2010* (Bologna: Damiani, 2011). Unless otherwise noted, all Casebere quotations are from this conversation. The initial version of the present chapter also appeared in this volume.

2. Casebere was also affected by the quality of televisual light, its broadcast glow, so distinct from the projected light of film. In some early installations he used light boxes in a way that evoked the formats of both television and advertising.

3. This is a central topic in the literature on Casebere, from my "Uncanny Images" (*Art in America* [November 1983]) to *James Casebere: The Spatial Uncanny* (Milan: Charta, 2001) and beyond.

4. Casebere evokes nine types of prison in this body of work (which predates recent studies of racial capitalism). *Georgian Jail Cages* (1993) is a related work, though it evokes less an architectural type than an oppressive apparatus in a system that treated prisoners effectively as slave crews on southern plantations in the late nineteenth century. Casebere acknowledges the influence of *Discipline and Punish: The Birth of the Prison* (1975) by Michel Foucault, but the emphasis of his prison pictures is different. Whereas Foucault focused on a panoptical regime of subjection that treated prisoners abstractly and alike, "race and class were still much more the issue" for Casebere. See *James Casebere: Asylum* (Santiago de Compostela: Centro Galego de Arte Contemporánea, 1999), 118.

5. Here as elsewhere Casebere reflects on the physical makeup of photography—on its materials of liquid, light, and paper. This reflection shifts with the dominance of digital images. How has this digitality affected the virtuality of his work, which once relied on our assumption that photographs were analog, grounded in an indexical relation to the world?

6. Of course, this typology of symbolic, real, and imaginary is drawn from Jacques Lacan. The dominance of the first two categories, in discussions of photography in particular, was signaled by the prominence of *Camera Lucida* (1980), where Roland Barthes proposed a theory of the photograph in two registers, the *studium* and the *punctum*, which are based on the symbolic and the real respectively.

7. Gaston Bachelard, *The Poetics of Space*, trans. Maria Jolas (Boston: Beacon Press, 1969), xii. See also Jean-Paul Sartre, *L'Imaginaire* (Paris, 1940).

8. Bachelard, *The Poetics of Space*, xxxi.

9. Ibid., xiv, xx.

10. In this way, conceptually, the simulacrum in Casebere is akin to what Deleuze describes in "Plato and the Simulacrum": "The simulacrum implies great distances, depths, and distances which the observer cannot dominate. It is because he cannot master them that he has an impression of resemblance. The simulacrum includes within itself the differential point of view, and the spectator is made part of the simulacrum which is transformed and deformed according to his point of view" (*October* 27 [Winter 1983]: 49). Bachelard has a similar thought (though it is phrased in benign terms) in *The Poetics of Space*: "Space that has been seized upon by the imagination cannot remain indifferent space subject to the measures and estimates of the surveyor. It has been lived in, not in its positivity, but with all the partiality of the imagination" (xxxii). The usurpation of reality by representation in Casebere is not only a function of the imaginary; it also reflects a social process, a becoming-image of the world in postwar consumerism, that is treated in different ways from Pop art to postmodern architecture. In this respect, interested through he is in the latter, Casebere provides a note of caution to the enthusiasms, say, of Robert Venturi and Denise Scott Brown.

11. There is a connection here to his contemporary Robert Gober, whose tableaux I discuss in terms of primal scenes in *Prosthetic Gods* (Cambridge, MA: MIT Press, 2002). Also see "Inexplicable Things" in this volume.

12. Bachelard, *The Poetics of Space*, xxxiii.

13. On this type of time see "Philosophical Objects" in this volume.

Chapter 22

1. In the dye-transfer process there are three printing matrices (one for each primary color) and gelatin is used to fix the colors, which possess more tonal range than those derived from other techniques. Eastman Kodak stopped production of the materials required for this process in 1994, and few printers retain the equipment and the expertise necessary to accomplish it. Demand discusses the making of *The Dailies* in *Thomas Demand: The Dailies* (Sydney: Kaldor Art Projects, 2012). The initial version of the present chapter appeared in Thomas Demand, *The Dailies* (London: Mack Books, 2023).

2. Coline Milliard, "Same Author, Different Form," *Artinfo UK*, April 18, 2012. Already implicit in "The Histories" is the claim that the little things of everyday life coexist with the grand events of official history.

3. On this point see Norman Bryson, *Looking at the Overlooked: Four Essays on Still Life Painting* (Cambridge, MA: Harvard University Press, 1990).

4. Georg Lukács discusses "second nature" in *The Theory of the Novel* (1916), as do Walter Benjamin and Theodor Adorno after him.

5. Demand laminates his photographs behind Plexiglas and mounts them on aluminum without frames; that is, he presents them as objects too.

6. Svetlana Alpers, *The Art of Describing: Dutch Art in the Seventeenth Century* (Chicago: University of Chicago Press, 1983). The models of window and mirror might not be as opposed as Alpers believes. In fact, Foucault and Marin saw them as complements that together constitute the great achievement of "classical representation," as epitomized, for Foucault, by Diego Velázquez in *Las Meninas* (1656) and, for Marin, by Nicolas Poussin in *Et in Arcadia Ego* (1655). Located between the Italian and the Dutch, the Spanish Velázquez and the French Poussin resolve the two kinds of picturing into one metapictorial type. See "In a Glass Darkly" in this volume.

7. See Michel Foucault, *The Order of Things: An Archaeology of the Human Sciences* (New York: Pantheon, 1970); Louis Marin, "Toward a Reading of the Visual Arts," in Susan Rubin Suleiman and Inge Crosman, eds., *The Reader in the Text: Essays on Audience and Interpretation* (Princeton: Princeton University Press, 1980); Svetlana Alpers, "Interpretation without Representation, or, The Viewing of *Las Meninas*," *Representations* 1 (Winter 1983); and Craig Owens, "Representation, Appropriation, and Power," *Art in America* 70, no. 5 (May 1982). Here I agree with Owens, whose dispute with Alpers on these points (he argued with Michael Fried as well) was a telling instance of the tension between art history and critical theory during the advent of postmodernist art.

8. The opposition between window and mirror in Alpers maps onto the one between theatricality and absorption in Fried, a great advocate for Demand. Yet both these models miss how Demand works to confuse such binaries.

9. For the persistence of these paradigms in the discourse of photography, see John Szarkowski, *Mirrors and Windows: American Photography since 1960* (New York: Museum of Modern Art, 1978).

10. Michael Fried, *Why Photography Matters as Never Before* (New Haven: Yale University Press, 2008), 271. Like painting, photography presents but one vantage, unlike sculpture, which is why the young Baudelaire dismissed sculpture as "tiresome" in his *Salon of 1846*. Both Fried and Demand have cited this argument.

11. Gravity and suspension are conditions negotiated by bodies and pictures alike, a sharing that might underline the subtle sympathy between the two that Demand is able to elicit.

12. For an excellent account of these old concerns, see Robin Kelsey, *Photography and the Art of Chance* (Cambridge, MA: Harvard University Press, 2015).

13. Roland Barthes, "The Reality Effect" (1968), in Barthes, *The Rustle of Language*, trans. Richard Howard (New York: Hill & Wang, 1986). "Semiotically," Barthes writes, "the 'concrete detail' is constituted by the *direct* collusion of a referent and a signifier; the signified is expelled from the sign, and with it, of course, the possibility of developing a *form of the signified*, i.e., narrative structure itself" (147). Here the detail almost obstructs meaning, and this opposition recalls not only that between "the world is seen" and "I see the world" but also that between description and narration, which Lukács used to distinguish naturalist fiction (which he deplored) from realist fiction (which he championed because it involves a narrative understanding of the social world). In this sense Demand is more realist than naturalist.

14. Demand in Milliard, "Same Author, Different Form."

15. Ezra Pound, "In a Station of the Metro" (1913); William Carlos Williams, "The Red Wheelbarrow" (1923).

16. Charles Baudelaire, "The Painter of Modern Life" (1863), in Baudelaire, *The Painter of Modern Life and Other Essays*, trans. and ed. Jonathan Mayne (London: Phaidon, 1964), 13. See "A Painter of Pop Life" in this volume.

17. Demand, in "A Conversation Between Alexander Kluge and Thomas Demand," in *Thomas Demand* (London: Serpentine Gallery, 2006), 51–112. Unless otherwise noted, all further Demand and Kluge quotations are from this text.

18. On this point see my *The First Pop Age: Painting and Subjectivity in the Art of Hamilton, Lichtenstein, Warhol, Richter, and Ruscha* (Princeton: Princeton University Press, 2012). As Demand has suggested on a few occasions, the "punctal" is not opposed to the banal.

19. See Andreas Ruby, "Memoryscapes," *Parkett* 62 (2001). "Something seems to stare back at us," Ralph Rugoff writes. "Rather than mirroring our gaze, these compositional black holes solicit the blind spots of our subjectivity. They do so, in part, by evoking that 'beyond'—that unknown other towards which desire ceaselessly circulates." Rugoff, "Instructions for Escape," in *Thomas Demand: Phototropy* (Bregenz: Kunsthaus Bregenz, 2004). Again, I see this "beyond" as touching on death more than desire.

20. See Bryson, *Looking at the Overlooked*.

21. On this connection see in particular Sigmund Freud, "Medusa's Head" (1922). For me the connection is summoned in *Daily #36* with its pieces of eggshell on a cutting board with a sharp knife nearby.

22. Jacques Lacan, *The Four Fundamental Concepts of Psychoanalysis*, trans. Alan Sheridan (New York: W. W. Norton, 1978), 77.

23. See Walter Benn Michaels, "Photographs and Fossils," in James Elkins, ed., *Photography Theory* (New York: Routledge, 2007).

24. Rugoff, "Instructions for Escape."

25. If Lacan understands the gaze as maleficent, Benjamin understands it as beneficent, at least when he thinks of aura as the capacity of an object to return our gaze. Tricking of our look is everywhere in Demand, and I see wilding in *Daily #19*, for example, and taming in *Daily #14*.

26. This artifice often takes the form of a reconstruction, a repetition aimed to actualize an event, whether historical or imagined. It is pervasive in recent art, performance, fiction, and other forms. See my "Real Fictions: Alternatives to Alternative Facts," *Artforum* (April 2017).

27. See Alexander Kluge and Oskar Negt, *History and Obstinacy*, ed. Devin Fore (New York: Zone Books, 2014). In his brilliant introduction Fore glosses "obstinacy" as follows: "The word *Eigensinn*—rendered variously into English as 'autonomy,' 'willfulness,' 'self-will,' and, here, 'obstinacy'—implies a degree of stubborn obtuseness, an imperviousness to directives from above. Hegel, for example, describes *Eigensinn* as 'a freedom' that is 'enmeshed in servitude.' Kluge, in contrast, describes *Eigensinn* as 'the guerrilla warfare [*Partisanentum*] of the mind.' Obstinacy is the underside of history" (36).

28. Implicitly Kluge, a legatee of the Frankfurt School, pushes back on the notion, advanced in the actor-network theory of Bruno Latour, that agency is distributed among people, things, and systems, even as he also pushes back on the fatalism of his own critical tradition. Demand seems to agree on both counts.

29. See Rem Koolhaas and Hal Foster, *Junkspace with Running Room* (London: Notting Hill Editions, 2013).

Chapter 23

1. "John Miller in Conversation with Beatrix Ruf," in Beatrix Ruf, ed., *John Miller: A Refusal to Accept Limits* (Zurich: Kunsthalle Zürich, 2009), 19–20. The initial version of the present chapter appeared in Alex Gartenfield, ed., *John Miller: I Stand, I Fall* (Miami: Institute of Contemporary Art, 2017).

2. John Miller, *The Ruin of Exchange and Other Writings on Art* (Zurich and Dijon: JRP/Ringier and Les presses du réel, 2012), 130.

3. John Miller, *The Price Club: Selected Writings (1977–1998)* (Geneva and Dijon: JRP Editions and Les presses du réel, 2000), 71.

4. Miller was later supported in this line of thinking by the media theorist Vilém Flusser, his *Towards a Philosophy of Photography* (1983) in particular.

5. "John Miller in Conversation with Beatrix Ruf," 20. Miller expanded on this point: "Pictures theory presumes that the camera is objective, whereas Kelley et al. think of the camera as embedded in deeper levels of mystification (similar to what Michael Taussig suggests in *Mimesis and Alterity*): that mimetic technologies are bound to magical thinking. Cue Flusser." Miller, e-mail to the author.

6. Miller, *The Ruin of Exchange*, 275.

7. Ibid. With "pictures of pictures" Miller wanted to create distance enough from the representations that they would read as versions of world views, that is, as ideologies.

8. "John Miller in Conversation with Beatrix Ruf," 20.

9. Ibid.

10. Miller, *The Ruin of Exchange*, 275. Allan McCollum created very different "surrogates" of painting and sculpture during these same years.

11. Ibid., 274.

12. "It was a discursive, field relationship," Miller comments, "like words in a dictionary" ("John Miller in Conversation with Beatrix Ruf," 21). At times, however, there is a tension in this posture between participant and observer, between demotic solidarity and sociological overview.

13. "Instead of subversion, I would assign the value of dysfunction to painting," Miller tells Liam Gillick in an interview. This calls up the avatar of the adolescent as dysfunctional adult often adopted by Kelley. See Liam Gillick, "John Miller," *Bomb* 118 (Winter 2012).

14. "John Miller in Conversation with Beatrix Ruf," 20. Mary Douglas offered this famous definition of dirt in *Purity and Danger: An Analysis of Concepts of Pollution and Taboo* (1966). On abject art see my *Bad New Days: Art, Criticism, Emergency* (London and New York: Verso, 2015).

15. Miller, *The Ruin of Exchange*, 330.

16. Ibid., 278.

17. That Miller paints his brushstroke on a mirror might also evoke—in order to question—the famous "mirror stage" of ego formation theorized by Jacques Lacan.

18. Miller positions his mannequins as our doubles, as in *My Friend*. The mannequin is figure of reification in Dada and of the uncanny in Surrealism. Miller assumes both attributes as given. "A mannequin is a display rack in human form," Miller states simply (Miller, *The Ruin of Exchange*, 352). Like Nauman, Miller often structures his works, or at least his titles, as jokes, especially those, like *Feet of Clay* (1988), that make the metaphorical literal, thus collapsing the high into the low. In *Now We're Big Potatoes* (1992), Miller has his mannequin literally step in shit substitute; hence my allusion to Bataille on the big toe as the body part that both supports our verticality and roots us in the earth. See "The Underside of Things" in this volume.

19. Another work, *I, a Man* (1986), presents an Ionic column that is also a capital *I* covered in brown impasto; it thus reminds us that architecture is also bound to the earth. So, too, it plays on *I-Box* (1962) by Robert Morris, a key piece that anticipates both Minimalism and body art.

20. Miller, *The Price Club*, 97. Miller grew up in Chagrin Falls, a small town near Cleveland and not far from Kent State, where *Partially Buried Woodshed* is located. The Kent State student shootings occurred on May 4, 1970 when Miller was a sophomore in high school.

21. Miller, *The Ruin of Exchange*, 345.

22. See "Every Sidewalk Is a Ray Gun Beach" in this volume.

23. With the title of another relief, *The Office Party and the Communist Party* (1991), Miller points, à la Guy Debord, to the emergence of one integrated market, one integrated spectacle, after the collapse of Communism in 1989 (again, "utopia is a space outside the market"). See "A Certain Practice of Life" in this volume.

24. "The ruin of exchange" is another Miller aphorism, this one inspired by his friend Nicolás Guagnini; see Miller, *The Ruin of Exchange*, 341.

25. Ibid., 351.

26. Miller, *The Price Club*, 96. On the connection between art and hierarchy, the sociologists Thorstein Veblen and Pierre Bourdieu became touchstones for Miller as well.

27. Also significant for Miller was that Kelley, in works like *Pay for Your Pleasure* (1988), had begun to "raise hard-headed questions about the efficacy of sublimation or, for that matter, of desublimation." Miller, *The Price Club*, 62, 105.

28. Ibid., 143.

29. "John Miller in Conversation with Beatrix Ruf," 22.

30. The title alludes to a 1929 painting by Salvador Dalí that is concerned with desire, emasculation, and punishment, which make it relevant to the televisual scenarios that concern Miller.

31. Miller, *The Ruin of Exchange*, 300.

32. Miller comments in the *Bomb* interview: "My most recent paintings, which are all titled *Everything Is Said*, show people crying on reality TV. Crying suggests the breakdown of subjectivity. It points to an apparatus-like quality where the subjectivity doesn't count for much." (Gillick, "John Miller.")

33. Hugo Ball, *Flight Out of Time: A Dada Diary* (1927), trans. Ann Raimes (New York: Viking Press, 1974), 51–52.

34. Ibid., 66. For my views on this mimetic exacerbation, see *Bad New Days*.

35. Gillick, "John Miller." He follows Benjamin here.

36. For more on this possibility, see Giorgio Agamben, *The Coming Community*, trans. Michael Hardt (Minneapolis: University of Minnesota Press, 1993).

37. Miller, *The Ruin of Exchange*, 136.

Chapter 24

1. Gober speaks of "jumping sculptural traditions" in Ann Temkin, ed., *The Heart Is Not a Metaphor* (New York: Museum of Modern Art, 2014), 144. The initial version of the present chapter appeared in *Artforum* (January 2015) as a review of his 2014 retrospective curated by Ann Temkin for the Museum of Modern Art. For an extended reflection on Gober, see my *Prosthetic Gods* (Cambridge, MA: MIT Press, 2004).

2. See "Oblique Looking" in this volume.

3. See Georges Bataille, "L'Esprit moderne et le jeu des transpositions," *Documents* 8 (1930).

4. Robert Gober, "Interview with Richard Flood," in Richard Flood, ed., *Robert Gober: Sculpture + Drawing* (Minneapolis: Walker Art Center, 1999), 125.

5. See Walter Benjamin, "The Storyteller," in *Selected Writings*, vol. 3: *1935–1938*, ed. Howard Eiland and Michael W. Jennings (Cambridge, MA: Harvard University Press, 2002).

6. Again, Gober is distinctive, yet that difference is produced in relation to the work of other artists that he develops and redirects. For example, an essay might be written on the replica placing Gober in relation to Vija Celmins, who, like Gober, uses the replica less to question originality than to explore similarity. Or an essay on the souvenir putting Gober in dialogue with Jasper Johns, who also treats traces of the body as palimpsests of memory. Or an essay on the part object as posed by Duchamp (*Étant donnés* is also a "diorama about contemporary human beings"), picked up by Johns, and elaborated by Gober. Or an essay on sexuality in art from Surrealism to feminism, clarifying how Gober queers the devices developed to probe gender and difference.

7. Along with the recursivity of this work, its reticence, which might be born of "the epistemology of the closet," recalls Johns. See "Watchman and Spy" in this volume.

Chapter 25

1. My epigraph comes from Rachel Kushner and Charles Ray, "1000 Words: Charles Ray Talks about *Hinoki*, 2007," *Artforum* (September 2007), 439. "The big lady" refers to the super-sized mannequin titled *Fall '91* (1992). The initial version of the present chapter appeared in Silvia Gaspardo Moro, ed., *Philosophical Objects: An Essay on the Sculpture of Charles Ray* (Los Angeles, 2019).

2. Robert Storr and Charles Ray, "Anxious Spaces," *Art in America* (November 1998), 143. Other critics, such as James Rondeau, John Kelsey, and Jack Bankowsky, aren't so averse to the imagistic dimension of the work.

3. This might also reaffirm the old opposition between formalism and iconography. The danger of the latter is clear enough; that of the former arises when, for example, we ignore that *Sleeping Woman* (2012) is based on a homeless person.

4. Charles Ray in James Rondeau, ed., *Charles Ray: Sculpture 1997–2014* (Chicago: Art Institute of Chicago, 2014), 138.

5. Charles Baudelaire, "A Philosophy of Toys," in *The Painter of Modern Life and Other Essays*, ed. Jonathan Mayne (London: Phaidon, 1964), 202–203. "This is the beginning of melancholy and gloom," Baudelaire concluded. For Freud such investigations have to do with the sexual curiosity of the child, which, in "On the Sexual Enlightenment of Children" (1908), he presented as the prototype of all intellectual work. This, too, seems relevant to Ray, who once commented that his mannequins involved fundamental questions of origin and identity—"where was my life made, did I make me or did someone else make me?" Lucinda Barnes, "Interview with Charles Ray," in *Charles Ray* (Newport Beach: Newport Harbor Art Museum, 1990), 9.

6. Kushner and Ray, "1000 Words," 439.

7. Ray in Rondeau, *Charles Ray: Sculpture 1997–2014*, 108.

8. Charles Ray, "There Is No Color in the Great Outdoors," in David Breslin, ed., *Raw Color: The Circles of David Smith* (Williamstown: Clark Art Institute, 2014), 45.

9. Ray in Rondeau, *Charles Ray: Sculpture 1997–2014*, 124.

10. Ray, "There Is No Color," 46.

11. Kushner and Ray, "1000 Words," 439. For Michael Fried embedment goes so far beyond installation as to cancel it, almost in a Heideggerian way: "Embedment, one might say, concerns the placement of a sculpture in the world rather than simply in a room." In *Four Honest Outlaws: Sala, Ray, Marioni, Gordon* (New Haven: Yale University Press, 2011), 101.

12. Fried, *Four Honest Outlaws*, 68.

13. Charles Ray and Michael Fried, "Early One Morning . . . ," *Tate Etc* 3 (Spring 2005): 51.

14. Fried claimed a phenomenological orientation for Caro (his early plasters and bronzes, the critic argued, convey what it feels like to be a body in action, holding a foot, taking off a shirt, and so on), while others such as Rosalind Krauss claimed this orientation for the Minimalists, who act directly on the bodies of viewers (too literally for Fried). Ray is closer to Caro here; about the boy in *The New Beetle* he comments: "He is lost in play, and soon the viewer is down there on the floor with him. With all sculpture, I am interested in where you find yourself in relationship to the object. If the object can move you physically from one position—one space—to another, it will also move you intellectually" (Ray in Rondeau, *Charles Ray: Sculpture 1997–2014*, 112). In a sense, not only are his sculptures figurative, but they also turn his viewers into figures, into live sculptures. Fried also pulls Ray toward Smith and Caro and away from the Minimalists through an opposition between the intentionality of the former and the indeterminacy of the latter. Yet there is little that is indeterminate about Minimalism; to suggest so is to collapse it too quickly into the tradition of Duchamp and Cage.

15. Fried admits that Ray doesn't always agree with him vis-à-vis Judd. Of *Untitled* (1968) Ray comments, "this sculpture is totally and completely embedded in the space of its existence" (Fried, *Four Honest Outlaws*, 115).

16. At one point Fried agrees: "If this seems dialectical with respect to both Caro and Minimalism/Literalism, it is" (ibid., 91). But so opposed is he to Minimalism that his reading doesn't sustain the dialectic that Ray projects.

17. Charles Ray in Paul Dickerson, "Charles Ray," *Bomb* 52 (Summer 1995).

18. All three exhibitions took place at the Matthew Marks Gallery in New York.

19. Ray in Rondeau, *Charles Ray: Sculpture 1997–2014*, 114.

20. The head of *Spinario* is not original, as is indicated by the fact that, even though the head is inclined, its hair does not hang down—a discrepancy that Ray maintained in *Shoe Tie*. *Sleeping Woman* also alludes, more specifically, to the recumbent Roman hermaphrodite in the Louvre.

21. Ray in Rondeau, *Charles Ray: Sculpture 1997–2014*, 130.

22. Charles Baudelaire, "Salon of 1846," in *The Mirror of Art*, ed. Jonathan Mayme (Garden City, NY: Doubleday, 1956), 83. Also see "The Artist as Anthologist" in this volume. "Exact imitation," Baudelaire continues, "spoils a memory." In a similar vein Richard Neer writes of

classical allusions in Ray: "Not much seems to depend on the specific iconographies of these ancient statues. . . . [I] am not completely sure that the similarities are even fully intended; in some ways I hope not" ("Tumbling into Time," in Rondeau, *Charles Ray: Sculpture 1997–2014*, 66–67).

23. Neer, "Tumbling into Time," 67.

24. Ray in Rondeau, *Charles Ray: Sculpture 1997–2014*, 126.

25. Ibid.

26. Kushner and Ray, "1000 Words," 439.

27. Ray in Rondeau, *Charles Ray: Sculpture 1997–2014*, 132.

28. Ibid., 136. In "Tumbling into Time" Neer also connects *Mime* to the recumbent *Giant* and *Amazon*, Roman versions of Greek originals in Pergamon.

29. Ray in Rondeau, *Charles Ray: Sculpture 1997–2014*, 106. The car was a Pontiac Grand Am.

30. Evoked here, too, are the sculptures of car scrap made by John Chamberlain as well as the silkscreens of car crashes produced by Andy Warhol. For me it also calls to mind the scene in the James Bond film *Goldfinger* (1964) in which a Lincoln Continental is crushed into a block with Napoleon Solo in it.

31. See Charles Baudelaire, "The Painter of Modern Life" (1863), in *The Painter of Modern Life and Other Essays*. Also see "A Painter of Pop Life" in this volume.

32. When Ray and I were boys, *The Lone Ranger* was still on TV, but even then it seemed a little ridiculous, and as a genre the Western was soon ripe for satire. If *Goldfinger* can be paired with *Baled Truck*, then one comparandum for *Horse and Rider* might be the sad-sack cowboy played by Lee Marvin in *Cat Ballou* (1965).

33. Ray in Rondeau, *Charles Ray: Sculpture 1997–2014*, 124.

34. See James Rondeau, "Alternative Americana: Two Public Sculptures by Charles Ray," in Rondeau, ed., *Charles Ray: Sculpture 1997–2014*.

35. Ray in Andree Russeth, "Shoeless Ray," *Observer Arts*, November 26, 2012, B10, as quoted in Neer, "Tumbling into Time," 68.

36. Ray quoted in ibid., 69.

37. See Quentin Meillassoux, *After Finitude*, trans. Ray Brassier (London: Bloomsbury, 2009).

38. Ray in Rondeau, *Charles Ray: Sculpture 1997–2014*, 110. Ray uses the word "Platonic" often, which suggests an idealism distant from Minimalist immanence.

39. Ray, "There Is No Color," 46–47.

40. Ibid., 47; Ray quoted in Jack Bankowsky, ed., *Fritsch/Koons/Ray: Sculpture after Sculpture* (Stockholm: Moderna Museet, 2014), 107. His interest in found objects and insistence on collaborative process also complicates authorship, and in turn this complication supports the effect of "tumbling into time."

Chapter 26

1. Gerhard Richter, *Text: Writings, Interviews and Letters 1961–2007*, ed. Dietmar Elger and Hans Ulrich Obrist (London: Thames & Hudson, 2009), 129; and Lucy Lippard, "Eccentric Abstraction," in *Changing: Essays in Art Criticism* (New York: E. P. Dutton, 1971). Also see "In a Glass Darkly" in this volume. The initial version of the present chapter was published in *Artforum* (December 2022) as a review of the retrospective *Cornelia Parker* curated by Andrea Schlieker for Tate Britain.

2. See Georges Bataille, "Primitive Art" (1930), in Bataille, *The Cradle of Humanity: Prehistoric Art and Culture*, ed. and trans. Stuart Kendall (New York: Zone Books, 2005).

3. Mignon Nixon, "Posing the Phallus," *October* 92 (Spring 2000).

Chapter 27

1. These phrases and others can be found in Ralph Rugoff et al., *Joy in People: Jeremy Deller* (London: Hayward Publishing, 2012). For an excellent survey see Ralph Rugoff, "Middle Class Hero," in that volume. The initial version of the present chapter appeared in *English Magic*, the pamphlet for the Deller exhibition of that title in the British Pavilion at the 2013 Venice Biennale.

2. Here the connection is clear to Andy Warhol, whom Deller encountered on a New York visit in 1986 at the age of twenty.

3. Stuart Hall, "Jeremy Deller's Political Imaginary," in Rugoff et al., *Joy in People*, 89. Deller not only delves into subcultures but also draws on projects (such as the aforementioned) concerned with these formations. In this respect one also thinks of critics like Dick Hebdige and Greil Marcus, whose own model of dissident culture as so many "lipstick traces" from Dada through Situationism to Punk resonates with Deller. More distantly, Deller has an affinity with William Morris, to whom he has devoted a number of pieces. Whereas Morris sought to restore craft from its degradation by capitalist industry, Deller seeks to find, in an industrial culture now decayed, a new source of folk expression.

4. Deller quoted in Rugoff et al., *Joy in People*, 66.

5. Rugoff, "Middle Class Hero," 10.

6. Deller quoted in Rugoff et al., *Joy in People*, 70.

7. Ibid., 98.

8. Ibid., 174. This notion of "cover" is close to that of "re-scenario" as practiced by Pierre Huyghe, Joachim Koester, Matthew Buckingham, and other artists of the same generation as Deller.

9. Unless otherwise specified, all quotations derive from e-mail exchanges with the artist.

Chapter 28

1. See David Joselit, "Rachel Harrison, Untranslatable," in Elisabeth Sussman and David Joselit, eds., *Rachel Harrison Life Hack* (New York: Whitney Museum of American Art, 2019), 251–258. The initial version of the present chapter appeared in *Artforum* (January 2020) as a review of *Rachel Harrison Life Hack*, curated by Sussman and Joselit for the Whitney Museum.

2. See Georges Bataille, "Formless," in Bataille, *Visions of Excess: Selected Writings, 1927–1939*, trans. Allan Stoekl (Minneapolis: University of Minnesota Press, 1985), and Julia Kristeva, *Powers of Horror: An Essay on Abjection*, trans. Leon Roudiez (New York: Columbia University Press, 1980).

3. To be fair, Joselit stresses "untranslatability" too.

4. See "Every Sidewalk Is a Ray Gun Beach" and "Perverse Pantomime" in this volume.

5. Ernst Mandel, *Late Capitalism*, trans. Joris De Bres (London: New Left Books, 1974).

6. Harrison rebaptizes the three graces as "Art, Sex, and Death" in a 2017 press release republished in *Rachel Harrison Life Hack*, 198–199.

7. To underscore the message about domestic labor, Harrison had the floor of the principal gallery in her Whitney Museum show diagrammed in white in a way that recalled the Lars von Triers film *Dogville* (2003), in which the Nicole Kidman character, on the run from the Mafia, is put to demeaning work by the good folk of a Colorado town.

8. Roland Barthes, *Mythologies*, trans. Annette Lavers (New York: Farrar, Straus and Giroux, 1972), 135; Carl Andre, *Cuts: Texts 1959–2004*, ed. James Meyer (Cambridge, MA: MIT Press, 2005), 30.

9. See "Perverse Pantomime."

10. Hugo Ball, *Flight Out of Time: A Dada Diary* (1927), trans. Ann Raimes (New York: Viking Press, 1974), 66 (the entry is dated June 12, 1916); Karl Marx, "A Contribution to the Critique of Hegel's Philosophy of Right" (1844), in Marx, *Early Writings*, trans. and ed. T. B. Bottomore (New York: McGraw Hill, 1964), 47 (translation modified). Also see my "Dada Mime," *October* 105 (Summer 2003).

11. Harrison, 2017 press release, in *Rachel Harrison Life Hack*, 198.

12. See "Oblique Looking" in this volume.

13. See Mignon Nixon, "Posing the Phallus," *October* 92 (Spring 2000). Also see "Lost and Found" in this volume.

14. Giorgio Agamben, *The Coming Community*, trans. Michael Hardt (Minneapolis: University of Minnesota Press, 1993), 50. Also see Fredric Jameson, "Utopia and Reification in Mass Culture," *Social Text* 1 (1979).

15. Claes Oldenberg quoted in Achim Hochdörfer, ed., *Claes Oldenburg: The Sixties* (Munich: Prestel, 2012), 154.

Chapter 29

1. See Mungo Thomson, *Time Life* (New York: Karma Books, 2023). The initial version of the present chapter was published in that catalogue.

2. Mungo Thomson, unpublished text on *Time Life*.

3. Ibid.

4. While *Flowers* recalls any number of Stan Brakhage films, *Color Guide* evokes *Color Aid* (1970–1971), a film in which Richard Serra flicks through the 220 color sheets included in a Color-aid box, a device for instruction about color. This suggests a further association with the Josef Albers classic, *The Interaction of Color* (1963), which Serra color-proofed for Albers while he was a graduate student at Yale.

5. On originality versus repetition in Rodin, see the title essay in Rosalind Krauss, *The Originality of the Avant-Garde and Other Modernist Myths* (Cambridge, MA: MIT Press, 1986). Also see "Made for Cutting" in this volume.

6. The literature on Muybridge, Marey, Taylor, and the Gilbreths is vast, but a good place to start is Sigfried Giedion, *Mechanization Takes Command* (Oxford: Oxford University Press, 1948). In *The Making of Incarnation* (2021) Tom McCarthy brilliantly dramatizes the historical trajectory from time-motion studies to image capture technologies today.

7. On televisual flow see Raymond Williams, *Television: Technology and Cultural Form* (New York: Schocken Books, 1975).

8. Marshall McLuhan, *Understanding Media: The Extensions of Man* (New York: McGraw Hill, 1964), and Lev Manovich, *The Language of New Media* (Cambridge, MA: MIT Press, 2001).

9. "I had to buy 2 copies of each book so I could have the front and back of every page," Thomson notes of the fifty-plus Rodin books that went into the making of *Sideways Thought*. "I then guillotined the spines off all the books and organized the pages into stacks of individual sculptures" (unpublished text on *Time Life*).

10. Self-improvement remains a huge industry, of course, now expanded into the less sanguine markets of "the care industry" in particular and of "human capital" in general, in which we figure as neoliberal entrepreneurs of our own ever-retooled skillsets.

11. *Time Life* reveals how often apparently "natural" activities are actually "cultural" techniques. The classic text on this subject is "Techniques of the Body" (1934) by Marcel Mauss.

12. On seeing as targeting, see Samuel Weber, *Targets of Opportunity: On the Militarization of Thinking* (New York: Fordham University Press, 2005). On targeting and testing in Pop art and beyond, see my *The First Pop Age: Painting and Subjectivity in the Art of Hamilton, Lichtenstein, Warhol, Richter, and Ruscha* (Princeton: Princeton University Press, 2011).

13. "Percussive" stems from the Latin *percutere*, "to shake through," which captures the effect of much of the music. The volumes might also be compared to "flicker" films, on the psychophysiology of which see Rosalind Krauss, "Pulse," in Yve-Alain Bois and Rosalind Krauss, *Formless: A User's Guide* (New York: Zone Books, 1997), 161–165.

14. Salomé Aguilera Skvirsky, *The Process Genre: Cinema and the Aesthetic of Labor* (Durham: Duke University Press, 2020), 16. Process films often "straddle two distinct modes of organizing labor that are rarely treated together: artisanal and industrial production" (4). The volumes add a third mode, digital production, reflecting on the first two.

15. Ibid., 3, 15, 34.

16. Skvirsky quotes Roland Barthes on the "genetic type" of illustrations used in the *Encyclopédie* of Diderot and D'Alembert: "The image is a kind of rational synopsis: it illustrates not only the object or its trajectory but also the very mind which conceives it" (ibid., 43). *Time Life* might be productively compared to other artistic critiques of modern labor such as *Semiotics of the Kitchen* (1975) by Martha Rosler. For a helpful overview of such work, see Helen Molesworth, *Work Ethic* (University Park: Penn State University Press, 2003).

17. Thomson, unpublished text on *Time Life*.

18. Ibid. Again, Thomson sees the *Time-Life* book series as an "analog prototype for the internet." The library and the museum each had an epistemological project, an imagined order, however flawed. Can the same be said of the internet as archive?

19. On this posthuman time see "Philosophical Objects" in this volume.

20. On machine vision as taken up in the work of Harun Farocki, Hito Steyerl, and Trevor Paglen, artists to whom Thomson can be related, see my *What Comes after Farce? Art and Criticism at a Time of Debacle* (London and New York: Verso Books, 2020).

Chapter 30

1. The initial version of the present chapter appeared in *Artforum* (October 2021) as a review of *Ed Atkins: Get Life/Love's Work*, curated by Massimiliano Gioni for the New Museum. In an excellent essay in the catalogue, Erika Balsom provides an overview of relevant works by Atkins. Unless otherwise noted, all quotations are from this catalogue, which includes two essays by Atkins, a conversation with Gioni, and a note by Mark Leckey.

2. The initial concept was to interview people in isolation—jailed, disabled, poor, old—but the pandemic made that scheme seem superfluous to Atkins. Nevertheless, *The Worm* is all about both the desire and the difficulty of connection. For the conversation, Atkins set up in a hotel room in Berlin while his mother remained in England. The data captured during the conversation was used to animate the avatar, though "it's my face that palpably lurks beneath the CG wireframe and JPEG skin."

3. Atkins uses the interview form as the basis of several videos. "For such a long time, I made these works alone, at a computer, interrogating myself with technologies that surveilled my every grimace. For me it was a pitched self-surveillance that ended up melodramatizing me to myself." Imagine the Warhol *Screen Tests* updated technologically, self-inflicted, and not at all silent.

4. Gillian Rose, *Love's Work: A Reckoning with Life* (New York: Schocken Books, 1995), 74. For Rose "love's work" is a reckoning with risk and loss. "Philosophy, ancient and modern, is born out of this condition of sadness" (124). This is also true of art for Atkins, at least in part.

5. These surrogates "descended, psychically, from that literal dead man who began this whole sorry mess for me. Making videos became about reparative mourning."

6. See my "Obscene, Abject, Traumatic," *October* 78 (Autumn 1996).

7. "The presumption of the project, from the beginning, was the accentuation of those aspects of life that elude technological remediation, recoupment, representation, rendering, capture. The work would try to rehearse freedoms by their omission from the remit of what's reproducible. In this, at least structurally, it would recapitulate the core thesis of my work."

8. Tacita Dean deploys media corpsing brilliantly in her 2015 film *Event for a Stage*. See my "Real Fictions," *Artforum* (April 2017).

9. "Analog flaws [are] re-created digitally in order to militate against the sterile horror of computer-generated nothings." In the film *Anomalisa* (2015) Charlie Kaufman also uses glitches in the animation—cracks in the avatar—to evoke the real. See Zadie Smith, "Windows on the Will," *New York Review of Books*, March 10, 2016.

10. For Atkins "the celluloidal story" has "the uncanny at its heart," and the digital image is even more "spectral"; its "persistent aping of analog reality means that the animation, the life, is doubly lost, doubly dead." In some ways Atkins continues, by digital means, the old cinematic fascination with ghosts, robots, and doubles of all sorts.

11. Walter Benjamin uses this phrase (without much explanation) in both "Little History of Photography" (1931) and "The Work of Art in the Age of Its Technological Reproducibility" (1935–1936).

12. Atkins continues in this vein: "I go after the idea that the tech believes it possible to convince us of its life, and that it always fails in this pursuit. That gap between the 'almost' and the 'never' is a promising, sad, mortal, and inimitable place."

13. See Giorgio Agamben, *Homo Sacer: Sovereign Power and Bare Life*, trans. Daniel Heller-Roazen (Stanford: Stanford University Press, 1998).

14. Atkins deals in "travesty" and "caricature" in his writing too: "Typically for me, the prose is purple, bathetic; mortifying, in retrospect." See Mike Spelinger, "Close without Saving," in Ed Atkins, *Seer Reader* (London: Koening Books, 2015). There is a connection to John Miller here as well; see "Perverse Pantomime" in this volume.

15. "I do think all this structural reflexivity I apparently demand of the medium is maybe a manifestation of the kinds of structural reflexivity that I try to undertake in my personal life."

16. In his novel *Klara and the Sun* (2021) Kazuo Ishiguro presents an AI avatar who develops an emotional maturity that the nominal humans around her either lack or have lost.

17. Perhaps another sign of an inability to think the social is the recent spread of autofiction; like much art, much literature has narrowed its scope to the personal.

18. See Leo Bersani and Ulysse Dutoit, *Arts of Impoverishment: Beckett, Rothko, Resnais* (Cambridge, MA: Harvard University Press, 1993), and Leo Bersani, *The Culture of Redemption* (Cambridge, MA: Harvard University Press, 1990). Atkins might reply that there's no contradiction here: love's work follows on loss. But might he then primordialize and hypostatize loss? "Loss is our exemplar," Atkins states, and he aims to render it "sublime."

Chapter 31

1. See Leonard Schwartz and Michael Hardt, "A Conversation with Michael Hardt on the Politics of Love," in *Pasts, Futures, and Aftermaths: Revisiting the Black Dada Reader*, by Adam Pendleton (London: Koenig Books, 2021); and Lauren Berlant and Michael Hardt, "No One Is Sovereign in Love," in Adam Pendleton, *Who Is Queen?* (New York: Museum of Modern Art, 2021). The initial version of the present chapter appeared in Meredith Malone et al., *Adam Pendleton: To Divide By* (St. Louis: Kemper Art Museum, 2023).

2. To continue with etymologies, "seminar" derives from the Latin *seminarium*, or seed plot, and "symposium" from the Greek *sumposion*, or drink taken with others.

3. Jenny Schlenzka, "What Can Black Dada Do for My Institution Do for My Institution Black Dada, Some Thoughts," in Adam Pendleton, *Black Dada Reader* (London: Koenig Books, 2017), 17.

4. Gilles Deleuze, "Three Questions about *Six Fois Deux*," in ibid., 82.

5. "I have a drive toward radical juxtapositions, toward making spaces as full as you can, with names and references and ideas and images," Pendleton has remarked, with Joan Jonas also in mind. "She has a drive toward the combinatorial as well. It's a poetics of disruption." "*Who Is Queen?* A Roundtable," in Pendleton, *Who Is Queen?*, 244.

6. Simone White, *Dear Angel of Death* (excerpt), in ibid., 103.

7. Stuart Comer, introduction to Pendleton, *Who Is Queen?*, 7.

8. "I have a problem with the historical understanding of what a manifesto is, and the 'Black Dada' text seeks to re-litigate that historical understanding. A manifesto is a monolith in a certain way—it's oriented in one direction—whereas the 'Black Dada' text splinters into many different directions." Pendleton in "Alec Mapes-Frances in Conversation with Adam Pendleton," in Alec Mapes-Frances, Adrienne Edwards, and Andréa Picard, *Adam Pendleton* (London: Phaidon, 2020), 8.

9. See Brent Hayes Edwards, *The Practice of Diaspora: Literature, Translation, and the Rise of Black Internationalism* (Cambridge, MA: Harvard University Press, 2003).

10. Michel Foucault, "Nietzsche, Genealogy, History," in *Language, Counter-Memory, Practice*, ed. Donald F. Bouchard (Ithaca, NY: Cornell University Press, 1977), 140, 154, 157. Also see "Made for Cutting" in this volume.

11. See Hortense J. Spillers, "Mama's Baby, Papa's Maybe: An American Grammar Book," *Diacritics* 17, no. 2 (Summer 1987).

12. Saidiya Hartman, "Venus in Two Acts," *Small Axe* 26 (June 2008).

13. Trajal Harrell, "Dance Q&A: Trajal Harrell Brings Voguing Downtown," in Pendleton, *Black Dada Reader*, 327; Alexis Pauline Gumbs, "From the Lab Notebooks of the Last Experiments," in Pendleton, *Who Is Queen?*, 130, 128. Some selections in the readers also reflect on semi-forgotten anthologies, exhibitions, and the like.

14. Adam Pendleton, "Introductory Note" (2018), in Mapes-Frances, Edwards, and Picard, *Adam Pendleton*, 132; Pendleton, "Black Dada," in *Black Dada Reader*, 333.

15. "Incomplete cube" alludes to a work by Sol LeWitt, *Incomplete Open Cubes* (1974), photographs of which Pendleton has used as the armature of his Black Dada paintings.

16. See Baudelaire, "The Salon of 1846," in Baudelaire, *The Mirror of Art*, ed. and trans. Jonathan Mayne (New York: Doubleday, 1956), and Aby Warburg, *Bilderatlas Mnemosyne* (Berlin: Hatje Cantz, 2020). Pendleton shares with Warburg an interest in the "afterlives" of art, and shares with Joan Jonas an interest in Warburg, whom he also evokes in *Pasts, Futures, and Aftermaths*.

17. Appositely here, Alec Mapes-Frances describes the Pendleton project as "a catalogue of scenes of representation." In "Alec Mapes-Frances in Conversation with Adam Pendleton," 13.

18. Jason Adams, "Occupy Time," in Pendleton, *Who Is Queen?*, 15.

19. See Adrienne Edwards, "Adam Pendleton: Here Is Your Language," in Mapes-Frances, Edwards, and Picard, *Adam Pendleton*, 36.

20. Roland Barthes, "The Death of the Author" (1968), in Barthes, *Image Music Text*, trans. Stephen Heath (New York: Hill & Wang, 1977), 146.

21. Adrienne Edwards, "The Struggle for Happiness, or What Is American about Black Dada," in Pendleton, *Black Dada Reader*, 30. Pendleton speaks of his readers as "only assembled in order to disassemble" in "Alec Mapes-Frances in Conversation with Adam Pendleton," 11. For a different version of such assembly, see "Happy Days" in this volume.

22. See "Made for Cutting" in this volume.

23. "Alec Mapes-Frances in Conversation with Adam Pendleton," 32.

24. Harrell, "Dance Q&A," 328.

25. Pendleton, "Black Dada," 338. See Tristan Tzara, "Monsieur Antipyrine's Manifesto" (1916), in Robert Motherwell, ed., *The Dada Painters and Poets: An Anthology* (Cambridge, MA: Harvard University Press, 1981), 75. Still to be explored in the Black Dada project (and elsewhere) are the colonialist-imperialist underpinnings of "european dada." Others have taken up this strategy of *détournement* vis-à-vis white avant-garde artists and thinkers. See, for example, Aria Dean, "Black Bataille," in *Bad Infinity: Selected Texts* (London: Sternberg Press, 2023).

26. See the excellent analysis in Tom McDonough, "BLACK DADA MIME," in Pendleton, *Black Dada Reader*. McDonough builds on my "Dada Mime," *October* 105 (Summer 2003).

27. Pendleton, "Black Dada," 344.

28. "I feel as though our consciousness is the result of appropriation. We are appropriated. We are, culture is, the result of that which has become networked throughout our history into the web/realm of culture." Adam Pendleton, in Gillian Sneed, "Interview with Adam Pendleton," *The Highlights* 9 (2008), thehighlights.org/wp/interview-with-adam-pendleton. On Pendleton and abstraction, see Adrienne Edwards, "Blackness in Abstraction," *Art in America*, January 5, 2015, https://www.artnews.com/art-in-america/features/blackness-in-abstraction-3-63053/. On Pendleton and appropriation, see Tom McDonough, "The Parallax View: The Art of Adam Pendleton," *Artforum* (November 2011). One could extend this list of *détournements* or queerings to graffiti and graphic design. The most striking definition of *détournement* in art remains that of Asger Jorn in "Détourned Painting" (1959):

> The future is made through relinquishing or sacrificing the past. He who possesses the past of a phenomenon also possesses the sources of its becoming. Europe will continue to be the source of modern development. Here, the only problem is to know who should have the right to the sacrifices and to the relinquishments of this past, that is, who will inherit the futurist power. I want to rejuvenate European culture. I begin with art. Our past is full of becoming. One needs only to crack open the shells. Détournement is a game born out of the capacity for devalorization. Only he who is able to devalorize can create new values. And only there where there is something to devalorize, that is, an already established value, can one engage in devalorization. It is up to us to devalorize or to be devalorized according to our ability to reinvest in our own culture. There remain only two possibilities for us in Europe: to be sacrificed or to sacrifice. It is up to you to choose between the historical monument and the act that merits it.

29. "Alec Mapes-Frances in Conversation with Adam Pendleton," 21.

30. Ibid. See Hito Steyerl, "In Defense of the Poor Image," *e-flux* 10 (November 2009).

31. "Alec Mapes-Frances in Conversation with Adam Pendleton," 30.

32. "*Who Is Queen?* A Roundtable," 241. "*Queen* . . . is all about being queer. . . . It really came out of this feeling or this sense of vulnerability, when someone thinks they can name you or claim you as something" (245). Like the artist Claire Fontaine, Pendleton speaks of the "refusal to be a subject" as a "strike" (246).

33. See Edwards, "Blackness in Abstraction."

34. This last phrase is a well-known Marxist/Situationist slogan.

35. Pendleton also insists on abstraction against the tendency to reduce Black art to either expressionistic or figurative modes. While Kerry James Marshall underscores the pictorial history of blackness as underpainting, Pendleton uses blackness as a mode of overpainting. Other analogues of his medium are hinted at in *Black Dada Reader* and elsewhere: for example, a letter from Félix González-Torres about the blank piece of paper as a "passport" on which to inscribe "life, love, memories, fears, voids, and unexpected reasons for being," or an agitated musical score by Julius Eastman. These are instances of black written on white, not the reverse, which Toni Morrison calls out as a dominant trope in American literature in *Playing in the Dark: Whiteness and the Literary Imagination* (1992). The recent discovery of a racist joke scrawled by Kazimir Malevich under his epochal *Black Square* (1915) now inflects this discussion as well.

36. Adam Pendleton, "Afterward," in *Black Dada Reader*, 348.

37. Pendleton, "Afterward," 347. "For the African in America, abstraction is the orienting fact of her existence, something to be overcome, either by refusing it, or by deploying it herself": Adam Pendleton, "Amiri Baraka (1934–2014)," in Mapes-Frances, Edwards, and Picard, *Adam Pendleton*, 130. In an "Introductory Note" to that volume, Pendleton adds: "Abstraction is the image of self-legislation" (132).

38. Fredric Jameson, *Valences of the Dialectic* (London and New York: Verso, 2009), 43, 13. Also see "Antinomic Modernism" in this volume.

Chapter 32

1. Guy Debord, *Correspondence: The Foundation of the Situationist International (June 1957–August 1960)*, trans. Stuart Kendall and John McHale (Los Angeles: Semiotext(e), 2009). Unless otherwise specified, all Debord quotations are from this text (all italics are in the original). The initial version of the present chapter appeared in the *London Review of Books* (March 12, 2009).

2. McKenzie Wark suggests "secretary" in her helpful introduction to Debord's *Correspondence*.

3. Michèle Bernstein quoted in Greil Marcus, *Lipstick Traces: A Secret History of the 20th Century* (Cambridge, MA: Harvard University Press, 1989), 181.

4. Guy Debord, *The Society of the Spectacle*, trans. Donald Nicholson-Smith (New York: Zone Books, 1994), 136 (italics in the original).

5. Bernstein, "In Praise of Pinot Gallizio" (1960), *October* 79 (Winter 1997): 94.

6. Asger Jorn, "Peinture détournée," in *Vingt peintures modifiées par Asger Jorn* (Paris: Galerie Rive Gauche, 1959), n.p.

7. "Definitions" (1958), in *Situationist International Anthology*, ed. and trans. Ken Knabb (Berkeley: Bureau of Public Secrets, 1981), 45.

8. Ibid.

9. Georg Lukács, *History and Class Consciousness*, trans. Rodney Livingstone (Cambridge, MA: MIT Press, 1986), 83.

10. Debord, *The Society of the Spectacle*, 24. This formula has long since become reversible. See my *The Art-Architecture Complex* (London and New York: Verso, 2011).

11. Michèle Bernstein, *All the King's Horses*, trans. John Kelsey (Los Angeles: Semiotext(e), 2008), 33. The Situationists used this exchange in détourned images like film stills.

12. Marcus, *Lipstick Traces*, 4.

13. Guy Debord, Attila Kotányi, and Raoul Vaneigem, "Theses on the Paris Commune," https://www.cddc.vt.edu/sionline/si/commune.html.

Chapter 33

1. See Susan Sontag, "Against Interpretation" and "Notes on 'Camp'" (both 1964), in *Against Interpretation* (New York: Farrar Straus & Giroux, 1966), 14, 288. The initial version of the present chapter appeared as a tribute to Sontag in *Artforum* (September 2005).

2. On this divergence also see "Made for Cutting" in this volume.

3. Margalita Fox, "Susan Sontag, a Social Critic with Verve, Dies at 71," *New York Times*, December 29, 2004.

4. See "Hyperbolic Criticism" in this volume.

5. Susan Sontag, "Remembering Barthes," *New York Review of Books*, May 15, 1980.

6. Theodor W. Adorno, "Cultural Criticism and Society" (1951), in *Prisms*, trans. Samuel and Shierry Weber (Cambridge MA: MIT Press, 1981), 19.

7. Sontag, *Against Interpretation*, viii. The Baudelaire line, "criticism must be passionate, personal, political," is from his "Salon of 1846."

8. Susan Sontag, "'Thinking against Oneself': Reflections on Cioran," in Sontag, *Styles of Radical Will* (New York: Dell Publishing, 1969), 75.

9. Sontag, *Against Interpretation*, 276.

10. Susan Sontag, "One Culture and the New Sensibility" (1965), in *Against Interpretation*, 302. The Arnold line is from *Culture and Anarchy: An Essay in Political and Social Criticism* (1869).

11. Norman Podhoretz, longtime editor of *Commentary*, told his version of this story in his memoir *Making It* (1967).

12. Charles McGrath, "A Rigorous Intellectual Dressed in Glamour," *New York Times*, December 29, 2004.

13. Fox, "Susan Sontag, A Social Critic with Verve, Dies at 71."

Chapter 34

1. See Michael Fried, "Art and Objecthood," *Artforum* (Summer 1967); Robert Morris, "Notes on Sculpture, Parts 1, 2, 3, 4," *Artforum* (February 1966, October 1966, Summer 1967, April 1969); and Rosalind Krauss, "Sense and Sensibility: Reflections on Post '60s' Sculpture," *Artforum* (November 1963). The initial version of the present chapter appeared in *Artforum* (September 2012).

2. Amy Newman, *Challenging Art: Artforum 1962–1974* (New York: Soho Press, 2000), 152, 187.

3. Ibid., 187.

4. See Tom Wolfe, *The Painted Word* (New York: Farrar, Straus & Giroux, 1975). Wolfe coined the anti-Semitic term "Cultureburg" to underscore what he saw as the undue influence of Clement Greenberg, Harold Rosenberg, and Leo Steinberg.

5. Newman, *Challenging Art*, 295 (italics in the original).

6. See Fried, "Three American Painters: Kenneth Noland, Jules Olitski, Frank Stella" (1965), in *Art and Objecthood* (Chicago: University of Chicago Press, 1998), and Donald Judd, "Specific Objects," *Arts Yearbook* (1965).

7. This charge ran the other way too: Fried accused Minimalists like Donald Judd and Larry Bell of the hypostatization of "literalness" in "Shape as Form: Frank Stella's Irregular Polygons" (1966), in *Art and Objecthood*, 88.

8. See Robert Morris, "Some Notes on the Phenomenology of Making: The Search for the Motivated," *Artforum* (April 1970). Arbitrariness emerged as a primary concern for modernists as soon as abstraction was broached: How to motivate the work of art once its grounding in the world was forgone? This provoked the insistence, on the part of Kandinsky

and others, on the "internal necessity" of the artist and/or the artwork. See "An Inventory of Encounters" in this volume.

9. Michael Fried, "Morris Louis," in *Art and Objecthood* (Chicago: University of Chicago Press, 1998), 101. "Compelling conviction" is a Friedian imperative. For his close interlocutor, the philosopher Stanley Cavell, this difficult situation *is* the modernist condition, and one purpose of modernist art is to test the limits of its meanings and the understanding of its viewers over and over again.

10. Thomas Crow, "These Collectors, They Talk about Baudrillard Now," in Hal Foster, ed., *Discussions in Contemporary Culture* (Seattle: Bay Press, 1987), 7.

11. Fried, "Three American Painters," 217–218.

Chapter 35

1. Krauss refers to the "Greenberger" gibe in "A View of Modernism" and speaks of her status as an "apostate" in *Perpetual Inventory* (Cambridge, MA: MIT Press, 2010), 116, 113. Unless otherwise noted, all other Krauss quotations are from "A View of Modernism," *Artforum* (September 1972). The initial version of the present chapter was my contribution to a panel honoring Krauss at the College Art Association convention in 2012.

2. Greenberg and Fried differed over Frank Stella, whose work troubled this historical logic for the former but not for the latter. See "Hyperbolic Criticism" in this volume.

3. The first assumption is often termed essentialist, the second historicist. See "An Inventory of Encounters" in this volume. Leo Steinberg countered this account, which he termed "preventive," in his "Reflections on the State of Criticism." This text appeared in *Artforum* (March 1972) several months before "A View of Modernism." (Steinberg also alleged there that this account "put all painting in [a] series.") Greenberg dismissed the general understanding of his position as a caricature in a 1978 addendum to his definitive statement, "Modernist Painting" (1960). See Clement Greenberg, *The Collected Essays and Criticism, Volume 4: Modernism with a Vengeance, 1957–1969*, ed. John O'Brian (Chicago: University of Chicago Press, 1993), 93–94.

4. This apparent objectivity, Krauss noted, was also a reaction against the subjective criticism common in the 1950s: hence again "the curiously dissociated tone" of her early criticism.

5. Alain Robbe-Grillet, "On Several Obsolete Notions" (1957), in *For a New Novel: Essays on Fiction*, trans. Richard Howard (New York: Grove Press, 1965), 32.

6. Like spatial perspective, this historical perspective places the subject in a position of authority.

7. See Clement Greenberg, "Towards a Newer Laocoön" (1940), in *The Collected Essays and Criticism, Volume 1: Perceptions and Judgments, 1939–1944*, ed. John O'Brian (Chicago: University of Chicago Press, 1993).

8. This line of thought culminated in the 1996 exhibition-cum-catalogue *L'Informe*, produced with Yve-Alain Bois, at the Centre Pompidou in Paris. Inspired by the Bataillean notion of the formless, *L'Informe* traced the intermittent eruption of antiformal impulses

across twentieth-century art. The project was also influenced by Denis Hollier, editor of the collected writings of Bataille and author of the essential book on his work, *Against Architecture*, trans. Betsy Wing (Cambridge, MA: MIT Press, 1989).

9. David Smith died in a car accident in 1965, which qualified him as a proper art-historical subject for a dissertation at Harvard—a small indication of the great difference between protocols in art history then and now.

10. Krauss first put forward this reading in "Sense and Sensibility: Reflection on Post '60s Sculpture," *Artforum* (November 1973).

11. See Michel Foucault, *Archaeology of Knowledge and The Discourse on Language*, trans A. M. Sheridan Smith (New York: Harper & Row, 1976), 126–131. Krauss refers to the notion of "historical *a priori*" in *Under Blue Cup* (Cambridge, MA: MIT Press, 2011), 15.

12. Krauss, *Perpetual Inventory*, 1. A previous flashpoint for Krauss and Michelson was the publication of an advertisement for a Lynda Benglis show in the November 1974 issue of *Artforum*, which presented her naked with a dildo. This was widely read as a parody of a poster for a prior Robert Morris show, which presented him in a Nazi helmet and brandishing a chain (Krauss took the photo).

13. There was a rhythm to transformative publications of American art criticism in the postwar period: Greenberg published *Art and Culture* in 1961, Leo Steinberg *Other Criteria: Confrontations with Twentieth-Century Art* in 1972, and Krauss *The Originality of the Avant-Garde and Other Modernist Myths* in 1985.

14. Rosalind Krauss, "The Originality of the Avant-Garde," in *The Originality of the Avant-Garde and Other Modernist Myths* (Cambridge, MA: MIT Press, 1985), 158.

15. Ibid., 162. In effect, Krauss read the paradigm of the grid through the notion of the picture developed by Douglas Crimp in "Pictures," *October* 8 (Spring 1979): "underneath a picture is always another picture."

16. Krauss, "Introduction," in *The Originality of the Avant-Garde*, 5.

17. Ibid., 1.

18. Claude Lévi-Strauss uses this phrase in *Totemism*, trans. Rodney Needham (Boston: Beacon Press, 1971), 89.

19. Krauss, "Introduction," 3.

20. See "*The Anti-Aesthetic* Then and Now" in this volume.

21. Krauss, "Notes on the Index, Part 1," in *The Originality of the Avant-Garde*, 198.

22. Krauss, "Notes on the Index, Part 2," in *The Originality of the Avant-Garde*, 212. In retrospect, the emphasis on the indexical might be seen, in part, as a defense against imminent dominance of the digital.

23. Ibid., 206.

24. See Rosalind Krauss, "Bachelors," *October* 52 (Spring1990), reprinted in Krauss, *Bachelors* (Cambridge, MA: MIT Press, 1999).

25. See Louis Althusser, *For Marx*, trans. Ben Brewster (London: New Left Books, 1977).

26. Jacques Lacan, "Signification of the Phallus," in *Écrits*, trans. Alan Sheridan (New York: W. W. Norton, 1977), 284. What "postdated" Freud was the reception of Saussure.

27. See in particular Rosalind Krauss, "The Motivation of the Sign," and Yve-Alain Bois, "The Semiology of Cubism," in Lynn Zelevansky, ed., *Picasso and Braque: A Symposium* (New York: Muscum of Modern Art, 1992).

28. For my version of this approach see "Interdependent Study" in this volume.

29. Michel Foucault, "Nietzsche, Genealogy, History," in *Language, Counter-Memory, Practice*, ed. Donald F. Bouchard (Ithaca: Cornell University Press, 1977), 154.

30. Walter Benjamin, "On the Concept of History" (1940), in *Selected Writings*, vol. 4: *1938–1940*, ed. Howard Eiland and Michael W. Jennings (Cambridge, MA: Harvard University Press, 2003), 390. Other key interventions in modernist art history are also informed by this "effective" relay between the historical and the critical.

31. The 2000s saw Krauss preoccupied with "the post-medium condition," which she disparaged, blaming the "dissolution" of the concept of the medium on the compound effects of Conceptualism, deconstruction, and postmodernism: Conceptualism because it shifted art practice from the specific (the individual media) to the general (art as such), deconstruction because it undermined "self-presence" in art, and postmodernism because it justified interdisciplinarity as such. Announced in *Voyage to the North Sea: Art in the Age of the Post-Medium Condition* (2000), this concern is central to both *Perpetual Inventory* (2010) and *Under Blue Cup* (2011). It can be seen as an apostasy from her apostasy, a reversion to the Greenbergian discourse of medium-specificity, but it can also be understood as a return (in the sense discussed above), a revisiting of an episteme in order to open it up, from the inside, to other possibilities. Thus Krauss redefined medium not as a traditional form to inherit (painting, sculpture, etc.) but as a "technical support" to adapt. In this account almost anything might qualify as a medium (her examples include the slide carrousel in the art of James Coleman and the car in the work of Ed Ruscha). Rather than posit an ontology of a medium and then disclose its primary and secondary attributes, the artist develops a set of rules that might ground a practice recursively and, in doing so, allow for invention and improvisation.

Chapter 36

1. Yve-Alain Bois, *An Oblique Autobiography* (New York: no place press, 2022); unless otherwise noted, all quotations are from this source. The initial version of the present chapter appeared in the *London Review of Books* (March 30, 2023).

2. See Jacques Derrida, "Restitutions," in Derrida, *The Truth in Painting*, trans. Geoff Bennington and Ian McLeod (Chicago: University of Chicago Press, 1987). Bois was chagrined that Derrida derided Meyer Schapiro to the extent that he did in the published essay.

3. Piet Mondrian, letter to James Johnson Sweeney, May 24, 1943, in *The New Art—The New Life: The Collected Writings of Piet Mondrian*, ed. and trans. Harry Holzman and Martin S. James (New York: Da Capo Press, 1993), 357.

4. Bois has written several essays on Kelly and has worked for many years on his catalogue raisonné.

5. See Clement Greenberg, "Modernist Painting" (1960), in *The Collected Essays and Criticism*, vol. 4: *Modernism with a Vengeance, 1957–1969*, ed. John O'Brian (Chicago: University of Chicago Press, 1993), 85–93.

6. See Leo Steinberg, *Other Criteria: Confrontations with Twentieth-Century Art* (Oxford: Oxford University Press, 1972). Also see "Watchman and Spy" in this volume.

7. See "Made for Cutting" in this volume.

8. Roland Barthes, "On *The Fashion System* and the Structural Analysis of Narrative" (1967), in Barthes, *The Grain of the Voice: Interviews 1962–1980*, trans. Linda Coverdale (New York: Hill & Wang, 1985), 50.

9. Alexandre Koyré quoted in Bois, *An Oblique Autobiography*, 300.

10. Walter Benjamin, "A Berlin Chronicle" (1932), in *Selected Writings*, vol. 2: *1927–1934*, ed. Michael W. Jennings, Howard Eiland, and Gary Smith (Cambridge, MA: Harvard University Press, 1999), 614. In many ways a maze is the opposite of an axonometric projection. In a maze one is plunged into a space-time experienced in constant transformation—hence its interest for Minimalists like Robert Morris—while an axonometric projection represents the object world at a distance, without distortion. At the same time, Lissitzky, an essential modernist for Bois, folds together the axonometric and the labyrinthine in some of his *Prouns*.

Chapter 37

1. Unless otherwise noted, all quotations are from T. J. Clark, *If These Apples Should Fall: Cézanne and the Present* (London: Thames & Hudson, 2022). The initial version of the present chapter appeared in the *London Review of Books* (December 1, 2022).

2. T. J. Clark, *Image of the People: Gustave Courbet and the 1848 Revolution* (1973; Princeton: Princeton University Press, 1982), 6.

3. Christopher S. Wood, "Paul de Man and Art History," *Flash Art News* (Summer 1995), 87–90.

4. T. J. Clark, "The Conditions of Artistic Creation," *Times Literary Supplement*, May 24, 1974, 561–562.

5. See T. J. Clark, "Clement Greenberg's Theory of Art," *Critical Inquiry* (September 1982), and Malcolm Bull, "Between the Cultures of Capital," *New Left Review* (September/October 2001).

6. See Theodor W. Adorno, "Late Style in Beethoven" (1937), in *Essays on Music*, ed. Richard Leppert, trans. Susan H. Gillespie (Berkeley: University of California Press, 2002).

7. See T. J. Clark, "For a Left with No Future," *New Left Review* (March/April 2012).

Chapter 38

1. Jonathan Crary, *Techniques of the Observer: On Vision and Modernity in the Nineteenth Century* (Cambridge, MA: MIT Press, 1990), 4. The initial version of the present chapter appeared in the *London Review of Books* (October 5, 2023).

2. Crary, *Techniques of the Observer*, 3.

3. Ibid., 14.

4. Ibid., 125, 127, 136, 150.

5. Jonathan Crary, *Suspensions of Perception: Attention, Spectacle, and Modern Culture* (Cambridge, MA: MIT Press, 1999), 3.

6. Ibid., 300, 297, 300.

7. Crary, *Techniques of the Observer*, 6.

8. Jonathan Crary, *24/7: Capitalism and the Ends of Sleep* (London and New York: Verso, 2013), 13, 43, 59, 33, 59, 73, 57.

9. Ibid., 63, 10, 25.

10. Jonathan Crary, *Scorched Earth: Beyond the Digital Age to a Post-Capitalist World* (London and New York: Verso, 2022), 34, 19, 9, 109, 118, 121.

11. Ibid., 123, 124, 32.

12. Jonathan Crary, *Tricks of the Light: Essays on Art and Spectacle* (New York: Zone Books, 2023), 215.

13. Ibid., 38.

14. Ibid., 81, 95, 81, 121.

15. Ibid., 128, 130, 131.

16. Ibid., 98, 104, 102, 103, 106.

17. Michel Foucault, *Discipline and Punish: The Birth of the Prison*, trans. Alan Sheridan (New York: Pantheon Books, 1977), 217.

18. Crary, *Tricks of the Light*, 135, 155.

19. Karl Marx, *Grundrisse*, trans. Martin Nicolaus (London: New Left Books, 1973), 335.

20. Crary, *Tricks of the Light*, 100,

21. Crary, *Suspensions of Perception*, 370.

22. Crary, *Scorched Earth*, 4.

Chapter 39

1. The initial version of the present chapter, which appeared in *October* 168 (Spring 2019), was my contribution to the fiftieth-anniversary celebration of the ISP at the Whitney Museum on October 19, 2018.

2. At the time CUNY graduate students included Benjamin Buchloh, Douglas Crimp, David Deitcher, Rosalyn Deutsche, Ewa Lajer-Burcharth, Craig Owens, and Abigail Solomon-Godeau, to name only several. See "Made for Cutting" in this volume.

3. Howard Singerman, "In Theory and Practice: A History of the Whitney Independent Study Program," *Artforum* (February 2004).

4. In my view the ISP suffered whenever (usually for budgetary reasons) this structure was not maintained.

5. See "Made for Cutting."

6. See my *Compulsive Beauty* (Cambridge, MA: MIT Press, 1993).

7. Michel Foucault, *Discipline and Punish: The Birth of the Prison*, trans. Alan Sheridan (New York: Pantheon Books, 1977), 31. Also see Foucault, "Nietzsche, Genealogy, History" (1971), in his *Language, Counter-Memory, Practice*, ed. Donald F. Bouchard (Ithaca: Cornell University Press, 1977).

8. Walter Benjamin, "On the Concept of History" (1940), in *Selected Writings*, vol. 4: *1938–1940*, ed. Howard Eiland and Michael W. Jennings (Cambridge: Harvard University Press, 2003), 390.

9. Grant Kester quoted in Singerman, "In Theory and Practice."

10. Clement Greenberg, "The Late Thirties in New York" (1957), in *Art and Culture* (Boston: Beacon Press, 1961), 230.

11. Michael Fried, "Three American Painters: Noland, Olitski, Stella" (1965), in *Art and Objecthood* (Chicago: University of Chicago Press, 1998), 218. See "Hyperbolic Criticism" in this volume.

12. As Marx wrote in "A Contribution to the Critique of Hegel's *Philosophy of Right*" (1844), "We are *philosophical* contemporaries of the present, without being its *historical* contemporaries."

13. See Vladimir Lenin, "Left-Wing Communism: An Infantile Disorder" (1920).

14. This point was made by Claire Pentecost at the ISP symposium on October 20, 2018.

15. Hal Foster, ed., *The Anti-Aesthetic: Essays on Postmodern Culture* (Port Townsend, WA: Bay Press, 1983), xvii. See "*The Anti-Aesthetic* Then and Now" in this volume.

16. Ben Lerner diagnoses this syndrome brilliantly in *The Hatred of Poetry* (New York: Farrar Straus & Giroux, 2016).

17. "Dadaism sought *to abolish art without realizing it*, and surrealism sought *to realize art without abolishing it*," Guy Debord writes in *The Society of Spectacle* (1967; trans. Donald Nicholson-Smith [New York: Zone Books, 1994], 136). Debord implies that, in its transformation of critical art into direct action, Situationism aimed to do both. See "A Certain Practice of Life" in this volume.

In the late 1990s, during the debate about "visual culture," I proposed the value of "strategic autonomy," which played on the notion of "strategic essentialism" once put forward by Gayatri Spivak. In the way that, for political reasons, an essential identity must be asserted at times, so, too, for cultural reasons, aesthetic autonomy must be claimed at times. Most artists, even those committed to political engagement, likely agree that the work that they do as artists is at least semi-autonomous, that they must develop their own languages first and foremost. Many critics probably think the same about their work.

18. This kind of query can also be taken up within novels, as when Jean Rhys imagines the life of Bertha Mason in *Wide Sargasso Sea* (1966), or, more recently, when Caryl Phillips does the same with Jean Rhys in *A View of The Empire at Sunset* (2018) or when Kamel Daoud elaborates on *The Stranger* in *The Meursault Investigation* (2013).

19. Singerman, "In Theory and Practice."

20. See "Antinomic Modernism" in this volume. Also see my "Modernism in a Non-Melancholic Key," *October* 186 (Fall 2023).

Chapter 40

1. The initial version of the present chapter appeared in *Artforum* (September 2023). Unless otherwise noted, all quotations are from *The Anti-Aesthetic: Essays on Postmodern Culture* (Port Townsend, WA: Bay Press, 1983). Its publisher, my great friend Thatcher Bailey, was crucial to the making of the book from first to last.

2. There was pushback on the Frampton essay from architect friends who didn't see critical regionalism as properly postmodernist, but what appealed to me was precisely its critical posture, which pointed to a "postmodernism of resistance."

3. "The logic of sculpture, it would seem, is inseparable from the logic of the monument," Krauss wrote in "Sculpture in the Expanded Field." "By virtue of this logic a sculpture is a commemorative representation. It sits in a particular place and speaks in a symbolical tongue about the meaning or use of that place." Two decades later Benjamin Buchloh offered this diabolical revision: "The logic of sculpture, it would seem, is inseparable from the logic of the commodity fetish. By virtue of this logic a sculpture is always already a fetishized object whose function is disavowal. It lacks any particular location and it is universally accessible. It speaks in a symbolic tongue about the meaning or use of the fetish." In "Sculpture: Publicity and the Poverty of Experience," in Buchloh, *Formalism and Historicity: Models and Methods in Twentieth-Century Art* (Cambridge, MA: MIT Press, 2015), 510.

4. See Algirdas Julien Greimas, *On Meaning: Selected Writings in Semiotic Theory*, trans. Paul J. Perron and Frank H. Collins (Minneapolis: University of Minnesota Press, 1987), including the foreword by Fredric Jameson. Recently, of course, "the logic of the monument" has been contested in very different ways.

5. Michel Foucault, "Fantasia of the Library," in Foucault, *Language, Counter-Memory, Practice*, trans. Donald F. Bouchard and Sherry Simon (Ithaca: Cornell University Press, 1977), 92.

6. It could be argued that Owens totalized in his own way, hypostatizing all authority as domination.

7. In a text on "post-criticism" for *The Anti-Aesthetic* Gregory Ulmer argued, after Rosalind Krauss, that critical theory had achieved a "paraliterary" status of its own, carrying over the modernist critique of representation, through the devices of collage and montage, into the domain of philosophy. Otherwise, I was stumped by how to treat postmodernist literature,

in large part because the writers associated with the category (such as Thomas Pynchon, William Gaddis, John Barth, Robert Coover, Donald Barthelme, Dion DeLillo, even William Burroughs and Amiri Baraka) were more ultramodernist than post-. The different arts do not necessarily develop synchronously.

8. Also contingent was my acquaintance with the authors. I knew Frampton from the Institute for Architecture and Urban Studies, and Krauss and Crimp from *October*. I worked alongside Owens at *Art in America*, and met Jameson through *Social Text*. I studied with Said at Columbia, and met Baudrillard on one of his trips to New York.

9. This problem isn't mitigated by the fact that Owens was gay. However, in the short time remaining to him—he died, far too young, in 1990—he did become an important voice in queer theory, which had only begun to emerge at the time of *The Anti-Aesthetic*.

10. See my "(Post)Modern Polemics," in *Recodings: Art, Spectacle, Cultural Politics* (Seattle: Bay Press, 1985).

11. Saidiya Hartman, *Wayward Lives, Beautiful Experiments: Intimate Histories of Social Upheaval* (New York: W. W. Norton, 2019), 33. Also see Christina Sharpe, "Beauty Is a Method," *e-flux* 105 (December 2019).

12. I allude here to my "Post-Critical?," in *Bad New Days* (London and New York: Verso, 2015); Eve Kosofsky Sedgwick, "Paranoid Reading and Reparative Reading, or, You're So Paranoid, You Probably Think This Essay Is About You," in Sedgwick, *Touching Feeling: Affect, Pedagogy, Performativity* (Durham: Duke University Press, 2003); and Leo Bersani, *The Culture of Redemption* (Cambridge, MA: Harvard University Press, 1990).

Index